Eurasia Twenty Years After

EURASIA
TWENTY YEARS AFTER

Edited by

Anita Sengupta
Suchandana Chatterjee
Susmita Bhattacharya

Maulana Abul Kalam Azad Institute of Asian Studies, Kolkata

SHIPRA

ISBN: 978-81-7541-639-0

First Published in India in 2012

Eurasia Twenty Years After

Published by:
SHIPRA PUBLICATIONS
H.O.: LG 18-19, Pankaj Central Market, Patparganj,
I.P. Ext., Delhi-110092, Tel: 91-11-2223 5152, 2223 6152
Br.Off.: 4617/18, Ansari Road, Darya Ganj,
New Delhi-110002, Tel: 6594 6453, 9810522367
E-mail: info@shiprapublications.com
www.shiprapublications.com

Contents

Societies in Motion

Resurgent Identities in Religion

Migration Patterns

Introduction: Perspectives on Twenty Years After

The year 2011 marks the twentieth anniversary of the disintegration of the Soviet Union. One of the major debates that have dominated global politics during the year has therefore centred round the fundamentally transformative events of December 1991. It has been twenty years since the disintegration of the Soviet Union but also twenty years since the appearance of fifteen new independent states in the global arena. Taking stock of the way in which not just the post Soviet space but also the Eurasian space has changed over the last twenty years has been attempted from a variety of perspectives that have taken note not just of political and economic concerns but also the entire gamut of experiences that differ from those of the Soviet period. With the emergence of new states there were attempts to analyse shifting legacies not only of the Soviet period but also those of the Ottoman, Tsarist, Mongol and Qing eras. Place names changed and new national monuments replaced Soviet era commemorative markers in many states. Cultural norms and beliefs, holiday rituals, modes of communication, state symbolism and popular historical narratives were altered in fundamental and obvious ways. Yet, in the continuing existence of fifteen sovereign states in the post Soviet space there remains the most visible legacy of the Soviet state and its nationality policy.

The twentieth anniversary occasioned a retrospective look at 1991. It also led to focus on developments within the post Soviet space in the twenty years that followed. On the one hand twenty years of the collapse of the Soviet Union generated debates over the causes and consequences of the collapse where the nature of the phenomenon was itself contested. Did 1991 imply the end of an era? Or was it simply the culmination of reforms that had begun much earlier under the label of *perestroika* by the last Soviet President Mikhail Gorbachev? Equally, the disintegration of the Soviet Union in December 1991 had already been presaged by a qualitative change in the nature of the country, reflected in continuing debates over changing the name of the new entity to something along the lines of a Union of Sovereign States. In examining the events of 1991 there also remains a permanent search for an interpretative framework. While there is no doubt that the Soviet Union collapsed as a result of its own contradictions, the nature of these contradictions themselves need to be explored. It is argued that the fundamental contradiction that precipitated the fall was the attempt to create an "alternative modernity." The central features of this alternative modernity included the abolition of the free market, the attempt to achieve direct expression of popular sovereignty as represented in the party-state, the inversion of typically modern forms of class hierarchy, and a permanently revisionist stance in international affairs, defined as the aspiration to revise the existing international order.

On the other hand debates have been generated on what the last two decades has meant for the emerging states, the individual and the international community. This has formed the subject of a number of discussions both within the post Soviet space and outside. From a broader perspective these have examined where the 'post Soviet' state situates itself today in terms of a global grid where ideological divisions are not as significant as strategic confrontations and where political and cultural alignments are still being redefined. The negotiation of value systems in crisis, changing cultural values, religious, ideological, economic collapse, as well as various degrees of recovery from that collapse have been deliberated on. From the perspective of the individuals within the space these have examined new understandings of his place within a redefined space in the face of social and economic transformations. These continuities and the ruptures have led to examinations of topics as wide ranging as the impact of the collapse on the postal system to the impact of the Soviet legacy on the development of human rights law in the post Soviet states. The sustainability of older forms and the viability of newer ones have been studied in analytic and comparative forms. Among the vast range of themes taken up for study the question of whether it is at all correct to speak of the former Soviet Union as a region has attracted the attention of analysts. In *Post-Imperium: A Eurasian Story*, for instance, the need for reformulating the idea of a post Soviet space is clear when Dmitri Trenin argues that Moscow needs to drop the notion of creating an exclusive power centre in the post-Soviet space. Like other former European empires, Russia has no choice but to reinvent itself as a global player and as part of a wider community.

This volume has been compiled out of presentations made at the International Seminar *Eurasia Twenty Years after: 1991 in Retrospect* organized by the Maulana Abul Kalam Azad Institute of Asian Studies in February 2011. It also includes articles that were commissioned from experts concerned in their particular fields of study. As a seminar organized in Kolkata it attempted to begin a debate on the ways in which the southern perspective on the region has essentially been different from the western one. In the course of the inaugural debate the perspective of a southern state looking to its north and north-west was therefore emphasized as the traditional way in which the region has been viewed. This is a tradition based on the sharing of a Turko-Iranian heritage and several diaspora sentiments common to South Asia and Central Asia. It is essentially a heritage that takes note of South Asia's northward gaze towards Eurasia that was based on trade and cultural connectivity between the two regions. This was a perspective that eminent historian and social scientist Professor Barun De, and Founder Director of the Institute, in the course of his reflections on the region emphasized. He argued for the necessity of developing a geo-cultural vision based on India's historical contacts with the Turko-Iranian civilization which is significantly different from the western world's geo-strategic vision. This western perspective is based on an orthodox meaning of geopolitics with overtones of conflict. He argued that these ought to be minimized. Alternative connotations based on linkages and connections between the states within the entire Euro-Asian region need to be researched and carefully worked out. Elaborating on the argument he pointed out that most western and westernized decolonization models (based on the maritime interests of the imperial powers) use the northern gaze southwards. As an example he quoted K.N. Pannikar's guiding premise in *Asia and Western Dominance*. If this perspective is inverted and if we scan the map of contemporary affairs from a middle southern position, i.e. looking north-west, then a reinterpretation of insights is possible. These alternative views on what used to be considered as Bactria and Sogdiana in ancient history and as Balkh, Badakhshan, Khorezm and Mawar-an-Nahr as well as Mughalistan further east in medieval times and the Trans-Pamir or Trans-Oxiana during the Tsarist and Soviet periods needs to be re-examined. From this revised position, one also needs to gauge the contacts between Central Asian and South Asian cultures and communities. A series of eastward and westward migration took place leading to intermingling of religion, faith and culture. The southward penetration of trade brought Ghazni Turan and the Mughal lands closer to Sindh, the Punjab, Kashmir and even the Deccan and Bengal, and vice-versa.

Such Asian links are intriguing and have their echoes in the post-Soviet period with Russia attempting to forge strategic alliances with China or Kazakhstan or realign with old Asian allies like India for creating a strategic space. Such pro-eastern options are juxtaposed to the Gorbachevian principle of looking west, though both options seem to have generated their own set of contradictions. These have encouraged alternative discourses that have shaped the course of new historiography in the region, argues Isenbike Togan. A people's history approach is the latest trend in Azerbaijan and Turkmenistan that have excluded or included certain communities in nationalist historiography. Thus, Chingizids, Timurids and Shaibanids were honoured in the Turkic historiography while the Kipchaks, who were the competitors of the Chingizids were excluded. Such radical approaches in historiography have not occurred in Russia, argued Tatiana Shaumian, the renowned Russian Orientalist who pointed to the continuity of tradition with regard to Tibet studies in Russia, revolving round the role of the Dalai Lama and his close coterie of Buryat and Kalmyk lama scholars especially Agvan Dorjiev in building up Buddhist connections in the trans-Himalayan sector.

The debate about the Soviet legacy continues. Scholars sometimes over-emphasize a "Soviet myth" that is all-pervading among the older generation and which tries to derive new strength from the Soviet ideal and values. This is puzzling for the new post-Soviet generation that fails to comprehend the myth. Oleg Donskikh's argument about the mythological aftermath of the post-Soviet era was echoed by Vsevolod Bashkuev in his description of myth-making in the ethnic nationalist discourse of Buryatia. The selective historical narrative in Buryatia has been critiqued by the new generation of historians to which Bashkuev belongs. Marina Baldano and Sveta Baldano are assertive about the making and unmaking of Buryat political culture, identifying distinct phases in Buryat political activism and the role of Buryat intellectuals in post-Soviet political space. Shifting patterns of Kyrgyz history-writing in the post-Soviet period also indicate similar silences in Kyrgyz history, argues Zuhra Altymshova. Citing archival sources as well as oral accounts in Kyrgyzstan, Altymshova reveals gaps in the official historiography about Soviet deportation project in the 1920s—'30s that exiled several Kyrgyz *kulaks* (rich peasants) as enemies of the state.

The year 1991 also marks a transition in terms of the education policies that have been adopted by the post-Soviet regimes. Uzbek and Turkmen history textbooks have been written from the perspective of an identity-story, showing an original interpretation that balances both the nationalist and the socialist interpretations, instead of juxtaposing them to each other, argues Büşra Ersanlı. Yunus Emre Gürbüz's article is about school history textbooks in Azerbaijan that reflect a similar revisionist approach. He perceives the potency of the territorial issue over Nagorno-Karabakh that the Turkish Azeris are extremely sensitive about. Denis Ananyev, in his profile of the academic environment in Siberia, indicates the history projects of the Institute of History, articulating the alternative paradigms that reflect diverse research traditions. The complementary nature of Russia's relations with her autochthonous population in Siberia has been studied in detail by historians associated with Novosibirsk's Institute of History of Russian Academy of Sciences. The three-volume *History of Siberia* is the product of this enterprise.

The section "Societies in Motion" deals with real life experiences, some positive and some negative, in the newly independent states of Central Asia. It is interesting to note how perceptions about state-society relations have been variously reflected in the writings in this volume. Shirin Akiner makes a distinction between past and present civil society projects in post-Soviet Uzbekistan. She idealizes the civil society model undertaken by the Fund Forum in Uzbekistan that tries to engage several associations in building harmony between state and society. Timur Dadabaev, on the other hand, while arguing that the *mahalla* in Uzbekistan has a role in creating an environment of social consent and new opportunities, in state-society relationships also notes the contradictions within this relationship. Similarly, Ilhan Sahin, in his field survey report on the Küntuu village in Kyrgyzstan, emphasizes the efficacy of rural management and survival of rural kinship ties in sustaining social structure in Kyrgyzstan and their usefulness in coping with social and economic problems in post-Soviet Kyrgyzstan. However, other articles note that urban-rural divide has led to disproportionate results. The hazards of uncontrolled urbanization in Kyrgyzstan have been pointed out by Kishimjan Eshenkulova. Her paper portrays the disparities in living patterns of the urban and the rural population that have also accentuated social tensions in Kyrgyzstan. Similar tensions have been replicated in the neighbouring republic of Uzbekistan. The shrinkage of urban space in Tashkent has created acute housing shortage in Tashkent, argues Hikoyat Salimova. Preeti Das looks into some of the historical facts which help in an understanding of the cultural identity of the Ukrainians and how it has been transformed over the years under Soviet influence.

Irrespective of social tension, cultural representations are varied in nature. The section "Cultural Representations" introduces an element of variety in post-Soviet Eurasia. Festivals and celebrations are integral to Russia's political culture, and in Buryatia too there have been special commemorative events not only in connection with religious ceremonies but also as cultural events (e.g. *Sabantui, Surkharban)* symbolizing the social interaction among all ethnic groups in Buryatia. Thus New Year and New Year's Eve are celebrated with as much enthusiasm as the Buddhist rituals in Ulan Ude. The *Sagaalgan* is also an event that idealizes the meeting of the *zemlyaki.* Rashmi Doraiswamy describes interesting features of the Kazakh New Wave Cinema and the way it has gained an international image. It is interesting to observe the importance of the space that culture occupies in this region, as well as the way the festivals insert themselves into the geopolitics of the region. Cultural discourses of the region are based on "affinities" that the Central Asian republics associate themselves with and the image of the popular is increasingly getting attention among the international audience. Ranjana Saxena points to the resurgence of literary debates in the post-Soviet period some of which originated in the Soviet era. She argues that homogenization of the Soviet socialist canon needs is a misnomer—the canon was questioned several times even during the Soviet period, though the process gained momentum at the height of Gorbachev's *perestroika.* The article by Dilorom Karomat and Nigora Khasanova emphasizes two related aspects of the musical culture of modern Uzbekistan as a mirror of musical culture: (1) contest and festivals; (2) condition of musical critique. Shakhym Gullyev, a musicologist from Turkmenistan, narrates his own experiences about musical art in Turkmenistan in the first decade since the disintegration of the USSR.

Social predicaments have been replicated at the political level with the "resurgence" of political Islam in the region. In the last two decades, this issue has played a significant role in the determination of the direction that politics has assumed. In certain cases political Islam has transformed itself by adapting to new circumstances while in others it has disrupted social cohesion resulting in fragmentation. From a perspective of transformation Pinar Akcali talks about, what she identifies as, one of the most important and unique actors of political Islam in Central Asia, the Tajik Islamic Renaissance Party (IRP). Through an examination of its policies, programme, and leaders and the role that it has been playing in the various stages of the political life of Tajikistan she argues that its ability to formulate different policies and assume different attitudes has enabled it to adjust to the conditions of the post Soviet era. P.L. Dash, on the other hand, talks about how present day radical Islam in Russia has created a schism within its own society, hopelessly divided along those who support terror acts and those who oppose it. In this context he talks about the recent trends of terror, invariably linked to Islamic groups across Eurasia. Debidatta A. Mohapatra also speaks about the different forms that revival of Islam has assumed in Russia and like Dash focuses on the North Caucasus. He brings to the forefront the question whether it is possible to think of Islam within a regional context. Similar questions are raised by Michael Fredholm in his analysis of the role of Uzbek Islamic extremists since the 1990s and the negative impact that they have had in the countries where they have acquired bases. In this context he makes a detailed analysis of the Islamic Movement of Uzbekistan and Islamic Jihad Union to show how the two groups have changed considerably in character and in terms of their membership on several occasions during the two decades. Didier Chaudet also examines the Islamic Movement of Uzbekistan in the Ferghana Valley, the Caucasus Emirate in Northern Caucasus, and the Islamic Jihad Union to demonstrate how foreign ideas found ways to influence local grievances, sometimes morphing them in a transnational fight. Both Fredholm and Chaudet argue that the broader regional threat emanates from Afghanistan, and this should be taken into account in any examination of the activities and membership of these organizations. The roots, they argue are local; however the influence of foreign elements cannot be disregarded. Arguing from a sociological viewpoint Darima Amogolonova notes that ideological rethinking, in poly-confessional Russia has led to politicization of religious issues and the incorporation of religion into ethno-national ideologies. Talking specifically about the Buryat situation, she argues that symbolism and religion has a somewhat different role in the region where Buddhism and Shamanism have played a significant role. She concludes that Buddhist ethics could be a salvation for Russia's ethnic problems and religious intolerance.

Such debates have continued in the context of transformation of structures and institutions. R.G. Gidadhubli looks into alternative economic models followed by Kazakhstan and Uzbekistan in the last twenty years. He argues that the Kazakh policy of participation in regional economic and political organizations has had a positive impact on the economic performance of Kazakhstan. On the other hand, the Uzbek policy of economic diversification and economic development for domestic needs has meant that Uzbekistan has suffered less from the global economic crisis. He also talks about the negative impact of certain problems arising out of the inability of the state to control factors like bribery, corruption and bureaucratic control. Mirzhoid Rakhimov examines institutional transformation in Uzbekistan from a political perspective. He argues that the experience of the last twenty years testifies to the fact that a difficult process of formation of a civil society in Uzbekistan is evolving. However, further liberalization of the country, creation of necessary preconditions of effective partnership among the state and society, and strong institutions of civil society remain important objectives for Uzbekistan. Rakhimov's ideas should be read along with the articles by Timur Dadabaev and Shirin Akiner in this volume for a deeper understanding of state-society relations in Uzbekistan and the various points of view from which they are being viewed. Ajay Patnaik examines the arrival of parliamentary democracy in Kyrgyzstan and the factors that created conditions for its establishment. While he looks into the Kyrgyz case he also examines why similar situations of discontent did not translate into movement away from Presidential systems in the other states. On the other hand, Marilisa Larusso points to the fragility of the situation in the Caucasus with the breakdown of trust among ethnic groups, inbuilt contradictions of the democratization process and certain "grey zones" which have made the environment undemocratic.

Eurasia's borderlands have also been in a state of flux. Intricacies of border management became evident in the wake of Soviet disintegration. Sometimes, local initiatives changed the character of Sino-Soviet rapprochement and Sino-Russian relations during 1983-93, confirms Sören Urbansky. Natalia Ryzhova also points to a series of similar informal mechanisms and illegal practices by Russian entrepreneurs in the Far East and the percolation of cross-border criminal activities in fish-trade which assumed the character of "poaching-trade" in the Amur and Khabarovsk regions. These tensions, argues Sharad Soni, are not revealed in the case of Mongolia, which is projected as a dynamic "Third Neighbour country" and is considered a safe bet by its global partners. Faced with domestic problems, Mongolia has adopted a favourable attitude to the world community in general, and East Asia in particular. Turkey too is a diplomatic favourite as far as the Central Asian republics which share a Turkish destiny are concerned, notes Roza Abdukulova. Issues of diplomacy are central to Indian think tanks' research and are suitable talking points for a discourse on Central Eurasian engagement, as Nivedita Kundu argues.

Diverse migration patterns also affect Asiatic Russia, Central Asia and the neighbourhood. The articles in the section on 'Migration Patterns' was presented in a symposium on *Migration and Demography in Asia: Comparative Trends* that followed the seminar. Viktor Dyatlov's article is a reality check on the Tajik labour migrants in Russia and their "ghettoization" that has practically peripheralized them in Russian society. Vladimir Isupov has also traced the irregular demographic trends in Northern Russia that has affected the overall demographic profile of Russia. His study is about external factors that have resulted in dramatic mortality rates in western Siberia since the beginning of the twentieth century and continued throughout the Soviet period. Yana Kuznetsova also holds age and sex factors responsible for the underdevelopment of Asiatic Russia. According to Sayan Darzhaev, demographic patterns have been so erratic in Eurasia that they have created social disparities and accentuated conflict in Russia and Central Asia. The negative features of migration are reflected in economic, cultural and psychological spheres as well.

This volume, in focusing on the two decades since 1991, which marked the demise of the Soviet Union, argues that the transformations that occurred since then constitute the essence of "a post-Soviet dispensation." The basic assumption is that changes were visible in politics and policies of the post-Soviet republics that reconstituted the erstwhile Soviet Union as the Commonwealth of Independent States and subsequently as regional organizations with "western" or "eastern" affiliations. The social and cultural manifestations of change—art forms like films, iconography, aesthetics, music, tourism, architecture and media also tend to reflect the changing psyche in the post Soviet space. The ways in which the newly independent states perceive themselves, i.e. as entities that are strictly "sovereign" or as cosmopolitan spaces with pan-Iranian/pan-Turkic/pan-Mongol linkages and sharing a Russian past, have also been re-evaluated. Similarly it examines the rhetoric invoking "national" sovereignty both in terms of its continuities and discontinuities which are today being reassessed in several ways. Here, one needs to take note of the fact that both the socialist choice and the Soviet memory of socialism remains vivid within the region. However, the last two decades have been years of the existence of the states as independent republics. Therefore the volume also focuses on how experiences of independence have been both similar and dissimilar for the former Soviet republics themselves. It addresses certain preconceived notions about the direction that the states would assume in terms of the ways in which relationships and identities have been reconfigured; structures have been institutionalized while issues like ethnicity still remain important. The wide gamut of impressions about Eurasia in this volume indicates sensitivities about this region. It also reflects the visibility of this region in international affairs.

The editors are grateful to Dilorom Karomat, Fellow, Maulana Abul Kalam Azad Institute and Aditi Bhaduri, Independent Researcher for the translation of some of the articles of this volume from Russian to English. The editors also wish to express their gratitude to Rita Bannerjee for copy editing the volume.

Legacies and Images of the Soviet and 'Post Soviet'

1

Mythological Aftermath of the Post-Soviet Era

Oleg A. Donskikh

Cassirer in his famous book, *The Myth of the State* noted, "Problems that had been unknown to the political thinkers of the eighteenth and nineteenth centuries came suddenly to the fore. Perhaps the most important and the most alarming feature in this development of modem political thought is the appearance of a new power: the power of mythical thought. The preponderance of mythical thought over rational thought in some of our modem political systems is obvious."[1] It is especially actual and dramatic for the Russian state, which has been living for the whole century in the kingdom of ideological myths. The objective of the paper is to analyse the situation from the standpoint of the contemporary mythology and the basic beliefs characteristic for the post-Soviet society, as they are represented in Russia after the "triumphant" crash of "actual socialism" taken in relation to economic life and to discuss the recent state of their interaction.

In order to define the role of mythology in different human societies Max Weber isolated at least two factors which, although functioning independently, can give the most important impetus to social development and gradation. These factors are: 1) economics, and 2) mythology (or religion).[2] According to his doctrine these factors interact in order to give meaning to social life and to produce ethical value. The examples of positive interaction can be found, for instance, in the history of England with its industrial development and practical attitude to labour in Protestant teaching. Soviet society manifested a very close alliance between economy and corresponding mythology of proletariat as a hegemonic power of social life. This alliance, however, proved to be a disaster both from a spiritual as well as from an economical point of view.

Mythology can be defined as a body of ideals, images and/or attitudes which are associated with the justification of social order and of individual life, and this justification in its turn shapes social and individual behaviour. Therefore, mythology can be regarded as genuine only if it is consciously or unconsciously taken by society as some kind of absolute and ultimate reality. The structure of mythology is quite complex and contains different levels of meanings. Myth, which is the vehicle of mythology, also requires a working definition. The use of the term "myth" implies stories or key statements, which express a significant belief transposed in an imaginative and symbolic manner, the basic structure on which a culture rests. Some authors emphasize the difference between myth and ideology, saying that "a myth proposes a story, whereas ideology has its roots in systematic ideas;" or, in other words, "all ideologies do have a mythological core, but in addition they build up conceptual edifices."[3] However, for the purposes of the paper I would use "mythology" and "ideology" as synonyms terms.[4]

Myth stands in opposition to history because of its timeless character. Myth does not know time as an arrow moving from the past to the future, but only as an arrow trying to escape from time by means of perpetual repetition, eternal renewal and recurrence. In as much as mythology is a necessary component of social life, it is a life-supporting mechanism of society, functioning as a kind of spiritual pivotal point. In order for society to survive mythology should stand in balance with economical life. And this balance can be different for different cultures.

Russian history provides us with the example of the situation when two mythologies characteristic for two different social groups could exist simultaneously for a long time. This situation was caused by the reforms of Peter the Great in the first quarter of the eighteenth century when the mythology borrowed from Western Europe was violently set off against traditional mythology inherited from the Muscovite state. Moreover, this foreign mythology from the very beginning was in strong opposition to any manifestations of what was regarded as backwardness of customary mentality and used every chance to challenge it.[5] Usually this coexistence of different mythologies marks a transitional period. However this cannot last for long and the bridges which would allow normal development should be established through inner restructuring. But in reality these mythologies were continuing to live completely alienated from each other. The traditional mythology was prevalent predominantly among the majority of the Russian population, i.e. for peasants who used to live in self-sufficient communities with customary laws, while liberal ideology (mythology) characterized the upper layer of aristocracy and the not of noble birth intelligentsia. The unresolved situation led to revolutions at the beginning of the twentieth century and the establishment of the Soviet state with its particular communist ideology.[6] The bearers of this ideology were revolutionaries, the extreme group of Russian intelligentsia, who promoted their beliefs after they came to power and created the Soviet state. Thus we will talk about the interaction of three mythologies: traditional, liberal and Soviet.

The Traditional Russian Mythology

The traditional mythology inherited from the Muscovite times was formed during the period of Mongol Yoke and acquired its peculiar features by the mid-sixteenth century. It was based on the ideals of *pravda* ("truth" and "justice") and *volya* ("will" and "freedom"). Basically this ideal was indifferent to economic life as such; it defined people's relationship with God and within the community rather than outlining any specific forms of economical activity. However indirectly it also influenced this activity through: 1) the ideal of political organization which was a righteous monarchy; 2) the specific attitude to the land the value which cannot be turned into private property; 3) through valuing personal relations over legal relations (Russian consciousness strictly separated *pravda* (truth) from *zakon*, i.e. law); and 4) valuing collectivism over individualism.[7] An important feature of this mythology was that it is turned towards past to the image of Christ and the corresponding events. It did not prescribe any progress in historical sense but rather the eternal self-improvement of the personality, and this striving was expressed by the great Russian writers, Tolstoy and Dostoevsky in particular.

The people regarded the relationship with the Tsar through the institution of community (*mir obshchina*). *Mir* ("world," "peace" and "agricultural community") possesses *volya* in the same way as the Tsar possesses *volya*. Otherwise their relationship would not make sense. However the nature of these *volyas* is different: the Tsar possesses *volya* because it has been given to him by God; *mir* possesses *volya* because it was established as an autonomous unity. The main goal and inspiration for both *volyas* is *pravda*, which is one and the only one God's *pravda*. The Tsar is regarded as an embodiment of this *pravda* on earth: "Where there is a Tsar, there is *Pravda*."[8] People's *pravda* in its turn can be found in their unity. This unity should be established on the basis of love which is *pravda* in human hearts. The Tsar's *pravda* is higher than that of the people: "If the people sin, the Tsar will atone for their sins by prayer, and if the Tsar sins, the people will not be able to atone for his sins by prayer."[9] This approach is apparently contrary to any theory of the origin of supreme power through delegation and as such stands aside of the democratic establishment of the authority in a way similar to the western election campaign. At the same time it accepts an idea of the "Assembly of the Land." This ideal shaped the core of traditional mythology and was in apparent correspondence with the economic life of the agricultural society.

Though not identified with economic activities, it created a balance between the collective ownership of the land by local peasant *mirs*, and the supreme power over the Russian land by Rurik's (later Romanov's) dynasty. It is essential that the very name of *Russian land* related the land to the ruling dynasty of *Russian* princes rather than to the population of this land.[10] The image was formed of the righteous Tsar who was beyond law and was responsible for the people before God. The legitimacy of the dynasty was also crucial based on the belief that only the legitimate Tsar could be genuinely righteous, and that was why the phenomenon of the false-Tsars played such a role in the Russian history. Thus, according to this mythology the land should not belong as such to people but to the state represented by Tsar, who was expressing and manifesting the will of the population. An important fact was that administration, bureaucracy, manifestation of legal relations based on laws, was taken as necessary yet evil medium between Tsar and people. The land was considered as belonging to the people of the country subordinated to the sovereign who is responsible for the people before God.

This Russian attitude to the land ownership intersected with the religious and mystical attitude to the land, which is taken as sacred.[11]

Russian consciousness strictly separated truth (*pravda*) from law (*zakon*). Initially these concepts were quite close to each other (though not defined properly), and the first code of laws was called *Pravda Russkaya*. Over the centuries *pravda* gradually gave way to *zakon*. At the same time *pravda* was joined with the Christian concept of a merciful God and through this secured a position beyond *zakon*. In the course of this development *pravda* moved closer to the concept of *svet* ("light" and "world") acquiring the significance and image of the supreme ethical value. The value of the concept of *pravda* predetermined (or rather reflected) a strong anti-state feeling and a cultural preference for the unity of personalities compared with the unity of citizens. Through this development *pravda* was moving closer and closer to the concept of *volya* which, in Russian consciousness, is "boundless, independent of any social or other restrictions." As an adjective it means "free, independent, autonomous, having power by himself." It is extremely significant that *volya* means freedom from *any* sort of dependence and responsibility. It is also important that *volya* bears the meaning of unrestricted inner freedom, freedom of soul; through this the social connotations of the word were linked with individual connotation. From the old times *volya* was associated with *mir,* and through this association it expressed united collective consciousness as opposed to a bondage brought about by political relations. Being allied with God's *pravda, volya* bypassed the legal relations and formed a direct link with the supreme secular power represented by the Tsar. The specifics of this relation lie in its personal rather than its legal nature. This relation between people and sovereign was based on feeling rather than on reason, and because of this the heart, symbolizing feelings, came to the fore compared with the mind. This personal attitude towards authority was conveyed onto other relations, which involved elements of legal system.

The Liberal Mythology

The Liberal mythology has made its appearance in the West since the Renaissance with the idea of progress and the corresponding infinite technological development under the F. Bacon's slogan "Knowledge is power." Reason *is believed* to replace belief. Man is taken as being reasonable and living in "the state of nature."[12] Society therefore is believed to be based on the contract which replaced the idea of the divine origin of the supreme authority.[13] This formed the core of the liberal democratic mythology of the modern times. The emphasis is on individualism with the core belief that the individual is more significant than civil society, and correspondingly, the civil society has to express the general will of individuals. The liberal mythology forms a specific attitude to economic life:

1. In order to be self-sufficient an individual should possess a property. The institution of private property is guaranteed by the state.[14]
2. The supreme authority of this state is founded and preserved through the agreement (contract) of the equal individuals in the form of democratic organization of political life, i.e. through delegation of the part of their own rights in the form of suffrage. In return the state (an elected government), executing the system of laws, guarantees life, liberty, and property of citizens.
3. Economic relations should be ruled by scientific methods, which include the theories at different levels. The idea of freedom enters the complex of these doctrines through the concept of market as the ultimate regulative factor. The Enlightenment myth of a just society based on science in

turn inspired science to look for a corresponding argument to justify itself and its "progressivist" thinking. Thus science voluntarily became a slave of myth.

The Soviet Mythology

The Soviet mythology contains various layers of meaning organized around the utopian image of the just communist society. These views was taken faithfully and religiously by some groups of Russian intelligentsia and put into action in the first quarter of the twentieth century. In relation to the economic life this mythology consists of the following:

1. Communist society does not know private property. Everything should belong to the state which expresses the general will of the population and the goods should be distributed in accordance with the principles of the justice.
2. The general will of the people is expressed by the communist party. The party deserves its leading position also for its collective wisdom and power.
3. This society, based on scientific principles offering prediction and providing recommendations which were of benefit to the working class, however gradually came to benefit so called "Soviet people as a new historical community."

The image of a communist society which does not have the antagonistic contradictions of the capitalist society has an extremely interesting and complicated history in western civilization going back to the Pythagorean doctrines, the utopias of the Renaissance, the socialistic utopias of the Enlightenment. In the nineteenth century the possibility of establishing a fair and just society is believed to be scientifically proved by Karl Marx. All the problems of the capitalist society were believed to be caused by the institution of private property which was responsible for the alienation of the working class from the results of their labour. It was also believed, as in liberal ideology, that Reason should replace Belief, or, in other words, Science should replace Religion. In Russia these concepts were combined with the belief of the moral supremacy of the lowest, uneducated part of the Russian population. Everything creative was to be made in the name of the poor and the underprivileged. These views was taken up by some groups of Russian intelligentsia and put into action in the first quarter of the twentieth century. The so-called "Soviet Society" which thus came into existence obviously had nothing in common with the principle of the *soviet* which in Russian means a form of collective administration with representation from all layers of the population. It was, paradoxically, under this name that the dictatorship of the communist party was established. Ironically, in the early years of the Revolution, the rebels against Bolshevik power had slogans like *For the Soviets without Communists*![15]

The Three Mythologies: A Review

These three mythologies—traditional, liberal and Soviet—stand in strong opposition to each other.

There are at least two significant points which differentiate traditional and liberal mythologies (keeping in mind that the society, in which the first mythology is inherent, is based on collective property while the second is based on private property).

1. Collectivism versus individualism. This, for instance, explains why the industrialization in Russia took its specific forms. Peter the First had to create factories using the serfdom-based labour, etc.
2. "*Pravda*" versus law. The emphasis on juridical relationship vis-à-vis personal relationship was always regarded as untrue. This contradiction cannot be avoided and cannot be resolved. This explains why till nowadays the juridical system is so ineffective. And also the values of spiritual life were regarded as being more important than values of economic life.

Traditional mythology seems to be closer to the Soviet mythology than to the liberal one on two points: 1) in negation of individualism, 2) in preference of the so called "class consciousness" (which is taken for truth and ultimate justice) to law. However, this closeness is quite superficial. The traditional worldview is organically inherited from feudal social life, while the Soviet ideology was growing as the negation of liberal ideology. Accordingly, the collective consciousness of peasant communities was secured by the financial responsibility of every member of the community ("*mir*"). But the class consciousness of the Soviet society was secured by the Marxist doctrine for which the communist party was responsible. Consequently, other classes were excluded as being alien to the proletarian consciousness; moreover, the majority of the working class was also excluded due to the fact that it did not match the demanded ideology. Similar considerations relate to the specific truth, which in traditional ideology is taken as divine and relating to the whole society from the last peasant to Tsar, yet in case of the Soviet ideology the truth was in disposal of a particular group which was standing beyond other groups including proletariat itself declared to be hegemonic.

Soviet mythology thus stood in opposition to both traditional and liberal ones.

1. It negated religious foundation of traditional worldview in favour to the "scientific" Marxist philosophy.
2. Though it represented itself as collectivistic way of thinking the majority of population was not able to recognize this.
3. It was in contrast to liberal mythology in the relation to private property. That is why the civil society in western sense of the word could not be created.
4. The emphasis on personal relations at the expense of the legal ones separated the traditional approach from both the liberal and the Soviet mythologies. In liberal mythology all human relations (including the relationship between family members) were based on law. From the traditional point of view this interaction should be based on love given through God's will, and this is impossible without free will of every individual.[16] However, at this point the traditional mythology is different from the Soviet mythology because the latter takes all the relationships as mediated by the state manifesting the general will.

Thus, all three ideologies stand in complicated interdependency. This leads to the situation that when one ideology comes to the fore it suppresses the others. This happened in Soviet time, which lasted for three generations. The principles shaping mythological picture is not subject to the categories of truth or falsity.[17] It simply belongs to another dimension of reality. The significant point to be made about the Soviet myth is that it was functioning to suppress the economic relations characteristic for the previous period, as well as the corresponding features of the everyday life of the Soviet people. The system grown on the Soviet myth was in disequilibrium with the economic and everyday life of the nation. The more the myth expanded, the more the economy shrank to the brink of disaster.

Also it should be taken into account that the construction of communist society demanded a lot of effort from the people, when the most independent and self-relating groups were suppressed and exterminated, and with its collapse the population has been left tired and spiritually devastated. The main contemporary diagnosis is that the post-Soviet Russian society is *the society with the gaping lack of genuine uniting mythology*, and this is a tragedy for the society. After *perestroika* it was believed that the liberal ideology with corresponding myths had again become predominant, since the disappointment in this ideology became quite obvious.[18] This disappointment goes along with the disillusionment in the behaviour of western countries. It was predominantly believed that as soon as Russia would drop the Soviet ideology it would become the welcomed part of the western world. However the real politics demonstrated quite the opposite situation, and the expansion of the NATO to the East as the answer to the dismissal of the Warsaw Pact, is only one, though significant, component of this.[19]

It is impossible to use accurate measures in relation to the actual mythological dimension of social reality. However, it seems plausible to presuppose that there are four groups of population separated by their different attitude to this dimension of social life. First, there is a large group of population, definitely forming the majority, which predominantly will just "go with the flow" and as such is quite indifferent to any mythology at all. Moreover, they are against it thinking that every general statement relating to society is false. Second, there are nationalists who do not form the unbroken group but sharing the mythology outlined earlier display all colours of the spectrum from narrow-minded chauvinistic groups with so called Black-Hundred ideology to the groups of intellectuals trying to renovate Slavophil mythology of the nineteenth century. Third, there are liberal thinking people who believe that Russia should follow the models of development presented by Western Europe and United States in particular. Fourth, there are people who are would like to revitalize the communist soviet mythology. It is interesting to note that while one generation earlier this mythology, which had been violently embodied in social life, suppressed all other myths, after the death of the state, which manifested and supported this mythology, did not come to the end but had to be revised in order to acquire a new strength.

The danger of contemporary situation lies in the intolerance of the outlined groups. They are perfectly convinced that only their mythology is correct and instead of the search for common ground are doing their best trying to suppress others, which leads to more and more gaping ideological chasm.

In order to prove this I would relate to the sociological research of modern Russian youth. Their image of the state of the time of Yeltsin is the following: unspiritual (81.8%), respect towards Orthodox church (58.3%), crisis (92.7%), difficult economic situation

(89.3%), uncertainty in relation to the future (93%), social injustice (85.6%), possibility to become rich (75.6%), ethnic conflicts (84.8%), bureaucracy (65.2%), criminal situation (95.8%), corruption, bribes (92.4%). "It is the image of the state which is in the situation of deep political and economical crisis, spiritually fallen and corrupted, completely alienated from its citizens."[20] The first years of Putin's presidency brought some hope, strengthening the state and providing some stability, however later the situation again became quite poor. According to different recent reviews about 70 per cent of adult population wishes to permanently migrate from Russia to other countries in contrast to about 20 per cent in 2004.

It is obvious that nothing can be built on this ground. That is why the search for the national idea and the corresponding ideology (mythology) is crucially important for Russia.

Notes and References

1. Ernst Cassirer, *The Myth of the State* (New Haven: Yale University Press 1946), 3.
2. Weber investigates religion from the point of view of sociologist, i.e. from the point of view of correlation between religion as a doctrine and social behaviour. See Max Weber, *The Protestant Ethics and the Spirit of Capitalism* (London and Boston: Unwin Hyman 1930).
3. Vladimir Tismaneanu, *Fantasies of Salvation. Democracy, Nationalism, and Myth in Post-Communist Europe* (Princeton, New Jersey: Princeton University Press 1998), 23.
4. The word "myth" is ambivalent as it contains in modern mentality two opposite meanings. It signifies "in everyday parlance either a traditional story commanding special respect or a widely disseminated falsehood." See Andrew Von Hendy, *The Modern Construction of Myth* (Bloomington: Indiana University Press 2001), 278. However, for the purposes of this paper we will take only the positive meaning leaving for the critics to take the negative ones.
5. Although this mythology was not completely unknown for Russian people, it was Peter who turned it into the sort of religion.
6. Apparently, the events of the twentieth century had different causes, among which one of the most obvious was, from ideological point of view, the clash of the intelligentsia's westernized convictions with the traditional worldview of the Russian peasantry.
7. This is apparently not a comprehensive list of factors which are influencing economic life.
8. The proverbs are taken from Dahl's dictionary: "Где царь, там и

правда". The truth is where the Tsar is.

9. "Народ согрешит – царь умолит, а царь согрешит – народ не умолит." If the people make a mistake, the Tsar forgives: if the Tsar makes a mistake the people do not forgive.
10. Later, with the establishment of the serfdom the system of the ownership of the land became more complicated. However it still kept the features of the previous state.
11. See for instance George P. Fedotov, *The Russian Religious Mind*, vol. 1 (Cambridge, Mass.: Harvard University Press 1946), 369-70.
12. Locke defined this state in the following words: "Men living together according to reason, without a common superior on earth, with authority to judge between them, are properly the state of nature." As quoted in B. Russell, *History of Western Philosophy* (London: Routledge, 2nd edition, reprinted in 1994), 602.
13. It is quite important that the contract in this regard from the very beginning was taken as a pure myth to justify an idea rather than any real contract in history of humankind.
14. Apparently the justification of the institution of private property is not a unique feature of modern society; it is known from the history of Sumer, etc., the unique is a combination of these beliefs, ideals and images.
15. The detailed picture of the Soviet mythology is presented see Oleg A. Donskikh "Soviet Mythology and Modern (Post-Soviet) Russia: An Excursion into the Problem of Myth and Human Society," *East Europe Forum. Working Papers Series*, No. 5, Melbourne, Monash University, Slavic section, 1996.
16. I wish to emphasize that this relates to the domain of values rather than to the domain of the social reality as such.
17. Therefore it could not be the topic for scientific studies (I mean not as a myth but as a naturally functioning structure); this provided great difficulties for the development of economic and sociological disciplines.
18. One of the most revealing examples is provided by Alexander Zinoviev, who was the uncompromising critic of the Soviet regime. He became dissident, yet after return to post-Soviet Russia published series of books criticizing the western way of life. In his book Zinoviev describes the collapse of the liberal mythology in favour of the Soviet one. See Alexander Zinoviev, *Russkaya tragediya. Gibel' utopia* (Moscow: Exmo, Algorithm 2003).
19. Michail Gorbachev in his interviews insists that the western leaders, including the president of the United States Bill Clinton promised to dismiss NATO.
20. M. Gorshkov and F. Sheregi, *The Youth of Russia: Sociological Portrait*, chapter 2 (Moscow: RAN 2010).

2

Mythmaking versus Forgetting in the Context of Post-Soviet Ethnic History in the Republic of Buryatiya, late 1980s-Early 2000s

Vsevolod Bashkuev

The *perestroika* years (1985 to 1991) marked a historical watershed in the fortunes of all nations of the Soviet Union. As the bonds of communist ideology weakened, the process of nationalist awakening began all across the country. This phenomenon manifested itself differently from region to region. In some cases, such as the Baltic republics, its ultimate goal was total sovereignty and eventual secession from the USSR, while in the case of others attention was mostly focused on the revival of nationalist ideology and religion. According to some scholars, this trend started after countrywide celebrations of the 1000th anniversary of Russia's revival in 1988.[1]

The process of national awakening began in Buryatiya around 1989 with publications by Buryat scholars on the national question.[2] The movements by nationalist intelligentsia in support of Buryat culture, language and tradition emerged simultaneously. The failure of the official Soviet ideology required urgent and flexible forms of ideology. The idea was to mobilize ethnicity by bringing Buryat communities together in a broad national revival project. Ethno-ideology was expressed through a new kind of national text: a colourful narrative with powerful imagery and broad historical associations serving as symbolic markers of ethnic and cultural collective memory.[3] This narrative, often referred to as "ethno-national discourse," was to a large extent a product of contemporary mythmaking.

The mechanisms of modern mythmaking in the context of Buryat national revival have been thoroughly studied in recent times. The Buryat ethno-nationalist discourse has revealed several features about this new myth. In order to find a solid spiritual foundation for ethnic unity, post-socialist Buryat ideologues, like their counterparts in other national regions, turned to history, traditional culture, folklore and religion. The belief was that the idea of unity was already embedded in the historical and cultural ancestral heritage.

However, after decades of being in oblivion, it needed to be either cleansed of unnecessary borrowings or reconstructed. In this process elements of traditional heritage were modified in accordance with contemporary realities. Hence, modern concepts and practices amalgamated with the "revived" heritage, producing what some scholars call "invented archaic,"[4] and others like Eric Hobsbawm terming it "the invention of traditions."[5] According to Hobsbawm, "inventing traditions ...is essentially a process of formalization and ritualization, characterized by reference to the past..." It happens more frequently during rapid societal transformations, when either old social patterns or institutional carriers and promulgators of "old traditions" can no longer adapt to new conditions or survive in them.[6] Ancient material is often used to reconstruct traditions for novel purposes. As Hobsbawm argues, "A large store of such materials is accumulated in the past of any society and an elaborate language of symbolic practice and communication is always available. Sometimes new traditions could be easily grafted on old ones, sometimes they could be devised by borrowing... from official ritual, symbolism and moral exhortation—religion and princely pomp, folklore and freemasonry..."[7]

The Buryat ethno-national discourse was constructed during such a period of transition when with old Soviet national patterns failing, ethnic elites began to search for new ones. Naturally, past historical events, characters, phenomena of traditional culture, spirituality and ancient mythology were picked up, cleansed of unnecessary (or undesired) details, modified to fit the context of modernity and used as mobilizing frames for the Buryat ethno-national revival. As Darima Amogolonova argues, where possible invented traditions tended to establish an unbreakable connection with the convenient historical past.[8]

The key element here was convenience. Not every historical event, character and phenomenon selected as a basis of new mythmaking was unequivocally positive or inspiring. Tragic moments and traumatic memories of the twentieth century often cemented the gaps in national unity better than ambiguous memories of heroic age. Martyrdom of the Buryat people written in the late 1980s–mid-1990s in certain contexts and situations worked more efficiently than any invented tradition or archaic element in mobilizing strong ethnic Buryat sentiment. At the same time, using this as a mobilizing frame essentially remained part and parcel of Buryat ethno-national discourse. Like other kinds of ethno-political mythmaking it served the goal of advancing the national revivalist project.

Certain moments in the ethnic history of Buryats were deliberately omitted from the ethno-national discourse. Some of them were "inconvenient" for the nascent narrative of new ethnic history since they evoked uncomfortable feelings of shame and confusion. On the other hand, their interpretation could lead to conclusions, contradictory to some recently actualized myths and therefore would be detrimental for the ethno-national mobilizing frames.

This paper aims to describe, analyse and juxtapose modern myths made for the Buryat national revival project and some "inconvenient" historical events or characters deliberately forgotten or omitted from the new historical narrative. For reasons of brevity I will narrow down the scope of this paper only to some contemporary myths that became pivotal in the Buryat ethno-national discourse. One of such invented traditions becoming an ethno-political mythologem is the legitimization of ethnic right over the territory manifested in the primordial origin myth.[9] Another powerful mythologem refers to ethno-genetic origin of Buryats and their connections with the glorious ancient empires of Xiongnu, Turks and Mongols under Genghis Khan. Since the latter association forms probably the most widely discussed and researched issue, I choose to briefly touch upon it.

A rather interesting mythologem was developed by contemporary intellectuals who were regarded as the academic and creative intelligentsia of the Buryat ethno-national discourse. Here, invented tradition encompassed not only relatively recent history and personalities, closely associated with the making of Buryat nation, but delved into the archaic past making it a vivid example of mythmaking in the ethno-national discourse. Contemplating about Buryat ethno-ideology it is impossible to skip Buryat martyrology that reached its climax in an irredentist "split-nation" ideologem, readily utilized in radical ethno-national discourse.

Different from ethno-national mythmaking is a contrasting case of forgetting, for example, the syphilis epidemic among the Buryats in the 1920s. On the eve of Buryat nation-building it was a big problem that required coordinated efforts by medical, educational and executive authorities. Eventually syphilis was eradicated. To fight it the Bolsheviks even had to compromise with the ideological opponents by summoning foreign medical expertise. However, very surprisingly this issue was forgotten and if in the 1920s it received significant attention of the mass media, academics and communist functionaries, after 1930 very few people knew of it. In the period of ethno national discourse formation this problem was almost completely avoided. Slight references to it appeared in the press in a context that was offensive to Buryat nationals and, thus, received angry comments by the ideologues of Buryat nationalist revival. However, there was no objective interpretation of this problem. I argue that this could be a case where deliberate forgetting becomes as an efficient means of ethno-national discourse similar to mythmaking, depending on the situation and the context.

The methodological basis of this paper rests upon several influential works on Buryat ethno-national discourse and national-cultural revival. The invention of tradition as presented by Eric Hobsbawm in the introductory article to his book *The Invention of Tradition* (2003) is actualized in the Buryat ethno-ideological context and interpreted in eloquent terms by the ethnologist Darima Amogolonova and a team of younger scholars in a volume entitled *Buryats: Socio-cultural Practices of the Transition Period* (2008). A slightly different view is presented in Elena Stroganova's monograph *Buryat National-Cultural Revival* (2001). The terms "invented tradition" used by Amogolonova and "invented archaic" used by Stroganova are interchangeable and arise from Hobsbawm's work. Keeping in mind references to antiquity I will prefer using Stroganova's term, while in other contexts the original term is more appropriate. "Mythmaking" will also be used as a collective term though it is essentially much broader and includes many other cases of mythologizing history and culture, from martyrology to historical fiction and speculation.

The term "forgetting" is borrowed from a small but influential article by Paul Connerton "Seven Types of Forgetting," published in *Memory Studies* in 2008.[10] The case of forgetting the epidemic of the 1920s has several forms, as outlined and described by Connerton. Surprisingly, during Buryat nation-building the problem that was so seriously taken by the Bolsheviks during the 1920s underwent severe forms of amnesia including forceful erasure during Stalinist era, with forgetting becoming a part of new identity formation, and forgetting as humiliated silence during the ethno-national revival of the late 1980s–mid-1990s.

In this paper, I argue that forgetting in the course of formation of a new ethno-national discourse is not a new concept and the syphilis epidemic of 1920s may be considered within the discourse of forgetting. Juxtaposition of mythmaking and forgetting, two strategies of ethno-national ideology, is a novel approach to the study of contemporary Buryat ethno-national discourse.

Mythmaking as a Strategy of Buryat Ethno-National Discourse

Geographical Space

Geographical space is probably the most important physical landmark of ethnic and national identity. As such, in the process of identity formation, geographical space is appropriated and legitimized. In the Buryat ethno-national discourse, the legitimization of ethnicity to territorial identity is a feature of national identity. According to Shirab Chimitdorjiev, one of the leading Buryat intellectuals:

> In ancient times Buryat tribes lived on the northern periphery of the Mongolian world in the region named Bargujin-Tukum on both shores of Lake Baikal. Bargujin-Tukum was the centre of the Mongolian-speaking world of Transbaikalia and a historical fatherland of ancient Mongolian-speaking old Buryat tribes of Barguts, Khori-Tumats, Ikires, and so on.[11]

Chimitdorjiev situated Buryat geographical space within the paradigm of spatial identity since antiquity and highlighted the pivotal position of the Baikal region in the Mongolian world. When contemporary geographers speak about the Baikal region they usually mean the entire drainage area of Lake Baikal including northern Mongolia, considered as the cradle of Genghis Khan's great empire. Moreover, the geographical term "Transbaikalia" is somewhat vague compared to "the Mongolian world" as it blends into this collective term. He thus combined both in the generic category "the Mongolian world of Transbaikalia" adding significance to an otherwise unobtrusive region.

Another intellectual leader of Buryat national revival Vasilii Naidakov went further by adding temporal dimensions of the mythologem developed by Chimitdorjiev:

> Buryats are the aboriginal, indigenous people that dwelt around Lake Baikal since the times immemorial in the territory of Cisbaikalia and Transbaikalia. ...And since the territory of the Republic of Buryatiya is situated in Transbaikalia, Buryats, who constitute only a quarter of the entire population of the Republic, a state within the Russian Federation, are the state-forming people, the titular nation that gave a name to the republic... The Buryat population of the Republic of Buryatiya forms the main diaspora of the nation—the people living in their state that is the centre of gravity for all Buryats.[12]

This statement has three interconnected meanings, one of which appeals to antiquity and origins, placing primordial right to own the ancestral land into the mythologized historical context. Another meaning is the present claim to political primacy of the Buryat minority group in the context of the modern state formed out of Buryat ancestral lands and named after the ethnonym "Buryat." The third is based on a futuristic notion since Buryatiya is viewed as a central rallying point for Buryats worldwide, a land where dreams of modern statehood and unity of all Buryats will eventually come true.

As Amogolonova argues, the concept of primordial right to dwell in ancestral lands is a constructed notion, subordinate to the logic of a myth, that is, the myth's ability to process and subject all content, including history. The above-mentioned examples display the continuity and complementarity of ideas and ideological constructs in the Buryat ethno-national discourse. Moreover, characteristic discreteness of a myth allows identifying great past with no less brilliant future using the present as a link.[13] As the mythologems suggest, the primordial right to own the ancestral lands comes from the ancestors of the modern-day Buryats and manifests itself in the restoration of Buryat statehood within the Russian Federation and will eventually lead on to the unification of all Buryats within a state that is built upon their ancestral lands.

Some Buryat national ideologues went so far to create spatial constructions under a vague collective term "Baikal Asia," sometimes expanding it to the entire Central Asian region. Irina Urbanaeva formulated an idea of the Baikal supra-ethnic tradition, rooted in "Baikal Asia," as a part of Central Asia, housing spiritual centres of all races. Idealizing this Central Asian spiritual unity, Urbanaeva came to the conclusion that the nomadic Central Asian tradition spread to the rest of the world all esoteric teachings originating from the Sky.[14] It was not simply a broad spatial expansion of mythologized Buryat geographical space, but an attempt to appropriate the origins of esoteric teachings that praise the Sky, locating them in the area of Buryat settlement. It was an extremely bold and powerful, yet scientifically ambiguous, ideological framework that still attracts intellectuals' attention.

Ethno-genetic Concepts of Buryat History as Mythmaking

The association of modern Buryats with ancient nomads inhabiting the areas around Lake Baikal was the basis of ethnic identity centred round territoriality. The authors of post-Soviet historiography wrote about civilizational unity of the Buryats and peoples of ancient nomadic empires. The period of the Mongolian empire created by Genghis Khan was referred to as the "golden age" of the Buryats. It is this empire that serves as a symbol of order and stability in the writings of contemporary Buryat ideologues. It is much more difficult, though, to give scientific grounds to genetic kinship of Buryats and the ancient population of the region.

The kinship ties of the Buryats to the Xiongnu empire is difficult to prove. There is no consensus on ethnic and linguistic lines and affiliations showing Xiongnu identity. However, acknowledging the complexity of this problem, Buryat scholars prefer articulating the Mongolian element. Some go so far as to state that though the Xiongnu were Turkic in origin their culture was shaped more by ancient tribes of Transbaikalia and Qalqa, i.e. ancestors of the Buryats. Referring to L.N. Gumilev, Alexander Elaev argues that the Xiongnu subjugated Mongolian tribes near Lake Baikal and for a millennium absorbed Mongolian cultural elements to form their own distinct culture.[15] It can be inferred from this viewpoint that the Xiongnu came to the lands inhabited by older tribes (ancestors of the Buryats) and over centuries borrowed so much from them that their own exterior and culture became more Mongolian than anything else. The logic of a myth is manifested here in two ways: a) the historical data are liberally interpreted to mean that the Xiongnu were Mongols; and b) the achievements of the Xiongnu are ascribed to long coexistence with older indigenous tribes.[16]

It is even more challenging to prove kinship of Buryats and Turks of the early medieval Turkic Kaganate. Yet here, like in the previous example, liberal interpretation of the historical information from ancient sources, archaeological findings and contemporary historiography allow comparison of Turkic and Buryat ancestor cults as well as linguistic similarities in old Turkic and old Mongolian languages. A genetic connection traced back to the ancient Mongolian Xianbei cultural environment is traced from the ancient Turks to the Cisbaikalian Buryats. According to Yulia Misyurkeeva, the ethno-genetic myth defines social and cultural boundaries and creates certain mutual group hierarchy based on such opposites as "earlier/later," "indigenous/alien," "conquered/conqueror," etc.

In the context of Buryat ethno-national discourse these opposite ideas tend to acquire political rather than purely cultural or historical connotations. The thesis about the indigenous character of Buryats in the lands of ethnic Buryatiya is a good example. It plays a major role in the politicization of the Buryat ethno-national discourse and demonstrates how ethno-historical and ethno-cultural mythmaking can acquire political connotation. Leaders of the Buryat ethno-national revival insisted that a term "indigenous people" should be used to refer only to Buryat population. As Pavel Varnavskii argues, attempts to legally institutionalize this term would have far-reaching political consequences. The urge of the Buryat ideologues to reserve the indigenous status only for the Buryats had both symbolical and instrumental purposes. It gave space to political preferences of the Buryat population in the republic,[17] primarily, during distribution of governmental posts.

One complex question still remains largely unanswered. It is the question whether the Buryats willingly or voluntarily joined the Russian state in the seventeenth century or they were conquered and colonized. Today, in the wake of the formal celebrations of the 350th anniversary of Buryatiya's voluntary entry into the Russian state, this question may be once again raised as it imbibes a lot of ethno-political sentiment.

Buryat National Intelligentsia as Carriers of Mythmaking

The Buryat national revivalist project is headed by national intellectuals such as scholars, artists, writers, and poets popularly called the scientific and creative intelligentsia. In the early twentieth century a few Buryat intellectuals launched the first wave of Buryat national awakening. At that time Russian Tsarist rule left no hope for progressive Buryat intellectuals to implement their ideas. Thus the first initiatives of national-cultural revival did not have any official recognition.

Contemporary intellectuals leading the post-*perestroika* Buryat national awakening movement in the late 1980s to the mid-1990s continued the legacy of the first Buryat "national democrats." They looked for comparable situations and hoped to find answers to difficult questions of ethno-nationalism. At the same time, they strove to recreate the ideological legacy of the Buryat national democrats in order to pass their knowledge to the Buryat people as well as to other nations. Reference to the past achievements was also gaining solid historical foundation.[18] In mythological terms, the famous Buryat personalities, charismatic intellectuals such as Tsyben Zhamtsarano, Elbeg-Dorji Rinchino, Bazar Baradiin, Gombojab Tsybikov and Agvan Dorjiev belonged to the pantheon of dynamic leadership. The leaders of the new ethno-national revivalist movement were blessed with their intellectual legacy.

Two problems were crucial to the role of the intelligentsia in the process of Buryat ethno-national revivalism. Scholars writing on this topic idealistically portrayed the national intelligentsia as the "brain, soul, and consciousness of the nation," "carrier of humanistic values," leaders of the nation and mediators of a globalized environment of human development and nationalist revival. They closely identified their own search with the goals of nationalist revival without taking into account the disagreement between the educated classes and the common folk in Russia. I.S. Urbanaeva was of the view that the intellectuals knew the way of reforming themselves.[19]

Mythmaking took place on the issue of the origin of the Buryat intellectual movement. An acceptable answer was the establishment of a certain hierarchical relationship between Russian and Buryat intelligentsia based on "who came first" principle. As Stroganova argues, in the conditions of high ethnic sensitivity even an implied suggestion that the national intelligentsia was a product of Russian culture, whose influence the Buryat ideologues tried hard to downplay, would be very painful. In one of his articles, Vasilii Naidakov categorically challenged the view that the intelligentsia was a Russian phenomenon, that it started with A.N. Radishchev or during the reign of Peter the Great, and so on. He contended that the creation of the intelligentsia predated the formation of Russia, probably in ancient Sumer, India or the mythical land Atlantis.[20] According to Naidakov, many large developed nations of Russia had their own national intelligentsia that initially formed around princely courts, khanates, temples and monasteries. Minority populations also had their ancient national cultures, nurtured their own national intelligentsia in the turbulent years of the early twentieth century. However, national calamity of revolution, civil war, and political repression decimated this minority group, putting pressure on the rest of the population. Yet, despite ideological control most representatives of the nationalist intelligentsia stayed loyal to their nationalist goals and exerted influence on the formation of national self-consciousness and mentality. This national intelligentsia headed national revival movements across the former USSR. In Buryatiya, having demonstrated its high moral and intellectual potential, it was highly accepted as the leader of the nationalist movement.[21]

This viewpoint, typical of the ethno-nationalist discourse of the 1990s, reveals the same patterns of mythmaking as the constructed notions legitimizing Buryat right to ancestral land. Associations range over various directions: from distant and mythical past (Atlantis, Sumer, and ancient India) to glorified national intelligentsia of the early twentieth century; victimized and ideologically indoctrinated Soviet intelligentsia to present-day intelligentsia that gives leadership to national revivalist movements and, finally, an intelligentsia that is hoped to lead the nation in the future. There is also an element of martyrdom when the narrative tends to be concerned with the period of repression and ideological pressure. In Stroganova's view, Buryatiya belongs to this cradle of ancient civilizations. Since India is the birthplace of Buddhism which is the official religion in Buryatiya, one notices a continuity of Buddhist tradition across nations and the wisdom of the Buryat intelligentsia are implied. The Sumerian hypothesis was borrowed from the worldview of the Kazakh writer Olzhas Suleimenov, but in Buryat ethno-national discourse it acquired its special character. The idea was that since the Buryat language belongs to the Altaic family and the latter display some genetic proximity to Sumerian, the Buryats must be accepted as the descendants of ancient Sumerians.[22]

In the modern age, such a hypothesis seems to be rather odd. Nevertheless it provides an excellent example how history and myth amalgamated into a single ethno-national discourse aimed at ethnic mobilization of the Buryats. Such examples clearly demonstrate that active mythmaking was an inseparable part of the Buryat ethno-national discourse. To a certain extent it still is, because mythmaking is a readily available, powerful and well-tested means of ethnic mobilization that is convincing and easily comprehensible. It is typical of profound societal transformations such as national-cultural revival and indispensable when convenient interpretations of history and tradition are sought.

However, as the scholar from Irkutsk rightly points out, a principal feature of "inventing traditions" the Buryat way was a rare occurrence of historical falsification. In the works of the ideologues of Buryat national revival a borderline between scientifically proven reconstruction of the past and its liberal modification was often hard to define. So it was overstepped almost unconsciously. This usually happened when attempts of historical reconstruction are consciously politicized to obtain ethno-political dividends.[23]

Epidemics and Mythmaking in Buryat-Mongolia

At this point I will turn to forgetting as another strategy of passing judgments on convenient historical "truths." In the context of Buryat ethno-national discourse forgetting can be viewed as an amplifier of "myth effect" since it helps to omit "inconvenient," "unattractive" chapters of ethnic history. At the same time forgetting is, by itself, a multifaceted phenomenon that plays its independent role in the creation of myths.

In the early 1920s the Bolsheviks embarked on what they conceived as rapid social modernization of non-Russian minorities of Siberia and Central Asia.[24] In doing so they were driven by geopolitical aims, of exporting proletarian revolution to the Orient, and their ideologically predetermined "civilising mission," the essence of which was "acculturation" of what they called "backward" Asian nationalities. Essentially Eurocentric, the Bolshevik programme of social modernization of national minorities aimed at radical improvement of their health, widespread cultural change as well as a reform of tradition and daily living practices according to Marxist-Leninist principles. The European medical, legal, economic and cultural practices were to replace what the Bolsheviks saw as "rudiments of the past" and "superstitions" meaning traditional lifestyle and religion.

This was a providential decision for Buryat-Mongolia. At the dawn of the 1920s her intelligentsia was actively involved in the Bolshevik-style modernization. Several reasons can explain this phenomenon. First of all, the Moscow leadership hoped that Buryat autonomy would become a showcase of successful socialist experiment and an incentive for Asiatic nations to start proletarian revolution.[25] Therefore, the region attracted special attention of Kremlin. Second, this thoroughly geopolitical goal was inseparable from the necessity to transform the traditional Buryat nomadic society into a "truly socialist nation." As mentioned above, this required rapid reform in the way the Bolsheviks saw fit. Years of war had shattered the already weak pre-revolutionary socio-economic infrastructure. Wartime damage was especially heavy in healthcare and education. Civilian population suffered enormously under various "governments" and "partisans," who often were simply outlaws disguising themselves as "revolutionaries." A significant part of the Buryat population migrated south to Mongolia. It is not surprising that old "scourge of the aborigines," such as syphilis, flourished on such appalling conditions.

The Bolsheviks ascribed prevalence of syphilis among Buryats to their terrible living conditions resulting from past discrimination by the imperial authorities. In their opinion syphilis was synonymous to poverty and backwardness. In remote areas of Buryat-Mongolia where no "modern" urban centres existed in the 1920s, syphilis was unanimously considered as endemic (non-venereal). The Soviet doctors described syphilis in Buryat-Mongolia as "household infection." In their view, the "cultural barbarianism" of nomadic life was the main factor in the spread of syphilis. Merely "acculturating" them without radically transforming their traditional lifestyle would not eradicate syphilis. So, cultural reform was to become part of the anti-syphilis campaign. In the Bolshevik strategy eradication of syphilis and sanitation of the indigenous population were impossible without systematic measures in education, sanitation, culture and large-scale implementation of the European biomedicine. Officials of the Buryat-Mongolian Commissariat of Public Health were anxious about long-term consequences of syphilis for the future generations. They warned that considering the low birth rate among the Buryat-Mongols (about 17.6 per 1000 compared to 45.5 per 1000 among the Russians in 1924),[26] widespread cases of syphilis could result in the extinction of the Buryats, or, at least, lead to a dramatic decrease in their numbers.[27] That scenario would be absolutely contrary to the Bolshevik vision of the socialist Buryat nation that was being showcased by the Communists.

To confront and solve this problem, the leadership of the Buryat-Mongolian republic with full support from Moscow embarked on a long and costly but, in the final analysis, effective anti-syphilis campaign. It comprised several stages, including thorough medical examinations of the population and painstaking research on the origins, characteristics, consequences, and treatment of syphilis of the Buryats and Russians. The results did not bring about simply scientific or clinical changes but a completely new thinking about the ways in which syphilis could be treated and thereby affect social transformation in different areas of Buryat-Mongolia.[28] Furthermore, the campaign involved vigorous propaganda in the field of personal hygiene as well as social education. The People's Commissariat of Public Health of the RSFSR summoned foreign experts, primarily from Germany. [29]

The character of the anti-syphilis campaign in Buryat-Mongolia was a well conceived ideological mobilizing frame that portrayed syphilis as the enemy and dark legacy of Tsarism. This implies that in the early Soviet social modernization discourse, the Bolshevik ideology combined with European concepts of hygiene. The combination of geopolitical aspirations and ideological designs with goals of social eugenics points to the fact that the Bolsheviks theorized of a utopian eugenics programme that would produce sane human beings over decades. At the same time, despite its obvious overall utopianism, once implemented, elements of this programme had far-reaching social and demographic effects. The anti-syphilis campaign in Buryat-Mongolia definitely was one such element that had high socio-historical importance for the emergent Buryat nation.

Forgetting the 1920 Epidemic in the Context of Post-Soviet Buryat Historiography: An Interpretation

The epidemic of the 1920s and the campaign against it for a long time was a taboo in Soviet and post-Soviet Buryat historiography. Probably the only work giving this problem due attention is a recent monograph by D. Batoev, N. Demkova and S. Batoev.[30]

Even though richly documented in the archives, the syphilis problem is only described in connection with professional activities of the first Buryat People's Commissar of Health A.T. Trubacheev. In most post-Soviet books on the history of Buryatiya this problem is euphemistically named "problem of social diseases." For example, the influential book by Alexander Elaev only mentions that "epidemics, venereal diseases, tuberculosis and high infant mortality were a scourge of Buryat population" and this refers to the imperial period, not the years of active nation-building after 1923.[31] Other ideologues of Buryat national revival refuted any references to "degrading Buryat-Mongolian people." For instance, Shirab Chimitdorjiev wrote:

> People never forget their spiritual and cultural heritage, their outstanding representatives… People reject persons lacking memory. Unfortunately, the "oblivious" can be easily met nowadays. Do these persons really think that before 1917 Buryat-Mongols were depopulating, wild and completely illiterate people?… Perhaps, one should prove with facts and show them that they are absolutely wrong…"[32]

While Chimitdorjiev wrote about the pre-revolutionary period, the problem of social diseases originated even earlier. Soviet specialists talked about a period from several decades to several centuries. Yet, this problem escaped the attention of the ideologues of Buryat national movement.

In my view, this situation can be explained differently. Based on the assumption that forgetting is not always related to failure, remembering and commemorating a virtue, Paul Connerton outlined in his "Seven Types of Forgetting" (2008) seven basic types of forgetting that human history displayed through the ages. He explains how "repressive erasure" appears in the history of totalitarian regimes, though it was known long before the twentieth century.[33] The anti-syphilis campaign took place in Buryatiya right before Stalin's great social experiments of collectivization and industrialization; subsequently there were open discussions of the most acute problems of national minorities, such as venereal diseases and several data about syphilis in Buryatiya were published. Syphilis was viewed as an obstacle to progress, especially on the road to communism, not as a legacy of the past, as was the case earlier. Gradually it became a taboo to speak about the subject. Memories of anti-syphilis campaign and the international cooperation to eradicate social diseases were totally suppressed.

Another type of forgetting is as follows:

> ...There is, for instance, the forgetting of the details of grandparents' lives that are not transmitted to grandchildren whose knowledge about grandparents might in no way conduce to, but rather detract from, the effective implementation of their present intentions... Not to forget might...provoke too much cognitive dissonance: better to consign some things to a shadow world...What is allowed to be forgotten provides living space for present projects.[34]

This type of forgetting is explained much by the mechanism of interaction between mythmaking and forgetting in the context of a new Buryat identity. In the context of ethno-national revival mythmaking defied weakness and imperfections as it gave a powerful boost to national consciousness and formation of a new Buryat identity. Memories about past sickness were allowed to be forgotten. Thus, forgetting freed living space and glorified the past and by associating it with the present it had an optimistic future.

Connerton's final analysis about forgetting fits the context of Buryat ethno-national discourse, i.e. "forgetting as humiliated silence." As the author puts it:

> This type of forgetting is certainly not solely, and may in large part be not at all, a matter of overt activity on the part of state apparatus. It is manifest in a widespread pattern of behaviour in civil society, and it is covert, unmarked and unacknowledged. Its most salient feature is humiliated silence.[35]

Many social problems that were a taboo in the Soviet socialist discourse prevented balanced discussion of health-related problems like syphilis even during the *perestroika* years. References to this problem immediately became political issues that threatened carefully constructed mythologems as part of the new ethno-national discourse. Silence and forgetting were more convenient exercises.

Conclusions

The Buryat national revival of the late twentieth century was a period full of promises, experimentation, conflict and compromise. It left a solid legacy that will, hopefully, reappear in new revivalist projects in the future. Mythmaking was an inseparable part of this process. It played a role in the consolidation of Buryat conscience. Many "invented traditions" came to stay as popular festivals, gatherings, holidays, and anniversaries.

Conscious and deliberate historical falsifications were not typical of "inventing traditions" in the Buryat way. The results were often dubious or debatable, and many contradictions were rectified as a result of collective scrutiny. Mythmaking as a strategy of national unification in the context of Buryat national revival proved effective. Forgetting formed an important part of the Buryat ethno-national discourse. In this context it was more a defensive strategy provoked by repressed memory. The most important problem of forgetting in this particular context is absence of historical lessons learnt from the described events of the 1920s.

Notes and References

1. E.A. Stroganova, *Buryatskoe natsional'no-kul'turnoe vozrozhdenie* (The national-cultural revival of the Buryats) (Moscow-Irkutsk: Natalis 2001), 58.
2. Stroganova, *Buryatskoe national*, 60.
3. D.D. Amogolonova, S.D. Batomunkuev, P.K. Varnavskii, V.V. Kuklina, Y.S. Misyurkeeva, M.M. Sodnompilova, *Buryaty: sotsiokul'turnye praktiki perekhodnogo perioda* (Buryats: socio-cultural practices of the transition period) (Irkutsk: SibPoligrafServis 2008), 14.
4. Stroganova, *Buryatskoe national*, 75-77.
5. Amogolonova et al,*Buryaty*, 16-17.
6. Eric Hobsbawm, Introduction to *The Invention of Tradition*, E. Hobsbawm and T. Ranger (eds) (Cambridge: Cambridge University Press 2003), 4-5.
7. Hobsbawm, Introduction to *The Invention of Tradition*, 6.
8. Amogolonova et al,*Buryaty*, 17.
9. Amogolonova et al,*Buryaty*, 18.
10. Paul Connerton, "Seven Types of Forgetting," *Memory Studies* 1, no. 59 (2008): 59-71.
11. S.B. Chimitdorjiev, *Buryat-mongoly: istoriya i sovremennost'* (The Buryat-Mongols: history and modernity) (Ulan-Ude 2000), 36.
12. V.T. Naidakov, "Problemy natsional'no-kul'turnogo razvitiya narodov

Respubliki Buryatiya (Problems of national-cultural development of the peoples of the Republic of Buryatiya)," *Buryatiya* (4 April 1997): 2.

13. Amogolonova et al,*Buryaty*, 19.
14. See for instance, I.S. Urbanaeva, *Chelovek u Baikala i mir Tsentral'noi Azii: filosofiya istorii* (A man by Lake Baikal and the world of Central Asia: philosophy of history) (Ulan-Ude 1995) and *Mongols'kii mir: chelovecheskoe litso istorii* (The Mongolian world: the human face of history) (Ulan-Ude 1992), 4-5, 54-55.
15. A.A. Elaev, *Buriatskii narod: stanovlenie, razvitie, samoopredelenie* (The making, development and self-determination of the Buryat people) (Moscow 2000), 29-30.
16. Amogolonova et al,*Buryaty*, 215-16.
17. Amogolonova et al,87-9.
18. Stroganova, *Buryatskoe national*, 68-9.
19. Stroganova, *Buryatskoe national*, 70.
20. V.T. Naidakov, "O sushchnosti i istorii intelligentsii (v poryadke diskussii)," in *Natsional'naya intelligentsiya, dukhovenstvo i problemy sotsial'nogo, natsional'nogo vozrozhdeniya narodov Respubliki Buryatiya* (National intelligentsia, clergy and the problems of social and national revival of the peoples of Buryatiya) (Ulan-Ude 1995), 6-7.
21. Naidakov, "O sushchnosti," 7-10.
22. Stroganova, *Buryatskoe national*, 72.
23. Stroganova, *Buryatskoe national*, 76.
24. For example, a detailed analysis of Soviet-style modernization of healthcare in Kazakhstan was done by Paula Michaels. See Paula A. Michaels, *Curative Powers: Medicine and Empire in Stalin's Central Asia* (Pittsburgh, PA: University of Pittsburgh Press 2003).
25. This idea is thoroughly discussed in Elaev, *Buriatskii narod*, 188.
26. Report by the representative of the Buryat-Mongolian ASSR at the All-Union Central Executive Committee Chenkirov and Deputy People's Commissar of Health of the BMASSR Zhinkin to the Department of Maternity and Childhood Protection of the People's Commissariat of Health of the RSFSR, 10 March 1926, *NARB*, R-661/1b/1/154.
27. V.N. Zhinkin, "Toward the question of the spread of syphilis in Buryatiya, 1926," *Natsional'nyi Arkhiv Respubliki Buryatiya* (National Archive of the Republic of Buryatiya), *NARB*, R-661/1b/1/
28. Francine Hirsch, *Empire of Nations: Ethnographic Knowledge and the Making of the Soviet Union* (Ithaca: Cornell University Press 2005), 245.
29. For an excellent rendering of history of the 1928 Soviet-German expedition, see Susan G. Solomon, "The Soviet-German Syphilis Expedition to Buriat-Mongolia, 1928: Scientific Research on National Minorities," *Slavic Review* 52, no. 2 (1993): 204-32.
30. D.B. Batoev, N.P. Demkova, S.D. Batoev, *Pervyi narkom Andrei Timofeevich Trubacheev v istorii zdravookhraneniya Buryatii* (The First

People's Commissar Andrei Timofeevich Trubacheev in the history of healthcare in Buryatiya) (Ulan-Ude 2009).

31. Elaev, *Buriatskii narod*, 204.
32. S.B. Chimitdorjiev, *Buryat-Mongoly: istoriya i sovremennost' Razdum'ya mongoloveda* (Ulan-Ude 2000), 4.
33. Connerton, "Seven Types of Forgetting," 60.
34. Connerton, "Seven Types of Forgetting," 63.
35. Connerton, "Seven Types of Forgetting," 67.

3

Soviet Deportation Policy of Nomadic Population in 1920–1930: The Case of Kyrgyzstan

Zuhra Altymyshova

In the era of Soviet rule the ideological restrictions imposed on historical scholarship made it difficult to study and draw correct conclusions about the development of the states under the Soviet Union. However, with the fall of the Soviet Union it is now possible to objectively research history. This has led to the emergence of new opinions and findings. Kyrgyz history during the Soviet period is a very important part of Kyrgyz history. Soviet Government was established in the region of what is now Kyrgyzstan in the middle of 1918. The Autonomous Soviet Socialist Republic of Turkestan was founded in 1918 and Kara Kyrgyz Autonomous Region was formed within the Russian Soviet Federative Socialist Republic (RSFSR) on 14 October 1924. On 25 May 1925 the official name of Kara Kyrgyz Autonomous Region was changed to Kyrgyz Autonomous Region. It was renamed Kyrgyz Autonomous Soviet Socialist Republic on the 1February 1926.

The policy of class differentiation was implemented from the beginning of Soviet rule. The responsibility of the communist party in Central Asia was to carry out a policy of class differentiation among local dwellers. At first, it was necessary to identify the upper classes among people so that class struggle could be carried out against them according to logic of the revolution. The terms "class" or "fighting against the class" were not clear for the majority of Kyrgyz people. Traditionally differentiation within villages was minimum; it the class concept that was to be realized since the propaganda around the revolution had influenced it.[1] The measures taken against wealthy people were also implemented in the Kyrgyz Autonomous Soviet Socialist Republic as a part of the USSR in the early Soviet years.

One of the methods to eliminate their influence in society was to deport some of them to other republics of the Soviet Union. Deportation was aimed at strengthening Sovietization by elimination of public, political, economic and tribal influences of the people. They were accused of participation in the Basmachi Movement, for slavery and carrying out anti-Soviet propaganda and of inciting tribal confrontation.

This article deals with the deportation process and deportee's life during exile. Apart from literature related to the problem, archival documents are of special interest for the study. Elderly people who had been exiled when they were children were interviewed. Their recollections, facts, and evidences during the interview were of great interest. Oral narratives have been checked and compared with official documents.

Deportation of *Bay-Manaps*

In Kyrgyzstan, wealthy people such as the *bay-manaps* were forced to leave their homeland in 1920–30. The word *baylik* in Kyrgyz language means "wealth," but the word "*bay*" besides meaning "rich" also means the man who has wealth and lives prosperously. The *manap* is a social category that ruled the Kyrgyzs before the Soviet period; they had a right to judge members of their tribe. There was a head *manap* of tribal consolidations in the northern part Kyrgyzstan and all the other *manaps* obeyed him. But South Kyrgyzstan did not have the social category of the *manap*.[2] Generally most of the *manaps* were tribal leaders. The *manaps* solved important political and economic problems. Before Soviet rule, the Russian empire relied on the *manaps* when ruling the region and the *manaps* were elected to local services. A famous ethnographer S.M. Abramzon indicated that very literate people were *manaps* till 1930 and most of them worked as teacher. Also between 1920 and 1930 there were *manaps* who worked in Soviet government bodies together with communists.[3]

The word *kulak* was used as a political term between 1920 and '30 and it meant well-off peasants who exploited people.[4] In general, everybody who was against collectivization was regarded as a "*kulak*." Rich people and *manaps* were considered to be *kulak* in Kyrgyzstan and this conception of the rich and *manap* changed to *kulak* and "exploiter." The terms *bay-manap* have been used together in literature since Soviet period. Resettling *bay-manaps* from Kyrgyzstan to other Soviet republics began in 1927. However, after studying archival and oral materials closely, it was discovered that the decision to resettle some of the most influential *manaps* was carried out from 1921 to 1927. But what happened to them is unknown even today.

Central Asian Bureau of Central Committee CPSU (b) adopted a resolution on the *manaps* on 27 January 1927. The aim of the resolution was to resettle the *manaps* who were leading group and tribal factionalism in the party and Soviet administration and to confiscate their property. CPSU(b) Kyrgyz Regional Committee was given responsibility to agitate people against the *manaps*.[5] Central Committee of the CPSU(b) Executive Office Kyrgyz District Committee came to the decision (27 March 1927) to deport 21 *bay-manaps* and this decision was realized in the spring of that year.[6] Unfortunately, there is no accurate information about the *bay-manaps*' destiny. We can only surmise that they had been exiled to Orenburg. The oral history materials given by Saparbek Musin[7] (September 2008) during his interview led to the discovery of this problem. The deported *bay-manaps*' life in exile was described in Ziyash Bektenov's in the work entitled *Memories about my Contemporaries*.[8]

Twenty-one *bay-manaps* were deported to the Halturino city of the region Kirov which was near Moscow. Since the climate of the Halturino was too cold, some people complained to Moscow, and then they were resettled to Ordo of the Orol region in Kazakhstan which was a desert and hot place. Being unable to endure such a hot place, they were again moved to Orenburg in 1929. In 1930 the *bay-manaps* were permitted to come to Chimkent city, later to Jambil city, then to Frunze in 1931. But they were not permitted to go back to the place where they were born. The *bay-manaps* had been living in Frunze till 1935 but they were under surveillance. Only in 1935 they could go back to their home villages. Among the 21 deported people in 1927 the story of Abdylda Musin is worth telling. He opened a butcher shop, sold meat and national drink *bozo*, he also went to Moscow, brought tea and goods then resold them to the Kazaks during exile. In this way he took care of the other *bay-manaps*.

On the 4 February 1929 Kyrgyz Soviet Socialist Autonomous Republic Central Executive Committee and Council of People's Commissars adopted a resolution on resettling from Naryn, Talas, Karakol and Osh region 44 families of *bay-manaps* who were regarded as obstacles to Sovietization and collectivization of the village because of their economic and social influence. In the resolution the *bay-manaps* were charged with agitating against Soviet Government, intensifying quarrel between tribes, creating obstacles to cultural and economic progress of the republic. They were deported to Orenburg city, Russia. According to a letter written by the deported Kyrgyz to

M. Kalinin who was Chairman of USSR Central Executive Committee (13 June 1929) the deported families experienced great hardship in Orenburg due to the lack of proper living conditions and unemployment.

The letter says:

> According to the resolution of Kyrgyz Soviet Socialist Autonomous Republic Central Executive Committee,[9] we were to be given land after resettling to Orenburg. But Central Executive Committee of Orenburg refused to give us land…These days we have nothing to live and in spite of the fact that we aren't guilty, about 200 people are experiencing a hard life in a foreign city. After confiscating our property, we had nothing to live on. There are too many unemployed people in Orenburg. There is nowhere to work and also we don't have any opportunity to work for a day. That's why if we stay in Orenburg we can die of hunger. [10]

Before the Soviet rule, most of the Kyrgyz, especially *bay-manaps*, used to keep cattle in high mountain areas and led a nomadic life. Therefore, city life of Orenburg seemed to be alien for their life style; in addition, the majority of the deported Kyrgyz had no qualification for any kind of job. At the end of the letter they requested permission to come back to their Motherland.[11] Were the Kyrgyzs requests carried out? M. Kalinin sent the letter to the Kyrgyz Soviet Socialist Autonomous Republic Central Executive Committee Frunze (the previous capital of Kyrgyzstan) on 19 June 1929. However, according to oral information their requests were not carried out; the deported people from Kyrgyzstan to Orenburg were allowed to return to their home country only after three years. Among the deportees were musician as Boogachy Jakypbekov and poet Kazybek Mambeteminov. Some old people died during the exile to Orenburg.

The state policy of "eradication of the kulaks as a class" was strengthened during forced collectivization of agriculture. The policy of eradication of the *kulaks* as a class was reflected in the decision of Central Committee VKP (b): "About rate of collectivization and steps to help for the state collective farm construction" dated 5 January 1930.[12] The programme started at the beginning of 1930. This meant alienation of land of the affluent, private property and their subsequent deportation. On 29 June 1931 Central Asian Bureau of the Central Committee CPSU(b) confirmed and sent the directive "About deportation of kulak families," and on the 21 July 1931 they sent instruction on carrying out deportation to the Kyrgyz District Committee of CPSU (b). According to the instruction 6 thousand families from Central Asia were to be exiled to the Ukraine and the North Caucasus; 700 families from Kyrgyzstan were among them. It was forbidden to confiscate property and deport *bays* or *kulaks* whose family members served in the Red Army, worked at the industrial enterprises and were highly skilled and experts working at factories, on construction of power stations and who took part in struggle against the Basmachi Movement. Also old people over 65, invalids and pregnant women without voluntary desire were not subjected to deportation.[13]

The *Kulaks* and Collectivization

Kulaks were divided into 3 categories.

- Category 1: Active part of counterrevolutionary *bay-kulaks*, members of the active counterrevolutionary organizations.
- Category 2: The richest *bays* and *kulaks* (*manaps*, tribal leaders, influential clergy).
- Category 3: All the other *bay-kulak's* families that could not be connected with the first two categories by their own signs.

The head of the family of the first category was sentenced to be sent to concentration camp, and their families were to be sent outside Kyrgyzstan at the same time with deported *kulaks* and their families of the 2nd category. The 2nd category representatives who were actively struggling against actions of Soviet rule were deported with families outside of republic and the rest were deported from the region where they had lived to specially allocated places inside Kyrgyzstan. The third category people were left in the same region but deported outside their villages, settlements.[14]

On August 1931, people who were accused of being *kulaks* from Isyk-Kul, Chuy and Naryn districts of Kyrgyzstan were exiled to the Ukraine. There were also Ukrainians from Kyrgyzstan among them but most of them were the Kyrgyzs. The people deported to Ukraine were given status as *labour settler* or *special settler.* There were human losses because of illness, famine and different climate. Deported people from Kyrgyzstan lived in Chalbasy Skadovsk region, Nikolayev district in the Ukraine (present Vinogradov village, Styuripinsk region, Kherson district). Chalbasy is situated 30 km from south to the Black Sea, 60 km from north to the Dnepr. From 1935 the economic life of the Kyrgyz improved. Deported people from

Kyrgyzstan were mainly engaged in agriculture. A *kollhoz* (collective farm) named *Noviy Put'* was organized in Chalbasy and farming area and cattle was allocated to this *kolkhoz*. Besides agriculture and cattle-breeding they worked in sewing and were occupied with shoe craft.[15] Children's home and school were opened in Chalbasy. According to the famous Kyrgyz musician Asankan Jumakmatov several children were taken to the children's home so that they would not be under their parents' influence.[16] While the Kyrgyzs were living in the Ukraine, they did not forget their national traditions. Children studied at the school and were educated in communism, but their parents taught them Kyrgyz tradition at home.[17]

The next deportation campaign was implemented in 1932. On 11 April 1932 Kyrgyz Regional Executive Bureau of CPSU (b) adopted a resolution of resettling *kulaks*' farms from south of Kyrgyzstan. Unfortunately, I was not able to find the original decision of 11 April 1932, in State Archives of Kyrgyzstan. So there are not many opportunities to research deportation problems of the *kulaks* from Kyrgyzstan in 1932 properly because of the lack of materials. Only in U. Asanbayev's work, it was indicated that 66 *kulaks*' farms from the region Aravan-Bura and 146 from the region Bazar Korgon were resettled. [18] They were probably deported to Ukraine, though this is a problem that would require additional research.

Some literate Kyrgyzs were victims of political repression carried out in 1938. It has been confirmed through interviews and documentary evidence from the State Derjavniy Archive of Kherson district in the Ukraine that 63 people were arrested from February to October in 1938. They were accused of organizing counter-revolutionary group that intended to disorganize kolkhoz *Noviy Put'* and renewal of old *bay-manap* rights and tribal influence,[19] carrying out anti-Soviet propaganda against activities of Soviet Government and *kolkhoz* system while they were living in the Ukraine in 1931-38.[20] Sixty one of them were sentenced to be shot, only two them (Baybosunov Arun and Januzarov Israil) were sentenced to be exiled for ten years. All of them were involved in criminal liability and were punished without sufficient evidence. Majority of the repressed Kyrgyzs and others were however rehabilitated in 1970.[21]

In August 1941during the World War II, 18-60 year old Kyrgyzs and Ukrainians from Kyrgyzstan were taken to fight in the war. Chalbasy was occupied by the Germans from August 1941 to November 1943. Before 1945, all the Kyrgyz returned to Motherland in different years. The Ukrainians who were deported with the Kyrgyz returned to Kyrgyzstan, too.

A special Republican and Regional Commissions were organized for carrying out displacing of the *kulaks*. *Troikas* were organized and consisted of representatives of the Kyrgyz Central Executive Committee, chairman of the Regional Executive Committee and the representatives of Department of State Political Administration (OGPU). *Troika* confirmed lists of people who were subjected to deportation and they made the last decision.

The results of my research show the instructions of the communist party on the deportation of the *kulaks* were implemented by breach of the laws by the local authorities themselves. For example, rules concerned with the government documents were not kept because of economic reason, but because of private and tribal relationship. As a result not only the wealthy category but middle class and the poor also suffered from this campaign due to different reasons. Some people were deported or their property confiscated because they were the others' opponent or due to the tribal relationships. People holding different Soviet state posts were exposed to deportation too. Sometimes the number of *kulaks* increased in some places. For example, in 1931 according to an order from the Centre 25 families from Jety-Oguz region had to be exiled. But *troika* added 5 more families so it became 30.[22] On determining of the *kulaks* to be deported different factors like personal hostility, mutual relations, squaring of accounts played an important role.[23] Ayish Akebay Kyzy, who was deported to the Ukraine and lived there until 1937, said that her father was only a middle peasant. Her elder sister married a man whom she did not love. Soon she declared that she would not live with her husband and came back to father's home. Then the brother of her husband who worked as a local Soviet leader accused the bride's father of being a *kulak* and all family members were exiled to Ukraine.[24]

Unbearable difficulties had risen as a result of quick and forcible collectivization and class struggle aggravation resulted in emigration to China and joining Basmachi groups voluntarily. Due to many breaches of laws and dispossession of the peasants who were not as rich as a *kulak*, people became disgruntled so much so that some people living near the state border moved to China with their families to show their protest at the end of 1920s. Another form of protest was the intensification of the Basmachi Movement at the end of the 1920 especially, in the south of Kyrgyzstan. Deportation process was accompanied with widespread governmental agitation against the *bay-manaps*. Regardless of this, analysis of archival documents shows that ordinary people did not take active part in this campaign work and demanded the release of people who were arrested. For example in1929, when Chokobay Sasyev was being arrested, the villagers wanted him to be released in the village Bel-Ayil in the region Osh. They said "either you will release Sasyev or you will arrest all of us."[25] In some places deportation campaign of ordinary people was regarded as detrimental for tribes.[26] There are reports of some local Soviet workers defending arrested people. There were measures taken for handing out properties of deported people to the poor in order to mitigate the people's opinion of the deportation campaign. However, such kind of attempts did not yield any results.[27] There was resolution of deporting farms of people who had 400 or more cattle in the nomadic region, who had 300 or more cattle in the semi-nomadic region. But this rule was not always kept. The property of exiled *kulaks* were completely confiscated like home, *yurta* (nomad's tend), stable, store house, trees, dishes, furniture, carpet, blanket, thick felt, mat, plough, harrow, wheel barrow.[28] Those confiscated items which were of historical and ethnographical value, were given to Central Frunze Museum.[29] Confiscated houses were used as a cultural-social office.

Conclusion

It is obvious that the Soviet Government solved its economic problem at the expense of stocks and properties confiscated from these people and also, they composed main stocks of *kolkhozes*. For example, to realize collectivization in 1927, 12 cartels[30] for cattle-breeding or agriculture were founded in the regions where deported *bay-manaps* lived before.[31] In 1929, 48 *kolkhozes* were organized based on confiscated property from deportees.[32] Oral records have corroborated with archival documents. According to government documents and historical works published during Soviet period, deportations of *bay-manaps* were regarded as "fair decision taken to release workers from exploitation and it assists to fortify Soviet's power." However, it cannot be disclaimed that deportation caused much suffer and deprivation of property.

It has been established that there was discrimination to deportee's children for many years during the Soviet period by the state organizations and higher educational institutions. It is a fact that most of the deportees lost their parents and close relatives in the exile. This campaign had negative consequences on Kyrgyz society from the moral, economic and cultural point that can be seen even today. New generations still do not know what happened to their deported grandparents.

Notes and References

1. I.S. Boljurova., "Vostok delo tonkoe; Pravda o manapah," *Respublica* 39 (1992).
2. *Kyrgyz Taryhy* (Bishkek 2003), 280.
3. S.M. Abramzon "Sovremennoe manapstvo v Kirgizii," *Sovetskaya Etnographia* 3-4 (1931): 47-54.
4. S.I. Ojegov, *Slovar Russkogo yazyka* (Moscow 1964), 303; K. Yudahin, *Oruscha—Kyrgyzcha sozduk* (Bishkek 2000), 314.
5. I. Ibraimov. *Borba partorganizatsii Kirgizii za podgotovku usloviy sploshnoy kollektivizatsii selskogo hozyastva 1926-1930 gg* (Frunze 1967), 121-22.
6. The Central State Archive of Political Documents of the Kyrgyz Republic, fund. 10, list. 1, file 97:122-23; The Central State Archive of the Kyrgyz Republic, fund. 21, list.15, file 39: 105, 238.
7. Saparbek Musin was born in Ordo in 1927. His father Abdylda Musin was among deported *manaps* in 1927.
8. Ziyash Bektenov, *Memories about My Contemporaries* (Bishkek 1992).
9. According to 7 point of the decision taken on the 4 February 1929 in Kyrgyz Soviet Socialist Autonomous Republic Central Executive Committee, the deportees were expected to be given plot in the region of RSFSR by fund of resettling colonization.
10. The Central State Archive of the Kyrgyz Republic, fund. 21, list 4, file 16: 53.
11. The Central State Archive of the Kyrgyz Republic, fund. 21, list 4, file16: 53-4.
12. J.S. Baktigulov, *Sosyalisticheskoe preobrazovaniye Kirgizskogo ayila (1928-1940)* (Frunze 1978), 135; *Izmeneniye sosyalno-classovoy struktury naseleniye Kirgizii v gody stroitelstva i uprochenie sosyalizma, (1917-1961)* (Frunze 1989), 146; The Central State Archive of Political Documents of the Kyrgyz Republic, fund.10, list 1, file 245: 2-8.
13. The Central State Archive of Political Documents of the Kyrgyz Republic, fund.10, list 1, file 363: 72-6.
14. The Central State Archive of Political Documents of the Kyrgyz Republic, fund.10, list 1, file 245: 2-3.
15. Interview with Asankul Alymbaev (1927-2007).
16. Interview with Asankan Jumakmatov (1923-2008).
17. Interviews with Asankul Alymbaev (1927-2007), Asankan Jumakmatov (1923-2008).
18. U. Asanbayev, *Sovety Kirgizii v borbe za stroitelstvo sotsializma (1929-1932 gg.)* (Frunze1968), 67.
19. The Derjavniy Archive of Kherson District (Ukraine), fund. 4033, list 5, file 233:100.

20. The Derjavniy Archive of Kherson District (Ukraine), fund. 4033, list 5, file 233: 217.
21. The Derjavniy Archive of Herson District (Ukraine), fund. 4033, list 4, file 584: 28.
22. The Central State Archive of Political Documents of the Kyrgyz Republic, fund.10, list1, file 363: 87.
23. A. Jumanaliev, *Politicheskaya istoriya Kyrgyzstana* (Bishkek 2005), 251.
24. Interview with Ayish Akebay Kyzy (1923).
25. *Sovetskaya Kirgizia*, no. 237. 17 October 1929.
26. The Central State Archive of Political Documents of the Kyrgyz Republic, fund. 10, list 1, file 201: 29.
27. D. Junushaliev, T. Koychuev, V. Ploskih and G. Junushalieva, "Traybalizm: Istoki i sostoyanie," in *Suverenniy Kirgizstan: Problemy traditsii I sosyalnoy selostnosti* (Bishkek 1999), 92.
28. The Central State Archive of the Kyrgyz Republic, fund. 21, list 15, file 39: 53.
29. The Central State Archive of the Kyrgyz Republic, fund. 21, list 15 file 44: 1; KR SD BMA, fund. 10, list 1, file104: 1-2.
30. *Artel* (Russian: артéль) is a general term for various cooperative associations. (From en.wikipedia.org).
31. The Central State Archive of the Kyrgyz Republic, fund. 21, list 15, file 39: 115-16.
32. D. Malabayev, *Ukrepleniye Sovetov Kirgizii v period stroitelstva sosyalizma* (Frunze 1969), 187.

4

The Soviet Republics in the Post-Soviet Space: Buryatiya in Search of Sovereignty

Marina N. Baldano, Svetlana V. Baldano

In the early 1990s, the need to comprehend the outcomes of ethno-national development during the Soviet era and formulate guidelines for the future was the task of undisputed priority to the Buryat national elite. Numerous meetings and congresses were held, research and journalistic texts appeared, resolutions and official documents were adopted, as well as parties and movements formed. The issues as regards native language as well as culture were discussed, and new versions of national history were constructed. The discussions on preservation, revival and development of national culture organically shifted to the debate on issues of statehood and nature of power.

The sources of such debates can be traced back to the end of the nineteenth and early twentieth centuries, when Buryatiya embarked on the path of modernization. The formation of the first generation of European-educated Buryat intellectuals was the most important constituent part of this process. This small but extremely active section with great intellectual potential made a huge contribution in laying the foundations of modern culture and social consciousness of the Buryat society.

The Buryat intellectuals not just in terpreted, constructed and studied the history of their people, but also worked out the plans for its preservation and further development. Actually, the discourse was about conscious and purposeful transformation of the tribal environment into a uniform cultural and political community that would successfully fit in with the processes of modernization. Essentially, it was a political project in which the great significance was attached to the formation of their own statehood, both as a necessary attribute and prerequisite for creating a nation.

Original Paper in Russian: *Sovetskie respubliki na postsovetskom prostranstve: Buryatiya v poiskakh suvreniteta*—Translated by Susmita Bhattacharya

"Creating a state in order to create a nation," was a widespread and intelligent strategy in the nineteenth century. The specific feature of "Pan-Mongolism" was that the nation was supposed to be formed on the basis of Mongolian historical and cultural commonality, for a long time resolutely divided by the state boundaries. Accordingly, the plan to create their own state inevitably presupposed large-scale geopolitical steps forward in the entire region. Some of such plan makers, by this time as politicians and statesmen, tried to put them into practice.

Even during the Soviet times, while giving special attention to involve the old intelligentsia in building socialism, the Soviet state, simultaneously, addressed another important issue—to train up the new intelligentsia. According to T. Martin, the well-known researcher on Soviet nationality policy, the crux of Soviet nationality policy was a contradiction between the support for nation-building on the one hand, and the need for centralization on the other.[1] The Soviet authorities encouraged ethnic particularism and *korenizatsiya* or *korenization*[2]—to build up administrative staff from the representatives of local ethnic groups.

The communist party defined a clear political line with regard to various categories of intellectuals. There was serious stratification among the Buryat intellectuals in two directions. The personalities united around the nationalist goals belonged to the first one. Around the second one rallied the Sovietized intelligentsia, supporters of the Soviet power and who mostly came from the toilers section of the Buryat population.

Buryat Nation

In the early 1990s, the plans of the early twentieth century were studied and discussed in the circles of Buryat intelligentsia. As a social group most prone to introspection, it turned to the historical experience, striving to find analogues of the evolved situation in the past, "making a start from the searches of the predecessors, to find ways to solve the urgent problems of today."[3]

During this period, the formation of a new state was going on in Russia and Boris Yeltsin's call in August 1990 to the autonomous republics to "swallow" as much sovereignty as they could, stimulated the vigorous political plans including those based on ethnic terms. In Buryatiya, as in the entire post-Soviet space, the key issue was sovereignty of the nation, most often not in the civic but in its ethnic sense. From here directly followed the question on the status of statehood of Buryatiya and/or the national status of the Buryat people. There were strong representations among a section of the adherents of "ethno-nation" that it cannot and should not be confined within the existing state boundaries. The representatives of the government as well as of the opposition parties and movements that had been formed took part in the struggle for the constitution, sovereignty, the place of Buryatiya within the country as well as in the world and its political system.

The centrifugal trends grew in the country. The decline of the authority of the communist party led to the weakening of power at the Centre. In the absence of guarantees of actual political, legal, military, economic, social, cultural and ecological security from the USSR as the supreme guarantor of the rights and freedoms of its constituent nations, the most politicized among them turned to political struggle for implementation of their right to national self-determination and, ultimately, for national sovereignty.

For realization of sovereignty and interests of Russia, the authority of the RSFSR came into conflict with the union bodies like the Supreme Soviet and the President of the USSR. In an effort to enlist the support or at least "expectant neutrality" from the governments of the republics within the RSFSR, it took the manifestations of ethno-political self-assertion and sovereignization of the former Russian autonomies quite favourably.[4] The processes that were going on in Russia, did not take long to have an impact on the political situation in Buryatiya. In September 1990, the republic's authorities started working out the draft of the Federal Treaty between the Buryat ASSR and RSFSR and the draft of the Declaration on State Sovereignty. Publications appeared in the press criticizing the status of the autonomous republic, the competence of which was being determined by those "from above" and the opportunities for effective use and development of her potential was restricted. Persistently were heard the propositions to decline the status of autonomous republic and adopt a Declaration on State Sovereignty. In the course of the debate different viewpoints came to light: from total denial to recognition of state sovereignty of the Republic, right up to the cessation of Buryatiya from the Federation.[5]

On 8 October 1990, the Supreme Soviet of the Buryat Autonomous Soviet Socialist Republic adopted the Declaration on State Sovereignty, which consolidated the new conceptual propositions concerning democracy, state power in the republic, territorial integrity, economic self-sufficiency, ecological security and national-cultural development of the peoples of Buryatiya.[6] The creators of the document, in an attempt to get away from selecting a specific people-cum-ethnos as the bearer of sovereignty, defined the people as a whole set of nations (ethnic groups),—the multinational people of Buryatiya. It was proclaimed in the Declaration that "The citizens of the Republic of all nationalities constitute the people of the Buryat SSR. The people of Buryatiya are the bearer of sovereignty and the sole source of state authority in the Republic."[7]

The Supreme Soviet of the Republic, taking into account the changes that had taken place, made a number of amendments to the text of the constitution in force (1978), aiming at consolidation and development of democratic reforms. In the Regulation of the Presidium of the Supreme Soviet of the Buryat SSR, approved in April 1991, its role and responsibility was increased. Some of the commissions of the Supreme Soviet of the Republic were transformed into committees. The Supreme Council undertook the basic regulatory functions that were previously prerogative of the *obkom*[8] of the party. Buryatiya started legalizing its status as a parliamentary republic.

While adopting these resolutions, not all the possible consequences, including the negative ones, were fully taken into account. The resolution of sovereignization adopted by the Supreme Soviet in conditions of euphoria neither fully reflected the mood of the entire population nor really came to be the democratic will of the people. The bulk of the population of the country as well as the republic advocated for preservation of the existing state structure of the country—the USSR. The proclamation of sovereignty was not done as a result of mature political and economic conditions of the republic, but under the influence of the political events that were taking place in the country in the early 1990s.[9]

The ruling elite were not politically consolidated; its division along the ideological and ethno-clan criteria was visible in the struggle for power that affected its ability to pursue its own independent political and economic policies in the republic and at the federal level. One of the reasons behind the division of the ruling elite on the basis of nationality was the removal of all obstacles and moral constraints in the struggle for political dominance. The rivalry of the ethnically oriented power groups, which were compelled to periodically appeal to the people, to certain extent had its impact on the inter-ethnic relations that until this time were in a state of relative peace.

The objective need for taking measures to restore the lost cultural traditions and language, which was not dictated by the political declarations, ripened and promoted the enhancement of activities of the Buryat population. In the spring of 1990 on the initiative of a group of scientific and creative intelligentsia the Public Council for coordination of revival and development of language, culture, traditions and customs of the Buryat people was formed. The first

All-Buryat Congress for consolidation and spiritual rebirth of the nation was opened on 22 February 1991 in Ulan-Ude.

At the Congress the main paper was presented by Professor T.M. Mikhailov (BION SO AN SSSR[10]), in which he analysed the history of the Buryat people, its culture, statehood, as well as the problems of the Buryat at the current phase. The Congress established the All-Buryat Association for Cultural Development (BACD/VARK[11]) and made an appeal to the Buryat people.

The significance of the First All-Buryat Congress was that the issues related to nationality policy, history, Buryat culture, language, which accumulated over many decades, were for the first time discussed collectively. And the establishment of the BACD/VARK in the form of a social organization became the first practical step towards consolidation of the Buryat people and revival of their culture, as well as a platform for debates, which identified both the cultural and political issues.

In 1992, the Supreme Soviet of the Republic adopted the Law "On languages of the people of the Republic of Buryatiya," which gave Buryat the status of state language along with Russian. The law guaranteed the right of all the peoples of Buryatiya to preserve their native language and to create conditions for its study and development.

With the proclamation of sovereignty Buryatiya started acquiring its own symbols of statehood, which, despite the changes that took place, reflected the ethnic specificity of the republic. In 1992, by a resolution of the Supreme Soviet of the Republic the national flag of the Republic of Buryatiya was approved. The adoption of the flag was preceded by a competition, the process and results of which were widely covered by the national mass media. The flag, which portrays a rectangular width with blue, yellow and white colours, with the state symbol "Soyombo" close to the flag-pole in the form of an image of the moon, the circle of the sun above it and the hearth with three tongues of flames, got reflection of the Buryat ethnic motifs and symbols of friendship among the peoples of the Republic of Buryatiya.

Federal Reforms and Buryatiya

The peak of development of federalism in Russia came during the years from 1990 to 1993. The tragic events of October 1993, when the Supreme Soviet of the Russian Federation was disbanded with the help of the armed forces, marked the end of dual power in Russia. There are many ways to evaluate it, but for the sake of justice we must admit that the end of the dual power initiated the restoration of governability by the state. This also coincided with the changes of political orientations of the vast majority of regional leaders. They already had firm foothold in their republics and did not need the support of the ethnic movements, considering them more as potential competitors rather than allies. The regional leaders started relying on the federal authorities in displacing the ethnic movements from the political stage. Some got posts in the regional bodies of power, some got chunks of privatized assets, and the others, being deprived of financial, and more importantly of information support of the regional authority, lost their influence in no time. Stratification took place among the intellectual elite: some joined politics and business, and others reverted back to science and academic world.

Radical legal reform of legislation in the sphere of state structure of the Russian Federation was carried out during this period. The Constitution Commission completed its work on the draft of new constitution of the Buryat SSR by the early 1994. In the course of nation-wide discussion of the draft of the Basic Law, more than one thousand comments and suggestions were received, reflecting different approaches to its separate clauses. However, the majority agreed on the general principles. The parties and movements exerted pressure for adopting one or the other formulas.

On 22 February 1994 as a result of the clause-by-clause discussion of the draft, the Supreme Soviet adopted the new constitution of the republic, which was based on the values of democracy, principle of separation of powers, strong guarantees of rights and freedoms of the citizens. The Constitution of 1994 consolidated the fundamental changes in public and state system of Buryatiya, which became a presidential republic. It was aimed at promoting market relations and consolidated the parity of all forms of ownership.

The contours of the new Russian state as a federation were basically affirmed by the mid-1990s. However, the lack of clear and definite prospects of federalism among the leaders engendered contradictory policy. Flirtation and concessions of the Centre during demarcation of subjects of joint jurisdiction as well as plenary powers to the regional authorities brought the existence of the state as an integrated whole to a dangerous point, and the Chechen war of 1994-96 exposed the problems in the sphere of ethnic relations.

In 1996, the work on the Concept of State Nationality Policy of the Russian Federation was completed, which was approved on 15 June 1996 by Decree no. 909 of the President of Russia. The work on the draft of the Republic's Concept of National Policy began at the initiative of the People's Khural[12] of Buryatiya. The variations of the draft were published for discussion in the republic's newspaper *Buryatiya*. The draft was discussed at the parliamentary hearings in the People's Khural with the participation of the representatives from social organizations. Being opponents, the groups of the draft designers persisted in their opposing views on the matters affecting the interests of the Buryat and Russian segments of the population. The reflection of their standpoint in the mass media had an impact on the ethno-political situation in the republic.

Buryat Identity and Inter ethnic Relations

The First Congress of the Peoples of Buryatiya was held on 4-5 April 1997 in Ulan-Ude. At the Congress, more than 500 delegates were elected from all the regions of the republic, government bodies, national-cultural associations, political parties and public organizations. According to the official documents, the basic idea of the Congress was to map out measures to strengthen the inter-ethnic harmony in the republic based on the study of ethnic problems.

The keynote speech was delivered by L. Potapov, the President of Buryatiya, elucidating at length the historical and contemporary aspects of interethnic relations.[13] Prof. V. Naidakov, the director of the Buryat Institute of Social Sciences, SB RAS, tried to express his stance on the understanding of what was meant by the "peoples of the Republic of Buryatiya." The question was raised about the criterion for categorizing people as indigenous or non-indigenous. The delegates and invitees, speaking at the Congress, discussed the problems of inter-ethnic relations, economic and social development of the republic. The Congress made recommendations and circulated it to the citizens of the Republic of Buryatiya.

After the Congress, the government of the republic adopted the Concept of Nationality Policy and established the Council of Nationalities for organizing dialogue between the ethnic communities and government bodies.

The Second All-Buryat Congress was held in March 1996. A paper entitled "Ob osnovnykh polozheniyakh kontseptsii vozroshdeniya buryatskogo naroda, ego kul'tury" (On the basic propositions of the concept of revival of Buryat people and their culture) was presented by Professor Yu. B. Randalov, the head of the department BISS SB RAS. At the Congress, the idea to form the *Kongress buryatskogo naroda* (KBN)[14] was made public, which coincided with the formation of the *Russkaya obschina*[15] of the Republic of Buryatiya that was the regional branch of the *Kongress russkikh obschin*[16] of D. Rogozin. This organization made the protection of civil rights of the Russian population of the republic as its main objective. S. Pronin, the Director General of the OJSC[17] "Amta," became the chairman of the "Russian Community" and V. Yakovlev, the secretary.

At the inaugural (constituent) Congress the KBN/CBP adopted the Decree, elected its governing bodies, and E.M. Egorov became its president. The Council of the Congress included well-known public figures and representatives of the state authorities as well as the local self-governments. The KBN/CBP set the followings as their main task: to protect the rights and interests of the Buryat people, consolidate and unify the efforts of all organizations for resolving their urgent problems, to strengthen inter-ethnic relations and friendship among the peoples, participate in the work of the government bodies and develop international relations.[18]

The 1990s became the renaissance of religious life in the spaces of former USSR. This process took place in Buryatiya*, along with Russia as a whole. The process of revival of Buddhism was marked by a surge of interest and growth of religiosity among the population of Buryatiya as well as by the restoration of old Buddhist temples and construction of new ones. In the early 1990s alone more than 20 *datsans*[19] were opened in the republic and the Buddhist Institute, "Dashi Choinkhorlin," which trained more than 100 students, the future priests-Lamas was opened under the *Tsentral'noe Dukhovnoe Upravlenie Buddistov* (Ts.DUB) (Central Spiritual Board of the Buddhists). The international and interregional connections between TsDUB and other Buddhist organizations became more active. Close contact was established with the fourteenth Dalai Lama, the spiritual and political leader of the Buddhist school of Gelugpa and the entire Tibetan Buddhism, whose visits to Buryatiya in these years contributed to the growth of authority and popularity of this religion among the population. Along with the Buddhist religious organizations different cultural, educational and social organizations, such as *Obschestvo druzei Tibeta*,[20] *Fondy Agvana Dorzhieva*,[21] *Akhalar*,[22] *Buddiissko-khristianskii soyuz*[23] and others started to emerge.

The political activities of the Buddhist clergy, who was trying to participate in public policy and activities of the representational government bodies, increased. In the year of 1989, for the first time in the entire history of Buddhism in Russia, Did-Hambo-Lama Erdem Tsybikzhapov was elected to the Supreme Soviet of the RSFSR, and Did-Hambo-Lama Dorzhezhap Markhaev, as a member of the Constitutional Assembly of the Russian Federation. In 1994, Lama

Fedor Samaev and Lama Matvei Rabdanov were elected in the People's Khural of the Republic of Buryatiya. In the1996 elections Lama Nimazhap Ilyukhinov was a candidate for the State Duma of the Federal Assembly of the Russian Federation. The political activities of the Buddhist priests/monks did not evoke any sharp condemnation; rather the general people of the Republic evaluated this development in different ways. Against the backdrop of the revival of Buddhism in Buryatiya, which became a part of culture, national psychology and way of life of the Buryat people, such unconventional forms of activities of individual lamas were considered by the public as a manifestation of activity of the Buddhist church and growth of its popularity.

Conclusion

The development of political milieu in the early 1990s went on by leaps and bounds, as there emerged the opportunity to speak about the problems accumulated over decades. The processes that were going on in Buryatiya led to the construction of foundations of political culture: the pre-election campaign, while not taking the character of confrontation, assumed ideological shades; the ideological concepts were adopted as weapon, and platforms were created for discussions.

It was a great step forward. However, the 2000s were characterized by unification of the constitutions and construction of vertical power. Putin's formula was perhaps justified considering the abstract interest in preserving the integrity of the Russian state. However, it went beyond the original scope as a result of levelling the role of the majority of the federal subjects including the ethnic ones. The contradictions were driven inwards. The recent developments in the Manezhnaya Square showed that the matter is not resolved and it needs to be addressed in a cardinal manner.

Notes and References

1. T. Martin, *The Affirmative Action Empire: Nations and Nationalism in the Soviet Union*, 1923-1939 (Ithaca and London: Cornell University Press 2001), 112.
2. The term means "Nativization" or "indigenization," or literally, "putting down roots." It was the early Soviet nationality policy promoted mostly in the 1920s, but with a continuing legacy in later years. The term derives. from the Russian term *korennoe naselenie* ("root population") for indigenous nationals—translator's note.

3. E.A. Stroganova, *Buryatskoe natsional'no-kul'turnoe vozrozhdenie* (Moscow and Irkutsk: Natalis, 2001), 68.
4. A.R. Aklaev, "Etnopoliticheskie konflikty v Rossiiskoi Federatsii i problemy legitimnosti vlasti," *Suverenitet i etnicheskoe samosoznanie: ideologiya i praktika* (Moscow: IEA Ran 1995), 20.
5. O.V. Khyshiktuev, *Konstitutsionno-pravovoi satus Respubliki Buryatiya* (Ulan Ude 1996), 76-7.
6. Sessiya Verkhovnogo Soveta Buryatskoi ASSR, Stenograficheskii otchet (Ulan Ude 1990), 27.
7. Khyshiktuev, *Konstitutsionno-pravovoi*, 80.
8. In Russian *Oblastnoi komitet* or *Oblast* means Regional Committee—translator's note.
9. A.A. Elaev, *Buryatiya: put'kavtonomii i gosudarstvennosti* (Moscow: Antal 1994), 102.
10. In Russian: *Buryatskii Institut Obschestvennykh Nauk, Sibirskoe Otdelenie Rossiiskoi Akedemii Nauk.* In English: BISS SB RAS, which stands for Buryat Institute of Social Sciences of the *Siberian Branch* of Russian Academy of Sciences—translator's note.
11. In Russian *Vseburyatskaya assotsiatsia razvitiya kul'tury*—translator's note.
12. The unicameral legislature of that Republic—translator's note.
13. *Materialyl s'ezda narodov Respubliki Buryatiya* (Ulan Ude 1997), 7.
14. Congress of the Buryat People or CBP—translator's note.
15. Russian Community—translator's note.
16. Congress of Russian Communities—translator's note.
17. Open Joint Stock Company—translator's note.
18. E.M. Egorov, "O kongresse buryatskogo naroda," *Sovremennoe polozhenie buryatskogo naroda i perspektivy ego razvitiya*, no. 2, Ulan Ude (1996): 19.
19. Buddhist monastery or temple—translator's note.
20. Society of the Friends of Tibet—translator's note.
21. Aghvan Dorzhiev Foundations—translator's note.
22. Buddhist ecological organization—translator's note.
23. Buddhist-Christian Alliance—translator's note.

History and Historiography

5

Twenty Years After: New Histories Emerging

Isenbike Togan

It is known that one of the great historians of Central Asia is V.V. Barthold whose works were published in the form of "collected works" during the Soviet era. These works were used in studies both in and outside of the USSR. He created a heritage in the study of the area, and thus had followers like V. Minorsky or Yuri Bregel, the former translating and annotating old texts of geography and the latter doing textual study as well as interpretative history. Needless to say manuals prepared by Bregel have become indispensable for research.[1] Another associate and a follower of Barthold was Zeki Velidi Togan to whose works there was no easy access in the Soviet Union. In the West and in Turkey where he lived he left his imprint by his discovery of manuscripts and his historical analysis. Although his studies on historical manuscripts appeared in different western languages, his studies on historical analysis which are mostly in book form appeared in Turkish. In his work he tried to understand Central Asian history within a system; hence these studies address different systemic problems related to Central Asian history. [2]

The only study that deals with this aspect of his studies is Lawrence Krader's article in which he compares the analyses of Radloff, Barthold and Zeki Velidi Togan. Zeki Velidi Togan's approach to Central Asian history has been adopted and transmitted by scholars who came to Istanbul to study with him.[3] Among others the then young scholars Franz Schurmann, Martin Dickson and Maso Mori stand out. The latter two have transmitted this outlook and understanding to their students. This outlook consists of a spirit looking from inside and reaching to the outside from there. In other words within this outlook study of local sources in their original form is imminent. Translations can be consulted if there are annotations. The understanding reached on the basis of local sources then needs to be put in juxtaposition with studies by contemporary scholars both local and global. In this case western scholarship and knowledge of western languages is also a must. In this way a student of Central Asian history can come to conclusions based on current methodologies in western scholarship. Zeki Velidi Togan elucidated these ideas in his work on methodology (*Tarihte Usul*) and applied them in his general history (*Umumi Türk Tarihine Giriş*) and in other works and studies. In its present form this approach requires a strong basis for textual study and use of all the tools of western scholarship.

At one time Princeton University where Martin Dickson used to teach was the center of such an outlook; now it is Chicago where John Woods and Cornell Fleischer, both students of Martin Dickson continue to pass on this outlook to their students. Their students like Evrim Binbas and Judith Pfeifer have become young scholars contributing to the history and historiography of the region. Such developments were not so prevalent during the Soviet times; Barthold's followers were mostly living outside; but Russian scholars like Akimushkin, Klyashtorny, Trepavlov kept the tradition alive.

After the dissolution of the Soviet Union this former trend was not continued so much; instead a new trend with a direct connection to the new situation emerged. One of the two different approaches within this trend was to find ways to discover oneself. In this connection the earlier Soviet historiography which emphasized modes of production in a nameless fashion was slowly replaced by a perception of history which would lead to self identification that could find and did find a parallel niche in western scholarship in social sciences concentrating on identity.

In a second approach, contextualization of the historical material as well as of historical developments became apparent. It is in this connection that history writing could serve as a guide for political culture. Just before the formation of the Soviet Union studies of this sort had shown a great interest in the political movements. Both in independent and autonomous republics the liberation movements of the early twentieth century found ardent researchers who were able to put these developments into a historical context. For instance in Bashkortostan the liberation movement at the beginning of the twentieth century was contextualized in terms of three agreements (compromises). The agreement with Ivan Grozny was seen a forerunner of these developments leading to the agreements with the Reds / Bolsheviks in 19 February 1919. Then, as a follow up to these developments, the agreements with Yeltsin can be put into a context. As we can see, this kind of historiography, this approach of contextualization which is still an issue—tough in different ways—could serve as a guide for political culture.

Trends

Trying to look back to the last two decades it has been observed that within the first decade the driving force among the independent as well as the autonomous republics was this great urge to assert oneself this took several shades. First there were studies on the prominent cultural heroes of the past; the nameless past was thus restored in a new fashion of biographical studies. Studies on Mir Jakub Dulatov, Ahmed Baitursun from Kazakhstan were accompanied by the publication of their collected works. The same attitude could be found in the cases of Mukhtar Auezov who was a prominent writer during the Soviet period, Behbudi in Uzbekistan and Makhdum Quli in Turkmenistan who were studied through biographical works. Special studies were devoted in Bashkortostan to three émigré scholars: Zeki Velidi Togan, Abdülkadir İnan and Galimjan Tagan.

Secondly the earlier emphasis on production and land as means of production shifted towards specific state traditions. Both of these issues, land and state traditions, functioned within the borders of the territorial state as understood in the present day. The emphasis on state traditions was to be seen both in independent and autonomous republics as could be observed in the examples from Uzbekistan and Bashkortostan.

In the second decade we witness another shift, this time from concerns on state and land to people. The first decade saw people being brought to the forefront but only as individual heroes of the pen or in clan, tribe affiliations. This trend continued well into the second decade. In the last ten years we also witnessed an emphasis on people becoming apparent in studies on local history. But the development emphasizing cultural identity is more pronounced in the studies in a fashion which shows individuals reaching out as cultural entities beyond the borders of the territorial state. This is especially apparent in the intellectual traditions like Jadidism or Sufism. While there are also studies showing an interest in "overseas" Uzbeks, Kyrgyz or Bashkorts, the most striking ones are those studies which emphasize social or political organizations with a sense of cultural belonging.[4]

The aim of this article is to examine two works from Turkmenistan (2009) and Azerbaijan (2010), both of which have been written by well known historians from respective academies, for a deeper understanding of the above mentioned connection. Although their audience is not the same, in terms of their outlook they represent a similar approach in looking at history in terms of a larger context, the first one in terms of Turkmen people and the second more in terms of socio-political organization of people. Both of the works deal with coexistence rather then domination, better to say, they are not under the shadow of theories of dominance as Colin Renfrew describes them.[5]

Contexts and Connections

The first is a textbook from Turkmenistan titled *Türkmenistanyň Taryhy*. X-XVI asyrlar, the author of which is Oraz Polat Ekäyev. Dealing with the tenth to sixteenth centuries the book is designed for the 8th graders.[6] Reading this book, what is most striking for a person and historian from Turkey is the fact that the history of the Turkic peoples dating this period is regarded as Turkmen history. In other words Turkmen identity provides an umbrella under which the Karakhanids as well as the Ottomans are regarded as Turkmen states. In essence this is exactly what we do in Turkey by looking at these states as Turkish or Turkic. In the introduction the author says that the history of Turkmen people will be studied in three stages, namely the periods of formation, expansion and occupation by foreign rule. The first stage (12–91) consists of states and tribes, for instance of the Ghaznevids and the Oghuz Turkmen tribes which later contributed to the formation of the Seljukids. The second stage (114–224) represents the expansion/spread of the Turkmen into Asia Minor, Iran, Caucasus and India and the states established there. The Turkmen who explored these new regions established first principalities and named them after the person who was the founder. The Ottomans are thus to be found under this category. They are called "Osmanlı türkmenleri döwleti (the state of the Ottoman Turkmens)" (165) appearing as one of the *many* Turkmen principalities.

The third stage (92–101 and 225–60) on the other hand, is described as the period under which the Turkmen—while still living in their fatherland—lost their independent state due to different reasons. We know that during this period the Turkmen were under the occupation of the Mongols, the Timurids, the Shaibanids and the Safavids. Here the vision differs from Turkey where these states are regarded as part of the history of the Turkic peoples. In Turkey Chingis Khan's state and empire is included into the pantheon with the claim that there were many Turkic elements within the army of conquest. Timurids and the Shaibanids are regarded as part of the pantheon because they were Turkic speaking and contributed to the development of Turkic and Turko-Islamic culture. The Turkmen, on the other hand, apparently exclude Turkic people whose language carries elements from Kipchaq. In Turkey only the Safavids are excluded from the pantheon. It is acknowledged that Shah Ismail was of Turkmen origin but the country is seen as Iranian. While apparently here the Ottoman heritage has influenced the present outlook, Shia and tribalism were not part of the Ottoman heritage and they have not been so under the historiography of the nation state. The Turkmen panthcon includes the non-Muslim Oghuz and their ancestors like the Karakhanids but excludes the Chingisids.

In Ekäyev's work in the first stage the Oghuz are described in detail as the main actors of deliberation. Whereas in western literature they would be referred to as a loose tribal confederation,[7] here they are regarded as "*Beyik oguz türkmen döwleti*/ the Greate Oghuz Turkmen State." They are seen as half nomadic and half sedentary and their way of governance is deliberation. They regard their social organization as consisting of 24 tribes (*taypa, boy*) and *they administer the state as a union of tribes* (21) which are divided into two groups, the well known *bozok* and the *üçok*. The tribal leaders are called "*beg*" and they are elected from the aristocracy of these tribes. The notion that the tribal confederation is regarded as a state and as part of the historical heritage and that they were governed by deliberation are also quite foreign to historiography in Turkey, where only states in the western sense are recognized, thanks also to the Ottoman heritage. Moreover in this Turkmen version these tribal groups are described with their handicraft activities which are geared to trade and they have been placed within the network of trade routes. Additionally the role of women in forging alliances is emphasized contributing to the sense of "people." Within that framework Osman the Karakhanid ruler is mentioned as son-in-law. In Turkey's historiography however, Ottoman sultans are never regarded as sons-in-law. They are seen as only wife takers. In other words Turkmen historiography seems to be less patriarchal and patrilineal.

In this account expansion is not described as something which is in the nature of the Turkmen (37). They also do not seem to be keen to bring "order" to others. On the contrary a reason is given for their dislocation. The migration leading to expansion is explained as the result of the western Karakhanid Sultan's policy who did not want them to settle in their earlier homeland. The Seljukids under Chaghri and Tughrul Begs were in the region of Transoxiana. The Karakhanid Ilek Nasr wanted to drive them out of this region as they were getting stronger. This is how they contacted the western Karakhanid ruler Bughra Khan who sounded favourable but encouraged them to go away to the west. It is to be noted here that high school students of Turkmenistan are learning about the western expansion and conquest in a different tone and manner than students in Turkey. Later the incident in which the Oghuz tribes took Sultan Sanjar prisoner is given quite a lengthy account (72–9) where not only the Sultan's but more so the Oghuz tribes' perspective is given. The whole incident is not portrayed as the "unruly Oghuz" rising against the Sultan. On the contrary their plight is described in detail. Especially descriptions as to how the Oghuz wanted to settle the affair and showed their willingness by placing their womenfolk and children to the front lines and offered 7 *batman* silver are striking. Sultan Sanjar seeing the situation wanted to forgive them but his advisers and close associates were against such a settlement. Finally after a number of other incidents when Sultan Sanjar's army went into a battle, the Oghuz tribes who were exasperated by that time, defeated the Sultan's army and took him prisoner.

This approach of giving a double sided perspective is also seen in the account on the Khwarezmshahs (Köneürgenç) who were conquered by Chingis Khan's army. First the Khwarezmshah state is put in context in terms of its location at the crossroads north-south and east-west trade. With that contextualization we understand the root of the problem for both sides. It was important for both parties to have a hold of this region. Moreover, Khwarazmshah Muhammed's mother is portrayed as the Kipchaq Khan Jahankishi's daughter who is described as a person with power and a penchant to rule. The state is described as being in a situation of dual administration (91). Seen from Khwarazm, Chingis Khan seems to emerge at about this time and the Khwarazmshah sent first an envoy which was well received by Chingis Khan. This was a moment when the two sides were collecting information about each other. When the envoys and the traders whom Chingis Khan sent were killed at Ortar, Chingis Khan requested that the killers be punished. However Khwarazmshah Muhammad was confident of his own superiority and valued himself highly thinking that he was the pillar of Islam. He was dreaming of conquering China and becoming the ruler of the most powerful empire of the world. Khwarazmshah being far detached from the reality killed the envoy of Chingis Khan who was sent with the request that the people involved in the Ortar incident be punished. The author says "with this act Khawarazmshah put himself into the position of a person who was not informed and who acts impulsively (ukypsyz, başarnyksyz: 93). In contrast to him Chingis Khan was well informed about the situation in the Köneürgench state. He was well aware of the dual administration as well as of the unskillful governance of the Khwarezmshah (94). Thus the later victory of Chingis Khan is portrayed by the author not as an onslaught, barbarian incursion, as ruthlessness of Chingis Khan, but as shortsightedness of the Khwaramshah ruler who in fact was a ruler of Turkmen people.

In the above study an extensive analysis and account of Orazpolat Egäyew's work has been attempted because a portrayal of historical events from two sides by weighing the actions against one another is not something we find in textbooks in Turkey or anywhere. Furthermore in this way there is no "enemy"—most often presented as the initiator of political action in Turkish historiography—but developments in history. The same attitude is prevalent in the 3rd section of the book dealing with the sixteenth century. There the Turkmen people are portrayed under foreign occupation; however we get a glimpse of the foreign rule in an indirect way. The Turkmen are not present there; the actors in the third part of the book are foreign rulers. Towards the end of the sixteenth century the author starts to speak of the Turkmen, preparing the reader for the seventeenth and eighteenth centuries when they emerge again under the Khanate of Khiva and Bukhara.

What is interesting is that the second book under discussion also has a broad outlook which is regional. It carries the title: *Selcuqilerden Osmanlılara*. The author of the book, Shahin Mustafayev does not deal with linguistic or cultural identity but socio-political make up within a region placed within the triangle of eastern Turkey, Azerbaijan and Iran.[8] S. Mustafayev sees a development of a political culture accompanied by a literary language. The argument is that this political culture is different from central and western Turkey where Ottoman norms took root. Turkish historiography looks at history from the vantage point of rising Ottomans. All the other principalities are regarded either as friends, allies who contributed to the rise of the Ottoman state or as adversaries who stood in the way. Mustafayev, on the other hand, sees a twosome development. The Ottomans achieved political centralization on the basis of incorporation of the conquered non-Muslim populations. The Turkmen tribes in eastern Turkey, on the other hand, were excluded as the beneficiaries of the new state. More importantly, they were also not keen to be administered by a centralized state structure. This conflict which looks like center-periphery struggle when seen from the Ottoman point of view is actually a competition between two systems. Until now, historians have analysed historical conflicts in eastern Turkey as occurring between individual rulers. However Mustafayev, on the basis of a long time research shows that these conflicts were ongoing (Yıldırım/Qadi Burhan al-Din, Mehmed II/Uzun Hasan; Selim the Grim/Shah Ismail; the Qaramanli have also been included into this struggle) and that these struggles ended with the victory of the Ottomans only in the west and not in fact in the east. Shahin

Mustafayev sees a cultural difference here which he calls "as a conflict between east and west" the west being western Anatolia and the Balkans, and the east, eastern Turkey and Azerbaijan. He sees the political culture belonging to this eastern ethno-cultural milieu as emanating from nomadic culture which has its roots in nomadism, in conflict and in competition with the sedentary culture. In this view the latter is inclusive and is thus of mixed population, and without the fetters of tribal affiliations is open to change and can easily adopt centralization. In contrast the eastern culture is exclusive, nomadic, tribal and conservative. It is not geared to centralization and domination but to coexistence.

Actually the argument of the book can also be extended to Central Asia, and in fact will also be useful for analysing the struggle between Temür and Bayezid at the beginning of the fourteenth century. This study also enables us to understand the bifurcation of the literary language into Ottoman and Chagatai in later centuries. Until that time there was one literary language defined as ancient and middle Turkic. This bifurcation set the trend in the following centuries.

Conclusions

These two studies offer a fresh look at the developments on the western parts of Central Asia (Transoxiana, Khorasan, Iran, Azerbaijan and eastern Turkey). Their importance arises from their unique position where they interpret history with local dynamics but in terms of a methodology that is universal. Although these works do not explore new manuscripts and bring forth new textual evidence to the foreground, they provide us with a new interpretation emanating from local circumstances where people play a significant role. It is to be noted that they emphasize coexistence rather than dominance. They apply this outlook also to the Ottomans whom they regard as one among many. It seems that coexistence emphasized by both authors is part of the cultural heritage where there were many principalities and khanates at about the same time, but it is also part of the present culture of Central Asia with the republics.

New textual evidence interwoven into a new outlook is also emerging. It is the old style textual study coupled with new interpretations. B.Babadjanov and G. Sultonova both from Uzbekistan seem to carry the torch in these kinds of studies. While Babadjanov unearths new manuscripts in relation to Sufi studies, there is also a lot of excitement and praise for his recent study on the Khoqand khanate. Gulchekhra Sultonova, a young scholar is dealing with commercial relations between Bukhara and the outside world. She is deciphering letters between different rulers.

The studies mentioned above cannot be generalized for the whole region. But they do provide us with clues of new interpretations for the future.

Notes and References

1. Most of the earlier works mentioned in this article are to be found in the bibliography published by Yuri Bregel in three volumes. See Yuri Bregel, *Bibliography of Islamic Central Asia*, 3 vols. (Bloomington, Ind.: Research Institute for Inner Asian Studies, Indiana University 1995).
2. Zeki Velidi Togan's collected works will appear in Turkish among İşbankası Kültür Yayınları, Istanbul and in Russian in Ufa, Bashkortostan (RF).
3. Lawrence Krader, "Feudalism and the Tatar Polity of the Middle Ages," *Comparative Studies in Society and Culture* 1(1958): 76–99.
4. Busra Ersanli conceptualizes these trends as "politics of culture/culture of politics" in her article.
5. Colin Renfrew, Introduction in *Peer Polity Interaction and Socio-political Change*, Colin Renfrew and John F. Cherry (eds.) Cambridge: Cambridge University Press 1986), 1–18.
6. Oraz Polat Ekäyev, *Türkmenistanyň Taryhy*. X.-XVI asyrlar (Asgabat: Türkmen döwlet nesryat gullugy 2009).
7. For confederations regarded as stemming from political culture see Ersanli's article in this volume. "Tools for epiphany in new histories in Central Asia. Sudden revelation but gradual change in history textbooks."
8. Shahin Mustafayev, *Selcuqilerden Osmanlılara*, Azerbaijan Milli Elmler Akademiyası, Bakı (2010).

6

Tibet in Soviet Studies

Tatiana Shaumian

Tibetan studies in Soviet Union and Russia have a long tradition of historical and cultural interaction. There has been a history of diplomatic and political contacts between Russia, China and Tibet as well. Studies also revolve round contacts between Russian Buddhists and the Tibetan temporal and spiritual leader, the Dalai Lama.

In Russia, almost 160,000 Buryats and 200,000 Kalmyks were adherents of Lamaism. These religious communities of Lamaists maintained regular links with Lhasa and went for pilgrimages to Tibet. It is known that in 1741 Lama Damba Darzha Zayayev of Tsongol Datsan in Trans-Baikalia had toured Tibet. On returning home he did much to spread Buddhism and also received the approval of Empress Catherine II for his *Regulations on Buddhist Clergymen in East Siberi'*.[1]

In 1891–94 Baza Monkochzhuev, a Kalmyk toured Tibet. His work, *Tale about a Journey in the Tibetan Land of the Malo-Dorbot —The Far-Eastern and Tibet Policies of the Russian Tsar* was translated and published in 1897 in Petersburg with notes by Prof. A. Pozdneev. In his preface Prof. Pozdneev wrote that of all countries of East Asia, Tibet "since the last quarter of the century has been a 'forbidden land' for the Europeans." He went on to say that Russia has for generations had a Mongolian population who are related to Tibet if not in language or mode of living, but in creed and religion, and this religious affinity had motivated them to maintain relations with Tibet from time immemorial. Scores of Buryats, according to Pozdneev, "are now rumoured go to Tibet annually to worship the sacred objects, to get initiated, and to improve their knowledge of the science."[2]

It was in the interest of the Tsarist government to demonstrate its "patronage" of the Buddhists, in order to help them to establish links with Tibet and thus consolidate their power in Siberia and the Trans-Baikal area and spread their influence in Mongolia. Many young Buryats were educated in Tibetan monasteries. Although this won them greater respect in their own country, the Tibetan authorities regarded them as foreigners and they were forced to live there illegally posing as Sikkimese and Nepalese pilgrims. This prompted the Russian authorities to activate their presence in Tibet on grounds of the necessity to safeguard the interests of their Buddhist subjects.

The AVPRI (Foreign Policy Archives of Russian Empire) preserves the unique documents: special Memoranda and Letters forwarded to Tsar Nicholas II by Foreign Ministers V.N. Lamsdorff and A.P. Izvolsky, which is indicative of an acute interest towards Tibetan affairs at the very top echelon of Russian politics. Of special value are letters handwritten by the Dalai Lama addressed to the Russian Tsar containing a request to take Tibet under his own patronage, and staff reports by Agvan Dorjieff, Plenipotentiary Envoy and confidential person of the Dalai Lama. The archives also preserve documents relating to the correspondence between foreign ministers and ambassadors of Russia, Great Britain and China, Russian consular officers in India, China, Mongolia, Britain and the Foreign Ministry, position papers by high-ranking Russian officers on the situation in Tibet and around it.

> The role of Russian travellers in the exploration of Central Asia and Tibet was immense. Since the beginning of the 1870s several expeditions were organized there by G.N. Potanin (1884—6), the results of whose investigations were set out in his work The Tangut-Tibetan Outskirts of China; the Grum-Grzhimaylo brothers (1886—90); V.A. Obruchev (1893-4), M.V. Pevtsov (1889-90), V.I. Roborovsky (1893—5). The travels of the distinguished traveller, N.P Przhevalsky (1876-8, 1879-80, 1883-5) won him fame. Particularly interesting were the travels in Tibet the descriptions of which were provided by P.K. Kozlov [3] and G.T. Tsybikov.[4]

P.K. Kozlov, member of the Imperial Russian Geographic Society, toured Tibet and Mongolia twice, in 1905 and 1909, and met the Dalai Lama. The principal purpose of his visits and books about them was, according to him, to establish firm Russian–Tibetan relations. The works of Kozlov are of great interest, providing as they do the "impressions" of a person directly witnessing events and having several meetings with the Dalai Lama. The author provides a brief history of Tibet and the Dalai Lamas, but does not discuss why the Tibetan authorities had at a certain time appealed to Russia for assistance or what Russia's real interests were in establishing relations with Tibet.

Between 1899 and1902 G.Tsybikov, a Buryat and Ovshe Norzunov, a Kalmyk visited Lhasa and other Tibetan holy places. Tsybikov was a highly educated person who had graduated from the Oriental Studies Department of the St. Petersburg University and was a Professor at the Oriental Studies Institute in Vladivostok. His work *Buddhist Pilgrim in Tibet's Sanctuaries* (1918) contains his diaries illustrated with unique photographs taken both by himself and O. Norzunov, which are of immense value. The book is a rich storehouse of the geography of Tibet, descriptions of its largest cities and monasteries and ways of life. He also provides a short history of Tibet and the Dalai Lama.

In that early period of Russian expansion in the Far East a Tibetan doctor, P. A. Badmayev played a certain role in determining Russian policy. He was a Buryat who had graduated from the Eastern Language Department of St. Petersburg University and was close to court circles. In addition to making "miraculous" medicines that was greatly admired in the court, he was also engaged in a big concessional business. As B. P. Semennikov writes in the Introduction to the collection of documents from Badmayev's archives, the Tibetan doctor "hardly belonged to the people, able to understand the complicated issues of policy;" "all his brains and energy Badmayev addressed to various shady transactions."[5] Badmayev based his fantastic plan on the belief that the Manchu dynasty would soon fall and that Russia should lose no time in stealing a march ahead of the western powers by organizing an uprising against the Manchus, overthrowing them, and annexing a considerable part of China, Tibet and Mongolia. On 3 May 1896, S. Witte reported to Nicholas II that "although the Buryats sent by Badmayev openly called themselves Russian subjects, they reached Lhasa and were received there with affection." He went on to say that "the geographical position of Tibet is politically of great importance to Russia, especially in view of the British attempt to penetrate into that country and bring it under their political and economic influence. Russia, according to my conviction, should make every effort to foil the British attempts to establish her influence in Tibet."[6]

The Buddhist Connection

The existence of Buddhist religious centres in Russian territory that maintained relationships with Mongolian and Tibetan monasteries provided a significant advantage to the Russian Buddhists over their western counterparts. Although since the end of the eighteenth century, Tibet had pursued a "policy of isolationism," and visits by foreigners to this place were banned, at the turn of the twentieth century Russian researchers did find a way of getting access to the region. They succeeded in moving into the Tibetan region under the guise of Buddhist pilgrims from Outer Mongolia, or posing as the Chinese emperor's subjects, as China under the rule of the Qing Dynasty had the status of a suzerain power over Tibet. Thus, in course of his explorations in Tibet between 1899 and 1902, Tsybikov reached Lhasa in August 1900. He brought 333 volumes of writings by Tibetan authors, rich archaeological and ethnographic material, artefacts and ritual objects for the Russian Academy of Sciences and Imperial Geographic Society. Owing to the pictures taken by Tsybikov and Ovshe Norzunov, the west got the first opportunity to get acquainted with the images of temples and monasteries in Lhasa, Tashilhumpo, Samye. The publication of Tsybikov's monograph entitled *A Buddhist Pilgrim to the Holy Place of Tibet* made headlines, as the subject of research had remained inaccessible to European researchers before.

The success of Tsybikov's mission gave a powerful impetus to researchers in collecting materials related to Buddhism. Having completed a four-year instruction course, students S.F. Oldenburg and F. I. Scherbatsky, B.B. Baradin and Ts.Zh. Zhamtsarano made several science expeditions into Buddhist temples (*datsans*) located in the Irkutsk province and Trans-Baikal territory. The data gathered by the young explorers demonstrated a high level of cultural development in the Buddhist regions inside Russia, which by the end of the nineteenth century had become major centres of knowledge, book printing, architecture and icon painting. Baradin managed to persuade one of the lamas of the Aginsky *datsan*, Danzen Zarbain, who had received higher confessional education at a tuition centre of the Gelugpa School associated with the Lavran Monastery, to get relocated and settle down in St. Petersburg. In a short time, St. Petersburg hosted a small Buddhist community, the bulk of which was comprised of ethnic Buryats, Kalmyks, merchants and craftsmen from Trans-Baikal territory, Astrakhan and Stavropol Provinces, lower-ranking Cossack officers and students.

Russian diplomacy and Russian readers displayed a keen interest in Tibet and its history. This is testified by the writings by foreign explorers and travellers that were published in the Russian language towards the end of the nineteenth and beginning of the twentieth centuries. Among them were *Unknown Asia—Travel to Tibet* by Gabriel Bonvalot (Tashkent 1897), *Journey to Lhasa and Central*

Tibet by Sarat Chandra Das (St. Petersburg 1906), L.A. Waddell's *Lhasa and Its Mysteries* (St. Petersburg 1906), *Tibet and its Heritage* based on works of F. Grenau and A. Landor (St. Petersburg 1904).

The plan of setting up a Great Buddhist Confederation centred on the cultural and economic issue of annexing Tibet and Mongolia to Russia and transforming St. Petersburg into a potential heartland of Buddhism in Europe was debated in the highest circles of power. In the late nineteenth century, with the support of Russian emperor Alexander III, P.A. Badmayev, made efforts to carry out these plans. In the twentieth century, Agvan Dorzhiev endeavoured to do the same under the patronage of Tsar Nicholas II. The economic substantiation for the Badmayev project was provided by the construction of two railways designed to connect Central Russia with the Far East; by contrast, Dorzhiev encouraged the establishment of a Trade and Industrial House that would spread its activities to Mongolia and Tibet.

The mentor of the latter project, Agvan Lobsan Dorzhiev, first came to St. Petersburg in 1898 as a member of the Tibetan legation. He was born in the village of Kara-Sibir, not far from Ulan-Ude, east of Lake Baikal, and at the age of 19, he joined pilgrims and left his home for Tibet. In 1888, having completed his studies in the Gomang College of the Gelugpa Drepung monastic university near Lhasa, with focus on philosophy, he attained the academic Buddhist degree of Geshe Lharampa (the highest level being Doctorate of Buddhist Philosophy). As an expert of Buddhist philosophy, Dorzhiev was admitted as the close entourage of the thirteenth Dalai Lama (1876–1933), to provide training to His Holiness in philosophical debates. Over the years, Dorzhiev earned the Dalai Lama's trust and became his close adviser and friend. Inside the Palace of the Supreme Ruler of Tibet, he created a Russophile movement, which had a strong impact on the Tibetan external policies for many years to come.[7]

In 1905, the thirteenth Dalai Lama repeatedly expressed his intention to take up residence in Russia, and the emperor Nicholas II offered his reassurances to Agvan Dorzhiev to the effect that "Buddhists in Russia could feel as safe as beneath a mighty eagle's wings." However, the idea of building up a Great Buddhist Confederation was never implemented. Nevertheless, the activities by Agvan Dorzhiev had strong appeal and worked towards rapprochement among the peoples of Russia, Mongolia and Tibet.

Due to the patronage of Prince E.E. Ukhtomsky, Count V.N. Lamsdorff and Foreign Minister A.P. Izvolsky, Agvan Dorzhiev was granted permission to meet Emperor Nicholas II and he won over the sympathy and favour of many influential persons from the elite sections of society. According to John Snelling, British expert on Buddhism, Dorzhiev's personality and argumentative style allowed him to obtain the highest favour from His Imperial Majesty who granted him the permission to build a Buddhist temple in the capital of the empire.[8]

The involvement of the leading figures in the Oriental Department, especially members of the Russian Academy of Sciences, in the *datsan* development project is the best evidence of the significance of the undertaking and huge enthusiasm among Orientalists, who were excited about the uniqueness of the project of interacting with the representatives of Buddhist culture and doing research on the lively traditions without leaving St. Petersburg. Even more promising, initially a classical Buddhist school was scheduled for construction alongside the temple as also a hostel for lamas, monarchs and probationers. Further developments were anticipated though the Buddhist centre did not have an effective role for a long time.

In the 1920s and the 1930s, due to the imposition of the militant atheist doctrine in the USSR, the existence of the Buddhist temple was becoming more and more difficult with each passing year. Finally after December 1933 the authorities declared lamas to be "socially dangerous elements" and "adversaries of socialist transformation." Massive arrests of the lamas began in the spring of 1935. Initially, they were deported to labour camps for three to five years; the repressions reached a climax in the autumn of 1937, when the last group of lamas and Buddhologists, comprising Bazar Baradin, Ts. Zhamtsarano and others, were detained and sentenced to execution by a firing squad. All of them are buried at an NKVD (secret police) cemetery in St.Petersburg, known as Levashovaskay Pustoch (barren land). The St. Petersburg Buddhological School founded by academician F.I. Scherbatsky were totally destroyed. Russian Buddhists were deprived of the possibility of visiting Tibet, while one of their most outstanding representatives, Tsanid-Hambo (Professor of Buddhist Metaphysics) Agvan Dorzhiev was persecuted for political reasons in the 1930s and died in police custody in a prison hospital at the age of 84 on 29 January 1938. After a 30-year battle to suppress the "reactionary clergy," Buddhist monasteries were practically destroyed and the clerical order of lamas was eliminated.

Accounts of Foreign Authors

The developments of the second decade of the twentieth century are obtained from the accounts of the foreign authors who visited Tibet in the aftermath of 1917 Revolution and from the subsequent translation of their works. The possible reason for this was that the new Soviet government apparently believed that it would be able to unite the people of the East around itself and encourage them to fight against imperialism. Having proclaimed the right of nations to self-determination, the Bolshevik leaders had assumed that they would have enough power to realistically sustain the Tibetan movement for independence, which was pronounced in 1913 after the Xinhai Revolution in China. In 1929, the travelogues by William McGovern *To Lhasa in Disguise* (M-L) were published, and in 1924 *In the Forbidden Land* by Arnold Henry Savage Landor (M-L) was released. The publications had lengthy forewords and epilogues that were drafted by Russian/Soviet authors E.S. Batenin, A. Ivin (W. McGovern), V.L. Kotovich (S.C. Das) and others.

Works by Soviet authors were also published at that time, for example, the articles in the *New Orient* magazine by L. Berlin (who was an analyst affiliated to the People's Commissariat for Foreign Affairs) entitled "Britain and Tibet"[9] and "Tsanid-Hambo Agvan Dorzhiev"[10] and by A. Popov, a Marxist historian entitled "Russia and Tibet."[11] Those articles were written on the basis of archival diplomatic documents and for the first time they furnished an objective assessment of Britain's expansionist plans in Tibet and the attempts made by Russian diplomacy to use the Tibetan issue for the purpose of obtaining certain advantages in other Asian regions. The relationship with Tibet was viewed through the prism of international developments in Asia and Europe. L. Berlin provided a positive acknowledgement of the actions accomplished by Agvan Dorzhiev, who had built up a pro-Russian lobby in Lhasa and thus for many years "had been restraining Britain from invading Tibet by putting it in confrontation with a competing Russia." At the same time, the controversy that has arisen between Britain and China factually liberated Tibet from centuries-old Chinese rule."[12]

Popov reviewed the Russian-Tibetan relationships within the context of a "big game," i.e. British–Russian rivalry in Central Asia. Relying on the documented sources from the Foreign Ministry archives of the Russian empire, Popov arrived at several conclusions: the close links between the Tibetan issue and Russia's policies in the Far East; the absence of Russia's business or strategic military interests in Tibet; discrimination between Tibetan and Mongolian issues in 1906 which resulted in the Anglo-Russian Convention of 1907.

Tibet-Russian Relations in the 1940s and After

In the late 1940s, the geopolitical situation in Asia changed dramatically. In 1947, India proclaimed its independence, and in 1949, the communist party came to power in China. Both of those events worked in favour of the Soviet leadership, although in different ways. Stalin was straightforward in endorsing the idea of a "peaceful liberation of Tibet," which was concluded in 1950. And precisely at that time, the Soviet leaders were prepared to formulate their position on the Tibetan issue as follows: "Tibet is an inalienable part of China, and its affairs fall into an exclusive jurisdiction of the Chinese government." The question of a possibility of proclaiming Tibet as a sovereign state was practically dismissed. On 23 May 1951, an "Agreement between the Central People's Government of China and Local Government of Tibet on Measures for the Peaceful Liberation of Tibet" was signed in Peking, which was approved by the Soviet leadership, and acknowledged in Delhi with the hope of its implementation. Moreover, on 29 April 1954, an "Agreement between the Republic of India and the People's Republic of China on Trade and Intercourse between Tibet Region of China and India" was concluded. Its relevance consisted in resolving a number of problems related to the trade operations between India and Tibet, the official recognition of Tibet as a part of China by India, and in designating six high-altitude passes/routes for travelling across the border. The five principles of peaceful co-existence set forth in the preamble of the Panchsheel agreement were later universally acknowledged as provisions related to the relationships between states belonging to different social systems. The actual recognition of the fact that Tibet was a part of China on behalf of the USSR and India has exerted a significant impact on the further development of Tibet and the fate of the Dalai Lama.

Shortly after the signature of the 1951 Agreement, the Peking authorities embarked on the reform of the conservative feudal theocratic system of governance in Tibet. The steps undertaken during the initial period had a positive effect, but were accompanied with human rights violations, public addresses containing outspoken declarations against the Lamaist clergy, a forceful assimilation of the Tibetan inhabitants by the Chinese, etc. That gave rise to the anti-Chinese protests, and as a retaliatory measure the Chinese troops were concentrating on the territory of Tibet, the construction of airfields, strategic roads, reinforcement of the old and building of the new border control stations, etc.

In the spring of 1959, isolated Tibetan protests evolved into an uprising against the Chinese authorities on 10 March, which was suppressed by Chinese troops. The Dalai Lama and more than six thousand Tibetans fled Tibet across high-mountain passes and entered the territory of India and other neighbouring states. Until this day, the

Tibetan High Priest has to be in exile in the city of Dharamsala in northern India, while overall there are now over 100 thousand refugees outside Tibet. The decision of the Indian Government to accept the Tibetan religious and secular leader as well as thousands of refugees, proceeding from humanitarian considerations, caused a wave of sharp protests from the Chinese side, which considered those actions as the policy of "Indian reactionaries," who had followed in the footsteps of British imperialists and demonstrated their "expansionistic ambitions" with regard to Tibet.

The attitude of the Soviet/Russian leadership towards the situation inside and around Tibet and the policies pursued by Peking had to take into account the interests of Russian Buddhists from Buryatiya, Kalmykia and Tuva. However, their traditional cultural and religious contacts with the Dalai Lama and Tibetan authorities were revived only during *perestroika* years in Russia. It should be noted that the Russian Government appeared to be in a precarious position: on the one hand, it was interested to retain its friendly ties with the Peking, while on the other hand, it was seeking to support the interests of its Buddhist nationals and facilitate their meetings with the Tibetan High Priest, who was considered to be a dissenter and an enemy of the Chinese people by Peking.

Recent Research

Referring to the research papers by the Soviet/Russian authors published in the first decades after the proclamation of the People's Republic of China and "peaceful annexation of Tibet to the People's Republic of China," the Tibetan revolt of 1959 and the escape of the Dalai Lama to India and subsequent developments, mention should be made of the articles, brochures and monographs by V.A. Bogoslovsky, B.P. Gurevich, G.M. Valiakhmetov, T.R. Rakhimov, A.M. Reshetov, A.G. Yakovlev, V.A. Krivtsov, L.N. Gumilyov, R.E. Pubayev, L. Duman, A.S. Martynov, although some of them did not deal explicitly with the role of Tibet in the international relations of Asia at the turn of the century. These works were published under conditions of strict censorship and was subject to the nature of relationships between the USSR and China, Communist Party of the USSR and Communist Party of China. Sometimes the books were published in an abridged form or bearing the stamp "Confidential." Thus, in the period of friendly relations, any criticism of the Peking leadership was banned, and that was the reason why many research papers were published in a substantially reduced format, involving deletions, and their authors were sometimes compelled to restrict the words that were not in conformity with the politically acceptable guidelines. Moreover, some works were not published at all or were only available for perusal in publications of restricted circulation or those designated "for official use" only. To avoid doubt, it should be noted that many of those writings were released afterwards and were widely available for the general public.

It is important to mention the work of B.P. Gurevich, a prominent Sinologist and the author of many historical chronicles dealing with issues of the Russian-Chinese borders, who prepared for publication volumes of archival documents that were unknown before. His work *The Liberation of Tibet,* published in 1958 tells us of the focus the work. Having worked with Gurevich for many years, I have reason to believe that he had profound knowledge of the issue and he gave ample evidence of that in his later works. As for *The Liberation of Tibet*, the question at issue was whether it could be published at all or it should be pigeonholed for a long time to come. It was not only Gurevich who found himself in such a situation. It was the fate of many authors, who produced their writings on critical problems related to current politics.

I would like to single out from the listed authors a monograph by V.P. Leontiev entitled *Foreign Expansion in Tibet* 1888–1919 (Moscow 1956) which narrates the military expedition of Francis Younghusband to Tibet in 1903–04. The book is based on the materials from the Archives of Foreign Policies of the Russian Empire (AVPRI), British diplomatic publications, media articles and diverse literature. Leontiev's advantage was that the topic of his research was based on the developments of a seemingly remote past, but even so, he still could not disregard it given the realities of the 1950s and the status of Soviet–Chinese relations during that period. The author in fact reflected the official Soviet stance that implied the recognition of Tibet as being a part of China, seeking to prove that the Anglo–Russian rivalry regarding Tibet was prompted by Russia's desire to win back Tibet from Britain for the benefit of China. Since that book was published in 1956, researchers were in a more beneficial position as they could gain access to the new, formerly inaccessible documents from the National Archive of India, and those materials allowed scholars to get a broader perspective, and in some cases, a radically new outlook on an array of problems related to the Asiatic affairs, including the issue of Tibet.

In the last two decades, after the formal end to censorship and availability of access to archival documents, the Russian scholars got their research works published without any restriction and were able to uphold their ideas about historical developments. With the opening of Russian borders and the adoption of the Soviet laws "On Freedom of Conscience and Religious Organizations" and "On Freedom of Religious Worship," the ideological stereotypes portraying religion as a rudimentary tool of spiritual life were ultimately brought to an end. It is significant to note that many Russian scholars were able to travel across China and Tibet, collect data in Tibetan and Chinese scientific centres, archives and libraries. The scientific investigation of Tibet was given importance: travel notes and fundamental research works and articles were encouraged in Russia's capital cities and regions with predominantly Buddhist population in Siberia and the Far East, and the public also got access to the local archives. The authors of the new published research papers endeavoured to assert their ideas of historic developments inside and outside Tibet and in some cases adhere to diametrically opposite views.

In the early 1990s, it was possible to release the translated versions of the writings of the Dalai Lama, e.g. his well-known autobiography *My Land and My People* (2000), *Freedom in Exile* (1992), and *Buddhism of Tibet* (1991) apart from his regular addresses on the anniversary of the 1959 Tibetan revolt and other writings on Tibetan Buddhism.

Speaking about the works by Russian researchers of Tibet, the works of E.A. Belov, who died prematurely, must be mentioned. His article "Tibetan Policies of Russia (1900-1914)" was published in the journal *Orient* based on archival documents.[13] He was the first author to have access to documents from the files of the Archives of Foreign Policy of the Russian Empire (AVPRI) e.g. *Mission in Peking*. According to Belov, Russia had pursued a fairly cautious policy towards Tibet, defending it from British aggression, but not advocating its separation from China. The pro-Russian position of the Dalai Lama helped Russia to "minimize and eventually contain the British expansion into Tibet." Belov notes quite justifiably that if Russia had no Tibetan policy of its own, it would not have concluded a separate agreement with Britain in 1907.

In 2005, my colleagues and I worked with Belov on the collection of documents entitled *Russia and Tibet. Collection of Archival Documents from 1900 through 1914*, which was published after his death in which we incorporated 122 original documents relating to the early twentieth century, including correspondences between the Russian Tsar and the Dalai Lama, reports and letters of Russian diplomatic representatives from London, Calcutta, Peking and Urga (Ulan Bator). These documents allow us to get a glimpse about the little known events in the history of international relations of Central Asia and the Far East. They also shed light on the significance of Tibet in Russia's foreign policy.

One of the most prolific authors writing on the history of Tibet and Russian-Tibetan relations is a researcher from St. Petersburg, Alexandre Andreyev, who published his work *From Baikal to the Holy Lhasa. New materials on Russian Expeditions to the Central Asia in the First half of the 20th century (Buryatiya, Mongolia, Tibet)* in 1997. He is also the author of several articles that were published in the journals *Problems of History, Buddhism in Russia, Aryavarta.* These articles describe the mission of a Russian agent to Tibet during 1869–73, the Mongol-Tibetan expedition of P.K. Kozlov (1923–26), the activities of a well-known doctor, Petr Badmayev and others. In 2003, Andreyev's major research *Soviet Russia and Tibet. The Debacle of Secret Diplomacy, 1918-1930s* was published in English by E.J. Brill in Leiden and Boston. The Russian version of that book was published in St. Petersburg in 2006 under the title *Tibet in the Russian Tsarist, Soviet and post-Soviet policy.* The book is an investigative account of the Soviet Foreign Ministry's efforts to involve Lhasa in Russia's politics. Examining the history of relations between Tsarist, Soviet and post-Soviet Russia and Tibet from the seventeenth century to the 1990s, the core of the narrative builds around the unknown story of negotiations between the Soviet Government and the thirteenth Dalai Lama as part of Russia's struggle against British imperialism in Asia.

One of the recent works that is worth mentioning is the writing of A.D. Tsendina entitled *The Land is called Tibet,* published in Moscow in 2002. The author analyses the political background of Tibet from ancient times until the middle of the twentieth century; the formation of the Tibetan ethnos, establishment of the theocratic monarchy, the beginnings of Manchurian suzerainty, struggle for independence, Chinese annexation. Tsendina treats the myths surrounding Tibet from a realistic perspective. Emphasizing the dramatic nature of the historical path of Tibet and making an attempt to identify its distinctive features as compared against other people's journeys, the author reveals its peculiarities, considers the circumstances that led to the emergence and facilitated the development of Tibetan religion and culture, showing the specific features of its history through its interaction with religion and its fight for the prevalence of independence and the reasons behind its loss. A precondition for writing such a book should have been visits to Tibet, and familiarization with its historical and cultural heritage.

It was only possible after changes in the relations between countries and peoples took place in the beginning of the new millennium. In conclusion, the author notes that "the Tibetans have always led a hard life. Hard, from the point of view of their struggle for bread, for survival under rigid natural conditions, and recently—for the possibility of being the masters of their own lives and living as they wish and deem right. But they have never lost the sense of their national dignity."[14]

The single Russian scholar who does not seriously consider the Anglo-Russian rivalries in the whole of Central Asia and Tibet is N.S. Kuleshov who wrote a book *Russia and Tibet in the early 20th Century,* which was published in 1992. He asserted that "Russia has not had any political, military, economic interests in Tibet, and has demonstrated its complete non-involvement in the handling of its problems." In his opinion, "there has been neither objective nor subjective causes that could have provided the ground to assume that the Russian government had certain incentives to conduct or plan any Tibetan policies."[15] The delegation of Agvan Dorzhiev to Russia is interpreted by Kuleshov as a religious mission only, although the archival documents testify to the effect that those trips were aimed at securing an agreement for a Russian protectorate over Tibet. The author disagrees about the suggestion that Russia and Britain used Tibet as "token money" in their diplomatic bargaining over their spheres of influence in Asia.

It can hardly be reasonable to go along with Kuleshov's assertions particularly as he argues that since the late eighteenth century until the Xinhai revolution, there had been no "formal suzerainty of China over Tibet—and that there is not a single document that would testify to the finalization of such suzerainty status of the Chinese."[16] As a matter of fact, no such document has ever existed, but China's suzerainty over Tibet was fairly explicit especially during the time of election of a new Dalai Lama, carried out with the direct participation of the Chinese *ambans*. Kuleshov's concept can be challenged with evidence in archival documents that is now accessible to researchers.

However, it should be acknowledged that the relations between Peking and Lhasa had a special and peculiar character. And it would be reasonable to agree on the viewpoint of Kuleshov who made pointed projections in the concluding chapter of his book:

> The *amban*, a representative of the Qing dynasty in Tibet, was not only a figure behind which stood the whole Empire, but also the ancient, rich Chinese civilization, whose part

> was represented by the Tibetans. It was not easy to break away from that civilization for the Tibetans. That is why even during the period of the most severe and cruel Tibetan-Chinese military confrontation during 1906-1912, the Chinese *amban* in Lhasa with a very limited military escort assigned to it, remained inviolable. The Chinese-Tibetan affinity that had been forged throughout history, exerted a restrictive influence on the armed resistance put up by the Tibetans against the Qing troops that resistance has not become an all-embracing national movement.[17]

In 2003, Russian Tibetologists A. Tsendina and A. Sazykin released a full version of Agvan Dorzhiev's autobiography entitled *Entertaining Notes. Description of a Round-the-World Trip* (1921) and which was translated from Mongolian to Russian. Of great interest are his records relating to his travel experiences and above all in Tibet. Although, apparently, basic events and facts depicted by Dorzhiev are well known, his own assessment, intriguing style of writing and vivacious presentation impart a specific significance to those events and the more so as they are narrated by someone who was directly involved in these developments.

Dorzhiev writes how he arrived in the "highland country, was enrolled in Gomang College of the Gelugpa Drepung monastery where he embarked on the path of religious service. At that time, however, all across Tibet there had been strict regulations to exclude disloyal students and Russian subjects were treated with particular incredulity and suspicion."

> We, who are called Buryats, are referred to here as Russian subjects. [That's why we] have been banned many times from entering Tibet. The reason for that is as follows. The country called England conquers poor people all across the golden land. Such is its inclination and disposition. [It] has resorted to various techniques—animosity and oppression—in order to make an incursion into Tibet from India. [Many people here] didn't know that Russia and England are two different nations, and because of that they banned Russian nationals from entering [their country]. I decided to explain this thing to them. I have pointed out to influential individuals many times that the geographical locations of Russia and England are different; these two states are completely different and separate from each other. [I also

> mentioned] that the two empires are not on very good terms [with each other]). Moreover, now that England wants to conquer Tibet, Russians are sure to give Tibet a helping hand. I kept on making my reports in the same manner and they started to listen to me. It was unreasonable of me to think that way: If Russia takes Tibet under [its] patronage, then the Buryats will have security for their religion too. And Tibet, having received such protection, will wrench itself free from the jaws of its foreign enemy.

Irina Garry from the Institute for Mongolian, Buddhist and Tibetan Studies in the Siberian branch of the Russian Academy of Sciences in Ulan-Ude (Buryatiya) published in 2009 the monograph *Buddhism and Politics in Tibetan Region of China (the second half of 20th to the beginning of 21st century)* based on documents collected from Chinese, Tibetan and British archives and the author's personal impressions and observations after visiting Tibet and China. Garry analyses the so called Tibet question, the Chinese policy in Tibet, struggle of Tibetan Diaspora for independence, the role of religion in social and political development of Tibet and so on. She considers the China–Tibetan dialogue and the perspectives of Tibetan autonomy within the framework of the history of the People's Republic of China. She writes:

> Tibet and Buryatiya are countries very closely related to each other. First of all, both regions share a common historical destiny of Tibet-Mongolian civilization which is rooted in Tibetan Buddhism and submission to the authority of His Holiness the Dalai Lama . ... Both regions passed through a similar history of persecution of religion and its subsequent revival . ... There are more than 200 Buddhist communities in Russia now.

She explained with restraint the features of Chinese policy towards Tibet, and did not directly criticize the annexation of Tibet as China announced it as an inalienable part of China. Such a point of view was also expressed by Sergey Kuzmin whose book *Hidden Tibet. History of Independence and Occupation* (2010) was a revelation. He writes that Tibet has never been a part of any other state and that the inclusion of Tibet into the People's Republic of China was not legitimate. Tibet is an occupied country. Kuzmin's book analyses the history of Tibet from ancient times, describes life of the Tibetans at the time of feudalism and socialism, suppression of national liberation movement, destruction of Tibetan civilization, etc. He recognized the significance of the preservation of Tibetan-Mongolian civilization which was possible only on the basis of cultural integration of Tibetan communities in India, Bhutan and Nepal.

Notes and References

1. The Zayayev diaries were published in the Buryat language by A.M. Pozdneev in 1900. See A.M.Pozdneev, *Mongolian Reader for Elementary Teaching* (St. Petersburg 1900).
2. A.M.Pozdneev, *Tale about a Journey in the Tibetan Land of the Malo-Dorbot Baza-Barshi* (St. Petersburg 1898), iii.
3. P. K. Kozlov, "The Dalai Lama of Tibet," *Historical Bulletin* 107 (1907); *Tibet and Dalai Lama* (Petrograd 1920); *Three Years of Travelling across Mongolia and Tibet* (St. Petersburg 1913); "The British Expedition in Tibet," *Historical Bulletin* (1907): 109.
4. G.S.Tsybikov, *Buddhist Pilgrim in Tibet Sanctuaries* (Petrograd 1919).
5. *Za kulisamy Tsarisma* (Behind the Scene of Tsarism), Archives of Tibetan Doctor Badmayev (Leningrad 1925), iii, iv.
6. Report of S. Witte to Nicholas II, 3 May 1896, 23–24.
7. Agvan Dorjieff's autobiography, AVPRI, Chinese Desk, File 1448, 162–7.
8. John Snelling, *Buddhism in Russia—The Story of Agvan Dorzhiev, Lhasa's Emissar to the Tsar* (Brisbane, Queensland: Element Books 1993), 131, 136–7.
9. L. Berlin, "Britain and Tibet," *New Orient*, no.2 (1922): 355–66.
10. Berlin, "Tsanid-Hambo Agvan Dorzhiev," *New Orient*, no.3 (1923):139–56.
11. A. Popov, "Russia and Tibet," *New Orient*, no.20–21(1928): 33–54.
12. Berlin, "Tsanid-Hambo Agvan Dorzhiev," 140.
13. E.A. Belov, "Tibetan Policies of Russia (1900-1914)," *Orient*, no.3 (1994): 99, 101.
14. A.D. Tsendina, *The Land is called Tibet* (Moscow 2002), 282.
15. N.S. Kuleshov, "Russia and Tibetan Crisis in the Early 20th Century," *Problems of History*, no.11 (1990); Kuleshov, *Russia and Tibet in the early 20th Century* (Moscow 1992).
16. Kuleshov, *Russia and Tibet,* 17.
17. Kuleshov, *Russia and Tibet,* 249.

7

Tools for Epiphany in New Histories in Central Asia: Sudden revelation but gradual change in history textbooks

Büşra Ersanlı

Declarations of or changes in identity stories in history textbooks always follow a political turmoil, or at least shifts of political system/ governments. After the demise of the Soviet Union, the ex-Soviet republics started to rewrite history textbooks to assert national independence and sovereignty. Since the nation-state formation euphoria spread to most nations in Europe during the late nineteenth and early twentieth centuries, all states pursued the same target: to write an integrated, central/mostly single identity-story to mobilize the peoples for durable independence and sovereignty through standardization. This target had both political and military connotations, either defensive or aggressive. The fashion was to produce new generations, well armed to defend their bordered states; and history education was one of the most widespread and relevant instruments used. To make one story of plural stories of different human communities was always a complex national duty but its political legitimacy was very high in Europe then.

USSR did not organize their state and society in exactly the same fashion. It was founded as a federal, socialist country with many nations; it recognized them culturally, ethnically and linguistically. These nations' attempts for one/single strong identity followed a different path under the banner of internationalism of the Soviet Communist Party. Thus standardization was not national in its conventional/European meaning. With growing complexity and degeneration of the system the different nations' nostalgia for single state adventure developed gradually, accelerated during the late 1950s and 74 years after the Bolshevik revolution the USSR disintegrated into 15 independent nations. In this process Central Asian countries just like the other erstwhile Soviet nations followed a similar course of rewriting their own identity-story, each with some different stress points, trying slightly different methods for change. None of them however could radically depart from their socialist tradition of writing history textbooks. There existed a gradual/evolutionary interpretation of "national in form and socialist in content."

In this paper my focus will be on the changes observed in Uzbek and Turkmen history textbooks in their quest for self-recognition, self-realization, or self image during the last two decades. It is notable for example that these two countries chose different heroes, concepts/events to highlight national self assertion to indicate the pride of new citizenship replacing or reinterpreting *homo-sovieticus*. While the Uzbeks chose Emir Timur of fourteenth century as the greatest hero symbolic of their national pride the Turkmens pointed to their contemporary leader Turkmenbashı. Furthermore these two countries had slightly different styles of referring to themselves as an ethnic group, as a nation, as a culture, as human geography, sometimes merging all these characteristics as a new political identity. The changes their ministries of education undertook in history education could be observed in the textbooks published between 1992–3 and 2010. I will take sample textbooks on national and world histories from the 1990s and 2000s to indicate the differences and styles of narratives in the process of change. Generally speaking the gradual change took place in three phases.

The first phase of change in history textbook production was reflected as "socialist in form and national in content" as reversed from the prior Soviet motto to create new generations. This meant that the authors were free but hasty in appending pages or paragraphs with local/national heroes and traditional/native concepts; but the method remained more or less the same using the periodization in line with historical materialism. For example in 1989 a "most recent history book" for 9th grades covered the concrete military and political conditions of capitalist world in strict chronological order starting with the Bolshevik revolution, explaining revolutions and anti imperialist and anti fascist struggles in the course of First and Second World Wars.[1] While this book takes up history solely as international history though not called world history, a few years later the same anti imperialist, freedom struggle is narrated from the perspective of the local people (Uzbeks) underlining the liberation movements and reform movements of their own, namely the Jadid movement,[2] which actually was a typical extension of the reform movement in nineteenth century Russian empire.

In the next phase after the mid–1990s there was an accentuated stress on selected events and heroes. During this phase historians tried to write textbooks and related complementary books conceptualizing history, sociology and politics around the ideational impact of chosen heroes or chosen names of their homeland, trying to focus on the nation, its emergence and contribution to the people. They criticized the earlier history writing with respect to periodization and territoriality; thus discussions and debates among historians became frequent. "Turkistan" along with Jadid movement became conspicuous not only in academic research and popular history but also in textbooks in Uzbekistan. This attempt did not create a completely new method but opened a route for new interpretations. Picking up a super hero (like the communist party) or a community of heroes (Jadids) was partly a continuity in history textbooks; but at the same time refusing radical/revolutionary change and following a soft, evolutionary pragmatic adaptation was a difference. This they found necessary to harmonize with the "global" era.

Finally during the 2000s self-recognition/revelation or self realization was clearly observed and any ideological method was denied, openly worded in recent Uzbek textbooks.[3] This was the stage when Uzbek and Turkmen textbooks could be differentiated clearly; the former following a progressive political state construction and the latter feeding on the dynamics of Turkmens as a widespread community in motion not only in the region but also around the world.[4] In neither of them there seems to be an outright condemnation of any phase in their histories. We could observe mainly a realist and pragmatic neutrality in placing themselves within world history textbooks (*Jahon Tarixi*: Uzbekistan and *Dunya Taryhy*: Turkmenistan) in a flexible, instrumental manner. Both countries pursued a vacillating journey out and around the European understanding of the nation state construction but they did not give in completely.

Marxist approach to history writing extended political identity to the international arena by asserting that whatever was national should remain as natural and cultural. Even after sovereignty and independence was declared by both Turkmenistan and Uzbekistan, while alternative regional and international alliances could portray pragmatic realist policies, in reformulating history narration, the cultural side of national identity could be found satisfactory enough. In this sense a methodological continuity was not totally abandoned. Historical materialism could be detected easily in history textbooks of both the 1990s and the 2000s, especially in chapters where economic and social history is taken up after the political, military and administrative narration of each historical era. This approach hardly complies with philosophical and mythical golden periods of the Uzbeks in the later middle ages or of the Turkmens in sixth–seventh centuries or in the eighteenth century. Rebirth or finding refuge in native golden ages contradicts linear progressive history. Therefore neither positivism nor historicism could be satisfactory for depicting the emerging historiography; a new critical romanticism probably would comply with local/regional cultural historiography. The major enemy is still the "oppressor," the imperialist powers holding the material and non-material sources and forces in hand, but it is more the Russian imperialism. In a way the former internationalism of the proletariat and the oppressed peoples today in their local/national colours are expressed as local/regional self-rule and would be welcomed as "glocalism."

All in all it is possible to argue that there exists an original interpretation slowly developing during the last two decades, balancing socialist historiography with that of competitive stately nation historiography. History textbooks in both countries have local and global features but the question is what to leave behind nation state historiography or territorial culture history. Is nation state historiography still the only universal way of self revelation or can territorial regional culture, ecology, anthropology be more relevant for an updated and upgraded "political" identity stories? The new interpretations in textbooks within this process of change lead to the above questions, and I believe that this is positive.

Turkmen History Books

For the coming years the Institute of History–Academy of Sciences/ Turkmenistan is preparing history books in three languages: Turkmen, Russian and English ("Turkmen history from ancient times to present day," "Famous people in Turkmen History," "Relations of Turkmens with Asia Minor and the Ottoman Empire" are some of them). This attempt can be viewed as a further demand for global recognition.

Turkmens throughout their history pursued a decentralized life in a temporary status within their tribal communities (*tire-taypa-xalk* according to their size and kinship relations[5] and *yurt, oba, il* and confederation according to their style of settlement and needs for settlement which was more often temporary). W. Irons studying Turkmen history assert their decentralized self-governing social organizations and see a link between desire for mobility and their understanding of freedom and individuality. This life style is reflected in their political organizations as well.[6] Their understanding of power and security is also related to their confederative lives. Their mobile nature with shifting alliances made them dynamic warriors. From sixteenth century onwards they fought against Nadir Shah, Khiva and Buhara Khanates and finally the Russians. They also fought for the states and the peoples they lived with, for example in Afghanistan just before independence. They struggled for unification in the past for alliances and immediate benefits and recently also for international statehood status.

Within this perspective their choice of names and their preferential periods/sources were as follows:

1. **Turkmen is** used as an ethnic community name; literary artistic past is shared with Turkey and other Turkic peoples and this goes back to sixth–eighth centuries. They assert that it is the Turkmens who contributed to the literature of all famous "common" poets like Fuzuli, Kaşgarlı Mahmut, Hoca Ahmet Yesevi, Yunus Emre, Burhanettin Sıvaslı, Nesimi, Novai, Karacaoğlan. But when they start their history book on "world history" they avoid the word Turkmen or Turkmenistan state for almost two pages.[7] There was a discussion among the historians writing history textbooks whether the national history books should be called "History of Turkmens" or "History of Tukmenistan;"[8] finally the latter title was chosen. During the first years of independence the title of textbooks was "Materials from Turkmenistan History" and later, "History of Turkmenistan."
2. **Mahdumkulu** is frequently mentioned as the most famous Turkmen poet and the outstanding member of the group of famous eighteenth century poets called *Yedigen* (the sevens), as symbols of golden ages of Turkmen identity (ethnic and linguistic) as a nation and also significant stage for inspiring unification of different clans (*taypas)*. This was particularly underlined in 1990s when the eighteenth century was covered extensively, within a special chapter in history books.[9]
3. ***Ruhname*** was written by Saparmurat Niyazov (Turkmenbashı) in 2000 and this book was published many times; it was also translated into different languages (Turkish in 2006). Style of epic in history is very conspicuous here; "thematic freedom" which was underlined by many Central Asian historians, calls for a philosopher king in this book. The book is an autobiography, a history book, an etiquette book, a mythology book, a guide for all tastes. While the name Turkmen goes back to sixth–seventh century according

to historians, Niyazov brought this 3000 years back. *Ruhname* opens up the third phase of history interpretation/analysis of the Turkmens.

4. The **horse** symbolizes the mobility, dynamism of power as a member of the household. Integration with nature/*ecological identity* and fusing this identity with mobile community traditions; family, nature, land and animals reflected through history of literary ethnography of the Turkmen people is a national heritage.[10] Both fauna and flora are essential ingredients of Turkmens' social mobile identity but this stress is mostly in etiquette (*edeb*) books rather than history books. However, the horse is present in all popular presentations of Turkmen identity and way of life.
5. Permanent **neutrality**, bilateral relations: Shifting alliances with different nations indicates permanent neutrality that could well signify free will to choose and act accordingly, taking dependency-free, mobile political decisions. Turkmenistan refrained from participating in any regional or multinational alliances or organizations. This foreign policy decision is also reflected in World History textbooks describing status of bilateral relations with Turkey, Pakistan and Iran for example; the narration of the three countries is in a factual, neutral and sincere tone, placing each in its special position with respect to Turkmenistan.[11]

This somewhat scattered process does not lead to a politically strong state developed in a chronological, progressive order, but gives reference to valued heroes, preferences of a community, their life styles and activities. Authoritarian subject culture is crowned by the place of *Ruhname* in education during the 2000s. Earlier during the 1990s the history books were partly loyal to the socialist interpretation/method; feudalism, the role of economic history and the discussion about the local and dynamic mobility of the Turkmens were underlined, in line with officially accepted local specificities. This was followed by Turkmens' struggles against "feudal states" (nineteenth century) and finally Russian empire, named as "colonial age." The eighteenth and nineteenth century history book has no ambition to cover Turkistan as a civilizational area with modernization and reform movements as in Uzbek history books, and suffices to mention the continuity of local/national arts during the colonial imperialist times (only handicrafts, rugs and silverware are mentioned).[12]

In the most recent History of Turkmenistan textbook covering tenth to sixteenth centuries, we observe that "turkmen" is used like a family name in the process of reconstruction of the new state. The word frequently refers either to the peoples of all Turkic origins or to political organizations ranging from small princedoms to Seljuk and Ottoman empires or to a sociological identity (In the last case the word is used after the names of historical heroes).[13] All the princedoms (*beylik*) mentioned in the book have their proper clan or family names but all the same Turkmen is added to the front of each as an adjective. The author when narrating the White Sheep and Black Sheep Princedoms or other "Turkmen origin" princedoms fighting with each other, implies that for all confrontations what is most important is their being ethnically Turkmen; neither their wars with one another nor their allying with other nations or regions counts as much.

This attitude was accentuated or inspired by *Ruhnama*, the book written by Saparmurat Niyazov for elevating the native spirit and national dynamism of the Turkmens. Niyazov wanted to ward off unwanted spirits with the force of this book. Roy Medvenev, eminent Russian historian argues that this book is a holy book because of two reasons: 1. Turkmens did not enjoy the modern historiographical and liberal concepts; and 2. Koran was never translated into Turkmen language. "*Ruhnama* is an epic, yet it is void of the aggression that permeated *The Short Course in the History of the Communist Party* (Bolsheviks)," says R. Medvedev. The author had studied the Soviet textbook used in St. Petersburg State University during late1940s or early 1950s.[14] In other words, Turkmens are considered to be lacking the two great frames of references for history writing, both the linear and the cyclical. Their alternative vision, *Ruhname* was accepted as an integral part of history teaching at all levels of education; it is officially required reading. As well known Niyazov/Turkmenbaşy also brought in his own family names to replace weekday names.

Drawing attention to "Turkmen" as a sociological identity of heroes and political organizations in Turkmen history is expressed as hero cult in world history books also. We see photos of all leaders of different countries, as extraordinary individuals who made history; among the 98 illustrations in the world history book 83 are photographs of political leaders. This emphasis on individual fame as driving force of contemporary history is different from that of Uzbek World History (*Jahon Tarixi*) books. Within the latter we also see illustrations of social events and actions, both agrarian and urban. Hero cult is demonstrated in a different style, infiltrated into progressive chapters as outstanding intellectual contribution of their leader, Karimov's proverbs.

Although there is an emphasis on state as a concept in Turkmen history textbooks and assertion that Turkmens were the people of many states, they remain always the people, as a mobile social reality of many states. "They prized mobility and viewed settled farming as an invitation to predatory behavior."[15] Their pride in having found many states is very different from our knowledge of the historiographical tradition of state building in the European sense in Turkey; Turkmens see the state as only one crucial aspect of human social activity and not the major one. They do not underline a single powerful state formation or a linear development leading to a single state within their history and territory. One can suggest that their historiographical vision is more confederative—which is not even sedentary—rather than "national" with a centralized political culture.

In connection to the concept of state and statehood, the impact of official Turkish nationalistic historiography is also quite conspicuous; the Turkish history textbooks cite from 12–20 states founded by the Turks, thinking the state foundation is the climax of human excellence; however the narration on Turkmen-origin state plurality is loose/flexible, sometimes even undecided in Turkmen textbooks. Although the Turkmen historians cite about 70 states, all these political structures seem to be secondary to their ethnic/clan/family names. Their status remains as "Turkmen" as a set of free mobile communities widespread within the region and beyond extending from India to Asia Minor. On the other hand it is obvious that they share many of these states with the Anatolian, Mesopotamian and Persian lands; for example, all Anatolian princedoms (*beylik*) before and during the consolidation of the Ottoman empire were common at least both to Turkey and Turkmenistan. Hence, the difference between these two countries could only be underlined by a different political culture; that which we can observe in the following words: "Döwlet gurjak bolsan Turkmeni çagyr" (If you want to create a state call the Turkmen).[16] The statement implies sharing political and military sentiments with different peoples/nations. The essential subject is Turkmen in action; the secondary subject is the state to be found, in fact by the Turkmens, preferably.

Uzbek Textbooks

Uzbeks' narration of their history claims a glorious cultural continuity crowned by a strong state created and solidified after the disintegration of the USSR. All secondary school books start with Karimov's (no photograph) statements relating to state building achievements in both History of Uzbekistan and world history books while Turkmenistan history books start with a poem and its author Turkmenbaşy's one page photograph.

The Uzbek history textbooks are named as Uzbekistan History (*Ozbekiston Tarixi*) taught as a distinct subject since late 1950s,[17] World History (*Jahon Tarixi*) and recommended history books for schools are called "homeland history" (*Watan Tarixi*)[18] indicating the significance of territoriality.

The starting point of Uzbek history writing goes back to the fifteenth century when history books on Turkistan in Persian and Arabic languages were translated to native Turkic and when Timur's son Ibrahim Sultan initiated a number of collected works to be written by Uzbek historians.[19] This historiographical enterprise was based on the need to narrate victories and accomplishments of the Timuride era. The political goal, besides legitimization, was to unite the fragmented peoples of Turkistan. In short, the political recognition of the era was sought for and is underlined in the post independence history textbooks along with the carefully placed building blocks of continuity especially with the Islamic and Asian civilization. Uzbeks are keen to avoid ruptures in their history narration; pragmatic reformism suits their historians more than radical change.

It is well known that history writing in the post Stalinist era revitalized traditions of Russian national historiography. The new historians after the Gorbachev era started to cling to the Jadid awakening both as a national revival and historiographical start for national self assertion. This was always coupled with the concept of Turkistan, introduced as an administrative regional unit by the Russian empire during late nineteenth century. Because the central point of Turkistan mostly overlaps with the geographical existence of Uzbekistan today they took pride in this concept as a national unifying symbol as well as hinting for aspirations of a regional power in Central Asia. During late 1990s, Uzbeks preferred the use of "Turkistan" to indicate a regional power base as a cultural centre and also as an initiation of regional alliances for contemporary requirements.[20] Timur and the Jadid movement articulated this aspiration. Recently even the Rashidov era which was related to corruption during the 1980s seems to be rehabilitated as one of the minor building blocks.

The Uzbeks in their post independence history textbooks draw attention to the single state created by the Uzbeks after the disintegration of the Soviet Union. Their references to the past heroic periods stand out as building blocks. In the history textbooks written during the 1990s accidental discontinuity sticks out as contextual implants of heroic resistance to Russia and the early Soviets, reformist movements in education, morals, conduct and traditions. This was criticized by some historians and there existed a debate on the issue of cultural identity and legal state identity as the basis for history education. *Watan Tarixi* books were written for this purpose; Halbayoglu said "'Watan Tarixi' should be elevated now to the status of legal statehood as an understanding and not be confined to cultural territorial history only."[21] Uzbek historians preferred a clearer European chronological order to nourish symbols of continuity. To underline their self realization as a political community they pinpointed the following concepts/events:

1. Taking pride in the **Islamic renaissance,** the *medrese* tradition and men of science of the twelfth and thirteenth centuries,[22] followed by Uzbek Khan's conversion to Islam. Islam is an integral part of the identity but its civilizational impact is more adopted by the textbooks than its sacred symbols and principles; the latter only became trendy during recent years as an everyday fashion.[23]
2. Making **Emir Timur** (fourteenth century), the greatest hero of the Uzbek past, a big museum was built crowning him for the 600th commemoration in 1996. Uzbeks were paying tribute to his busts and sculptures just like to those of Lenin before, bringing the newly wedded couples to this site. In 1994 national history books had already started covering the Timuride era extensively[24] and in 1996 the Academy of Sciences published a special history book devoted to Emir Timur and Ulugbek.[25] In Turkmen history textbooks however, Emir Timur is named Timurlane (Agsak Timur) against whom the northern Turkmens had fought.[26] Within the Timuride era science and literary achievements were worth noting. Ali Shir Navai (fifteenth century), the most celebrated literary hero has always been associated with the continuity and strength of the Uzbek language as a very important element of national identity; 1993 project on "common Turkic language" was based on this heritage of Navai's literary work which is believed to have inspired Gaspirali in publishing *Tercüman.* This journal had played a great role in helping the communication of Turkic peoples during the second half nineteenth century.
3. The historiographic role of the **Jadid movement** is very significant, because it was asserted by mid 1990s by the Academy of Sciences that modern historiographical understanding was initiated by the Jadid intellectuals/ historians of Uzbekistan.[27] This specific reform movement

was taken as a building block for further development, a complementary progressive stage inspired by the Russian reform movement. In the history textbooks however Jadid movement coexists with Russian empire's imperialistic policies during the second half of nineteenth century[28] essentially as an opposing force.

4. Devotion to historiographical work and encouraging research under the name of **Turkistan** (studies, research) especially in 1995–8 was very easily observed in all academic activities, conferences, national and international publications. The identity of Turkistan is portrayed in a flexible, intercultural and even inter-heroes (sharing the glory of cross-cultural heroes) style.[29] A special focus on the nineteenth century shows the Uzbek's interests in modern reforms and also creates opportunity to underline self recognition against Russian/ Soviet rule, thus guides strengthening state with the nation.
5. Shifting stress points in compliance with the changing alliances with the USA, the RF, CIS, or EU or combinations of some of them. The elevation of the role of USA in world politics is very conspicuous in 11th grade history textbooks; concluding chapter on the achievements of world states in technology, communication and arts; there exists a hierarchical order here on the contributions of world states: USA is first in everything, then comes western Europe UK, Germany and France, then USSR within which Uzbek literature and art is mentioned, then finally Asia (Turkey is in this section), Africa and Latin America.[30]

In all of the above phases of history Karimov stands out not only as a political leader but also an intellectual guide for comprehending the building blocks in history textbooks as well as following all recent developments in the world both in theory and practice.

In world history books we observe a close attention paid to the new values and new interpretations of world politics with the aim to adapt them into their own national narration. Humanism, democratization and globalization are underlined in analysing the first half of the twentieth century, worded by Karimov as: "a controversy/struggle between democracy and totalitarianism; between humanism and fascism and between global perspective and discrimination…."[31]

Uzbekistan history textbooks for 11th grades are on Independent Uzbekistan period. This period in early 2000s are based on international relations of Uzbekistan with a method which is highly strategic and the alliance with the USA can easily be detected in the last chapter on "regional adventures and international terrorism," the chapter just before that is "Silk Road = development road."[32] There seems to be an enthusiasm for maintaining a firm status within the world economic market. Although Uzbeks' Karimov sought shifting alliances with RF, USA, EU he was successful in balancing them off by mid 2000s.

In *O'zbekiston Tarixi* for 9th grade covering the nineteenth century, held to be the most important period, there were other changes within 2000s (2002 and 2010 particularly). The tables of contents in both are very similar: territory and society in Central Asia, socio-economic life, civilization, ethnic make-up, land and water policies, Karakalpaks, then the Jadid intellectuals and Turkistan. However, when we observe closely we see two differences in the most recent 2010 textbook. In the first place the new one uses modern interactive method encouraging the participation of the students: it is simply written, well illustrated and each chapter followed by exercises for remembering, knowing who you are, summarizing, questions and answers. Secondly and more importantly, the new books give lesser stress to governments and administration history or war history, but more to social history and significantly, it is not always coupled with economic history.[33] In general we observe that Uzbek historians working for the Ministry of Education pay special attention to nineteenth century putting more effort to develop both the content and method of 9th grade history textbooks.

Concluding Remarks

The Soviet Union did not disintegrate through any kind of revolution; this was an evolutionary change that forced the communist leaders to adopt new policies. Post Soviet independence, as reflected in textbooks has not created a political nationalism in the form of nation-state standardization. Time and again many specialists of education from all over Central Asia expressed their concern to train standard people. They reject Soviet standardization of education in the modernist sense. Standardization of education in the traditional nation-state building does not satisfy the needs of interdependence in world politics, could easily freeze the quest for change and betterment in history textbooks, and would shadow the contribution of local/territorial inventions of plural renaissance within each bordered area.

In both countries' history narration cultural identity overpowers or rather shapes state identity and state continuity. Uzbekistan has always been an urban cultural centre appealing to Muslim countries as well as to other USSR republics during the Soviet times. Uzbek historians much more than the Turkmens have underlined the road to state building in accordance with western historiographical tradition thanks to Jadids' attempts for modern history writing. The confederative community culture among the Turkmens had created another way of telling stories of the "*taypas*" brought together as "Turkmens" in motion. However, both countries feeding on a specific national culture localized/territorialized different phases of historical ventures; Turkmens of different locations of the world were seen as a motor in the national focus in modern Turkmenistan and Uzbeks in Turkistan feeding on its theological, cultural, scientific, artistic past.

In a way they are trying to create a new culture of political history with their specific styles of history narration. In other words they might end up moving away from politics of local culture to create a historiographical tradition of local politics. Uzbekistan and Turkmenistan are developing a set of new values for interpreting their national history, which is not entirely conventional.

Notes and References

1. *Eng Yangi Tarix, 1917-1939*, "O'kıtuvcı," (Toshkent 1989).
2. *Ozbekiston Tarixi 8*, "O'kıtuvcı" (Toshkent 1994). This book takes up the late nineteenth and early twentieth century. Out of 250 pages nearly 160 pages are allotted to liberation movements and Jadid reforms. Social and economic life is narrated solely from the aspect of class analysis, economic and social problems come to the agenda outside of "national consciousness." Insurrections and Islamic reform at times stand out as if they are the main themes of a parallel history.
3. *O'zbekiston Tarixi Klas 11* (2003), 46–51.
4. Marat Durdıev, Şehrat Kadirov, *Dunyadaki Turkmenler, Tarihi Demografik Sın* (Turkmens in the World) (Aşgabat, "Kharp", 1991). This booklet was one of the first books to assert Turkmens' widespread existence after the sovereignty was declared. The late Marat Durdıev, well known archeologist in a private interview in November 1993 in Aşgabat, underlined the mobile nature of the nation also taking pride in this. In his book Turkmens demography is outlined in 13 different countries, USSR, Turkmenistan, Eastern Tacikistan, Uzbekistan, Kazakistan, Stavropol and Astrahan Turkmens, Crimea, China, Afganistan, Iraq, Syria, Turkey and Iran. This "Turkmens everywhere" approach became a part of history textbooks especially during the 2000s.
5. Murat Annanepesov, M. Atagariyev, *Türkmenistan'ın Tarihinden Materyaller* (*X-XVI. Asırlar*) (Aşgabat: Magarif 1995), 95-105.

6. William Irons, *The Yomut Turkmen: A Study of Social Organization Among a Central Asian Turkic Speaking Population* (Ann Arbor: The University of Michigan1975), 39-81.
7. Contrary to this all Uzbek history textbooks on world history start their introduction with the Uzbek state and leader Karimov in the first or second sentences.
8. Büşra Ersanlı, "Azerbaycan, Özbekistan ve Türkmenistan'da Eğitim ve Kültür Politikaları" (Education and Culture Policies), in *Bağımsızlığın Ilk Yılları: Azerbaycan, Kazakistan, Kırgızistan, Özbekistan ve Türkmenistan* (The First Years of Independence: Azerbaijan, Kazahkstan, Kyrgysztan, Uzbekistan and Turkmenistan), B.Ersanlı-Behar (ed.) (Ankara: TC Kültür Bakanlığı HAGEM Yayınları 1994), 186
9. Ersanlı, "Azerbaycan, Özbekistan ve Türkmenistan'da," *Bağımsızlığın*, 183,197.
10. Umur Esen, *Türkmen Aganın Edebi* (Marı: Marı Velayat Mugallimleri Kamilleştiriş İnstitutu 1994).
11. Orazpolat Ekayew, *Türkmenistanyn Tarihi* (Aşgabat: Turkmen döwlet neşiryat gullugy 2009), 184–20.
12. Annanepesov, *Turkmenistanın Tarihinden Materyaller*, 63–68, 192–207.
13. Ekayew, *Türkmenistanyn*, 44, 54, 67, 179, 183, 212, 214, 260; for "Turkmen" as surnames of heroes and for warring see 182–89.
14. Roi Medvedev, "History and Myths," *Russia in Global Affairs*, no. 3 (July–Sep 2006).
15. "History," in *Turkmenistan in Perspective*, chapter 3 (Curriculum Development Division, Education Technology Division, Defense Language Institute Foreign Language Centre 2008) 15.
16. Ekayew, *Türkmenistanyn*,8.
17. Shoshana Keller, "Story, Time, and Dependent Nationhood in the Uzbek History Curriculum," *Slavic Review* 66, no. 2 (Summer 2007): 257.
18. Turkmen history books were called during the 1990s as "Materials from Turkmen's History," exhibiting caution not to depart radically from the Soviet historiographical tradition. An example of *Watan Tarixi* in Uzbekistan was published in 1997 as a recommended book for both secondary and higher education students. This 500 page book also has a chapter on the academia (6 pages) and historiography (8 pages). See Ş. Karimov, R. Şamsuddinov, *Watan Tarixi Birinci Kitab* (Toshkent, "Okıtuvcu" 1997), 463-76.
19. Büşra Ersanlı, "History Textbooks as Reflections of the Political-self: Turkey (1930s and 1990s) and Uzbekistan (1990s)," *International Journal of Middle Eastern Studies* 34 (2002): 338.
20. Uzbekistan was recognized as a historic Muslim cultural center by the Soviet regime also. B. Ersanlı, "Yeni Bağımsızlık ve Ulusun Adı: Özbek Milliyetçiliği" (New Independence and the name of the nation: Uzbek nationalism), *Akademik Araştırmalar Dergisi* 2, no.6 (2000): 67–79.

21. S. Halbayoglu, "O'zbekiston'da Milli Tarix, öğretim ve ders kitaplarını yaratısh sorunları" (National History in Uzbekistan; problems confronted while preparing history textbooks). Paper read at the Second International History Congress, *History Education and the 'Other'*, organized by Türkiye Ekonomik ve Toplumsal Tarih Vakfı, İstanbul, June 1995
22. W.K. Medlin and W.M. Carpenter, *Education and Development in Central Asia* (Leiden: Brill 1971).
23. There also examples of recent oral history books written by Uzbeks. One is women's oral history published in Moscow, analysing and comparing recent past and present in Uzbek life from women's perspective. Among their complaints are: "dialogue is less," "inequality between men and women is very sharp," "spiritual values are lost," "religion is lived as a fashion not as a value system for better lives," "social life has lost vigor compared even to the 1990s." See Marfua Tohtakhodzhayeva, *XX vek v vospominaniakh, ustnykh istoriiakh, pis'makh i dnevnikakh zhenshchin Uzbekistana* (Moscow: Natalis 2008), 178–88.
24. A. P. Muhammadjonov, *Ozbekiston Tarixi 6* (Toshkent, "Okıtuvcı" 1994). This book covers fifth to sixteenth centuries and one third of the book is spared to the Timuride era covering all political, economic, social and cultural developments.
25. Ahmadali Askarov (ed.), *Timur ve Ulugbek Davri Tarixi* (History of Timur and Ulgbek's Times) (Toshkent: Komuslar Bosh Taxririyatı 1996).
26. Ekayew, *Türkmenistanyn*, 229–32.
27. D. Alimova, *XX. Asrın Dastlabkı Ottuz Yıllıgıda Ozbekiston'da Tarix Feni,* 2 vols. (Toshkent: Ozbekiston Respublikası Fenler Akademiası "Fen" Noshriyatı 1994).
28. G. A. Hidoyatov and V. A. Kostetskiy, *O'zbekiston Tarixi*, 9 (Toshkent, "O'zinkomsentr" 2002), 85–6.
29. Ersanlı, "History Textbooks," 343.
30. G. Hidoyatov, *Jahon Tarixi 11, Eng Yengi Tarix (1945-2002)* (Toshkent: "Sharq" Nashriyot 2004), 378–400.
31. G. Hidoyatov, *Jahon Tarixi 10* (Toshkent: "Sharq" Nashriyot 2003), 5.
32. Hidoyatov, *Jahon Tarixi 11*, 319–29.
33. Hidoyatov and Kostetskiy, *O'zbekiston Tarixi 9* and Soyiphan Tillaboyev and Akbar Zamanov, *O'zbekiston Tarixi, 9-sınf* (Toshkent: "Sharq" nashriyot 2010).

8

From Soviet Historiography to National Historiography: Continuities and Discontinuities in Azerbaijani Historiography

Y. Emre Gürbüz

The dissolution of the USSR brought new challenges to the newly independent republics. One of those problems was constructing a proud identity for the citizens, and to replace the venture of "*homo sovieticus*" with this new identity. This task created a new challenge for the elites of the independent Republic of Azerbaijan. Because of the fact that they were going through a period of founding a nation-state, the new identity was also related to forming a historical national identity, which was already undertaken during the Soviet period. This time, however, it had to be realized within a different paradigm and with different priorities.

In this study the continuities and discontinuities in Azerbaijani historiography will be analysed. Education in history is one of the most crucial sources of a state in constructing an identity, and for this study history textbooks will be the main source of analysis. The history textbooks give clues about the idea of identity. Who are "we" are and how do "we" perceive ourselves? In history textbooks the past is being shaped in a certain way in order to train the future generations, i.e. the students. Definitely not everything in textbooks is taken and remembered by the students as they are, but still they form the basis of the citizens' shared knowledge, thus creating the common, national/international reflexes. The dates, names even events learned at school might be forgotten, but the basic ideas remain, as they present clues about the identity at a time, when a young person needs it the most. This process makes history education a crucial field for a state in constructing a common identity for the citizens.

It is also a relatively protected area closed to international academic circles, as they are written only in the national languages. The history textbooks are not translated to other languages, and they cannot be analysed nor criticized by people not knowing the language.

They are not academically evaluated, and they rarely rely on references to validate their thesis. Their power for persuasion comes from the authority preparing and lecturing these courses that is the state authority itself. Not only the language barrier prevents their evaluation in international academic circles, but in some countries it also forbidden to take them away from the country or they are not sold in bookshops but distributed by the ministry to the students to be returned at the end of the year.

Azerbaijani historiography at the turn of the independence did not make the first paces following the sovereignty but it already had a fair tradition in history, which left its traces on recent historiography. Azerbaijan's break from the Soviet past was sharper than most other Soviet republics, because Azerbaijan experienced a strong nationalist unrest and opposition to the Soviet rule following the Nagorno-Karabagh conflict with the Armenian SSR and Moscow's intervention. Moscow was not able to deal with the Nagorno-Karabagh conflict and rising nationalism, which escalated to the killing of 132 Azerbaijani protestors by Soviet troops in January 1990. Right after the sovereignty the government of independent Azerbaijan distanced itself from Moscow, unlike other Caucasian and Central Asian post-Soviet republics. Later Azerbaijan adjusted its relations with Russia. After nearly two decades, however, there is still some continuity with the Soviet methodology of historiography.

During the Soviet period historiography was based on historical materialism and in order to support a national identity within the republican borders the history was examined and taught on a territorial basis. After independence the territorial approach of history proved to be the most persistent element in understanding the past but in a different context due to the changing realities. Here the continuities and discontinuities will be sought to be examined thematically under topics like periodization, territoriality, ethnogenesis, the friends and enemies in history, religion and methodology.

Periodization

During the Soviet era the periodization was organized in a certain way to demonstrate the progress of humanity from *primitive communal society* to socialism. This evolutionary progress had to prove the linear advancement of humanity, giving self-esteem to citizens of the USSR, who were on a more developed stage of history than the people in capitalist countries. The final step would be communism, which would inevitably follow the socialist period. *Class war* was considered to be the *engine of history* as it was formulated by Karl Marx and Friedrich Engels. The history books and atlases exemplified the long struggle of exploited classes against the exploiters and the progressive advancement of humanity through these wars and revolutions. Azerbaijani history itself was not the main concern of history education, but world history and the history of the USSR beginning with the Russian history was the basic path of history. The tools and methods of classifying the past still inspire writing of recent history textbooks, especially about feudalism. The debate about feudalism is definitely not restricted to Marxism, but there are other alternatives to feudalism, such as the *Asiatic Mode of Production* or the terminology can be totally neglected. This example, however, is directly borrowed from the Soviet school textbooks on history.

The first chapter of the recent seventh class textbook is called "Feudal Relationships in Azerbaijan."[1] Other chapters carry names related to "invasions," established states and assaults on Azerbaijan. But the events are generally discussed within the problem of centralization-decentralization, which is a tool applied to determine the level of feudalism in historical materialist periodization. Like feudalism Azerbaijani historiography, however, took it from historical materialism. It is still applied in understanding the historical processes, probably because of the fact that it is also related to the process of state formation. For modern Azerbaijan, which is establishing a state apparatus, it is of utmost importance to find and present the roots of statehood in Azerbaijan. The notions of centralization and state formation debate offer some insight for the recent process of Azerbaijan's centralization and state formation.

As this new state is a nation-state, it is also important to prove the presence of Azerbaijani/Turkic peoples in Azerbaijan. History, which was expected to show the progress of humanity towards communism in the Soviet period, is now a source for demonstrating the progression of Azerbaijani nationhood and statehood. Thus it can be argued that some tools of historical materialism are still in use, as they are applicable to the new paradigm.

Territoriality

Territoriality has also been reshaped in a similar way to periodization. During the Soviet period not only the borders of the recent republics were drawn, but through historiography some feeling of belonging to that territory was also shaped. Each republic studied the past and the cultures of the peoples within their particular Soviet Socialist Republic's borders. All the peoples who lived within those borders were accepted as their ancestors and their artefacts as theirs, whereas other peoples and achievements beyond those borders were abandoned to related republics. This can be very natural for some other peoples living on the same territory for millennia, but here we speak about Turkic peoples, who mostly shared a nomadic past as mixed and mobile tribes. Territoriality was accepted by the Azerbaijanis as well. After nearly two decades, it is still in continuity with the Soviet period. This time, however, it is not the space creating the Azerbaijani people and culture in time but the space retrospectively redefined as Turkic/ Turkish. Today, territoriality and nationalism are amalgamated and the main emphasis has been shifted to proving the existence of Turkish tribes in Azerbaijan starting from the ancient ages. In a hypothetical, non-territorial, lineage-based nationalist evaluation of history the main course of history would be the migration of Turkic tribes to today's Azerbaijan as it is in the case of Turkey's history education.

Other than the Soviet legacy the territorial conflict with Armenia is probably another factor reinforcing the need for proving the perennial existence of Azerbaijani/Turkic tribes in greater Azerbaijan. The ancient states that were part of what is modern Azerbaijan are also accepted as Azerbaijani/Turkic achievements. For example, the finding of the state of Albania, which was included in today's Republic of Azerbaijan in the ancient ages (fourth century BC), is introduced as a Turkic tribe.[2]

The amalgamation of the Soviet territoriality with the new nationalist approach creates both chronological and spatial expansion that is the extension of the historical field of interest. Azerbaijani historiography is not only delimited to the borders of the recent Republic of Azerbaijan but it also covers neighbouring areas ruled by former—real or hypothetical—Azerbaijani/Turkic rulers. This includes Iranian Azerbaijan with its centre in Tabriz. For example the ancient Atropatena state, which was founded in today's Iranian Azerbaijan, is also introduced in a section with the subtitle "the Invasion of Atropatena by Sassanids" (Map 1).[3]

This interest in "Southern Azerbaijan" continues until the last book, where each section about Azerbaijan is followed by sections on "Southern Azerbaijan," such as "National Liberation Movement in Southern Azerbaijan," "Southern Azerbaijan in 20s and 30s," "Cultural Life in Southern Azerbaijan," "Southern Azerbaijan during the Second World War," "Southern Azerbaijan between the Second Half of 40s till 70s" and "Southern Azerbaijan at the End of 70s till 90s."[4]

Ethnogenesis

Another significant issue of the Soviet period was ethnogenesis. For

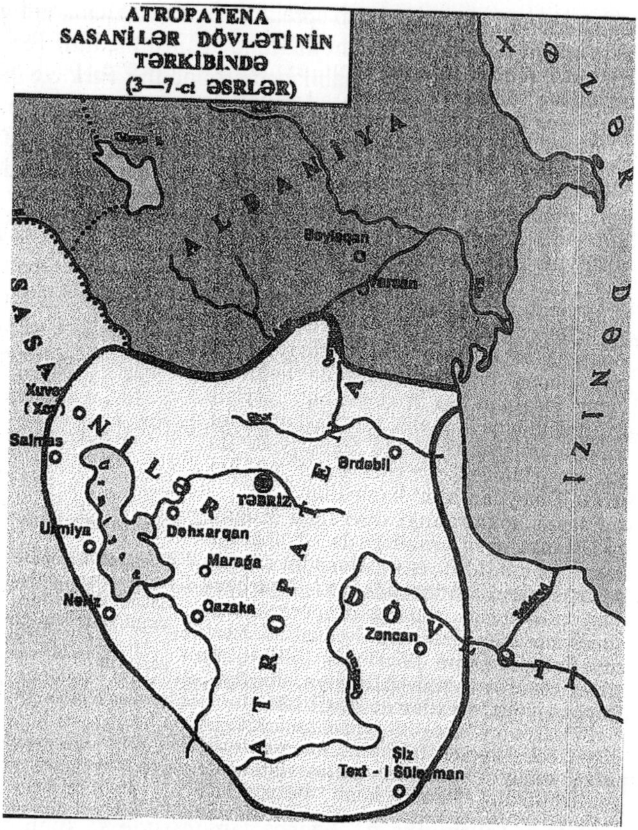

Map 1. Atropena under the Control of the Sassanid State in the 3-7th Century

Source: Y.M. Mahmudlu and Y. Yusipov (eds.), *Azərbaycan Tarixi, 7-ci Sinif Ümumtəhsil Məktəbleri üçün Dərslik*: 12 (History of Azerbaijan, Textbook for 7th Grade General Schools)

the Soviet scholars the definition of nation, nationality, people, ethnic group, etc., was a very strict task. All the people of the USSR obtained special political and cultural rights according to its level in the progression of nationhood. This was reflected in history in the formulation of ethnogenesis that is the formation process of a certain nation. Both in the Soviet period and now it is important to determine, when the Azerbaijanis came into being, who were the subjects of the nation, and what were the factors solidifying the "national unity." For Azerbaijanis ethnogenesis was the solidification of the Azerbaijani population under the umbrella of the already existing Turkic tribes.

Turks were the only ethnic group spread over Azerbaijan, and when the solidification to protect the motherland against the intruders was required, the unification was established around the Turkic tribes.

Under the subtitle of "the Role of Turkic Tribes in the Formation of Azerbaijani People" it is stated that ethnogenesis was established in the early Middle Ages as a result of incorporation of already existing and migrating Turkic tribes. The argument is as follows:

The majority of the ethnic groups living in Azerbaijan (Alban, Qarqar, Uti, Sovde, Sakasen, Hun, Girdiman) were Turkic. In ancient and early Middle Ages there were two great migrations to Azerbaijan. In the first migration Turkic Cimmerian, Scythian, Sak tribes settled in Azerbaijan. The second migration enabled the settlement of Turkic Huns (Kengerli, Pechenek, Bulgar, Onogur, Sabir, Hun, Herlat, Oghuz, etc.). The migrating tribes were ethnically and linguistically close to local Turkic population. The Oghuz Turks built the majority among the Turkic tribes.[5]

It is also stated that in the ancient ages the population in the territory of conflict between Azerbaijan and Armenia, i.e. the Nagorna Karabagh region, was "the Turkic Alban, Qarqar, Hun and Khazars."[6] The Armenian population of Nagorna Karabagh is explained as an outcome of the conversion of the "feudal elites of the mountainous parts of Karabagh" to Christianity.[7] We will return to this issue under the title on religion.

The Friends and Enemies in History

In the history textbooks of Azerbaijan intruders, such as the Armenians, Georgians, Byzantine, Arabs, Persians and Russia are considered as enemies. It is underlined that from ancient ages onwards the Azerbaijani people had fought against them in order to defend their country. The periods under the control of Persians or Arabs/ Caliphate are called as "invasion." The general argument is, however, that they had some positive influence in history as they helped the solidification of the national amalgamation or unity; when all peoples of Azerbaijan were fighting united against the invaders, this resulted in the unification under the common Turkish umbrella.

The period under the Russian Tsardom is termed as colonization. Although it is negatively evaluated, the developments and modernization of Azerbaijan is also mentioned in chapters. The division of Azerbaijan into Northern (Russian) and Southern (Persian) happened in this period, which was just another unwelcomed outcome of colonial rule. The Soviet period, which is covered in the book for the 11th year, is also portrayed negatively with reference to liberation, resistance and suppression. One of the titles is "April Invasion and the End of Azerbaijan People's Republic"[8] and followed by titles, such as "Resistance Movement and Uprisings against the Soviet Rule."[9] Another issue in this book is that of forced migration of Azerbaijanis from Western Azerbaijan, assaults on territorial integrity and "Armenization" of Azerbaijani territories. Azerbaijan had been divided by the struggles between the colonial forces, and then during the Soviet period Azerbaijan lost its historical territories to Armenians.[10] This was another legacy of the Soviet period, which produced lasting troubles for Azerbaijan. This acute problem is a very sensitive issue and mentioning it as one of the outcomes of the Soviet period increases the power of disapproval for the period.

On the other hand the relations with the Ottoman empire present an interesting example. Despite the fact that the Ottomans were long-time enemies of some "Azerbaijani" states, they are not considered as enemies. The Ottoman attacks are again mentioned as "invasion," but the wars with the Ottoman empire are not condemned. Today the official proclamation of Azerbaijan and Turkey is that they are "one nation [in] two states." The past wars are also perceived in a similar way as those between two brothers. The Akkoyunlu ruler Uzun Hasan (1468-78), who is honoured as a ruler during whose time Azerbaijan "advanced to a new level by joining the world political arena,"[11] was decisively defeated by the Ottoman ruler Mehmed the Conqueror. The battle is summarized under the title "the Ottoman Akkoyunlu Wars and Their Negative Effect on the General Turkish Unity."[12] The title clearly shows the main concern here: Turkish unity. The evaluation differs from the discourse on assaults and invasions applied to other "invaders."

According to the section another negative effect of the battle was the decentralization of the state by feudal lords.[13] As has been mentioned above the centralization process of the state and the decentralizing forces constitute a very significant dynamic in the assessment of the past. The main task today is the founding of a nation-state. In the evaluation of the negative outcomes of the war with the Ottomans, those outcomes are presented in relation to the "broader" national identity and state formation.

A more critical issue for Azerbaijan is the battle between the founder of the glorious Safevid state, Shah Ismail, and the Ottoman ruler Selim the Grim. Shah Ismail is a very important figure for Azerbaijani history, because he started from Eastern Anatolia with Turcoman warriors and conquered all Persian territories and parts of Central Asia (see Map 2). He founded the Safavid dynasty, which

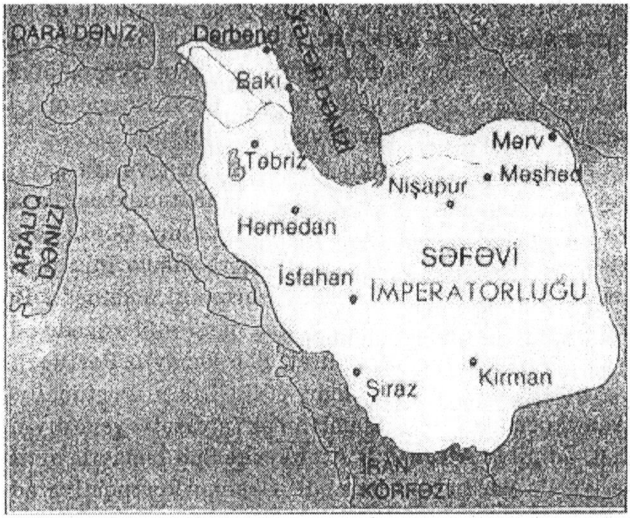

Map 2. Safavid Empire

Source: Y.M. Mahmudlu and Ə. Ə. Qocayev (eds.), *Orta əsrlər Tarixi, 8-ci Sinif Ümumtəhsil Məktəbleri üçün Dərslik* (History of the Middle Ages, Textbook for 8th Grade General Schools) (Baky: Maarif Nə şriyyatı 2001), 289.

ruled over Iran from its capital in Tabriz. This dynasty was also responsible for the permanent Shiification of Iran and Azerbaijan. He was also a popular poet writing in Turkish. There is also a chapter devoted to him in the literature textbook for the ninth class.[14] All those characteristics, like being a glorious conqueror, leader of the Turcoman warrior clans, an empire-builder, a religious leader, a cornerstone in Shiification, a Turkish poet, make him a unique and splendid figure for the Azerbaijani history.

For the Azerbaijani history textbooks the most significant point about the period of Shah Ismail is the centralization and state-formation in Azerbaijan. In both history textbooks "History of Azerbaijan"[15] and "History of the Middle Ages,"[16] which covers the world history at that period, Shah Ismail is introduced as the person, whose period was a cornerstone in the centralization of Azerbaijan. In the following citation from the book "History of Middle Ages"[17] the result of Shah Ismail's glorious attacks summarizes the general perception of Shah Ismail in history. Now Safavid empire was a powerful, Azerbaijani-Turkish empire, not just covering Azerbaijani territories but also all of Iran, Arabian Iraq and Kurdistan. The establishment of Safavid empire is an exceptional event in the

Azerbaijani history; this re-foundation of the lost state tradition meant the unification of all Azerbaijan under a single state.[18]

The notions to be underlined here are "Turkish," "greater territories," "lost state," "state establishment," "unification of all Azerbaijan." Those are the notions defining the greatness for Azerbaijan. Shah Ismail's period is the only period in history, when all of those were achieved. It, however, should also be mentioned that this period does not acquire a special status as the "golden age." A proud reference point in the past is psychologically also a necessity for strengthening the self-esteem. Shah Ismail's swift rise to power came to an end after the disheartening defeat by the Ottoman Empire. Despite this fact the Ottoman Empire is not mentioned as negative as other "enemies" of Azerbaijan. It is written that:

> In [the Battle of] Çaldıran it was the Turkish world in particular and Islamic world in general, which were defeated. Unlike all catastrophes before, this massacre of brothers occurred at a time, when western colonizers were establishing their hegemony in the East. Thus, Çaldıran was the defeat of the whole Turkish-Islamic world and the glory of the western diplomacy.[19]

Despite the fact that the war was with the Ottomans, the main enemies here were the westerners taking advantage of the war. The Ottomans and Safavids, on the other hand, were just "brothers in arms," but with a twist of fate they had ended up on different sides of the front falling prey to the rise of the West.[20] Beside these issues it is also interesting are the omissions. As I have mentioned earlier, Shah Ismail is also responsible for the Shiification of Iran and Azerbaijan. Shia identity is the main factor differentiating Azerbaijanis from other Turkic groups, especially from their Turkish Sunni neighbours in Eastern Anatolia. Thus, his achievement has become a cornerstone in the formation of Azerbaijani nationhood. Because the history is being rewritten in a mainly nationalistic perspective today, it can be expected that Shah Ismail's role in Shiification would become the main factor in introducing him. Here, however, the greater Turkish nationalism is more appreciated than Shiification. This can also be understood as a result of the Soviet scientific attack on religion, which might have been replaced by a secular nationalism.

Religion

Religion is generally understood as one of the unifying factors in the formation of the Azerbaijani identity. Azerbaijanis were continuously in conflict with different religions but especially with Christianity, practiced by the Armenians, Georgians, the Roman Empire and Byzantium. Azerbaijanis were first united under the Zoroastrianism, and then under the Islam. The Arabs, who brought Islam to Azerbaijani territories, however, are defined as invaders and Zoroastrian rulers resisting Arab "invaders" bringing Islam are celebrated as patriots, but it should also be mentioned that Islam itself has not been looked upon negatively. This is in continuity with the Soviet "patriotic" assessment of the past. The famous fighter Babek is a heroic figure, whose legendary struggle against the Caliphate is defined against the "invaders." The book devotes 16 pages to the legendary fight of Babek against the Arab invaders.[21]

Another Soviet continuity with the past historiography is seen in the evaluation of Mazdek and Manichaeism. In a long paragraph Manichaeism is celebrated as a movement "against the feudality of upper classes" "for the establishment of a just society based on equality in property." It is underlined that according to Mazdek "God gave human beings property so that they can share it among themselves."[22] Here religion is not only understood on a materialist basis but also within the tradition of the egalitarian struggle of the human kind. This is one of the rare passages devoted to define a belief system.

After the conversion to Islam, it became the solidifying factor for the Azerbaijani identity. It is stated that "the Arab armies achieved to invade Azerbaijan after many struggles of nearly hundred years,"[23] and only after the Arabs had perceived that they had to deal with Azerbaijanis appropriately.[24] The factors leading to the acceptance of Islam are defined as: the people were permitted to keep their customs and traditions; the taxes were lower than the Sassanid period; the political stability accomplished after the elimination of the multitude of religions; national unity; the more humanitarian, optimistic, objective and just characteristics of the new religion.[25] Some of the Alban population living in north western Azerbaijan, however, had converted to Christianity. They belonged to a different Christian Church from the Georgians and Armenians, but which was sought to be assimilated through the attacks of the Georgian and Armenian churches. It is stated that they had some success, which resulted in the assimilation of some Turks by them, and especially in (Nagorno-) Karabagh. The presence of the Christian-Armenian population of the conflicted territory of Nagorno-Karabagh, which was claimed to be originally Turkish, is explained within this discourse of conversion to Christianity. This history of Christianity and its assimilation underlines the importance of Islam in the formation of the Azerbaijani identity from the opposite view.

Another interesting issue about religion is about the encounter of the Sunni Turks of the Ottoman Empire and Shia, i.e. Azerbaijani Turks of Shah Ismail. As mentioned above Shia identity is one of the most significant characteristics of the Azerbaijani identity, and it is Shah Ismail, who is who responsible for that. A brief evaluation of Shiification can now be attempted.

> In order to reach his military-political objectives Shah Ismail started to pull wider masses to his side. He used Shia as a tool on that purpose. After the establishment of his rule he announced Shia as the hegemonic sect in all Safavid territories. This was a great historical process. The transformation of Shia to official state religion by the Azerbaijani Turkish Safavids divided the whole Turkish world and even the Islamic world to two fronts. The western diplomacy lucratively utilized that to establish its hegemony in the East.[26]

Here Shiification is first understood as a pragmatic tool to control masses for political ambitions, which can be related to the general perception of historical materialism for religion, but the last sentence underlines a different issue: the fatal division of the Turks. Consequently, the West had benefited from the division of the Turks, which should be a lesson learnt from history. The main characteristic going towards the making the Azerbaijani people, Shiaism, was not considered as a formative factor but on the contrary is it introduced as a destructive force. Turkish unity is perceived as the main factor, which would help to promote the further development. Nationalism does not only enlarge the territorial aspect or deepen the historical roots but it also supersedes the religious differences created ages ago.

Methodological Continuities

There are some methodological continuities worth underling separately. The materialist approach is in continuity with the previous period, as it was exemplified in the case of Shah Ismail. While his religious status is more emphasized and also the division to different Islamic sects is considered as the main factor of the struggle in Turkey, worldly matters are on the forefront in Azerbaijan. Shah Ismail's aim is declared as opening a window to the Mediterranean by conquering Syria.[27]

Generally struggles are perceived to be conditioned by the economic substructure, which corresponds to historical materialism.

Religious reasons, political rivalry for extending territories or other potential political reasons, such as the intrigues of the West are either not mentioned or they are mentioned as extensions of economic reasons. In the example of the struggle between the Ottomans and the Safavids, the reason for the western intrigues as well as the result of "the war between two brothers" is presented within the similar historical materialist approach as "the suitable conditions for colonial invasions in the Near East, Middle East and Indian Ocean in the first period of accumulation of capital were created."[28]

The same trend is also seen in other chapters, where nearly every section starts with the economic or socio-economic structure, followed by political developments, such as wars, and the final chapter is generally devoted to "civilization," which covers the scientific-technological developments, education and cultural life.[29] Also the sections devoted to political, technological and cultural developments are displayed through the economic perspective. The reforms are for example explained within the context of the class war between the aristocracy and bourgeoisie or bourgeoisie and proletariat. Before the rise of bourgeoisie the focal point is on the feudality as mentioned above.[30]

The linear, progressive understanding of historical materialism is also clear in the evaluation of the past. It is reflected in the periodization mentioned above, but this is not limited with the stages in the history. Nearly all events, even the invasions are considered to have had some positive effects. The invasions, for example, helped to the unification of the Azerbaijani society against the common enemy, thus leading to the establishment of a national identity. Furthermore the invasion was followed by a stability and centralization period. This can be understood within the optimistic view to the history that it is a progressive movement for the better.

Conclusion

It can be argued that generally the tools and methods of historical materialist analysis seem to be in continuity with the Soviet period. They also, however, have catered to changing needs. The aim of the independent Republic of Azerbaijan is to form a state and a new identity as a nation. This nation, however, is not only the Azerbaijani nation but the Turkish nation in general of which Azerbaijanis are understood as an inseparable part. Every issue analysed in this essay is refashioned within this new identity formation. The periodization still uses formulations of the Soviet past, but this time they are used for demonstrating the progress of the Azerbaijani Turkish nation. The Soviet stress on territoriality seems to be enduring the changes, but it is now a tool for underlining the perennial Turkish presence in wider Azerbaijan, due to the requirements of claiming the historical right for conflicted territories with Armenia. Additionally, the territory of interest has been enlarged parallel to the new emphasis on nation, and it became the land of all Azeri people, including Iranian Azeri people.

Ethnogenesis was also an important tool in Soviet historiography, which is in continuity but was reshaped according to recent necessities. It is argued that Azerbaijan was always a land with some Turkic tribes, along with sporadic non-Turkic tribes. Arrival of further Turkic migrants created the recent Azerbaijani Turkish identity. In evaluating the friends and enemies patriotism is mixed with Turkish nationalism. All foreign attacks are called "invasion" including the armies of the Caliphate, but excluding Selchukids, who were Oghuz Turks. Also the presentation of the wars with the Ottomans differentiates them from others. Here it is the division of the Turks, which is condemned more than the "invasion" of the Ottomans the Azerbaijani territories.

Religion is also assessed similarly. It is either a force beyond patriotism against foreign intruders, or a unifying factor, or a factor leading to assimilation by Christian Armenians, or a dividing factor for the Turks. It is not a belief system in itself but some contributing factor to another material issue, generally related to the fluctuations in the formation of the national identity. The traces of the historical materialist approach, such as the class struggle, centralization-decentralization of the state in the discussion of feudality, the linear, progressive march of history, are seen in recent textbooks as well. Most of them, however, are this time applied to explain the process of the formation of the nation or to prove the presence of a centralized state apparatus in the past or to underline the centralization of the state or formation of a unified nation.

The approach during the Soviet period was formulated as "national in form, socialist in content." The recent history textbooks have generally been written by the same cadres or those who were educated during that period. They are accustomed to the application of these tools, and these tools and methods do not appear to be conflicting with the recent requirements of the state and nation-building. Thus, these tools and methods are still in use but this time within a different paradigm emphasizing the perennial nature of the nation, its land and state formation.

Notes and References

1. Y.M. Mahmudlu and Y. Yusipov (eds.), *Azərbaycan Tarixi, 7-ci Sinif Ümumtəhsil Məktəbleri üçün Dərslik* (History of Azerbaijan, Textbook for 7th Grade General Schools) (Baky: Tahsil Nəşriyyatı 2002), 7.
2. Mahmudlu and Yusipov, *Azərbaycan Tarixi*, 18, 20.
3. Mahmudlu and Yusipov, *Azərbaycan Tarixi*, 11.
4. S. Kəndilov and I. Məmədovun (eds.), *Azərbaycan Tarixi, 11-ci Sinif Ümumtəhsil Məktəbleri üçün Dərslik* (History of Azerbaijan, Textbook for 11th Grade General Schools) (Baky: Çaşıoğlu 2002), 348-9.
5. Mahmudlu and Yusipov, *Azərbaycan Tarixi*, 40-41
6. Mahmudlu and Yusipov, *Azərbaycan Tarixi*, 18.
7. Mahmudlu and Yusipov, *Azərbaycan Tarixi*, 23.
8. Kəndilov and Məmədovun, *Azərbaycan Tarixi,* 62-74.
9. Kəndilov and Məmədovun, *Azərbaycan Tarixi,* 109-19.
10. Kəndilov and Məmədovun, *Azərbaycan Tarixi,* 119-25.
11. Y.M. Mahmudlu and E.E. Kocayev (eds.), *Orta Asrlar Tarihi, 8-ci Sinif Ümumtehsil Mektebleri üçün Derslik* (History of the Middle Ages, Textbook for 8th Grade General Schools) (Baky: Maarif Neşriyyatı, Bakı 2001), 60-62.
12. Mahmudlu and Kocayev, *Orta Asrlar Tarihi*, 152.
13. Mahmudlu and Kocayev, *Orta Asrlar Tarihi*, 156.
14. Ə. Səfərli and X. Yusufli (eds.), *Ədəbiyyat IX Sinif Üçün Dərslik* (Textbook for Literature 9th Grade) (Baky: Təhsil Nəşriyyatı 2002), 184.
15. Yaqub Mahmudlu and Süleyman Məmmədov (eds.), *Azərbaycan Tarixi 8-ci Sinif üçün Derslik* (History of Azerbaijan, Textbook for 8th Grade General Schools) (Baky: Təhsil Nəşriyyatı 2001),181-82. It should be mentioned here that in this book the stress in the centralization is more on the objective conditions. The internal factors were ripe to pass to the upper stage of the evolutionary development, and the Ottomans brought about the external factor pushing the Azerbaijanis to stick together for unity and centralization.
16. Y.M. Mahmudlu and Ə.Ə. Qocayev (eds.), *Orta Əsrlər Tarixi, 8-ci Sinif Ümumtəhsil Məktəbleri üçün Dərslik* (History of the Middle Ages, Textbook for 8th Grade General Schools) (Baky: Maarif Nəşriyyatı 2001), 288.
17. Mahmudlu and Qocayev, *Orta əsrlər Tarixi,* 288.
18. Mahmudlu and Qocayev, *Orta əsrlər Tarixi,* 288.
19. Mahmudlu and Qocayev, *Orta əsrlər Tarixi,* 280.
20. Turkey and the Ottoman Empire are taught in a relatively positive manner and with more pages devoted to their history than to any other state in history.
21. Mahmudlu and Yusipov, *Azərbaycan Tarixi,* 73-88.
22. Mahmudlu and Yusipov, *Azərbaycan Tarixi,* 30.

23. Mahmudlu and Yusipov, *Azərbaycan Tarixi,* 59.
24. Mahmudlu and Yusipov, *Azərbaycan Tarixi,* 59.
25. Mahmudlu and Yusipov, *Azərbaycan Tarixi,* 59-61.
26. Mahmudlu and Qocayev, *Orta əsrlər Tarixi,* 288-9.
27. Mahmudlu and Qocayev, *Orta əsrlər Tarixi,,* 290.
28. Mahmudlu and Qocayev, *Orta əsrlər Tarixi,* 292.
29. See for example the subsections for England, Italy, Austria-Hungary, USA, Latin America, Turkey, Central Asia Kazakhstan, the Crimea, Volga, Sibir Turks, Iran, China and Japan in T.T. Vəliyev, R.C. Süleyman (eds.), *Yeni Tarix, Ymumtəhsil* [sic] *Məktəblerinin 10-cu Sinfi üçün Dərslik* (New History, Textbook for 10th Grade General Schools) (Baky: Çaşıoğlu 2002).
30. Vəliyev and Süleyman, *Yeni Tarix.*

9

The New Edition of the History of Siberia: Reviewing and Summarizing Trends in Contemporary Siberian Historiography*

Denis Ananyev

In the last thirty years, socio-political, socio-economic and ethno-cultural interaction has taken place. Under conditions of globalization it is not only necessary to determine the prospects of development of humanity and that of individual countries and regions, but is also important to show the legitimacy in civilizational processes, taking a fresh look at the historical events and phenomena.

At the beginning of the twenty-first century Siberia became one of the regions that attracted increased interest of authors, who were writing about energy security of states, a more equitable distribution of resources, about the role of regions in the labour economy and their influence on global politics. In spite of the increasing significance of Siberia for the prospects of Russia's development, the economy of the region is still weakly diversified, and the energy and raw material sector is based on traditional methods of technology, which create obstacles in the way of speedy reform. All this makes the study of historical experience of the 'discovery' and opening up of a place, the evaluation of historical risks, short term and long term effects and missed opportunities in the aspect of development of Siberia in various periods of its history extremely important. The study of problems, associated with the various periods of "Russian colonization" of Northern Asia, is necessary for a greater and objective evaluation of the modern situation in Siberia and in the Far East.

The relevance of the given problem is determined by the role which Siberia played in the past in Russia, and also continues to play in the present. The accession of the region to the Russian state

---

* Supported by RFH (Grant no 11-01-00242a)

possessed geopolitical significance, since Russia did not only acquire a huge territory, but practically inexhaustible natural resources, and became a part of the Asia Pacific Region. Siberia experienced the socio-economic, cultural and political traditions of Europe and Asia, accumulated enormous potential, without the rational use of which Russia could not effectively interact with the representatives of different cultural and historical traditions. No less is the importance to study the unique historical experience of the ways in which Siberia's economic potential was revealed.

The Siberian problematic is important from the point of view of internal administration in the historiography of the region, the definition of the perspectives of its further development. From the end of the 1980s, historical Siberian Studies, like Russian historical science as a whole, is going through a transitional phase, conditioned by the rejection from a single methodological paradigm (and in fact—the postulates of Marxism and historical materialism) and the search for new, alternative theoretical methodological approaches, which allow a fresh look at the problems of social development.

Along with working on new conceptual approaches, historians have also widened the circle of investigation. But a total break with research traditions, obviously, did not occur. Historians continue to work out traditional themes, connected to the study of moving forces of colonization of Siberia, with the question of inter-relation of the policies of state and mass local movements, about the course and culmination of agrarian and trade-industrial development of the east of Russia, about the character of the interaction of the Russians with diverse ethnic groups. The relevance of questions related to settlers' movement, of the evolution of the forms of economic activities of different groups of rural and urban populations, was not lost either.

In the modern period it is necessary to systematize and rethink over accumulated historical experiences, especially considering the fundamental difficulties in charting a history of Siberia (edited by A.P. Okladnikov)[1] that was published in the middle of the '60s of the twentieth century. The last decade was marked by significant accretion of historical knowledge, new sources were explored and conducted in the scientific circulation, and newer aspects of the history of Siberia that were not reviewed earlier by historians, appeared.

Conceptualization of the New "History of Siberia"

At present, the Institute of History of SO RAN in Novosibirsk is working on a 3-volume monograph, entitled "History of Siberia," which will accumulate the findings of earlier works related to various periods of development in historical sciences. The project is premised on the territorial trajectory of the Siberian region as a wide, historically formed territorial unit stretching from the eastern borders of Urals to the Pacific Ocean, including within it the Russian Far East. The history of Northern Asian micro-region will be perceived from ancient times till the beginning of the twenty-first century.

The newness of the given task is defined by 1) accumulation of historiography-related material over the past four decades; 2) the working out of a new conceptual framework of the given problems; 3) the analysis of a vast chronological framework; 4) the spectrum of basic elements of the historical process; 5) the research of the development and balancing of state and regional interests; 6) emphasizing new paradigms in the understanding of the factors of development of Russian statehood; 7) the combination of historical and geo-political analysis; 8) pointing to the gaps in historiography.

In the course of the work, the main thrust should be placed on the representation of processes and phenomena, having a global as well as Russian significance and exerting significant influence on the economic, political and socio-cultural development of Siberian region on the whole. According to the view of group of authors, events have become important as historical milestones in the history of Siberia that impact on the general Russian and global processes in various periods of historical development. The present publication will help to reflect on the integration of functions of the eastern regions of the country, their role in the economic, demographic, political and socio-cultural processes of the development of the Russian state. "The History of Siberia" is also called upon to liquidate the several gaps in the history of Siberia, facilitating the formation of a scientifically grounded approach to native and regional history.

The first volume "*Sibir v drevnosty I srednevekovye*" (edited by academician A.P. Derevyanko) will be dedicated to the archaeological investigations. The second volume is "*Sibir v novoe vremya (1581-February 1917)*" and its main editor is academician N.N. Pokrovsky. The third volume "*Sibir v noveishee vremya* (1917—to the beginning of 21st century)" edited by V.A. Lamin will be research-based of concrete and historical character. On the basis of these volumes the problematic-chronological principle of statement of the material will be determined. The main editor of the series will be academician A.P. Derevyanko.

The object of research is Siberia, both specific historical and cultural, ethno-social and economic and geographical region of Russia. The subject field of survey will include periods of growth of the region and the main structural elements of the historical process, which reflect the historical reality and historiographical traditions.

Methodology

Siberian studies will always be at the centre of attention as both native, and western researchers have demonstrated various approaches for the study of Siberia. There is no simple or universal solution, but two main views can be delineated. The first group of researchers relied on "Europeanization" of the colonies, understanding in this the simple production, reflection of traditional way of life, transported to the colony from the metropolis. The other group of historians concentrated on the unique specificities of colonized territories, which transformed the earlier way of life and created new geographical, economic and cultural milieu. The first approach was adopted by native/domestic authors, who have studied the history of conquest of Siberia, and also by their western colleagues, who have written about "Russian eastern expansion" in Northern Asia. The second approach often is associated with the theory of "frontier" theorized by Eurasian scientists, and the geopolitical theory of "heartland," etc.

At the same time the majority of researchers have underscored the key role that the Russian state played in opening up Siberia to it. The first historian of Siberian colonization G.F. Miller was also the author of the idea about the decisive role of the state in the conquest and settlement of Siberia. In the nineteenth century this idea was reiterated by Russian historians—the representatives of so called "state schools." In their works, they viewed the history of Russia as the history of uninterrupted colonization, when its penetration into Siberia was only part of this process. At the same time they, undoubtedly, considered Russia to be a part of European civilization, and accordingly, the usage of the term "Europeanization" was fully justified.

During Soviet times, researchers, adopting the Marxist formation approach, in essence, did not go beyond the "colonization" theory, changing only the evaluation of the effects of colonization. In the 1920s-'30s, Soviet historians mainly wrote about the negative impact of tsarist colonial policy, i.e. about mainly the positive aspects of opening up Siberia by the Russians. The logical result of colonization theory is represented by the concept of "modernization," used in the context of a later period of the history of discovery of Siberia.

In the last few decades Siberian studies have become popular, research being conducted with an inter-disciplinary approach (ethno-history, historical anthropology, adaptation approach, oral history, etc.), which also finds its reflection in the pages of the new edition of *Istoriya Sibiri*. Apart from this, along with the realization of the general aims and concrete tasks together with the traditional resources and methods for historians of analytical works there is also a plan to adopt the method and approaches of related sciences: economy, social psychology, statistics.

Authors' Collective

For the preparation of the generalized scientific work on the history of Siberia, there are some necessary prerequisites. In the region there exists a strong scientific tradition of historical research. The centre of organization of historical sciences in Siberia is the Institute for Archaeology and Ethnography and the Institute of History of the Siberian Section of the Russian Academy of Sciences. In these institutions four members of RAN work, there are more than 60 doctors and 100 candidates of historical sciences.

The present project is both research oriented and coordinates the preparation of the volume in a chronological as well thematic format. The participants of the project possess an experience of research and scientifically organized activity, and also necessary qualifications and have participated in the preparation of collected works as well as research projects, including projects supported by RGNF.

The members of the collective have prepared and published a three volume *Istoricheskaya Entsiklopedia Sibiri*,[2] and also a series of monographs and articles on the history of Siberia. In 2010 the participants of the project conducted a preparatory survey work necessary for the realization of the project. The structure of the publication has been worked out by a circle of specialists decided the main research questions. Information about the preparation of *Istoriya Sibiri* has been sent to several academic institutions of Siberia.

Apart from the institutes of the Novosibirsk scientific centre the others participating in the project are: Institute of History, Archeology and Ethnography of the Nations of Far East of the Far-eastern Department of RAN (Vladivostok), the Institute of History and Archaeology of the Ural Department of RAN (Ekaterinburg), Institute of Mongolian Studies, Buddhism and Tibetology of the Siberian Department of RAN (Ulan Ude), Institute of Humanitarian Research and Problems of Small Nations of Northern Siberian Department of RAN (Yakutsk), Tuvinsky Institute of Humanitarin Research (Kyzyl), Hakasky Scientific and Research Institute of History, Language and Literature (Abakan), Altaisky Scientific Research Institute of History, Language and Literature (Gorno-Altaisk).

Large groups of historians are working in all the universities of the centres of the region. The Institute of History of the SO RAN is the main centre that has united several researchers and is coordinating the preparation of the second and third volumes of *Istoriya Sibiri*. At present the work is being carried out together with the Amur, Keremovsky and Blagoveshensky State Pedagogical Universities, the Irkutsk State University, the Krasnoyarsky State Pedagogical University, the Kemerovsky State University, the Novosibirsky State University and State Pedagogical University, Omsk State University, the Tyumen State University. Based on requirements, others scientific and research and educational institutions of the Altai State University, Kuzbasskaya State Pedagogical Academy, Tomsk University, Ural State University are also involved.

Area Focus : Archaeology

The first volume of the publication, which will reflect the ancient history of Siberia, has attempted to reconstruct the appropriation by archaic people of a significant region of Eurasia, the specifics of the formation and evolution of regional cultures of primitive humans, which occurred under conditions of inaccessible, periodically changing natural and climatic systems.

Since antiquity, the paths of human migration have crisscrossed the northern territories of Eurasia. In spite of inhospitable climate, this region always attracted attention. Throughout the entire course of the history of Siberia migratory waves of European and Asian tribes and nations flowed across its space. All this resulted in Siberia becoming a kind of "floating kettle," which integrated on its territory peoples of various nationalities, religions and cultures. In essence, it manifested a kind or sample of modern globalizing world. The Siberian regional model of this world, its historical experience of a sufficiently long existence, as never before is relevant and important for today's global community.

A part of the project, the ancient history of Siberia (volume 1), is dedicated to the reconstruction of the subsequent appropriation by archaic groups of people of a significant region of Eurasia, the specifics of the formation and evolution of regional cultures of primitive humans, which occurred under conditions of inaccessible, periodically changing natural and climatic systems. The work proposes an analysis of the numerous minerals, natural and anthropogenic objects, the linkages and totality of which allows the consideration also of humans, their culture, their results, social environment and habitation environment as a single system.

Till the 1960s there was a widespread opinion that Siberia and the Far East began to be inhabited only during the state of final inclusion (18-20 thousand years ago) of lower Paleolithic culture. Modern empirical and theoretical achievements of archaeology establish that the first and most ancient colonisation of Siberia during the time of the lower Paleolithic is almost 0.8 million years ago. In Siberian sites weapons of this time have been discovered, which are the earliest symbols of human culture, formed in the one type of environment of Homo Erectus—*Homo ergaster* (archaic form of African Homo Erectus), the remains of which were discovered in the outside the limits of the African continent.

The spatial reconstruction of the most ancient migrations, involves one more migratory wave of ancient hominids, who could have, in later evolutions appeared to be Homo sapiens in Eurasia, partially in Siberia, but already from the Middle East. The beginning of such a movement, according to modern data, is dated as being 450-350 thousand years ago, and its result was the mechanical transfer and resultant distribution of late Paleolithic culture.

The next stage of the ancient history of Siberia corresponds to Acheulian epoch (early Stone Age/Lower Paleolithic Age). The authors of the project offer an analysis of the epochs, whose culture has succeeded the ancient local Acheulian prototypes. Characterizing the later Paleolethic stage of the ancient Stone Age of Siberia, authors of the project pay great attention to the character of the transition from the medium to the higher Paleolithic. It is acknowledged that the carriers of the later Paleolithic culture are anatomically modern humans (Homo sapiens sapiens), who have in comparison with the earlier representatives of the clan of Homo have had fundamental changes in the norms social behaviour, in their thought process and social organization.

The following discoveries about middle Paleolithic and early upper Paleolithic show that Northern Asia represents one of the regions where later Paleolithic culture appeared which transformed itself from the culture of medium Paleolithics. The unexpected early growth of early Upper Paleolithic remnants of the monuments of the Altai allows the review of all concepts of the genesis of the first development of the cultures of the Upper Paleolithic of the Eurasian type. The cited results in the work of the genome expertise of the odontological material from the caves of Altai answer the question, as to which biological specifics of their ancestors did the carriers of Asian and South Siberian paleolithics inherit.

Characterizing the final stage of the Upper Paleolithics of Siberia, corresponding to the intervals 21,000-10,000 years ago, the authors of the project observe that this time was the special time in the ancient history of Siberia, which reflects the process of a high unification of culture of the region, and first of all, of the South Pole. This condition of culture is not repeated in the future history of Northern Asia.

Characterizing the earlier Holocene material of Siberia and the Far East, which synchronises with the Mesolithic and Neolithic epochs of Eurasia, the authors of the project pay special attention to the cultural norms of the population of the region, inhabiting it 10,000-5000 years ago, the analysis of the housing constructions, the details of the heating systems and the organizations of the spaces, as well as the economy. The production of ceramics in the societies of the Far East is specially analysed, whose age indices exceed 13 thousand year cycles.

These materials have a global historical significance and allow principally new solutions to the problems of the genesis and development of the ceramic production in the east of Asia. In the last thirty years huge archeological material was accumulated, which was connected to the period of Paleometals (Bronze and early Iron age) and the middle ages of Siberia. With its interpretation, the main direction was taken by the complex multi-disciplinary research of the material of the culture, its chronology and ethnic history of the population of this region of Asia. Presently it is obvious, that the working out the problem ethno-genesis and of the historical destinies of the population of either region, through a combination of archaeology, physical anthropology and molecular genetics, opens a wide perspective for the reconstruction of the cultural and ethnogenesis, migrations of people, and also of the structure of inter-group relations.

The presence of unique, archaeological and anthropological sources in the Bronze epoch, the experience of receiving the chain of ancient DNA from bone fabric, and also the possibility of conducting a comparative analysis of the received information with the world data banks allowed the implementation of unique research, which is not comparable to any other practice.

As was established, the population in the Bronze Age of Western Siberia, especially of its steppe regions, felt the impact of cultural and biological influence through the territory of Altai and the steppes of Northern Kazakhstan. In the mitochondrial genomes of the autochthonous population of mountainous Altai only West European genetic pool was discovered, which leads to the conclusion that genetic belonging is related to the gene pool of European populations.

The mixture of western and eastern gene waves on the mountainous territory of Altai speaks of the Iron Age in Pazyryksky culture. The European component, discovered in the anthropological composition of the tribes of 2000 BC, is witness to the possibility of linkages between the tribes of mountainous Altai with the cattle rearing population of Central Asia. The details of the Paleolithic Age also give evidence about the existence of such ties.

Considering the specifics of the ancient history of the population of Siberia based on archaeological sources, the main content of the archaeological cultures of Siberian region from the Neolithic Age to the later middle ages can be affirmed. The contemporary results of the study of ancient history that the publication deals with are more significant than the chronological periods. However, all the problems raised in this or that degree reflect the processes, occurring today in global archaeology.

The first section of the first volume is dedicated to the history of the development of climate and nature amongst anthropogenists (authors S.V. and V.S. Zykyna, M.V. Shunkov, I.U. Slyusarenko, S.K. Vasilyev). The second section is dedicated to the archaeology of Siberia in the Paleolithic era (authors writing on this section are academicians P.P. Derevyanko, S.V. Markin, A.V. Tabarev, G.I. Medvedyev, M.V. Shunkov, N.I. Drozdov). The third chapter is called *Sibir v epokhu Neolita* (authors writing on this are V.V. Vorbov, A.V. Tabarev, V.E. Medvedev, U.F. Kiryushin, T.A. Chikisheva, I.V. Aseev, A.N. Alexeiv, S.V. Alkin, A.A. Vasilyevsky). The fourth section has been dedicated to the Bronze Age, whose authors are academicians V.I. Molodin, V.V. Bobrov, U.F. Kiryushin, T.A. Chikisheva, O.I. Goryunova, A.N. Alekseev, A.A. Vasilyevsky, A.P. Borodovsky, L.N. Malynkova, O.I. Novikova.

The early Iron Age and the Middle Ages are reviewed in the fifth and sixth sections (the authors are U.S. Khudyakov, O.A. Mitko, V.I. Molodin, N.V. Polosmak, U.S. Khudyakov, T.A. Chikisheva, D.V. Cheremisin, I.V. Aseev, E.I. Derevyanko, V.E. Medvedev, S.P. Nesterov, A.A. Vasilyevsky, D.V. Pozdnyakov, A.I. Solovyev, E.S,. Bogdanov, S.V. Alkin, A.P. Borodovsky). The last and seventh section of the first tome, written by A.V. Baulo and D.V. Pozdnyakov, look at the archaeology of the nations of Siberia in the New Age.

History of Siberia: 16th to Early 20th Centuries

In the last half century the country's historical science fruitfully has worked on the problems of the moving force in the beginning of the century of opening up Siberia, the questions about the correlations between the policies of the state and local movements of the people, about the role of social consciousness, about the paths of agricultural, territorial and trade and industrial appropriation of the east of Russia, about the character of the inter-relations between Russians and ethnic groups of Siberians, about the role of external policy problems etc. Significant success was achieved in the study of migratory and settler movement, the evolution of forms of economic activities of various groups of rural and urban populations.

With the Novosibirsk archaeological expeditions, and the formation of archaeological investigation centres, is linked the renewed interest in the history of the Russian Orthodox religion in Siberia, the history of the Old Believers in the middle of the 1960s. This historians and Siberian experts analysed the problems of religious and political social consciousness, the various forms of social protest of the population of Siberia in seventeenth-beginning of twentieth centuries.

In the second half of the 1980s, a search for new methodologies and approaches began, the alternatives to the dominant orthodox view, the scope of research problematic was increased. Modern historical research is dedicated to the problems of state directives, to the questions of Siberian urbanization, the history of native peoples of Siberia, their ethnic composition, numbers, settlements, spiritual and material cultures; to the problems, connected with the problems of the realization of Stolypin's agrarian reforms, of socio-political lives of the region. The history of the Church and various faiths has become extremely popular subject in the last few decades.

A notable contribution in the working of the problems of the history of Siberia in the second half of the sixteenth-beginning of the twentieth century has been made by western researchers, first of all by the representatives of the Anglo-American and German historians. Soviet historiography has traditionally underscored the narrowness of the sources of the bases and the ideological tendencies of the works of Western Siberian specialists. But along with this, it is necessary to note the conceptual variety of foreign researches, the significance of the worked out theoretical methodological approaches which have been used in the Western historical sciences, and which has allowed solid and all-rounded analysis of the historical sources available to us.

In the main structure of the second volume, named "*Sibir v Novoe Vremya*," a chronological principle is followed. Content wise the volume consists of four sections, dedicated to the history of the main periods of development of Siberia in the period under review: the first section is dedicated to the history of unifying and discovery of Siberia in the end of sixteenth-seventieth centuries; the second section involves the period of the beginning of eighteenth century till 1820s; the third section involves the period from 1820s till the beginning of the 1880s; the fourth section—from the end of the ninteenth century till February 1917. Each of the mentioned sections in its turn is divided into 8-10 basic thematic groups: "Demographic and migration processes," "Economic Development," "Communications," "Social set up, population groups," "State governance," "Development of Faiths," "Culture, education, science," "Socio-political life," "Government policies in the region," "Politics towards the aboriginal ethnicities." In a series of sections more detailed thematically or chronological stories have been delineated as paragraphs.

Redaction colleagues of the second volume include academician of RAN N.N. Pokrovsky (main editor), M.V. Shilovsky (Main deputy editor), A.H. Elert (Main deputy editor), D.A. Ananyev (main secretary), L.I. Gallyamova, O.N. Kationov, N.P. Matkhanova, A.V. Remnev, O.I. Sergeev, V.A. Skubnevsky. The first section is dedicated to the expedition of Ermak and the beginning of the discovery of Siberia (end of sixteenth/seventeenth centuries). The authors are D.A. Ananyev, A.A. Borisov, L.I, Zhurova, N.D. Zolnikova, O.N. Kationov, A.I. Poberezhnikov, academician N.N. Pokrovsky, D.A. Redin, I.R. Sokolovsky, L.I. Sherstova, A.P. Yarkov.

Amongst the stories reviewed in the first chapter are: the question about the role of Ermak, the merchants Stroganovs, Cossacks and martial bands in the accession of Siberia, the basis of islands and cities; the inter-relations between Russians and aboriginal population and *yasak* taxation; questions of demography, problem of relations between the state and voluntary colonization, Siberian exile. The chapters also takes a look at the social setup of Siberia and the biggest national revolt in the eighteenth century; the genesis and development of land cultivation, reform of U.A. Suleshov; the characteristics of trade, business, artisans, traders, communication is also looked at. Special sections are dedicated o the problems of the administration of Siberia; to foreign policy and borders; to the history of Christianity in the region, the questions regarding history of Old Believers, the spread of Islam and Buddism; the problems of cultural development.

The second chapter is dedicated to the socio-economic development of society, to the system of governance and culture in the beginning of eighteenth century–1820s, (authors are D.A. Ananyev, L.I. Galyamova, E.M. Glavatskaya., Zhurova L.I, N.D.

Zolnikova, O.N. Katianov, A.K. Kirillov, E.V. Komleva, T.S. Maмsik, N.P. Matkhanova, academician N.N. Pokrovsky, A.I. Savin, T.N. Soboleva, L.I. Sherstova, M.V. Shilovsky, A.K. Elert, A.P. Yarkov).

Among narratives, that are included in the second chapter are: the demographic and migratory processes, movement of population to the south and to the south-east of Siberia; the history of exile; the development of communications, defense and development of Moscow-Siberian tracts, evolution of the society in conditions of absolute monarchy, history of social protests, the Pugachev mutiny, creation of cabinet metallurgic complex in the Altai and in Zabaikal; the role of Russian and American companies in the discovery of Pacific coast and of Russian America; the administrative reforms of Peter I till the beginning of nineteenth century; Siberian Cossacks and the creation of regular military formations; growth of religion; the history of academic expeditions, appearance of scientific ethnography, Siberian studies etc.

The third chapter of the second volume is called "*Obshchestvo, ekonomika, pravitelstvennaya politika and kultura v 1820*-e-*nachale 1880*-x *gg.*" (authors are D.A. Ananyev, L.I. Gallyamova, G.M. Glavatskaya, U.M. Goncharov, E.A. Degaltseva, V.A. Zverev, N.D. Zolnikova, O.N. Kaтionov, A.K. Kirillov, T.S. Mamik, N.P. Matkhanova, academician N.N. Pokrovsky, A.V. Remnev, T.M. Stepanskaya, N.N. Pokrovsky, L.E. Fetisova, L.I. Sherstova, M.V. Shilovsky, À.P. Yarkov).

The main attention is given to problems like the settlement policy of the monarch, the role of the exiles and banishment in the development of the region, technical discoveries in water transport and its development, development of telegraph, economic opening of Siberia and the Far East, development of gold industry, the cracks in the main industrial complex and the change in the economic activities in Altai; changes in the governmental politics in the region, the activities of 1st and 2nd Siberian Committees, revision and reform of M.M. Speransky; "*Ustav ob inorodtsakh* (Charter about Foreigners)" and the real practice of international relations.

In the sections on the second half of the nineteenth century, subjects that were included are: the accession of Kazakhstan to the conclusive formation of borders with China, the sale of Russian America to US and the liquidation of Russian-American companies, the formation of Priamurskaya Governor Generalate, the creation of Separate Siberian Corpus, military formations, Siberian flotilla, reforms of 1860-1880s in Asian Russia, the history of political and criminal exiles (Dekabrists, Petrashevets, Poles), nature of Sakhalin exile system, creation of local intelligentsia, history of Siberian regionalism, creation of first stationary scientific institution (institutions of IRGO, museums), etc.

The fourth chapter is on the land in the nineteenth-twenteenth centuries: the core socio-political turmoil and the authors are N.A. Belyaeva, S.I. Boyakova, L.I, Gallyamova, E.M. Glavatskaya, U.M. Goncharov, E.A. Degaltseva, V.A. Zvereev, T.Y. Ikkonikova, A.K. Kirillov, academician N.N. Pokrovsky, A.V. Remnev, D.G. Simonov, V.A. Skubnevsky, T.M. Stepanskaya, L.E. Fetisova, L.I. Sherstova, M.V. Shilovsky, A.P. Yarkov.

The main descriptions of the fourth chapter are related to the construction and exploitation of TransSiberia, KVZD, which branched out from it, Amur railways, Chelyabinsky Customs stop; Northern Sea Route and Porto Franco in the mouth of the Ob, Yenisei, Lena in the Far East; the demographic and migratory processes, settlement policy, stages, methods of conducting results. The Stolpin agrarian reforms, land distribution, sedentarization of foreigners, rise of agricultural production, butter making, cooperatives, state regulation of economic development of the territory, strengthening of state interference in the economic processes in the years of the First World War, organization of governorship in the Far East, the establishment of protectorate over Tuva, liquidation of West Siberian Governor Generalate and the creation of the Steppe Governor Generalate.

Moreover, special attention has been paid to the evolution of the governmental policies in relation to the aboriginal ethnicities, to their socio-economic development, formation of national elites and national movements; the formations of diaspora in the course of mass resettlements (German, Baltic, European, etc.) and the creation of national cultural unions, socio-political lives of the region, formation of organizations of political parties, protest activities, activities of representatives of Siberian regions, participation of Siberians in the elections and work of State Duma (First to Fourth Duma Councils); Russo-Japanese war of 1904-05 and the First Russian Revolution, movement for the introduction of the *zemstvo*; history of the First World War, the establishment of first educational institutions, the activities of non-political social formations and their roles in the development of cultures of the region, etc.

History of Siberia in the Soviet Period

In the second half of the tweentieth century native historians and Siberian experts was sincere about topics like the revolution of 1917 and the civil war, questions of history of party organization, history of the working class of Siberia, industrial and transport development of the region, history of cooperatives, peasants and agriculture, problem of socio-cultural development. Significant attention of historians was paid to the study of the role of Siberians and the Siberian strength in the years of the Great Patriotic War. The accumulated experience was reflected in the pages of the fundamental multi-volume publication "*Istoriya Sibiri*", "*Istoria Rabochego Klassa Sibiri*" and "*Istoria Khrestyanstva Sibiri*" as well as in other works of this type.

Modern research on the Soviet period is characterized by conceptual variety, the widening of the source base, references to earlier "closed" topics. The most consequential was the study of activities of the anti-Bolshevik government of 1918-1920, the peasant uprising of 1920-1922, the functioning of economic mechanism in the years of NEP, cooperatives, taxes and duties of peasants, *kulakization* and other forms of repressive policies of the Stalin regime, including mass deportations, daily lives of the urban population, demographic catastrophe, establishment and development military-industrial complex, scientific and educational potential.

Many works have followed in detail the scenarios and models (projects) of economic growth of Siberia, which the Soviet Government and society tried to help by modernization. Researchers came to the conclusion that the socio-economic development of the region in the Soviet period distinguished itself by a high rate, played an important strategic role in the years of the Second World War and in conditions of geopolitical confrontation of USSR and USA in the second half of the century.

The history of the Soviet period is the subject of the third volume "*Sibir v Noveishee Vremya.*" The first chapter touches on the problematic of history of the revolution of 1917 and the civil war in Siberia (authors are V.M. Rynkov, D.G. Simonov, V.I. Shishkin). The main sections are dedicated to themes like the February revolution, the breakup of the old State apparatus, the creation of new organs of power and governance, dual power in Siberia, formation of organs of self-governance, self-rule, establishment of Soviet authority, anti-Bolshevik resistance, formation of armed forces of the counter-revolution, Siberian Oblastnaya Duma, establishment of Temporary All Russian Government, the political regime of Kolchak, the destruction of the Kolchak army, militant communism, history of Far Eastern republics, demographic and migratory processes.

The second chapter is on the New Economic Policy (NEP) and the authors are L.I. Gallyamova, E.V. Demchik, V.A. Ilyinikh, V.A.

Isupov, A.A. Nikolaev, S.A. Papkov, L.I. Proskurina, A.I. Savin, V.L. Soskin. The main questions, which were touched on in the second chapter are changes in the administrative department of Siberia in 1920s; development of party-state apparatus; inner-party fights; "rejuvenating" the Russian Orthodox Church, anti-religious and national policies, history of peasantry and agriculture, consumer and agricultural cooperatives, development of industry and transportation, "dawn" of private industry and trade, cultural politics of the Soviet authority, socio-demographic development, etc.

The third chapter is on the period of forced modernization in 1929-1941 (the authors are M.M. Efemkin, M.M., B.I. Isaev, V.A. Isupov, V.A. Ilynikh, S.A. Krasilnikov, S.A. Papkov, L.I. Pystina, A.I. Savin, V.L. Soskin, A.I. Timoshenko, E.N. Chernolutskaya). In the articles, the questions that are raised are industrialization, working out and realization of the Five Year Plans, creation of second coal and metallurgical base in the USSR, transport regimes, problems of history of collectivization, the period of *kolkhoz* building, de-kulakization, changes in governing system, national and territorial organization, the fight with non-conformity/dissent and growth of repression, history of "cultural revolution;" demographic situation of 1930s, process of forced urbanization and decrease in numbers of rural population.

The fourth chapter is on the history of Siberia in the years of the Second World War (authors are S.S. Bukin, V.I. Golikov, V.A. Isupov, V.A. Ilyinikh, L.I. Pystya L.I, R.E. Romanov, I.M. Savitsky, D.G. Simonov, G.A. Tkacheva). The chapter characterizes the international situation in the east of the USSR on the eve of and at the beginning of the period of the Second World War; and touches on the history of armed conflicts on the islands of Khasan and the river Khalkhin Gol; it looks into the questions of the war preparedness of the industry and transport; the hardening of labour laws, calls and mobilization of population into armed forces at the beginning of the war, the history of formation of military brigades and sub-brigades, the 24th and 59th armies, Siberian voluntary corps, the participation of Siberians in the war activities, industrial development of the Siberian rear, creation of defence industry, situation of agriculture.

The history of Siberia in the final period (1946 to the middle of 1950s) is the subject of the fifth chapter (authors are S.N. Andreenkov, S.S. Bukin, A.S. Bashuk, A.A. Dolgolyuk, V.A. Isupov, S.G. Kovalenko, A.B. Konovalev, L.M. Medvedeva, I.M. Savitsky, E.N. Chernolutskaya). The chapter deals with the changes in the system of governance, socio-political life, administrative set up of

Siberia and Far East in the post-war period; it touches upon topics like industrial development of the region, conversion of production, production and social adaptation of frontier people, the condition of villages after the end of the war, the growth of the system of education, the influence of ideological factors on the development of high schools, creation of branches of AN USSR in Siberia, changes in the dynamics of birth rates and deaths among the population, the expansion of the system of coerced labour and its crisis.

In the sixth chapter, named "*Reformy serediny 1950*-х-*nachala 1960*-х гг" (authors are S.N. Andreenkov, E.T. Artyomov, S.S. Bukin, A.A. Dolgolyuk, V.A. Isupov, A.B. Konovalov, N.A. Kupershtokh, L.M. Medvedyeva, I.M. Savitsky, A.I. Timoshenko), an analysis of the changes in the socio-political life of the country and region after the death of I.V. Stalin; followed by the administrative reforms, the history of the liquidation of the gulags, changes in the composition of governing cadres, reforms of the party and state structures at the beginning of 1960s, campaign against atheism, reform of the system of economic governance (*sovnarkhozy*); the project of acquiring new regions and the beginning of the move of industry to the East, change in the mechanism of stimulation of agriculture, development of grain culture, conducting the corn campaign, campaign for the increase of production of animal products, also looked at are regional aspects of scientific and technical policies, the history of creation of SORAN USSR, the changes in the sphere of higher education, of polytechnic education, main tendencies of socio-demographic development.

The seventh chapter deals with the history of Siberia in the second half of the 1960s–end of 1980s (authors are E.T. Artyomov, A.S. Bashuk, O.B. Dashinamjilov, A.A. Dolgolyuk, M.M. Efimkin, V.A. Ilyinikh, I.B. Karpunina, A.A. Kiselnikov, V.I. Kozodoi, A.B. Konovalov, N.A. Kupershtokh, member-correspondent of RAN V.A. Lamin, L.N. Lopatin, V.G. Makarenko, A.P. Melentyeva, I.M. Savitsky, A.I. Timoshenko, L.E. Fetisova). Some of the main themes are: changes in the composition of governing cadres, industrial development and scientific and technical progress, development of defence and civil sectors, oil and gas complex in Eastern Siberian TPK; electrification of railways, the construction of Baikal-Amur railways; the dynamics of agricultural production, formation of new scientific centres, the accumulation of negative factors in the demographic development; "*perestroika*" and the systematic crisis of the Soviet society; problems of economic development, attempts at reforming the agrarian sector, new processes in the socio-political life.

The eighth and final chapter is dedicated to the post-Soviet period (authors are S.S. Bukin, A.S. Bashuk, A.V. Druzyaka, V.A. Isupov, I.B. Karpunina, V.I. Kozodoi, V.G. Makarenko, V.U. Malov, A.I, Melentyeva, S.V. Novikov, A.G. Osipov, L.E. Fetisova). The chapter looks at the changes in governance at home in the 1980–'90s; also described are the negative features of the Soviet system, political reforms, problems of international relations and sovereignty of territory, national politics, there is an analysis on the history of the party setup and transition to political pluralism, the social results of transformation of economy, the history of privatization, formation of market institutes, impact of systemic crisis on the development of science, the changes in the social structure, demographic catastrophe.

On the whole, the new publication *Istorii Sibiri* showcases the modern level of scientific investigations, and also indicates the prospects of further development of historical Siberian studies. No less importantly the other task is also presented—the popularization of accumulated scientific knowledge, disseminating the results of researchers to the largest audience, both in Russia as well as outside it. For the writing of this text, material of the booklet *Istoriya Sibiri* has been used (which is in print and the authors are D.A. Ananyev, V.A. Ilyinikh, S.V. Markin, S.P. Nesterov, D.G. Simonov).

Notes

1. A.P. Okladnikov ed. *Istoria Sibiri s drevneishikh vremyon do nashikh dnei*, 5 vols, (Leningrad: Nauka, 1968-1969).
2. *Istoricheskaya Entsiklopedia Sibiri*, 3 vols., Novosibirsk; *Istoricheskoye nasledie Sibiri*, 2010.

References

1. *Istoriografiya sovetskoi Sibiri (1917-1945)* (Novosibirsk 1968); M. Ye. Plotnikova, *Sovietskaya istoriografiya Grazhdanskoi voiny v Sibiri (1919-pervaia polovina 1930-kh godov)* (Tomsk: Tomsk University Press 1974); *Istoriografiya krestianstva sovetskoi Sibiri* (Novosibirsk: Nauka 1976); *Istoriografiya kulturi i intelligentsia sovetskoi Sibiri*, (Novosibirsk: Nauka 1978); V.T. Aniskov, *Podvig sovetskogo krestianstva v Velikoi Otechestvennoi voine: Istoriograficheskii ocherk.* (Moscow: Mysl 1979); *Istoriografiya Sibiri (sovetskii period)* (Novosibirsk: Nauka 1980); N.Ya. Gushchin, A.S. Moskovskii, V.L. Soskin, *Istoriografiya Sibiri (sovetskii period)* (Novosibirsk: Nauka 1980); *Rabochii klass Sibiri v dooktyabrskii period* (Novosibirsk: Nauka 1982); *Rabochii klass Sibiri v period stroitelstva*

sotsialisma (1917-1937) (Novosibirsk: Nauka 1982); *Krestianstvo Sibiri v epokhu kapitalisma,* (Novosibirsk 1983); *Krestianstvo Sibiri v period stroitelstva sotsialisma (1917-1937)*(Novosibirsk: Nauka 1983); *Rabocii klass Sibiri v period uprochenia i rasvitiya sotsialisma* (Novosibirsk: Nauka 1984); *Istoriografiya rabochego klassa Dalnego Vostoka SSSR* (Vladivostok 1985); *Krestianstvo Sibiri v period uprocheniia i razvitiia sotsialisma* (Novosibirsk: Nauka 1985); A.L. Volchenko, A.S. Moskovskii, *Ocherki istoriografii rabochego klassa Sibiri. 1917-1937* (Novosibirsk: Nauka 1986); *Rabochii klass Sibiri, 1961-1980* (Novosibirsk: Nauka 1986); N.Ya. Gushchin, V.A. Zhdanov, *Kritika burzhuaznikh kontseptsii istorii sovetskoi sibirskoi derevni* (Novosibirsk 1987); *Krestianstvo i selskoe khoziaistvo Sibiri. 1960-1980-e gg.*, (Novosibirsk: Nauka 1991); V.L. Soskin, *Sovremennaia istoriografiia sovetskoi intelligentsii Rossii*, (Novosibirsk: Nauka 1996); T.A. Nemchinova. *Sovremennaia istoriografiia belogo dvizheniia v Sibiri* (Ulan-Ude 2002); A.A. Nikolaev, *Osnovnie vidy kooperatsii v Rossii: istoriko-teoreticheskii ocherk* (Novosibirsk 2007).

2. A.I. Andreev, *Ocherki po istocnikivedeniyu Sibiri* (Moscow, Leningrad 1965); M.M. Gromyko, *Zapadnaia Sibir v XVIII v. Russkoe naselenie i zemledelcheskoe osvoenie* Vol. 1 and 2 (Novosibirsk 1960–1965); V.G. Mirzoev, *Istoriogragiia Sibiri (Domarksistskii period),* (Moscow 1970); A.A. Preobrazhenskii, *Ural i Zapadnaia Sibir v kontse XVI-nachale XVIII veka* (Moscow 1972); N.A. Minenko, *Severo-Zapadnaia Sibir v XVIII-pervoi polovine XIX veka* (Novosibirsk 1975); *Krestianstvo Sibiri v epokhu feodalizma*, (Novosibirsk 1982); L.M. Goriushkin, N.A. Minenko, *Istoriografiia Sibiri dooktiabrskogo perioda (konets XVI-nachalo XX v.)* (Novosibirsk 1984); D.A. Anan'ev, Ye.V. Komleva, D.V. Raev et al., *"Novie zemli" i osvoenie Sibiri v XVII-XIX vv. Ocherki istorii i istoriografii* (Novosibirsk: Sova 2006).

Societies in Motion

10

Civil Society in Uzbekistan: Continuity and Innovation

Shirin Akiner

Civil society in Uzbekistan is rooted in a variety of traditions and experiences. In the twenty years since independence considerable attention has been devoted to this sector. How one assesses its strengths or weaknesses depends very largely on what one understands by the term "civil society." This paper has two aims: one is to map out some of the contextual issues; the other is to look at the work of a specific organization, the Uzbek Charitable Foundation Fund Forum. This is a cross-sectoral initiative that, in a relatively short period of time, has succeeded in generating a notable degree of civic activism. It represents an innovative model of international approaches to social development in combination with indigenous values and customs. The first section looks at the evolution of the concept of "civil society" and its incorporation into international aid and development policies. The second section looks at the Uzbek context, outlining the range of civil society activity. The third section summarizes the aims and objectives of the Fund Forum. In the final sections, some of the challenges of modern society are discussed, in a general sense and with specific reference to Uzbekistan.

Civil Society: From Concept to Prescriptive Policy

Confused (and Confusing) Definitions

To describe the Fund Forum as a "civil society institution" inevitably raises the question as to what is meant by "civil society." There is no simple answer to this: the term has been re-defined and re-appropriated, expanded and contracted many times over, spawning controversy, debate and competing interpretations. Some interpretations of civil society focus almost exclusively on the role of voluntary and community organizations, while others frame it more broadly to encompass the whole gamut of formal and informal interaction:

> Civil society...is composed of voluntary associations ranging from local community groups to faith based groups, to trade unions, to large non-governmental organisations that operate on a national and/or international scale. It can include political parties, committed to the development of a state, and radical groups who position themselves in opposition to such objectives—and in extreme cases, seek to overthrow the ruling order.[1]

Some definitions include yet more elements. As one author put it: "Civil society has become a conceptual rag bag, consisting of households, religious denominations, and each and every activity which is not of the state."[2]

This confusion over terms of reference obscures the fact that beneath the academic disputes there is an important layer of social activity that deserves serious attention. The nature of this activity—the range of actors and stake-holders, organizational structures and capabilities—varies from society to society, shaped by the specific cultural-historical framework. Attempts to impose a normative understanding of what "civil society" *ought* to be like, regardless of local context, are futile. Such approaches, based on superficial generalizations, are not only misleading in a theoretical sense, they also foster naive policy making. Thus, the way in which the term is commonly used today generates obfuscation rather than clarification. To understand how this has come about it is necessary to take account of the long and complex evolution of the concept. A summary of the developments most relevant to the present discussion are set out below.

History of an Idea

The theoretical genealogy of the term, as it is generally understood today, is European. Its origins can be traced back to Greek and Roman philosophy, when thinkers such as Socrates, Plato and Aristotle sought to elaborate the notion of a good and just society; Cicero is generally credited with coining the term *societas civilis* ("civil society"). After the adoption of Christianity, European ideas on the ordering of society were informed by theological arguments on the relationship between the Human and the Divine. On the social level, this was accompanied by a culture of public and private philanthropy, with emphasis on communal, mutual support activities (confraternities, for example).

In the sixteenth century, Protestants such as Martin Luther and Jean Calvin openly challenged the supreme power of the Church, insisting instead on the role of the individual believer. From then onwards, debates on the nature of authority, and the "contract" between the governing and the governed, shifted steadily from the religious domain to the secular. In the Age of Reason in the seventeenth century and more especially in the Enlightenment of the eighteenth century, philosophers in France, England and Scotland grappled with notions of the rights and interests of the citizen within the state polity. This theme became more prominent in the industrializing world of the nineteenth and twentieth centuries, with major figures such as Hegel, Alexis de Tocqueville and Karl Marx analysing the relationship between the public and private spheres, the state and civil (or "civilian") society.

A new strain of thought was added by the Italian Marxist Antonio Gramsci, who recognized the dual potential of civil society: a conduit through which the state could win the support of its citizens, but also a revolutionary force to defend the people against predatory exploitation by the state and the market. Imprisoned by Mussolini, Gramsci died in 1937. In the ensuing fifty-odd years the dominant theoretical concern was the confrontation between capitalism and communism. The concept of civil society seemed irrelevant to this polemic and the term itself was virtually forgotten. Then, in the last quarter of the twentieth century, it was suddenly rediscovered and given a powerful new lease of life, becoming the mobilizing inspiration for opposition movements not only in Eastern Europe, but also in Latin America and Africa. The fall of the Berlin Wall and subsequent disintegration of the Soviet Union seemed self-evident proof of the transformative power of civil society. Those who had suffered under repressive regimes, as well as those in the West who had opposed them, shared this euphoric vision of "citizen power."

National and international donor agencies rapidly came to regard civil society as a prerequisite for democratization, good governance and development. This view coincided with the foreign policy objectives of the United States, the one remaining superpower, which advocated the promotion of these same goals on a global scale. Not surprisingly, "civil society" became an ultra-fashionable topic for research, as evidenced by a burgeoning scholarly literature, numerous research and teaching programmes, and grant-funded projects.[3] Concurrently, there was a mushrooming of donor-funded facilities and initiatives to strengthen civil society in target populations in the developing world, likewise in former socialist countries. For the most part, these activities were directed at the support of non-governmental organisations (NGOs).[4] Consequently, "civil society" came to be understood, and measured and assessed, by the number of such organizations in a given state. Programmes to promote the rule of law and other aspects of good governance were also initiated, but tended to receive less publicity. Moreover, owing to organizational as well as funding problems, they often failed to make a significant impact.

Reality Checks

The "honeymoon period for civil society and the aid industry" which in the early 1990s had seemed to promise so much, did not last long.[5] Rather than offering a fast track to democratization and the growth of a market economy, by the mid-1990s civil society projects were regarded with mounting suspicion in former Soviet republics, likewise in other parts of aid-receiving countries.[6] There were many reasons for this. One was that the availability of foreign funding prompted a massive surge in the formation of NGOs. Frequently, however, little thought was given by either grant-providers or grant-recipients as to whether their projects corresponded to local needs, were sensitive to local customs and importantly, were well regarded by the local population. This lack of engagement with the community meant that many NGOs were ineffective. There were of course some that did make a valuable contribution but in general, rather than being seen as channels for civic activity, they were regarded as money-making enterprises for the lucky (and/or privileged) few who managed to secure access to donor funds.

Meanwhile, local constituencies in recipient countries began to question the "efficiency, flexibility and probity of NGOs."[7] In donor agencies, too, there was growing unease about the relatively limited success of their interventions. Thus, in the span of a decade, enthusiasm for civil society projects was, in many quarters, giving way to the realization it was not yielding the anticipated results. Worse, in some cases such activities were actually contributing to the emergence of a more closed environment. Host states, both at government and at grassroots level, became increasingly hostile towards foreign-backed NGOs, which they believed had been co-opted by external agencies intent on pursuing their own agenda rather than responding to needs on the ground.[8] Attitudes such as these reflected the failure of the donor community to "indigenise" their programmes by creating a real sense of local ownership and legitimacy. This in turn began to call into question the validity of the assumption that the current western understanding of the "civil society/ state" paradigm is universally applicable.

Currently, much of this discussion focuses on Africa.[9] However, similar issues are debated with regard to the Islamic world. A striking aspect of this discourse is the extent to which it is dominated by misunderstandings, preconceived judgments and careless generalizations.[10] There is frequently an added barrier to mutual comprehension and that is the casual, almost instinctive, belief in the superiority of western cultural values, political institutions and economic models. Concomitantly, there is a tendency to ignore, or underestimate, the strengths and merits of other systems. This hinders genuine dialogue and fosters confrontation rather than cooperation. To gain an insight into how other societies function, it is important to understand their historical legacy, likewise their cultural and intellectual traditions.[11] Equally, it requires a more pluralistic and critical interpretation of the European-American experience. This means moving beyond simplistic, normative paradigms (largely shaped by modern Eurocommunism) and instead, locating the concept of civil society, that is to say, the totality of voluntary civic actions, within a broader social and ethical framework.

The Uzbek Experience

Discussions on civil society development in Uzbekistan tend to fall into two camps. One embodies the revolutionary aspect of Gramsci's analysis and evaluates civil society institutions by the extent to which they contest the power of the state and succeed in "rolling back" its authority. In this interpretation, civil society is primarily concerned with political empowerment and, by extension, represents a way of mobilizing political opposition. This thinking informs much of the foreign commentary on Uzbek civil society; a number of Uzbek scholars (particularly those who have studied aboard) hold similar views.[12] Their assessment of the situation is predictably pessimistic, since they rarely find signs that civil society in Uzbekistan is fulfilling this "radical" mission. However, as Gramsci pointed out, civil society can also play a very different, contradictory role—a dichotomy that reflects the fluid, constantly evolving nature of the relationship between state and society. The two spheres are not intrinsically confrontational: they can be cooperative or mutually reinforcing in order to further the common good. When viewed from this perspective, the outlook in Uzbekistan is far from bleak: there is a positive interaction and engagement between many different types of civic organizations and associations. They can be divided into three categories: modern, formal institutions; traditional, community-based organisations and customs; and religious practices.

The Soviet Legacy

The formal institutions of civil society in modern Uzbek society are rooted in the Soviet experience, and more especially in the developmental policies of that era. The objective was the rapid modernization of the entire Central Asian region. Consequently, shortly after the establishment of Soviet rule, a comprehensive programme of social, cultural and economic transformation was launched. Priorities included the emancipation of women (gender equality before the law, in education and in employment), education (free, compulsory and universal), and the delivery of professional health care and sanitary facilities. European-style higher educational facilities and advanced research institutes replaced Islamic centres of learning. A similar process of "Europeanisation" took place in many other spheres. In the arts, for example, traditional forms of music, literature, dance and painting were neglected or deliberately eradicated. In their place, "advanced" Soviet/western arts such as theatre, ballet, opera and orchestral music were introduced. Other fundamental changes that occurred at this time included the establishment of modern state institutions, the transformation of the economy through industrial development and the introduction of new practices in agriculture.

These and many other changes in society were driven and funded by the state, under the leadership of the communist party. Consequently, institution-building in every sphere was permeated by ideology. This included not only the chain of communist party organizations, but also a broad spectrum of related bodies such as professional/trade unions, youth organizations, women's committees, libraries, sports clubs, hobby groups and so on. The cooptation of the local intellectual and leadership elites played a crucial role in indigenizing the system. Central Asians were quick to join the state and party organs and were incorporated into the administration at all levels of responsibility. Likewise, they eagerly embraced the new educational and cultural opportunities. Several Central Asians made their mark among the Soviet Union's outstanding doctors, scientists, ballet dancers, opera singers, athletes and other high achievers. In scope and pace of implementation the Soviet modernization programme in Central Asia was unique. It brought truly remarkable results, raising the level of development far above that of neighbouring countries. However, it was an uneven, flawed process. Along with the undeniable successes, there were also negative consequences, notably in the damage inflicted on the natural environment, and the undermining of inherited cultural, religious and linguistic identities.

In terms of civil society development, the Soviet legacy was on the whole more beneficial than is sometimes acknowledged. In political terms it was certainly constrained by a rigid ideological framework, but in practical terms it encouraged a high degree of civic activism. Both men and women participated in semi-state/semi-voluntary organizations not only as members, but also in leadership roles. This gave them invaluable experience in the administrative, managerial and presentational skills that were required to plan and implement various enterprises. It also provided an insight into social issues, such as the need to cater for the physical and cultural development of young people through sporting events and other forms of group activity. After independence, the professionalism that had been gained in these types of activities provided the organizational base (and personnel) for the development of new civic institutions.

Independence: A New Chapter in Civil Society Development

In the early 1990s, Uzbėkistan, together with the other Central Asian states, received "tens of millions of dollars, pounds, marks, and francs" in foreign aid to accelerate the development of civil society.[13] The emphasis was on the creation of NGOs, which came to be regarded as virtually synonymous with democratization and liberalization. Immediately, there was a proliferation of foreign-funded, and sometimes foreign-staffed, organizations of this type. Yet quantity was no guarantee of quality. Some NGOs did do useful work, but many others failed to undertake any meaningful activity. Soon, western analysts were frankly acknowledging that "a good part of this [NGO] community has come into being in order to take advantage of the sudden wealth of funding opportunities brought by the major multilateral and bilateral development programmes."[14] This raised serious doubts about the effectiveness as well as the sustainability of these organizations. Moreover, and perhaps more significantly, the majority of these organizations failed to win the respect and trust of the local communities. This was not unique to Uzbekistan: as mentioned above, there was a similar "backlash" reaction to foreign-sponsored NGOs in many parts of the world, for largely the same reasons.[15]

Meanwhile, Uzbekistan was creating a legal infrastructure for the regulation of public (non-state) associations. It adopted the law "On Public Associations" on 15 February 1991 (before the collapse of the Soviet Union) to cover socio-political movements as well as non-profit/nongovernmental organizations. It specified the activities that public associations were allowed to undertake. In 1996 a separate law "On Political Parties" was adopted. The Human Rights Commission of Uzbekistan, headed by a parliamentary Ombudsman, had already been created the previous year, with the brief to respond to citizens' complaints. Western opinion at this time was largely supportive of Uzbekistan's policies towards non-state organizations; as one legal specialist commented, Uzbekistan was "generous in permitting registration of NGOs except when it views the conduct of such NGOs as hostile and political."[16] Within less than a decade this had changed very substantially. In December 2005 Uzbekistan adopted a Code of Administrative Liability. In the following months, a number of prominent foreign NGOs and media organizations were accused of failing to comply with this law and their registration was either withdrawn or not renewed.[17] Each side was convinced that the other was pursuing a malevolent agenda. The number of foreign NGOs was greatly reduced after this. However, those that did remain continued to make an important contribution to Uzbek society through a range of programmes and activities.

Alongside the foreign-backed NGOs in Uzbekistan, local civil society institutions were also emerging. Voluntary bodies, described as "non-profit organizations" (NPO) rather than "non-governmental organizations" were formed in order to address community needs. In 2011, there were over 5,600 NGOs/NPOs in Uzbekistan.[18] This number continues to expand. Such organizations are involved in a variety of sectors, including health care, education, social protection, human rights, and environmental protection. Some of these NGOs/NPOs are new initiatives. The Uzbekistan Association of Businesswomen, for example, established in 1991 by 12 female entrepreneurs, is a self-funding organization that provides professional training and assistance for fledgling businesswomen. Other organizations, especially those involved in youth activities and women's issues, resemble Soviet-era institutions but with a different ethical-cultural content and a different set of priorities. An interesting example of community action is the formation of housing associations (condominiums) to manage the maintenance and servicing of apartment blocks. These groups were created when, soon after independence, all such buildings were privatized and residents had to assume responsibility for the upkeep of communal property.[19]

In the 1990s, many of those who participated in NGO/NPO activities had previously been engaged in Soviet state-civic bodies and so were able to draw upon that experience. Gradually, however, younger people, including several who had studied abroad, became involved in this sector, introducing new perspectives. Women play a major part in the voluntary sector; several of the most successful enterprises have been founded and directed by women. This is partly related to employment patterns (and opportunities), but it also reflects a strong caring ethos. Arguably, this has helped to shape the cooperative, non-confrontational approach of these organizations. This is reflected in the importance that is given to building partnerships. Project partners include ministries and other state entities (particularly in the spheres of health care and education), as well as commercial enterprises (e.g. banks and business corporations). The state supports and encourages these private-public partnerships by providing generous tax concessions for charitable donations and projects.[20] Joint ventures with foreign partners have also been developed. Some of these partner organizations have representation in Uzbekistan (e.g. the British Council, the Konrad Adenauer Stiftung), while others are based in their home country and cooperate on a project-oriented basis.

Traditional Institutions

One of the most distinctive features of Uzbek life is the vibrancy of its traditional institutions and customs. These indigenous manifestations of civil society are the mechanisms whereby society's values and beliefs are consolidated and handed on from one generation to the next. They serve as the informal regulators of society, enhancing social cohesion, acting as a gauge of personal trust and reputation, identifying community needs and resolving conflicts. Documentary evidence allows these institutions to be traced back to the nineteenth century, but they are undoubtedly much older.[21] Yet they are by no means static, ossified formalities: on the contrary, they are constantly changing and adapting to new social, political and economic circumstances. This resilience has enabled them to preserve a sense of shared identity throughout the huge upheavals of recent history.

The most structured of these traditional institutions is the *mahalla* (neighbourhood). Its geographic locus is a defined physical area, such as a street, a neighbourhood or even an apartment block; within this space, the inhabitants are bound together by a strong "micro-identity." The socio-demographic size of the *mahalla* varies, ranging from small groups of families to clusters of around 1,500 households.[22] There is a high degree of voluntary self-regulation and self-administration within such communities. The smooth and effective functioning of these entities has traditionally been overseen by a committee consisting of the most respected members of society. In the past this was an unpaid, but highly prestigious position. It is now remunerated by the state, but is still regarded as a commitment that requires great moral integrity. Traditionally, the main role of the *mahalla* was to deal with community needs, including charitable support for the vulnerable, dispute resolution, care of the environment, and organization of community celebrations. Since independence, some additional administrative duties have been added on behalf of the state, such as the payment of child benefits and other social welfare allowances. This enlarged role is part of the government's programme of decentralization. It aims to develop a sustainable system of community organizsations by strengthening and empowering local governance capacity. This process was initiated in the early 1990s and intensified in 2003, which was declared the Year of the Mahalla.[23]

Community solidarity, as a principle of social organization, is constantly reinforced by group activities. The institution of *hashar*, for example, is a voluntary task force that comes together to carry out a specific communal project, such as renovating a historic monument, clearing a waste site or helping a neighbour to build an extension to the family home. Several forms of group activity are related to life-cycle ceremonies, marking turning points such as birth, circumcision, marriage and death. Typically, these events are attended by large congregations of guests (often numbering a hundred or more). Preparations for such undertakings require a major input of communal effort, all of which is discussed and agreed in advance. Then, the etiquette of the occasion—the exchange of salutations and gifts, the sharing of a meal, the communication of family news—follows established patterns of behaviour. These gatherings are not mere entertainment, but constitute a physical as well as a social form of bonding. They engender mutual awareness, concern and responsibility. For the young, this is the training ground where they learn norms of courtesy and respect. For the older generation it is a reaffirmation that they are still valued members of society. There are many other channels of interaction. The *gap* (literally "conversation"), for example, is a regular gathering of friends of the same age who are bound by a shared experience, such as having been classmates at school, colleagues at work, etc. Whatever differences may have emerged over the years in the financial standing and social status of members of the group, within the *gap* they meet on a strict basis of equality and mutual trust.[24] So, the *gap* not only maintains social cohesion across social and economic boundaries, but it is also a space within which views reflecting different perspectives may be exchanged.[25]

The Religious Legacy

The religious history of Uzbekistan is long and diverse. Many of the world's great faiths have been practised here, including Zoroastrianism, Buddhism, Judaism and various forms of Christianity. For well over a millennium, however, the dominant religion has been Islam. Islamic culture and scholarship melded with local customs and beliefs to create the value system and norms of conduct that have shaped community life. During the Soviet period all forms of religion were repressed, likewise many national customs. However, they survived in people's way of thinking and behaving. Since independence, the role of Islam as an integral part of Uzbek culture and spirituality has been given due recognition and respect. As President Karimov expressed it, "We cannot imagine our nation without this sacred religion…religious values and Islamic notions are an inalienable part of our life."[26] This is not an exaggeration: the civic virtues that are most prized in Uzbek society are rooted in the teachings of Islam. Thus, there are many passages in the Quran, and many sayings of the Prophet (*hadith*), that emphasize the importance of such qualities as civility, compassion, charity, filial duty and care of orphans. Even Uzbeks who do not consider themselves to be devout believers would nevertheless regard these values as "typical" national characteristics.

The link between Uzbek civic culture and Islamic ethics is not confined to a generalized identification with the religion. Several of the most renowned Muslim authorities on jurisprudence and Qur'anic exegesis were natives of this region, as is evidenced by their names. To mention but a few, they include Imam al-Bukhari (AD 810-870), revered by the worldwide Muslim community as the compiler of the most authentic collection of *hadith*; the prolific writer Abu Mansur al-Maturidi (c. AD 853-944), born near Samarkand; and Burhanuddin al-Marghinani (AD 1135-1197) from the Ferghana Valley, author of the monumental work *al-Hidaya* ("The Guidance"). Founders of two of the most important Sufi orders also came from here: the visionary teacher Najmuddin Kubra (AD 1145-1220) from Khorezm, whose disciples formed the Kubrawi *tariqa*; and Bahauddin Naqshband Bukhari (AD 1318-1389) from Bukhara, the spiritual father of the Naqshbandi *tariqa*. During the Soviet period these scholars were known to Muslims around the world, but almost entirely erased from local memory within Uzbekistan. In the past two decades, however, great efforts have been made to popularize knowledge of their legacy here, in their birth-place, through publications of their writings, the restoration of monuments associated with them, and by celebrations of events connected with their lives. In this way, the learned intellectual legacy of the region has been reunited with popular practice.

The official reinstatement of Islam as a vital element in Uzbek culture and society has meant that ceremonies with a religious connotation are now being openly and enthusiastically celebrated. Again, as with the neighbourhood activities discussed above, they serve to enhance social cohesion and to reinforce shared values and patterns of behaviour. Up to 4,000 Muslims from Uzbekistan now go on the *haj* to Mecca every year; during the Soviet period only a small group of handpicked individuals was allowed to go. The local mosque is the centre of public prayer services and religious festivals. It also engages in religious instruction, charitable work and a range of community welfare projects. During Ramadan, large numbers of people come to the mosque to break the fast together. On these occasions gifts of food and other useful items are distributed to the elderly, the sick and those in need. More intimate religious activities involving a close circle of friends, such as pilgrimages to the tomb of a local saint, or ritual recitations in honour of the life of the Prophet, are also gaining in popularity.

These traditions—community self-governance and self-help, underpinned by religious precepts and practices—have helped to form a mind-set that is characterized by a strong social conscience. Thus, civic activism in Uzbekistan is an intrinsic part of the social fabric, an expression of deeply engrained values and modes of behaviour. The importance of an ethical framework as the basis for the "good society" has been recognized in many cultures. St. Thomas Aquinas (1225-1274), drawing on a line of moral philosophy that stretches back to Aristotle, used the maxim *actio sequitur esse* ("action follows being") to explicate the connection between our behaviour and our moral being.[27] Current debates on "civil society" tend to overlook this crucial element: institutions and legal safeguards are essential, but of themselves are never sufficient. Ultimately, what matters is the "human factor"—the way in which the individual acts.

The Fund Forum: A Symbiotic Concept of Civil Society

As the preceding section indicates, there is a strong vein of civic activity in Uzbekistan. It is characterized by a high degree of voluntary personal commitment and a sense of communal responsibility. However, there are relatively few linkages between the modern and the traditional structures, although the same sets of individuals may be involved in both spheres. The *mahalla* is an exceptional example of an informal community organization being transformed into a more formal branch of local governance. The novel contribution of the Fund Forum is that it draws on the strengths of traditional customs and practices and combines them with the professional skills and experience of modern institutions. Moreover, although it does not espouse a religious agenda, it does respect and support some undertakings that have a religious significance, particularly those of a philanthropic nature.

Genesis

The "Fund Forum" was the brainchild of Gulnara Karimova and a group of like-minded individuals. Concerned that Uzbekistan's national culture, arts and traditions were being marginalized and neglected at home and abroad, they decided take steps to reverse this trend. They devised the idea of a "Forum"—an open, flexible structure that could encompass a range of activities. This was an ambitious plan and could not be undertaken on a haphazard basis: it would require a sustained programme of projects. This in turn required a sound institutional base. To this end, the "Fund Forum" was established in March 2004 as an independent, non-state charitable foundation.

During that year (March-December 2004), the Fund Forum organized around 14 events, including concerts, theatrical performances, book fairs, displays of arts and crafts, and exhibitions of paintings. They were held in Uzbekistan and in various Russian cities; there was also one exhibition in the Egyptian capital. The following year, the number of undertakings more than doubled; in addition to venues in Uzbekistan and Russia, events were also held in China, Japan and Italy. The main emphasis was still on the propagation of Uzbek culture, but there was interest, too, in bringing foreign artists and performers to Uzbekistan to create a culture of dialogue and of interchange.

Such events served as a showcase for Uzbekistan's culture, a platform for the country's young talent and a space for intercultural debate. However, these activities would not, on their own, be sufficient to achieve the aims of the Fund Forum. It became clear that there was a need for a broader vision of development and engagement to encompass the whole of Uzbek society. So, projects to stimulate interest in the arts and crafts were accompanied by efforts to address wider social needs. The chief target for these activities was the youth, but there was a keen awareness of the importance of empowering women to play a more active role in society. This entailed projects that were specific to their needs, such as advice on health and child care, as well as better access to education, professional training and micro-financing. Providing additional social support for the vulnerable and the disadvantaged, such as the elderly, the sick and the handicapped, and families with limited incomes but many dependents, also became a key concern.

Structure

As the scale and variety of the work of the Fund Forum expanded, so too did its structure. The Forum has become the nucleus around which a number of sub-groups have been formed. Some of these are single-purpose bodies, engaged in such activities as the running of an annual festival or sporting event. Others have a larger thematic remit, such as charitable work, youth projects or gender and family issues. Each body has its own priorities and areas of interest. They plan and implement their particular undertakings, but retain close links with the main Fund Forum nucleus. Moreover, when there are projects which involve a number of different elements, requiring different types of input, there is strong cooperation between the various sub-groups.

Currently, the main "satellite bodies" are:

- "Ray of Love" (*Mehr nuri*): founded in mid-2004, the primary focus is the support and sponsorship of charitable projects in the social welfare sphere;
- Women's Assembly: founded in 2005, prioritizes projects related to the welfare of women and families; undertakings include professional training and education for women, raising knowledge of their legal rights, and offering practical and emotional support; particular attention is devoted to health issues and to child care;
- "Voice of the Future" (*Kelajak ovozi*): founded in 2006, its activities are mainly devoted to the promotion of talented young people (musicians, sportsmen, inventors and so on); undertakings include youth forums, public debates, video-conferences, seminars and media training sessions; it organises sport and recreational activities, as well as social awareness campaigns;
- Fund for the Support of Social Initiatives: also founded in 2006, promotes a wide range of activities, including humanitarian aid, ancillary welfare support, the provision of micro-credits for women (especially farmers and agricultural workers) and environmental awareness schemes; it also seeks to promote inclusive education (e.g. for handicapped children).

Organization

The strategic planning and decision-making hub of the Forum is the Steering Committee. Headed by Dr. Gulnara Karimova, it comprises ten members—leading cultural figures and scholars in Uzbekistan and abroad. The Steering Committee meets at regular intervals to assess progress and to agree new undertakings. Non-members, including representatives of partner organizations, may be invited to participate in these deliberations. There are also specialized Working Groups composed of elected representatives with relevant professional expertise. They are responsible for the practical issues of project implementation. A similar administrative-steering structure is repeated in the sub-groups.

Much effort has been devoted to developing cooperative ties with other organizations. This is not a new approach. As mentioned above, other civil society institutions in Uzbekistan have adopted a similar strategy. However, the Fund Forum has been unusually assiduous in forging such partnerships and has created effective working relationships with a wide range of public and private bodies within the country. At state level, these include relevant ministerial organs (Ministries of Health, of Public Education, regional governments, etc.), as well as many provincial and district public-sector facilities (e.g. universities, institutes and health centres). In the commercial sector, the Forum and its sub-groups collaborate with a variety of business enterprises, sometimes on a one-off sponsorship basis, at other times as longer-term undertakings. Among them are "Ferghana Azot," "Andijan Telekom" and "Uzexpomarkaz." A number of financial institutions also support the work of the Fund Forum, including micro-financing organizations, credit unions and numerous banks. Yet another layer of cooperation is provided by the partnerships have been formed with official bodies such as the Women's Committee of Uzbekistan, the Muslim Board of Uzbekistan, and so on. In sum total, these relationships not only extend the outreach capacity of the Fund Forum, they also serve to embed it firmly in society by forming a network of relationships based on collaboration and interdependence.

Similar importance has been attached to developing links with international partners. These, too, are very varied in terms of size, structure and remit. In 2007 the Fund Forum signed a Memorandum of Mutual Understanding with UNESCO and in 2010, was granted Special Consultative Status with the UN Economic and Social Council. In July 2011 the Forum sent delegates to participate in a high-level meeting on youth, convened by the UN General Assembly as part of the International Year of Youth. There has also been cooperation with UNICEF and UNDP. Relations with individual countries are conducted with official organisations such as the British Council, Goethe Institute, United States Agency for International Development (USAID), Japan International Cooperation Agency (JICA), Turkish International Cooperation and Development Agency (TIKA) and Korea International Cooperation Agency (KOICA), usually on the basis of memoranda of cooperation. However, both the Forum and its sub-groups also participate in individual projects with small NGO partners in other countries, including Austria, Russia, Switzerland and United Kingdom. Foreign embassies sometimes help to sponsor particular charitable events, as do foreign commercial enterprises. Importantly, the Fund Forum not only collaborates with foreign organizations on its own territory. It has opened offices in other countries (as of 2011 in Beijing, Berlin, Geneva, Madrid, Moscow, New York, Paris, Tokyo and Vienna) in order to facilitate international contacts. Moreover, Fund Forum members regularly take part in international events in other countries.

Taking Stock

It is seven years since the founding of the Fund Forum. A great deal has been achieved during this period. The organization has grown dramatically, extending its activities far beyond the original concept of reviving Uzbekistan's traditional cultural and artistic heritage. Today (autumn 2011), in addition to supporting the development of all forms of traditional arts, music and dance, it also promotes contemporary international styles in the visual and performing arts, in fashion design and in architecture. It nurtures scientific and technological innovation and helps to find financial backing for the implementation of promising inventions; it provides practical assistance for fledgling entrepreneurs of all ages, including those for whom it represents a second or third career. There are many projects devoted to youth development, education and sport; environmental protection and the development of alternative sources of energy (notably, solar and wind); health care, poverty alleviation and care for the elderly and infirm. Help for women, as mentioned above, is also a priority area; there are projects dedicated to providing targeted practical training as well as social and psychological support.

One of the most successful of the Fund Forum's initiatives has been the nationwide campaign to raise awareness of breast cancer. This is a multi-faceted (and on-going) undertaking, involving breast screening, follow-up medical treatment where appropriate, counselling, nutritional advice and in mastectomy cases, fashion and beauty advice.

The professional staff not only gives their time free of charge, but work at the weekends and on holidays when it is easier for women to attend the clinics. The results are striking. There are obvious health benefits, but there is also a psychological bonus in that it makes women, especially in poorer, rural communities, feel valued by society: if they are worth this amount of attention, they must count for something.[28]

This impressive burgeoning of activities is the outcome of a number of factors. Firstly, the work of the Fund Forum is rooted in a holistic view of society which encompasses both physical and spiritual aspects of wellbeing. Secondly, it draws on the values of traditional civic life, including community solidarity and responsibility; self-help and self-governance. This encourages volunteerism as a means to resolve common problems as well as to help those in need. Thirdly, it has adopted a strongly collaborative approach, which has an amplifying effect on all its undertakings. Fourthly, it has understood the need to incorporate modern institutional models into its organizational structure, in order to function efficiently not only within the national context but also, and increasingly, with partners round the world. This twin-track approach, combining traditional experience with contemporary international practice, has given the Fund Forum considerable flexibility and resilience.

Perhaps the organization's most important characteristic is that it has a realistic vision of its capabilities. As the founder of the Forum, Gulnara Karimova put it: "We cannot do the undo-able." Thus, it does not seek to solve all the country's socio-economic problems. It does not launch sweeping programmes. Rather, what it can do, and what it does extraordinarily well, is to act as a mobilizing agent, inspiring and enthusing those with whom it works. Instead of handing out generous grants, the Forum provides seed-funding, combined with practical help and advice. It provides short training courses to impart particular skills (e.g. public speaking, writing business plans, making feature clips for television) and opportunities to meet others with similar interests. Through concerts, fashion and art displays, sports contests and other such activities, it showcases new talents. Underlying all these activities is the aim to motivate the beneficiaries to stand on their own feet, to seek their own solutions and to follow their own dreams. A number of experienced professionals, Uzbeks as well as foreigners, who have taken part in these projects, have expressed their admiration for what the Forum is doing. These are not idle compliments: anyone who, like the author of this paper, has witnessed these events, spoken to the participants and looked at their accomplishments cannot fail to be moved and impressed by the results.[29]

The Fund Forum already has much to be proud of, but if it is to continue to develop successfully there are issues that must be addressed. One is the need for adequate and sustainable funding. Currently, all the activities of the Forum and its sub-groups are financed by grants from national and international organizations, private and public sponsors, charitable donations and fund-raising events. The administrative costs of the organization are low, owing to the small number of full-time staff and the many unpaid volunteers. Also, several projects are self-contained events, requiring little in terms of capital expenditure. Nevertheless, in the longer term, if the Forum is to progress beyond the present *ad hoc* approach to its operations, it will need to establish a more secure financial base. A second issue that is emerging is the need for more trained professionals to oversee larger and more complex projects and to administer the growing network of international contacts and activities. A third issue is the need for better monitoring and evaluation of projects. Although the intention is good, the implementation may not always live up to expectations. Finally, the Forum has been striving to extend its outreach beyond the cities and towns to include remoter rural settlements. This is already happening, but more needs to be done if it is to function as a truly inclusive, nationwide organization.

Challenges: Global and Local

Societies round the world, in all ages, have faced challenges to their security, prosperity and stable development. Today, however, we live in a time of unprecedented levels of change, risk and vulnerability. Globalization is drawing us closer together, increasing our interdependence and inter-connectivity. Rapid advances in science and technology are opening new horizons, delivering unimagined benefits. Yet they also bring incalculable dangers. Threats, too, are constantly evolving and spreading beyond national boundaries. They take many forms: natural and manmade environmental hazards; pandemics that spread lethal diseases to plants, livestock and human beings; illegal migration; transnational crimes such as drug trafficking and terrorism; global economic crises, fluctuating commodity prices, the rising cost of food and energy. No country is immune to these problems. Equally, no country has found the answer to creating the "just" and "good" society. A sound political system, robust institutions and a strong legal framework are important instruments of state management, but by themselves they are not sufficient to produce an equitable, well-functioning society. The social and economic stresses of contemporary life have resulted in high levels of anxiety, depression and alienation. This phenomenon is particularly marked in the most industrialized countries of the world, where the social fabric has been weakened to such an extent that the notion of community spirit has almost ceased to exist.

So what of civil society? What role is it playing in the face of these challenges? In one country at least these issues are being addressed head on: in the 1980s, British Prime Minister Mrs. Thatcher stated firmly that there was "no such thing as society." Ten years later, a new generation of politicians was witnessing the effects of the loss of social cohesion. Pride in the disintegration of society was now giving way to concern about a "broken society."[30] It was against this background that in 2010, the British Conservative Party launched its concept of the "Big Society." The objective was to create a climate that would empower local communities, and would "take power away from the politicians and give it to people."[31] It proposed such measures as transferring power from central to local government (localism and devolution), encouraging people to take an active role in their communities (i.e. volunteerism), supporting cooperatives, charities and social enterprises, and other such local activities. Two points stand out from this manifesto: firstly, that the very values that donor agencies have been urging on host communities in the developing world under the rubric of "civil society building" are in fact under threat in a "mature democracy" such as Britain; secondly, that the proposed "Big Society" agenda is very similar to what is already being done in Uzbekistan. This does not mean that either "civil society" or the "big society" have all the answers, but it does mean that community values, community bonds, are a vital part of creating a caring, humane environment.

Uzbekistan, in its modern form of statehood, is just twenty years old. It has rich human and natural resources, but by international standards of economic development it is not a wealthy country. A doubly landlocked country, two thirds of its territory lies in the arid zone; almost half its population is under 20 years of age.[32] One could list at great length the inherent disadvantages of its geographic, not to mention geopolitical, location. Not surprisingly, it faces many problems. What is important, however, is that it is striving to resolve them. There are no ready, global prescriptions that suit every society. Each country and each situation must be looked at within its own historical and socio-economic context.

A case in point is the issue of child labour in Uzbekistan. This has attracted much negative comment in some countries and has resulted in boycotts of Uzbek cotton production. Yet the issue is not as clear cut as it may appear. In the opinion of this author, based on first-hand experience of working in the fields, the situation has been seriously misrepresented.[33] The legal position is clear: child labour is prohibited in Uzbekistan. Nevertheless, it does happen that within communities, especially in remote areas, children aged 12 years and above do work in the fields during harvest time. However, this is nothing like the relentless sweated labour, twelve hours or more a day, seven days a week all year round, that one find in many developing countries. This is seasonal work, undertaken with classmates, school teachers and other familiar adults (usually relatives). Of course it is physical labour and it could be argued that it is bad for children's development. Yet there are other considerations to be taken into account. Firstly, by the very nature of the agricultural cycle, cotton picking lasts a relatively short time. If one checks the educational standards of these children, they are not only on a par with those in developed countries, but often considerably higher. Secondly, in Uzbekistan, as in other countries with a large agricultural sector (including several European states), there is a tradition of children helping to bring in the harvest, be it of potatoes, hops or any other local crop.

In Uzbekistan almost every adult, no matter what their socio-economic status, will have participated in this work.[34] It falls within the tradition of *hashar* (communal labour) mentioned above. This does not necessarily make it right, but anyone who genuinely cares about the welfare of children should reflect on the priorities of their society. Today, in many parts of the developed world formal child labour has been virtually eradicated, but illegal sexual exploitation for money is widespread, likewise physical and emotional abuse. Chronic child obesity and its mirror image anorexia, along with numerous other instances of dangerous trends in children's behaviour, are all too common. Practices such as these raise fundamental questions about basic attitudes to children. Every society, every family, no doubt wants to provide their young with the best care and the best opportunities in life—but "the best" may take many different guises. It is unhelpful and dishonest to single out particular incidents without reference to the larger cultural, social and economic framework.

The issue of child labour is relevant to a discussion of the objectives of the Fund Forum, since a large part of its activities are directed towards creating an enabling environment for young people. This inevitably raises the question as to the stance the Forum takes on matters relating to child welfare in a general as well as a specific sense. The answer is implicit in the way in which the Forum seeks to implement its mission. It is not a campaigning organization and it does not initiate protest movements against perceived wrongs. Instead, it focuses on giving people of all ages and backgrounds the support and the personal confidence to bring about change for the better by their own actions. This approach, evolutionary not revolutionary, will seem to some to be ineffective and even pusillanimous. Certainly it is not designed to win accolades from those who want instant reform. Yet in the longer term, it is surely the only way to effect genuine, lasting improvements in society. It is for this reason that the Fund Forum places such emphasis on inculcating a positive attitude towards voluntary activities. This includes being prepared to devote unpaid personal time and energy to community work. This type of altruism has become unfashionable, and indeed controversial, in some parts of the world. To take again the example of Britain, one of the criticisms of the "big society" concept was that by stressing the role of volunteerism it was providing an excuse for economic exploitation.[35] This debate links back directly to the good governance of society: what are the responsibilities of the individual? What is the optimal balance between opposing and sometimes contradictory assumptions regarding the common good? Any serious attempt to answer such questions must look beyond ideological prescriptions to the total balance of positive and negative factors within society.

Pooling Resources

A well-known *hadith* reminds us that wisdom knows no geographic boundaries: "Seek knowledge even if it lies in China." There are no perfect solutions to the complex social, economic, environmental and ethical challenges that we all face, but the pooling of experiences and resources helps us to find better ways of tackling our common concerns. Stereotypes and preconceived notions about "the others" should be set aside. Cooperation, whether in the form of long-term joint projects or more modest exchanges, leads to better mutual understanding and may perhaps suggest novel solutions to familiar problems. The Fund Forum is very open to such contacts. It is still a very young organization and has much to gain from the experience of working with more established bodies. At the same time, it has interesting perspectives of its own to share with partners at home and abroad. It has moved beyond conventional approaches to civil society development and is seeking to create an innovative symbiosis of traditional practices and modern institutional structures. The most vivid testimony is the reality on the ground, encapsulated in the projects that are being undertaken with such energy, excitement and imagination. The Fund Forum does not pretend to provide all the answers but the model of civic engagement that it is developing has the potential to make a real contribution to this society. It might also be a worthwhile example for other countries to study and to consider if, and how, it could be adopted elsewhere. Four hundred years ago John Donne, cleric and poet, wrote:

> No man is an Island, entire of itself; every man is a piece of the Continent, a part of the main…any man's death diminishes me, because I am involved in Mankind.

We are all "a part of the main" and so it matters that we should try to engage with one another in a positive, constructive manner.

Notes and References

1. S. Daly and J. Howell, *For the Common Good? The Changing Role of Civil Society in the UK and Ireland*, Democracy and Civil Society Programme, Carnegie UK Trust, June 2006, 14.
2. N. Chandoke, *State and Civil Society: Explorations in Political Theory* (New Delhi: Sage Publications Pvt. Ltd 1995), 38.
3. The Centre for Civil Society (CCS), established at the London School of Economics, was one of the most interesting of these ventures. The CCS gained an international reputation for its postgraduate programmes and for its research output. However, the Centre closed in 2010—possibly an indication of changing circumstances and funding priorities. Several of the papers cited below were published by the CCS and are still available (July 2011) at http://www2.lse.ac.uk/CCS/home.aspx.
4. Jude Howell, Armine Ishkanian, Ebenezer Obadare, Hakan Seckinelgin, and Marlies Glasius, *The Backlash against Civil Society in the Wake of the Long War on Terror,* Civil Society Working Paper No 26, CCS-LSE, 2006. [eprints.lse.ac.uk/13205/].
5. Howell et al, *The Backlash against Civil Society.*
6. Howell et al, *The Backlash against Civil Society.*
7. Howell et al, *The Backlash against Civil Society.*
8. Howell et al, *The Backlash against Civil Society.*
9. David Lewis, *Civil society in non-western contexts: Reflections on the 'usefulness' of a concept Civil Society*, Civil Society Working Paper No 13, CCS-LSE, 2001 [http://eprints.lse.ac.uk/29052/].
10. Amyn Sajoo (ed.), *Civil Society in the Muslim World: Contemporary Perspectives* (London: I.B. Tauris 2002), 149-93.
11. Mohammed Arkoun, "Locating Civil Society in Islamic Contexts," in Sajoo, *Civil Society in the Muslim World*, 35-60, particularly 35-39. See also C. Hann and E. Dunn (eds.), *Civil Society: Challenging Western Models* (London: Routledge 1996).

12. A balanced assessment of these processes is given by Masaru Suda, *The Politics of Civil Society, Mahalla and NGOs: Uzbekistan* [http://src-h.slav.hokudai.ac.jp/coe21/publish/no10_ses/12_suda.pdf].
13. S. Frederick Starr, "Civil Society in Central Asia," in *Civil Society in Central Asia*, M. Holt Ruffin and Daniel Waugh (eds.), Center for Civil Society International, Central Asia-Caucasus Institute (Seattle/London: University of Washington Press 1999), 29.
14. Scott Horton and Alla Kazakina, "The Legal Regulation of NGOs," in Ruffin and Waugh (ed.) *Civil Society in Central Asia*, 35
15. See further Howell et al, *The Backlash against Civil Society*.
16. Horton and Kazakina, "The Legal Regulation of NGOs," in *Civil Society in Central Asia*, 43.
17. Howell et al, *The Backlash against Civil Society*, 12.
18. According to data from Uzbek Ministry of Justice, as of 1 July 2011, there were 5,650 registered NNOs.
19. *UNDP Human Development Report: Uzbekistan-2005*, 69.
20. Chapter 26, article 157, *Tax Code of the Republic of Uzbekistan*, 15 March 2011.
21. Suda, *The Politics of Civil Society*.
22. *UNDP Human Development Report*, 66.
23. Every year particular issues are highlighted as priority activities for the state and for citizens.
24. Alisher Faizullaev writes perceptively on these traditions. See for example his paper *Gap,* 19 August 2010, available at: [http://alisher-faiz.net/2010/08/gap]; and on "Morning Plov," *Druzhba narodov*, 2011, no. 7 [http://magazines.russ.ru/druzhba/2011/7/fa10.html].
25. Arnaud Ruffier provides an illuminating study of these institutions and customs in his thesis *To'y, gap, ziyofat et bayram*: *espaces de construction des identitités et des solidaritiés en Ouzbékistan* (Ecole des Hautes Etudes en Science Sociales 2002); a shortened version was published in book form under the title *Samarcande-Identités et espaces festifs en Ouzbékistan* (Montreuil: Aux lieux d'e^tre 2007).
26. Speech of President Karimov at the inauguration of the Tashkent Islamic University in 1999. A collection of his speeches and a chronology of events connected with Islam are given in *Islamic Spirit in the Life of the Uzbeks* (Tashkent: Islamic University Publishing House 2005).
27. See St. Thomas Aquinas, *Summa Theologica*, particularly II/1, which discusses "Human Acts."
28. The author visited several clinics in various parts of Uzbekistan and Karakalpakstan in August 2010 and spoke to patients, as well as to doctors, nutritionists and other professionals. Without exception, the feedback was extremely positive.
29. Over the past few years the author has travelled by road over a good part of Uzbekistan, visiting projects and talking to the beneficiaries of

the Fund Forum in towns as well as small villages in the heart of the countryside.

30. Richard Wilkinson and Kate Pickett, "A broken society, yes, But broken by Thatcher," *The Guardian*, 29 January 2010.
31. See report of David Cameron's speech on 18 May 2010 [http://www.number10.gov.uk/news/big-society/]
32. See the *CIA Factbook 2011*, under 'Uzbekistan' for country data [https://www.cia.gov/library/publications/the-world-factbook/geos/uz.html].
33. Travelling through the Ferghana valley at harvest time in 2010, the author saw children picking cotton. She asked the driver to stop the car, went into the field and asked the nearest adult if she could join them. Her request was met with surprise, but granted. The women helped her to put on the harvesters' apron and showed her what to do. Her clumsiness, like her poor grammar, evoked much laughter, but she was accepted as one of the team. In size she was the same height as the children (5 ft.), but not so strong. The experience was important for the insight it gave into the nature of the work—arduous, but not unduly tiring even for someone many decades older than anyone else in the field. Also, it gave an invaluable insight into the mood in the field, which was more relaxed and good-humoured than an outsider might have expected.
34. As confirmed by numerous personal discussions with senior government ministers and other 'elite' members of society.
35. The Archbishop of Canterbury was amongst those who expressed such concerns about this policy [http://www.archbishopofcanterbury.org/articles.php/571/how-should-churches-respond-to-the-big-society-rowan-williams].

11

Between the State and Society: Position of *Mahallas* in Uzbekistan

Timur Dadabaev

The Central Asian states are presently at the stage of implementing structural reforms and are in a state of transition to new forms of society-building. They face a number of challenges such as preservation of peace, "de-ideologization," democratization, and "market-ization" of their societies. In order to deal with these challenges, the majority of Central Asian states follow the top-to-bottom scheme of decision-making in their approaches to dealing with various issues in their societies. On many occasions, it leaves the public disengaged and detached. This, in turn, results in ineffective and counter-productive policy outcomes with respect to initially pursued goals. There are, however, indigenous institutions in the region, which prove to be highly efficient and offer many options in addressing social, economic and political conundrums, primarily at the community level.

This paper will focus on one such indigenous institution: the neighbourhood community, or *mahalla*. While Central Asian local communities, like *mahalla*, have gained considerable footing in recent years, there is no consensus yet on what is the role of these communities in the construction of the new states and societies of the region. Their potential is not properly researched and therefore, is poorly realized. The main thrust of this paper is to suggest that community represents one of a few effective traditional substitutes to unite representative of various ethnic and religious groups through creation of common identity based on the shared residence criteria. In addition, while Central Asia faces all possible evils such as environmental hazards and economic shortcomings, these problems cannot be addressed without localizing public dissatisfaction and creating public consent within the smaller communities like *mahalla*. Yet, throughout the history of existence of these communities, political authorities often attempted to manipulate these institutions in order to enhance their legitimacy in the eyes of their population and other governments. Thus, this study will investigate the *mahalla* neighbourhood communities in the context of other social and political organizations.

The main sets of questions that this essay aims to address are the following. Firstly, what is the relationship between *mahalla* and political authority? Secondly, is *mahalla* a government-affiliated unit or non-governmental (unofficial) indigenous network? If both exist within the same space/locality, what is the relationship and difference between the two? What is the nature of their public support?

Mahalla: Resident Community and its Expressions

The *mahalla* stands for residents quarters in the city, its community and self-governing administrative unit of the residents which exercised significant influence in Uzbekistan during pre-Soviet, Soviet and post-Soviet periods. By its design, each *mahalla* is managed by a group of recognized elders referred to as *aksakal* (directly translated as "white beard"). Interestingly, prior to current system of appointments of the *aksakals,* these individuals were chosen to lead their communities on an unofficial basis and were later recognized by an executive authority or government office. In the later years after the independence of Uzbekistan and institutionalization of the *mahalla*, leaders of *mahalla* are normally elected in their communities and then need to be officially appointed as the leaders of their *mahalla* by the administration of a city. Before revolution and establishment of Central Asian republics, the job of elder consisted of various functions, such as the collection of taxes, conveyance of orders, maintaining of security, arbitration of disputes between residents, and guardianship of orphans and widows. However, with the establishment of Soviet administration, *mahalla*'s functions were decreased mainly consisting of communal mutual support and the duties of supporting initiatives of the Soviet Government. With post-Soviet transformation of *mahalla*, its duties were gradually increased to transform *mahalla* from unofficial voluntary association of residents into official administrative unit of the city.

While the official process of institutionalization of *mahalla* in the post-Soviet environment is discussed in the sections below, the consistent elements of "unofficial" *mahalla* traditionally consisted of informal network of residents, information sharing and voluntary mutual support system. In this sense, *mahalla* historically used to be primarily a unit of identity which served as a basis for effective self-governance. As opposed to modern-day *mahallas* which consist of more than 500 households, traditional residential quarters and communities normally consisting of less number of households with no certain criteria existent to qualify them as one *mahalla*. Such compact residential quarters made the task of keeping close contacts and information exchange much easier and faster. Also, due to the existence of various traditions and unofficial social engagements, associations within *mahalla* have proven to be much stronger than any alternative attachments (such as socialist organizations, comrade councils, etc.), which were intentionally introduced into the society by various governmental initiatives over various periods of time. The "*gap*" ("*gashtak*"), "*guzar*" and "*chaikhona*" can be mentioned as engagements and shared spaces of information exchange and communication of the *mahalla* residents.

For instance, the "*gap*" is an Uzbek term which stands for "word" or "talking." In the context of *mahalla*, the "*gap*" stands for the unofficial association among small group residents who would visit each other's home, and have small talk-parties while having dinner together. In most cases, the "*gap*" was performed by men and women separately. Each such group had a leader or an organizer called differently in various locations but often referred to as the *jo'ra boshi*. The costs of the "*gap*" was either rotated around the members by each member of the "*gap*" having to cover costs of one such meeting in a year or shared by participants at the end of each meeting by giving some money to the convener. In the Soviet and post-Soviet times, normally, the total amount given by the participants exceeded the total cost of the dinner prepared by the convener, which further added to the motivations of the participants in participating and convening the meetings. However, money has never been a primary motivating factor and social networking within the area of ones' residence were always prioritized much higher than any possible financial gains.[1]

In addition to the social networking through the "*gap*" there were some other ways for residents to meet, form and share their common identity. One such example is the meeting space of "*guzar*" which existed as a place in each resident community to exchange information and strengthen relationships between people. Historically, the "*guzar*" was a place where services provided to the residents of the *mahalla*, such as shopping streets were concentrated. Small markets existed as important consisting elements of the "*guzars*" and people were able to acquire all their daily necessities without going to large bazaars (large markets). Also, there were small squares which existed in the "*guzars*" where people could gather and have small talk and share their news. "*Chaikhonas*" (teahouses) which were built in the centre of the *mahalla* were often part of these "*guzars*" serving as another venue for the exchange of information and forming common vision and shared values of the community. Frequently, "*chaikhonas*" served as places where the "*gaps*" and other *mahalla* related activites were performed.[2]

In addition to information exchange and the strengthening of identities, there were some traditional structures used in the *mahalla* as methods of the mutual support. One of them was called the "*khashar.*" The "*khashar*" stood for the voluntary mutual support provided by residents of the same community to each other in maintaining their livelihoods. A typical example of "*khashar*" was an assistance of neighbours when someone rebuilt an old house or built a new home. In such cases, residents of the same *mahalla* would voluntarily gather mainly on the weekends to help with the construction. The residents, who received the help, were morally obliged to help in return when other residents built a new home in the future.

The "*khashars*" were praised even during the period of the Soviet Union, and it was reported in the newspapers and media in those days, that the Soviet administration had to accept the aspect of mutual assistance of residents of *mahalla* as a positive element of neighborhood association.

> We have good customs. One of this is the *khashar*. For example, when people were facing very difficult tasks, such as building a home or digging a well, the neighbors were the first to help. Naturally this is done for free, and is the conduct of a friend. This is the khashar.[3]

Such assistance extended not only to in the cases of construction but was also demonstrated when residents were faced with the task of conducting big ceremonies and events. Conducting them without assistance of other residents would put too heavy burden on one family and therefore the role of community assistance in helping in organizing of weddings, funerals and related events was instrumental. While the forms of mutual assistance and functions of *mahalla* listed above have been typical throughout *mahalla* existence, these were much more diverse in the period prior to the formation of Soviet Central Asian republics. In the conditions of the limited governmental support, *mahallas* historically served as units which were called upon to regulate relations and solve problems between residents as exemplified in the cases discussed in the next section.

Contested Nature of Composition and the Functions of Pre-Soviet *Mahalla*

In the literature on *mahalla*, various criteria are emphasized as the ones which were used by residents when choosing their place of residence and on how neighborhoods were formed in Central Asia. Very often the names of *mahallas* included references to the ethnicity, social stratification and other features related to the residents of these communities. Occupation-based communities were historically present in Central Asian cities and it was not uncommon to find quarters named after a particular specialty or profession in almost all cities of the region. As some scholars noted, the common area of residence of traders or craftsmen indicates that quarters or *mahallas* were often regarded by residents not just a place of residence but also as place of work.[4] In addition, such quarters did not only provide for the well being of the traders and craftsmen but also were a way to provide for security and political influence. Many of these quarters had their gates which were locked at nights in order to provide security to the residents from looters and robbers.

Scholars suggest that heads of such quarters or leaders might have been the heads of the productions.[5] From analysis of academic work of medieval scholars, Belenitski and his colleagues note that in Merv for instance, there were separate quarters of leather craftsmen, jewelers, carpenters, those involved in money exchange, and that in the city or its surroundings, there was a slope of shoemakers and repairers.[6] They further suggest that there also existed such quarters as those of bakery builders. In addition to these specialties, quarters and gates of traders are also mentioned in several writings. For instance there were gate of grass traders and gates of scene makers in Bukhara. Samarkand had quarters of metal craftsmen. In Randzhed (Ferghana), one could see quarters of shoemakers and repairers. There were quarters of meat sellers and cloth traders in Tashan, etc.[7]

However, the connection of occupation with the residential neighbourhood communities is still not very clear and leaves many questions open. When analysing the notions of quarters, gates and streets mentioned above, scholars noted the lack of clarity in defining the difference between these three categories of residential areas in CA cities.[8] Such confusion of terms, according to Belenitski, made it difficult to understand whether specialized marketplaces existed alongside the quarters, hence residences of craftsmen or both existed in the same space. As he suggests, if market places existed separately from a place of residence of craftsmen, then it can be asserted that professional activities did not necessarily take place in the quarter where craftsmen lived. Therefore, Belenetski and his colleagues posed questions about whether quarters should be considered as places of residence of people of particular occupation/specialty, whether these were areas of their professional activity or whether these areas were the places where people lived and worked while trading in the market places.[9] In this regard Belenitski expresses his concern with the uncertainty around the question of whether residences in medieval Central Asia were at all based on the common occupation or profession or quarters where people of common profession resided were just coincidentally populated by residents that way. He supports the view that although the quarters populated mainly by the people of the same profession indeed existed in Central Asia, they can be explained not so much by the desire of these people to live in the same place but more by the fact that production facilities might have been placed in the same area, and therefore living nearby was a comfortable option.[10] He further suggested that such notions as *mahalla* were quite big in the scale and therefore, included not one but several streets. Some of these streets might have included people of the same profession but the neighbouring ones were populated by people of completely different specialties. He regretfully suggested that the average or standard size of medieval Central Asian *mahalla* was not known, which further complicates the understanding of how it was populated. Judging from Nishapur's size, he suggests that 44 *mahallas* there were located on the territory of 1000 hectares with the population of the city equaling around 100-120,000. Through simple calculation he guessed that the average size of *mahalla* was 25 hectare with population of 2.5 thousands. However, in Bukhara he suggests, the principle of "one quarter-one profession" existed for a long time. He further suggests that while the territory of Nishapura is smaller than that of Bukhara, the overall number of *mahallas* in Bukhara was 217, almost 5 times more than that in Nishapura in tenth-eleventh centuries.[11] He further attempted to support his argument that people of one quarter did not necessarily settle according to the professional belonging by citing an example of Samarkand (Afrasiyab) where craftsmen and their workshops were located chaotically without certain order or rule.

In terms of functions of *mahallas* mentioned above, there were certain problem-solving functions of pre-Soviet *mahallas* which lost their importance in the Soviet and post-Soviet contexts. One of such functions was related to irrigation. The bulk of literature on the traditional community-based system of irrigation and the role of *mahalla* in this process comes from the writings of Russian travelers and civil servants who traveled or were stationed in Turkistan and other city states at the end of eighteenth and the beginning nineteenth century.[12] It is well-known that by the beginning of nineteenth century certain authority over water management in the localities was entrusted with personal from among local population often referred to as "Aryq-oqsoqol." The title of "aryq-oqsoqol" is compiled of word "*aryq*" implying small canal and "*oqsoqol*" referring to elder in the traditional local community. Therefore, Aryq-oqsoqols were water administrators at the local level, who not only distributed the water according to the size of the plot of each member of the local community but also made sure that no injustice occurs in the process. These people were not just entrusted with power of administering local water distribution but were the people whose social stature left no doubt in minds of community residents that injustice would not be tolerated. In addition to the distribution of water, Aryq-oqsoqols were also responsible for mobilizing people to rebuild decaying dams, cleaning the canals and paving new canals to the distanced areas and plots of land.[13] Logistic capacity of the Aryq-oqsoqols was limited. Thus they had several assistants called Mirabs who helped them with distribution of water and maintenance of water-related facilities within entrusted community or territory. Sometimes, Aryq-oqsoqols administered distribution of water among several communities or villages. In such a case, each Mirab was entrusted one village or community or one canal line/system.[14]

The local system of irrigation in Central Asian city-states (like Bukhara, Tashkent and others) was based on two pillars: private and community-based ones. Private water consumption was possible in Bukhara and surrounding areas when the villager or other consumer paves a smaller water-way from a bigger canal or river for his land-plot without asking for an assistance of the community or neighbours. By committing to an individual water management and administration, the individual also had an obligation to periodically clean all the water-ways and canals leading to his land-plot without assistance of the community. This was a rare case though. Community-based water consumption was much more attractive option because it was more rewarding in terms of labour-commitment required from an individual member of the community and as an outcome, implied more water for a land plot. In this sense, the community-based water consumption in Bukhara was a consequence and an outcome of the difficulties encountered in the process of building irrigation facilities and infrastructure for individual use. Therefore, it was profitable for individual community members to unite their efforts and resources in building and administering water facilities, which was impossible to do through individual efforts.

The community-based water consumption system had several specific features. Firstly, it was guided by the Adat customary law.[15]

According to it, each community member involved in agricultural production had a right for a part of water of the canal required to produce a harvest and feed one's family. Also customary law implied that in order not to lose water as an outcome of evaporation and over-excessive filtration, irrigation system of the area in particular community should not be divided into small constantly functioning water-ways and canals to each land-plot. Instead, peasants had to maintain the water-flow of the canal (without taking the water into their own plots) and wait in line for their own turn, which was clearly determined and followed.

The order of water distribution was also a well-calculated system of community-based water consumption and management in the Bukhara area. According to customary law, the right of every member of community for water was in direct relation to the quantity of the water in the canal or basin and number of people claiming that water. The right of a community member for part of the water in the canal was referred to as "*suv*" (water). In calculating how much water should be distributed to the members of community the following formula was used: the available water was divided into the number of community members claiming the water, with one unit implying one hour of water consumption. After this calculation was done, the number of land-plot owners was grouped according to the proximity of their land. The main principle in this process was to group community members into groups so that the total right of each group for water was equal to the 24 hour period. This is normally a period for the duration of which the water from the canal is channeled into the land of a particular group, while other groups await their turn. Logofet demonstrated how the system worked by saying that most canals consisted of 144 *suv* (water rights) which implied that 144 land-owners had the right to use the water. The time for which every land-owner was allowed to use the water was calculated by dividing the number of minutes in 24 hours (1440) into the number of land-owners (144). As an outcome of such calculation, theoretically, each land-owner was allocated 10 minutes of water flow into their land every day.[16] However, in practical terms, it was very difficult to divide people into users per hours because of the large number of such users. Therefore, the villagers or community-members were divided into several groups, with each group being allocated water for one day (24 hours). Each group waited for its turn in the line. Such lining up was referred to as "*peikal*."

The distribution of water among the members of each "*peikal*" was made by the decided time, by measuring the time according to the change of shadow or movement of stars, if at night. Logofet noted several methods of determining without a watch the exact time of when water should have been switched to another land-owner though he did not provide details of the methods. The water right measured in "*suv*" was not a constant measure but fluctuated according to the quantity of water in the canal. However, the aim of setting such mechanism was to guarantee that every land-owner receives an amount of water that he required in order to irrigate a land plot and provide for the family's well being.

If the land-owner did not use the water during his turn, his right to use water is transferred to the next in line or whose land is located in the downstream of the canal. At the same time, intentional attempt to or unintentional appropriation of water without proper procedure or right was considered a criminal act and one had to pay penalty for the amount for which the damage has been made to the community or to the individual land-owner.

Soviet Authorities and *Mahalla*

The Soviet policy towards *mahalla* is to some extent the colonial pattern of administration in which colonizing power maintains the indigenous structure which can serve its interests and benefit its power.[17] Prior to the revolution, by and large *mahallas* maintained certain degree of independence from the city administrations, while being reliant on them for the functions mentioned above. The Soviet policy towards *mahalla*, especially in the aftermath of the revolution was somewhat ambiguous. On the one hand the Soviet approach to *mahalla* in the early years after Russian revolution was to diminish its significance in order to eliminate any alternatives to the Soviet institutions. On the other hand, Soviet authorities realized that doing so required time and could not be achieved overnight.[18] Therefore, they applied a dual policy of firstly using tools which *mahallas* offered to propagate Socialist ideas and later as this work progressed, weaken the influence of *mahallas* on the masses.[19]

This policy was started in 1922, when the People's Commissariat for Internal Affairs (NKVD) of Turkistan sent a recommendation note (memorandum) to the various Soviet bodies and revolutionary committee (*revolyutsion ko'mita*) suggesting usage of *mahallas* for the purposes of delivering to the masses the ideas of Soviet state building.[20] In order to do so, it was also recommended to reorganize *chaikhonas* (tea houses) into something referred to as "red chaikhonas" and to use these spaces, where local populations often gathers and exchanges information, to more effectively inform masses of the advantages of the Soviet and Socialist state building processes.

In order to turn these *chaikhonas* into "red chaikhonas" it was recommended to create small library corners in those tea houses with Soviet magazines, books and posters made available in them for wider distribution of information.

In addition to this, in 1924, the communist party appealed to men with a "strong sense of responsibility" to join the Soviet "*gaps*" (traditional custom of small talk while having dinner together), to have political discussions.[21] The expectation was to use social networking of *gaps* for the purpose of creating a Soviet-minded people with strong attachments to the ideas of new administration of the region. In addition, groups for women were also created both within the structure of *mahallas* to deal with the issues of women and their so-called liberation.[22] In 1932, several legislative documents were adopted to stipulate the standing of *mahalla* residentional neighborhood committees.[23] This eased the image of severe opposition of the Soviet authorities and the *mahalla* by 1938, and the *mahalla* were allowed to play certain, yet not very significant, social roles.[24] After a number of years, additional power was outwardly given to the *mahalla* by the re-evaluation of the history and the political system which started with the campaign of Khrushchev in 1959.[25] Although the supreme council of the Uzbek Soviet Socialist Republic established a law regarding the "*Mahalla* Committees" in 1961, it did not expand much the rights and roles played by *mahallas*.

As is well-known, city administration and executive powers were given to the Soviet councils established and functioning at various (regional, city, district, etc.) levels and the *mahalla* committees were positioned under the jurisdiction of the executive committee in the districts of each city. A *mahalla* representatives did not play significant roles in these schemes and were often required to appear for some particular instructions to the executive committees of each district without which, they had little power or authority even to deal with the issues of a particular concern to their own communities. Within the Soviet executive committees, representatives of various *mahallas* constituted the council which existed at the city and the district levels.

Originally, the purpose of such institution was to serve as the channel of dialogue between the *mahalla* representatives and the Soviet authorities. However, the committee turned into no more than a structure to give instruction to the *mahalla* representatives by the Soviet administration.[26] The formation and approval of the *mahalla* was determined by an executive committee which was a governmental agency in each district, and the existence of the *mahalla* was not recognized without its decision.[27] In contrast to the current 10,000 *mahallas* which exist in Uzbekistan, the number of *mahallas* according to the data of some cities in 1961 indicated that there were 270 or more in Tashkent, 131 in Samarkand, 45 in Nukus, 42 in Namangan, 41 in Andijan and 48[28] in Kokand.[29]

Although the structure shown above existed, same individuals could be members of various groups within *mahalla*'s structure at the same time as belonging to the groups was rather free. The activities of the *mahalla* of this period were performed voluntarily, and participation was not an obligation of the residents. The activity of each organization which consists of the *mahalla* committee was mainly related to culture, sports and improvements in the living environment of the neighbourhood. Only organizations, such as the "neighborhood watch" and "Comrades Court" performed activities in close cooperation with governmental agencies, and both organizations received instructions from the police, public prosecutor's office and the court.

Through the creation of such structure, the Soviet administration limited the social roles of the *mahalla*, while at the same time, using the *mahalla* to achieve governmental goals of socialist state-building and diminishing non-socialist attachment of residential or religious nature. The *mahalla* became a social organization whose existence was subordinated to the purposes of the Soviet administration, rather than an autonomous organization of self-governance by the residents.

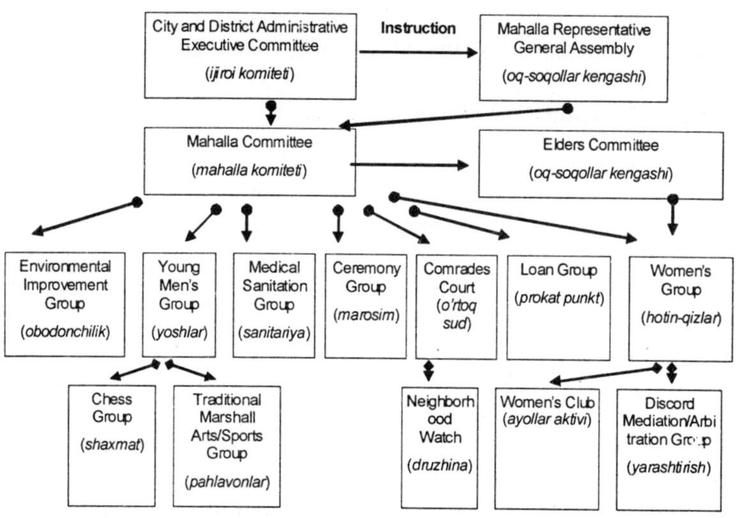

Figure 1. Structure of *Mahalla* Committee in the 1970s
(Example of *Mahalla* named after 40th anniversary of October Revolution)

It can be asserted with a certain degree of confidence that the *mahalla* of this period was different from that which used to traditionally exist in this region prior to the establishment of Soviet administration. Under the new Soviet regulations of *mahalla*, their purpose was not so much as to self-govern but rather to self-control and self-monitor.[30] The purpose of the strict control was not limited to the monitoring of suspicious anti-Soviet activities but also extended to the monitoring of household tax payments on to crops in their yards and livestock in early stages of the existence of the Soviet administration.[31]

Out of the traditional functions which were left to *mahallas* were those connected to various ceremonies and events. But even those were not conducted with the support of the administrative unit of *mahalla* but rather by the community and elders who considered participation and management of funerals, weddings and other ceremonies their ethical and religious obligation and not the legal duty. In this sense, while the self-government function of *mahalla* has been lost and transferred to the Soviet authorities, the identity-attachment of residents has still been preserved through activities of an official nature such as *gaps*, *khashars* and various ceremonies which were conducted as a part of community life.

The *mahalla* continued to exist, and maintained relations of the residents and supported their livelihood. The structure of the human network, exchange of information and mutual support based on the morals, educational roles, Islamic customs and neighboring communities were inherited by the residents, and the *mahalla* was informally maintained by the efforts of the residents.

Institutionalizing Post-Soviet *Mahalla*

With the end of the Soviet Union and the dawning of the era of *perestroika*, there was a steady trend to re-examine the functions of the *mahalla* and the values that this neighbourhood format embodied. As a result, the *mahalla* made a return to play an active role in the society. The independence of Uzbekistan from the Soviet Union further spurred this trend. The *mahalla* first earned attention as the venue for carrying on ethnic and Islamic values, with their resurrection was supported not only by the president and government but also by the nationalistic intelligentsia. This was because the *mahalla* itself was an expression of the unique identity of Uzbek culture, and a tradition that having withstood the oppression of the Soviet era deserved to be protected.

At a later stage, however, the government began to stress those aspects of neighbourhoods that promoted inter-ethnic dialogue and helped to stabilize the society, rather than promoting the fact that the *mahalla* was a socio-cultural tradition of the Uzbek people. The aim of this shift was to use the traditional mechanism of the *mahalla* to alleviate and stabilize the tensions existing between different ethnic groups, the decline in the standard of living and people's dissatisfaction and anxiety, seen in society directly after the achieving independence. Towards that end, the government of Uzbekistan re-organized the institution of *mahalla*, establishing its executive committee, setting the budget, personnel and defining their duties. With the decline in the standards of living after the collapse of the Soviet Union and growing tension in the political environment, most notably the rise of Islamic extremists, the duties of *mahalla* increased. This resulted in the process of de-facto transition of *mahalla* institution from an unofficial network of residents to a rather "official" social institution.

This process of transforming the *mahalla* into an official institution has not been conducted at once and has been a reactive process towards changing internal and international environment that Uzbekistan faced over the years of independence. As is outlined above, Uzbek Government even prior to independence recognized the positive influence of *mahalla* as an institution which contributed to the preservation of Uzbek culture. It also recognized the fact that although *mahalla* residential communities historically were the feature of Uzbek ethnicity, they were rarely exclusive ones offering an opportunity to reside to people of various ethnic groups willing to live in and live by the rules of the community. This process of recognition of the importance of the *mahalla* continued into the post-Soviet period of independence of Uzbekistan. Almost immediately following the independence of Uzbekistan, the *Uzbekistan Mahalla Philanthropic Foundation* was established through a presidential decree. The degree further enhanced *mahalla* functions and duties such as social support of decreasing living standards of population. Each *mahalla* was supposed to receive funds to perform this duty. Government justified this move by suggesting that residential councils know better who to support in their communities and that *mahalla* were historically had such functions. By doing so, the government officially recognized the *mahalla* as a traditional mutual assistance institution, and moved to particularly bolster the support functions designed to address needs of the socially disadvantaged.

In mid-1990s, with increasing social and security-related pressures on the government, it offered additional functions and duties to the residential communities which this time were expanded to include duties and responsibility to enhance the public order of each residential area in the face of the rise of Islamic extremists and terrorism. In order to do so, the *mahalla posboni* (neighbourhood watch) system was established in 1999 for which some amount of money has been allocated to respective *mahallas*. The logic behind this move was to deal with security concerns at the local level and delegate the duties of prevention and early warning of terrorist activities at the community level. With the pronouncement of 2003 as a "The Year of *Mahalla*," the government further diversified *mahalla*'s functions to include not only social, economic and security issues but also turning it into a fully-fledged administrative unit responsible for all aspects of residential life of people which include residents' registration, hosting the house/apartment owners' association, supervising payments of communal fees and communicating on behalf of citizens with the government and on behalf of government to the residents.

As explained above, while the Soviet era *mahalla* were unofficial community organizations based on traditional ties between people, the situation in current-day Uzbekistan is marked by the steady evolution of *mahalla* into what might be described as "official" *mahalla*. The aim of the government in promoting this trend is to organize the *mahalla* to help compensate for the inadequacies of administrative function, thereby having various different issues resolved at the resident level. Also at work here is the vision of relying on the efforts of residents to curb government expenditures in order to generate greater results with a limited budget. There is also much for the residents to gain if they subscribe to the government's logic. The role to be played by *mahalla* is likewise considerable in terms of bringing stability to the state of public security, with the government also embracing high hopes for the contributions by *mahalla* in that field as well.

While ideally, these measures to enhance the community functions needed to be understood as positive developments leading to de-centralization of authority and power in the country, there are few conceptual and logistical problems that such innovations bring with them thus questioning the rationale behind the idea of transfer of multiple functions and duties to the institution which used to be rather a unit of identity and voluntary mutual support. This move to institutionalize the status for the *mahalla* is not necessarily producing the anticipated results.

Firstly, there seems a lack of transparency in the relations between the *mahalla* and the governmental institutions and bodies. The *mahalla* survived the Soviet era and managed to maintain its traditional functions for the very reason that it kept a certain distance from the government and its functions were based on voluntary participation by residents. Under the present-day *mahalla*, which have been transformed into "official" institution, the *mahalla* executive committees have effectively become administrative organs. Although they are supposed to act on behalf of residents, frequently there seem to be instances of proactive governmental participation in the elections, policymaking and general activities of the *mahalla* executive committees, leading to the erroneous impression that those committees function more as government subcontractor bodies than as resident self-governance organizations. There are demands, therefore, for clarification of the ties between the *mahalla* executive committees and the national and local governments.

Secondly, while the *mahalla* executive committees have been given legal rights and independence, the *mahalla* have yet to attain financial self-reliance and independence without which it has to heavily rely upon governmental financing. In the absence of firm legal foundations for independent decision making and execution of *mahallas* mentioned above, such financial dependence may result in victimization of *mahalla* and the abuse of authority by other institutions and agencies. In addition to that, there are also obvious gaps between the revenue sources supplied to *mahalla* through government budgeting and the duties that the *mahalla* are required to perform. In other words, the allocations offered to *mahalla* fall far behind what the government expects them to do. In the conditions of perceived governmental guidance of these institutions and their financial dependence on the government, it is highly likely that the resident *mahalla* executive committees will come to be perceived by residents as part of the governmental institution than local resident self-government units. In its own turn, this leads to isolation of *mahalla* officials and decrease of the efficiency of this institution.

The third problem consists of the gaps in how residents actually view the *mahalla*. Attitudes of residents toward the *mahalla*, and how they participate in these community organizations, are definitely not one and the same. For that matter, the very structure of the *mahalla* has conveyed the right to make such choices to the residents. From days of old, people who have viewed participation in *mahalla* as leading to their own benefit, or who believe the *mahalla* to be a part of their own sub-identity have taken active part in it. Those who do not subscribe to that viewpoint, meanwhile, have had the freedom not to participate. However, there is now the fear that as the move by the government to make the *mahalla* "official" and "organized" picks up steam, the decisions handed down by the *mahalla* will become involved with the lives of all residents, causing people to lose the right to choose whether or not to participate or to decide for themselves to what degree they wish to take part. In particular, as the *mahalla* steering committees have come to undertake welfare work, audit functions and various other duties in recent years, people have come to sense fewer and fewer differences between these steering committees and government administrative agencies. Large numbers of residents now point out the possibility that this type of shift to "official" status for the *mahalla* will damage the traditional image of the *mahalla* (of being based on spontaneous actions) that has existed from long ago.

Conclusion

Neighbourhood communities, exemplified by *mahalla*, have traditionally played significant roles in the lives of people in Central Asia and in Uzbekistan in particular during the pre-Soviet, Soviet and post-Soviet periods. Historically, they were the institutions which united people at the local level and served as a mobilization force when such need arose. In this sense, they represented the grass roots organizations of residents who not only united their resources for the problem-solving purposes but primarily shared common values. Because of such appeal authorities in pre-Soviet, Soviet and post-Soviet contexts, were tempted to utilize this institution for their purpose by granting or omitting certain powers of the residential communities.

There are several conclusions that can be made on the evolution of the modern *mahalla* in Central Asia in general as an indigenous institution of local self-government and as an element of local civil society. Firstly, this study argues that there are several forms of expressions of the *mahalla*'s existence. This study attempts to determine not only the forms of "official" and "unofficial" *mahalla* but also the different roles the two played in citizen's participation in local governance: the first, being a part of local government unit and the second, an identity agent and more "unfocussed," more tied to particular concerns and to a certain degree more partisan. This research also tries to demonstrate that while in the Soviet times, *mahalla* used to be placed outside the hierarchy of power, in the post-Soviet setting *mahalla* has been incorporated into local government structures.

At the administrative level, the Government of Uzbekistan attempted to build on the legacy of the traditional *mahalla* by institutionalizing its structures and functions and integrating *mahalla* into the structure of administrative bodies. Although not fully absorbed, *mahalla* committees, which oversee the functioning of *mahallas* are de-facto part of the overall administrative system and often serve as assistants of the executive branch of power or policy. This has both positive and negative aspects.

Among the negative aspects, the lack of privacy, problems in human relations and extension of the powers of *mahalla* committees frequently resulted in rejection of their initiatives by the residents. But in general, people remain somewhat tolerant to the *mahalla* with some particular members taking active part in strengthening *mahalla* functions. Rational and positive side of such engagement between government and local form of self-governance are often justified by the fact that the *mahalla* represents members of their communities and are closer to the needs and concerns of their residents. In this sense, if properly framed, financially supported and legally protected, these institutions can play a constructive role in defending the rights of communities as institutions of public participation and in the self-management of their resident areas. Therefore, issues such as the financial, legal and social preparedness of the *mahalla* to take up the roles entrusted to it by the government, building constructive equal partnerships between *mahalla* and governmental institutions and merging the "official" and "unofficial" parts of *mahalla* into one remain detrimental to the success and sustainability of this scheme.

Notes and References

1. K. Rakhimov "Makhalla, nachalo nachal: Obychai i sud'ba," *Nauka i Religiia*, no. 9 (1989), str.28-29.
2. *Makhallada Tarbiia*, (Toshkent: Yosh gvardiia 1970).
3. Yu Kotler, "Makhallia reshaet i deistvuet," *Sovetskij Soyuz*, no. 12, s.33.
4. A.M. Belenitski, I.B. Bentovich and O.G. Bol'shakov, "Chislennost' Naseleniia," in *Srednevekovyj Gorod Srednej Azii* (Leningrad: Nauka 1973), chapter 5: 298.
5. Belenitski et al, *Srednevekovyj Gorod*, 299.
6. Belenitski et al, *Srednevekovyj Gorod*, 299.
7. For details see Belenitski *et al.*, *Srednevekovyj Gorod*, 300.
8. Belenitski et al, *Srednevekovyj Gorod*, 300.
9. Belenitski et al, *Srednevekovyj Gorod*, 300.
10. Belenitski et al, *Srednevekovyj Gorod*, 334-35.
11. Belenitski et al, *Srednevekovyj Gorod*, 335.
12. D.N. Logofet', *Buharskoe Hanstvo: Pod Russkim Protektoratom*, Tom II (St.Petersburg: Izdal V. Berezovskij 1911), 77.
13. Logofet', *Buharskoe Hanstvo*, 81-82.

14. Logofet', *Buharskoe Hanstvo*, 82.
15. Logofet', *Buharskoe Hanstvo*, 82-83.
16. D.N. Logofet', *Buharskoe Hanstvo*, 83.
17. Yurii Kulchik, Andrei Fadin, and Victor Sagdeev, *Central Asia After the Empire* (London: Pluto Press 1996), 10.
18. O Umarkhodzhaeva, "Makhallinskii Komitet dejstvuet," *Agitator Uzbekistana*, no. 17 (1987): 26.
19. David MacKenzie Abramson, *From Soviet To Mahalla: Community and Transition in Post-Soviet Uzbekistan* (*From Soviet To Mahalla*), unpublished Ph.D. Dissertation, UMI Microfilm, Indiana University, 1998, p. 61.
20. David MacKenzie Abramson, *From Soviet To Mahalla: Community and Transition in Post-Soviet Uzbekistan,* Ph.D. Dissertation, UMI Microfilm, Indiana University, 1998, 72.
21. Abramson, *From Soviet to Mahalla*, 71.
22. G'ulomov, *Mahalla-Fuqarolik Zhamiiatning Asosi* (Tashkent: Adolat 2003), 31.
23. "Polozhenie o makhallinskikh (kvartal'nykh) komitetakh v gorodakh Uzbekistana," *Sbornik Ustavov*, no. 17 (1932), str.113; "Polozhenie ob Obschikh Sobraniyakh (Skhodakh) Grazhdan v Sel'skikh Mestnostyakh Uzbekskoi SSR Utverzhdeno Ukazom Prezidiuma Verkhovnogo Soveta Uzbekskoi SSR, 30 avgusta 1961," *Spravochnik Aktivista-Obschestvennika: Sbornik ustavov I polozhenii samodeiatel'nykh organizatsii trudyaschikhsya* (Tashkent 1963), str.182-94; "Polozhenie o Makhallinskikh komitetakh Tashkenta," *Vechernyi Tashkent* (19 oktiabria 1990), str.2.
24. G'ulomov, *Mahalla-Fuqarolik*, 31.
25. Abramson, *From Soviet to Mahalla*, 72.
26. "Makhallinskie komitety Tashkenta: Tsyfry i fakty," *Agitator Uzbekistana*, no. 7 (1990), str.22-25.
27. K. Kamilov, "O roli makhallinskikh (kvartal'nykh) komitetov v sovremennyi period (v gorodakh Uzbekistana)," *Obschestvennye nauki v Uzbekistane,* no. 2 (1961), s.59-60.
28. Kotler, "Makhallia reshaet i deistvuet."
29. Kamilov "O roli makhallinskikh."
30. "Polozhenie ob Obschikh," str.188-191.
31. *Sotsialisticheskie Obriady v Zhizn'* (Tashkent 1987), str.14.

For further reading see:

Caroline Humphrey, *Karl Marx Collective: Economy, Society, and Religion in a Siberian Collective Farm* (Cambridge University Press 1983).

Caroline Humphrey, *Marx Went Away but Karl Stayed Behind* (Ann Arbor: University of Michigan Press 1998).

Denis Kandiyoti, "Rural livelihoods and social networks in Uzbekistan: perspectives from Andijan," *Central Asian Survey* 17, no. 4 (1998): 561-78.

Georg Paul Geiss, "Mahalla and Kinship Relations: A Study on Residential Communal Commitment Structures in Central Asia of the 19th century," *Central Asian Survey* 20, no. 1 (2001): 97-106.

Hisao Komatsu, "Maharra ni kansuru no-to—O.A.Suharewano fi-rudo waku kara-," *Ajia-Afurika gengo bunka kennkyu* 16 (1978): 179-215.

J. Critchlow, *Nationalism in Uzbekistan: A Soviet Republic's Road to Sovereignty* (Boulder: Westview Press 1991).

Johan, M. Rasanayagam, "Spheres of communal participation: placing the state within local modes of interaction in rural Uzbekistan," *Central Asian Survey* 21, no. 1 (2002): 55-70.

Johan, M. Rasanayagam, *The Moral Construction of the State in Uzbekistan: Its construction within concepts of community and interaction at the local level,* Ph.D. dissertation, Cambridge University, Kings College, 2002.

John Micklewright, Aline Coudouel, and Sheila Marnie, *Targeting and Self-Targeting in a Transitional Economy: The Mahalla Social Assistance Scheme in Uzbekistan*, January 2001.

Lidmila Polonskaya, and Alexei Makashenko, *Islam in Central Asia* (Reading 1994).

Nancy Lubin, "Islam and Ethnic Identity in Central Asia: A View from Below," in *Islam in the Soviet Union: From World War II to Perestroika (Gorbachev)*, Yaacob Ro'i (New York: Columbia University Press 1994).

O.A. Suhareva, *Kvartal'naya Obshina Pozdnefeodal'nogo Goroda Buhari (V svyazi s istoriei kvartalov),* (Moskwa: Nauka 1976).

Ozod Husanov, *Mustaqillik va Mahallyi Hokimyat (huquqyi, tashiqiliy masalalar va muammolar*) (Toshkent: Sharq 1996).

Pak Chan Kyu, *Obshina v Azii: Tipologicheskie harakteristiki obshinnih struktur Kitaiskoi Narodnoi Respubliki, Respubliki Koreya I Respubliki Uzbekistana, Dissertatsiya na soiskanie stepeni kandidata istoricheskih nauk* (Moskwa: MGU 1998).

Sergei Polyakov and Martha Olcott (eds.), *Everyday Islam: Religion and Tradition in Rural Central Asia* (New York: Sharpe 1992).

Sh.G. Ochilov, "Iz opita razvitiya obshestvennogo samoupravleniya v Uzbekistane," *Obshestveniie Nauki v Uzbekistane*, no. 8 (1990).

Spravochnik Aktivista-Obschestvennika: Sbornik ustavov I polozhenii samodeiatel'nykh organizatsii trudyaschikhsya (Tashkent 1963).

W. Eric Sievers, "Uzbekistan's Mahalla: From Soviet to Absolutist Residential Community Associations," *The Journal of International and Comparative Law* 2 (2002).

Yaacob Ro'i, *Islam in the Soviet Union: From World War II to Perestroika (Gorbachev)* (New York: Columbia University Press 1994).

12

Kinship Relations in Kyrgyzstan Following the Transition Period: The Case of Küntuu Village

İlhan Şahin

The Kyrgyz people represent one of the most ancient nations of Central Asia. They are a people who have preserved the traditional features of nomadic lifestyle even until today. Besides, they still retain a strong social structure based on a traditional lineage system. As far as is known, before 1917 they had a very strong inner relationship based on a social and administrative structure called *uruu* or *uruk*, which means clan or kin groupings. But after the establishment of the Soviet rule, the above-mentioned kin grouping system with its active inner relationships was maintained locally in accordance with the ideological policy of the Soviet regime. This brought about a weakening of the traditional kinship structure. The local administrations of the Soviet rule called *kolkhozes* and *sovkhozes* took all the power in their hands. Later on, as the Soviet system fell, local Soviet authorities lost their powers and functions legally, and within this context the people returned to their kin grouping structures in order to cope with the social and economic problems of post-Soviet Kyrgyzstan.

This paper focuses on kinship relations of the Kyrgyz people after the collapse of the Soviet Union. It seeks to emphasis on how the Kyrgyz people tried to return to their primordial past which remained buried under the Soviet regime. Research for the paper is mainly based on fieldwork materials gathered on the spot in Küntuu village in 2009–10 and will focus on kinship relations after the transition period with special reference to Küntuu village. We will also introduce some basic information related to the establishment and social structure of this village. Here, I particularly would like to emphasize that this represents micro-level research based on a specific point in kinship relations after 1991. The study of a specific point may appear unimportant, but it must be emphasized that it is impossible to reach general conclusions without accomplishing this type of research in depth.

Brief History of the Village

Küntuu is one of the villages of the Sokuluk raion in Chüy (Chuy) *oblast* and lies at a distance of 10 kilometres from the capital city, Bishkek, at the foot of the Ala Too (Ala Mountain). According to historical sources and traces, the history of Küntuu village begins from about 1932. Before this time a large Kyrgyz nomadic group called *Solto uruu*, *On Kanat* (Right Wing), was living in the Chüy valley. Specifically, the area occupied by Küntuu village had been used by the Küntuu people who belonged to the Solto uruu as well.[1] Soviet rule at first established and formed a *kolkhoz* (collective farm) called Kenesh[2] in this area in 1932. Besides, two other *kolkhozes* called Kirov[3] and Molotov[4] were established at that time in this same vicinity. This shows that the *kolkhoz* played a very important role in the foundation of the first type of villages during Soviet rule.

The *kolkhoz* on which we focus was called Kenesh for a while. In 1946 it came to be known as Kaganovich.[5] In 1958 those three *kolkhozes*—Kaganovich, Kirov and Molotov—were combined into a *sovkhoz* called Kirov. Kaganovich became the main administration centre of the Kirov Sovkhoz. After 1991, the village which previously carried the name Kenesh, and later on Kaganovich, started to be called Küntuu. The name *Küntuu* comes from a nomadic community which belonged as a sub-tribe to the *Solto uruu*. According to genealogical trees and interviews with informants, Küntuu was the name of the elder of three sons of Solto named Küntuu, Kultuu and Chaa.[6] Actually, Küntuu is the ancestor of this community. Also, the present Küntuu community in the village consists of three lineage groupings known Chong Murun, Dandybay and Kulboldu. As far as can be concluded from interviews with informants, these three brothers were the sons of Küntuu.[7] From these brothers Chong Murun had three sons named Balvak, Tökö and Nadır; Dandybay had two sons, Abek and Taylak; Kulboldu had six sons, Ernazar, Shükür, Satımkul, Jolumbet, Kızıl Kulboldu and Chanach. Kulboldu's descendents later comprised the largest group in the village.

After the collapse of the Soviet Union, the inhabitants of the village held a meeting dealing with several issues. Here they discussed about social and economic issues and tried to solve them. At the meeting the *aksakal*s (distinguished village elders who were respected) suggested changing the name of the village according to their lineage. All the participants agreed. From that time onwards the village has carried the name *Küntuu.*

I argue here that the first change in the village after the transition became the new name of the village in accordance with ancestral traditions. It should be emphasized that this reflects not only a "return to the past" but also the first sparks of kinship relations after independence.

Currently the village inhabitants consider themselves descendants of a man named Küntuu and his descendants who lived many generations before. Therefore, the people in the village call themselves *Küntuu eli* which means people of Küntuu. Some elderly residents said that the name Küntuu consists of "kün," which means "sun," and "tuu," which means birth. This refers to the current residents of the village who have been accepted as the real people of the village.

Changes and Social Networks after 1990

Before 1991 the total population of Küntuu village consisted of about 600 *tütüns* (households). Approximately, 40 per cent of these *tütüns* were Kyrgyz, 33 per cent Russians and 27 per cent Nemis (Germans), Uyghurs (Uigur), Tatars and Dargins, originally from the people of the Caucasus. This situation indicates that Küntuu was a multi-national *kolkhoz* at that time.

The collapse of the Soviet Union in 1990 brought a lot of unexpected social, economic administrative and political problems. Kyrgyzstan had been displaying symptoms of stagnation and negative effects in all spheres of life. Cattle-breeding, animal husbandry and agriculture totally collapsed, and administrational power became decentralized. Almost the same unwanted issues were reflected in Küntuu. As one of the first symptoms of these negative effects, non-Kyrgyz representatives began to leave the village. Russians migrated to Russia, Nemis to European countries and other nationalities like Tatars, Dargins and Uyghurs moved to other villages in the province where most of inhabitants consisted of their own nationalities.[8] As the local people in the village explained, those ethnic Russians and Nemis, seeing no future for themselves in their villages, sold all their belongings, including their homes at a very low price and migrated elsewhere.[9] Their homes were usually bought by the locals. After these migrations, only five or six Russian families remained in the village. Also, other nationalities consisted of only a couple of families. As a result of emigration, the structure of the village, which had earlier consisted of different nationalities, changed so that it currently consists mostly of Kyrgyz.

Along with these migration movements following the transition period, people faced many different social and economic problems characteristic of a free market economy. People in rural areas started to move to urban areas seeking jobs and battling for survival. Chüy province, specifically the capital Bishkek and its surroundings became very attractive places to live. Küntuu, being very close to Bishkek, lies within this attractive area. In this connection, the first settlements in the village were from other provinces. Settlers or families who emigrated from other provinces started to come in about 1988. The first settlers of the village before and after 1990, having health problems, came from Chatkal *raion*, Jalalabad *oblast* in 1988.[10] Another family came from Jumgal district, Naryn province, in 1992 because of heart problems of the husband in the family.[11] Outside of these families, also because of social and economic reasons, other families started to emigrate to the village from other provinces such as Osh, Jalalabad, Yssykkul, Talas and Naryn during the transition period. At the end of these emigration movements, Küntuu village had approximately 800 *tütüns* (households) and still has that many today. More than 300 *tütüns* belong to the Küntuu people. The rest emigrated from other provinces to the village. This is also evidence of the change that took place in the structure of the village.

Social Networks

Social and economic changes, migrations from other regions or provinces and other kinds of problems mostly affected kinship relations in Küntuu village in the post-Soviet period. There surfaced two different kinds of social networks after 1990. These two networks were both based on the neighbourhood within the village, but varied according to the peoples' backgrounds. In this connection, the first social network was called uruu yntymagı (lineage network) and the second is named jerdesh yntymagı (network of fellow countrymen). The difference between them is that first is based on the lineage network of the local community, while the second is a social network based on people or families who came from other provinces; otherwise it is a newly created network of migrants. So, according to our observations made through on-the-spot research, we can argue that there are two types of relationships or social networks in the village on which this article tries to focus.

Uruu Yntymagı (Lineage Network)

In the case of Küntuu village, *uruu yntymagı* means lineage based on kinship of social solidarity. This solidarity is based physically on a *köchö*, a street which is about 300-600 metres in length. Each of one of the *köchö*s (streets) in the village has a special name. At the same time, each one of them is inhabited mostly by the specific lineages. Lineages are settled according to street, and they are known as being mostly street-focused. The social principle of some streets in Kuntuu village is: "one *köchö* (street) represents one lineage grouping."

One of the largest lineage groupings is on a street is called Chong Murun. The families of this street are the households of that lineage, and they have a special kinship name called Chong Murun yntymagı. Chong Murun is the second largest lineage, and it belonged to the Küntuu nomadic group. They have their own rules and principles. The social structure of this street is not homogenous, as it is generally assumed. Thus, in the 1930s, a family from Sarybagysh uruu came to the village and settled on the street where the inhabitants are from the Chong Murun lineage. So, the family who is from another region actually entered the social network of "Chong Murun yntymagı." What is important here is that currently this family has been accepted by the street inhabitants and they see themselves as members of the Chong Murun.[12] Another migrant of village settled on a street called Sadovaya in 1988. This street was occupied by the Dandybay lineage. Dandybay is the largest lineage grouping in the village. Several months after they settled, some people from Dandybay visited and invited them to join *Dandybay yntymag*, which means social and economic solidarity of street families based on the kinship relation of the Dandybay lineage. The family accepted them and joined the group, and took part in almost all the social events of the street families.[13] These examples could be a sign of not only of the emergence and formation of a nomadic group but also the social structure.

Jerdesh Yntymagı

Jerdesh Yntymagı is another type of kinship relation in the village that has been there since 1990. *Jerdesh* means "solidarity of fellow countrymen." It is used in general for folks from the same province which is a key to the formation of the network. *Yntymak* means "solidarity." Hence, the widespread usage of the term *jerdesh yntymagı*, that indicates a social network of a group of people, was formed among the countrymen from the same province or region in the case of Küntuu village.

Solidarity of fellow countrymen in the village took place according to the provinces of the country. Currently families from only six provinces live in the village, though there are seven provinces, such as Naryn, Talas, Osh, Jalalabad, Batken, Yssykul and Chüy. Families from each of the provinces comprised the above mentioned social solidarity jerdesh yntymagı but are called by different names like *Naryndyktar*, *Talastyktar, Oshtuktar, Batkendikter*, etc. These names are given to them according to the provinces they came from, and they indicate their regional identity with respect to the social, economic and political issues within the Küntuu village.

These social groups in the village were formed in later years following the fall of the Soviet Union. Many families from far away regions of the country started to move to the central provinces with all their family members and belongings. Zamira Sopubekova, a current inhabitant of Küntuu village came here with her family in the year 2000. Before coming, she was working as a teacher at a secondary school in the Alay region in Osh province. As she had told us, she and her family had to leave school due to many social and economic problems after the collapse. So, she moved with her family to Chüy province in 1995 to earn a living.[14] She said that her family stayed in Kemin region for approximately four years. During that time, they grew beets and earned money by trading. Then, they bought a house for $1,500 (1 USD = 17 *soms* at that time) from a Kyrgyz family who had previously bought it from a Tatar family Families and people who migrated with these kinds of problems mostly settled in the central province of Chüy. The capital city of Bishkek is situated there, and market relations are much more developed. Those families today have their own small social groups and functions in the social life of the village.

At present, there are four social groups of fellow countrymen from the provinces of Naryn, Talas, Osh and Batken. The families from each of these provinces created their own social groups, and the number of families grew from 20 to 100 *tütüns* (households). Each group has their own leaders called *topbashy,* which means group leader who was elected for his personal competence and leadership ability. For instance, one of the informants, Toktomurat Mankiyev, who is currently the leader of *Oshtuktar* told us that his group consists of 24 families.[15] He has been leading this group since 2000 or right after his arrival in the village. As he had explained, he was chosen as a leader because he was a school teacher during the Soviet period; in other words he is an educated person.[16]

Today members of the social group *Oshtuktar,* meets regularly twice a year, on 31 August which is celebrated as the day of independence for the Kyrgyz people and on *Nuvruz*. In their meetings they celebrate the day sitting at a coffee house or restaurant. In addition, the 24 families help each other in bad and good days providing moral and financial support. For instance, in case of sad events like death or accident and on happy occasions like the birth of a child, marriage or buying a new car, each of families of Oshtuktar provide 500 *som*s under the leadership of Toktomurat Mankiev.[17] He does this job voluntarily and is responsible for organizing such kinds of social events for his group.

The case of Oshtuktar is an example of the kinship relations and it can be defined as close kinship. Since this is a small group consisting of 24 families, the relationship here developed quite closely. But in other groups, the kinship or the social relation changes according to the size of families, for example, Naryndyktar, who migrated from Naryn province to the village, call themselves *Naryndyktar* (People from Naryn). The group of Naryndyktar has about 100 *tütüns* (households). All of them came to the village after 1990 and currently share solidarity among them. If we compare the Naryndyktar group with other groups in the village, they are larger than the others. All of the families of Naryndyktar cannot come together in one place nor can they keep close relationships among themselves due to their larger population. Therefore, they are divided into two inner groups. Each group consists of approximately 50 families. As this number is still too large to have a permanent relation among these families, they are divided into two other inner groups again. One is a distant relation, another is close relation. In this connection, an informant among them told us that: "when one of the groups get together for only big social ceremonies like the death of person, we hardly have good relations with those families. We come together with all of them only when *Kishi ölgöndö* or somebody dies."[18] As the informant explained, this is a distant relation called *katysh*, which is based on 50 families, and they communicate occasionally such as in case of a funeral. In these cases, the leader of Naryndyktar, Sadybakas, collects 100 *som*s per family and give it to a member of the family to help organize the funeral. This is a very small financial aid, but in one way it represents moral support. But what is important here is that all the Naryndyktar, or those 50 families, keep the same kin relations they had before. The families from the same province do not divide themselves according to the districts or villages in their original province. This reflects a type of distant relationship.

It was disclosed by one of the informants from this group that 20 or 25 families have close communication with one another. They maintain close contacts with all members and try to follow all family events. In social ceremonies like marriage and death those families under the leadership of Sadybakas take part in the ceremonies, bringing moral and financial support to the ceremony holder. For instance, in these kinds of events each family brings 1,000 *som*s as financial support. If some of them organize a party commemorating a birth, or something of this kind, each family in the group contributes 1,000 *soms* to the family.[19]

Other Changes in the Village

We could observe some other changes in the village. One of them is about personal names. Prior to 1990 Soviet influence resulted in the naming of people with non-traditional names such as Sovietbek, Siezdbek, Melis, Sovkhozbek, Kolkhozbek, etc. In 1958 when the *kolkhoz* in the village became a sovkhoz, those born in this year were named "Sovkhozbek." This indicates that the system of *kolkhozes* of sovkhozes greatly influenced the process of giving names to people. But since 1991 the Kyrgyz people began to name their children according to their traditions, such names as Barsbek, Baytur, Atay, etc.

Other observations made in the village of Küntuu brought to light the existence of two cemeteries that were there before 1991, in accordance with their faith. After Christian migrations, the Muslim cemetery proved to be insufficient, so they decided to construct a new one for those people who came to the village after 1993. It should be also noted that close family members are buried closer to one another.

Local Administration in Social Network

There are about 15 *topbashys* or leaders of social groups in Küntuu village. Eleven of them are leaders of lineage groupings or nomadic groups known as *uruu* or *uruk*. Four of them are the leaders of the groups who came from other provinces. Following the transition period, *aiyl ökmöt* was established in the new administration system of Kyrgyzstan, and Küntuu village became the centre of the *aiyl ökmöt* (village government). The *aiyl ökmöt* consists of five villages: Shalta, Dostuk, Chong Jar, Kichi Shalta and Küntuu. The head of local administration is called *ökmöt* or *aiyl ökmötü*; he has an *orun basar* (vice government). Also, there are two official heads called *aiyl bashchysy* in the *aiyl ökmöt*. One of them is in charge of the Shalta and Dostuk, another is Chong Jar and Kichi Shalta. In addition to these, the *aiyl deputattary* (village deputies) consist of other formal groups under the village head.

As one of the informants told us that the head of the village always keeps good relations with the local leaders of social groups. The head gets in touch with the leaders several times a month to get advice and cope with some of the social problems of the village.[20] The current head of the village, Talaybek Korgoldoyev, confirmed this information during our conversation. Also he added some other relations in his interaction with the local leaders. As he explained, there are two informal groups under the village head. Those are *aiyl aksakaldary* (respectful and distinguished persons) of the village and *topbashchylar* (leaders of groups). Each of these groups consists of 7-15 persons, and they occasionally come together according to the social, economic and political problems of the village. For instance, as the head said, *aiyl deputattary* or the village deputies meet several times a month in the office of village head where they talk and discuss problems, like expenses, budget, sale, and other kinds of organizational problems.[21] This means that in case of absence of central support of the government, the head tries to solve local issues himself with the support of the deputies. The other group called *aiyl aksakaldary* is the group that helps the local administration to solve the legal issues of the village. The last group *topbashchylar* or the group leaders interact with the leaders of the local social network functions as an active network helping the local administration to cope with social problems in the village.

Conclusion

In conclusion, we can say that some initial changes occurred in the village of Küntuu after the transition period. For example, during this period almost all non-Kyrgyz nationalities emigrated from the village for social and economic reasons. On the other hand, other families started to emigrate to the village from other provinces such as Osh, Jalalabad, Issykkul, Talas and Naryn during the transition period. Along with this immigration or settlement process in the village, different types of kinship relations started to appear, such as close kin, distant kin, as well as the neighbourhood. The fundamental factors of these kin relations are based on being from the same place, belonging to the same lineage grouping and settling on the same street. Currently we can say that all the people of village are very happy and satisfied with their lives because the network which is based on different types of kinship relations provides them social and economic solidarity. This is a real portrait of Küntuu village, as well as many other villages in rural places of Kyrgyzstan, on how the people have been coping with the social and economic problems of their daily life in the framework of the weakened support of the government. People who lead the social groups and who are in those groups are overcoming their hardships and are creating social networks like *Naryndyktar, Talastyktar*, *Oshtuktar*, etc. It is clear from the interviews and conversations with the head and the other people as well as observations in the field that the local administration, as the face of the government, leads the village through the financial and moral support of the social groups.

Notes and References

1. For a field study on the geographical distribution, genealogy and ethnography of the Solto uruu in the 1950s, see S.M. Abramzon, "Etnicheskiy Sostav Kirgizskogo Naseleniya Jevernoy Kirgizii," *Trudı Kirgizskoy Arheologo-Etnograficheskoy Ekspedichii* 4 (Moskva 1960): 22-31.
2. The word "*kenesh*" is a direct translation of the word "soviet" which means in particular "advice" or "consul."
3. Sergei Kirov (1886-1934), a famous member of the CPSU.
4. Vyacheslav Molotov (1890-1986), foreign minister of Soviet Union between 1939 and 1949.
5. Lazar Kaganovich (1893-1991), a well-known member of the CPSU.
6. In addition to these brothers, Abramzon gives the name of one more brother, Aytuu. See Abramzon, "Etnicheskiy Sostav Kirgizskogo," 22-23 (genealogical listing).
7. On the other hand, the sons of the Küntuu are given by Abramzon as five persons Kulboldu, Chong Murun, Tonbay, Kara Mergen and Baygana. See Abramzon, "Etnicheskiy Sostav Kirgizskogo," 22-23 (list of genealogy).
8. Jaychybek Moldaliyev (1958-) is an inhabitant of Küntuu village, Sokuluk *raion* (district), Chüy Province: first interview on 17 November 2010, Küntuu village, Kyrgyzstan.
9. Interview with Moldaliyev.
10. Osmonkul Kazakbayev (1960-) is a migrant from Jalalabad province, Chatkal *raion*, Aktash village: interview on 29 January 2011, Küntuu village, Kyrgyzstan; Kunduzbübü Azırankulova (1960-) is originally from Jalalabad province, Chatkal *raion*, Aktash village: interview on 29 January 2011, Küntuu village Kyrgyzstan.
11. Osmonaly Kydyraliyev (1950-) is a migrant from Naryn province, Jumgal *raion*, Minkush village: interview on 29 January 2011, Küntuu village, Kyrgyzstan; Atyrkül Musayeva (1953-) is originally from Naryn province, Jumgal *raion*, Minkush village: interview on 29 January 2011, Küntuu village, Kyrgyzstan.
12. Moldaliyev: second interview on 29 January 2011, Küntuu village, Kyrgyzstan.
13. Interview with Kazakbayev.
14. Zamira Sopubekova (1952-) is a current inhabitant of Küntuu village, Sokuluk *raion*, Chüy province: interview on 25 March 2011, Küntuu village, Kyrgyzstan.

15. Toktomurat Mankiyev (1945-) is a current inhabitant of Küntuu village, Sokuluk *raion*, Chüy province: interview on 25 March 2011, Küntuu village, Kyrgyzstan.
16. Interview with Mankiyev.
17. Interview with Mankiyev.
18. Interview with Musayeva.
19. Interview with Kydyraliyev.
20. Erkinbek Abyrahmanov (1966-) is a current inhabitant of Küntuu village, Sokuluk *raion*, Chüy province: interview on 25 March 2011, Küntuu village, Kyrgyzstan.
21. Talaybek Korgoldoyev (1968-) is a current head of Küntuu village, Sokuluk raion, Chüy province: interview on 25 March 2011, Küntuu village, Kyrgyzstan.

13

Urbanization and the Process of Cultural Change in Kyrgyzstan

Kishimjan Eshenkulova

With the collapse of the Soviet Union in 1991, the Central Asian Republics were faced with challenges in all areas—political, economic, social, and cultural, etc. Reforms in the fields of policy, economy, agriculture, and education were implemented in response to these challenges. However, many reform policies failed and this, combined with political and economic instability, has caused a dramatic crisis.[1] The crisis manifested itself in Central Asia in the post-Soviet period by its effects on the values and life styles of Central Asian society. The crisis led to social depression, shock and then change in all areas. These political, economic, social and cultural challenges, crisis and changes have been observed not only by Central Asian researchers, but also by foreign researchers. The researchers are trying to understand and describe the reasons for the problems. However, these problems appear to be much more complicated than initially expected.

In this paper, using the case-study of the Kyrgyz Republic, two main problems have been focused on: (1) the existence of uncontrolled urbanization; and (2) cultural change in the post-Soviet period. The main objective of this paper is to explain the reasons for uncontrolled urbanization, urbanization problems, cultural changes, and the relations between urban and traditional cultures, as well as to analyse the challenges and changes involved in this process.

Uncontrolled Urbanization: Challenges and Change

The Kyrgyz Republic is a small Central Asian country sharing its borders with China, Kazakhstan, Uzbekistan, and Tajikistan. According to the US Bureau of the Census (July 2010), the population of the Kyrgyz Republic is 5,508,626.[2] Its capital is Bishkek with an official population of 819.000, though other estimates suggest a figure in excess of 1 million.[3] About two thirds of the populations live in rural and one third in urban areas in Kyrgyzstan. According to statistics of 2008, the urban population is 36.28 per cent of the total population[4] and the rate of urbanization is 1.6per cent as measured by the annual rate of change (2005-10 est.).[5]

Concepts of urban and rural areas are often interpreted in different ways in national and disciplinary contexts. There is no global definition for urban and rural. There are differences between urban and rural settlements on account of resources, facilities, demands and aspirations. There are also national differences in the characteristics that distinguish urban from rural areas. The distinction between the urban and the rural population is not yet amenable to a single definition that would be applicable to all countries or, for the most part, even to the countries within a region. In some countries the definition of urban is related to a specific number of inhabitants. In other countries urban could also be defined by local town plans. The definition of urban varies in European countries, as also in Central Asia. In post-Soviet Central Asian countries the definition still follows the two Soviet definitions of urban settlement, i.e. cities and urban-type localities. The urban-type localities are "officially designated as such, usually according to the criteria of number of inhabitants and predominance of agricultural, or number of non-agricultural workers and their families."[6] In accordance with the 2008 Law on Administrative and Territorial Subdivision of Kyrgyzstan, urban-type settlements are those that comprise economically significant facilities, such as industrial plants, railway stations, and construction sites, etc., as well as settlements with a recreational potential with a population

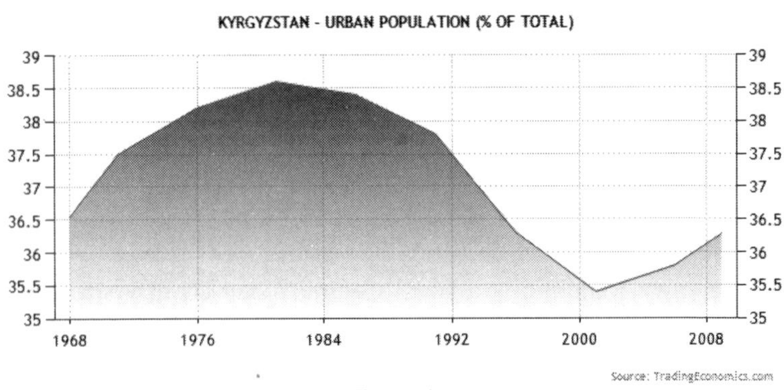

Figure 1

of at least 2,000. In exceptional cases, administrative, economic and cultural centres with a potential for economical development and population growth can be classified as urban-type settlements.[7]

In Central Asia a rapidly growing urbanization process appeared after the Soviet breakup in 1991. Urbanization is a process with a complex pattern of forces which drives the development. In this region the main driving forces are economic (oil, gold, gas resources, the free market economy, unemployment) and political (war and conflicts). Because of these reasons in Central Asia there occurred two types of urbanization; modernized (for example, Astana) and uncontrolled urbanization (Bishkek). After the Soviet period, the process of uncontrolled urbanization became a widespread characteristic across all the regions of Kyrgyzstan, albeit to differing degrees of intensity. The reasons for this process varied from region to region. Kyrgyzstan was faced with two main problems: de-urbanization and hyper-urbanization.[8] These problems were brought about by population displacement caused mainly by the closing down of mining enterprises, fabric production, light manufacturing, light industrial sectors, and factories in what were essentially "mono-sector" towns.

Parallel with the de-urbanization of small and medium towns, there was hyper-urbanization of large cities, such as the capital city Bishkek, as well as the city of Osh. New settlements appeared around these cities as a result of *en masse* migration of the population.[9] Socio-economic challenges and unemployment factors triggered the migration process and two kinds of migration are identified:

1. Internal migration from rural localities to urban areas, where the rural population is attracted by the higher living standards in urban areas or forced by the poor conditions in rural areas, to migrate to the cities. Some people residing in the smaller urban-type localities also migrate to the larger cities.
2. International migration where migration to other countries due to impoverished socio-economic living standards or ethnic conflicts in Kyrgyzstan. The rate of emigration abroad, especially to Russia and Kazakhstan has been increasing every year.

The rates of migration, unemployment and poverty in Kyrgyzstan are given in the Table 1.

Table 1: Migration, Unemployment and Poverty in Kyrgyzstan Net Migration Rate:-2.58 migrant(s)/1,000 populations (2010 est.)

Year	Net Migration Rate	Percent Change	Date of Information
2008	-2.55		2008 est.
2009	-2.57	0.78 %	2009 est.
2010	-2.58	0.39 %	2010 est.

Source:, CIA World Factbook_http://www.indexmundi.com/kyrgyzstan/net_migration_rate.html_01.02.2011

Unemployment Rate: 18% (2004 est.)

Year	Unemployment Rate	Percent Change	Date of Information
2003	7.20 %		1999 est
2004	7.20 %	0.00 %	1999 est
2005	18.00 %	150.00 %	2004 est
2006	18.00 %	0.00 %	2004 est
2007	18.00 %	0.00 %	2004 est
2008	18.00 %	0.00 %	2004 est
2009	18.00 %	0.00 %	2004 est
2010	18.00 %	0.00 %	2004 est

Source: CIA World Factbook http://www.indexmundi.com/kyrgyzstan/unemployment_rate.html_01.02.2011

Percentage of Population below National Poverty Line

Year	Rural Value	Urban Value	Total Value
2003	51	41.2	47.6
2004	57.5	35.7	49.9
2005	50.8	29.8	43.1

Source: United Nations Statistics Division,_http://www.indexmundi.com/kyrgyzstan/percentage-of-population-below-national-poverty-line.html_01.02.2011

Because of socio-economic challenges in rural and urban-type areas, there has been widespread population movement to the large cities in the country as well as to other countries since 1991 and this migration to the urban centres has caused uncontrolled urbanization and environmental unsustainability in Bishkek and Osh. Parallel with this there are other problems associated with urbanization. The reasons for the problems associated with urbanization can be summarized as follows:

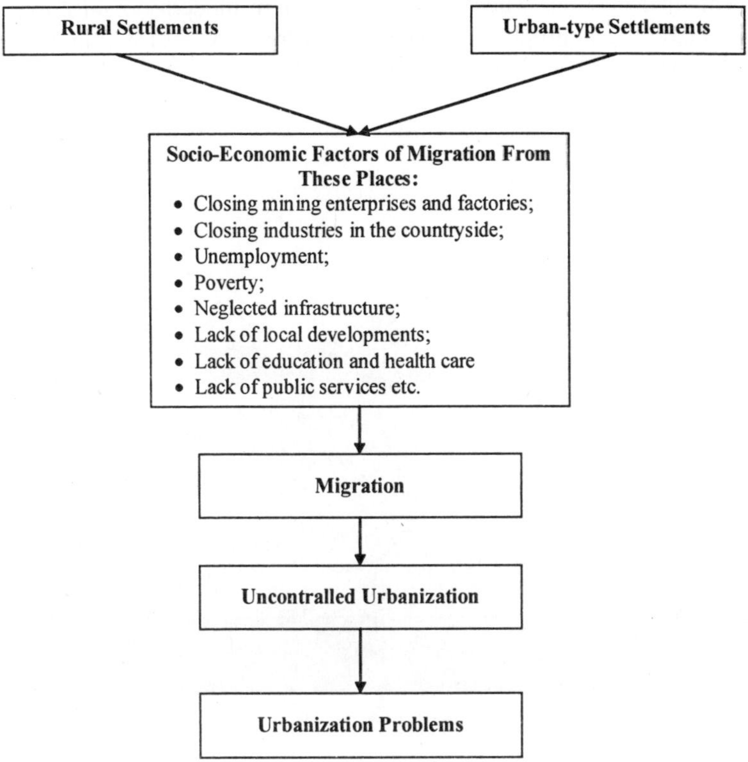

Uncontrolled urbanization occurred in two ways. On the one hand, western or modern style buildings and planning models, i.e. shopping centres, business centres and underground car parks and residential houses in utilitarian skyscrapers or single-use skyscrapers emerged horizontally or vertically. However, most of these modern style buildings are unplanned and do not correspond with city planning regulations. On the other hand, the migrants from rural or urban-type areas started building their houses on land which were not identified for this purpose and was generally owned by the state. The illegal areas, which began to surround cities within a very short time, have become the major source of accommodation for the poorer sections of the general population and new migrants. The majority of newly built settlements are characterized by a lack of social and economic infrastructure and public services such as roads, public transport, health care, schools, energy supply and public utilities. Such an environment is accompanied by high levels of unemployment, poverty, morbidity rate and crime. As mentioned by Kreir when referring to western modern urbanization, this kind of uncontrolled urbanization in Kyrgyzstan is also ultimately anti-urban, anti-social and anti-ecological.[10]

Figure 2: Rural-type Urbanization in Bishkek

Both these two styles of uncontrolled urbanization process have led to many problems in the last 20 years. During this period of rapid change many of the bigger cities in Kyrgyzstan lost many of the original characteristics which they had enjoyed prior to the events of 1991. Western-style new shopping and business centres are producing a new urban consumer identity; the urban landscape is changing rapidly due to "trend" and "brand" instead of preserving the uniqueness of a naturally developing city. The management of public and urban services is increasingly left to the private sector. This situation has brought about a rapid erosion of historical-cultural values. Therefore, in recent years, the main reasons of loss of the historical-cultural values in the cities in Kyrgyzstan are uncontrolled and unhealthy urbanization policies.

Figure 3: Modern Type Urbanization in Bishkek

The lack of macro-level planning, as well as gaps in the relevant legal regulations, a heavy bureaucracy, a lack of urban planning and control systems, uncontrolled land usurpation, unhealthy and awkward construction systems and an irregular and inadequate transport network have all caused an unhealthy environment and often ugly appearance of many new buildings. Ultimately around 50 new residential districts occupying around 1/3 of the size of Bishkek has grown outwards from the centre of the city. This development is what we call "uncontrolled urbanization" or "suburbanization" or "ruralization" rather than urbanization.

The two types of uncontrolled urbanization in Kyrgyzstan can be summarized as follows. Neither process is under the control of the government or by the urban planners and architects. It has led to unhealthy construction. Unhealthy and unplanned piles of stone and clay have increased in number and damaged the green areas. Buildings have been constructed near sites of historical value and originality with scant regard for the aesthetic aspects involved. The emergence of unplanned urbanization has changed the face of the city and destroyed the historical and cultural values of the city. Yet the culture of a city is one of the main factors in preserving the continuity of the city and its structures. Because it is a fact that culture shapes the urban, similarly the urban builds the culture of the society, so the urban areas are always hallmarks of culture.

Urban Culture and the Process of Cultural Change

Culture, cultural change, cultural clash and all types of cultural problems have been studied by the scholars. However, there is no accepted and agreed common definition of culture. The definition of culture changes depending on any given society's values as well as other elements such as their life style, goals, customs, traditions, sense, behaviour, belief, thought, knowledge, art and material objects that are passed from person to person or from one generation to the next generation in a society. These values and elements are not stable. While the values and elements change, the culture of society also changes. The speed of cultural change depends on time and place, or on features of the society. When the changes seem to emerge slowly, "continuity" prevails and when continuity ceases in periods of depression "changes" emerge.[11] For Simmel, "after every change arise the new cultural forms."[12] These forms affect a society positively or negatively.

Since 1991, Kyrgyzstan has experienced a state of unstable and erratic change. The problems of Kyrgyz society arose from this unstable economic, political, social and cultural change. After the collapse of the Soviet Union, Kyrgyz society experienced its own cultural crisis, in particular, an inability to overcome the crisis in economic and social fields, which first brought cultural crisis and then cultural change. It is difficult to explain this cultural change because it is dissimilar to either the modern or postmodern cultural change. It may be possible to identify a "post-Soviet cultural change process" generally, but this is also not clear. Kyrgyz society's cultural change is different even when compared to its neighbours. To find out these causes requires deep and serious research into this field.

The urban culture on one hand is closely associated with the rural culture, but on the other hand it was also influenced by external cultures. Therefore, the urban culture has undergone changes. This has occurred in two ways. Firstly, the modern style culture is accepted by some within Kyrgyz society and adopted regardless of whether or not it conforms to national values and traditional social forms of settlement. Secondly, the social life styles and culture observed in the rural areas have become a part of the city. In addition, in post-independence Kyrgyzstan there has been a polarization of rich and poor. The former are wealthy and their living standards increase socio-economically, the latter, are impoverished and locked in a cycle of poverty. As a result, within the city there have emerged both the enriched and the impoverished urbanized populations with differing cultures reflecting differing levels of wealth and poverty.

In this study, bazaars and shopping centres in Kyrgyzstan were selected as important places where urbanization and cultural changes can be observed clearly. As we know, metropolis' and big cities are always centres of the monetary economy and of the manufacturer and the consumer. The monetary economy and the sovereignty of the mind are deeply bound up with each other. However, the development of a monetary economy in Bishkek has been different from the western one.

Prior to 1991, in all cities across Kyrgyzstan any goods or products could be purchased from simple Soviet-style outlets like *Tsum, Detskiy Mir*, *Gastronorm*, etc., while fruits and vegetables were sold at bazaars. After 1991, many factories and industrial processes struggled to remain viable and pay their workers' wages. As a result of this people started to receive goods at their workplaces instead of a monetary wage. For example, a worker employed at a sugar factory received sugar to the amount corresponding to their salary; a shoe factory worker, instead of his salary, was given a few pairs of shoes. So, people tried to sell these products during this crisis. In this process, everything had been moved to the streets and street trade evolved. All of this led to the bazaars being seen as "the gate of hope," and it led to the formation of a bazaar culture. As a result of this "bazaar culture" has emerged the street sale (fair), *kamok* (single house-type shop), and bazaars in general. The initiators of this type of urban bazaar culture are a small number of the newly enriched, middle, and lower classes. Later on, trade centres were built indicating a transition of the street trade to the trade centre. Nowadays we can say that these four type of trades are still functioning and there are some similarities and differencies on the products and customer-seller relations (Figure 4).

Most of the employees in the bazaars came from the various regions of Kyrgyzstan. Therefore, the bazaars were places where region or sub-cultures overlap and sometimes integrate and interact with the culture of the city. Therefore, the use of local cultures and regional dialects can easily be witnessed. Although elements of local culture are dominant in the bazaars, the language used is mostly Kyrgyz. One of the most interesting aspects in this process has been the effects that this interaction has had upon those who have arrived in the cities from the village as well as the impact which they in turn

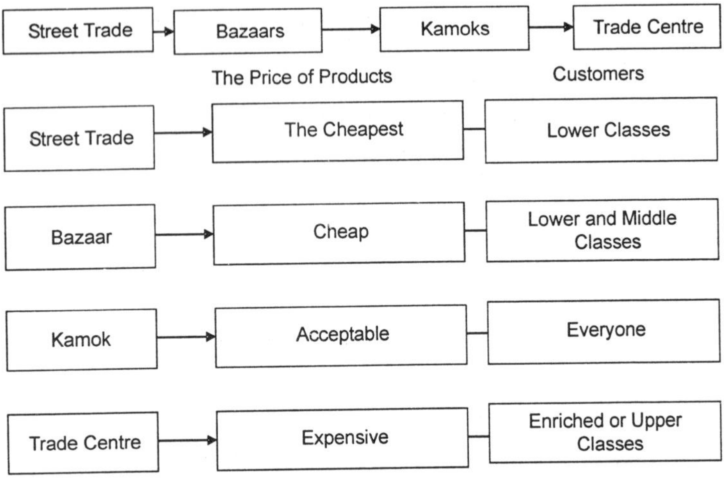

Figure 4: Relation between the different trade centres products and customer-seller relations.

have upon the city-dwellers. This has led to some interesting cultural exchanges.

By way of contrast, modern style trade centers, like *Beta Stores*, *Dordoy Plaza*, and *Vefa Centre* have also emerged. The modern culture and consumer mentality is more dominant in such shopping centers. These types of places are for the much more moneyed classes. The vendor-customer relationship exhibited in the shopping centers is akin to the Western behaviour model. Many places still use the Russian language as the language of the elite and people attempt to comply with this in order to appear more "cultured." This behaviour is reflected both by the vendor and the customer, especially in such places as a Pizza Hut, Imperia Pizza, Domino, Begemot and other western-style service places western culture is adopted by the customers. In this context of cultural globalization, namely, "the same kind of life, the same kind of talk, entertainment and rest, dressing, feeding" briefly the same consumer culture is widespread. As a result, individuals or the people that are within a consuming society are molded into similar styles of dressing, eating, leisure time spending and so on. Local music is more listened to in the bazaars, while classic and contemporary western songs are more popular at the modern shopping centres. This will influence their respective appeal to customers and to an extent determine the audience.

In addition, one of the most influential patterns of the cultural shift is, regardless of social classes or sector, is an attempt to identify with what is abroad and to look like foreigners. This has brought a desire to resemble westerners and an attraction to "brand" fashion. This interest to be dressed in "branded" clothes or to possess brand goods is evident regardless of social state. All ages appear to be influenced, though it is particularly strong amongst the young people. While middle-aged and older people can be more resistant and act measurably in the face of such situations and changes of this type, young people tend to accept the rapid cultural change. These young people experience positive or negative effects of foreign cultures in the process of cultural change. Especially in recent times, many young people, who underemphasized the values of their own national identities, have attached themselves to "planned networks" that seek to build a strong culture of domination and superiority or, in other words, "culture colonization."

Cultural change is reflected in the language, too. During the Soviet era Russian, as an official language dominated in official areas, in the institutions of higher education, and in cities, while the Kyrgyz language used to be a language used mainly in rural schools and villages. Therefore, Russian was a language that a villager had to know in order to make social progress. After independence, the Kyrgyz language began to develop in two directions. First, Russian and western words began to infiltrate the Kyrgyz language. Secondly, words from the Turkic languages and words previously used only in rural regions began to be used. As a result of this, while the local urban population is trying to learn Kyrgyz, urbanized peasants are trying to learn Russian. This can clearly be seen in the bazaars.

One more issue deserves to be mentioned here. It is that in this new urbanization and cultural change processes national values, clothing, food and goods have started to be given considerable importance. Recently efforts to revitalize and modernize the national culture have been increasing. It is possible to see in the shopping centers and restaurants which increasingly are offering national products and dishes. This is another product of the revived cultural change seen in cities since 1991.

Conclusion

In this article I have tried to explain the uncontrolled urbanization and cultural change which the people of Kyrgyzstan have experienced since 1991. In big cities they are still continuing uncontrolled urbanization. With the growth of migration and uncontrolled urbanization, the problems of urbanization and environmental pollution are increasing.

Cultural change of Kyrgyz society is an ongoing process. Incomprehensible, complicated and constantly changing types of cultures have emerged, whilst individual estrangement has also developed. As mentioned above it is rather difficult to explain or to define these types of cultural change of Kyrgyz society. Nevertheless, this cultural change can be variously termed as "culture of poverty," "culture of riches," "cultural colonization" and so on.

As a result of all these changes the Kyrgyz Government and non-government organizations need to take various measures to control and if possible solve the resulting problems of today as well as those one can predict for tomorrow. These new types of urban culture should be studied widely in order to understand society as a whole within twenty-first century Kyrgyzstan.

Notes and References

1. It is important here to refer to Habermas' definition of the concept of crisis. Habermas provides a useful taxonomy of systemic crisis comprising of a fourfold classification of economic crisis, rationality crisis, legitimization crisis, and motivation crisis. According to Habermas, an economic crisis, termed a "realization crisis" by him, may be a recession, an economic depression, or an inflationary phenomenon. A rationality crisis is a breakdown of the "rational administrative" practices necessary to maintain the economy in due course. This can be interpreted as the inability of the government in a crisis situation, to properly manage and regulate the economic system. A legitimization crisis is characterized by a breakdown in the level of public support, credibility, and trust in the existing institutions. A motivation crisis is a crisis in the realms of values, cultures, traditions, and norms within society. See C. Moser and C. McIlwaine, *Urban Poor Perceptions of Violence and Exclusion in Colombia* (Washington: World Bank 2000). After the breakdown of the Soviet Union, Central Asian society experienced all aspects of this definition.
2. http://www.indexmundi.com/kyrgyzstan/population.html_02.02.2011
3. A. Matveeva, *Kyrgyzstan in Crisis: Permanent Revolution and the Curse of Nationalism*, CSRC Working Paper 79, 2010, 2.
4. http://www.tradingeconomics.com/kyrgyzstan/urban-population-percent-of-total-wb-data.html
5. CIA World Factbook http://www.indexmundi.com/kyrgyzstan.html_01.02.2011
6. U. Akerlund et al, *Urban and Peri-urban Forestry and Greening in West and Central Asia: Experiences, Constraints and Prospects*, LSP Working Paper 36, Access to Natural Resources Sub-Programme, 2006,

http://www.fao.org/es/esw/lsp/cd/img/docs/LSPWP37.pdf_15.01.2011

7. Law on Administrative and Territorial Subdivision of Kyrgyz Republic, 25.04.2008 No. 65 (Закон Кыргызской Республики от 25 апреля 2008 года N 65 «Об административно-территориальном устройстве Кыргызской Республики»), http://namsu.org.kg
8. *Kyrgyzstan Country Profile*, United Nations, Johannesburg Summit 2002, 10.
9. *Kyrgyzstan Country Profile*, United Nations, Johannesburg Summit 2002, 10.
10. D. Harvey, *Postmodernliğin Durumu* (İstanbul: Metis Yayınları 2006), s. 85.
11. B. Güvenç, *İnsan ve Kültür* (İstanbul: Remzi Kitabevi 1999), 290.
12. G. Simmel, *Modern Kültürde Çatışma* (İstanbul: İletişim Yayınları 2004), 60.

14

Young People's Quest for Affordable Housing in Tashkent: The Transformation of Housing in Independent Uzbekistan

Hikoyat Salimova

In the Soviet Union, the state provided free housing for young people as part of remuneration for their labour at state enterprises. Under Khrushchev's reforms the central government set a goal to provide each family with a dwelling of minimal standards.[1] In two decades starting from the 1960s, the system eradicated most of the housing deficit that had persisted since the 1930s. When the Uzbek Soviet Socialist Republic became independent in 1991, housing was not of much significance to the state, since most its citizens had been already provided with dwellings.

The housing situation in Uzbekistan has changed drastically during the last decade. When the world housing prices boomed in the first half of the 2000s, this trend also reached Uzbekistan by 2006.[2] Such a rapid increase in housing prices made most housing in Tashkent unaffordable for young people. Moreover, the demand for housing is increasing continuously in urban cores due to migration from rural areas and natural population growth while the supply of new housing has slowed immensely. In case of Tashkent, significant in-migration also comes from provinces. The Uzbek capital headquarters most of the foreign companies and international organizations that offer higher salaries than state enterprises; and the majority of universities, including the best ones, are also located here. These are two major factors for attracting intelligent young people from all over the country.

Since these newcomers usually have low or no incomes, they need affordable housing; however, their options are quite limited. As a result of the 1990s' legislation on privatization, only strategically important enterprises remained fully state-owned, and even these are financially incapable of constructing houses in the necessary quantities. The emerging private sector does not provide housing for its employees either. The new state has no capacity to provide free housing for all citizens at its own expense. A few new developers build luxury housing where there is some profit; yet such housing is unaffordable for most Uzbek citizens, especially for the youth.

Once the old housing stock was privatized, the current residents became full owners of their apartments.[3] Therefore, the most affected were the new house seekers, in particular young adults establishing their first individual households. Responding to the lack of a formal housing market, the people who buy and sell residential dwellings have developed a fringe housing market. The place that was used by the buyers and sellers (in a broader sense) in Tashkent to meet on a daily basis, as any other marketplace, developed into an informal housing market, *Kvartirniy Bazaar* (Russian for "Apartment Market"). Started on an informal basis, after a few years this market was taken over by the city administration, first by moving it to a new location and then by transferring it under the guidance of *Goskomimuschestvo* (The State Properties Committee) in 2008. Albeit these opportunities were created by people and, partially, the government, the younger generation with a desire to establish their own households, families, and homes, separate from their parents', have almost no formal means for implementing their dreams.

Theoretical Framework and Methodology

This article spells out the major concepts and findings of my thesis that investigates how young Uzbeks in Tashkent find or create their own housing, exercising their "agency." The notion of people's agency has been explored by a number of scholars from different fields.[4] This work is premised on the idea that people are not passive recipients of external ideas; they have agency, see alternatives, and create their own options.[5] Focusing on social space of housing, I critically build on Nihal Perera's (2009) argument on "familiarizing space" by ordinary people and the "people's processes" of space making. The interviewed young people cope with and negotiate existing housing conditions and develop their own alternatives to fulfill their own housing needs. The individual stories of these Tashkent youths reveal how they struggle to improve their livelihoods and particularly enhance their income and security by deploying their social, technical and imaginative capacities. Arjun Appadurai argues "all human beings extend and struggle to extend their chances of survival, to improve their horizons of possibility and to enhance their wealth and security."[6] So, these young people also find the means within their surroundings, both physical and social. Their hometown connections, families and friends help them to establish their homes.

Initially, I conducted a sample survey among Tashkent residents, which was followed up by detailed interviews of 21 selected young people who have lived in the capital for at least four years. Some of them have left the city already, while others still live there; some managed to get their own housing, while others found ways to cope with the situation, or created their own spaces. This research is built upon the housing stories of these young citizens of Uzbekistan from different backgrounds. Both survey and interviews reveal the larger picture behind the quest for housing in post-Soviet Tashkent, especially from the youths' perspective.

Findings and Analysis

Survey

The survey findings demonstrate that the majority of young people who obtained their own housing achieved this with help from parents, relatives and friends. Out of 111 respondents, only one indicated the use of the formal mortgage system *Ipoteka*, introduced in late 2006.[7] Many were distrustful towards this mechanism, stating that such loans were inaccessible for the general public; the borrower must have a stable and above-average salary in order to be able to meet monthly installments.[8] The young people indicated not having enough money even for initial home down payments, so they have to seek informal financial aid from their social networks. In fact, studies by international organizations of the housing sector in Uzbekistan[9] also support this finding, stating that housing, as well as newly introduced mortgages are still unaffordable for the majority of citizens.

More than 71per cent of respondents indicated that they would like to improve their housing situations; in particular most expressed a desire to purchase their own dwelling. Considering that this sample falls in the 18 to 34 age group, it is fair to assume that these people are still looking for affordable housing. A significant number of respondents also noted that they desired either to repair the current dwelling or relocate closer to the centre of the city. Central placement seems to be crucial in young people's choice of housing location.

Natives, Migrants and Locals

Based on Owen's[10] criteria for analysing the interviews, which include recurrence, repetition, and forcefulness, I created categories in order to classify responses. As these categories are common among the general population, I draw my conclusion about the housing situation in Uzbekistan from this analysis. The house-seekers initially were divided into two categories, Tashkent natives and migrants, since they have quite different experiences. The first ones usually have fewer difficulties with initial housing because they live at their parents' house for an extended period. Nonetheless, this factor does not completely exclude them from similar obstacles as in case of migrants in finding affordable housing of their own. Tashkent natives also have to look for informal means to obtain their own housing as they establish separate households.

Tashkent hosts the majority of universities in the country and therefore attracts a large number of high school graduates from all provinces. Migration is fostered by the youth who come to the city for better employment as well. Basically, these reasons are similar to commonly described factors in migration theory.[11] This analysis revealed that compared to the "natives," migrants searching for affordable housing face more obstacles that are determined by regional peculiarities. These include city registration required to live and work in the city, lack of influence due to nepotism and regionalism,[12] limited social networks, and other stigma related to migrant workers whom identifies as a "floating population."[13] Despite these barriers a significant number of migrants manage to find ways to establish their livelihoods in Tashkent.

Separate from these two major groups, I also identified "the locals," who moved to Tashkent as children because of their parents' decision; their experience exemplifies a combination of the natives' and migrants' stories. These young people do not have all the benefits of the natives; however, they are not as deprived of certain privileges as the migrants. In particular, due to longer term of residence in Tashkent, the locals have been able to overcome many housing obstacles, either through their family or by themselves.

In relevance to homeownership, I categorized respondents as family residents who still live at their parents' or relatives' house, homeowners who managed to purchase housing of their own, and renters who are temporary tenants. Many interviewees fit into a combination of different groups, so I used their longest stay to define the category they belong to, but in their stories I bring up all the experiences they had regarding their housing quest in Tashkent. As the short-term residents, i.e. migrants, experienced the most diverse journeys till they got to their present housing, these stories provide the worst characteristics of housing problem and therefore represent a larger group.

Housing Quality

With respect to housing preferences, the quality of the dwelling and the location played a major role in determining the young people's satisfaction with their housing. For example, as survey respondents these interviewees prefer to live closer to the urban centre. However, due to non-affordability, some of them had to compromise on living conditions such that some situations even caused health problems. Most offices, universities, department stores, embassies and government organizations, theatres and museums, night clubs and restaurants, sport complexes, and other places of attraction are localized in the city centre. In Uzbekistan these are the spaces of the youth concentration; therefore, the young people prefer living closer to the urban core. Yet, such attraction to the central location, despite unfavourable—including uninhabitable—living conditions, might be relevant only to single youth who have not yet established their own families. Those with children prioritize the quality of the dwelling because this affects their offspring.

A significant portion of the housing stock in Tashkent was built during the Soviet era, and most houses have not received proper maintenance since independence; at present such apartment complexes mostly are in deteriorating condition.[14] Furthermore, living conditions are predominantly determined by the type of housing: whether it is a detached house, an apartment complex or a dormitory. Privately owned detached houses are maintained according to the owners' incomes; some can afford regular—usually annual—repairs, while others who struggle to meet basic needs in food and clothing push aside housing maintenance until "better times." Apartment complexes differ because renovations are required for the entire building, and not all its residents can meet the costs; even if they pay maintenance fees to association of homeowners, the latter might not fulfill its obligations as required. Most Soviet-built housing stock had already served its useful life and needs major renovations. Many houses have problems with pipes for heating and water supply, which leak inside the apartments and to the neighbours' apartments below. Moreover, these service problems were often present even before the residents moved in, because inspection committees were forced to submit incomplete buildings due to deadline pressures.[15] Some detached private houses of old construction also lack basic amenities (water, sewage, and/or gas). In fact, only newly-built luxury apartment complexes and western-style detached houses have properly functioning amenities. Constant problems with leaks, insulation, and air-conditioning make the living conditions a top priority for many of respondents and interviewees. The cost of repairs is usually high for low-earning youth in Uzbekistan. Besides, the temporary tenants do not usually invest in repairs and renovations, unless they are sure to stay in the rented place for a while which is very rare. Homebuyers estimate the cost of repairs and renovations before purchasing.

Despite dissatisfaction with the surrounding environment, the interviewees did not anticipate moving to different places, or they postponed relocation until they could find other suitable places for living. The reasons were identified as financial constraints and lack of information on available rental housing. The better living conditions require higher rents or dwelling prices. Therefore, the respondents had to tolerate the existing conditions. At the same time, a number of respondents demanded that the government provide improvements, as it used to during Soviet rule. This recalls the old mindset that was nurtured during the Soviet period, when the state was in charge of every aspect of citizens' life including provision and maintenance of housing.[16]

Transformations in Tashkent Housing

The housing constraints force Tashkent residents to become creative. The limited living space and the desire for personal touches in their housing lead people to make changes within their means. Under such circumstances people use their imagination and find alternatives. Some of these include the transformation of auxiliary spaces, such as balconies and loggias, into more useful space, such as kitchens, dining rooms, or even bedrooms. One of the most used methods is enclosing and winterizing open balconies and loggias. The mild winters in Uzbekistan, unlike northern republics of the former Soviet Union, make this possible (Figures 1 and 2).

Such physical transformations are also observed in traditional *mahallas*.[17] Modernizing traditional courtyard houses (*hovlis*) within this transformation process resulted in creating new hybrid houses that incorporate many features of western houses yet still have the spirit of typical local houses. Similar to the example of *havelis* in New Delhi that were described by Joyti Hosagrahar,[18] Uzbek *hovlis* equipped with western amenities create "indigenous modernity" in modern architecture in Uzbekistan (Figure 3). Although these houses might not appear as typical western houses, the understanding of such design is so-called 'Euro'-style, which indicates high quality imported materials and furnishing used construction and decoration of the house. I refer to such practices as hybrid spaces; they do not represent one pure style, but are infused with different trends, developed locally.

Figure 1. Multi-storey apartment complex with winterized balconies
Personal photograph by the author. 2010.

Figure 2. Balcony renovated in 'Euro'-style.
Personal photograph by the author. 2010.

The notion of transformation is relevant not only to physical space, but also to the cultural aspect of Uzbek society. Under cultural transformation I refer to the "modernization" of the Uzbek society under Tsarist Russia and, later, Soviet rule. As Jeff Sahadeo discusses, General Kaufman carried out a grandiose plan to transform Tashkent into an exemplar of western high culture, which would serve as a "model city."[19] This resulted in not only attracting westerners to the New City of Tashkent, but also changed the attitudes among rich local Uzbeks who then have strived to live in this "Russian Tashkent." Some of them even abandoned their traditional courtyard houses, which were both culturally and climatically comfortable, and moved to new houses introduced by the Russians. Eventually, through ideological pressing[20] and incentives, the Soviets managed to get the majority of the population into apartments. These new dwellings were much smaller than the average traditional Uzbek courtyard house, but they were more advantageous with regard to providing better amenities than old houses, including running tap water, hot water, heating, gas, and central sewage. More significantly, they represented the contemporary hegemonic notion of modernity.

Although Uzbeks agreed to move to the apartments, they did not and could not fully comply with the lifestyle imposed by the Soviets and created their own hybrid spaces within the "Soviet housing." In *Post-Colonial Transformation*, Bill Ashcroft argues, that through representation, "imitation," and, most importantly, cultural identity, "colonized peoples [...] transformed those [external] processes into culturally appropriate vehicles."[21] Modern Uzbeks, too, who moved to apartments, transformed the given spaces: they brought "pieces" of their old lifestyle (*homtakhta, kurpacha, topchon*)[22] and created rooms in the so-called "national" style. Not only is traditional interior design comfortable for Uzbeks, but it is also significantly cheaper than imported furniture and appliances that cost significant sums. Since the Soviet times, families have collected money over years or even a decade to purchase a television, a refrigerator, a *stenka*,[23] or even bedroom furniture. This cost is seen by some as a reason for furnishing apartments in traditional style (Figure 4).

However, even those who could afford the hegemonic Soviet lifestyle, i.e. the relatively richer citizens who purchased such furniture, had one room furnished in "national" style. This room was usually the loggia, the most underutilized space in most apartments. In rich people's apartments the traditional room served for daily uses and family gatherings. As practice demonstrates, among Uzbek families this is the most frequently used space, where the entire family has meals and

Figure 3. Western style house in Tashkent.
Digital image from www.makler.uz

Figure 4. Traditional Uzbek interior design.
Digital image from www.makler.uz

spends free time, while the "western" living room is used only for receiving guests. Thus, cultural transformation accompanied physical transformation of place and space. Although the Uzbek people and their dwellings "Europeanized," this process was never complete; modernization established a new combination of European and traditional Uzbek social traits and spaces, creating a new hybrid Uzbek modernity.

Search for Housing and Social Networking

The housing stock in Tashkent is diverse and affords a range of budget dwelling options. These include detached houses, apartment complexes of Soviet era, factory/plant or university dormitories as temporary housing, newly built apartment complexes, and houses in Western style. However, the process of finding a dwelling is not simple in Uzbekistan; during the Soviet times there was no established housing market. Although the *Kvartirniy Bazaar* was created within the last decade, it is still not fully developed. As this is a fringe market, the unavailability of affordable housing is exacerbated by the lack of information. Prior to its establishment, most housing transactions in Tashkent were conducted through social networking, using word of mouth, neighbors, friends and acquaintances, extended family and relatives' connections in order to find housing. In fact, these methods are still prioritized; people trust their social networks. Yet, as some respondents indicated, the *Kvartirniy Bazaar* is also widely used to find housing, especially among migrants from provinces who have limited or no connections in Tashkent.

Furthermore, social capital and social energy are significant to the stories of these young people. As in most of developing countries, people in Uzbekistan heavily rely on their social networks when they lack the capacity of their own. Such instances include weddings, higher education, the purchase of a car, as well as housing. The latter is usually the most expensive and, therefore, requires social capital the most. Drawing on Norman Uphoff's explanation of social energy[24] and Robert Putnam's evaluation of social capital,[25] I consider that this factor representing a strong community asset for young people in Tashkent. Most of my interviewees and survey respondents indicated that they received help from their social networks in search purchase and/or building of housing. Such close family relationship demonstrates the positive effects of traditions in modern society of Uzbekistan. In regard to the housing after the collapse of the Soviet system, some of old traditions had been revived, including *hashar*, community volunteer work for construction, renovation and improvement of living environment. In Tashkent this practice is mostly used for helping the neighbors and relatives with labour work in their home improvements.

Ethnicity and Identity

Although it was not explicitly demonstrated in the survey, several comments in the interviews raised the issue of ethnicity and identity, as another strong factor for housing choices of people in Tashkent. Such remarks, as "I wanted to live among Muslim [Uzbeks]," "I chose this district because it is more Europeanized [where many Russian-speaking population live]" or "because there are many Koreans" support the argument of ethnicity as an important determinant in regards to the preferences for housing choices young people make. Uzbekistan, and in particular Tashkent, has a multiethnic population. While the history of these ethnic groups intertwines, there is still clear distinction among different ethnicities, and they cannot be considered as a homogeneous society. Therefore, the widely-used practice of the Soviet system providing everyone the same housing needs to be revised under new circumstances. People have more freedom to make their own choices in independent Uzbekistan since the adoption of the law "On Destatization and Privatization" (1991) allowed them to privatize their apartments and become full owners. This led to open exchange and sell-purchase of housing, so people started moving closer to their relatives, which fostered development of ethnic enclaves. One such distinctive group is the Koreans; among all ethnic groups in Uzbekistan they are the most enclosed due to the history of their relocation to Central Asia.[26]

Natural and Social Environments

Many respondents, both in the survey and interviews, expressed their concerns about the natural environment in Tashkent. This was especially noticeable among those respondents, who have children in their households. They complained about air pollution and trash on the streets and in parks; nonetheless, they continued to live in those districts because at the moment they were willing to tolerate such inconveniences. They believe once they move into other dwelling in the future these concerns will be taken into account.

More than natural environment, my interest was focused on the social environments that the youths described to me. A number of renters had to change their place of residence due to problems in their surroundings. One woman told about pressure from male residents in a dormitory, another told about constant inspection of her living space by the landlady, and even a male respondent complained about intrusion in his life either by landlord or by his relatives, at whose apartment he lived. Within such conflicts of opinions, the discourse of modernity also takes place. Many respondents, as representatives of the Uzbekistan's youth, experienced struggles based on the notion of "Europeanized," or as locally known "Russified" lifestyle. Such cases are common especially among modern Uzbeks, who are in between traditional and modern ways of life. As one Uzbek young man pointed out, he would like to purchase his own apartment next to his parents' so that he still would be able to take care of his elderly parents according to the customs, but at the same time enjoy the semi-privacy with his own nuclear family that he plans to have in the future.

Gender and Housing

Gender has also been a significant factor in regard to housing provision and household interactions. Uzbekistan is largely a Muslim society, and this has influence even on non-Muslim population. Traditions in Muslim societies dictate female to male subordination.[27] Many female respondents faced gender discrimination at various housing situations without full realization of this fact. Among a few examples from interviews leading to this conclusion are the boys' control of girls' behaviour in a student dormitory, a married female's experience of being on maternity leave and, consequently, her lack of financial security and full dependence on husband's decisions, or another young woman's housing providence and security by the family, in particular her brother and uncle. This post-Soviet transition from relative gender equality achieved during Soviet era to more male-dominating society is still evolving.[28] Along with reviving Muslim roots after gaining independence the positions of women in Uzbek society was re-considered under the new paradigm. Now the Islamic pressure on women, especially young ones, has increased, and remarkably, not only from males' side, but also by females themselves.[29] Thus, as it was demonstrated on examples from my interviews, gender roles re-define housing situation in modern Uzbekistan. Women may own a dwelling, yet they are still supervised either by husbands or other male relatives.

Conclusion

The housing transformations in Tashkent after independence demonstrate modern changes in Central Asian cities, exposing their hybridity. These are no longer pure Uzbek, or Soviet, or western cities; the post-Soviet city incorporates all the historic trends that have occurred in Uzbekistan. The young people in this region are facing new challenges that are based on their past, both traditional Muslim and the Soviet experiences and, concurrently, mixed with the modern influence from the West. As the result of such trends, housing in Tashkent is also transforming and shaping into the unique forms that incorporate the attributes of these different influences. Perera argues that ordinary people create spaces for their own cultural practices and daily activities, modifying and adjusting their social and physical contexts.[30] In Henri Lefebvre's terms,[31] I refer to the people's conversion of abstract space into lived spaces; dwellings that these youths obtain or temporarily live in are not merely physical spaces, but are their living environments where various activities are taking place without specific or only one use; these activities, like sleeping, eating, resting, studying or working, often overlap in the presented stories. The house-seekers, who wish to rent, look after, or, earn some money, create their own housing options. This paper reveals, as in Goh's and Perera's works, that the ordinary people do see options and create their own livelihoods and spaces within the given conditions. However, their perspective is yet to be heard and appreciated by professional planners and architects.

Notes and References

1. S. Chernik, *O Razvitii Zhilishchnogo Stroitel'stva v Uzbekistane* (The Development of Housing Construction in Uzbekistan) (Tashkent: State Publishing Agency of the Uzbek S.S.R. 1957).
2. Data collected from online analytical articles from real estate agencies in Uzbekistan, such as Ansher Capital, Avesta Research Center, Lebed Kapital Invest, Toshkent Rielt, UzRe, and the interview with Murad Abduhakimov, the SKS Consulting Director, by Andrei Kudryashov of 26 July 2006.
3. During the Soviet era a small percentage of detached houses were privately owned, and all apartments were built and owned by the state enterprises. See G.D. Andrusz, *Housing and Urban Development in the U.S.S.R.* (Albany: State University of New York Press 1984).
4. For example, see A. Appadurai, *Modernity at Large: Cultural Dimensions of Globalization* (Minneapolis, Minnesota: University of Minnesota Press 2003); A. Giddens, *The Constitution of Society: Outline of the Theory of Structuration* (California: University of California Press 1984); J.C. Scott, *Weapons of the Weak: Everyday Forms of Peasant Resistance* (Connecticut: Courier Companies, Inc. 1985).

5. Appadurai, *Modernity at Large*; B-L. Goh, *Modern Dreams: An Inquiry into Power, Cultural Production, and the Cityscape in Contemporary Urban Penang, Malaysia* (Ithaca: Cornell Southeast Asia Programme Publications 2002); N. Perera, "People's Spaces: Familiarization, Subject Formation and Emergent Spaces in Colombo," *Planning Theory* 8, no. 1 (2009): 51-75.
6. A. Appadurai, "Contemporary Asian Modernities: Transnationality, Interculturality and Hybridity," conference on *Asian Modernity*, Hong Kong, 9-10 September 2006.
7. The law of the Republic of Uzbekistan "On Mortgage" was adopted on 5 October 2006, but some mortgage credits have been issued since 2005. Uzbekistan Today Information Agency, 2006.
8. Uzbekistan citizens who are on monthly payroll are not guaranteed to receive their salary in a timely manner, a fact that also jeopardizes their ability to meet monthly mortgage installments. Radio Free Europe Radio Liberty, 2005.
9. *Addressing Urban Poverty in Uzbekistan in the Context of the Economic Crisis*, United Nations Development Programme, Center for Economic Research and UN-Habitant (Tashkent 2010); *Housing Finance Development in Uzbekistan*, World Bank (Tashkent 2007).
10. W.F. Owen, "Interpretive Themes in Relational Communication," *Quarterly Journal of Speech* 70 (1984): 274-87.
11. E. Lee, "A Theory of Migration," *Demography* 3, no. 1 (1966): 47-57.
12. Regionalism and nepotism had been highlighted as some of the dangers for development in modern Uzbek society by the President I.A. Karimov in *Uzbekistan on the Threshold of the Twenty-First Century* (1998).
13. L. Zhang, *Strangers in the City: Reconfiguration of Space, Power, and Social Networks within China's Floating Population* (California: Stanford University Press 2001).
14. M. Tokhtakhodzhaeva, "Tashkent: Three Capitals, Three Worlds," in *Urban Life in Post-Soviet Asia*, Catherine Alexander, Victor Buchlli, and Caroline Humphrey (eds.) (London: USL Press 2007).
15. A.J. DiMaio Jr., *Soviet Urban Housing: Problems and Policies* (New York: Praeger Publishers 1974).
16. G.D. Andrusz, *Housing and Urban Development in the U.S.S.R.* (Albany: State University of New York Press 1984).
17. *Mahalla* is a traditional Uzbek neighborhood.
18. J. Hosagrahar, *Indigenous Modernities: Negotiating Architecture and Urbanism* (London: Routledge 2005).
19. J. Sahadeo, *Russian Colonial Society in Tashkent* (Bloomington: Indiana University Press 2010).
20. The Uzbek movie "*Mahallada Duv-Duv Gap*" (1960) directed by Shukhrat Abbosov demonstrates the deteriorating conditions of the traditional courtyard houses in the old city of Tashkent and the brand

new apartment complexes built next to these houses with all the necessary amenities. Moreover, the young people in the movie who built them eventually moved in these apartments, and some also invited their elderly parents to live with them.

21. B. Ashcroft, *Post-Colonial Transformation* (London: Routledge 2001), 5.
22. *Homtakhta*-a low dining table; *kurpacha*-a long and narrow padded quilt; *topchon*-a platform for setting kurpachas and other interior stuff.
23. *Stenka*-a furniture set from the Soviet times that consist of bookshelves, cupboard, television stand, wardrobe, and other uses.
24. N. Uphoff, *Learning from Gal Oya: Possibilities for Participatory Development and Post-Newtonian Social Science* (London: IT Publications Ltd. 1996).
25. R. Putnam, *Bowling Alone: The Collapse and Revival of American Community* (New York: Simon & Schuster 2000).
26. Resul Yalçin, "Ethnic Minorities in Uzbekistan: The Case of Koreans," *International Journal of Central Asian Studies* 4 (1999). Available online at http://www.iacd.or.kr/pdf/journal/04/4-04.pdf.
27. D. Spain, *Gendered Spaces* (Chapel Hill: University of North Carolina Press 1992).
28. P.M. Stronski, *Forging a Soviet City: Tashkent 1937-1966*, unpublished PhD dissertation, Stanford University, Stanford, California. 2003.
29. M. Tokhtakhodzhaeva, The Re-Islamization of Society and the Position of Women in Post-Soviet Uzbekistan (Folkestone: Global Oriental 2008).
30. Perera, "People's Spaces."
31. H. Lefebvre, *The Production of Space*, D. Nicholson-Smith (trans.) (Cornwall: Blackwell Publishing 1991 [1905]).

15

Identity of Ukrainians: A Historical Perspective

Preeti Das

> *We can flourish under free and independent development of Russian and Ukrainian cultures.*[1]
>
> —Hetman Skoropadski

Did globalization lead to transition of societies? Did the influx of globalization lead to adoption of newer ideologies within the societies? Indeed it did. So how have these changes been any different from earlier transition in societies, say in the twentieth century? Reflection would suggest that technological advancements particularly in the field of communication have played the role of a catalyst to bring about these changes. Besides, the velocity of change or the process of amalgamation of cultures has been far higher and quicker than ever before. So has this been for the better for the society? One would find it hard to deny that these changes have brought about betterment of society but along with it they have also brought in their share of problems or issues. One of the issues that have surfaced on account of these changes has been the fear of insecurity especially amongst the smaller communities that their own identities may get lost in the din of the larger, more powerful communities. Several such examples have been documented, such as disappearing minority groups like Finno-Ugric, Tibetans, Kosovars, etc. This feeling of insecurity is but natural unless the communities are recognized and are included as part of the overall change and growth. Ongoing researches after the disintegration of USSR of eastern European regions certainly have come across the problems of transition from communism. Attempts are being made to study the processes of transition based on the concepts like modernization as well as on the geopolitical or geo-cultural level.

Twenty years have been passed since Ukraine got its independence; nevertheless the Soviet ideology has left its imprint on the psychology of people. As per the Ukraine demographic profile the total estimated population of Ukraine in July 2011 is 45,134,707; of this 15,282,749 is the male population and 16,673,641 female. 70.8 per cent of the total population falls in the age group between 15 to 64 years whereas only 13.7 per cent are in the age group 0-14 years (Figure 1).

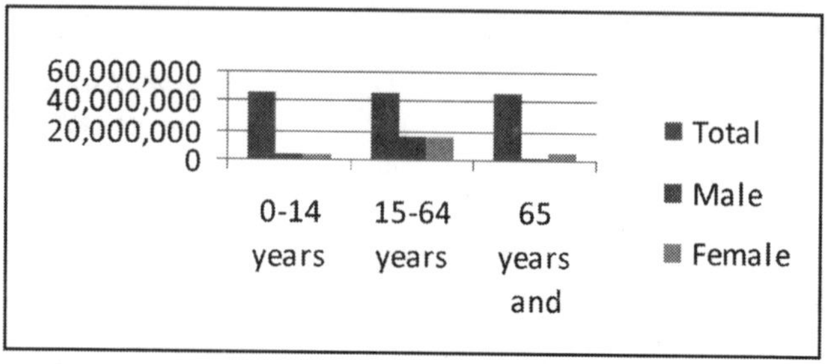

Figure 1. Population in Different Age Groups
Source: http://www.indexmundi.com/ukraine/demographics_profile.html

Apart from this the ethnic composition of the country projects that 77 per cent of the population are Ukrainians whereas the Crimean Tatars comprises only 0.5 per cent (Figure 2).

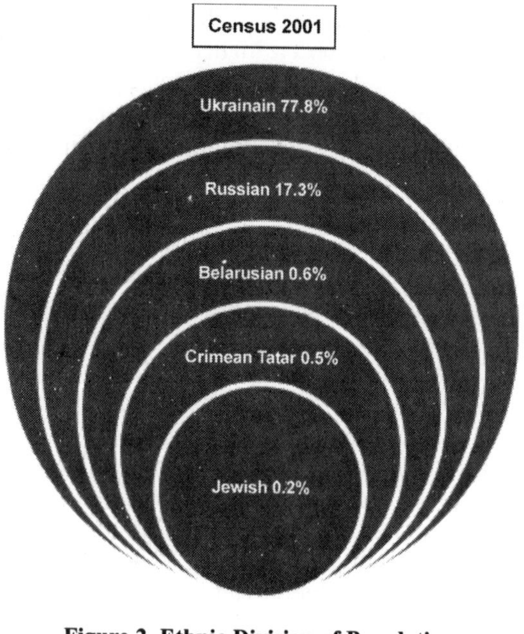

Figure 2. Ethnic Division of Population

However Crimean Tatars have increasingly been drawing the attention of authorities in the process of nation building.

The population data portrays that the majority of the population who are victims of identity crisis are youngsters or those born and brought up during Soviet period. Hence it is crucial that the reflection upon identity crisis is all encompassing. From Soviet period the Ukrainian society and history was studied as inseparable part of Russian history despite having its own sub-identity. It is only after disintegration that understanding "exclusively Ukrainian society and culture" required a fresh look not only on Ukrainian but also on Russian and Byelorussian history. It would seem natural that three people sharing common history and source of culture and statehood should have logically cultural unanimity at its base. However, it is not so. Ukrainians claim their monopoly over the culture and statehood of the "*Kievan Rus*" and deny others any rights to it.

The end of cold war changed the world from bi-polar to multi-polar one. However the major structural or cultural changes started only after 1991, i.e. with the nation building process of disintegrated nations.[2] The root of the present identity crisis lies in the socio-cultural structure of the past. Various debates and discourses have come up dealing with the question: what should be the future policies and regulations of sovereign Ukraine. In the article "Which national idea do we need?" (*Какая национальная идея нам нужна?*)[3] the author blames the opposition for not creating a powerful front capable of suspending the clan of yellow-orange revolutions. According to the article it is for the first time during Kravchuk and Kuchma that the ruling elite realized the future of Ukrainian society in so-called "national idea" the essence of which consisted in the people of Ukraine—national and state policies should be developed uniformly. Nonetheless it is not an easy task to name communities or groups which come under mainstream groups of communities.

Thus, today when we say "Ukrainian Identity" what do we mean: is it to do with political demography, or it is linguistic, religious, ethnic, cultural identity of certain groups residing within Ukrainian territory. Should we look at Ukrainian identity as part of European identity, or "Ukrainian Identity" of pre Soviet period or Ukrainians as Slovaks? Ethnic unrest in present Ukraine has divided it into "West" and "East" creating major cultural barriers among people residing in the country. The group belonging to West associate themselves more with Europeans. However the ground reality is that it should be looked upon from the "nation-building" perspective keeping in mind all the socio-cultural or historical ups and downs of the region. As per 1989 census Ukrainians are 73 per cent of the population whereas Russians are 22 per cent; however more Ukrainians live in rural areas in comparison to Russians. After the collapse of Soviet Union the Jews were permitted to emigrate decreasing their population from 2,919 in 1989 to 918 in 1994. Similarly the Crimean Tatars deported in 1944 were permitted to return back (nearly 250,000) in 1996. However, presently approximately 220-250 thousand Crimean Tatars still live outside Crimea.

With regard to the "National idea" of the country C. Ekelchik in his work "Nationality of Ukrainians, Byelorussians and Slovaks" (2001) explains the formation of national identities of three nations not only from the politico-social-historical point of view but also from the cultural point of view. For preserving national and territorial unity of Ukraine as a multiethnic secular state in the process of achieving strategic (geopolitics) interests it should achieve economic, cultural and political successes, providing stable growth and well-being of the citizens, as well as regions and the shaping of its ethnos.

Understanding Culture

The notion of culture employed by the intellectuals in the nineteenth century has acquired a different meaning. One of the most appropriate definitions which convey the meaning of culture has been given by M. Arnold: "culture as the great help out of our present difficulties; culture being pursuit of our total perfection by means of getting to know, on all the matters which most concern us, the best which has been thought and said in the world; and through this knowledge, turning a stream of fresh and free thought upon our stock notions and habits..."[4] Thus culture is not only something which is passed on from one generation to the other but it is also acquired based on the surroundings by "turning a stream of fresh and free thought." By his definition culture is also concerned with the overall behaviour and perfection of mankind.

This perfection or the behavioural aspect depends upon inner knowledge and understanding of an individual and certainly not always can be imposed from outside. The same is also supported by the arguments of Einstein, "Peace cannot be kept by force. It can only be achieved by understanding."[5] Hence, the understanding between the communities can be developed only through culture as it lies at the base of human behaviour. However, the dichotomy is that the development of culture is through the constant interaction with the surroundings and many a times these very interactions complicate the issues related to identity. Apart from this the dominant culture of a particular region makes it difficult for some to say something different from the dominant one. Many a times the dominant culture works against them.

Language and culture is a part of an overall historical process and change. Among them religion is one of the most sensitive and important. At some point it did play a very crucial role as far as education and improvement of lifestyle of people is concerned. As the language and culture could not remain unchanged for long the changes in religious practices and beliefs also took place. However, historically these (changes in religious practices) have been the key part of policies of ruling authorities which determined the religious sect to be followed, indirectly guiding the direction of cultural growth. The process of democratization and liberalization across the world provided freedom to individuals and communities as far as the religious beliefs are concerned. With the development of multicultural societies and intermingling of people belonging to different cultures unique features of culture have been generated. On the one hand it tries to retain its originality and on the other it adopts new ideas from the other cultures. This process contributed in generating fear among smaller communities of losing their identity. Awakened by the process of globalization and liberalization the populations of Crimean Tatar who constituted 0.5 per cent and Jews who constituted 0.2 per cent have tried to restore their lost cultural practices creating unrest among the rest.

Historical Perspective

Independent Ukraine in 1991was left with the fresh wounds by the Soviet propaganda which tried to exploit people in every possible way including emotionally. A call for construction of "One United Nation" touched the heart of the people and they concentrated fully in this effort. In this regard the works of social activists of second half of twenty-first century are significant, as they touched upon the issues relevant even today specially the relation between "East" and the "West." It was also during this time that the communities and ethnic groups tried to trace their roots while referring to identity issues. The Ukrainian national awakening, which began before its neighbouring countries can be said to have started by the first half of nineteenth century. Besides as constructivists put it, "It is important to show how social facts are constituted by shared ideas because this may reveal new possibilities for change."[6] Cultural activities and interactions took place during eighteenth century mainly through the church. The literature did contain scholastic and religious disputes.

Many works in Russian language reflected upon Ukrainian customs, history and folklore. Nikolai Gogol was one of the most famous writers.

Ukraine has always been part of major historical events and constant battles beginning from "*Kievan Rus*." The country has been divided in parts under different empires for long time: western Ukraine under Austro-Hungarian empire while the eastern part has been under the Russian empire. As a result of Polish-Sweden intervention Russia lost a huge part of its territory—lands bordering the Gulf of Finland and parts which it had acquired in sixteenth century along with some of ancient Russian territories. It is towards end of the seventeenth century that Russia could get back these territories. This was the period when Russian acquired the Left-Bank of Ukraine, Kiev and Slovobod Ukraine till Sea of Azov.

In 1648 the Hetman of Left-Bank of Ukraine Bohdan Khmelintski approached Russia with the request to merge "Little Russia" into Russia. This period also witnessed various coalitions and shifting alliances in the region. Swedish-Ukrainian coalition was made against Russia in 1657 and by 1663 there emerged two groups of Hetmans in Ukraine, one on the left bank of Dnepr in coalition with Russia and the other on the right bank against Russia. The immediate aftermath of the northern war in 1720 saw prohibition of use of Ukrainian language followed by administrative and socio-economic reforms of Katherine II leading to liquidation of Hetman ship in Ukraine in 1764. With the exile of Kalnyshevskii and some other Cossacks the land was given to Russian nobles. Cossacks were thrown out and those who were willing to stay were forced to join Russian forces. Many Cossacks who were forced to leave the country settled in Turkey near Danube which later merged into Russian regime. Ukrainian Church autonomy got abolished.

Following by the partitions of Poland (1772, 1793 and 1795) Ukraine was occupied by two major empires—Russians and Austrians. Galicia, Bukovina and Carpathian Ukraine were incorporated into the Austro-Hungarian (Habsburg) empire and the rest of Ukraine became part of Russia. The Austro-Hungarian and Russian powers were very strong and divided Ukrainian population could not raise their voice against any one of them to regain freedom and self determination. Nevertheless under Austria conditions of the region began to improve, whereas the life under Russian occupation deteriorated. This resulted in resurgence of Ukrainian culture and beginning of well organized political activities first in western Ukraine. Also in western Ukraine the educational reforms of 1775 allowed for the instructions in Ukrainian language; however the favour was given to Poles.

Thus these were some of the historical events which served as base for Ukrainian identity. In comparison with its neighbouring country Byelorussians and Moldavians the undercurrents of Ukrainian national identity came into existence much earlier. According to Bodyanski it had a very clear anti Polish and anti Russian direction.[7] Other than this the Ukrainian experience of political war at the time of revolution of 1848 also contributed significantly in the formation of Ukrainian identity.

Here it might be relevant to reemphasize one of conclusions of M. Grokh that national movements began only a generation after liquidation of serfdom. Some historical factors which show the continuity in accelerating the national movement and contributed to the formation of Ukrainian national identity are as follows.

1. Declaration of Ukrainian independence and creation of Ukrainian National Republic on 22 January 1918 after the revolutionary process of February and October 1917, which destroyed a monarchy and Russian empire.
2. The disintegration of Austro-Hungarian empire led to the creation of the West Ukrainian National Republic on 1 November 1918. However, this existed independently only for eight months.
3. The small military struggles of 1917-21 played important role in spreading national consciousness on all layers of the Ukrainian society.

The ethno-social structure of the population in Ukraine also contributed in the formation of Ukrainian cultural and religious identity. The research of V. Kabuzana and G. Makhnovoi shows that by the mid nineteenth century on the left bank (*Levoberejhe*) Ukrainians were 98.1per cent of the population[8] and the ethnic composition of Catholics and Jews in Ukraine was 4.24 per cent and 6.25 per cent. The number of Cossacks of "Little Russia" as per the Okladnaya book (Окладная книга 1834)[9] decreased to 12.35 per cent of the total population and by 1858 almost all Cossacks of "Little Russia" were transformed into state peasants. This caused a severe impact on the Cossacks both socially and emotionally.

The situation in Crimean peninsula is altogether different. Crimean peninsula which has been an integral part of Ukraine, despite being close to Ukraine geographically has had Turkish political influence for most of the time. It was during Crimean Khanate (fifteenth to eighteenth century) the assimilation of various languages, culture and tribes resulted in the formation of Crimean Tatar. This period also witnessed the complete Islamization of Crimean population and thousands of Christians were displaced (1778). The community known as Crimean Tatars included Turkic and non-Turkic ethnic groups having a very powerful and a well developed cultural belief and language. There were many fortresses and castles built by Tauro-Scythians, Greeks and Goths in Crimea which was used as a refuge for the people of nearby villages during war. The presence of different tribes and communities has found reflections in Crimean architecture.

The burning of Crimean villages (more than 200) with majority Tatars population resulted in mass deportation of Crimean Tatars during 1944. The communist policy was to rebuild Crimea in the Russian way of life. Today, since the deported Crimean Tatars have been permitted to return home it will require huge financial investments for the restoration of religious mosques, schools, etc. This is contradicting with the interests of local Russians residing since the 1940s.

A broad overview on the history of some of the major ethnic groups of present Ukraine with different life style, cultural and religious practice shows that the root to identity crisis lies deep in historical past. Ukraine has throughout been multicultural in its ethnic composition. It is not easy at the formation stage of nation-building to bypass the past strained interrelation between different ethnic groups of Ukraine.

Cultural Policies of Bolsheviks during 1920s

Cultural policies of Bolsheviks were based on two major principles: first, having ideological-political control over cultural and spiritual sphere with intensions to form socialist culture; and second, the overall enhancement of cultural level of population. They declared themselves atheist and attacked all religious institutions. In 1918 a decree on the separation of church from state and schools was issued. Thus began large scale shut down all the religious institutions, destruction of temples and arrest of the people. In 1922 the Glavlit was created as special censor body to take control of all the publications.

Due to this education in Ukraine suffered during 1917-20. There was also a fight between different political groups which led to the emergence of new Ukrainian schools with the compulsory courses on Ukrainian history, language and geography of Ukraine. Bolsheviks tried to alter the educational programmes for their own benefit, i.e. they tried to inculcate the idea of socialism. The Soviet authorities cautiously in the name of national unified life tried to eradicate the ukrainazation of educational institutions. Those who did not follow the instructions of Bolsheviks regime were either forced to or were dismissed. "Prosvit" the national cultural and education organization, which was very popular in villages and brought together Ukrainian people, was destroyed.

Since the educational reforms of Bolsheviks was done with intension to strengthen its regime and induce their ideology by 1920 the number of school in the region increased. A vigorous movement started for higher education. This movement was not limited to any particular group of people, involving both the working class as well as peasantry. However the higher institutions of national education required a certain level of knowledge. So special workers schools were opened. Some experts of Ukrainian Academy of Sciences which was created during Hetman period had to emigrate.

Despite all this when literary works of writers and poets suffered the poets like P. Tichin, V. Saussure, V. Chumak did come up with their passion for Ukrainian identity. Many poets like O. Olec had to leave the country. A lot of effort was made by P. Skoropadskii. Ukrainian universities, libraries and theatres were opened. New musical-drama institutions and creative collective groups appeared in Ukraine during 1919-20. In spite of all the prohibitions the work of new drama theatre named after I.Franko organized a collective composition led by Lec Kurbasov, which included famous artists like A. Marjanenko, Borisoglebski, M. Leontovich, B.Ljatoshinsk became very popular. Other than this owing to the efforts of mainline artists in Kiev by the end 1917 Ukrainian academy of arts came up which tried to assemble renowned artists. Awareness was also generated through the paintings of artists like M. Boichuk, F. Krichevskie, A. Murashka and others which reflect upon Hetman rule, State Emblem, military forms, etc.

At the time of revolution and liberation struggle Ukrainian believers and clergy aspired to have their own independent (self-ruled) church. However Russian Orthodox Church did not want to lose the control over former imperial empire. In order to proclaim self-rule over Ukrainian Orthodox Church the Bolshevik Party developed a struggle against religion and church. This became a major part of the Ukrainian national-liberation movement. Thus irrespective of rigid policies of ruling authorities a strong desire to preserve exclusive cultural Ukrainian identity prevailed.

Conclusion

Thus the roots of the Ukrainian identity are far more deep rooted and complex than it seems to be. Since a larger part of Ukraine has been part of its neighbouring countries for a very long time it did have a very deep socio-cultural impact too. Foreign occupation precipitated migration and rapid assimilation. The marriages between different nationalities were prevalent; however on paper only one nationality could be mentioned. As per the survey conducted by World Bank nearly one-sixth of the population is of Ukrainian/Russian ancestry, however many chose Russian nationality during census.[10]

Another aspect that needs consideration is the link of some of the conflicts of modern Ukrainian society due to reiteration of historical unrest and dissatisfaction among certain groups. History has brought them close to each other; nonetheless there has been significant difference among communities in the past. Today, since the inter-ethnic conflicts in modern societies across the world has broadened, it becomes important to work out certain precautionary methods to curtail or at least to identify zones with potential conflicts. This will help to adopt appropriate methodology for political decision making. Experience of many western countries also projects that granting some political and language rights to national minorities and ethnic groups helps to resolve the tension to a great extent. Thus recognition of ethno-cultural existence of these groups and providing a suitable atmosphere and sufficient funding for the development of groups relatively smaller in number could be a step in resolving the conflicts to an extent. For example for the settlement of Crimean Tatars along with recognizing their territorial claim also requires financial support for the development of religious institutions.

The task of nation building was not simple for Ukrainians also as apart from differences in cultural beliefs and values of these communities which has gone through various ups and downs in the past, historically their mutual interaction had witnessed various battles where they were objects under some or the other power. To keep all the communities united in one nation with a feeling of oneness across the nation leads to debate on the question of what should be the "National Ideology" of Ukraine. However this task is not as simple as it seems to be. Benedict Anderson mentioned in his *Imagined Communities*, "...the nation-ness is the most universally legitimate value in the political life of our time... But if the facts are clear their explanation remains a matter of long standing dispute." He also emphasized that "...nationalism has to be understood by aligning it, not with self-consciously held political ideologies, but with the large cultural systems that preceded it, out of which—as well as against which—it came into being."

It leads to the question: to what extent the cultural beliefs of ethnic groups or the communities residing in Ukraine have been preserved in its pre-Soviet form? It needs to be looked at various levels. For example at the historical level it is the oral history of the communities, at socio-cultural level it is the cultural differences, family traditions and religion and at political level it is the representation and role of the regions in administration, their cultural division. As some ethnic groups had very well developed socio-cultural set up that played the role of state also. Apart from this the social consciousness, stereotypes, fears from assimilation and demographic changes need to be taken care of.[11] Ukrainian literature and culture was suppressed but the same was the case for the rest of the regions as well including sub-ethnic groups of the country. It is the strength of their culture and ideology which produced a strong effect on formation of consciousness of youngsters like T. Shevchenko.

Throughout its historical development multinational Ukraine developed along the lines of a uniform Slavic state. As one Russian researcher commented, "It is sad that only tragically historical events—invasion of Tatar-Mongols from the east and Poles from the west have put on a side the Kiev Russia and tried in a germ to destroy the general Slavic roots, leading to ethnic identification of our people."

Notes and Reference

1. http://kro-krim.narod.ru/PUBLIK/UKR2/skoropaz.htm
2. Alexander Wendt, *Social Theory of International Politics* (London: Cambridge Univ. Press 1999), 314.
3. http://news2000.com.ua/news/proisshestvija/157700
4. Lesley Johunson, *The Cultural Critics—From Mathew Arnold to Raymond Williams* (London: Routledge and Kegan Paul 1979), 28.
5. Collected Quotes from Albert Einstein.
6. Wendt, *Social Theory of International Politics*, 314.
7. O. Bodyanski, "Istoria Russo."
8. Quote from Pavel Tereshkovich, "Ukrainians and Belarusians: Comparative analysis of formation of nations on the basis of history of Central and Eastern Europe of Nineteenth-Twentieth Century," *Political Science* 17, no. 2, Simferopol (2004): 20.
9. Tereshkovich, "Ukrainians and Belarusians."
10. Stephen Rapawy, *Ethnic Reidentification in Ukraine*, available from http://www.census.gov/ipc/www/ebspr98a.html
11. O.A. Gabrileyan "Система раннего предупреждения межэтнических конфликтов в Крыму" (System for warning in advance about interethnic conflicts in Crimea), *Political Science* 16, no. 1, Simferopol (2003): 3-20.

Resurgent Identities in Religion

16

Political Islam in Central Asia: The Case of the Tajik Islamic Renaissance Party

Pinar Akcali

This article aims to focus on one of the most important and unique actors of political Islam in Central Asia, the Tajik Islamic Renaissance Party (IRP), by taking a general look at its policies, programme, and leaders on the one hand, and the role that it has been playing in the various stages of the political life of Tajikistan on the other. In this framework, the party will be analysed in four different time periods: 1) the pre-1991 era; 2) the early months of independence; 3) the civil war era; and 4) the post civil war era. It will be argued that being a pragmatic political party, the Tajik IRP adapted to the new circumstances of each of these periods, formulated different policies and engaged in different attitudes, enabling it to adjust to the post-Soviet era conditions as one of the most important political actors in the country. In fact, Tajikistan in general and the Tajik IRP in particular are important, as they hold "the key to an understanding of the tendencies within political Islam in Central Asia as a whole."[1]

According to Anna Zelkina, Islamic revival in the region manifested itself in four general forms: 1) Islam is incorporated to the agenda of secular political parties; 2) government's appeal to Islam as a source of legitimacy; 3) official Islamic institutions attempt to become independent religious and political forces; and 4) active Islamic groups emerged within unofficial and reformist Islam.[2] One major factor that makes the Tajik IRP unique is related to this analysis: it actually overlapped with all of these four forms in various contexts and at various times. It incorporated secularism into its agenda; the government in Tajikistan had to accept the party as a legal and/or legitimate source to appeal to; official Islamic institution in the country in its attempt to become an independent religious and political force inevitably had to cooperate and negotiate with the party; and finally the IRP emerged as the most active Islamic group the roots of which could be traced to unofficial Islam.

The Tajik IRP had been an influential political actor in Tajikistan since the early 1990s, an exception not only for the Central Asian region, but for most parts of the Muslim world. Despite the fact that the party would be finally legalized in 1997 as a result of the peace agreement that ended the civil war, it had played a major role in the pre-war coalition, civil war, negotiations, and post-war political arrangements.[3] As Dmitri Trenin suggests, "Tajikistan is the only country in Central Asia where Islamists sit in parliament and in the cabinet, not in prison."[4] As will be further analysed below, the Tajik IRP could successfully bring together different groups and actors as well as seemingly irreconcilable ideologies in its attempts to share political power in the country. Ahmed Rashid suggests that this inclusive and conciliatory attitude of Tajik Islamists make them much different than any other Islamic group in the region, especially the radical militant ones such as the Wahhabis, the Taliban, and the Islamic Movement of Uzbekistan (IMU). In order to look further into such characteristics of the Tajik IRP, it is now necessary to focus on the party within the framework of the various periods in which it had been active.

Pre-1991 Era: Islamic Legacy in Tajikistan and the Roots of the IRP

In order to understand the uniqueness and importance of the Tajik IRP in the post-Soviet era, it is inevitable to look at the roots of this party. In this context, it must be emphasized that Tajikistan is a country in which Islamic heritage is very strong. It must be pointed out that Tajikistan was the centre of the anti-Soviet Basmachi rebellion of the early 1920s that was mostly a religious reaction against the atheist regime.[5] According to Monica Whitlock, "the shadow of the Basmachi wars lingered longer [in Tajikistan] than it did elsewhere."[6] Islam never stopped being a major social force during the Soviet era and it continued to be influenced by the activities of underground spiritual leaders such as Mullah Muhammad Rustamov Hindustani. Born in Kokand in 1892, Hindustani studied in Afghanistan and India before he finally moved to Dushanbe in 1947. Hindustani would stay there until his death in 1989.[7] According to Lena Jonson, his pupils were influential in spreading the Islamic message during these years.[8] Towards the end of the decade, the process of Islamic revival would accelerate especially in rural areas where Islamic education of small children was intensified by unofficial mullahs.[9] As one observer suggested, "The training was intensive, and so profoundly affected the consciousness of the children that upon coming to conventional Soviet schools, they even read Cyrillic from right to left."[10] Most of the future leaders of the Tajik IRP such as Muhammad Sharif Himmatzoda, Davlat Usmon and Said Abdullah Nuri would emerge as young and underground activists during the last decades of the Soviet Union.[11] Many scholars have pointed out that in rural areas of Tajikistan secret religious activities of unofficial clergy continued almost uninterrupted during the Soviet era.[12] Tea houses known as *chaikhonas* and clubs were secretly converted into temporary prayer houses,[13] whereas in remote areas many mosques had never been "formally" closed down.[14]

When the Soviet Union invaded Afghanistan in 1979, Islamic revival in Tajikistan gained a new momentum. Among both the Soviet Red Army soldiers and the administrative staff sent to this country there were many Tajiks who were expected to help the Soviet-backed Afghan Government.[15] However, once they arrived in Afghanistan, these Tajiks were observed to establish close ties with the local population as well as the mujahidin groups.[16] As Ahmed Rashid suggested, taking the opportunity to be in the region, hundreds of Tajiks secretly travelled to Pakistan and Saudi Arabia either to study or to be trained as guerrilla fighters so that they could help the mujahidin.[17]

It was against such a background that the Tajik IRP emerged. At first, it was a regional branch of the all-Union Islamic Renaissance Party that had been established in June 1990 in Astrakhan, Russia. The Tajik IRP was formed in late 1990 and was formally registered in October 1991, only to be banned shortly after.[18] However, as will be explained in the coming parts, it would continue to play a major role in the political developments of the post-Soviet era in Tajikistan.

Early Months of Independence: IRP during the Prelude to Civil War

The Tajik IRP emerged as one of the most influential actors of the political scenery in the early months of 1992. The party took the lead in the anti-governmental demonstrations held during the month of March as a result of which President Rakhman Nabiev agreed to establish a coalition government in which the opposition groups (including the Tajik IRP) were also to be represented.[19] However, this government was not recognized by all regions and clans in the country, resulting in the eruption of a civil war which would last for five years between 1992 and 1997.[20] The Tajik IRP, the major actor of the bloc that was composed of all anti-governmental parties, took the lead in the formation of the United Tajik Opposition (UTO).[21] Organized basically in the economically and politically disadvantaged regions of the country such as the Gorno-Bahakhshan, Kyrgan-Tyube, the Karatagin and the Tavildara valleys, the UTO fought against the pro-communist clans from Khojend and Kulab,[22] now united under the new president of the country Emomali Rakhmon[23] who had come to power in December 1992.[24] As soon as he became the new leader of Tajikistan, Rakhmon started to repress the opposition.[25] According to Muhiddin Kabiri of the Tajik IRP, such an attitude would contribute to the escalation of the civil war:

> The political elite of Tajikistan, educated within a totalitarian system, resisted handing over power to the new political forces. These forces were, in turn, inexperienced. The combination of the lack of readiness on behalf of the country's leaders to accept changes along with ambitious but inexperienced new political forces brought Tajikistan to civil war.[26]

When we look at the general attitude of the Tajik IRP in the early months of independence, it is possible to observe one dominant trend: the party had a relatively more cooperative and conciliatory attitude as opposed to the pre-independence era. This trend can be observed in three major areas: 1) the programme of the party; 2) its attitude toward other political actors; and 3) its attitude towards official Islam.

The programme of the Tajik IRP openly declared that it was a "socio-political organization based on Islamic faith, consisting of faith in one God and in the prophetic mission of Mohammed" and that it had the goal of "moral revival of the citizens of the republic, and a political and moral awakening aimed at the incorporation of the fundamentals of Islam into the life of the Muslims of the republic."[27] Abdullah Dadkhuda, the party secretary in charge of education and propaganda, indicated that the IRP wanted an Islamic government where the orders of God, the sacred Qur'an, the teaching and the knowledge of the prophet would be the principal elements. He suggested that there had to be a parliament because the Qur'an encouraged collective consultation.[28] Another major figure of the party, Davlat Usmon stated the following about the goals of the party in an interview conducted in late 1992 as follows:

> We seek to establish a democratic regime and achieve full independence. We also want to be allowed to teach people Islam, which they have been denied for seventy years. We

> are not calling for the establishment of an Islamic state in Tajikistan, as most people are ignorant of Islam, and in order for us to be able to do that we must teach people Islam, since we do not want to establish Islamic rule by force. God willing, we will achieve Islamic rule in the future in one way or another.[29]

Even though there was an emphasis on the establishment of an Islamic state in an unforeseeable future, the leaders of the IRP did not make this as their first priority; they rather focused on the introduction of a democratic parliamentary political system and basic human rights for Tajikistan.[30] The leaders would also explicitly state that they would use only peaceful and legal methods to reach their goals.[31] Therefore at least in the short run the goals and methods of the party were quite similar to other opposition forces in Tajikistan, especially to the secular, democratic groups. The party was against any political group having a monopoly of political power. As such, the Tajik IRP also had a positive and cooperative attitude toward other political actors in the country, including the communists.[32] Therefore, in the early months of independence, the Tajik IRP attempted to remain legal and sought recognition of the authorities.

It must also be kept in mind that during this time, the Tajik IRP took the lead in bringing together all the opposition groups around common goals such as a new constitution, multi-party system and the formation of a broader coalition government.[33] When eventually Nabiev had set up the national reconciliation government with 24 cabinet members, there were eight were from the opposition, including the ministries of interior, security, education, foreign affairs and defence.[34] Davlat Usmon was appointed vice-premier and it was agreed that he would be the government spokesman. In a protocol signed by the president, the council of ministers and the members of the opposition (including the IRP), it was stated that equal rights should exist for all political organizations and groups and that political parties and organizations could operate within the framework of law.[35]

Finally the relatively more cooperative attitude of the Tajik IRP during the early months of independence can also be observed in terms of its relations with the official Islamic institution. This attitude is mostly seen in the incorporation of *Qazi* Haji Akbar Turajonzoda, the most senior Muslim cleric in the country and the head of the Tajik *Qaziyat*[36] to the ranks of the Tajik IRP.[37] Turajonzoda was born in 1954 to a family of respected Sufi clerics. He received his education first with his father and maternal grandfather who taught him Persian language and poetry as well as the Qur'an. When he turned 18, he went to Bukhara, Uzbekistan to study at the Mir-e Arab Madrasa. Upon his graduation in 1976, he went to Tashkent to study further in the Tashkent Muftiyat.[38] He would later go to the Amman University that further broadened his knowledge of Islamic law and foreign languages.[39] He would eventually be appointed the Qazi of Tajikistan in 1988. One year later he was elected to the Supreme Soviet in Moscow.[40] Coming from within the Soviet establishment, Turajonzoda did not have any goal of creating an Islamic state. He would openly declare that the Tajik IRP was not seeking to create such a state but just trying to restore peace and reconciliation in the country.[41] On several occasions, Turajonzoda stated that he favoured a secular and democratic state in which religion would be separated from politics.[42] According to him Islam was not a barrier to democracy and it was possible to have them both.[43] His priority was to train clerics who would then teach Islamic principles to the Tajik people.[44] Working within the legal system of the Soviet Union, he established an Islamic Institute in Dushanbe in 1990.

Despite the fact that Turajonzoda emerged as one of the most influential figures of the Tajik IRP, there were several other prominent actors within the ranks of the party who had come from much different backgrounds and from the ranks of unofficial religious circles.[45] For example, one of the most influential leaders was Mullah Said Abdullah Nuri, born in 1947 in Tavildara in the Garm region. Nuri was educated as an unregistered cleric by his father, who after retiring from his job as a state farm director had become a self appointed mullah.[46] Nuri would be arrested many times by the Soviet authorities during the 1970s and 1980s.[47]

Although these two actors came from different backgrounds and religious traditions, they cooperated under the roof of the Tajik IRP during the early months of independence. This cooperation, together with the cooperation of IRP with other oppositional groups in Tajikistan would continue during the civil war years as well.

The Civil War Era: IRP as the Major Opposition Party

The civil war years (1992-97) would open up a new chapter for the Tajik IRP, which would now emerge as the major opposition party within the UTO. In this era, most of the prominent leaders of the party would either retreat to remote areas of Tajikistan such as the Pamir mountains or go into exile in other countries such as Afghanistan, Pakistan, Iran, Saudi Arabia and Russia. Among these countries, Afghanistan stands out as the most important case, as the

Tajik IRP would set up bases in Kunduz and Taloqan in which Tajik refugees who had escaped from the war or political repression would be trained, armed, and sent back to Tajikistan to join the war against President Rakhmon.[48] In this era, Ahmad Shah Masud, an ethnic Tajik who had fought the Soviets in Afghanistan, financially supported the IRP and helped the party to coordinate guerrilla actions.[49] The civil war years saw increasing contacts and mutual support between the members of the Tajik IRP and the Afghan mujahidin groups. In various "guerrilla warfare training centres" tens of thousands of Tajik refugees were being trained under the guidance of mujahidin leaders in coordination with IPR's best known leaders such as Turajonzoda, Usmon, and Himmatzoda.[50] During the civil war, the UTO would continue its guerrilla attacks against the Rakhmon government. At first, the government refused to deal with the opposition. Eventually acknowledging the fact that UTO was a major challenge to his rule, Rakhmon agreed to start negotiations with it. This change of attitude was mainly due to two factors. First, the government could not stop the attacks. Second, Russia, which was providing most of the border troops located on the Afghan-Tajik border became increasingly uncomfortable with the situation and pressured the Tajik Government to solve the conflict as soon as possible.

The Tajik IRP played a very visible role during the negotiations, acting as the main representative of the UTO. It seemed to receive de facto recognition from both Dushanbe and from international organizations such as the United Nations. According to the head of a UN delegation who travelled to Tajik refugee camps in north Afghanistan in March 1995, it was impossible to settle the problem without the participation of the UTO.[51] The Tajik Government also seemed to accept the importance of the IRP. In April 1995, President Rakhmon stated that he was ready to meet with the leader of the opposition, Said Abdullah Nuri "at any time, any place" with the purpose of "preventing further conflict situations on the Tajik-Afghan border, establishing and achieving peace, and consolidating stability."[52]

As a result of several rounds of talks, which took place in Moscow, Teheran, Islamabad, Kabul, Almaty, and Ashgabat, a peace agreement was signed on 27 June 1997 that ended the civil war. That would start yet another important chapter for the Tajik IRP.

Post Civil War Era: Challenges to the IRP

In the post civil war era, the IRP was considered by some scholars as a "major political force"[53] or "the most prominent opposition party."[54] The peace agreement legalized the party and gave the UTO members the opportunity to be represented in the new coalition government by a ratio of 30 per cent.[55] The IRP guerrilla fighters were incorporated into the Tajik army under UN supervision.[56] It seemed as if a new era with better and improved opportunities would begin for the Tajik IRP. However, February 2000 parliamentary elections indicated that the party's options to be an influential actor were indeed limited. In these elections, the Tajik IRP could get only 7.5 per cent of the votes and win two seats in the parliament.[57] It was suggested that by the spring of 2001, it became obvious that the party's influence had declined and that it had no new economic and political plan to appeal to the people.[58] It also lost most of its previous posts in the 1997 coalition government and public opinion polls indicated a weakened support for the party.[59] The 2005 parliamentary elections produced the same results for the party: it could pass the 5 per cent threshold but could again get only two seats.[60]

There are two main reasons why the IRP's support has eroded in the post-1997 era. One is the internal splits that the party suffered from; the other is the repressive attitude of the Rakhmon regime.

In terms of internal splits in the party some scholars suggest that the party is still seen as a clan-based organization representing only the interests of particular regions of the country that had supported it before and during the civil war.[61] As such, it does not represent the whole people and only has "very localized followings."[62] According to Lena Jonson, the results of the 2000 and 2005 elections indicated the regional support base of the IRP. In these elections, people from the Faizabad, Kafarnihan, Garm, Vaksh, Kabodiyan and Isfara as well as Kulyab, Sogh (or Khojend) and Gorno-Badakhshan voted for the party.[63]

But perhaps a more important reason of splits is related to the moderate and cooperative attitude of the party leadership in the post war era. Part of the reason why such an attitude would be adapted was the civil war itself. As Ahmed Rashid suggested, "War weariness had destroyed any desire for radical political change."[64] As such, the post-war IRP had the basic intention of contributing to the process of consolidation in the country. So, despite the fact that the 2000 elections were a major disappointment for the party, its leader Said Abdullah Nuri declared that the IRP accepted the results and that the peace process was irreversible.[65] In the post civil war era the party leadership had a "rather passive" attitude and went "to great lengths to demonstrate... willingness to cooperate with the Rahmonov regime."[66] In this framework, it acted as a modern political party that respected the secular constitution of Tajikistan.[67] According to the new charter of the Tajik IRP accepted in 1999, the party aims to "develop Islamic, national and human values in society."[68] Acknowledging the fact that Islam has a major role in Tajikistan as part of national and cultural identity as well as spiritual awakening, the party nevertheless seems to be committed to the democratic development, justice, equality, peace and human rights.[69] There is no reference to the creation of an Islamic state its programme; as such it is "not an anti-systemic party."[70]

This tendency was clearly seen in the speeches or attitudes of the party's leaders. For example, Nuri, the chairman of the party between 1999 and 2006 explicitly rejected an Islamic republic as in Iran, sharia rule as in Taliban's Afghanistan, or caliphate.[71] He had a moderate attitude and believed in the importance of "constructive dialogue" with other secular groups in the country.[72] Likewise, Muhiddin Kabiri, who is the chairman of the party since Nuri's death in 2006, advocated that the Tajik IRP should be transformed into a modern party similar to the Christian democratic parties of Europe, respecting both religious values and secular political system.[73]

However, this moderate and cooperative attitude has met with resistance from both the more conservative leaders and low level rank and file members of the party on the one hand, and some voters on the other.[74] These groups have started to find moderate leaders such as Turajonzoda, Nuri and Kabiri too soft and demanded more radical strategies to be adapted.[75] In this context, Himmatzoda, a founding member of the IRP and its chairman until 1999 is a noteworthy figure, as he never gave up his intention of establishing an Islamic state in Tajikistan. Likewise, Mirzo Ziya is considered as one of the most radical young activists of the party, believed to help the militants of the IMU in establishing training camps in Tajikistan.[76] These types of internal divisions in the Tajik IRP further contribute to the decline in party's effectiveness and credibility as a strong political actor as it once used to be.

One other important political group that both contributes to the internal divisions of the IRP and benefits from these divisions is the Hizb ut-Tahrir. Founded originally in 1950 in Jerusalem, it spread to several Muslim countries as well as Europe. In Central Asia, the party is considered to be one of the most important radical groups and it has become increasingly active since the late 1990s. In Tajikistan the party seems to be especially active in Khojend and Dushanbe.[77] As such, the Tajik Government made many arrests since the early 2000s against the members of the group.[78] According to Shirin Akiner,[79] there is not much of reliable information about Hizb ut-Tahrir's ties to the Tajik IRP, but some reports indicate that the organization "launched an aggressive campaign" to recruit the disenchanted members of the IRP to its ranks.[80] Some IRP leaders, such as Kabiri, accept the fact that some of the young Tajiks who "were just children during the civil war and are [now] being introduced to the Islamic teaching for the first time" through the channel of Hizb ut-Tahrir have been joining the party.[81] As such, the Hizb ut-Tahrir has emerged as another rival for the IRP, further reducing its appeal among the population.[82]

In addition to the internal splits that weakened the party, the Tajik IRP also suffered from President Rakhmon's repressive policies. Since the early 2000s, Rakhmon has been conducting a very active campaign to marginalize his political opponents.[83] In this context, the Tajik IRP, being the main opposition party with a high potential to emerge as a real power contender for Rakhmon, was at the very target.[84] The 9/11 attacks and the international anti-terrorism campaign that began in autumn 2001 gave the president another justification to scrutinize the Tajik IRP. Rakhmon began his own campaign to fight terrorism and religious extremism, which resulted in various sentences given to several opposition figures, including the ones from the IRP.[85] One such incident took place in August 2002 in the northern district of Isfara, a stronghold of the IRP, when ten imams were banned from service as they were also members of the party. This was a violation of the constitution which prohibited the religious leaders to participate into political activities.[86] President Rakhmon accused the IRP of engaging in similar activities such as the IMU and Hizb ut-Tahrir.[87] In 2004 two IRP leaders, who had been arrested a year ago, were sentenced to long prison terms on various charges, including forming a criminal group, illegal border crossing, polygamy, murder, and rape of a minor.[88]

This general attitude on the part of Rakhmon regarding all opposition groups, including the IRP, has not changed much in the last couple of years as well. His attempt to consolidate political power in the post of presidency is also reflected in his attitude regarding the local leaders. He constantly shifts their positions so that they would not be able to form local-based allegiances and develop social networks around them.[89] He appoints to important posts his own relatives or people from his home town Dangara. These people do whatever they can to make sure that they stay within the clientalistic network of the president.[90] In this general framework, the country's economic resources are also shared among a limited number of people who are believed to have an oligarchic control over these resources.[91]

Under such conditions, the chance of the Tajik IRP to be a real opposition party with a serious chance of coming to power seems little. As the last two presidential elections in the country held in 1999 and 2006 indicated, the candidate of the IRP lost to Rakhmon, who got a solid majority of votes in both cases. The same thing happened in the last two parliamentary elections as well, the IRP winning only two seats in the parliament both in 2005 and 2010.[92]

Conclusion

Tajikistan's IRP proved itself to be an important and key political actor until the 2000 elections. As was explained above, the party had played a major role in the process of disintegration of the Soviet Union, in the early months of independence, in the first coalition government established in early 1992, the civil war, and the negotiations that led to the signing of the peace treaty of 1997. The party had a key role in the post war coalition government as well. In that sense the Tajik case represented a more inclusive political system that had the potential of solving problems via cooperation and mutual understanding. As Kabiri indicated, "Giving official status to a political party that had a religious character brought peace and stability to Tajikistan."[93] Furthermore, as the Tajik IRP had developed pragmatic and realistic policies that fitted well within the requirements of each different time period that was analysed in the article, it has also proven to be a resilient political party that could continue to exist in the system for more than two decades. Before the war and during the negotiations, the party had a more radical and harsh attitude, whereas before the war and after the war it had a more collaborative and moderate position. In other words, whenever given a chance to exist legally in the political system, the IRP had a softer attitude, but whenever it was oppressed or outlawed, it resorted to more radical measures. This attitude resulted in two related outcomes that seem to somehow produce a paradoxical situation. On the one hand, it allowed the party to be flexible enough to be the main opposition group over the last two decades; on the other, this flexibility has resulted in a certain loss of support among the people as well as splits in the party. When combined with the post war tendency of power consolidation on the part of Rakhmon and the rising popularity of more radical organizations such as the Hizb ut-Tahrir, the future chances of the Tajik IRP to increase its popular support seems to be rather bleak.

Notes and References

1. Anna Zelkina, "Islam and Security in the New States of Central Asia: How Genuine is the Islamic Threat?" *Religion, State and Society* 27, nos. 3-4 (1999): 362.

2. Zelkina, "Islam and Security."
3. Lena Jonson, *Tajikistan in the New Central Asia: Politics, Great Power Rivalry and Radical Islam* (London: I.B. Tauris 2006), 128; Ahmed Rashid, *Jihad: The Rise of Militant Islam in Central* Asia (New Haven, Connecticut: Yale University Press 2002), 105; Brent Hierman, "What was the Election to US? Clientalism and Political Trust amongst Ethnic Uzbeks in Kyrgyzstan and Tajikistan," *Nationalities* Papers 38, no. 2 (2010): 256.
4. Dmitri Trenin, "Russia and Central Asia: Interest, Policies, and Prospects," in *Central Asia: Views from Washington, Moscow and Beijing*, Eugene Rumer, Dmitri Trenin and Huasheng Zhao (eds.) (New York: M.E. Sharpe 2007), 91.
5. Michael Rywkin, *Moscow's Muslim Challenge* (New York: M.E. Sharpe 1990), 42.
6. Monica Whitlock, *Land beyond the River: The Untold Story of Central Asia* (New York: Thomas Dunne Books 2002), 79-80.
7. Shirin Akiner, "The Politicisation of Islam in Postsoviet Central Asia," *Religion, State and Society* 31, no. 2 (2003): 98.
8. Jonson, *Tajikistan in the New Central Asia*, 162.
9. Yaacov Ro'i, *Islam in the Soviet Union: From Second World War to Gorbachev* (London: Hurst and Company 2000), 357; Shirin Akiner, *Tajikistan: Disintegration or Reconciliation* (Great Britain: Royal Institute of International Affairs 2001), 30.
10. Dmitri Mikulski, "Central Asian Alternatives: The Islamic Revival Party of Tajikistan (History of Creation, Structure, Ideological Principles)," *Vostok*, no. 6 (November-December 1994), quoted in *FBIS-SOV Daily Report*, 7 April 1995, 94.
11. Sophie Roche, "From Youth Bulge to Conflict: the Case of Tajikistan," *Central Asian Survey* 29, no. 4 (2010): 411; Jonson, *Tajikistan in the New Central Asia*, 154; Dilip Hiro, *Between Marx and Muhammed: The Changing Face of Central Asia* (London: Harper Collins Publishers 1995), 193; Mikulski, "Central Asian Alternatives," 94.
12. Yaacov Ro'i, *Islam in the Soviet Union: From Second World War to Gorbachev* (London: Hurst and Company 2000), 327; Akiner, *Tajikistan*, 29; Ahmed Rashid, *Jihad*, 40.
13. Akiner, *Tajikistan*, 29.
14. Ro'i, *Islam in the Soviet Union*, 58.
15. Colette Harris, *Muslim Youth: Tensions and Transitions in Tajikistan* (Boulder: Westview Press 2006), 29-30; Glenn E. Curtis, *Kazakhstan, Kyrgyzstan, Tajikistan, Turkmenistan and Uzbekistan: Country Studies* (USA: Federal Research Division Library 1996), 281.
16. Whitlock, *Land beyond the River*, 131.
17. Rashid, *Jihad*, 44.
18. Akiner, *Tajikistan*, 30; Curtis, *Kazakhstan, Kyrgyzstan, Tajikistan*, 274; Jonson, *Tajikistan in the New Central Asia*, 153-54.

19. Barnett R. Rubin, "Tajikistan: From Soviet Republic to Russian-Uzbek Protectorate," in *Central Asia and the World: Kazakhstan, Uzbekistan, Tajikistan, Kyrgyzstan and Turkmenistan*, Michael Mandelbaum (ed.) (New York: Council on Foreign Relations Books 1994), 213.
20. Michael Kort, *Central Asian Republics* (New York: Facts on File 2004), 167; Michael Hall, "Tajikistan at the Crossroads of Democracy," in *Prospects for Democracy in Central Asia*, Birgit N. Schlyter (ed.) (Stockholm: Alfa Print 2005), 25-26.
21. Susan Clark, "The Central Asian States: Defining Security Priorities and Developing Military Forces," in Mandelbaum (ed.), *Central Asia and the World*, 188; Karen Dawisha and Bruce Parrott, *Russia and the New States of Eurasia: The Politics of Upheaval* (Cambridge: Cambridge University Press 1994), 1.
22. Rashid, *Jihad*, 90.
23. His surname was "Rakhmonov" until 2007, the year in which he ordered his countrymen to drop Russian-style surnames. He also removed the Russian suffix "-ov" from his surname (http://news.bbc.co.uk/2/hi/asia-pacific/country_profiles/1296639.stm). However, for the purpose of consistency, in this article "Rakhman" would be used, unless taken from a source.
24. Jonson, *Tajikistan in the New Central Asia*, 41; Stina Torjesen and S. Neil MacFarlene, "R Before D: the Case of Post Conflict Reintegration in Tajikistan," *Conflict, Security and Development* 7, no. 2 (2007): 314; Michael Hall, "Tajikistan at the Crossroads of Democracy," in Schlyter (ed.), *Prospects for Democracy in Central Asia*, 26.
25. Richard Pomfret, *The Central Asian Economies since Independence* (New Jersey: Princeton University Press 2006), 63; Martha Brill Olcott, "Ceremony and Substance: The Illusion of Unity in Central Asia," in Mandelbaum (ed.), *Central Asia and the World*, 33; Michael Kort, *Central Asian Republics* (New York: Facts on File 2004), 167; Hall, "Tajikistan at the Crossroads of Democracy," in Schlyter (ed.), *Prospects for Democracy in Central Asia*, 173.
26. Muhittin Kabiri, "The Tajik Experience of a Multiparty System—Exception or Norm?" in Schlyter (ed.), *Prospects for Democracy in Central Asia*, 22.
27. Mikulski, "Central Asian Alternatives," 94.
28. Shahrbanou Tadjbaksh, "The Tajik Spring of 1991," *Central Asia Monitor*, no. 2: 25.
29. *Al-Hayah*, 11 December 1992, 8, quoted in *FBIS-SOV Daily Report*, 16 December 1992, 48.
30. *FBIS-SOV Daily Report*, 1 October 1992, 75; Mehrdad Haghayeghi, *Islam and Politics in Central Asia* (New York: St. Martin's Press 1995), 88.
31. *FBIS-SOV Daily Report*, 19 May 1992, 43; Robin Wright, "Report from Turkestan," *The New Yorker*, 6 April 1992, 74.

32. Aziz Niyazi, "The Year of Tumult: Tajikistan After February 1990," in *State, Religion and Society in Central Asia: A Post-Soviet Critique*, Vitaly Naumkin (ed.) (Reading: Ithaca Press 1993), 282; Alexei V. Malashenko, "Religious and Political Change in Soviet Moslem Regions," in Naumkin (ed.), *State, Religion and Society in Central Asia*, 172.
33. *Central Asia Brief*, no. 2 (1992): 5
34. *Central Asia Brief*, no. 2 (1992): 5.
35. *FBIS-SOV Daily Report*, 7 May 1992, 53.
36. *Qaziyat* or *muftiyat* referred to the Muslim Spiritual Directorate in Tajikistan, the backbone of official Islam in the republic.
37. Rashid, *Jihad*, 140.
38. Whitlock, *Land beyond the River*, 143-44.
39. Akiner, *Tajikistan*, 31.
40. Rashid, *Jihad*, 100.
41. Boris Rumer, "Disintegration and Reintegration in Central Asia: Dynamics and Prospects," in *Central Asia in Transition: Dilemmas of Political and Economic Development*, Boris Rumer (ed.) (New York: M.E. Sharpe 1996), 54.
42. *FBIS-SOV Daily Report*, 8 July 1992, 73.
43. Malcolm Gray, "Shedding the Past," *Maclean's*, 25 November 1991, 35
44. Akiner, *Tajikistan*, 31.
45. Akiner, *Tajikistan*, 31.
46. Hiro, *Between Marx and Muhammed*, 195.
47. Rashid, *Jihad*, 97-8; Whitlock, *Land beyond the River*, 142; *FBIS-SOV Daily Report*, 15 March 1994, 40; Yaacov Roi', "The Islamic Influence in Nationalism in Soviet Central Asia," *Problems of Communism* 39, no. 4 (1990): 61.
48. Rashid, *Jihad*, 103-04.
49. Ahmed Rashid, *The Resurgence of Central Asia: Islam or Nationalism* (Karachi: Oxford University Press 1998), 215; Giampaolo Capisani, *The Handbook of Central Asia: A Comprehensive Survey of the New Republics* (London: I.B. Tauris 2000), 169.
50. Rashid, *The Resurgence of Central Asia*, 159-60.
51. *FBIS-SOV Daily Report*, 14 March 1995, 85
52. *FBIS-SOV Daily Report*, 24 April 1995, 83
53. Erica Marat, "Imagined Past, Uncertain Future: The Creation of National Ideologies in Kyrgyzstan and Tajikistan," *Problems of Post-Communism* 55, no. 1 (2008): 18.
54. John Heathershaw, "Tajikistan's Virtual Politics of Peace," *Europe-Asia Studies* 61, no. 7 (2009): 1327.
55. Brent Hierman, "What was the Election to US?" 256; İhsan Yılmaz, "An Islamist Party, Constraints, Opportunities and Transformation to Post-Islamism: The Tajik Case," *Uluslararası Hukuk ve Politika* 5, no. 18 (2009):141.

56. Rashid, *Jihad*, 105, 235.
57. Rashid, *Jihad*, 100; Yılmaz, "An Islamist Party," 141.
58. Rashid, *Jihad*, 112-13.
59. Akiner, *Tajikistan*, 67; Jonson, *Tajikistan in the New Central Asia*, 130.
60. Yılmaz, "An Islamist Party," 34-128, 141.
61. Rashid, *Jihad*, 108; Emmanuel Karagiannis, "The Challenge of Radical Islam in Tajikistan: Hizb ut-Tahrir al Islami," *Nationalities Papers* 34, no. 1 (2006): 10.
62. Brent Hierman, "What was the Election to US?" 256.
63. Jonson, *Tajikistan in the New Central Asia*, 155.
64. Rashid, *Jihad*, 113.
65. Ian Jeffries, *The Caucasus and Central Asian Republics at the Turn of the Twenty-first Century: A Guide to Economies in Transition* (London: Routledge 2003), 29.
66. Hall, "Tajikistan at the Crossroads of Democracy," in Schlyter (ed.), *Prospects for Democracy in Central Asia*, 31.
67. Jonson, *Tajikistan in the New Central Asia*, 154.
68. Karagiannis, "The Challenge of Radical Islam in Tajikistan," 12.
69. Karagiannis, "The Challenge of Radical Islam in Tajikistan,"12; Yılmaz, "An Islamist Party," 142-43.
70. Yılmaz, "An Islamist Party," 142.
71. Yılmaz, "An Islamist Party," 142.
72. Akiner, *Tajikistan*, 67.
73. Yılmaz, "An Islamist Party," 11-155, 142.
74. Hall, "Tajikistan at the Crossroads of Democracy," in Schlyter (ed.), *Prospects for Democracy in Central Asia*, 31; Karagiannis, "The Challenge of Radical Islam in Tajikistan," 13-14.
75. In an extreme case of such a reaction, hard-line members of the IRP who found Turajonzoda too moderate attempted to assassinate him in Dushanbe in February 2000 (26-108).
76. Akiner, *Tajikistan*, 68.
77. Rashid, *Jihad*, 124; Akiner, *Tajikistan*, 69. For a detailed account of the party in Tajikistan see Karagiannis, "The Challenge of Radical Islam in Tajikistan," 1-20.
78. Karagiannis, "The Challenge of Radical Islam in Tajikistan," 4.
79. Akiner, *Tajikistan*, 69.
80. Karagiannis, "The Challenge of Radical Islam in Tajikistan," 8.
81. Rashid, *Jihad*, 131-32.
82. Rashid, *Jihad*, 111.
83. Rashid, *Jihad*, 132.
84. Erica Marat, *The Military and the State in Central Asia: From Red Army to Independence* (Great Britain: Routledge 2010), 74; Hall, "Tajikistan at the Crossroads of Democracy," in Schlyter (ed.), *Prospects for Democracy in Central Asia*, 31.

85. Rashid, *Jihad*, 132.
86. Karagiannis, "The Challenge of Radical Islam in Tajikistan," 14.
87. Rashid, *Jihad*, 134.
88. Pomfret, *The Central Asian Economies Since Independence*, 64.
89. Rashid, *Jihad*, 30.
90. Hierman, "What was the Election to US?" 256-7.
91. Sumie Nakaya, "Aid and Transition from a War Economy to an Oligarchy in Post-Soviet Tajikistan," *Central Asian Survey* 28, no. 3 (2009): 259.
92. https://www.cia.gov/library/publications/the-world-factbook/geos/ti.html (retrieved 5 May); "Islamic Renaissance Party of Tajikistan. Background Information Summaries, 2010." International Security and Counter Terrorism Reference Center. Available from http://ehis.ebscohost.com/eds/detail?sid=8556d663-0151-4638-b139fa57f8ca82bd%40sessionmgr4&vid=3&hid=20&bdata=JnNpdGU9ZWRzLWxpdmU%3d#db=tsh&AN=55741365 (retrieved 5 May 2011).
93. Muhittin Kabiri, "The Tajik Experience of a Multiparty System—Exception or Norm?" in Schlyter (ed.), *Prospects for Democracy in Central Asia*, 22.

17

Terror, Islam and Imperatives of Reconciliation in Eurasia

P.L. Dash

During the time when Mikhail Gorbachev was ruling the Soviet Union and ethno-national upheavals were sweeping across Soviet territory, a cryptic caption to a cartoon said: "the army is Soviet, the territory is Uzbek and the language is Russian." This small caption depicted the heterogeneity facing the then Soviet society. The moot question is the divisive tendencies such connotations attribute to human relations in a seemingly homogenous society, where cultural clashes become inevitable on grounds of ethnicity, nationalism, language and religion; and that too in a complex and globalizing world. It is simply because a certain group in a given society contemptuously differentiate between themselves and other groups within the same society on grounds of speaking a different tongue, writing in a different script from left to right, professing a different religion, following different cultural mores and leading a different way of life. Such feelings provide a fecund ground for mutual hostility, animosity that finally leads to cultural clashes even among the people professing the same religion. In Pakistan, Afghanistan and all across the Muslim world, Muslims are killing Muslims and that too in the name of *jihad* and Islam, whose very name embodies peace. This mutual hostility is more dangerous to peaceful coexistence, more pernicious to the well being of the society and worrisomely oriented toward economic non-development.

When Samuel Huntington, the reputed political scientist, formulated his thesis of "Clash of Civilizations" he clearly meant clashes could take place along the cultural fault-lines where it could be Islam verses the West and Islam verses the rest; but he could not fathom the depth of hostility among Muslims themselves that would pit them against their co-religious brethrens within the same society. The focus of this paper is to analyse and assess how present day radical Islam has created a schism within its own society, hopelessly divided along those who support terror acts and those who oppose it tooth and nail, and how rapprochement among many incongruent groups is essential. More alarming is the recent trend of terror invariably being linked to Islamic groups and that too concentrated in a single flashpoint of Eurasia. Spread across a swathe of triangular landmass covering the Af-Pak tangle to Xinjiang uprising to intractable Chechnya, the terrorist activities are too heinous and too truculent to be borne with by any civilized society.

Many Faces of Terror

Beginning this millennium, as Vladimir Putin piloted Russia from uncertainty and chaos to stability and prosperity, he created hope for many a Russian heart. The first term of his Presidency passed off well, setting the ball to roll for the second term. The Chechen war entered into a decisive phase with junior Kadyrov on the saddle of state responsibility through an election patronized by the Kremlin. Putin effectively arranged for peace through the rebel leader ruling the republic. He bought peace for Russia and for himself that lasted for a few years. However, this peace was like an ephemeral bubble; terror has spread by leaps and bound, bringing agony to millions of Russians. The rebels regrouped and their women brigade called Black Widows wreaked havoc as suicide bombers across Russia seeking revenge against the atrocious elimination of their husbands by Russian security forces.

A quick look at some of the tragic incidences in Russia of the past decade seems appropriate here. Terror as an unseen enemy has been outmaneuvering the security forces year after year. On 5 February 2001, explosive devices placed under a bench on the platform of Berorusskaya station went off, injuring 15 people. On July 2003 a Chechen woman detonated a suicide belt at a rock concert that killed over a dozen spectators. The police said a second woman's bomb, waiting nearby, failed to explode or else the casualties could have been higher. In December 2003, the widow of a Chechen guerrilla commander blew herself up in Moscow, killing six and injuring many. Since Caucasian women in large number have taken recourse to terrorist strikes, the terminology "black widow" came into vogue. On 6 February 2004, a suicide bomber from north Caucasus sets off a device in the morning rush hours in a train travelling between Avtozavodskaya and Paveletskaya stations, killing more than 40 people and injuring over 100. On 30 August 2004, a Chechen female suicide bomber blew up herself outside Ryzhsky Bokjal, killing 10 people and injuring more than 50. An unknown Islamic group, supporting Chechen rebels, claimed responsibility.[1]

Five years after Putin bought peace in Chechnya, the most horrendous terrorist act happened on 1 September 2004 on the opening day of a new academic year, when armed terrorists took more than 1000 school children and teachers hostage for three days in Beslan, North Ossetia. The hostage taking led to intervention of Russian security forces and the result was over 300 children and adults killed. In November 2009, a bomb blast derailed a train, travelling between Moscow and St. Petersburg in rural European Russia. It killed 26 people.[2] On 29 March 2010, suicide bombers brought their terror acts close to the Kremlin and exploded bombs at two major Metro stations: Lubyanka close to the FSB office and Park Kulturi in the heart of Moscow. Varying figures put 38-40 people killed and hundreds injured. On 24 January 2011 Moscow's busiest airport, Domodedovo, witnessed a terror blitzkrieg that instantly killed 35 people, maimed a dozen more and injured around 300, all innocent civilians, awaiting in the welcome hall to receive their relatives.[3]

The list is thus endless. The above examples are only those that represent the wide spectrum of terror strikes. Russia has witnessed numerous other serious acts of terror. A good example is the theatre hostage taking in Moscow a few years ago, when security forces tunneled into the ventilation system in the metro to spray Pentanol gas on the terrorists inside the theatre and after paralyzing them flushed out dead bodies. All terrorists and some 200 spectators were dead in the process. Moscow has also witnessed bombing of residential apartments in Moscow. In all these terror acts, Moscow has been the main target because the Caucasian terror groups, encouraged by leaders of world *jihad*, wish to send a clear message to the Kremlin. As Chechen leader, Doku Umarov put on his blog in February 2010: "If the Russians think that the war is happening only on TV, and it will not touch them, we are going to show them this war will return to their homes."[4] The statement is indicative of the determination of Islamic terrorists to teach Russia a lesson so that Russia never forgets what Islam is, what is *jihad*, who are Muslims and what their commitment to the cause of *jihad* is. All these put together bind Russia in a knot with the Muslim world. Thus will the crescent forever clash with the cross through *jihad*?

In the two decades following the disintegration of the Soviet Union, free from fear of repression by the state, terrorists and separatists from southern Russia have pushed the country as much into chaos as to a virtual terrorist cauldron. Islamists have joined hands with money launderers and drug traffickers to profiteer from the messy situation and launch terrorist attacks against the Russians in the name of *jihad*. Often billboards and death graffiti are pasted on the walls of city Metro, thus spreading panic and fear among people with their announcements: "Allah Ho Akbar and death to the Russians."[5] They have taken a democratizing Russia too much for granted and are possibly rendering a disservice to the nation by serving as tangible impediments to the process of democratic transformations. The problem is further compounded by the involvement of *jihadists* from all cross the world to launch attack on the Christians, who they consider as "infidels." For Russia under the Putin-Medvedev dispensation and even beyond, Islamism continues to pose a paramount challenge to overcome. Thus Russia is located on the precipice of an Islamic cliff across its southern underbelly, thereby endangering its very existence as a multi-cultural and secular entity.

The Complexities

The fact that Russia is a vast country straddling across eleven time zones makes it one of the world's most diverse landmasses. It is a multicultural polity embracing a number of religions. In the East Buddhism, in the South Islam, and across mainland Russia Christian Orthodoxy have always entwined Russia with a diverse cultural ethos. To pinpoint singularly at any religion will be nothing less than foolhardy. While it would be wrong to pinpoint to Islam as a divisive religion, given the fact that Islam has been inflicting physical damage to the Russian psyche, it is also true that it is increasingly becoming synonymous with terror. Should Islam ever render itself synonymous with terror or Muslims with terrorists, Islam's very meaning will be lost forever in the wave of sweeping multiculturalism.

The pragmatic mosaic of religious complexities in Eurasia is best demonstrated by the following circles that entail multi-religiosity and multi-cultural ethos. The inevitability of reconciliation with various *Mazhabs* is particularly essential, when the world is increasingly becoming a global village with distance disappearing, knowledge predominating and information technology bringing people closer than ever before in human history (Figure 1).

A Few Questions

Given that Islam as a faith is preeminently prevalent across Eurasia and Africa, added importance is attached to distinguishing bad

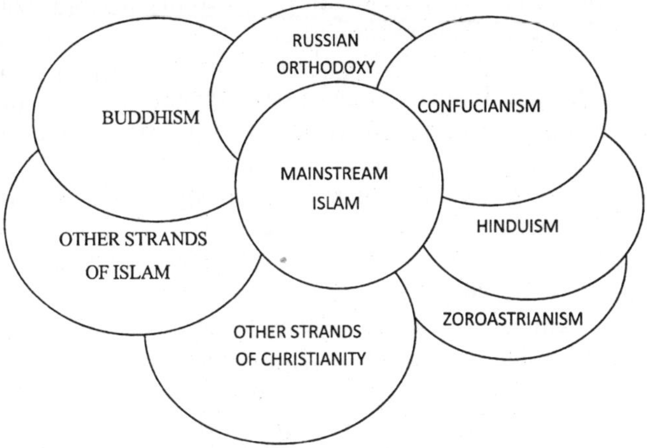

Figure 1. Eight major religions converging on Eurasia

elements from the good elements. The bad elements are Al Qaeda and all terrorists inspired by it and the good elements are apostles of true Islam, who stand for peace and progress. The contradiction between followers of good and followers of the evil is the inherent puzzle within the Muslim society. Riddled with underdevelopment despite having enormous energy reserves, none of the West Asian and Middle Eastern Muslim countries are considered developed. From the 1960s when these countries had experienced oil boom up to the present they have not been able to develop either economically or socially. Had they spent a fragment of the oil revenue they have earned all through these years, they could have transformed their societies and their lot too. Alas! They remain woefully poor and undeveloped. Developing a show case city in the capital is no evidence of real development. The moot question is that of governance: when kingdoms have perished everywhere, will they last long in Saudi Arabia or elsewhere? The rulers must understand that bitterness and tears of the people have congealed in to hatred and perpetration of terror acts is a way of expressing that hatred.

This leads one to ask a few pertinent questions in order to find out how Islam could be a resourceful religion to be harnessed for the benefit of mankind. Firstly, can the world isolate Islam by talking in terms of Islam verses the rest and Islam verses the West?[6] Certainly not. The answer to this question would be an antithesis to Huntington that mandates the modern world to find ways of embracing Islam for developmental goals. What one could isolate in Islam are the elements of the ilk of Atta, who blazed planes through the twin towers in September 2001 from rest of the Muslims who despised that tragic event.

Secondly, can Islam go against modernity? The world was shocked when the Taliban flogged a few women in an open stadium and it was televised all over the world. This had preceded atrocious attitude to female nurses and teachers who were summarily sacked from their jobs after the Taliban takeover in Afghanistan. If a society does not respect its women, the mothers and sisters, who bind the bonds of love in the society, that society is certainly doomed. Similarly, when a girl in the streets of Srinagar was shot on her thigh because she was walking clad on a pair of jeans, the atrocities are monstrous. Or if a modern nation destroys its cultural heritage as did the Taliban in Bamiyan and evince intolerance due to lack of deference to another faith, the act assumes horrendous proportion of stupidity and it deserves condemnation. Since most Islamic countries are underdeveloped, they must focus on development rather than misuse religion.

Thirdly, how to engage Islam in positive economic development? This is the question that has been haunting many for decades. The roots of terror lie in economic woes. The economic asymmetry between the rulers and the ruled within the Muslim society itself, and the social dichotomy between the elite and laymen are worrisome developments in the Muslim world. Since the oil boom of the 1960s, the kings, emirs and sheikhs of the oil rich Arab countries have deposited their wealth in the western banks, not caring for the needs of their people. Not for too long can countries survive on cruel methods of autocracy, plutocracy or aristocracy. They must think in terms of democracy based on its basic ideas of liberty, equality and fraternity. Look at the events in Tunisia, Egypt, Syria, Yemen and elsewhere. All these are outcome of the yawning gap between the rulers and the ruled.

Fourthly, what sort of governance model has Islam been searching for? In the nineteenth and early twentieth century, there were liberal trends in Islam in Iran, Egypt and Turkey. If Kemal Ataturk's Turkish Republic could become an embodiment of a thoroughly secular regime in contemporary history, why not Saudi Arabia, Iran, Afghanistan or Pakistan? Shorn off societal tolerance and heavily laden with hatred towards other faiths, today's radical Islam has engaged itself in a quest that detests modernity, the rights of women as in western societies; in short modernity has become the culprit and the West is at the base of it. *Jihad* thus becomes a mission of conversion until adherents and followers of all other faiths follow the line of Islam. Such a governance method is infeasible, far too impractical and precisely well nigh impossible. This was why Francis Fukuyama had written that "radical Islamists, intolerant of all diversity and dissent, have become the fascists of our day."[7] These fascists must not emerge victor; they ought to be vanquished.

Fifthly, who are the stakeholders? As terrorist activities have stepped up in Islam in a big way, particularly since the aftermath of 9/11, several stakeholders have appeared on the scene. For the first time a world religion is being misinterpreted to justify terror in the name of *jihad*. For the first time Islam has pitted itself against the West in a decisive manner, in a focused way to take revenge through terror acts. It is for the first time the adherents of all other religions have been termed as infidels-Christians, Hindus, Jews *et al.*[8] It is for the first time a world religion has taken recourse to unjustified acts of terror, which is proscribed by their own religion. The quantum of funds at the disposal of Islamic zealots to unleash their campaign against all so called infidels is pegged at $35 billion by various sources and it is a huge sum that knits together a network world wide which is too formidable to handle. From here stems the perception that everyone is a stakeholder because everyone's existence is in danger, even those of the Islamists themselves, whose leaders are often running as fugitives and rumoured to have possessed even nuclear devices. The entire humanity becomes stakeholders because Islam today is pervasive from Morocco to Indonesia and from Xinjiang to Sri Lanka. Of the 42 existing international terrorist organizations, as detailed by the USA, 27 organizations are radical Islamist. Of the 191 UN member states 57 are members of the OIC. 900 million people living in Islamic countries and getting their higher education in more than 500 universities located on one fifth of the world's territory, plus 400 more millions living in the non-Islamic world, Muslims constitute an integral part of any society. The imperatives for a rapprochement with Islam is urgent because there is an underlying current to subvert the adherents of Islam by interpreting it the wrong way; the reason is majority of the followers are poor, illiterate and ill educated and they are into the politicized Islam. Lenin had once termed: "an illiterate man stands outside politics."

Al Qaeda Menace

The Al Qaeda connection to Islam and terrorism has added a new twist to the interpretation of Islam. The organizational genesis of Al Qaeda goes back to 1985, the year Gorbachev became General Secretary of the CPSU and the Soviet entanglement in Afghanistan was at its peak. The first organization was known as Maktab-al-Khidamat (MAK). Organized with the active help of a Muslim Brotherhood leader, Abdulla Azzam, the organization soon spread its tentacles from Afghanistan to US, Egypt, Saudi Arabia, Pakistan and elsewhere. Its main objective was to unleash a *jihad* against the Soviets in Afghanistan. The organization sheltered and transported clandestinely individuals from over 50 odd countries, provided them food and clothing and began training them to fight what it called the "Infidel Atheists." It set up paramilitary training camps in Afghanistan and Pakistan and particularly in the fluid tribal regions of Waziristan and on the territory of Pak Occupied Kashmir. It flanked India and Pakistan on the one side on the north western regions of Kashmir and on the NWFP of Pakistan: both regions have extremely difficult terrain, high mountains and no vegetation. The camps trained 10,000 Arabs, half of whom came from Saudi Arabia, 3000 were Algerians, 2000 Egyptians and numerous numbers were from Yemen, Pakistan, Syria and other Muslim countries. The ideas of Islam appealed to them. And youngsters, jobless, unemployed and aspiring to become something, thronged to the training camps to be recruited as interns in terrorist activities.

The monetary aspect was far too alluring. A stipend of nearly $100 per day was given to teenaged young Muslim trainee, which was paid in cash for his devotion to Islam to undertake *jihad*. The youth were far from understanding the essence of this money; more so from where it came. This is how a well-knitted network sprang up to pit the Russians in Afghanistan against a vicious *jihad* culture funded by the United States through Pakistan, where hundreds of terrorist training camps mushroomed to continue their campaign. It is these well-trained cadres in the hands of Al Qaeda leadership that switched to fight the West in the aftermath of 9/11. It is these cadres concentrated in the fluid zone of Waziristan, who have been fighting the Americans along the Durand line. Inspired by the ideology of Al Qaeda and supported by the ISI of Pakistan, it is these cadres, who also have been waging a war against India unleashing terror across the territory from Kashmir to Guwahati, from Jaipur to Bangalore and from Delhi to Mumbai.

If the Soviet withdrawal from Afghanistan was any indicator to stop fueling the aspirations of these youngsters to hoist the flag if Islam everywhere, the legitimate question to be asked is who would finance them in their mission? As Pakistan continued to milk the American cow in some pretext or the other, it channelized most of the funds it obtained from the US in stationing the *jihadists*, who were by now actively into formation of various religious groups within Pakistan and Afghanistan. The vacuum that the Soviet withdrawal created in Afghanistan provided the golden opportunity to Taliban to capture power in that country, quickly regroup solidly around Osama bin Laden and continue the ultimate mission of *jihad.* From there on Al Qaeda has never looked back and its financial health looked rosy forever.

By indulging in all kinds of nefarious activities such as narcotic trade and money laundering, Al Qaeda further enriched itself so much so it nurtured the hope of teaching a lesson to the United States. It prepared meticulously to target the most powerful country on earth and carried out the attack on the twin towers, on Pentagon and on White House fairly successfully in what we know today as the gory incidence of 9/11 that claimed more than 3000 lives in the US. Once accomplished, the mission virtually choked the lifeline of money supply to the *jihadists* from the US channel. However, by now, the *jihad* child was grown up enough to raise his own money and sustain itself independently. This is precisely why the ISI of Pakistan and Al-Qaeda based in Afghanistan have successfully hoodwinked the US on all occasions, siphoned off US funds via Pakistan and continued to play truant not only for the US, but also for all in the South Asian region. Let us hark back to those televised pictures of the Mulla Omar on Pakistan TV, advocating *jihad* to all against the West in the immediate aftermath of 9/11. Without a tandem between the ISI and Al Qaeda such televised programmes were well nigh impossible and they continued until Musharraf made u-turn to side with the US to fight terrorism. The man, who watered, tendered and fostered terrorism to grow, carefully nurtured and clandestinely harbored it, suddenly became the animus of terror along with the US; and fairly surprisingly the US believed in Musharraf. The rest is history and the result is the continuing Af-Pak imbroglio without any solution in sight. But their spillover effects are felt everywhere—from New York to New Delhi, from Britain to Bangladesh and from Moscow to Mumbai.

Synergy as Safeguard

The current hotspot of terror is Afghanistan, the Taliban haven and narcotic hub of the world. Everyone has been concerned about a peaceful solution to the Afghan crisis since the Taliban appeared there after Soviet withdrawal, disappeared after October 2001 attack by the allied forces and now reappeared with the help of ISI-Al Qaeda combine, making three things synonymous: Al Qaeda, Taliban and Islam. It is these three elements Russia wants to engage in constructive dialogue for development for the future prosperity of Afghanistan. Results, however, have been not so forthcoming. With terror and turmoil sweeping across the country development has been put on the back burner. Engineers and technical hands helping Afghanistan in infrastructure building, whether from Japan, China or India, are being killed by Islamists, Afghanistan has turned out to be a danger zone for international community. Although it is not the placed here to argue about the viability of American forces staying back in Afghanistan as guarantor of peace and development, things are not as simple as the world thinks them to be. Afghanistan is a complex country and to engage it in peaceful development requires tenacity and years of hard work in the direction of capacity building, which the Russians did for a decade in 1980-89 and the Americans have been doing since October 2001. The need of the time is to embrace Afghanistan within the orbit of globalization and development. If the Islamic component cannot be eschewed, it must be incorporated into that development process. Three things are significant in this context.

First, the challenges of regional cooperation are too formidable, but not entirely unmanageable. The economic imperatives of integrating Afghanistan, one of the poorest countries in the world, to the process of globalization are trammeled by divisive ethnic culture and woeful underdevelopment.[9] Both these aspects cannot be overcome overnight. Extension of help by all in this regard in the right direction may well take years before they bear fruit. However, external help alone will not suffice. Capacity building in all spheres of human endeavour must be undertaken with participation of interested countries within the UN framework and beyond to put the Islamic countries in general and Afghanistan in particular, into the fast track of sustainable economic development as enunciated in the UN millennium goals.

Secondly, here in the process of economic development Islam comes as a potential hindrance. And here Islam ought to be engaged and the followers of Islam made to see the veracity of the enormous challenge facing their country in the comity of nations in modern world. Thus we confront not only Islam but a complex gamut of cultural issues closely linked to the societal ethos of Islam in Afghanistan, and for that matter all underdeveloped Muslim societies. Modernity versus Islam is once again the issue that has to be addressed. If the Taliban and Al Qaeda have Islam as their instrument to oppose modernity, the entire world has modernity as the anathema to Islam. The Islamic clerics can play here a pivotal role to influence the masses, wean them away from fragmentation to unity and mobilize them for constructive ventures of nation building.

The third factor is social fragmentation. Muslim society is stratified and scattered with many internal contradictions. On all issues society is not united. There are vast differences in the mindset of the people, their standard of living, their economic orientation and specifics of their economic and social development.[10] Using Islam for destructive activities or unleashing terror in the name of Islam is as blasphemous as committing a heinous religious crime against humanity. The Taliban and Al Qaeda elements have been usurping Islam for their own aggrandizement and not for the benefits of Muslims of the world. They are socially so fragmented that they are away from their own people and living in inaccessible mountains, away from others in the world and in obscurity as fugitives, away from the mainstay of development and democracy and leading life in jungles, far away from modernity, and certainly away from all that Russia or the Western world wishes to achieve.

Conclusion

The diversity of Russia geographically situated across eleven time zones and living in unity through centuries is evident of its tolerance with multi-ethnicity and multi-religious environ. Compared to Russia's vastness and religious diversity, Al Qaeda and Taliban are intolerant zealots, who may ultimately prove to be an ephemeral phenomenon in a given time and space. The web and tide they generate through terrorist activities by killing innocent civilians are testimony of their disdain for humanity that does have a place in Islam. Abhorrence and tolerance are two contradictory trends in modern Islam, seemingly hard to reconcile, but surely tolerance has more sympathizers, who herald a way to cooperation, rapprochement and reconciliation even with those who spread the gospel of hatred against so called infidels, although the preachers themselves sit on the zenith of blasphemy. The Russians and the Americans are infidels, but not the arms they produce, which *jihadists* and terrorists use. This makes us believe that only around 70 years ago Italy, Germany and France were fighting wars among each other, Seventy years later we find them united in the European Union, endearing borderless travel and embracing a common currency. Who knows seventy years from now or even earlier the Islamic world will be united with the western world? Just a decade onto this century, the way political upheavals have been sweeping the Arab world, demanding regime change, it would not be audacious to think about English poet Shelly, who wrote in his famous Ode to the West Wind: "If Winter comes, can Spring be far behind?"

Notes and References

1. Alexander Osipovich, "Tears and Rage," *Hindustan Times*, New Delhi (30 March 2010): 19.
2. "In Moscow, We live on powder keg," *The Times of India*, New Delhi (30 March 2010): 16.
3. P.L. Dash, "Caucasus Terror Cradle?" *Defence and Security Alert, Russia Special*, New Delhi (February 2011): 8
4. *The Times of India*, New Delhi (30 March 2010): 16.
5. *The Times of India*, New Delhi (6 April 2010): 17.
6. See Samuel P. Huntington, "The Age of Muslim Wars: A Wave of Violence Pitting Muslims against each other and against the West," *Newsweek*, Special Davos edition (December 2001-February 2002): 8-13.
7. Francis Fukuyama, "Today's New Fascists; their Target the Modern World," *Newsweek*, Special Davos edition, (December 2001-February 2002): 54.
8. For a detail discussion on a book summary, see P. Zolotarev, "Islamic Factor and International Terrorism," *Russia and the Islamic World* 7, no. 205 (2009): 155-76.
9. For a comprehensive study of the situation in Ferghana valley and elsewhere in Central Asia, see Anara Tabyshalieva, *The Challenge of Regional Cooperation in Central Asia* (Washington: Peacework, US Institute of Peace 1999).
10. Islamskii Mir: "Ostayushyee Razvitie I Musulmanskii Radikalizm," *Russia i Musulmanskii Mir* 5, no. 191 (2008): 152-76. Debate summary of IMEMO, Moscow.

18

The Role of Uzbek Islamic Extremists in the Civil Wars of Tajikistan, Afghanistan and Pakistan

Michael Fredholm

The Islamic Movement of Uzbekistan: Origins of the Movement

The Islamic Movement of Uzbekistan (IMU), or *O'zbekiston Islomiy Harakati* as it is known locally (*Harakat ul-Islamiyyah* in Arabic),[1] had its origin in the Islamic movement called *Adolat* ("Justice"), a faction of a larger group known as *Islom lashkarlari* ("Islamic Warriors"), which arose in the city of Namangan in the Uzbekistani part of the Ferghana valley in about 1990 as a response to what was perceived as widespread corruption and social injustice exposed by the liberal *perestroika* era as well as the resurgence in Islamic activities no longer prohibited by the Soviet Government. The movement was reportedly founded, or at least inspired, by Abdulhakim Qori. Supported by men such as Obidkhon Qori Nazarov from Tashkent, and Umarkhon Domla and Davudkhon Qori from Namangan, who also contributed funds from their mosques, the movement grew rapidly.

However, funded by sources in Saudi Arabia, the movement became increasingly radicalized by the variety of Salafism known as Wahhabism, thus producing a form of Islamic extremism by then rare in the Central Asian region. Yet, few of the movement's members had the theological skills to recognize the differences in various types of Islam, so these names are of little value in analysing their religious beliefs. For practical purposes, perhaps the definition of Islamic extremism proposed by the Council of the Muftis (Islamic religious leaders) of Russia on 30 June 2000 is the best one. The Council then singled out as extremist those movements that (1) rejected the basic Islamic traditions, (2) claimed the right to brand as "non-Muslims" traditional believers who happened to disagree with their interpretation of Islamic law, and (3) claimed the right to kill "infidels" including traditional Muslims who had failed to side with them.[2] This will be the definition of Islamic extremism adopted here, since it subsumes all varieties of Sunni extremism, whether referred to as Salafi or Wahhabi.

The movement came was led by two young men: the college drop-out and local mullah Tohir Yo'ldosh and the former conscript soldier Jumaboy Hojiyev (later known as Juma Namangani or, at times, Tojiboy). In January 1990, Yo'ldosh renamed the movement *Islom adolati* ("Islamic Justice") and introduced the taking of an oath of allegiance (*bayah*) by its members, promising to introduce Islamic law first in Namangan, then the rest of Uzbekistan. In the same year, the movement built the first of several mosques and madrasahs. Of the various centres, Yo'ldosh operated out of the Otavalikhon mosque in Namangan. From November 1991 to the spring of 1992, the movement, which primarily consisted of unemployed young men, perhaps as many as five thousand altogether (although other reports indicate numbers ranging from three to five hundred active members only), went on to organize protest meetings and occupy government buildings. The movement formed its own vigilante religious police force, the most militant of which became known as *yurishlar* ("conquerors"), which administered summary justice in the streets. Each member was paid a salary from mosque funds as well as taxes imposed on local traders. In April 1991, President Karimov, arriving to talk to the militants, was shouted down. Tohir Yo'ldosh even grabbed the microphone from the president's hands, shouting "No! Now and here, I'm the ruler! You can talk only when I allow you! Now, shut up and listen!" In December 1991, militants occupied the headquarters of the Communist Party of Uzbekistan (CPU) in Namangan. Among many demands, they wanted the government to immediately proclaim the establishment of an Islamic state, use Islamic law as the only legal system, cease to orient the country towards Turkey, and introduce separate schools for boys and girls. They also began to refer to themselves as *mujohidlar* (mujahidin). Yo'ldosh assumed the title *bosh amir* ("commander-in-chief"). Branches of Adolat rose across the Ferghana valley, in Andijon, Margilan, Kuva, Farghona, and Osh (in Kyrgyzstan).[3]

Tohir (or Tohirjon) Abduhalilovich Yo'ldosh (also known in Russian as Tahir Yuldashev and in Arabic as Muhammad Tahir Farooq (Farukh in Russian), was born in 1967 in Namangan.[4] His father died when he was five, and he was brought up by his mother, Karomat Asqarova.[5] An early member of the Uzbekistani branch of the All-Union Islamic Renaissance Party (IRP), founded in

Astrakhan in June 1990, he had grown disillusioned with this party's refusal to demand an Islamic state. Together with other likeminded young Uzbeks, Yo'ldosh formed Adolat as a platform for his demand for an Islamic revolution.[6]

Jumaboy Ahmadjonovich Hojiyev, an ethnic Uzbek born in 1967 in Namangan, graduated from agricultural vocational school before he was drafted into the Soviet army in 1987. He reportedly served as an airborne soldier in Afghanistan during the last phase of the Soviet war there, eventually becoming promoted to sergeant. However, this elite airborne episode too may be a part of the myth that soon grew around his person. He is said to have become interested in Islam during his term in Afghanistan.[7]

Adolat was banned in March 1992, and the Uzbekistani Government restored order, dissolving the movement. Several Adolat leaders, including Yo'ldosh and Hojiyev, who now took the name Juma Namangani after his hometown, in 1992 fled to Tajikistan, where they joined the Tajikistani branch of the IRP, which by then was preparing to launch a violent civil war in Tajikistan.[8] There the two young men embarked upon very different careers, although aiming for the same broad goals. Yo'ldosh began what can only be called a political career, while Namangani became a guerrilla leader. Their militant activities took them first to Tajikistan, then Afghanistan, where they formed the Islamic Movement of Uzbekistan (IMU) in 1998. The history of their activities there, the death of Namangani in battle against the American-led invasion of Afghanistan in late 2001, and the flight of the IMU survivors into Pakistan has been told elsewhere and will not be repeated here.[9]

The Surviving IMU Networks in Central Asia

To the surprise of many, it soon turned out the IMU had survived in Central Asia as well as in Pakistan. Details are sketchy, but a few facts can be ascertained. In Uzbekistan, militants believed to have been members of the IMU by mid-2003 still remained in the south, in the Surkhondaryo (Surkhandarya) province, where the IMU had been known to have sleeper cells as late as in 2001.[10] The IMU had also survived in Kyrgyzstan. Several alleged IMU bombings took place in Kyrgyzstan during 2002 and 2003. In the United States, the State Department issued several warnings, possibly based on American intelligence information, that the IMU might attack American citizens in Uzbekistan and Kyrgyzstan.[11]

Other alleged IMU incidents took place in Tajikistan. In January and June 2005, explosions occurred near the Ministry of Emergency

Situations in Dushanbe, for which Tajikistan accused the IMU of involvement. On 25 January 2006, a small group of militants managed to free a prison inmate from Ghayroghum district of Soghd province in northern Tajikistan, who was accused of links with the IMU, killing the prison director in the process. The group then disappeared by car towards the nearby border with Kyrgyzstan, where they presumably went into hiding. However, there remains some doubt whether the militants in fact belonged to the IMU. Suspicions have also been directed towards another organization, Bayat ("Oath of Allegiance"), which had been accused of the murder of a Baptist missionary which took place on 12 January 2004 and subsequently several arson attacks of homes and shops of sellers of alcohol as well as local mosques in Chorkuh, Isfara district. A number of Bayat members were reported once to have been members of the IRPT.[12]

There may also have been a connection between the IMU and the Andijon affair on 13 May 2005.[13] Although there is no evidence that the IMU was directly involved in the events on that day, the Uzbekistani Prosecutor-General's office on 16 September 2005 noted that a certain Ilhom Hojiyev in April 2005 had smuggled up to $200,000 into Uzbekistan in support of the group involved in the affair.[14] Whether this Ilhom Hojiyev was the relative of the late Namangani who previously had joined Yo'ldosh in Pakistan is unknown, but the Uzbekistani investigators may have thought so, since they also requested Kyrgyzstan to return a certain Dilshod Hojiyev, who had sought asylum there after the Andijon affair. A criminal case was opened against him in Uzbekistan, while several human rights organizations expressed their rage that the Kyrgyzstanis considered handing him and three other named Uzbekistani citizens over to Uzbekistan for criminal charges. Again it is unknown whether this Dilshod Hojiyev was the same man who was the son-in-law and second-in-command of Yo'ldosh, and also the one in charge of IMU finances, or merely an unfortunate bystander who happened to have the same name.[15] Yet, the fact that his name was on the list of four named suspects requested by Uzbekistan certainly indicates that the Uzbekistani investigators thought that he belonged to the IMU.

On 12 May 2006, militants from Tajikistan reportedly associated with the IMU attacked a Tajikistani border post and a Kyrgyzstani customs office, presumably to acquire weapons. Four militants were killed and one captured. Tajikistani law enforcement noted that their captive was a member of the IMU and was on the wanted list. In early 2008, one of the remaining wanted gunmen, alleged IMU activist Abdulhai Yuldashev, was arrested in southern Kyrgyzstan. Three other gunmen remained wanted, two of them Tajikistani citizens and one a Kyrgyzstani.[16] It is difficult to assess whether these and several other acts of violence attributed to the IMU in the Central Asian republics were planned acts of terrorism or merely the side effects of continued drug smuggling activities.

In 2006, Yo'ldosh issued statements to the Muslims of Central Asia on three occasions, speaking in Uzbek. Interestingly, he devoted considerable time towards a refutation of the ideology of the Hizb ut-Tahrir. He also denounced the perpetrators of the March and April 2004 suicide bombings in Tashkent and Bukhara, that is, the IJU, severely. He may have felt that he was losing support in his Central Asian core territories due to his long absence and the comparable success of other Islamic groups there. Indeed, in August 2005, dozens of people who claimed to be former IMU members rallied at the Dutch embassy in Tehran to demand refugee status.[17] Yet more Uzbek Muslims contacted other European countries for the same purpose.[18] However, Yo'ldosh also denounced the presidents of Uzbekistan, Kyrgyzstan, and Tajikistan, and wowed vengeance for the Muslims killed in Andijon in 2005,[19] a statement that may support the supposition that the IMU had provided funding there in anticipation of the affair.

The IMU in Waziristan

The IMU also suffered an uneasy existence in Waziristan. Already in June 2002, Pakistani security forces killed six alleged IMU members in South Waziristan and Kohat after they had killed a policeman and an intelligence officer.[20] Further conflicts soon followed. The fighting with Pakistani security forces around Wana in South Waziristan became particularly severe in March 2004, and a general Pakistani offensive followed from late 2003 onwards.[21] In Afghanistan, the IMU had been protected by the Taliban. In Pakistan, the IMU henceforth fell under the protection of the Mehsuds, a powerful local tribe which dominated South Waziristan. In particular, the IMU became associated with the important Taliban-supporter Baitullah Mehsud, who led large numbers of Pakistani Taliban and soon came into conflict with the Pakistan Army. The IMU henceforth became as closely allied to the Pakistani Taliban as it had been to the Afghan Taliban. Yo'ldosh was reportedly present as a witness to the 2006 peace agreement between the Pakistan Army and the Taliban in South Waziristan. In December 2007, Baitullah Mehsud formed the Tehrik-e-Taliban Pakistan (TTP), which he then led from its formation until his death in a CIA drone attack in September 2009. The IMU supported the TTP in its various activities, for instance by sending fighters to Swat when the Mehsud ally Maulana Fazlullah began his militant activities there. The IMU also retained its international networks. For instance, several Uighurs train with the IMU in South Waziristan, before they reportedly returned to China to attack targets in Xinjiang.[22]

However, problems soon arose in the relationship between the IMU and local Pashtuns in Waziristan. The exact cause for this largely remains unknown, although it seems likely that the IMU was caught up in internecine rivalry within the local Ahmadzai Wazirs, many of whom were hostile to the Mehsuds.[23] In March 2007, Uzbek extremists and local Pashtun militants clashed in the town of Azam Varsak in South Waziristan, close to the Afghan border. At least 15 people died as a result of the fight, and the IMU was forced to leave its bases in and around Wana, at least for the time being.[24]

In January 2008, Yo'ldosh confirmed his support for Baitullah Mehsud, calling for intensified *jihad* against the Pakistani security forces.[25] Following Baitullah Mehsud's death in September 2009, Yo'ldosh reiterated his support for the new TTP leader, Hakimullah Mehsud.[26] However, on 26 September 2009, Yo'ldosh was himself mortally wounded in a CIA drone attack in South Waziristan.[27] He reportedly died on 1 October and was replaced as head of the IMU by Usman Jan, the group's until then deputy leader.[28] Usman Jan was in his turn targeted by a CIA drone in January 2010, but he may have survived the attack.[29] On 17 August 2010, the IMU finally confirmed the death of Yo'ldosh, and announced that he had been replaced as Amir by one Usmon Odil (Usman Adil), presumably the Usman Jan already mentioned.[30]

The IMU Networks in Europe

Despite the IMU's operations in Waziristan and apparent activities in the Central Asian republics, the organization had not neglected the war in Afghanistan, which it continued to fight, either in rivalry or cooperation with another Uzbek group, the IJU. The IMU also did not neglect its supporters elsewhere. It soon became clear that the IMU had at its disposal networks of supporters and activists in Turkey and Europe as well as in Central Asia. In May 2008, French, German, and Dutch security agencies reported that they had detained ten individuals, most of them of Turkish background, on suspicion of running a network to send money to the IMU. The network had been led by Irfan Demirta°, of Turkish and Dutch origin.[31] Although this particular network was broken up, it seems likely that the IMU still enjoys the assistance of support networks in Turkey and Western Europe. In September 2008, for instance, the IMU posted a German-language propaganda video on the Internet in support of the Afghan Taliban. The IMU asked Muslim men and women to come to join the *jihad*.[32] This may have been a deliberate attempt to copy the success of the IJU in attracting German-speaking recruits. It may also have been a sign of increased cooperation between the two groups.

The Islamic Jihad Union: The Younger Generation of Uzbek Extremists Comes of Age

Following the Taliban defeat in Afghanistan and their 2001/2002 rout into Pakistan, the surviving Uzbek extremist leaders within the IMU could not agree on how best to continue the holy war. Some IMU leaders stayed with Yo'ldosh, who hid in South Waziristan and henceforth appeared to concentrate on the war in Afghanistan and local rivalries in Pakistan. Others, led by Najmiddin Jalolov and Suhail Buranov, in presumably early 2002 withdrew to North Waziristan. There, most likely in March 2002, they founded a new group, which later came to be called the Islamic Jihad Union.[33] Unlike Yo'ldosh, Jalolov and Buranov seem to have been more interested in global *jihad* of the type waged by Al-Qaida.[34]

Najmiddin Kamolitdinovich Jalolov (born in 1972 in Andijon; alias Abu Yahya Muhammad Fatih, Muhammad Foteh Bukhoriy, and Abdurakhmon; Fatih or Foteh signifies "Conqueror") appears to have been a member of the IMU since at least the late 1990s and perhaps from the outset. He was known to have been trained at Al-Qaida camps, presumably in Afghanistan. Jalolov was sentenced to death by an Uzbekistani court in 2000 for his role in the 1999 Tashkent bombings but was never apprehended. Jalolov now appointed as his deputy another Uzbek named Suhail Fatilloyevich Buranov (born in 1983 in Tashkent; alias Sohail Mansur, alias Abu Huzaifa). Buranov was known to have been trained at an Al-Qaida camp in Khost province, Afghanistan. Criminal charges had been filed against him in 2000, which would seem to confirm that he too then belonged to the IMU.[35] However, considering his young age at the time, he is unlikely to have been a founding member.

The core of the IJU accordingly consisted of former IMU members who had broken away from Yo'ldosh to work more closely with Al-Qaida against its global rather than regional enemies.[36] The IJU had its headquarters and ran training camps in North Waziristan (in Mir Ali), unlike those of the IMU which were located in South Waziristan (around Wana). While the IMU turned towards the

Mehsuds for protection, the IJU instead became the junior partner in an alliance with the Haqqani network (a fundamentally autonomous wing of the Afghan Taliban movement based in Miram Shah, the administrative centre of North Waziristan, and named after its leader, Jalaluddin Haqqani) and Al-Qaida.[37] The relationship with Al-Qaida with time became increasingly public. In late January 2008, Abu Laith al-Libi, the Libyan liaison officer between the Al-Qaida leadership and the IJU, was killed in a CIA drone attack in Pakistan. The IJU confirmed his death, referring to him as "our Shaikh."[38] The IJU again acknowledged its relationship with Al-Qaida in a video communiqué on 5 June 2009, showing several IJU commanders with another Libyan Al-Qaida member, Abu Yahya al-Libi.[39]

Even so, it was soon shown that the IJU, first known to outsiders simply as the Islamic Jihad Group, was even more involved in the Central Asian republics than the IMU. Indeed, the IJU, as it became known in 2005 in the American and British lists of banned terrorist organizations, first rose to fame only for a series of plots to use suicide bombers in Uzbekistan.[40] The IJU is generally believed to have been behind the suicide bombings in Tashkent and Bukhara in March and April 2004, in which both male and female suicide bombers were used, and almost certainly conducted the coordinated suicide bombing attacks in Tashkent on 30 July 2004 against the American and Israeli embassies and the office of the Uzbekistani Prosecutor General, all for which the IJU claimed responsibility.[41]

In the trials that followed the events and arrests of 2004, the evidence presented indicated that a radical Jamoat group led by one Farkhad Kazabkhayev had been operating in Tashkent, Bukhara, and Samarkand since 2000. The trial proceedings also indicated that others, including overall leader Jalolov based in Waziristan, may have played a role linking this Jamoat with a network that facilitated the movement of small amounts of weapons and men to training camps in Pakistan.[42] There was also an IJU cell in Kazakhstan, headed by Akhmed Biymurzayev (Ahmad Bekmirzayev) and Zhakshybek Biymurzayev. The former died in the attacks in Uzbekistan. The latter had apparently received training in Afghanistan, and had played a significant role in the IMU incursions into the Batken region in 1999 and 2000, which if correct would have made him yet another early IMU member who had changed his allegiance to the IJU, presumably along with Jalolov and Buranov.[43] Several Kazakh members of the cell had been trained in Shymkent in southern Kazakhstan.[44]

On the eve of the Andijon affair on 13 May 2005, the IJU rapidly posted a communiqué on the Internet, in which it expressed its support for any uprising against the Uzbekistani Government, declared war on the Karimov Government, and called on all Muslims to join in the attack. The statement, which was written in vague terms and signified no particular knowledge of the events in Andijon, was signed by the Amir of the IJU, Muhammad Foteh Bukhoriy, that is, Jalolov.[45] The United States and Israeli embassies in Tashkent took the threat from the IJU very seriously. In response to a "specific terrorist threat" the two embassies in early June 2005 withdrew non-essential staff from the country.[46]

The IJU Networks in Europe

The IJU then turned its attention towards Europe. On 4 September 2007, a plot to attack possibly Frankfurt airport and an American air base in Germany was foiled with the arrest of three men, two of them German converts to Islam, Fritz Gelowicz and Daniel Schneider and the third a Turk, Adem Yılmaz. The group, which became known in the media as the "Sauerland cell," had trained in Pakistan and had links with the IJU. Later on, a German Turk, Atilla Selek, was arrested as well.[47] On 11 September 2007, the IJU posted a communiqué on a Turkish web site which stated that the three men arrested in Germany had planned attacks on the Ramstein air base and the United States and Uzbekistani consulates in Germany.[48] The IJU had by then come to rely on several Turkish-language web sites.[49] In them, the IJU used a Turkish name, İslami Cihad İttehadi (ICI, translated by the group into English as Ittihad Islamic Jihad).

It soon became clear that the "Sauerland cell" formed part of a larger group, consisting of about thirty extremists, mostly ethnic Turks living in Germany but also several converts. Between ten and twenty of them had participated in terrorist training in IJU camps in Pakistan. This was unprecedented, since ethnic Turks in Europe had not earlier been seen to turn to extremism. Now several were reported to have been to IJU camps in North Waziristan.[50] Previously, IJU recruits had been sent to commit terrorist acts in Central Asia or to participate in guerrilla warfare in Afghanistan; now the IJU had trained European recruits and dispatched them back to Europe to engage in terrorism there.

The IJU networks in Europe were not confined to Germany. In April 2009, Turkish security forces arrested over thirty militant extremists, most of them allegedly IJU members, including the IJU leader in Turkey, Mahmut Kaplan alias Abu Muhammad.[51] IJU networks may have existed in other countries too, since in May 2008, as noted, French, German, and Dutch security agencies detained several people, most of them of Turkish origin, for suspicion of supporting the IMU.[52] It does not seem too far-fetched to argue that in communities where one Uzbek group would have supporters, another one would most likely find a few of its own.

The IJU Media Wings

The IJU maintained a quite professional media wing, known as Badr at-Tawhid ("Full Moon of Monotheism"). The group also published in German and Turkish with another media outfit, Elif Medya.[53] Both seem to have understood what kind of media strategy goes down well in the West. The media campaign focused on fighting crusaders, which appealed to an extremist Muslim audience, and to fight dictatorships such as those of Central Asia, which appealed to the western media. The IJU in October 2009 even claimed not to be connected to Al-Qaida, so as to present itself in better light to a western audience.[54]

Badr at-Tawhid by early 2010 seemed to have some relationship to yet another jihadist web site, tawba.info, allegedly produced by the Jamaat Bulgar group of Russian-speaking Islamic extremists.[55] This was unsurprising, since already in 2007 Andrey Batalov, a Russian convert to Islam, had been arrested in Afghanistan, disguised by a burqa, in a truck loaded with explosives. He admitted to having received some kind of training in presumably an IJU camp in North Waziristan, although he claimed that he had never intended to take part in fighting.[56] Indeed, the IJU made considerable efforts to maintain contacts and recruits in many different countries and among many different ethnic backgrounds. In May 2007, Jalolov in an interview confirmed that the IJU had been in contact and worked on common targets with *jihadists* from the Caucasus.[57]

The IJU and Pakistan

Despite its apparent focus on Europe and Turkey, the IJU true to its allegiance to Waziristani militants remained engaged in hostilities with Pakistani security forces. In October 2006, three Pakistanis trained and supported by the IJU and its leader Jalolov went so far as to attempt improvised explosive devices (IED) attacks on government targets in the Pakistani capital of Islamabad.[58] In October 2007, the Pakistan Army launched an offensive against Uzbek fighters in Mir Ali in North Waziristan. The IJU was also active elsewhere in Pakistan. The group claimed to have attacked Pakistani military targets in Swat in late 2007.[59] Jalolov was killed on 14 September 2009 in North Waziristan in a CIA drone attack. He was replaced as Amir by Abdullah Fatih.[60]

The IJU (and IMU?) in the Central Asian Republics

From 2009, Uzbek terrorism appeared to have returned to its place of birth. On 25-26 May 2009, several attacks took place in Uzbekistan. A police checkpoint was attacked in Khonobod on the border with Kyrgyzstan and bombings occurred in nearby Andijon. The IJU claimed responsibility for the attacks a few days later.[61] In July, the IJU again voiced its support for jihad against Uzbekistan.[62] On 23 June 2009, Kyrgyzstan claimed to have killed five IMU terrorists in a special operation.[63] On 29 August 2009, a series of shootings took place in Tashkent, in which one alleged IMU member was killed.[64] In early June 2010, Tajikistan too claimed to have killed two IMU members in a special operation.[65] It is hard to assess the level of involvement, if any, of the IJU or IMU in these events. Both organizations have expressed their participation in and support for *jihad* against the governments of Uzbekistan, Kyrgyzstan, and Tajikistan. Both organizations certainly appear to have networks in place in these countries. Since the IJU split from the IMU, there exists the possibility that individuals cooperate with each other, even if they have given their allegiance to separate groups. There is also the possibility that security organs may mistake members of one organization for that of the other. On the other hand, there is some doubt whether all these incidents were properly attributed by the law enforcement organs of the countries involved. The temptation to label regular violent crime as terrorism may be strong. It may even be that individual IMU and IJU members have turned to regular crime to fund their activities, or even to support themselves. As described elsewhere,[66] the IMU once played a substantial role in narcotics trafficking out of Central Asia. The two groups may still be involved in such activities.[67]

The IJU's Recruitment in Turkey and Europe and the Concept of Jihad Tourism

Arguably, the main impact of the IJU has been as a promoter of international *jihad* and facilitator for extremist recruits from Turkey and Europe who wish to fight in Afghanistan. The memoirs of the German convert and IJU recruit Eric Breininger (who died in action on 28 April 2010[68]) give a vivid description of how new recruits from Turkey and Europe from the mid-2000s onwards reached the IJU training camps in Waziristan. Recruits to Waziristan first travelled by air to Iran (for which they needed a visa, something that caused difficulties for Breininger and his friend, the German-Lebanese Hussayn al-Mallah, although they eventually got 7-day transit visas upon landing in Tehran). Then they would board a domestic flight or bus from Tehran to Bam, from which they continued to Zahedan. There the recruits typically changed their names or adopted *noms de guerre*, apparently due to the fact that there the clandestine part of their journey began. Having arrived in Zahedan, they would take a taxi to a certain mosque (possibly the large Makki Mosque, reportedly an important centre for IJU logistics[69]), where a contact was waiting. This contact brought them to a safe house inhabited by facilitators (*ansar*), where they would wait a few days until a small group of recruits had shown up. The group would travel together along the apparently usual route, by bus across the Iranian-Pakistani border. Foreign-looking recruits such as Germans would instead travel in a private car to the Iranian-Pakistani border, hiding in burqas while crossing since women were usually not searched. From the border, they would then take one of the waiting Pakistani taxis to a certain hotel, while a native facilitator bought bus tickets and then put them on a bus to presumably Quetta. Foreign-looking recruits would remain in burqas during the ride. Upon arrival, other facilitators would meet them and take them to a safe house, where they finally could get out of their burqas. From there, the final leg of the journey was by car along a mountain road to a house belonging to yet other facilitators, this time of the IJU. Judging from Breininger's memoirs, it is quite possibly that all other facilitators met during the journey were freelancers rather than IJU members, if so presumably part of regular smuggling networks that moved recruits for money (although the IJU may well have been the ultimate broker and financier of the journey). At the IJU safe house, the new recruits would await other recruits, from countries as far apart as Turkey and Tajikistan, after which they went as a group to the training camp.[70]

To hide foreign *jihadists* in burqas was by then standard operating procedure for both the IJU and IMU. In addition to the already mentioned Breininger and the Russian Batalov, who both hid in burqas, the IMU in a 2008 interview pointed out that a dark-skinned Sudanese too had been successfully smuggled into Pakistan by the same means.[71] The same method was again used in June 2010, when another suspected IJU recruit from Germany was detained in Bannu district, north-western Pakistan, travelling from Mir Ali to Peshawar with a fake Pakistani passport and a burqa to hide his foreign appearance.[72]

In fact, so many German and German-speaking recruits reached the IJU that Breininger and friends founded the "Deutsche Taliban Mujahideen" (German Taliban Mujahidin), in total 6 men, with a certain

Abu Ishaaq al-Muhajir elected Amir.[73] This was not all, however. Breininger wanted unmarried Muslim girls to travel to their camp, so they all could get married. The girls would also learn to use weapons, "just like the mujahidin." Then the newly-weds, he argued, would raise a new generation of mujahidin who would know Arabic, Turkish, English, Pashto, Urdu, and the mother tongue of the parents, in his case German. The children would learn Islam and temper their bodies through sports and martial arts, and early on learn the use of weapons and military tactics. This would, he planned, produce a new "generation of terrorists" whose names did not exist in any security service data base.[74]

Indeed, from the mid-to late 2000s a growing number of Islamic extremists from Germany, including converts but many of Turkish or North African descent, travelled to Waziristan. Swedish extremists too joined them, as did several of apparently Kurdish extraction, although their choice of names alone cannot tell whether they were Kurds from Europe, Turkey, Iraq, or Iran. Some commentators even referred to the establishment of *jihadist* village of European fighters.[75] The white-faced European recruits had a reputation as dedicated fighters, since for them, unless with less obviously foreign faces, it took some perseverance to reach Waziristan. Indeed, in July 2008 complaints were voiced in an IJU communiqué that too many new recruits, in particular among Turks, were useless as *jihadist* fighters, since "they grew up in a democratic society" and therefore were prone to discuss commands rather than accepting and obeying them without questions. Furthermore, many had come to the IJU only to prove to their friends back home that they were more religious than them, or had come to escape social or other secular problems. Many were indeed no more than *jihad* tourists, who had come to Afghanistan only so that they could tell stirring tales of their exploits when they returned home to friends and family.[76]

The IMU and IJU in Afghanistan

The fact that both the IMU and IJU continued to maintain networks for recruitment and presumably smuggling in the Central Asian republics and in Europe did not mean that they neglected the war in Afghanistan. Both groups continued to support *jihadist* activities against Afghan security forces and foreign troops there. On 3 January 2008, the IJU claimed to have attacked British troops in Paktika province, Afghanistan. On 3 March, the IJU announced on a Turkish web site that a second-generation Turk living in Germany had carried out a suicide attack on American and Afghan troops in the same province. In April, this was followed by a video call for *jihad* by Eric Breininger, the German convert then in an IJU camp in Waziristan.[77] Then the IJU claimed responsibility for two other suicide attacks (on 31 May and 4 June) in Jalalabad city and Khost province, respectively, the first on an American convoy and the second on a military post.[78] In the same year, the IJU also claimed responsibility for several additional attacks in Paktika and Paktia provinces.[79] There was then no longer any question of whether the IJU had begun to participate in the war in Afghanistan, at least in the named provinces, which formed part of the region traditionally dominated by the group's protector in Waziristan, the Haqqani network.[80] However, from 2009, if not before, the IJU was also active in Kunduz province, further to the north. On 12 May 2009, two IJU operatives were arrested there.[81]

This was a new development, since the IJU had not previously been known to fight in northern Afghanistan. However, later in the year, it seems that the IMU too had moved combat teams there. By October and November 2009, several reports mentioned that IMU fighters (usually only referred to as "Uzbeks and Chechens") had been killed in Kunduz, fighting German and Afghan troops.[82] Whether the attribution by the security forces of these "Uzbeks and Chechens" to the IMU was correct remains unknown and should not be taken for granted, even though the IMU had a long history of fighting in Afghanistan.[83] Be that as it may, in December 2009 further details from the north followed. The Afghan National Security Directorate's press service stated that four IMU fighters led by Hafiz Nurillah, a resident of Faryab province, had been arrested.[84] If correct, this would indicate that the IMU by then had acquired local roots in northern Afghanistan. In January 2010, reports suggested that armed groups comprising Chechens, Uzbeks, and Tajiks had moved into positions in Ghowr-Teppa, Kunduz province. Whether they belonged to the IMU or IJU was unknown; yet, the participation of Tajiks, and their identification as such by Afghan security forces, again suggested that networks that included both local militants as well as foreign fighters may have been formed.[85] By February 2010, IMU fighters were reported in Jowzjan province too.[86] By April 2010, IMU fighters were noted in Baghlan province as well as in Kunduz province.[87] In Baghlan province, the government forces had in May 2010 not yet gained control over the Ahmadzai area of Dahan-e Ghowri District, where Pakistani, Chechen, Uzbek, and other foreign fighters were reported as being part of the resistance.[88] By June 2010, IMU fighters were reported even in the hitherto fairly calm Balkh province.[89]

Concluding Remarks

This brief history of the IMU and IJU shows that the two groups changed considerably in character on several occasions during the two decades in which their members have engaged in violence. Yet, many of their goals, tactics, and means of finance remained the same. The IMU and IJU accordingly remain a source of violence and instability in their many and varied areas of operations. Although the eyes of the world are focused on Afghanistan and Pakistan, it will not be enough to ensure stability there (in itself a difficult task). Tajikistan, Kyrgyzstan, and to some extent Uzbekistan remain fragile states with militant networks closely connected to those south of their borders. Uzbek extremists have played major roles in civil conflicts, such as in Tajikistan, Afghanistan, and Pakistan, and in transnational narcotics smuggling. In civil conflicts, they have indeed played the role of a foreign legion. Uzbek extremists have also encouraged further radicalization as far as away as in Turkey, Russia, and Europe. The existence of IJU and IMU bases in Waziristan has encouraged jihad tourism from Europe and Turkey to Pakistan and Afghanistan.

The IMU and IJU have been rivals for funds and recruits; however, now all original leaders are dead. It is likely that the causes of rivalry between the IMU and IJU will have died with them. The survivors will probably cooperate or even merge, since their networks already seem to overlap in many places and some of their members very possibly already collaborate on an individual basis. Any increased level of cooperation will probably be seen first in Afghanistan. The IMU and IJU have been a catalyst for terror and instability. Their propensity for violence should not be ignored, nor their effect in pushing state structures into excessive repression in the name of combating terrorism. Indeed, the activities of Uzbek extremists have been central to the retention, and even strengthening, of authoritarianism within the Central Asian state structures, thereby directly preventing these states from acquiring any increased level of democracy and popular legitimacy. This was attained by the extremists through the role of catalyst rather than through direct participation in government. As in many other countries, including outside the region, the state confronted with terrorism responded with the tools at its disposal, including increased powers to the security services and harsher legislation. Although neither the IMU nor IJU ever stood a chance of assuming power in Central Asia, their negative impact on state development there, and elsewhere, has been considerable. Whether their present terrorist activities in Europe will result in sufficient violence to cause a similar response there remains to be seen.

Notes and References

1. See the movement's web site, www.furqon.com; International Crisis Group (ICG), *Central Asia: Islamist Mobilisation and Regional Security*, ICG Asia Report 14, Osh/Brussels, 1 March 2001, 4. The present report is an updated and expanded version of the chapters on the IMU and IJU in Michael Fredholm, *Islamic Extremism as a Political Force in Central Asia: A Comparative Study of Central Asian Extremist Movements*, Asian Cultures and Modernity 12 (Stockholm: Stockholm University, October 2006).
2. Alexander Ignatenko, "Islamic Radicalism: A Cold War By-Product," *Central Asia and the Caucasus* 1 (2001): 101-12. See also Fredholm, *Islamic Extremism.*
3. On the origin of the movement, see Mehrdad Haghayeghi, *Islam and Politics in Central Asia* (New York: St. Martin's Press 1995), 93-4; William Fierman, "Political Development in Uzbekistan: Democratization?" in *Conflict, Cleavage, and Change in Central Asia and the Caucasus*, Karen Dawisha and Bruce Parrott (eds.) (Cambridge: Cambridge University Press 1997), 382; Bakhtiar Babadzhanov [Babajanov], "Islam in Uzbekistan: From the Struggle for 'Religious Purity' to Political Activism," in *Central Asia: A Gathering Storm?* Boris Rumer (ed.) (London: M.E. Sharpe 2002), 315-16, 328 n.55; Ahmed Rashid, *Jihad: The Rise of Militant Islam in Central* Asia (New Haven: Yale University Press 2002), 137-40; Vitaly V. Naumkin, *Radical Islam in Central Asia: Between Pen and Rifle* (Lanham, Maryland: Rowman and Littlefield 2005), 66-7; Bahtijar Babadžanov [Babajanov], "Le jihad comme idéologie de l''Autre' et de 'l'Exilé' à travers l'étude de documents du Mouvement islamique d'Ouzbekistan," *Cahiers d'Asie centrale* 15/16 (2007): 141-66. The words of Yo'ldosh are translated from Babadžanov, 150.
4. Yo'ldosh was born on 2 October 1967. Official records, Uzbekistan; Interpol web site, www.interpol.int.
5. Rashid, *Jihad,* 146. She publicly disowned her son in 1999.
6. Rashid, *Jihad,* 138-9; Ahmed Rashid, "Heart of Darkness," *Far Eastern Economic Review* (5 August 1999): 8-12; Ahmed Rashid, "The Taliban: Exporting Extremism," *Foreign Affairs* (November/December 1999): 22-35; Ahmed Rashid, "From Deobandism to Batken: Adventures of an Islamic Heritage," CACI Forum Transcription, 13 April 2000.
7. Orozbek Moldaliev, "An Incongruous War in the Valley of Poison: The Religious Conflict in Southern Kyrgyzstan," *Central Asia and the Caucasus* 1 (2000): 11-20; Rashid, "From Deobandism to Batken," *Washington Post,* 10 November 2001; Rashid, *Jihad*, 137-8. Some report his year of birth as 1968. Other reports indicate that Hojiyev was born in 1967: see Vitaly V. Naumkin, *Militant Islam in Central*

Asia: The Case of the Islamic Movement of Uzbekistan, Berkeley Programme in Soviet and Post-Soviet Studies, Working Paper (Berkeley: University of California 2003), 22; or 1969: see Naumkin, *Radical Islam*, 68. He reportedly returned from Afghanistan in 1988, which would seem to suggest the earlier year as his year of birth. Hojiyev was later publicly disowned by his sister Makhbuba Ahmedova and his brother Nasyr Hojiyev (both arrested in 2000). Soon after, so did his mother. Rashid, *Jihad*, 147.

8. Rashid, *Jihad*, 140.
9. Fredholm, *Islamic Extremism.*
10. Esmer Islamov, "Sightings of IMU Militants Reported in Remote Area of Uzbekistan," *Eurasia Insight* (9 July 2003). www.eurasianet.org.
11. Richard Weitz, "Storm Clouds over Central Asia: Revival of the Islamic Movement of Uzbekistan (IMU)?" *Studies in Conflict and Terrorism* 27, no. 6 (2004): 512-13.
12. Zafar Abdullaev, "Tajikistan: Concern at New Islamic Group," *IWPR's Reporting Central Asia* 280 (27 April 2004); Zoya Pylenko, "Suspected IMU Member Escapes from Tajik Prison," *Central Asia-Caucasus Analyst* (22 February 2006).
13. On the events in Andijon, see Shirin Akiner, "Violence in Andijan, 13 May 2005," London 7 June 2005. Her report was subsequently published as Shirin Akiner, *Violence in Andijan, 13 May 2005: An Independent Assessment* (Washington DC and Uppsala: Central Asia-Caucasus Institute and Silk Road Studies Programme, July 2005). The media's somewhat one-sided focus on repression in the Central Asian states, in particular in Uzbekistan, has influenced the international community in several ways. First, any information received from Central Asian law enforcement organs will routinely be treated as unsubstantiated, regardless of content. While it has to be said that such information at times is biased and incorrect, it would appear unwise to disregard all information derived from these sources simply because they have received a bad press. Second, the way the situation in Uzbekistan in particular has been framed in the western media means that western governments only with great difficulty, or not at all, can refuse asylum to Uzbekistani citizens, even if they are known or suspected terrorists, since there are difficulties in separating *bona fide* refugees escaping from persecution by authoritarian government from terrorists and extremists fleeing from *bona fide* Central Asian counter-terrorism efforts.
14. Interfax, 20 September 2005.
15. RFE/RL *Newsline*, 13 June 2005; IWPR, *Reporting Central Asia* 387, 15 June 2005.
16. *Kommersant,* 13 May 2006; IWPR, *Reporting Central Asia* 448, 19 June 2006; Sanobar Shermatova, "IMU may return into politics only if

and when the existing geopolitical parity in Central Asia is ruined," Ferghana.ru, 8 February 2008. The captive was identified as 30-year-old Abdurahim Khojayev from the Syrdarya region of Uzbekistan. His name is a common one, but it is possible that the Kyrgyzstanis, perhaps wrongly, connected him with the already mentioned IMU leader Ilhom Hojiyev, alias Commander Abdurahmon, the relative of the late Namangani.

17. Ikbaldjon Mirsayitov, "The Islamic Movement of Uzbekistan: Development Stages and Its Present State," *Central Asia and the Caucasus* 42 (2006): 110-14. The video statements were issued on 10 January, in August, and on 11 September 2006. The IMU maintains a web site in Uzbek: www.furqon.com.
18. In Sweden, e.g., no less than 530 people born in Uzbekistan received asylum in 2005. In comparison, in the period 1994-2001 this number varied between 16 and 32 per year, rising to between 57 and 120 annually in the period 2002-04. SCB national statistics.
19. Ferghana.ru, 13 September 2006.
20. Weitz, "Storm Clouds," 510.
21. Mike Redman, "Central Asian Militant Group Remains Active in Pakistan," *Eurasia Insight* (24 March 2004) (www.eurasianet.org); Daan van der Schriek, "War in Waziristan," *Central Asia-Caucasus Analyst* (3 November 2004).
22. See, e.g., *Daily Times* (Pakistan), 3 October 2009.
23. See, e.g., Guido Steinberg, *A Turkish al-Qaeda: The Islamic Jihad Union and the Internationalization of Uzbek Jihadism,* Center for Contemporary Conflict, n.d. (July 2008).
24. See, e.g., RIA Novosti, 8 March 2007.
25. See, e.g., Steinberg, *A Turkish al-Qaeda.*
26. Yo'ldosh was, for instance, shown with Hakimullah Mehsud in a video released by the IMU's media wing, Studio Jundullah. NEFA Foundation web site, www.nefafoundation.org.
27. See, e.g., *Daily Times* (Pakistan), 3 October 2009; Jim Nichols, *Central Asia's Security: Issues and Implications for U.S. Interests,* Congressional Research Service Report RL30294, 11 March 2010, 9.
28. *Hindustan Times,* 3 October 2009. There have been conflicting reports on both the date of the drone attack and on whether Yo'ldosh survived or not. However, the appointment of a new head would seem to confirm his death before this date.
29. *USA Today,* 17 January 2010; *Dawn,* 18 January 2010.
30. IMU web site, http://furqon.com.
31. Europe1 (www.europe1.fr), 19 July 2008; AFP, 20 July 2008.
32. NEFA Foundation web site, www.nefafoundation.org; NEFA release date 29 January 2009, original date September 2008.
33. IJU: *Islomiy Jihod Ittihodi,* or *Itihaad al-Jihad al-Islami,* perhaps more

correctly translated as the Alliance of Islamic Jihad; its original name was *Jamaat al-Jihad al-Islami,* Society of Islamic Jihad, or simply *Jamoat* in Uzbek.

34. Europol, *TE-SAT 2008: EU Terrorism Situation and Trend Report* (The Hague: European Police Office, 2008), 18. The IJU eventually confirmed that the group had been established in 2002. Michail Logvinov, "Islamische Dschihad-Union," *Die Kriminalpolizei* (March 2010), citing an IJU communiqué dated 31 May 2007 (www.sehadetzamani.com).
35. Jalolov was born on 1 April 1972, Buranov on 11 October 1983. Details on the various names, aliases, and addresses of the IJU leaders, and criminal charges against them, were published in, among others, United Nations Security Council Al-Qaida and Taliban Sanctions Committee, SC/9396, 23 April 2008; United States Department of the Treasury, press release hp-1035, 18 June 2008; Office of Foreign Assets Control, Specially Designated Nationals and Blocked Persons: Financial Institution Letter FIL-60-2008 (Washington, DC: Federal Deposit Insurance Corporation (FDIC), 26 June 2008).
36. In June 2008, an IJU video claimed that one Uzbek IJU member had taken part already in IMU's 1999 attack in Kyrgyzstan, and later had fought in Afghanistan against the Northern Alliance and then against Coalition forces. Nichols, *Central Asia's Security,* 9.
37. See, e.g., Steinberg, *A Turkish al-Qaeda.*
38. He was probably killed on 29 January 2008 in North Waziristan, according to the Pakistani military. See, CNN, 31 January 2008; Steinberg, *A Turkish al-Qaeda.*
39. *Der Spiegel* (www.spiegel.de), 5 June 2009.
40. See the presentation to the British Parliament by Home Office Minister Hazel Blears, 13 October 2005.
41. Press statement by Richard Boucher, spokesman for the Department of State, Washington DC, 26 May 2005, upon the inclusion of the group in the list of specially designated global terrorist organizations under Executive Order 13224. For a brief summary of the suicide bombings in March and April 2004, see RFE/RL *Central Asia Report* 4, nos.14, 15, 33 (7 April 2004, 14 April 2004, 1 September 2004); Artie McConnell, "Tashkent Bombings Signal Rise in Islamist Activities," *Jane's Intelligence Review* (May 2004): 14-17. The group claimed responsibility for the March and April 2004 attacks in a communiqué conveyed by an opponent of the Karimov Government in exile, Hazratqul Khudoyberdi, through the web site, www.centrasia.ru, 3 April 2004. The group claimed responsibility for the 30 July 2004 attacks in a second communiqué, signed by Deputy Amir Sayfurrahmon and again conveyed by Hazratqul Khudoyberdi through the web site, www.centrasia.ru, 31 July 2004.

42. AP, 27 July 2004; Cerwyn Moore, "Uzbek Terror Networks: Germany, Jamoat and the IJU," *Terrorism Monitor* 5, no. 21 (November 2007). Yet another member was mentioned as being called Abu Muhammad.
43. Naumkin, *Radical Islam*, 117; IWPR, *Reporting Central Asia* 380 (20 May 2005); Marat Yermukanov, "Kazakh Security Services Trumpet Victory over 'Al-Qaida Members'," *Central Asia-Caucasus Analyst* 3 (November 2004).
44. See Steinberg, *A Turkish al-Qaeda.*
45. The communiqué was as before conveyed by Hazratqul Khudoyberdi through the web site, www.centrasia.ru, 13 May 2005.
46. Reuters, 6 June 2005. On 2 June 2005, the United States Department of State issued a travel warning due to the sudden terrorist threat.
47. See *Economist*, 8 September 2007; *Der Spiegel*, 12 September 2007, 9 October 2007 (www.spiegel.de). The group was reportedly first identified by the NSA. The operation was later handled by a joint CIA and German task force set up in Berlin. See also Moore, "Uzbek Terror Networks;" Logvinov, "Islamische Dschihad-Union."
48. *Der Spiegel,* 12 September 2007 (www.spiegel.de); IJU communiqué, 11 September 2007 (www.sehadetvakti.com).
49. The 11 September 2007 communiqué was posted on www.sehadetvakti.com ("Time for Martyrdom"), now defunct. The IJU has also posted information on www.sehadetzamani.com (in Turkish) and the more general jihadist web sites www.sodiqlar.com (in Uzbek) and www.cihaderi.net (in Turkish). The first communiqué posted on Turkish web sites seems to be dated April 2007. Logvinov, "Islamische Dschihad-Union."
50. See Steinberg, *A Turkish al-Qaeda.*
51. *Turkish Weekly,* 21 April 2009 (www.turkishweekly.net).
52. Europe1 (www.europe1.fr), 19 July 2008; AFP, 20 July 2008.
53. See the movement's various web sites.
54. Thomas M. Sanderson, Daniel Kimmage, and David A. Gordon, *From the Ferghana Valley to South Waziristan: The Evolving Threat of Central Asian Jihadists* (Washington DC: Center for Strategic and International Studies, March 2010), 12, citing www.sehadetzamani.com, 22 October 2009.
55. The group's web site, http://tawba.info/ru.
56. *New York Times,* 30 October 2007. Batalov's case can be found among the secret US military reports covering the war in Afghanistan that in July 2010 were exposed by the Wiki leaks web site (http://wikileaks.org/wiki/Afghan_War_Diary,_2004-2010). See Report Key 759114F2-5F50-4303-B45F-790FEE8B7526, document AFG20070826n804. According to this initial report, Batalov was unknowingly going to be used as a suicide bomber.
57. NEFA Foundation web site, www.nefafoundation.org; NEFA release date, 23 September 2009, original date 31 May 2007.

58. *Dawn*, 4 November 2006.
59. IJU communiqué, 19 December 2007 (www.sehadetvakti.com). See Steinberg, *A Turkish al-Qaeda*; Ronald Sandee, *The Islamic Jihad Union (IJU)*, NEFA Foundation, 14 October 2008, 15.
60. GEO TV Pakistan (www.geo.tv), 17 September 2009; Bill Roggio, "Two al Qaeda Leaders Reported Killed in North Waziristan Strike," *Long War Journal* (www.longwarjournal.org) (16 September 2009); Badr at-Tawheed communiqué, 27 September 2009 (www.sehadetzamani.com).
61. RIA Novosti, 26 May 2009; Deirdre Tynan, "Uzbekistan: Kyrgyz Officials Deny Islamic Militant Raids Originated in Kyrgyzstan," *Eurasia Insight* (www.eurasianet.org) (27 May 2009); *Der Spiegel* (www.spiegel.de), 5 June 2009. See also Nichols, *Central Asia's Security*, 6.
62. In a communiqué dated 3 July 2009. Logvinov, "Islamische Dschihad-Union."
63. Roman Muzalevsky, "Kyrgyz Operation Against IMU Reveals Growing Terrorist Threat," *Central Asia-Caucasus Analyst* (1 July 2009).
64. Deirdre Tynan, "Uzbekistan: Authorities Link Tashkent Shootout in August to Islamic Movement of Uzbekistan," *Eurasia Insight* (www.eurasianet.org) (9 September 2009).
65. Interfax, 4 June 2010. The same news report indicated that some 15 suspected members of the IMU were convicted in Tajikistan each year.
66. Fredholm, *Islamic Extremism*.
67. For a list of terrorist attacks in Tajikistan, Kyrgyzstan, and Uzbekistan in the period 2004-09, not all of which can be attributed to the IMU or IJU, see Sanderson, Kimmage, and Gordon, *From the Ferghana Valley to South Waziristan*, 27-9.
68. Abdul Ghaffar El Almani [Eric Breininger], *Mein Weg nach Jannah* (ElifMedya, posted online on 5 May 2010), 106.
69. Sandee, *Islamic Jihad Union*, 11. Sandee does not provide a source for this statement, and Breininger never identifies the mosque in his memoirs.
70. Abdul Ghaffar El Almani [Eric Breininger], *Mein Weg*, 82-5.
71. NEFA Foundation web site, www.nefafoundation.org; NEFA release date 29 January 2009, original date September 2008.
72. BBC News, 22 June 2010.
73. El Almani [Eric Breininger], *Mein Weg*, 102.
74. El Almani [Eric Breininger], *Mein Weg*, 103-04. The implication of this, and his choice of languages, is that he also foresaw attacks in Germany itself.
75. *Daily Telegraph* (www.telegraph.co.uk), 25 September 2009.
76. Logvinov, "Islamische Dschihad-Union," citing an IJU communiqué dated 23 July 2008 (www.sehadetzamani.com).
77. IJU communiqué, 3 March 2008. The suicide bomber, Cüneyt Çiftçi, had lived in Germany until April 2007. *Der Spiegel* (www.spiegel.de),

15 March 2009; Logvinov, "Islamische Dschihad-Union." See also Steinberg, *A Turkish al-Qaeda*; Sandee, *Islamic Jihad Union*, 15.

78. IJU communiqués, 1 June 2008, 5 June 2008 (http://sodiqlar.narod.ru). Judging from the chosen names of the suicide bombers, Said Kurdi and Abu Muslim Kurdi, they were presumably of Kurdish origin. The Jalalabad attack killed a US Marine. NPR (www.npr.org), 31 May 2008.
79. Sandee, *Islamic Jihad Union*, 16-17; based on IJU communiqués.
80. Thomas Ruttig, "Loya Paktia's Insurgency: The Haqqani Network as an Autonomous Entity," in *Decoding the New Taliban: Insights from the Afghan Field*, Antonio Giustozzi (ed.) (London: Hurst & Company 2009), 57-88.
81. Kunduz Executive Summary, 15 September 2009 (Programme for Culture and Conflict Studies).
82. See *Afghan Islamic Press news agency* (Peshawar), 11 October 2009; Reuters, 20 October 2009; *Pajhwok Afghan News* (Kabul), 5 November 2009.
83. Doubts on whether the Afghan security forces in fact could correctly identify what they customarily referred to as "Uzbeks and Chechens" were also expressed by foreign intelligence officers in Afghanistan, for instance among the secret US military reports exposed by the Wiki leaks web site. See Report Key EDD3627E-B5D4-417E-B0B6-CBEDA3B8F08F, document AFG20071009n1041. According to this report, "PRT CO spoke with ANP 6 today regarding his comments in an open source report on the 5 OCT air strike in Sarobi. In the source, ANP 6 stated that 16 Uzbek fighters were killed and one was captured; however, this conflicted with TF Eagles own assessment of the fighters and the BDA. ANP 6 received his intelligence from the Sarobi Chief of Police, and it seems likely that the COP and the locals assumed the fighters were Uzbeks only because they did not speak Pashto. TF Eagle identified the fighters as Turkish based off of SIGINT and the 1 captured EWIA."
84. Arzu TV (Mazar-e Sharif), 3 December 2009.
85. *Avesta* (Dushanbe), 22 January 2010, citing the governor of Kunduz province. The Tajiks may of course have come from Tajikistan.
86. Shamshad TV (Kabul), 10 February 2010, citing the governor of Jowzjan province.
87. Arzu TV (Mazar-e Sharif), 15 April 2010, citing General Gholam Sakhi, deputy commander of Shahin Military Corps No 209 in northern Afghanistan.
88. *Afghan Islamic Press news agency* (Peshawar), 17 May 2010, citing Morad Ali Morad, commander of Shahin Military Corps No 209.
89. Arzu TV (Mazar-e Sharif), 22 June 2010, citing General Abdol Rauf Taj, commander of the Balkh provincial police.

19

No Iron Curtain Against the South: *Jihadi* Influence in the Post-Soviet Space and its Potential for Conflict

Didier Chaudet

When one thinks about the fall of the "Iron Curtain," the images of the Berlin Wall naturally come to mind. But the fact is that the ideological and political "Iron Curtain" was shielding as much as possible the entire Soviet territory from foreign influence. Hence, when the USSR fell apart, new and different ideas came not only from the west but also from the south. The most radical form of *jihadism* has appeared in different parts of the former USSR.

The focus here will be on the impact of what appears to have been, first and foremost, foreign ideas, which found ways to influence local grievances, sometimes morphing them in a transnational fight. The Islamic Movement of Uzbekistan in the Ferghana Valley, the Caucasus Emirate in Northern Caucasus, and the Islamic Jihad Union (sometimes dubbed as the "Turkic Al Qaeda") are examples of such a fact. But the irony here is that even if the ideas can be seen as having been imported into the Soviet Union, the *jihadists* have been able to have an impact in Central Asia not simply because the Iron Curtain was gone. In fact, their impact has been possible because this Curtain did not disappear from the mind of a section of the leadership in the post-Soviet space, making them unable to deal adequately with the threat. Of course, the *jihadist* problem has not been the only source. As much as the issue is not only foreign, it cannot be seen as only local. The regional threat is Afghanistan, and more broadly speaking, the Af-Pak region. But ultimately, if the foreign influences have worsened the problem, the local problems also need to have focus and be dealt with accordingly.

To demonstrate this approach, I will focus first on what make the *jihadist* issue a local one in Russia and Central Asia. Then, it will be shown how foreign influences have indeed an impact on local Eurasian issues, with a particular focus on the Af-Pak region.

Local Roots: *Jihadi* influence in Russia and Central Asia

In the Arab world as in the post-Soviet space, local leaders often blame the West for every political trouble on their territories. But a simple analysis of internal political, economic, and social issues of those countries is enough to prove that often problems do not arise entirely due to external intervention. Of course, part of those problems cannot be attributed to bad government only. Some issues the post-Soviet space has to deal with have ancient roots. But still, one can see that internal factors have facilitated the growth of *jihadism* in Russia and Central Asia.

The Russian Situation

Jihadism in Russia grew due to two main elements that are at the core of Russian identity: first, an ambivalent relationship to local Islam, that is, in fact linked to the tense relations between the centre and a periphery—the case of North Caucasus may be cited here; and second, the desire of the elite to make sure Russia is acknowledged as a great power, at any cost.

Indeed, to say the least, Russia's Muslims have faced a historically difficult problem—the symbol representing the Orthodox Church itself is an issue—a cross on top of a crescent-planted after Ivan the Terrible's victory over the Tatars.[1] At present, tensions between a section of the Russian population and the Russian Muslim community exist due to the fears regarding the growing Muslim population. The official figures indicate a population of around 40 million.[2] However, according to the 2002 census, released in 2005, one finds that there are no more than 1,464 million Russian Muslims in a country with 138.7 million citizens. Besides, since 1999, the Slavic areas in Russia have seen a demographic growth and a parallel decrease of the Muslim minorities. It has been speculated that after 2016–17, after some increase, the Russian Muslim population will indeed decrease.[3] But even the projected increase will not mean much, because the Muslim population in Russia is extremely secular. It is even more the case when one focuses on the second largest ethnic group in Russia, the Tatar (5.5 million in total, 3 million in Tatarstan itself).[4]

Hence it seems that the ambivalent Russian relationship towards local Islam has no strong roots in reality. But more importantly, the

Kremlin has no particular problem towards Islam in Russia as a whole. What external actors see sometimes as "Islamophobia" seems to be, in fact, a "Caucasus-phobia." According to some Russian analysts, two-third of the Russian population is, in fact, Caucasus-phobic. This hatred is said to be stronger than the xenophobic attitude towards the Central Asian migrants.[5] And it is based on historical animosity. The Russian conquest of the area in the nineteenth century was colonization at its worst. Besides, the Chechens did not, like most of the other ethnic groups in Russia, share a strong nationalist sentiment even as partners during the Second World War or the Great Patriotic War as it is called in Russia. Instead, like some other minority groups, under suspicion of being sympathetic to the Germans, the Chechens have been deported to Central Asia. In February 1944, 100, 000 Chechens died during this deportation process. It explains why, with the fall of the USSR, the Chechens were so eager to get independence from the Kremlin. And it also explains why the Russians never wanted the Chechen moderates to have an upper hand. The First Chechen War (1994–96) was concluded by the negotiations of Khasavyurt (31 August 1996). This accord recognized Chechnya as a subject under international law. This law sought to regulate the relationship between Moscow and Grozny. It was a *de facto* recognition of Chechen independence.[6] But excluding the south, the new independent republic was surrounded by Russia. It had been crippled by war, and from an economic point of view, to oppose Moscow would have been pure madness. The Kremlin had a chance to stabilize the Chechen entity, maybe renegotiate its status in the future, and make sure the moderates, and not the *jihadists*, would have the upper hand. But it was not the Russian choice. Immediately after the accord, Moscow has pressurized other countries to sever diplomatic relations with the Chechen government. Without recognition from the international community or from the Kremlin,[7] the Caucasians in general, and the Chechens in particular, supported the cause of the *jihadis*.

Apart from this particular tension with the Caucasus, one should keep in mind Russia's compulsions to show its strength as a great power. According to the perception of the Russian elites, to maintain a great power status, show of strength was a must and any means can be used.[8] Hence, the very idea of compromise with the Chechens was not an option, because it would signify an undesirable status. Because Chechnya was seen as a "state within a state" that was not following Russian law, it appeared as a threat for national status, and was treated accordingly by President Putin.[9] Such an attitude favoured use of brute force as the only means to deal with Chechnya. It also favored rigid centralization. President Putin wanted to make everybody forget about the Yeltsin era, a time when Moscow had to negotiate with regional authorities. Such an authoritarian move was motivated by the memory of Yugoslavia. But this approach meant disregarding local specificities as in Dagestan that made the importance of local laws essential.[10] More importantly, it meant the organization of a quasi-feudal system: the local leaders are committed to Moscow but they are all powerful on their territories. They are often corrupt, do not hesitate to use brute force, and focused primarily on monopolizing the political and economic opportunities. Ramzan Kadyrov is a perfect illustration here: he was accepted to be a Chechen who would lead the war against the "rebels." At present 95 per cent of Chechnya's budget (US $2,48 billion) comes from the centre, but fund embezzlement is extremely pronounced.[11] But at the same time, Kadyrov is locally very powerful and cannot be touched, even by the Kremlin.[12] Such a situation means that the Kremlin has put itself in a situation of never-ending war, without having the tools to change policy.

The Central Asian Situation

However, Russia has not been an exception in terms of bad governance. Central Asian leaders also chose to be repressive in order to deal with any dissent. And as a result, they have bred the same kind of radicalism.

Of course, the entire situation cannot be blamed on the post-Soviet rulers. They had a nearly impossible political and economic situation at the beginning of the 1990s. Historically, already since the pre-Soviet, Tsarist times, Central Asia has been a producer of raw materials for Russia. All the industrial products came from the core of the Empire, to this periphery. After the fall of the USSR, and end of Soviet discipline the industries in Central Asia moved to Russia, or fell apart through lack of competitiveness or investment. For example, the Kyrgyz people were often working for the production of Soviet naval equipment.[13] The gap between rich and poor widened. And the richest were seldom honest. Mafia organizations became powerful in this area. They targeted the weakest in their own societies, for example women from the rural areas. Central Asian women have been lured overseas, mostly in the Middle East and in other CIS states.[14] Such a situation added to the misery of the "new poor" in Central Asia.[15] The dismissal of the Soviet empire was a "tragedy" according to President Putin and this has been all too real for them. They lost access to functioning public services (health, education, in particular). Borders that existed only on paper became real, and made trade very difficult. Many of them, like the industrial and construction workers, suffered due to severance of their links with Russia. Others were *budjetniki*, or budget workers, employed by firms that were funded by the Soviet state. There are also the average farm workers, as the fall of the Soviet Union also strongly affected agriculture. Last, but not least, one could add the young generation who were not lucky enough. The demographic explosion all over Central Asia, at a time of economic, social and political turmoil, made them natural victims of the post-Soviet chaos and an easy prey for radical movements with a strong ideology.

But the situation has been made worse with the Central Asian regimes choosing repression instead of compromise. It instigated local *jihadism*. The standing example is Uzbekistan, where the Uzbeki *jihadi* movement that became known as the IMU (Islamic Movement of Uzbekistan), emerged. At first, it emerged as a small movement of young men influenced by Islamist ideas who organized themselves in the Ferghana Valley, in order to pressurize the government to deal with rising price of common goods and to fight crime. They also wanted Islam to fill the ideological void after the fall of communism. It does not seem that they had a clear vision of what an Islamic republic would be, but it seemed basically a remedy, for them, of the ills of their times (corruption, criminality, the disappearance of public services). In the face of such opposition, at first, the Uzbek regime simply defended itself against any alternative influence in the Tashkent area. But the radical voices in Ferghana tried to connect with the rest of the opposition, whether they were moderate Islamists or secular nationalists and democrats.[16] It was a clear threat against power that was exercised by President Islam Karimov and the elites around him. The regime chose extreme repression as a way of defense. By 1993 any opposition element that was in jail was exiled. Even outside Uzbekistan, the regime tracked down opposition groups located anywhere within Central Asia. Imprisonment and exile made the IMU the strongest opponent of Tashkent and unwilling to negotiate any deal. Because of the political choices of the Uzbek regime, a compromise like the one that ended the Tajik civil war (1992–97) was impossible. Hence the only answer of the IMU was violence against the Uzbek state, particularly as the attacks between 1999 and 2001 revealed.[17]

Broadly speaking, Central Asian regimes have largely targeted Islamic and Islamist groups that were not under governmental control. They targeted clearly non-violent groups, like the HT (Hizb ut-Tahrir, or Party of Liberation) and the TJ (Tabligh Jamaat). Indeed, there are more members of HT in jail than from any other organization. And in late 2004, in Uzbekistan, the TJ is perceived as a terrorist organization that was supported by western NGOs.[18] HT is an extremist group whose ideology is transnational—calling for a new transnational Caliphate that would not be part of the UN, and would refuse to have any diplomatic relations with any "imperialist" power, in particular the US. Besides, the Ḥizb believes in the "inevitability" of the clash of civilizations.[19] But at the same time, it did not evolve as a violent movement after the Iraq War, even if some of its members wanted to.[20] The TJ can be accused even less of being dangerous for the Central Asian states. It preaches return to Muslim forms of governance. From their point of view, the goal is not to impose *sharia* by force, but make the individual apply the *sharia* to himself.[21] Hence such an ideology is seen to be dangerous politically for the Central Asian regimes. They have been able to attract a sizeable number of people: 15,000 to 20,000 members for HT in Central Asia at the beginning of the years 2000s [22] and 10,000 TJ members in Kyrgyzstan only.[23] Hence they are persecuted because they are the few of the religious/political institutions that are not under government control. Such an approach has clearly resulted in radicalization that can assume dangerous proportions in the long run.

Foreign Influence

It is evident that *jihadism* in Central Asia has local roots. To claim that external forces have damaged internal security that is actually caused by militant groups would not be entirely true. But it does not mean that foreign countries and ideologies do not have an impact. Such an impact can be serious.

First, it is important to understand the impact of the global *jihadi* community and ideology on local tensions in the post-Soviet space. In Russia, one could argue that *jihadism* has "hijacked," at least partially, the local Chechen fight. It needed a new battleground and the first Chechen war happened at a very convenient time. At the beginning of the 1990s, the *jihadis* who had fought the Soviets in the 1980s felt deserted. What ensued after Soviet forces left Afghanistan was a terrible civil war in which the mujahidins were the worst persecutors.[24] The "Afghan-Arabs" were looking for another *jihad* to fight and seek redress and the fight for Chechen independence became very popular. Indeed, in *jihadi* circles, the distant enemy was not necessarily the US but any great power. And with the fall of the USSR, a sizeable number of *jihadis* saw in the new Russia a power weak enough to be the perfect target. This was the thought of Ibn

Khattab, the charismatic leader of the foreign fighters and the *jihadists* in Chechnya. Osama Bin Laden tried to convince him to follow his *jihad* against the US specifically. But Ibn Khattab declined, seeing this idea as unrealistic. In the 1990s, the vision of Ibn Khattab was clearly the one that seemed to be more attractive. Indeed, even Al Zawahiri, a close follower of Bin Laden in Sudan, did not follow the leader of Al Qaeda in Afghanistan in spring 1996. Originally, he was close to the vision of Russia as the distant enemy that as a great power that already suffered defeat (withdrawal from Afghanistan) and was weakened by the end of the Cold War, and therefore looked like an interesting target. The goal was, from his point of view, to help the fragmentation of Russia through troubles in Northern Caucasus, in order to facilitate on this part of territory, the formation of an Islamic Republic that would give shelter to the *jihadis*. He preferred to go to Chechnya, in order to create his own independent organization, targeting the Russian state. His attempt was a total disaster, and the Russians put him in jail for several months. After this bad experience, he returned to Bin Laden and followed his ideals.[25] Extreme nationalists on the Chechen side, like Shamil Basaev, were eager to follow the *jihadi* fight if it meant to receive support, and in particular money, for their war of independence.[26]

But the "hijacking" has not been possible only because the Chechen cause has been, for a while, fashionable among international *jihadists*. They made themselves extremely useful to the Chechens, in a way the international community could not or would not. The Afghan-Arabs were approximately 300 in number in August 1995. This group has not been essential for the fight by itself. But they were able to attract young local recruits through money, weapons, and their military experience. Soon, an alliance between local Islamists or extreme nationalists and their foreign mentors took place, making the influence of *jihadism* more important for Chechnya than it was originally envisaged. After the first war, the *jihadis* were able to take control of the training camps of the new Chechen "army." Quickly the training became not only military but political. Radical clerics from Pakistan and Saudi Arabia were invited to supervise the soldiers ideologically and religiously.[27] Between the two wars, the *jihadis* truly became part of the political spectrum in the area. They gave their support to the most extreme kind of nationalism in Chechnya, the one with a pan-Caucasian agenda. The threat to the territories east and west of the quasi-independent regions like Dagestan was real. The incursion of followers of Basayev and Ibn Khattab in the latter half of August 1999 was a proof of the seriousness of the issue.

It helped fuel Russian intransigence, breeding a vicious circle that nurtured the second Chechen war, and the weakening of the moderates in the Chechen resistance. Nowadays the upper echelons of the opposition on the ground are dominated by people influenced by the original *jihadi* vision, coupled with a pan-Caucasian/extreme nationalist approach. Supporting this fact is the new situation of the resistance, which is not only composed of Chechens, but also of other inhabitants of the region. Since the "abolition" of the Chechen Republic of Ichkeria in October 2007, with a declaration of its leader, Doku Umarov, the rebels have been fighting in the name of the Caucasus Emirate.[28]

In Central Asia, at least among the most violent groups, the foreign ideological influence of *jihadism* has not been not negligible, especially after 9/11. Part of the Uzbek *jihadis* felt disoriented with the failure of the Taliban in Afghanistan, and also tired to fight the Uzbek regime of President Islam Karimov that did not accept their local political agendas which could destabilize Uzbekistan. But others have been more radicalized by the repression by the state, and grew closer to the Al Qaeda, and its ideology. The best example of this influence has been the Islamic Jihad Union (IJU). They split from the IMU in 2002, partly for ideological differences. The IJU adopted the transnational vision of Bin Laden, and focused on Central Asia as a whole, and for a while, on Pakistan when it had a safe haven in the tribal areas. The IJU embraced the vision of a war against the distant enemy. The best example of that has been the terrorist plot against Germany, stopped before its completion in September 2007. The IJU appeared then as a true "Turkic Al Qaeda," with leaders being still Uzbeks, and based in Waziristan, but with foot soldiers being Turkish, German-Turkish, and German converts. Besides, in 2004, the IJU has been the first to use suicide bombing on Central Asian soil, and to target specifically symbols of the distant enemy, i.e. the American and Israeli embassies. Hence, here also, one can see the adoption by Central Asians of methods, and conceived of extremist versions overseas.

But it is important to notice that *jihadism* as a global ideology, nurtured by inner debates about ideology, made the Uzbek rebels move away from Islamic nationalism already before 9/11.[29] Primary evidence shows that contrary to the Tajik Islamists, the members of the IMU already accepted the idea promoted by Khattab or Bin Laden, that the "near enemy" President Islam Karimov was not the only enemy. They adopted the view that as their Uzbek President, the US, Russia, Christians broadly speaking, and Jews as a whole, were enemies that deserved to be targeted.[30] It appears already that the choice between a true Islamic nationalist agenda and a radical *jihadi* vision was made in summer 1999. One of the leaders, Tahir Yuldashev, wanted to use seized Japanese hostages to force Islam Karimov to negotiate a political settlement, like the one the Tajik Islamists got in 1997. The military leader of the IMU, Juma Namangani, refused, preferred a ransom, and a consistent fight to death against the regime, without any compromise. Such an extremist approach is an indication of the politicized vision of *jihadi* ideology. The post-9/11 environment made only the *jihadis* stronger.[31]

The Af-Pak Region

It appears that indeed, the influence from the *jihadi* international community have spiraled local tensions in the post-Soviet space. It is now clear that this influence, especially from the Af-Pak region, has made things worse.

In a way, it is not that astonishing. Because of geographic and human proximity, Afghanistan has always had some impact on Central Asia. The Tajiks and the Uzbeks are important minorities in Afghanistan. For political reasons, this country has often been a refuge for political dissidents coming from the north. It has been the case for the emirates of Bukhara and Khiva where after the Russian revolution the Basmachis infiltrated taking advantage of the Russian civil war. Since the fall of the USSR, it has been the case for the Islamic Revival Party of Tajikistan (in the northern part of the country, supported as much by Massoud as by Helmkatyar) and for the Islamic Movement of Uzbekistan (supported by the Taliban). The most dangerous expression of *jihadism* in Central Asia, the IMU has made Afghan a safe haven. Until 1999 the rebels had been sheltered in Tavildara, 170 southeast of Dushanbe. But after their 1999 attacks the Tajiks pressurized them to leave. Since that time onwards, they were based in Afghanistan and stayed close to Central Asia and were able to continue their attacks against the regime of Islam Karimov till 2001.[32]

But the Af-Pak region has been a strong ideological influence on Central Asian *jihadis*. Already during the 1980s, the Afghan *jihad* was an important voice on the religious debate in Central Asia, against the communists by supporting unofficial Islam. This debate expressed the divide among generations. The older one, which still had in mind the terrible Soviet repression, insisted that the real "holy war" was first and foremost a fight against oneself. For the younger generation that was impressed by the Afghan mujahidin, it was an

Islamic duty to support a real, violent opposition to the adversary, i.e. the Soviet state. Those "reformists" proclaimed their desire for an Islamic state, sometimes without understanding the implications of the concept. The best example of that is Abdullah Saidov. He tried to organize people in order to ask for the establishment of an Islamic republic at the 27th Congress of the communist party.[33] Such an extravagant plea is just an example of the fact that the events in Afghanistan had definitely an impact on the Central Asians. But Pakistan's situation is also of importance here. First some Central Asians found refuge on Pashtun territories, and settled in the tribal areas in Pakistan, during the 1980s.[34] Others came later, when they were targeted in Central Asia, in particular in Uzbekistan and Tajikistan, as part of the opposition or as too devout. There they were accepted by Deobandi *madarsas*, [35] i.e. the same religious school that trained and took care of the mujahidin during fights against the Soviets and subsequently also nurtured the Taliban. They found there an ideological environment that clearly radicalized them. Islamabad promised the independent post-Soviet regimes that Central Asian radicals would not be allowed in those *madarsas*. But it has been unable to keep its promise.[36] Moreover, under the protection of the Taliban the Central Asian rebels have been in contact with international *jihadis*. Some ideologues were able to infuse the IMU with a more radical vision than the simple desire to destabilize President Karimov's regime. One example of such an influence is Abu Mu'ab al-Suri. This *jihadi* ideologue and strategist thought Afghanistan was part of the rebels' regional fight targeted at Central Asia's authoritarian regimes. This kind of *jihad* was of primary importance for extremists like Suri. He was in contact with Uzbek fighters, and was integrated to their style of training. He even claimed that his former students were the ones responsible for the attacks against Uzbekistan in 2004.[37]

Last, the Af-Pak area has been a shelter for men and money for the IMU. Indeed, this group seems to have controlled, at least for a time, no less than 70 per cent drug trade going from Afghanistan to the north through Central Asia.[38] This source of founds explain how the IMU has been able to have access to weapons of good quality, and probably why the Uzbek *jihadis* are still active today.

One does have a skeptical approach about the Chechen presence in the Af-Pak region—unlike the Central Asians who were prominent in the ex-Silk Road. Not one Chechen has been captured by the coalition forces. It makes sense: even if some Chechens have been influenced by the *jihadi* approach, Chechnya is a nation of no more than one million people that are already at war with Russia. It is difficult to imagine they would have men to spare on a fight far away, not directly connected with their national interests.[39] But for Russia, the issue has relevance, as it threatens directly its "backyard." When the US and its allies withdraw from the Af-Pak region, Moscow will have to prove its status of great power, and its claims to have its own version of the Monroe doctrine, by being active against threats coming from the South.

Hence, the foreign influences do not entirely come from the west but still, they cannot totally be seen as secondary. The Af-Pak is particularly important: as a safe haven, as a source of trouble (*jihadism* and drug trafficking in particular), and as the cradle of international *jihadism*, it cannot be seen as a perfect neighbourhood. Foreign influences in general, and the Af-Pak in particular, may have not endangered security in Russia and Central Asia but have partially nurtured the divisive and radical forces. Besides, they also can instigate the Russian and Central Asian regimes to use the excuse of the "foreign plot" to avoid dealing with the real issues that have surfaced at home.

Conclusion

Despite such a situation, it clearly appears that security situation related to *jihadism* will not improve without clear-cut political reforms in Russia and in Central Asia. There is a need for the local leaders to destroy the "Iron Curtain" from the perspective of security and politics. Indeed, repression against violent groups is unavoidable. It would be erroneous for the international community to wait for Dmitri Medvedev and the Central Asian presidents to stop targeting terrorists. Still, as this paper examines, it is a grossly mistaken suggestion that in Eurasia there are only *jihadists* "on the other side." First and foremost, there are civilians who are eager for peace and recognition of some political, social, and economic demands. There are also leaders with nationalist or moderate Islamist inclinations who could be integrated into open-ended political game. Maybe it is on this issue that reform is necessary. Of course, here, the idea is not to promote "democracy" as a concept that would solve all problems. The issue here is more precise. In Russia, at least in the North Caucasus and in the Central Asian republics, political and economic issues raised by average citizens are not necessarily listened to by the local and national elites. Part of the unheard voices is coming from people who are more religious, more detached from the former Soviet vision of religion. Those citizens are not necessarily prone to violence. But as in the Middle East during the second half of the twentieth century, the impossibility of any kind of legal and non-violent opposition can radicalize people that could be included in the political spectrum otherwise. It appears that if Russia and Central Asia want to deal with the problem, they should not only track down die-hard terrorists and denounce foreign influences. They should also learn to accept reforms in their own political systems in order to give all their citizens a voice.

Notes and References

1. Andrew McGregor, "Cross Under the Crescent: Shamil Basaev's Orthodox Enemy," *North Caucasus Weekly* 7, no. 4 (2006).
2. Shireen T. Hunter, *Islam in Russia. The Politics of Identity and Security* (New York: M.E. Sharpe 2004), 158 and 176.
3. Judyth Twigg, "Differential Demographics. Russia's Muslims and Slavic Populations," *PONARS Policy Memo no.388* (December 2005. www.csis.org.
4. See on this subject, for example, Fred Hilgemann, *Le Tatarstan, pays des musulmans de Russie* (*Tatarstan, Country of the Russian Muslims*) (Paris: Autrement–Frontières 2007), 80–1 and 103.
5. Aleksei Malashenko, "Islam, the Way We See It," *Russia in Global Affairs* 4, no.4 (October/December 2006): 31.
6. Robert Cottrel, "Chechnya: How Russia Lost," *New York Review of Books* 45, no.14 (24 September 1998).
7. Robert J. Art and Louise Richardson, *Democracy and Counterterrorism. Lessons from the past* (Washington D.C. : United States Institute for Peace 2007), 403.
8. Hunter, *Islam in Russia*, 136.
9. Omar Ashour, "Security, Oil, and Internal Politics: The Causes of the Russo-Chechen Conflicts," *Studies in Conflict and Terrorism* 27 (2004):133.
10. Gordon M. Hahn, *Russia's Islamic Threat* (London, New Haven: Columbia University Press 2007), 112.
11. "What Direction for Chechnya," *RFE/RL*, 8 July 2008.
12. Aslan Doukaev, "A State Within a State," *RFE/RL*, 31 October 2008.
13. Mehdi Parvizi Amineh and Henk Houweling (ed.), *Central Eurasia in Global Politics. Conflict, Security and Development* (Leiden: Brill 2005),146–53.
14. See Farideh Heyat, "Re-Islamisation in Kyrgyzstan: gender, new poverty and moral dimension," *Central Asian Survey* 23, no. 3–4 (December 2004): 280.
15. For a complete analysis of the "new poor," see Alisher Ilkhamov, "Impoverishment of the masses in the transition period: signs of an

emerging 'new poor' identity in Uzbekistan, " *Central Asian Survey* 20, no.1: 33–54.

16. Vitaly V. Naumkin, *Radical Islam in Central Asia. Between Pen and Rifle* (New York : Rowman & Littlefield 2005), 70.
17. For more informations on the IMU in the 1990s, see Didier Chaudet, "Islamist Terrorism in Greater Central Asia: The 'Al-Qaedaization' of Uzbek Jihadism," *Russie.Nei.Visions*, no. 35 (December 2008): 10–14.
18. Gulnora Saidazimova, "Tabligh Jamaat Group Added to Uzbek Government's Blacklist," *RFE/RL*, 20 December 2004.
19. See Hizb ut-Tahrir, *The Inevitability of the Clash of Civilizations* (London: Al Khilafah Publications 2002), 63.
20. Alisher Khamidov, "Hizb ut-Tahrir Faces Internal Split in Central Asia," *Eurasianet* (20 October 2003).
21. On this subject, see for example Yoginder Sikand, *The Origins and Development of the Tablighi-jama'at (1920-2000)* (New Dehli: Orient Longman 2002), in particular 261–3.
22. International Crisis Group, *Radical Islam in Central Asia : Responding to Hizb ut-Tahrir*, no. 58 (Osh/Brussels: ICG/Asia Report, June 2003): 17.
23. Igor Rotar, "Pakistani Islamic Missionary Group Established a strong presence in Central Asia," *Eurasianet* (23 July 2007).
24. Tim Bird and Alex Marshall, *Afghanistan. How the West Lost Its Way* (New Haven, London: Yale University Press 2011), 32.
25. Steve Coll, *Ghost Wars* (New York : Penguin Press 2004), 382.
26. "Obituary: Shamil Basaeyev," *BBC World*, 10 July 2006.
27. Lorenzo Vidino, "The Arab Foreign Fighters and the Sacralization of the Chechen Conflict," *Al Nakhlah* (Spring 2006): 2.
28. Scott Steward and Ben West, "The Caucasus Emirate," *Stratfor* (15 April 2010).
29. *Jihadism* has a transnational agenda. Islamo-nationalism is, in fact, promotion of nationalism with an Islamist political program. It is limited in space, and focus on an existing nation in particular.
30. Martha Brill Olcott and Bakhtiyar Babajanov, "The Terrorist Notebooks," *Foreign Policy* (April 2003): 38.
31. On this subject, see for example Guido Steinberg, "A Turkish al-Qaeda: The Islamic Jihad Union and the Internationalization of Uzbek Jihadism," *Strategic Insight*, Center for Contemporary Conflict, July 2008, 3-8.
32. Rohan Gunaratna, *Inside Al Qaeda. Global Network of Terror* (New York: Columbia University Press 2002), 170.
33. Adeeeb Khalid, *Islam after Communism. Religion and Politics in Central Asia* (Berkeley: University of California Press 2007), 145–6.
34. "Ethnic Rifts Tearing at Al-Qaeda May Have Led to al-Libbi Capture," *Associated Press*, 11 May 2005.
35. Here I choose to use the term "madaris" for the plural of madrasah, following here the logic of the original language (here Arabic). It is

the same approach that explains why one talks about Taliban (plural) but Talib (singular).

36. Ahmed Rashid, *Jihad. The Rise of Militant Islam in Central Asia* (New Haven and London : Yale University Press 2002), 212–13.
37. Brynjar Lia, *Architect of Global Jihad. The Life of Al Qaeda Strategic Abu Mus'ab al Suri* (New York: Columbia University Press 2008), 262–3.
38. Gretchen Peters, *Seeds of Terror. How Heroin is Bankrolling the Taliban and Al Qaeda* (New York : St Martin's Press 2009), 130.
39. Brian Glyn Williams, "On the Trails of the 'Lions of Islam': A History of Foreign Fighters in Afghanistan and Pakistan, 1980-2010," paper presented at the Foreign Policy Research Institute Conference, Washington D.C., 27 September 2010, 16.

20

Islam in Post-Soviet Russia, its Resurgence and Impact with Reference to Chechnya

Debidatta Aurobinda Mahapatra

The article aims at exploring one of the least researched aspects of Russian politics and society. In the 1990s after the Soviet collapse, Russia attempted at a process of reconciliation with Islam. Islam is officially recognized as one of Russia's four principal religions, along with Orthodox Christianity, Buddhism and Judaism. Russia's recent membership of Organization of Islamic Conference also reflects the factoring of Islam in its policy making. However, in Russia there appears two contradictory trends are emerging simultaneously. While the state has attempted to reconcile with the rising Islamic movements in some ways, the increasing trend of radical Islamization in the south has become evident in post-Soviet Russia. Keeping in view these post-Soviet developments, this article focuses on the situation and location of Russian Muslims in post-Soviet discourse, with particular focus on the conflict in Chechnya. It also focuses the impact of radicalization of Islam in Northern Caucasus and the Russia's response to radical Islam in that area. The essay argues that in conflict situations like in Chechnya, the situation has become further complicated, mainly owing two factors. First, it is the impact of rising Islamic fundamentalism; and second, the transformation of the Chechen movement from a home grown movement to an international *jihadist* movement. Hence, while applying the historical analytical perspective to track the genesis of Islamic radicalism in Russia with particular focus on Chechnya, the article also takes into account the broader picture of Islam in Russia in the post-Soviet scenario, and how the multidimensional equations between the multiethnic personality of Russia and assertion on part of Islam have made the Russian case an interesting aspect in social analysis and one of the fundamental issues in the post-Soviet Russia.

Islam in Russia: An Overview

After collapse of the Soviet Union, religion, in particular Islam has come to play a significant role in Russia. It is thus important to understand the current state of Islam in order to understand politics in Russia. Two different processes characterize religion and society in Russia: firstly, there has been a desecularization of the Russian politics, and secondly, there are also many changes occurring within Russian Islam thus impacting the contours of religion discourse. The post-cold war Russia has been undergoing religious transformation that is likely to have not only the national consequences but also greater implications for the international community. The collapse of the Soviet Union in 1991 created an ideological vacuum to be filled up by various forces, including that of religion. The revival of religion thus led to mixing of spheres that were previously subsumed by the Soviet state: religious, social, political, and economic. In this broader context, the revival of Islam in the Russian state has taken not a unilinear path; rather it has taken different shapes in different regions of Russia. The desecularization of society has brought with it the potential for conflict both within religions and within society as a whole. The fact that religious identities remained dormant during Soviet times makes the situation even more unstable as religious consciousness bursts onto the scene. The North Caucasus has obviously seen the results of this volatility, but other places, where religions have in the past peacefully coexisted, show a new potential for violence. While relations between Orthodox Christians and Muslims in Siberia have traditionally been peaceful, the confluence of the new waves of these two faiths presents a dangerous situation especially if latent tensions are allowed to grow unchecked.

Russia's demographic dynamics too have contributed to the scenario in which Islam in Russia is viewed with suspicion, particularly by sections of ethnic Russians. The country's 2002 census[1] shows that the national fertility rate is 1.5 children per woman, far below the 2.1 children per woman needed to maintain the country's population of about 143 million. The rate in Moscow is even lower, at 1.1 children per woman. But in case of people professing Islam the trend is different. The fertility rate for Tatars living in Moscow, for example, is six children per woman, while the Chechen and Ingush communities are averaging 10 children per woman. And hundreds of thousands of Muslims from Tajikistan, Uzbekistan and Kazakhstan have been flocking to Russia in search of work. Since 1989, Russia's Muslim population has increased by 40 per cent to about 25 million. By 2015, Muslims would likely make up a majority of Russia's conscript army, and by 2020 a fifth of the population. Islam is currently the second most widely professed religion in Russian federation, only behind Orthodox Christianity. Muslim communities are concentrated among minority nationalities residing between the Black Sea and the Caspian Sea: Adyghe, Balkars, Chechens, Circassians, Ingush, Kabardin, Karachay, and numerous Dagestani peoples. Also, in the middle of the Volga Basin reside populations of Tatars and Bashkirs, the majority of whom are Muslims. The majority of Muslims in Russia adhere to the Sunni branch of Islam. About 2 per cent of them are Shia Muslims. In a few areas, notably Chechnya, there is a tradition of Sunni Sufism. Russia's Muslims are extremely diverse, including Volga Tatars, the myriad ethnicities of the North Caucasus and newly arrived immigrants from the former Soviet republics of Central Asia. But they all share an important demographic fact that their birth rates are far higher than that of adherents of Russia's Christian Orthodox.

Islam in Russia is growing more rapidly than Orthodox Christianity. In fact, Moscow now has a Muslim population second only to Istanbul amongst European nations. Some analysts have predicted a Muslim majority in Russia by mid twenty-first century. According to the last census in 2002, about 14.5 million of Russia's 144 million people were ethnic Muslims. The changing balance has impacted the demographic composition of Russia. However, the worrisome factor appears not in the rise in the number of people professing Islam but in the rise of militancy in the name of Islam, and fear of such militancy. Russia after the Soviet collapse, especially during the period of Boris Yeltsin, attempted at a process of reconciliation with the Islam. The number of Muslims allowed making pilgrimages to Mecca increased sharply in 1990s. In 1995 the newly established Union of Muslims of Russia, led by Imam Khatyb Mukaddas of Tatarstan, began organizing a movement aimed at improving inter-ethnic understanding and ending Russians' misconception of Islam. A record 18,000 Russian Muslim pilgrims from all over the country attended the Hajj in Mecca, Saudi Arabia in 2006.

Islam in Russia has undergone transformation not only due to the influences from outside; their local variations too have their bearings on its changing course. Though the West Asian influence has been felt more acutely in recent years in North Caucasus than other Muslim regions of Russia, the traditional, Hanafi Islam still plays a role. Local traditions remain dominant in the Tatar region, where imams are hostile toward outside influences, especially those from Azerbaijan and Kazakhstan, although Kazakh influence, given the expanding community of immigrants, is growing. Meanwhile, in the North Caucasus, representatives of traditional Islam are becoming more aggressive. Islam too is affected by the local community perception of and orientation to the outside world. Thus, in the Northern Caucasus, there is a fusion and mixing of ethnicity and Islam. Many communities manipulate and adapt Islam in order to fight for their rights. Given the multiple layers of change and factors leading to change in Russia's Islamic community, it is important to think about the boundaries and continuities between these different levels. In this context these questions appear prominent. Is it really possible to think of Islam in a regional context? What are the influences on the Islamic community especially in the Russian context? How do practitioners and non-practitioners of Islam perceive each other in Russia?

The recent years have witnessed secular nationalist movements in Russia beginning to use religious slogans. Indeed, Islamic protests are becoming common in political activity throughout the North Caucasus. Moreover, residents of the North Caucasus are turning to religious organization as a provider of social, not just spiritual goods. With this trend, arises a set of questions: What has caused the frustration with secular movements and values? How has religion come to be a legitimate provider of social goods? Some of these questions can be answered through an examination of the changing dimensions of Islam in Russian society.

Islamic Factor in North Caucasus

The conflicts in the northern Caucasus region of Russia including Chechnya have been impacted by the radical version of Islam;[2] for instance, Chechen separatists among other methods exhorted to the slogan Islam in danger to wrest control of the Caucasus from Russia. They endeavored to instill a radical version to buttress the separatist movement. However, this was not widely accepted among the region's comparatively secular Muslims. Many Russians associate Islam with extremists from Chechnya or other parts of North Caucasus, who have carried out dozens of bombings and other attacks against public officials and properties as well as civilians. Separatism began in Chechnya as a largely nationalist movement, but was increasingly influenced by the ideas of radical Islamist organizations such as Al Qaeda. Rebel leaders like late Shamil Basayev or the current Chechen radical leader Doku Umarov were actively recruiting militants across the region in the name of Islam. The recent years have witnessed straining of inter-ethnic and inter-religious relations. There have been instances when Muslims are increasingly viewed with suspicion because of the radicalization of Chechnya and other republics. They are denounced as Wahhabis, followers of the puritanical sect from Saudi Arabia, a word that has been popular in Russia recently. The enmities in the North Caucasus, migration issues and international relations all have been significantly influenced by religion dynamics in the region. The Russian federal authorities and their separatist opponents liked to hint, at the end of the 1990s, that the Chechen war was a conflict between civilizations. The Chechen war had different, specific, causes of its own, but it did fit into the general line of inter-religious friction and added fuel to fire.[3]

Bringing into analysis, though briefly, the Soviet disintegration scenario and how then Boris Yeltsin government met the scenario of parade of sovereignty as disgruntled regions demanded independence would help factoring the complex nature of religion and separatism in post-Soviet Russia from a proper perspective. With the breakup of the Soviet Union in 1991, the former Union Republics became independent but the Autonomous Republics like Chechnya were not granted the right to independent status. They were incorporated into the Russian Federation, which was strongly desisted by some leaders from Autonomous Republics. Dzokhar Dudayev, on 1 November 1991, declared independence of Chechnya. Dudayev, a former Major General in Soviet Air Force had sheltered this ambition even before the disintegration of the Soviet Union. For instance, before the disintegration of the Soviet Union when Gorbachev sent troops to Baltic states to deal with secession problems they failed to reach Estonia because the local air base commander, Dudayev did not allow landing rights to the Soviet air planes to undertake the operation.[4] After the disintegration of the Soviet Union, Dudayev took advantage of the fragile character of the Russian polity and declared independence.

In order to streamline the functioning of the federal polity and meet the demands of separation from various republics, Yeltsin adopted the federal treaty on 31 March 1992. Chechnya, under the leadership of Dudayev, refused to sign the treaty. As per the provisions of the treaty, the republics were given the status of "sovereign republics within the Russian Federation"[5] with property rights over land and natural resources on their territory. The treaty[6] recognized two different categories of "subjects of the Federation": twenty-one republics and sixty-eight administrative territorial regions. The republics were given rights over their natural resources, external trade and internal budgets. Two republics, Chechnya and Tatarstan refused to sign the treaty as they insisted on a fuller statement of independence from Moscow. Yeltsin could handle the

Tatarstan demand by signing a treaty with it in February 1994. By the end of 1995 Moscow signed similar documents with six other republics, Kabardino-Balkaria, Bashkortostan, North-Ossetia, Sakha/Yakutia, Buryatiya and Udmurtia. Moscow could tackle the separatist demands from various republics successfully but it failed in the case of Chechnya. The next decade witnessed two violent wars between Russia and Chechen militants without any conclusive resolution of the conflict, partly due to the failure of the peace agreement called Khasavyurt agreement, and also due to the intransigence of the militants to abide by the rules of the Russian federation. According to one string of argument, despite a religious revival in Chechnya at the time, initially Islam played a marginal role in the ideology of Chechen separatists. It was after nearly ten years of conflict and chaos that both, political and radical Islam, which was perhaps earlier dormant, have become part of the ideology and working method of many Chechen fighters and politicians though these trends are quite alien to the Sufi Chechens.[7]

In most likelihood, the internal impetus toward Islamization of the Chechen separatist movement did not come from the Chechen population in general but rather from a group of warlords and politicians who acquired prominent positions in Chechnya because of the war. The group that included Shamil Basaev, Salman Raduev, Arbi, Movsar Baraev, Movladi Udugov and Zelimkhan Yandarabiev, underwent a process of radicalization/Islamization during the first war (1994-96). They justified the Islamization of the separatist movement. Yandarabiev, in an interview to a Russian journalist in 2001, stated: "Islamic fundamentalism is not dangerous. It's partnership, international relations. You don't consider a problem that Western investors tour Russia, do you? One cannot divide help into help from Wahhabis and help from others…"[8]

Chechnya's status as a republic within the Russian Federation was affirmed by the Russian Constitution in 2003 despite the opposition from the militants. In 2002, especially after the siege of one Moscow theatre, Putin announced a referendum to be held in Chechnya in March 2003 on a proposed new constitution that affirmed Chechnya's status as a republic within the Russian Federation. As per official estimation there was higher voter turnout and majority of the voters were in favour of the constitution. Under the new constitution, Chechnya is allowed autonomy and elected government under federal law.

The common perception of the Russian Orthodox Church community is that the government's policy towards Islam in the

Northern Caucasus and elsewhere has been largely successful. There seems to be a momentary respite from the all out conflict in the North Caucasus, but in reality, the radicalization of Islam continues and threatening processes have simply gone underground. It appears as the violent conflict of about two decades brought the realization that the radicalization of Islam cannot be checked by any repressive measures but by a reconciliation process, initiated by the state by taking into account the perspectives of all stakeholders. Before waging any "war on terrorism," it is important to realize that not all of "radical Islam" is violent and ask the question of what turns "radicals" to violence.[9] Once these questions have been answered, especially in a Eurasian context, one can begin to craft a sound policy to address the conflicts in the region as a whole and in Russia in particular. But, the crucial dilemma still remains as no party in these conflicts appear to have factored these complex issues in their strategies towards conflict resolution.

Internationalization of the Conflict

As indicated earlier, it was only in its later phase that radicalism in the Chechen movement acquired international dimensions. The most visible turning point of this transformation is the Chechen incursion into Dagestan in August 1999 led by Abdur Rahman Khattab and Shamil Basayev. Khattab, a Jordanian, had fought the Soviet forces in Afghanistan alongside Al Qaeda leader Osama bin Laden. Alexander Vershbow, then US Ambassador to Russia, shortly after 11 September 2001 attack in the US said, "We have long recognized that Osama bin Laden and other international networks have been fuelling the flames in Chechnya, including the involvement of foreign commanders like Khattab."[10] As per reports, a Moroccan man charged with abetting the hijackers of planes in 9/11 incident told a German court in October 2002 that the plot's ringleader, Muhammad Ata, initially planned to join the fight in Chechnya. Zacarias Moussaoui, whom the US authorities have charged with being the "20th hijacker" in the 11 September attacks, was reported by the *Wall Street Journal* to be formerly "a recruiter for Al-Qaeda-backed rebels in Chechnya." Chechen rebels reportedly fought alongside Al Qaeda and Taliban forces against the US-backed Northern Alliance in late 2001. Russian authorities, including Prime Minister Vladimir Putin, have repeatedly stressed the involvement of international terrorists and bin Laden's associates in Chechnya. Sergei Ivanov, former Defence Minister of Russia, claimed that a videotape of Khattab meeting with bin Laden has been found in Afghanistan. The Russian Government has claimed that as many as 200 terrorist groups were trying to get their hands on Russian nuclear materials. In the past three years alone, Russian authorities reportedly have broken up 601 nuclear-smuggling deals.[11]

Though the second Chechen war of 1999 brought into picture the overt radicalization of the conflict in Chechnya to its peak, it could be safely assumed that the culmination point had its earlier traces. For instance, in 1992, Islam was pronounced state religion by the Chechen constitution, adopted by the separatists under the leadership of Dudayev. In the summer of 1996, sharia based criminal law was passed by the local parliament in then de facto independent Chechnya. That criminal code was copied from a Sudanese act. In spring 1997, the first public execution took place and was telecast by Russian television. In 1997-98, Dagestan influenced by radical Islamists began applying sharia law in direct contradiction to the Constitution of the Russian Federation. However, Russian leader Vladimir Putin could successfully utilize the 9/11 incident to Russia's advantage towards containing radicalism. He linked the incident and the terror situation in Chechnya. "We face a common foe," he told the German parliament. As a result, there was a discernable difference in the American policy towards Chechnya before and after the 9/11. Before the incident, the US was harsh in criticizing human rights violation in Chechnya and the "mid-level Bush administration officials met with Chechen representatives with hopes of understanding their approach to a political settlement to the conflict." After the incident, President Bush and the US officials eased their criticism of Russia's policy on Chechnya: "While Western Governments have generally supported Russia's right to keep itself in one piece and subdue the Chechen rebellion, they have also said that Russia has committed massive human rights abuses in Chechnya—a theme that's now being downplayed."

The Moscow theatre hostage crisis of October 2002 made deep impact on the counter-terrorism policy of Russia. It was a major terrorist operation, which brought into picture the terrorists' objectives in clear terms. Russia utilized the occasion and pronounced its right on extra-territorial use of force against terrorists and their supporters. The bravado that "we are more keen on dying than you are keen on living," definitely puzzled the Russian leaders, though Putin handled the situation with apt strategy and his KGB background might have helped him in this regard. On the released video, a spokeswoman for Chechen fighters who held 800 hostages in the theatre, pronounced the destiny of Chechnya and Chechens, which needs quotation at length:[12]

> Every nation has the right to its fate. Russia has taken away

> this right from the Chechens and today we want to reclaim these rights, which God has given us (in the same way he has given it to other nations). God has given us the right of freedom and the right to choose our destiny. And the Russian occupiers have flooded our land with our children's blood. And we have longed for a just solution. People are unaware of the innocent who are dying in Chechnya: the sheikhs, the women, the children and the weak ones. And therefore, we have chosen this approach. This approach is for the freedom of the Chechen people and there is no difference in where we die, and therefore we have decided to die here, in Moscow. And we will take with us the lives of hundreds of sinners. If we die, others will come/follow us—our brothers and sisters who are willing to sacrifice their lives (in God's way) to liberate their nation. Our nationalists have died but people have said that they (the nationalists) are terrorists and criminals. But the truth is Russia is the true criminal.

The October 2002 incident impacted Russia's neighbours. Azerbaijan shut down a Chechen representative office in Baku. Georgian politicians were nervous lest the Russian troops cross the border and enter the Pankisi Gorge. According to Ariel Cohen, after the 1996 Russian troop withdrawal, organized crime and Islamic extremists have turned Chechnya into a haven for kidnappers for ransom, slave traders, and murderers of nuns and foreign aid workers. Shamil Basayev pushed President Maskhadov into adopting repressive sharia laws. Maskhadov could not forestall the invasion of Dagestan in July 1999 led by Basayev and Khattab—an invasion, which ended Chechnya's de-facto independence. Besides the political implications, the October 2002 attack also had wider economic implications. The leaders in Moscow were apprehensive of such terrorist strikes in future and moreover, any possible entity of a Caliphate as dreamed by Islamic extremists spreading from Black sea to Caspian Sea would pose a great concern regarding energy security of Russia in the region. The rhetoric about creation of a Chechen-led Caliphate "from sea to shining sea," i.e., from the Black Sea to the Caspian created panic among the leaders in Russia, Dagestan, Azerbaijan and Georgia. A radical and impoverished Islamic state in Europe, on the doorstep of Russia and the weak South Caucasus states would unquestionably be dangerous as it would act as a destabilising factor, and scare off the investors who otherwise could improve the lives of millions of people in the region.

The reported admission of the radical Chechen, Shamil Basayev in organizing the Beslan tragedy reinforces the theory of Chechen involvement in terrorist activities in Russia. In a letter posted on 17 September 2004 *Kavkaz Tsentr* website, Basayev purportedly said that he had sent a letter to Putin "proposing independence (for Chechnya) in exchange of security."[13] The Chechen involvement in the Beslan tragedy has further been confirmed by the identification of 11 hostage-takers as Ingush-Chechen. The only militant captured alive from amongst the hostage-takers was a Chechen, named Nur-pasi Kuvayev.[14] Putin and Foreign Minister, Sergei Lavrov have claimed that the attackers included several Arab Muslims. This claim, though not fully confirmed yet, has some elements of truth as one Arab mercenary was arrested on 17 September 2004 while trying to cross the Russian border.[15] Besides revealing the international character of terrorism, the Beslan episode added some new dimensions to the terrorist strategy. First, "the terrorists have crossed all the thresholds."[16] They are no more content in targeting government institutions and buildings but schools, restaurants, buses and other soft targets. Targeting children at the Beslan school is a testimony to this new development. Second, they have sought to hurt not only the visible things but also the mass psychology. The video footage of grieving mothers of the dead or dying children, all seem part of the strategy to hurt the psychology of the masses and to spread the feeling of insecurity among them. Third, they sought to adopt a novel strategy by attacking a school in North Ossetia, the Russian republic dominated by Christian population but surrounded by republics with Muslim majority population. Any Christian-Islam colouring of the situation, the terrorists might have intended, would instigate communal passion, thus furthering their cause of destabilizing the Russian Federation.

There is another reason behind Moscow's non-acceptance of the demands of the Chechen separatists. It may encourage other separatist groups in other republics to adopt the violent path for the fulfilment of their demands. This would also nullify all the efforts made by the Yeltsin government to accommodate the separatist demands in other republics within the federal framework. Another factor that has motivated Russia to adopt strong measures against the separatists in Chechnya is the likely conversion of the region into a hub of international terrorism. A brand of Islamic radicalism called Wahhabism has already engulfed Chechen society and spread to other regions, thus raising the fear of Moscow.

Citing the figures of Russian Foreign Ministry, a news agency reports that 561 acts of terrorism were registered in Russia in 2003, an increase of 55.8 per cent compared to 2002. Four hundred of the attacks took place in the southern federal district, including 386 in the Chechen Republic.[17] The agency further reports that more than 200 people were killed as a result of terrorist attacks and more than 600 were wounded. Russia passed several antiterrorism laws in 2003 and 2004, facilitated effective interdiction of terrorist finance flows by becoming a full member of the Financial Action Task Force (FATF). In February 2004, the Russian Supreme Court issued an official government list of 15 terrorist organizations, the first of its kind in Russia and an important step toward implementation of counterterrorism statutes. Following the promulgation of the list, the 15 organizations were prohibited from engaging in any financial activities.

In the case of Russia a trend that has been increasingly in vogue is the assertion of the Orthodox Church as the supreme religious authority and as a force to be reckoned with. During the second Chechen campaign, Russian Orthodox priests were present in the units of the federal forces. After the introduction of *perestroika* in 1980s hundreds of Orthodox churches, mosques, Armenian-Gregorian churches, synagogues, etc., were built. The recent Islamic extremism seemed to have impacted the religious balance in the Russian society as well. The conflict in Chechnya has intensified religious sentiments among the local Russian inhabitants. The emergence of militant Islamism in North Caucasus has created anxiety for Russian population. "Chechen Muslim militants have waged a fierce struggle against Russian Orthodox priests by kidnapping, torturing and killing them."[18] This trend of inter-religious rivalry may further worsen the situation in Russia and for its leaders it may bring difficult problems.

The terrorist attack at Domodedovo airport in Moscow on 25 January 2011 can also be characterized as another inhuman act perpetrated by the terrorists. If the reports are to be believed, it is the Chechen radicals who committed this act. The Chechen terrorist leader, Doku Umarov claimed responsibility for this attack, and threatened more such attacks in near future. His words, "the war will come to your streets, and you will feel it in your own lives and on your own skin"[19] reflected violence not only of plans and strategies but also in psychology of the Chechen separatist leaders. The attack reportedly killed 34 innocent civilians from different nations, besides injuring more than 150 people. Perhaps the attack and the selection of venue and time were aimed at creating disturbances and infuse fear in the Russian polity and society in a hectic year. This year Russia is going to have parliament elections, and the next year it will have the presidential elections. The Russian President, Dmitry Medvedev has already announced the cancellation of his trip to World Economic Forum at

Davos, held in the same month, where he was supposed to portray Russia as a booming investment destination. Domodedovo airport, one of the biggest airports in the world with modern facilities and technologies, was targeted to show that the militants are formidable in their designs and strategies, and also by targeting nationals from different countries, the attack probably aimed at reducing the confidence of other countries over the Russian security system.

However, the attack was nothing but another step to show how the militants used all kinds of violent methods to make their presence felt. There cannot be any justification of such violent activities like terrorism, whether perpetrated by a small group or a large group, or even by a state. In case of Russia the situation appears protracted due to its multi-ethnic and pluralistic nature. In fact it is the case with any country having a multiethnic and pluralistic character. It is natural that in a vast and diverse country like Russia, there will be competing demands from various regions to assert their rights. In a federal and pluralistic country, there can be mechanisms to address the grievances for different regions. Perhaps keeping that in mind, the former Russian President, Boris Yeltsin had signed a special treaty with Tatarstan, another republic of Russian federation, in 1994 to address its concerns. But in case of Chechnya, as mentioned earlier, the situation has become further complicated, mainly owing to the impact of rising Islamic fundamentalism, and in the transformation of the Chechen movement from a home grown movement to an international *jihadist* movement. As a result, no peace mechanism worked in the case of Chechnya, and various agreements like the Khasavyurt agreement of 2006 failed to achieve any result. Hence, when in 2007 the Chechen radical leader Doku Umarov proclaimed Caucasian Caliphate, it was more motivated by these above two factors, than the genuine concerns of the local people of Chechnya.

Conclusion

As the discussion above shows, Islam in Russia has sprung up in the discourse particularly in the aftermath of the demise of the Soviet Union. Though Islam could coexist with other religions of Russia and evolve its numerous forms and traditions, this divergence in Russian variety of Islam came to sharp focus in the post-cold war period. The emergence of new nation states in the post-Soviet space in a way bolstered new identities, which took into its ambit many divisions including religion. This religion aspect when combined with territory and territorial aspirations emerged strong and further provided rallying point for the assertion of religious identity, more visible in the peripheries like the North Caucasus region.

More importantly the emergence of new nation states also led to emergence of new tensions earlier managed or subdued by the erstwhile command structure, which could enmesh in its ambit diverse frictions and fractions in the overarching socialist ideal. The breakup of the Soviet Union opened up the fissures, latent as well as potent, thus making the appearance as well as assertions of these divisions more prominent. Hence the rise of extremism and religious assertion cannot be seen in isolation to situations inherent in the collapse of the Soviet Union. Equally importantly the lack of a smooth democratic transition from socialism to capitalist democracy, and also the fragile nation building process in the post-Soviet states have well contributed to this fragile scenario, which provided enough rationale as well as locale to the diverse aspirations enmeshed with different clans, religions, and sectarian identities to come forth. All the nation states in the post-Soviet space are to a degree authoritarian despite the claims of being "sovereign" democracy or real democracy, and this authoritarian system has driven the leaders to adopt religious symbols and dogmas to draw legitimacy and to further their reign.

Besides the inherent weakness and the political façades, the economic underdevelopment, the poor management of resources, and high rate of corruption and also population growth play a role in the rise of religion as unit of bargaining. Religion emerges as a rallying point for the poor people to assert for their rights. In this context, various religious organizations with their charitable trust have provided enough rationale to the aspirations of the poor people to rise to the occasion that religion is in danger for economic reasons. Regarding external factors and their role in promoting religion and religious fundamentalism, some crucial points need to be emphasized. Religion does play a role, and external factors also influence the playing of the religion card; but it is the fertile nature, or rather the receptivity of the sections of people that enable the external factors to play a crucial role in igniting the religious passion of the people. The religious organizations distribute propaganda literature, and also aid to complete the process of social mobilization in the margins of Russia. Religion in this context plays a role of social mobilization, and in the context of Islam it transcends barriers.

A balanced approach is needed for maintenance of religious harmony and coexistence in multiethnic and pluralistic societies like Russia. The rising tide of radicalism is not the issue of mere religion, it rather encompasses in its fold myriad incongruities and frictions which need to be studied in depth and dealt with. However, the fact remains that the radicalization of Islam or for that matter any religion cannot be tackled by mere repressive measures but by a reconciliation process, initiated by the state and supported by the conscientious people across divides. The Chechen quagmire brings forth this cardinal principle of conflict resolution and the urgency of its application starkly.

Notes and References

1. For some of the details see, Michael Mainville, "Russia has a Muslim Dilemma," *San Francisco Chronicle*, 19 November 2006. Also available at http://www.sfgate.com/cgibin/article.cgi?f=/c/a/2006/11/19/MNGJGMFUVG1.DTL
2. For an elaborate study of the Chechen conflict see, Debidatta Aurobinda Mahapatra and Seema Shekhawat, *Conflict in Kashmir and Chechnya: Political and Humanitarian Dimensions* (New Delhi: Lancers Publishers 2007).
3. Alexey Malashenko, *The Clash is for Real,* Carnegie Moscow Center Briefing 9, no. 4 (2007): 5.
4. John Colarusso, "Chechnya: The War without Winners," *Current History* 94, no. 594 (1995): 329.
5. Quoted in Steven Solnick, "Will Russia Survive? Centre and Periphery in the Russian Federation," in *Post-Soviet Political Order: Conflict and State Building*, Barnett R. Rubin and Jack Snyder (eds.) (London: Routledge 1998), 64. In this article the author has dealt with the federation treaty at length.
6. Yeltsin in fact had adopted three different kinds of federation treaties to deal with different kinds of constituents of the Russian federation: one with autonomous republics, another with lesser autonomous okrugs, and another with oblasts and krais.
7. Julie Wilhelmsen, "Between a Rock and a Hard Place: The Islamisation of the Chechen Separatist Movement," *Europe-Asia Studies* 57, no. 1 (2005): 35.
8. Quoted in Wilhelmsen, "Between a Rock and a Hard Place," 40.
9. Personal Interview with Alexy Malashenko, Co-Chair, Religion, Society and Security Programme at Carnegie Moscow Centre, 8 September 2010. Prof. Malashenko is of the view that all "radical" Islam is not "extreme" Islam which pushes adherents towards violent methods for conflict resolution.
10. Quoted in *http://groups.msn.com/UnitedAgainstTerrorism/terrorist groups.msnw?action=get_message&mview =0&ID_Message=4183&LastModified=4675437613027745643.*

11. "Has al-Qaeda operated in Chechnya?" *http://cfrterrorism.org/coalition/russia2.html.*
12. Yuri N. Maltsev, "Russia's War on Chechnya," *http://www.mises.org/fullstory.aspx?control=1080.*
13. *The Hindu*, 18 September 2004.
14. *http://www.guardian.co.uk/russia/article/o,2763,1302692,00html.*
15. *The Hindu*, 18 September 2004.
16. This view has been expressed by Jonathan Stevenson, terror expert at the International Institute of Strategic Studies, London. Quoted in Pramit Pal Chaudhuri, "Soft Targets, Deadly Results," *Hindustan Times*, 5 September 2004.
17. Roman Kupchinsky, "The Losing Battle against Terrorism and Insurgency in Russia," *Radio Free Europe Radio Liberty* 4, no. 17 (2004). Also available at http://www.rferl.org/content/article/1342345.html
18. Vyachslav Avyutsky, "Confessional Geopolitics in the South of Russia and the North Caucasus," *Russia and Moslem World* 3, no. 141(2004): 7.
19. http://www.thesundayleader.lk/2011/01/25/suicide-blast-in-russia-kills-34/

21

Politicization of Religion in the Context of Ethno Cultural Revival in Buryatiya

Darima Amogolonova

Religious revival and rise of religiosity among the population of post Soviet Russia have drawn the attention of both Russian and foreign researchers.[1] In Buryatiya, the problems have been studied mainly within the framework of sociology and religious studies[2]—these researches characterize religious processes and allow the observation of certain dynamics in the social mood concerning religion. The social significance of such research lies in looking for ways to explain and analyse the current state of affairs and the social atmosphere in Russia that depends on both individual and public consciousness.

The post Soviet realities, in which radical change in the attitudes to religion and religious institutions is most evident, is unprecedented in the sense that within a very short period the state became critical towards atheism. The state thus showed that social transformations in Russia were irrevocably democratic as freedom of worship concerned every common person unlike other expressions of modernization. The revived and "rehabilitated" religion was expected to fill a spiritual vacuum; besides, the religion (the Russian Orthodoxy first) was intended to play a major role in the growing Russian nationalist ideas. Such ideological rethinking, with simultaneous absence of all-Russian social concepts aimed at the future, in poly-confessional Russia has led to politicization of religious issues and has incorporated religion into ethno-national ideologies.

Role of Religion Reconsidered

If we agree that *perestroika* in the USSR has really inspired religious revival then we must also recognize that hopes for role of religion in social improvement were decreasing and political romanticism was tending to decline. B. Dubin argues in his paper on popular religious culture in modern Russia that the number of those who think that religion (Christianity) promotes better social health is steadily decreasing. He says, "The prevailing part of Russians either think that the church is of little importance in the everyday life of people or find it difficult to answer this question."[3] Paradoxically, the number of those who identify themselves as believers has gradually increased. I propose to identify this phenomenon as "de-secularization"—a term that was coined by Peter Berger. De-secularization, to him, reflects the changing character of secularization in a methodological sense. As early as 1966, jointly with T. Lukman, he argued that modernization inevitably leads to secularization of the public mind because science not only removes the sacred from everyday life but also the supporting knowledge from the world.[4]

However, since the 1990s, Berger's point of view has essentially changed. He "returned" religion to the world with the following explanation: "My point is that the assumption that we live in the secular world is false. The world today…is as furiously religious as it ever was, and in some places more so then ever."[5] Berger's ideas that secularization was always the ideology of elites that never influenced the public mind appeared to be productive in the methodological sense and in the context of post Soviet socio-cultural processes. Certainly, we must keep in mind that after decades of radical atheism and general religious ignorance, there are few true believers in Russia; religious indifference, a result of Soviet modernization, is characteristic for the most people. Therefore, we can hardly expect that the situation would swiftly transform into a certain religious fundamentalism, which has the potential of politicization that could lead to a religious war. Given the post Soviet practices, one must recognize that religion does not play a significant role in the everyday life.

Simultaneously, there is no doubt that the process of returning of religion in Russia is taking place. It would be a simplification to connect this process only with destruction of former political ideology (materialistic and atheistic), which had certain religious features.[6] De-secularization today does not mean replacement of the Soviet belief with religion because "the epoch of developed socialism" and the ideals of socialism are being critically evaluated. One can notice even a certain similarity between secularization of the European modernization (as defined by Berger as a component of elite culture)[7] and adherence of the Soviet elites to the atheist viewpoint. Really speaking, European modernization implied secularization as separation of church from the state; while for public consciousness, this separation meant no more then division of secular and religious spheres. The term "Soviet religion" applied to "believers" who had reverential belief in omnipotent and omniscient communist party's leaders. Later, liberalization as during the thaw period, brought atheism before public consciousness, and most of the Soviet citizens understood that communist ideas bore real fruits for the communist bureaucracy but not so much for the common people. From the 1950s, de-secularization of Soviet ideology was growing which initiated interest in traditional religions, though this did not simultaneously result in the revival of religiosity. In this connection, I would disagree with the assessment that "post-1989, the structures and ideologies of communism imploded, releasing space for religion that had not existed for several generations."[8] As far as Russian Orthodoxy is concerned, the number of believers in the USSR, according to both western and unofficial Soviet sources was usually cited between 30 million and 50 million; the actual number was presumably higher and could be around 55-60 million.[9]

Ethno-nationalism and Religion

Spontaneous and nearly uncontrolled *conditional* religious feelings in the late Soviet period became a reality during the post Soviet period. No wonder, the new elite saw in religion and religious institutions a strong mechanism for strengthening their positions. The instrumental approach towards post Soviet religious revival reveals purposeful move to the definite, though still not formulated, ideological programme that is aimed at negation of the Soviet heritage. The new national idea with its appeal to humanistic ideals of the Russian ethnic culture and former greatness of the Russian state unavoidably includes religion (and this must be the Russian Orthodoxy, the ethnic religion of the majority) as one of the principal components of national self-consciousness. In this instrumental sense the national religion as the integrating factor does not need restoration of basic (world outlook and compensatory) functions of religion; moreover, in terms of nationalist identity, the religious beliefs do not play a special role. The situation is comparable to situations in the nineteenth and twentieth centuries when, as Urs Altermatt marked, nationalism had taken the place of religion and national feelings began to fulfill the integrative function of religion.[10] To analyse post Soviet socio-cultural processes, we could adopt Altermatt's idea and conclude that modern Russia faces the opposite tendency, when nationalism is to be replaced by religion.

During the period of manifestation of ethno-nationalism and over criticism of both Soviet ideology and imperial history of Russia, the ethnic elite promoted large-scale politicization of culture. In public consciousness, this resulted in the stable mythologem/ideologem about indissoluble connection between ethno-political independence and preservation of national traditions. Besides, the hierarchical status of religion was established by the Preamble to the Federal Law on religions and religious associations (Special role of Orthodoxy in the history of Russia and in the establishment and development of its spirituality and culture) and the list of Russia's confessions (Christianity to "other religions" like Islam, Buddhism, Judaism, etc., that constitute an integral part of the historical heritage of the peoples of Russia").[11] It served the ideas that (a) besides the Orthodox Church, there were religions of ethnic minorities; (b) ethnic groups have a minor position in the hierarchical ladder; (c) the groups must take care of their own ethno-national religions while the state is mostly interested in Christian Orthodoxy, which, according to the Preamble to the Law, is undoubtedly the state religion (though the state is declared to be secular).

Since 2000, theoretically speaking, Russia has shown de-politicization of ethno-social practices. It means that ethno-national rhetoric and agitation "went out of political fashion;" thus, religious values, which have been understood as a fundamental component of national culture, have become the major markers of national space. Religious identity provides spiritual, moral and ideological basis for feelings of commonness on "blood and soil" on national memory and purposes. No wonder that sociological researches of 1990s in the territory of ethnic Buryatiya showed increase in number of Buryat who indicated their confessional status—61.2 per cent identified themselves as Buddhists, 21.9 per cent as Shamanists, 0.4 per cent as Russian Orthodox.[12] These figures have remained almost unchanging in the surveys throughout 2000s. It is worth marking that in the poll of 2009, the variants for non-atheists were for the first time differentiated as "I believe more likely" and "I believe." The total number of believers (despite the doubts they have about religious affiliation) appeared to be higher then at the polls of 1990s.

Table 1. Percentage of Believers and Non-Believers in Buryatiya

Variants of choice	*City (in %)*		*Village (in %)*	
	Men	*Women*	*Men*	*Women*
More likely I believe	42.9	41.1	38.1	36.7
I believe	36.7	55.3	52.4	54.4

Source: D.C. Budaeva *et al.*, *Voprosy sohraneniya i razvitiya tolerantnosti, problemy grazhdanskoi aktivnosti naseleniya Respubliki Buryatiya*, 48.

Political conditionality of religious choice can be traced to the considerable difference in the figures that concerned replies given by the representatives of different generations: for example, 75 per cent of young Buryat men from the city have chosen the option "I am a believer" (none in this group chose the option "atheist" or "more likely I do not believe") whereas among Buryat men of the age group 60 and more, 37.5 per cent ranked themselves as atheists. We can see the undoubted connection between revived interest to the "religion of ancestors" and modern ethno-nationalist ideology, in which religion plays a major integrative role. Therefore, the question of religious belief, i.e. world outlook function of religion, is disputable. Buryat sociologist I.E. Elaeva proposes an interesting approach to the problem that removes the contradiction between religious affiliation and religious faith: "it is quite possible to identify a person as a believer if he/she considers him (her) self to be so."[13]

Re-Inventing Ethnicity

The Buryat national heritage, having been "invented" by the leaders of post Soviet ethnic revival, emanates from the argument that during Soviet socialist modernization, the Buryats nearly completely lost their traditional economy and culture. The process of socialist modernization included in particular *etatization* of ethnicity and *ethnicization* of the communist state machinery. Though this concerned all ethnic groups, the situation of the Buryats was specific to the Siberian ethnic groups: the Buryats were more successful in all levels of education and urbanization. Correspondingly, the scenario, which was pessimistically treated by the national leaders of pre-revolutionary and early Soviet periods,[14] was different: the ethnocultural characteristics and peculiarities were pushed aside to the periphery of economic and cultural processes. Certainly, these changes have been witnessed in the religious sphere too.

When we analyse the ideology of the present-day Buryat national leaders, we can easily see that they did not invent something new; they are arguing with concepts they inherited from their predecessors. The essential difference is that the earlier leaders hypothesized about destruction of traditions while the contemporary political leaders are hypothesizing about the ruination of indigenous Buryat ethnicity (at least they think so). However, since *perestroika*, the creators of Buryat ideology have not lost hopes about restoration of national heritage by means of returning to Buryat ethnic consciousness (*re-ethnicization*).[15] The proposed programme is on the one hand wide-scale and ambitious, and on the other hand, too speculative and hardly practicable. Re-ethnicization implies a large spectrum of action—returning to nomadic stockbreeding, widening of the functional sphere of the Buryat language, revival of religious-spiritual culture. Revival of nomadic stockbreeding was doomed to failure from the beginning; ethnic language remained restricted to the family with steady narrowing of its social basis in favour of Russian. Thus, considering economic and cultural (linguistic) aspects of re-ethnicization, we tend to make a conclusion that ethno-nationalist agitation had no practical response.

Symbolism and Religion

The situation with religion is different. Affiliation to the Buddhist or shamanic community (or both of them) does not imply any sacramental ritual or regular participation in religious life. Actually, for years the former ideas about traditional religious beliefs signify *genetic* ties between Buryats and Buddhism: "The majority of Buddhists in Buryatiya are Buddhists by birth."[16] Therefore, a mythologem about inborn Buryat religiosity makes religious belief and nominal (declarative) religious identification synonymous; religion, first, acquires rigid ethnic borders and, second, becomes a symbolical marker that does not need even superficial knowledge about dogmatics. Therefore, in mass consciousness Buryats primordially correspond to Buddhism, and Russians to Orthodoxy.[17]

From the point of view of political ideology, because of its clan and family limitation Shamanism cannot be considered as a tool for all-Buryat ethno-national integration. On the other hand, Buddhism can easily fulfill this task. Moreover, the national leaders hoped to use religious resources for restoring the historical and cultural identity with Mongols and even with the whole Central Asian communality. Thus, religion appeared to be an effective instrument for revitalization of historical memory, with simultaneous fulfilling of a special function of today—answering the challenges of globalization that concerns spiritual sphere also.[18] Certainly, popularity of Buddhism among the Buryats is due to public statements of the Buddhist hierarchs, who include Buryats in the space of common culture because of genetic and world outlook similarity. The Dalai Lama in particular says, "... we, the inhabitants of Tibet, consider the people living in Buryatiya, Chita and Kalmykia as our twin brothers and sisters. Tibetans and Mongols have much in common; besides food and garment customs, people of these regions are devoted to Avalokiteshvara."[19]

Politicization of Religion

The integrative function of religion combined with cultural differentiation actions inspired by the national leaders was manifested in full by the political activities from 1989 to 2000. Similarly, to other administrative and political subjects of the Russian Federation with mixed ethnic cultures, religious revival in Buryatiya in external expressions obviously showed politicization (nationalization) of religion among both Buryats and Russians. The result is more important: under the slogans of religious values, every inhabited place of the republic, either rural or urban, is dotted with Buddhist, Shamanist and Orthodox symbols (*suburgans-stupas*, *oboo*-hips of stones, and crosses), sometimes very close to each other. All these would be ethnographic specimens of Buryatiya emphasizing peaceful coexistence of cultures, but in reality, it points to the political context: verbal marking of the territory in the poly-confessional society unavoidably gives birth to tension and mutual distrust.

Within the last years of Soviet era and beginning of post Soviet period, amidst active discussions about destiny of the nation, the topic of inseparability of the Russian culture from Orthodoxy inspired naive hopes for renewal of Christianity in Russia. In other words, in the construction of the national idea, the Orthodoxy was considered as a necessary integrating force. The negative results of politicization of the orthodoxy have deeper impact in the ethno-national regions of Russia especially because of the already existing mistrust between Russians and non-Russians.

In the early 1990s, the latent conflict between Russians and titular nationalities began to take the form of ethno-cultural opposition. In the marking of their own spaces, religious traditions and symbols were used indirectly; nevertheless, cultural confrontation initiated by the leaders of ethnic mobilization meant politicization of religion. For Buryatiya, in which political elites represent peaceful coexistence of Russians and Buryats, the actions aimed at a Russian restoration through Orthodoxy created nervousness on the Buryat side. Such actions of the Trans Baikalia Cossacks raised apprehensions—their members have put on the Cossack military uniform decorated with predecessors' imperial awards, sabres, and they organized marches in Ulan-Ude with written and oral slogans about reviving the city's historical name Verkheudinsk.[20] A memorial stone put up in the place of Udinskoye winter-hut (laid by Russian Cossacks-pioneers in 1666) pointed at revitalization of historical memory and had a political undertone. However, sometime later when the Orthodox cross was set up on the stone, the Russian space of Ulan-Ude was automatically recognized.

The leaders of the Orthodox Church in Buryatiya have, through their publications emphasized the religious factor as strengthening Russian ethnic identity. The Prior of the St. Odigitria Cathedral, Eugenie Startsev wrote: "The Russian people, who are now coming back to the sources, will find forces for revival only in the Orthodox belief of their pious ancestors."[21] She also sees in Orthodoxy a fully formulated national idea that unites ethnic Russians.[22]

Markers of Tradition

The principal ideology that is the marker of Buryat space is the Procession of Geser's Banner (1991-95) over all ethnic Buryat territories. Several events surrounding the *Geseriad* became symbolically meaningful. The consecration of Geser's Banner became a symbol of all-Buryat unity. Wooden posts (*serges*)[23] to hold the Geser Banner (*Geserei Serge*) were set up along the whole route of the procession, symbolically marking the territory as owned by the indivisible Buryat people. This festival had a religious component because of the participation of the clergy, construction of a Geser temple (supposing religious worshipping), and numerous rituals of religious sacralization according to both Shamanic and Buddhist traditions.

The politicization of traditional Buryat beliefs within the framework of institutionalized religious communities had no manifestation. Nevertheless, since the painful Buryat experience of the merger of two Buryat autonomous districts (Ust'-Ordinsky and Aginsky) with Irkutsk and Chita regions respectively, contradictions between the organizations of Shamanic revival and independent shamans deepened. The independent and famous woman-shaman Nadezhda Stepanova appointed holding of all-Buryat spring *tailagan* (shamanic ritual) under the slogan "Let us protect Ust'-Orda!" in 19 March 2006. She addressed the shamanic communities and organizations all over ethnic Buryatiya to support the idea and participate in the event with collective incantations to prevent merging. In particular, she said, "All those who want to 'to stand for himself' and to preserve autonomy may arrive for the *tailagan*... After Ust'-Orda, the same fate can be with Aga,[24] and then with the entire Buryat Republic."[25]

However, shamanic organizations refused to support such an individual call. Strong opinion was voiced by Budazhap Shiretorov, the vice-chairman of *Tengri*, the religious community of shamans. He said, "We are out of politics. Shamans should not define borders of territories because our task is to work with people and to help the people."[26]

The official Buddhist clergy showed a similar position in connection with the dispossession faced by the Buryat districts regarding their autonomous status. In the official discourse of the traditional *sangha* of Russia, the issue of merger was not heard. However, the lamas expressed their negative opinions in private. Some of them dared to speak out to the mass media, for example, Dzhampa Tinlei, a widely known teacher of Buddhist philosophy and one of the representatives of the Dalai Lama in Russia, said, "Enlargement of regions will prevent spiritual development of Buryatiya. Disappearance of unique and original culture of Buryatiya will be a tragedy both for Russia and for the whole world."[27]

The loyalty of the Buddhist clergy to the Russian state dates back to the imperial times when besides spiritual duties the Buddhist church was responsible for various administrative and economic affairs. Participation in political life was at that time limited to the faithful and was visible especially during official visits and celebrations both in the Buryat territories and in the capital city Ulan Ude. Thus, the Buddhist patriarchs were well aware of the political situation in Russia and always firmly supported the monarchy (the Russian emperors were called White Tsars and incarnations of God).

Despite Soviet atheist instructions, the Buddhist church was prominent in Buryatiya—it was founded in the Tsarist era. Its adaptation to Soviet socialism was not easy. The present-day model of behaviour towards Russian authorities reminds one of old well-tested relations with imperial power. Honest exercising of state-protective function of religion does not allow the officially recognized clergy to come into contradictions with the state policy. Simultaneously, the old experience in politics is now expressing itself in the wide participation of clergy in democratic institutions (elective bodies of federal and local level). The traditional Buddhist *sangha* of Russia fulfills the state-protective and regulative functions of religion by means of both support to the state and constant reminding the common people the tragic events in Russia's Buddhist history during the Soviet period.

Thus, after decades of persecution, post Soviet religious revival is being expressed through active discussions in political and cultural events, besides getting widespread coverage in the electronic media. The topics are various but strikingly similar in their anti-Soviet criticism: destruction of clergy and places of worship, persecution of believers, moral behaviour, elimination of ethno-national culture and so on. Buddhist revival along with ethnic mobilization is a multilayered phenomenon with distinguishable stages reflective of internal dynamics in the ethno-political process in Russia as a whole and in Buryatiya in particular. The features of this revivalist trend are de-politicization of ethnicity and interaction between the people and the national elite who adapted to slogans about Buryat unity and impending disaster of disintegration and destruction. At present, religion is only a matter of social practice, which allows manifestation of politicized ethnicity. Such ideology was born in the *perestroika* period and ethnic nationalists now prefer to keep quiet. Hambo Lama Ayusheev's [28] statements sound rather topical: "having taken the place of the former ideologists, the clergy became elite."[29]

Buryat ethno-political discourse in the first decade in the post Soviet period was refracted by the public statements of Hambo Lama Ayusheev. Of course, there have been revisions since then and his pronouncements are not as emotional and sensational as they were in the period of ethnic mobilization. In his defense of Buryat ethnic differentiation, Ayusheev preaches the original forms of Buryat identity that can be preserved by returning to pastoral stockbreeding. In his opinion, urban dwellers could have a flock of sheep in the rural areas and the clergy should ascribe to Buryat, not Tibetan rituals for holding religious services in the *datsans.* [30]

The Itigelov Phenomenon

While arguing against the impracticability of Buryat ideology for true national integration, the leaders complained about the absence of charismatic personalities. They said that it was Soviet power that deprived Buryats of committed people and this is an urgent task. The search was focused on history, both distant (Mongol empire) and Soviet. Despite great interest in a new interpretation of historical events and figures as well as the wide use of artistic and historical themes, especially the legend of Chingiz Khan as the central figure in the discourse of Buryat elites, it did not become a unifying symbol for Buryats to the same extent as in modern Mongolia. Yet the concerns were the same—the idea of uniting Buryats (Buryat-Mongols) and Mongols of sovereign Mongolia. For public consciousness, the idea about the integrative role of the Buddhist religion appeared to be much more attractive and productive. Numerous statements by both the clergy and believers aimed at representing Buddhism as a national religion, symbolizing the idea of a Buryat nation: "The *sangha* is the only thing that truly unites the Buryat nation."[31] The elites' desire for charismatic leadership was met in 2002 when a great event took place—the traditional *sangha* of Russia found the burial place of the Hambo Lama XII Dashi Dorzho Itigelov. His sensational "return" to the material world of the Buryats instilled new life to the Buryat national idea. His personality, biography, devotedness and miracles of his life (including his

"*Samadhi*" for 75 years) immediately made him a demi-god among the Buryats and a source of sustenance among his people. He became that very charismatic leader who symbolized Buryats' uniqueness. It does not matter whether people believe in the miracle or prefer to look for a rational explanation; in any case, they all feel their personal involvement in the miracle revolving round Itigelov who was (or is) a Buryat. Itigelov as a national symbol is much more important. Itigelov's miraculous return has restored faith in the Buddhist *sangha*. He was recognized as the reincarnation of the first Hambo Lama Zayaev; he was found and revived by the lamas of the Ivolginski *datsan*. Now, he is like a living legend that lives in the specially constructed palace in the territory of this *datsan* and thus Itigelov is considered as a property of the traditional *sangha*. Pilgrimage to Itigelov's sanctuary has become the most attractive part of popular Buddhist rituals. Lamas together with mass media are actively creating mythological plots composed of mixture of Buddhist dogma, miracle stories that are shown as happenings in Itigelov's earth life and his present-day ability to bring relief from suffering and dangers. Sensational and unsolved miracles of Hambo Lama Itigelov's return had a variety of consequences. Nationalist ideology in Buryatiya revolved round the Itigelov phenomenon and strengthened the Buryats' sense of ethnic belonging. This is proved by sociological data of 2002-05 when people, after Itigelov's return, increasingly identified themselves as Buryats on cultural-religious principles. Moreover, the number of those who believe that support to religion is the most important condition for revival of the nation increased by 2.5 per cent.[32] The miracle had resonance in Russia and in some countries abroad where efforts are on for strengthening the authority of Hambo Lama Ayusheev and the position of the *sangha*. The new proposal was to consider Buryat Buddhism as a special and independent branch of northern Buddhism. The idea that increasingly gained ground was that while Russia is the centre of Orthodox Church, Buryatiya is the centre of Buddhism independent of China and Mongolia, and the construction of the Buryats' *we-image* implies that in Buryatiya, ethnic Buryats are the focus of Buddhist spirituality.

Conclusion

The lack of true religious belief and the substitution by religious eclectics and superstitions has become a significant question for religious leaders of different confessions. For most Buryats, participation in the rituals has become an important but occasional matter—sometimes they merely emulate the religious actions and behaviour of older generations. This is what M. Billig calls "banal nationalism."[33] The Dalai Lama paid attention to this situation that is common for all modern and post-modern societies. Addressing the Buryat Buddhists, he said that it was not proper to reduce Buddhism to a mere chanting of prayers or practice of simple rituals. The profound knowledge of Dharma has to be abiding for all religious Buddhists.[34] This speech of The Dalai Lama fulfils my research's agenda—that social identification cannot be the substitute of religious obligations. Buddhism has been educative for the younger generation and Buddhist culture could even help in overcoming ignorance and getting profound cultural knowledge. Besides, Buddhist ethics could be a salvation for Russia's ethnic problems and religious intolerance. Thus besides the purely religious aspect (faith), Buddhism could contribute to moral improvement in both Buryatiya and Russia.

Notes and References

1. See for example Boris Dubin, "Massovaya religioznaya kul'tura v Rossii (tendencii i itogi 1990-h godov)" (Mass religious culture in Russia (tendencies and results of 1990-es), *Vestnik obshestvennogo mneniya: Dannye. Analiz. Diskussii* 3, no. 71 (2004): 35-44; J-E. Lane, S. Ersson, *Culture and Politics. A Comparative Approach* (Burlington: Ashgate Publishing Company 2005); Zoe Knox, *Russian Society and the Orthodox Church* (New York: Routledge Curzon 2005).
2. Ayuna Bil'trikova, *Buryatskaya nacional'naya intelligenciya na sovremennom etape* (Buryat national intelligentsia at the present stage) (Ulan-Ude 2001); D.C. Budaeva, Z.R. Merdygeev, N.C. Hanturgaeva, L.M. Itigilova, *Voprosy sohraneniya i razvitiya tolerantnosti, problemy grazhdanskoi aktivnosti naseleniya Respubliki Buryatiya* (Questions of preservation and development of tolerance, problem of civil activity of the population of the Buryat Republic) (Ulan-Ude: Izdatel'stvo BGU 2010); I.N. Dashibalova, "Problemy izmereniya etnicheskih stereotipov buryat v social'nom vremeni" (Problems of measurement of the Buryat ethnic stereotypes in the social time), in ? *Problemy izmenenii social'nyh otnoshenii sredi narodov Baikal'skogo regiona (teoretiko-empiricheskie aspekty* (Ulan-Ude: Izdatel'stvo BNTs SO RAN 2004), 112-21; Irina Elaeva "Buryaty: repertuar identichnostey v sovremennom sotsiokulturnom kontekste" (Buryats: repertoire of identities in the modern sociocultural context), in *Buryatskaya etnichnost' v kontekste sociokulturnoi modernizatsii (postsovetskii period)*, T.D. Skrynnikova (ed.) (Irkutsk: Izdatel'stvo Radian 2005), chapter 2.
3. Dubin, "Massovaya religioznaya kul'tura v Rossii," 39.

4. P. Berger, T. Luckman, *Sotsial'noye konstruirovaniye real'nosti. Traktat po sociologii znaniya* (The Social Construction of Reality: A Treatise in the Sociology of Knowledge), E. Rutkevich (trans.) (Moscow: Medium 1995), 137.
5. Peter Berger, "The Desecularization of the World: A Global Overview," in *The Desecularization of the World. Resurgent Religion and World Politics*, P.L. Berger (ed.) (Washington D.C.: Ethics and Public Policy Center 1999), 2-3.
6. G. Weigel insists on religious character of communist ideology, which, he thinks, being both secular and false religion, possesses all elements of a traditional religion. Those who were united by common revolutionary Marxist-Leninist faith in communism find this religious community as extremely attractive. See George Weigel, *The Final Revolution: The Resistance Church and the Collapse of Communism* (New York: Oxford University Press 1992), 11-12.
7. Peter Berger, "The Desecularization of the World," 10-11.
8. Grace Davie, *The Sociology of Religion* (London: Sage Publications 2008), 163.
9. Zoe Knox, *Russian Society and the Orthodox Church. Religion in Russia after communism* (New York: Routledge Curzon 2005), 5. Let us add that the 1937 Soviet population census only asked respondents to state their religion.
10. Urs Altermatt, *Ethnonatsionalism v Evrope* (Ethnonationalism in Europe), S.B. Bazarnova (trans.) (Moscow: RGGU 2000), 140-41.
11. Rossiiskaia Federatsiia Federal'nyi zakon, 'O svobode sovesti i o religioznykh ob'edineniiakh' (The Federal Law On Freedom of Conscience and Religious Associations), *Rossiiskaia gazeta*, 1 October 1997: 2-3.
12. Aleksandr Mahachkeev, *Portret iyerarha. XXIV Pandito Hambo Lama Damba Ayusheev* (Portrait of the Hierarch. Pandito Hambo XXIV Damba Ayusheev) (Ulan-Ude: Tipogragia NovaPrint 2010), 20.
13. Elaeva "Buryaty," 214.
14. Tsyben Zhamtsarano, "Buryatskoye narodnicheskoye dvizheniye i yego kritik" (Buryat Narodnik movement and its Critic), *Sibirskiye voprosy*, no. 24 (1907): 15-20; R.D. Nimayev (ed.), *E-D Rinchino: dokumenty, statyi, pis'ma* (E.-D. Rinchino: Documents, Articles, and Letters) (Ulan-Ude: Redaktsionno-izdatel'skii otdel Minpechati Respubliki Buryatiya 1994).
15. For my ideas about re-ethnicization see Darima Amogolonova, *Sovremennaya buryatskaya etnosfera: diskursy, paradigmy, sociokul'turnyye praktiki* (Modern Buryat Ethnosphere: Discourses, Paradigms, and Sociocultural Practices) (Ulan-Ude: Izdatel'stvo BGU 2008), 44.
16. M. Saidukova, "Robert Turman: ya mechtayu snyat' fil'm o buryatskom lame" (Robert Turman: 'I dream of shooting a film about Buryat lama'), *Inform Polis*, no. 1 (2006): 11.

17. I have left aside a discussion on the topic about inveigling of relatively big number of Buryats and ethnic Russians into the non-traditional for Buryatiya religious communities such as Bahai, Evangelists, Catholics, Mormons, etc.
18. Pavel Varnavski considers this aspect of the Buddhist revival in Buryatiya in his paper "Strategii konstruirovaniya sociokul'turnyh granic v sovremennom diskurse buryatskoi etnichnosti" (Strategies of constructing socio-cultural boundaries in the modern discourse of Buryat ethnicity), *Problemy istorii, filologii, kul'tury*, vol. 70 (2008): 254-67.
19. "Shes't' dnei" (Six days), *Nowhere* (1991): 3.
20. Ulan-Ude (Buryat: Red Uda-river) is a name of the capital city of the Buryat Republic received in 1934 after renaming of Verkhneudinsk (Russian: city on Upper Uda-river), that had existed as a city from the second half of eighteenth century.
21. Evgenie Startsev, "Slovo redaktora" (Word of the Editor), *Troickoe Slovo Zabaikal'ya* 3-6, no. 1 (2001): 4.
22. Startsev, "Krepkaya osnova" (Strong basis), Troickoe *Slovo Zabaikal'ya* 4-9, no. 4 (2005): 6.
23. *Serge* (Сэргэ) (literally: tether) is a post usually 1.7-1. 9 meters in height, decorated at the top with a curved ornament. The *serge* was an object of worship and symbolized well-being and social status of a Buryat and his family. Establishing a *serge* fixed a man's rights to a territory; the wooden posts symbolized that this land has an owner.
24. Nadezhda Stepanova's forecasting was correct: merging of Aginski Buryat Autonomous district with Chita region took place in a year after merging of Ust'-Orda with Irkutsk region.
25. Baikal-media Consulting (2008). Available from http://baikal-media.com. cited 18 February 2010.
26. "Kto balamutit narod? Uzh tochno—nie shamany" (Who agitates the people? It is exactly not shamans), *Argumenty i Fakty v Buryatii*, no. 12 (2006):1.
27. "Uchitel' vyshel v svet" (The Teacher went out to the world), *Argumenty i Fakty v Buryatii*, no. 24 (2005): 1.
28. Damba Ayusheev is the twenty-fourth Hambo Lama. He was elected to this position on 28 April 1995. In accordance to this status, he is the Chairman of the Traditional Buddhist Sangha of Russia.
29. Cited in Mahachkeev, *Portret iyerarha*, 142.
30. Cited in Mahachkeev, *Portret iyerarha*, 183, 164.
31. Dara Anzhilova, "Istoricheskiy syezd Sanghi" (Historical Congress of the Sangha), *Argumenty i Fakty v Buryatii*, no. 18 (2008): 1.
32. Elaeva "Buryaty," 149.
33. Michael Billig, *Banal Nationalism* (London: Sage Publications 1995).
34. "Obrasheniye Dalai Lamy XIV k buddistam Buryatii" (Dalai Lama XIV Address to the Buddhists of Buryatiya), *Ugai Zam*, no. 30 (2011): 1.

Institutions and Structures

22

Central Asian States: Alternative Models of Economic Development

R.G. Gidadhubli

After the breakup of the Soviet Union, the Central Asian States (CAS) as all other former Soviet Republics were in the process of transition from the former communist system to political democracy and market economy. This process had been difficult and painful particularly to the CAS which were relatively less developed as compared to republics in the western part and were politically and economically more dependent upon the centre. Moreover, under the former system of central political and economic control, they had least exposure of independently managing political and economic affairs such as foreign policy issues and carrying out foreign trade. Hence the impact of political vacuum caused by the dissolution of the USSR was very severe and consequences on the economy in the early 1990s were unprecedented resulting in sharp decline in Gross Domestic Product, industrial and agricultural production, hyper inflation, high level of unemployment and so on.

Notwithstanding these adverse conditions of historic proportions, being politically independent and sovereign, each of the CAS made attempts to evolve their own path of transition. An effort has been made in this paper to examine and evaluate economic policies and performance with special reference to Uzbekistan and Kazakhstan, which followed their own models of development. However, a brief review of economic performance at a macro level during the last decade seems to be in order. Having overcome the crisis conditions of the 1990s, all the five CAS showed positive GDP growth during the period 2000-04 (Table 1). In the case of the Kyrgyz Republic and Uzbekistan average annual GDP growth rates were modest below 5 per cent. Tajikistan recorded nearly 10 per cent and Kazakhstan above 10 per cent average annual growth in that period. Turkmenistan recorded over 17 per cent annual GDP growth rates during this period and as per the country's official data the country did not experience economic crisis and hence is an exception among the Commonwealth of Independent States (CIS). But during the last five years which also includes two to three years of global financial crisis and recession, there are high fluctuations in the annual GDP growth rates in the case of Kyrgyz Republic, Kazakhstan and Tajikistan. Low and even negative growth rates are recorded during the last two years particularly in 2009 which has been due to the impact of global financial crisis and sharp decline in international pries for oil and natural gas. In contrast to that both Turkmenistan and Uzbekistan have maintained relatively stable growth rates notwithstanding annual fluctuations.

Table 1. Growth Rates of Gross Domestic Product of Central Asian States

Country	2000-04	2005	2006	2007	2008	2009	2010(Est)
Kyrgyzstan	4.9	-0.2	3.1	8.5	7.6	0.9	0.9
Kazakhstan	10.4	9.7	10.7	8.9	3.2	-2.0	1.5
Tajikistan	9.7	6.7	7.0	7.8	7.9	2.0	3.0
Turkmenistan	17.3	13.0	11.4	11.6	9.8	6.9	7.0
Uzbekistan	4.8	7.0	7.3	9.5	9.0	7.0	7.0

Source: Official data and data from reports on internet on Central Asian States.

Essence of Uzbek Economic Development Model

After independence, the Uzbek leaders analysed the experience of economic reforms and development of neighbouring countries such as Russia, Turkey, China, Iran, Malaysia as various alternatives for choosing its own course of economic development. There was growing realization that the Russian model of "Shock Therapy" adopted by Boris Yeltsin had resulted in deep crisis for the Russian economy; this had created criticism and controversy among some former republics of the USSR which were also in the process of transition. Being aware of this fact the leadership of Uzbekistan was not in favour of "Shock Therapy" as a model for its economic development of the country. After deliberations, they worked out their own path of economic development known as the "Uzbek Model." The President of Uzbekistan Islam Karimov spelt out the main principles on which this model was based, the essential features of which are the following:

- de-ideologization of the economy;
- primacy of economics over politics;
- state to remain the chief for the management of the economy;
- strong social policy.

It was contended that the "Uzbek model" was needed so that the country gradually introduced market economic principles in order to avoid social dislocation. In this context it may be worthwhile to mention that the specialists from the IMF and the World Bank were advising these economies in transition to dismantle the old system as quickly as possible, which was also interpreted as transition in one-go. But some leaders including Islam Karimov, knowing their local conditions and concerned about social and economic consequences of such a path of transition, were not in favour of change in one-go as they were.

The Uzbek leaders have consistently maintained that the Uzbek Model had a positive impact on the economy. For instance, it has been argued that up to the second half of the 1990s the economic crisis was largely averted by Uzbekistan which had affected other countries in transition. This is evident from the decline in GDP growth rates in the Central Asian states during the decade of the1990s—GDP declined by 49 per cent in Tajikistan, 48 per cent in Kyrgyzstan, and 43 per cent in Kazakhstan. As compared to these countries there was somewhat smaller contraction in Turkmenistan at about 19 per cent and especially Uzbekistan 17 per cent. Hence in his book *Uzbekistan on the Threshold of the Twenty First Century*, Islam Karimov asserted that Uzbek economic reforms were based on solid principles. In fact there was appreciation of this model as a sound policy by some international financial institutions and economists including Vladimir Kolesnikov of Russia and Fredrick Starr of the USA. Considering political and economic development of Uzbekistan in the early 1990s following its own model, even the US policy makers opined "Uzbekistan was an island of stability in the ocean of instability." At that time the USA also extended substantial economic assistance through massive investment in joint ventures, which gave moral support to the Uzbek leadership. Similarly, the Uzbek leaders have again claimed that Uzbekistan was able to avert economic decline to a great extent during the global financial crisis in 2009 thanks to the model of development adopted by the country, whereas Russia and many other countries could not.

Objectively analysing the economic development process in the country, it may be stated that there are contentions and controversies so far as the Uzbek model of development is concerned between critics and supporters of Uzbek policy makers. For instance, there are many western critics including Andrew Apostolou of UK who have opined that the Uzbek Model was a mistake. It has been argued that the claim of high growth performance of the Uzbek Model depended upon the government subsidies, which supported the industrial production and the social welfare network and hence it was not sustainable in the long run. Secondly, in the opinion of some experts, since 1996 the economic system had been gradually collapsing under its own weight of subsidies and controls. Thirdly, on the type of economic reforms implemented in Uzbekistan through the Uzbek Model, some western critics have opined that the political system prevailing in the country was dominated by vested interests at all levels that had a considerable investment in retaining the "status quo," which possibly meant that of the Soviet era. In 2003 a leading European Think Tank had warned that Uzbekistan needed to undertake reforms or face economic upheaval.

Some important economic aspects of Uzbek Model may be pointed out.

1. In the Uzbek model of economic development, as opined by some analysts, foreign trade was not given due priority in the initial phase. In fact by adopting the policy of import substitution and imposing high taxes on imports, the Uzbek government had tried to protect the domestic producers. This is evident from the reduction of area under cotton, which was a major item of export earning hard currency and the country had a comparative advantage. But the leaders adopted policy of increasing area under food grains although yields were low as compared to cotton but the objective was to make the country self sufficient and reducing imports of wheat from Kazakhstan.
2. Besides that there were high indirect taxes on imported goods as a result of differentiated application of excise duties, which restricted imports in the county. According to some western experts, restrictions on trade imposed even in 2002 including some punitive tariffs, severely affected the Uzbek economy. In 2005 tariffs in Uzbekistan were about 30 per cent as compared to 15 per cent in Tajikistan and Kyrgyz Republic.

Some economists have opined that Uzbekistan adopted several administrative policy measures, which were not rational and they served to push trade out of the country into Kazakhstan and the Kyrgyz Republic. Thus official and legal channels of foreign trade were affected much to the disadvantage of the economy. Moreover, it led to cross border outflow of hard currency. Because even conservative estimates suggested that total cross-border outflow of hard currency was reaching at about US $ 100 million per month.

Economic Performance

On the basis of what is stated above let us examine the economic performance of Uzbekistan. As pointed out earlier, economic growth in Uzbekistan during the first decade of independence was modest and deep crisis was certainly averted. In fact, the Uzbek economy having undergone post-Soviet crisis up to 1995, was able to enjoy stable, albeit modest growth between 1996 and 2002 when annual GDP growth rates were low in the range of 4-5 per cent. American Prof. Spechler has called this "period of lean years" during which Uzbekistan was able to rely on the sale of cotton, gold, metals and minerals to earn much needed hard currency to sustain economic growth. As per official data economic growth picked up between 2002-06 when annual GDP growth rates were about 5-7 per cent. During the subsequent period of 2007 and 2008, there was significant rise in GDP growth rates of 9-11 per cent in Uzbekistan among the Central Asian States Uzbekistan apart from Turkmenistan.

But there are variations between official claims and assessments of economic analysts. For instance during the period 2000-06 as compared to many CIS countries including Russia, Kazakhstan, etc., overall growth performance of Uzbekistan economy was less impressive. During the period 2000-04 Uzbekistan had the lowest GDP annual growth rates of just about 4.8 per cent as compared to over 10 per cent in Kazakhstan and Tajikistan and over 17 per cent in Turkmenistan. It was also stated that economic growth hardly kept pace with population growth. Moreover, unemployment was rife and poverty was deepening. Similarly, disagreeing with the high claim with regard to Uzbek Model on the issue of global recession, in 2009 Farangis Najibullah has opined that Karimov has omitted glaring failures of Uzbek Model including the fact that substantial section of the population have lived in poverty and several thousands of Uzbeks have left the country for jobs outside mainly to Kazakhstan, Russia, etc. It is also important to note that contrary to the claim of Karimov about rising income of the population and their overall welfare, economic gap between urban population and large section of rural population has been widening over the last two decades.

Reacting to these criticisms there is a different argument made by the Uzbek leaders who have claimed that during the last decade economy has been stabilized and policy measures have been taken to reform the economy. Hence the arguments and contentions of western critics are not acceptable to the Uzbek leaders and economists. For instance, it is pointed out that the Government of Uzbekistan has been actively engaged in implementing a "comprehensive privatization programme for 2006-08." This policy measure envisaged privatization of more than 1,500 enterprises, including enterprises in strategic sectors such as energy, chemical and transport. According to Uzbek reports in 2006 more than 600 enterprises were privatized. It is reported that this policy measure has helped the government to get privatization revenues that were 20 per cent higher than in 2005. Hence as per Uzbek official sources by the end of 2006 the private sector's contribution to GDP reached 79.4 per cent.

But contrary to these claims, in the opinion of some western specialists, reliable information on Uzbekistan economy has been lacking and that official data is not necessarily reliable. For instance, it may be worthwhile to note that in the latest book entitled *The World Economic Crisis* by Islam Karimov it has been pointed out that Uzbekistan has weathered the global financial crisis and was projecting a robust economic growth in 2010. But as commented by Laurie Rich, in the report published on 17 December 2009 by the credit ratings agency Standard and Poor's there is total rejection of such a such a rosy picture and a much darker picture of the Uzbek economy has been painted. Similarly, while appreciating overall economic development in Uzbekistan in 2006, the IMF evaluated its economic growth rate at 6-7 per cent, which was lower than the official estimate. For instance, it is pointed out that the claim of comparatively high growth despite global recession in 2009 was partly due to the fact that Uzbekistan was isolated from global economy and hence recession had not impacted that country as it had done to most of the countries in the world. Similarly, as per independent estimates the inflation rate in Uzbekistan was higher than official estimates reaching double digit figures of 20-22 per cent while as per official figures inflation ranged between 7-8 per cent during the period 2006 to 2009. Another indicator of the problems facing the country has been the depreciation of its national currency Som. In August 2009 the Uzbek Som continued to depreciate through the crawling peg arrangement, trading at UZS 1,494 per US dollar. Finance experts forecasted further depreciation during 2010 and even beyond.

In addition to what is stated above it may be worthwhile to point out that according to one western critical analysis made in 2007, Uzbekistan had made the least progress in transforming its centrally-managed, planned economy to a market-based one among the former Soviet states. It is also pointed out that the government had demonstrated little commitment to much needed structural reforms and hence there were strong views that the country could face a stagnating economy. As has been observed, the trade regime remained highly restrictive and only a few large-scale enterprises had been privatized. Moreover, the agricultural sector has been under full state control. According to Angelnia Ksravaeva, the economy rested on two main export commodities, namely gold and cotton fibre, which boosted in recent years thanks to increase in world market prices. However, there was lack of diversification which made the economy extremely susceptible to external shocks. In her assessment, annual GDP had been growing steadily at an average 4 per cent during 1996-2003 peaking at around 7 per cent in 2004 and 2005. Contrary to these views, addressing the nation on the eve of 2010, Islam Karimov stated, "the circumstances proved that the way Uzbekistan has chosen was the most correct and realistic. While transforming from administrative system to market economy, we have followed the principle 'Do not destroy old house before building a new one. We chose evolutional and step-by-step way of reforms."

External Assistance

External assistance has played an important part in the economic development of all the former Soviet republics including Uzbekistan and Kazakhstan. But the scale and quantum was different depending upon the policies pursued by the recipient country. Being a relatively less developed country, domestic resources were inadequate and hence Uzbekistan badly needed external economic assistance after the Soviet break-up for its transition to market economic system. After gaining independence Uzbekistan became a member of various international financial institutions such as the World Bank, IMF, International Finance Corporation (IFC), Asian Development Bank (ADB), etc. Hence Uzbekistan has been able to get assistance, both financial and technical, from these institutions, which has immensely helped economic development of the country. For instance, during the last two decades, the IFC has extended economic assistance of about $ 68 million and arranged $ 13 million syndication. The IFC has extended assistance especially to promote Small and Medium Enterprises (SMEs) and develop financial markets through various banks in Uzbekistan (National Bank of Uzbekistan, Asaka Bank, etc.). For example, in 2002 the IFC helped to develop new leasing legislation which improved considerably financing options for SMEs, and in 2005 with IFC support, seven new Presidential decrees were adopted to help improve the business-enabling environment for SMEs. Moreover, the IFC has been active through what is known as the organization known as Private Enterprise Partnership of Central Asia which has helped improving financial intermediation for micro and small business enterprises. According to press reports as of January 2007, the IFC portfolio stood at US $16 million, with 88 per cent in financial markets and 12 per cent in the real sector.

Since investment from western countries was declining during the last decade mainly due to certain of its own policies, Uzbekistan made efforts to get investment from Russia, China and even Kazakhstan. Events at Andijan also adversely impacted political and economic ties with the West. During the last couple of years situation seems to have improved and Uzbekistan has been able to attract foreign investment in its economic development. According to Uzbek reports during 2007 foreign investment was of the order of $ 4.3 bln. which facilitated the country to complete 300 large projects. In 2008 according to official sources there was 40 per cent increase in foreign investment amounting to about $ 5.4 bln out of which FDI was $ 1.5 bln. This shows that stable economic growth of Uzbekistan has attracted foreign investment into this Central Asian country. The government expected 80 projects to be implemented including construction of industrial objects. The objective of the state was to utilize foreign investment for modernization of several enterprises. This trend seems to have continued in 2009.

In spite of this as stated by several analysts, Uzbekistan lagged much behind many other states including Kazakhstan with regard to external assistance including foreign direct investment (FDI). It is observed that per capita foreign investment was very low in Uzbekistan as compared to Kazakhstan. For instance, in the opinion of some analysts and also as per report of the European Bank for Reconstruction and Development (EBRD), foreign direct investment (FDI) per capita in Uzbekistan was the lowest and in Kazakhstan it was the highest among the CAS. The reason for this is as follows. Firstly, it was noted in this connection that investment climate in Uzbekistan was least favourable among the Central Asian countries. Secondly, in the aftermath of Andijan events Uzbekistan's political ties were under severe strain with the USA and West European countries. Thirdly, the policy of Uzbekistan Government in 2006 forced Newmout, the USA gold mining joint venture firm to close down its operations, an enterprise which was one of the earliest and most prestigious in Uzbekistan. Same was the case with British owned Oxus Mining firm and South Korean UzDaewoo automobile firm. Fourthly, the performance of many enterprises was not satisfactory. For instance, the ADB also reported that while it had funded Uzbekistan 90 projects of SME, many were not operating well. In view of this it may be stated that Uzbek leaders have to make sustained efforts to undertake liberal policy measures and improve investment climate to attract FDI to ensure economic growth in the medium and long run.

Kazakhstan's Developmental Model

Unlike Uzbekistan, Kazakhstan did make a brief experimentation with Shock Therapy after the Soviet breakup. Subsequently, Kazakhstan has essentially followed the path of gradual reforms. The leaders of the country have stated and consistently pursued the policy of economic liberalization with regard to privatization, opening up of the economy for foreign investment and so on. Thanks to huge exports of oil and natural gas at the then prevailing high international prices, country has recorded about 6-8 per cent average annual growth rates over the past decade and now boasts per capita gross domestic product of more than $9,000, a twelve fold increase compared with 1994 and four times that of Egypt in 2010. The high level of living standards in Kazakhstan has been the envy of some of its neighbours. It has been opined by analysts that prior to the global economic recession, there was reasonably high growth in the Kazak economy during the major part of the last decade unlike in the case of Uzbekistan. An idea about the economic development of Kazakhstan during the period till 2007 can be had from the data given in Table 2.

Table 2. Economic Development of Kazakhstan

	2004	*2005*	*2006*	*2007*
GDP*	5,870	7,591	10,214	12,726
Industrial Production*	3,734	5,124	6,433	7,704
Investment*	1,531	2,205	2,810	3,234
Percentage of Unemployment	1.5	1.2	0.9	0.7
Average Monthly Salary**	32.6	44.9	53.5	66.9
State Reserves***	9,277	7,069	19,127	17,392
Exchange Rate to US$	136	132	126	122

* in Billion Tenge

** in Tenge

*** in Million $

Source: *Sovremenny Kazakhstan* (Modern Kazakhstan: Strategy of Success) (Almaty 2008), 93

It is evident from the data that GDP in Tenge which is the national currency of the country, jumped from 5,870 billion in 2004 to over 12, 726 billion in 2007, which means more than two fold increase in four years. Same is the case with industrial production and investment in the country. The hard currency reserves of Kazakhstan shot up reaching the highest level of over nineteen thousand million dollars in 2006 which was more than double than that in 2004. This high growth was not there in the case of Uzbekistan. Needless to state that oil factor has played a crucial role in the Kazak economy. When the country became independent there was total state control over the economy and there was absence of entrepreneurial class. But by 2011 Kazakhstan has private sector with 700 thousand small and medium-size business enterprises, which are the backbone of its economy. Kazak analysts claim that this has enabled the country to build a strong economy. Apart from that the state has share in management and stake in large enterprises of hydrocarbon resources, mineral resources, etc.

The main sources of economic growth of Kazakhstan have been hydrocarbon energy, minerals and metals. The importance of oil factor in the economic development of Kazakhstan is evident from the following. During the period 2000-07 when there was consistent rise in the prices for oil and natural gas in the global market, which are the main items of export of Kazakhstan, the economy was booming with high annual GDP growth of 9-10 per cent. More importantly there was huge inflow of petrodollars into the country. Hence the Kazak president Nazarbaev was quite confident when he stated that his aim was to transform his country into one of the "50 most competitive, dynamically developing countries in the world" within the next decade, that is, by 2015. In order to achieve this objective it was stated that the government's principle aim should be "creating favourable institutional and economic conditions to raise Kazakhstan's competitiveness in the international arena, as well as living standards." There was optimism even among many western economic experts including Edward Parker who was the head of the London based agency known as Emerging Europe Sovereign of Fitch Rating in 2007. At the Kazakhstan investment conference held in London in March 2007 many analysts also supported such assessment. It was known that the engine of Kazakhstan economic growth was its abundant oil and natural gas resources. After the Soviet breakup major oil importing countries of the West were keen to utilize this source of energy as an additional one to that of the Middle East. Hence Kazakhstan had the distinction of high rating in 2006 and was put on par with Russia in terms of Global Competitiveness Index. It is significant to note that UNCTAD also supported this position of Kazakhstan's economic performance having examined growth process of economy during the previous decade. In view of this the Kazak leaders had reason to be satisfied with the economic policy of the country. Hence the country also worked out 10-year plan covering 2006-2015 during which economic growth would multiply and so also various branches of economy. But the sharp decline in economic growth due to decline in international oil prices and global recession in 2008 and 2009 have forced Kazakh leaders to revise their economic strategy and estimates of growth targets downwards for 2015. In 2010 the country had partly overcome these recessionary trends and growth has picked up thanks to policy of diversification of economy. Hence on 28 January 2011, Nazarbaev in his State of the Nation address which was based on "Country's Development Programme 2020," stated that his priorities will be to continue programmes of sustainable economic development.

There is also realization on the part of leaders that some regions of the country are not well developed. For instance, the southern part of Kazakhstan is energy deficient as a result of which the region's economic development has suffered. It has to depend upon import of energy from northern parts of the country or import from Uzbekistan. An important dimension of economic development is that in March 2011 to meet its energy needs the Kazak leaders have entered into a joint venture with company known as Central Asia Green Power which is a Turkish subsidiary of Italy's Relight Group. With investment of one billion dollars, this enterprise proposes to utilize the renewable wind energy as a source to meet energy needs of its southern region. This project is worth appreciating because if it succeeds that will open new possibilities for other Central Asian States including Tajikistan and Kyrgyz Republic which are also energy deficient.

Kazakhstan economic growth model and close interaction with the western countries led the country to become the rotating chairman of the Organization of the Security Cooperation of Europe (OSCE). This is the only country among the former Soviet states to have received this honour. In fact since 2006 the Kazak leaders worked hard so that their country got a chance to become a rotating chairman of the OSCE. It was obvious that the objective was to enhance the country's global standing. In support of the Kazak claim, the Belgian Foreign Minister Karel de Gucht, the former OSCE chairman-in-office, characterized Kazakhstan's bid as "both a challenge and an opportunity." He even added that Kazakhstan was the "worthiest candidate" in Central Asia, which he described as a "very important" region and for the first time a country east of Vienna, was to chair the European organization. Their objective was achieved in 2009 and Kazakhstan completed its task of annual chairmanship in 2010. It is important to note that the Kazak leaders have the objective of the membership of WTO which is yet to materialize.

Notwithstanding several economic achievements what are stated above, overdependence of Kazakhstan on energy sector has its own disadvantage. This became evident with the downturn in oil prices in 2008 and global financial crisis, which were least expected by the Kazak leaders. Hence contrary to the high hopes, sharp decline in oil price in the global market from about $ 150 per barrel in 2007 to below $50 per barrels in 2008 very adversely affected the economy which is evident from decline in GDP to – 2 per cent in 2009. Even in 2010 GDP growth rate has been low. As a result of this there was overall adverse impact on other sectors as well such as industry, agriculture, trade, banking, etc. Foreign exchange reserves also declined. All these affected the country's financial condition. In October 2010 the international rating agency Standard and Poor downgraded Astana's sovereign credit rating to BBB-, the lowest grade category. Hence there is realization of the part of the leaders of the country that overdependence on oil has not been a rational decision for the country. As opined by some international finance experts Kazakhstan banks resorted to rapid rate of borrowing and the country was unable to take timely corrective steps. Hence the economy became a victim of negative developments during global financial crisis. However, it needs to be added that the country has the potentiality for economic development and strengthen the economic base by following policy of diversification.

Some Concluding Observations

From what is stated above some concluding observations can be made. There are some distinctive features in the two models of economic development of Uzbekistan and Kazakhstan. A comparative analysis of economic development strategy and policies of the two countries indicates that in this regard Uzbekistan seems to be less consistent as compared to Kazakhstan. This is evident from the following. Firstly, Uzbekistan has been found to be changing its alignments between major powers namely Russia and USA during the last two decades. For instance, in the early 1990s Uzbekistan was very critical of Russia and was closely aligned with the USA. But subsequent to the Andijan event in 2005, Uzbekistan went totally against USA and West in general. During the last couple of years the relations have improved and in January 2011 Islam Karimov addressed the members of the European Union and invited their greater participation in the economic development of Uzbekistan. While some analysts might explain such changes in alignments in terms of the country pursuing its own national interest, it is needless to state that such extremities in alignments in foreign policies have impacted adversely on the economic development of Uzbekistan.

Secondly, there has been lack of consistency with regard Uzbekistan's policy for opening the economy for foreign investment. This is very evident in the case of Zaravshan Newmont Gold Mine American company. In the early 1990s when Uzbekistan wanted Newmont company to invest in its old gold mine and bring in advance technology for recovering gold, there was a hype created for foreign companies as well to invest in the country. But within a short of period of time the company was asked to wind up. Such abrupt policy changes have adversely affected foreign investment climate in the country and economic development in general. Thirdly, in the aftermath of the Soviet breakup, Uzbekistan was a member of the regional grouping known as GUUAM, which was a rival organization to that set up Russia, Kazakhstan, etc. Perhaps subsequently there was a realization by the Uzbek leaders that their interest was not served by its association with that regional organization. Hence there has been a change and Uzbekistan discontinued its membership. Fourthly, it needs to be stated that state control over the economy is relatively more in the case of Uzbekistan than in the case of Kazakhstan. Similarly, even as both Uzbekistan and Kazakhstan have been characterized by authoritarianism, Uzbekistan has greater degree of this phenomenon than Kazakhstan.

At the same time there are some common features. In the case of Kazakhstan the country has been very keen in inviting foreign capital and technology for the development of energy sector in the early 1990s. To a great extent it has succeeded. But during the last decade the policy of 'Resource Nationalism' followed by the Kazak leaders led to discouragement of inflow of foreign capital. This was evident in the case of Eni oil firm which was forced to reduce its share in the energy sector of Kazakhstan. Barring such few instances the leadership of Kazakhstan has been fairly consistent with regard to policies and ties with Russia in particular and the West in general.

For instance, in 2007 when Kazakhstan was seeking chairmanship of OSCE there were speculations as to whether there will be change in its policies since the country had to conform to European Union policies. At that time the Kazak foreign minister Marat Tazhin stated on 6 December 2007 that there would be no change. According to him Russia had been and would remain strategic partner and that energy policy would remain "clear and transparent." At the same time it is understandable that Kazakhstan has been guided by its own national interest. This is evident from the Kazakh participation in the Baku-

Tbilisi-Ceyhan pipeline project and the development of the planned Turkmenistan-Uzbekistan-Kazakhstan-China gas pipeline even as the country has been closely tied up with Russia in the energy sector.

It is important to note that China has also emerged as a major partner in the Kazak economy. China has become an importer of oil and gas, uranium (55 thousand tons to be supplied) and other mineral resources. China's CNPC oil firm has close links with the Kazak energy sector. In turn China has over 1, 000 joint ventures in Kazakhstan and Nazrbaev during his visit to Beijing in February 2011 has offered one million hectares of land to China on 99 years of lease. In turn without interfering in Kazakhstan's internal affairs, China has been consistently offering huge credits to Kazakhstan to overcome economic problems, infrastructure development, etc. India and Kazakhstan also have cordial relations. Thus in essence Kazakhstan has been more stable and consistent in its policies than Uzbekistan concerning external political and economic relations both at the regional and global level, which has brought good dividends for the economic development of the country.

For further reading see

A. Bedrintsev, "Uzbekistan in International Relations: Integrative Interaction," *World Economy and International Relations*, no. 2 (1999). (In Russian).

A.Gafurov, D Hakimov and A Urinov "Structural Changes in the Economy and Policy of Uzbekistan," in Central Asia Since Independence, K. Warikoo and Mahavir Singh (eds.), Maulana Abul Kalam Azad Institute of Asian Studies, Kolkata, 2004.

Andrew Apostolou, "The Mistake of the Uzbek Economic Model," *Central Asia Monitor*, no. 2 (1998).

Country Report on Uzbekistan, Economic Intelligence Unit, London, UK, 3rd quarter 1999 and 2nd quarter 2000.

Imtiyaz Ul Haq, "Economic Transition in Central Asian Republics: Problems and Prospects," in *Central Asia Continuity and Change*, Mushtaq Kaw (ed.), Center of Central Asian Studies, University of Kashmir, 1999.

Islam Karimov, *Uzbekistan: on the Threshold of the Twenty-first Century* (Richmond, UK: Curzon1997).

L.A. Chernykh, "Kazakhstan-Russia Relations," in *India-Kazakhstan Perspectives*, K Santhnam, Kurlay Baizakova and Ramakant Dwivedi (eds.), The India-Central Asia Foundation, New Delhi and Al-Farabi Kazakh National University, Almaty, 2007.

Laurie Rich, "Uzbekistan: International Institutions Skeptical on Uzbek Economy," *Eurasia Net Archive* (21 December 2009).

M.T. Laumulin, A.S. Kaukenov et al., "Foreign Political Course of Kazakhstan," in *Modern Kazakhstan Strategy of Success* (Almaty 2008).

Mahmud Hadjimetov, "The Global Financial and Economic Crisis: The Case of Uzbekistan," Eurasia *Net* (4 June 2009).

R.G.Gidadhubli, "Economic Transition in Uzbekistan," *Economic and Political Weekly* (5 February 1994).

Vladimir Koslenikov, "Uzbek Model of Development," *Russia and Islamic World* 1, no. 115 (2002). (In Russian).

23

Dialectics of Transition in Central Asia: Kyrgyzstan's Move to Parliamentary Democracy

Ajay Kumar Patnaik

The story of transition in post-Soviet Central Asia is a story of failed expectations. At the time of independence there was a huge expectation that the new states would move from a centralized command system to a liberal democratic polity. The end of command-administrative dispensation would usher in an era of prosperity for the people after years of economic stagnation. The experience of the last two decades shows that on both these counts the states have failed to deliver. In a curious departure from the Soviet legacy, the states have shed the paternalistic role that the Soviet state played in terms of providing a certain level of economic and social security to the population. At the same time the authoritarian aspect of the Soviet state has been retained and in some cases strengthened. This contradiction between welfare functions and authoritarianism in the role of the state has been a defining feature of transition in more or less all the post-Soviet states, especially in Central Asia.

According to Pauline Jones Luong, the Soviet system directly shaped societal expectations of the proper role of the state through what can be understood as a form of "social contract" between state and society. This was an implicit agreement that the state would provide for society's basic economic needs in exchange for its political acquiescence.[1] The Soviet state's authoritarianism was in a way legitimized by its distributive and redistributive functions. The successor states, however, are in the danger of losing legitimacy on this count. Some of the richer states have acquired the characteristics of a "rentier state," where the profits from natural resources are controlled and distributed among a small elite aimed at strengthening patron-client relationships. This helps create short-term regime stability but may not be enough in the long-run. This has been demonstrated by the experience of Kyrgyzstan.

State Failure in Kyrgyzstan

Kyrgyzstan was the most likely country in the post-Soviet space to have a successful popular protest movement. Like most other states the objective conditions were there. However, it is the subjective factor that marked Kyrgyzstan out from the rest. It had a relatively more liberal polity and the most liberal free market economy. The economic transition resulted in huge socio-economic deprivation and social discontent. With a stronger civil society network, popular anger found expression through anti-government protests that swept the incumbent President Akaev from power in 2005. The so called "Tulip Revolution" was supposed to be the antithesis of a system that in its eagerness to move faster to a free market economy failed to protect the vulnerable and in fact widened the gulf between the rich and the poor.

Transition from a centrally planned economy to a market-oriented one was both complex and painful. The situation was quite bad by the time the "Tulip Revolution" took place in 2005. The official rate of unemployment in Kyrgyzstan was 18 per cent in 2004. In rural areas, long-term unemployment exceeded 70 per cent, especially among the youth. The fall in employment and real wage, combined with declining spending in social sector and the removal of subsidies brought down real wages, increased unemployment and under-employment that affected the general living standard of the masses.

Kyrgyzstan largely removed subsidies for food, housing, transport, and other items in 1994 and these were replaced by targeted cash payments. Pomfret cites surveys in Kyrgyzstan in 1993 and 1996 which showed strong evidence of decline in social protection offered by the state, and of the increased cost of raising children as benefits such as kindergarten or school meals, etc., previously provided by the state or the workplace had disappeared. Households with many adults or pensioners were also more poorly placed in 1996 than in 1993, indicating that the value of the generous Soviet-era pension was being eroded. Reduced human capital not only harmed growth prospects, the emergence of alienated population challenged political stability.[2]

In Kyrgyzstan, the neo-liberal economic reforms resulted in a rapidly widening gap between rich and poor and greater distress for many. An FAO study of four Ali Okmots in the beginning of 2004 (Kara Alma, Kyzl Ungur, Arslanbob and Kaba) showed that the share of the extremely poor and poor was 49 per cent, 37.8 per cent, 44 per cent and 42 per cent respectively.[3] In 2001 around 50 per cent were classified by official estimates as poor and 13 per cent as extremely poor. In Jalalabad province in the south, the share of the population classified as poor was as high as 55 per cent, with per capita annual income of 3,854 Soms or monthly income of about 320 Soms, which was only 37.4 per cent of the national average.[4]

According to Timothy Edmunds the actual division in Central Asia has been between power and powerlessness. A small group enjoys power, while the rest of the population cutting across ethnic groups belong to the category that has been deprived since independence. Edmunds also underlined that the asymmetric distribution of power and resources might give rise to parochialism unless attended to seriously.[5] The average poverty level was very high at more than 43 per cent in 2005. In rural areas the poverty level was much higher at 50.8 per cent.[6]

The patron-client framework in which centre-periphery power relations are exercised in Central Asia depend to a large extent on the republican centre's ability to distribute wealth, favours and appointments. Failure to do so, according to Anna Matveeva, could create alternative power centres and lead to political instability.[7] For example, an important factor in mobilization against the Akaev regime was the regional discontent, which took concrete shape after the Asky shooting of 2002, when six people died in police firing on a crowd of demonstrators in southern Kyrgyzstan. The symbolic representative of the south, Prime Minister Bakiev, resigned in the aftermath of the event and the regional division heightened leading up to the parliamentary elections in 2005.

An interesting study by the Ferghana Valley Working Group of the Centre for Preventive Action indicated the intra-regional problems that had cropped up in all the three countries that share the Ferghana valley. Given high population density and rural-agricultural nature of the valley region, especially in the Kyrgyz and Uzbek part, these intra-regional problems could prove to be difficult unless addressed properly.[8] While the states were withdrawing more and more from the social sector, the concentration of political power in the Centre created tensions. In some cases globalization has created financial centres away from the resource rich areas, creating regional friction.

In Kyrgyzstan, according to the above report, the decision to end agricultural subsidies in 1998 exacerbated regional differences. The north was already getting most of the foreign investment. Given the already low income levels in south Kyrgyzstan and the ethnic split there between the Uzbeks and the Kyrgyz, the government's policy of decentralizing service delivery—shifting responsibility for the social safety net, education and health care from the national to the local and regional levels—was causing considerable friction.[9]

The failure of the local labour market in some Central Asian states to provide jobs resulted in large-scale migration. The decline of real wages in Kyrgyzstan and Tajikistan, the growing unemployment, especially among the youth in these two states and Uzbekistan, and the restrictions on trade and commerce in Uzbekistan, have pushed younger workers to migrate to Russia and other CIS states. According to official statistics, 30,000 Kyrgyz migrants worked in Russia in 2005. But unofficial sources in both Russia and Kyrgyzstan put the number between 200,000 and 500,000, which means that around 5-10 per cent of the total population of Kyrgyzstan worked in Russia.[10]

Kyrgyzstan implemented the IMF and World Bank prescribed reforms. This created greater social discontent among the population. As recognition of its free market and liberal economic reforms, Kyrgyzstan was dubbed as the "Island of Democracy." Ironically it was a region where authoritarianism prevailed otherwise. It was rewarded with WTO membership, while the rest were denied entry. By the time President Akaev was ousted, Kyrgyzstan was one of the poorest and the most debt-ridden state in the region.

Tulip Revolution: The Real Issues

Kyrgyzstan was the most liberal country in the region in all aspects. The civil society and the press were quite vibrant and were instrumental in mobilizing the human agency that is essential for a successful change of leadership. In its eagerness to curry favour with the West, the Akaev regime allowed the civil society to expand without much restriction. The American and other western-funded NGOs were allowed to work

Table 1: External Debt as Percentage of GDP, 1993-2005

Country	*1993*	*1998*	*2002*	*2005*
Kazakhstan	7	28	71	8.2
Kyrgyzstan	16	91	112	89.8
Tajikistan	23	94	95	47.1
Turkmenistan	6.79	NA	6.1	
Uzbekistan	5.21	58	29.9	

Source: Richard Pomfret, *The Central Asian Economies since Independence* (Princeton and Oxford: Princeton University Press 2006) 12; and *Regional Economic Outlook, Middle East and Central Asia*, IMF, September 2006.

freely in the republic to the extent that on 17 April 2000, the then US Secretary of State Madeline Albright could talk behind closed doors to leaders of opposition and NGO representatives within the framework of her official itinerary. The same August, two newspapers, *Dzany Muun* and *Demos Time*, supported and funded by US-based Democratic Organization were allowed to be launched in southern Kyrgyzstan.[11]

Despite the controversies surrounding the 2005 parliamentary elections, a number of actual opposition parties were allowed to contest and there were numerous observers from OSCE. More than half the seats (39 out of 75) went to second round and candidates who faced second round run-off included the President's daughter. Voting was moderate at 60 per cent in the first round and 54.5 per cent in the second round. Thus, Kyrgyz elections had a better record than parliamentary elections held in other states around that time. Yet, the allegations of unfair elections grew louder with the West and its supported NGOs joining in. While Kyrgyzstan faced turmoil, most of the other states in the region with more authoritarian dispensation were insulated from such upheavals.

The Kyrgyz experience thus shows that it is not so much the issue of authoritarianism that would arouse popular discontent but the failure of the state to redistribute wealth and meet the socio-economic needs of the population. Despite being more liberal than most other post-Soviet states, Kyrgyz leadership paid the price of rolling back the welfare functions of the state and increasingly using traditional regional-clan networks to distribute shrinking resources. President Akaev appointed northerners to key positions even in the south. Akaev was outside the communist party political hierarchy and lacked a patronage network of his own. He was thus accused of seeking to create a power base of his own in his home province of Naryn by aligning with old Soviet era party leader and Brezhnevite party boss Usubaliev and his network. This was reflected in the record support he received in the 1995 Presidential elections with 97 per cent of the votes in the Naryn region against his opponent Masaliev. In contrast Akaev secured less than 54 per cent votes in the Osh region.[12]

While Kyrgyz people wallowed in poverty, the leadership was busy in rolling back the state from much of its social responsibility. The regional clientelist network could not ensure regime stability any longer. Feeling insecure the leadership resorted to more authoritarian practices like clamping down on opposition leaders and press. With a strong civil society, this trend of less welfare and more authoritarian functions of the state could not last long. Popular protests paralysed the government in 2005 leading to the ouster of President

Akaev. The regime change was popularized by the West as "Tulip Revolution".

From "Revolution" to "Revolution"

The so-called "Tulip Revolution" did not mark a radical departure either in social or in economic terms. Many scholars do not believe that the "colour revolutions" in post-Soviet space were about democracy and think that these were all related to geopolitics. A close ally in terms of implementing free market reforms and later extending air base facility to the West, Kyrgyz leader Akaev was dumped when the regime was already facing a crisis of legitimacy.

The forces that came to power following the ouster of Akaev were not committed to revolutionary socio-economic transformation. Supported by western governments and NGOs funded by the West, the new regime continued with the same system, with a new patronage network.

The data in Table 2 demonstrates that there was hardly any change of direction. On some counts like spending on subsidies or salaries, government expenditure actually declined as a share of GDP. Indebtedness remained a huge problem. Share of unemployed working-age population (those above 15 years of age) remained unchanged between 2005 and 2008 at 42 per cent.[13]

The failure to address the issue of democratization following Akaev's ouster was also a huge blow to popular expectations. The parliamentary elections held after two years were so managed that one pro-government party secured about three-fourth of seats. The regime that replaced Akaev also failed to address the deteriorating socio-economic situation; neither did it move towards a more liberal polity. The popular frustration that was building up found expression in the events of April 2010, when masses of protesters defied the security forces to surround the centres of power in Bishkek. The feeling that they could do it again, after having done so in 2005, was the most potent factor in the success of the protest movement.

The popular protest in April 2010 was more spontaneous and the orchestration that was present in 2005 was missing. Even the western governments were surprised by the events of 2010. The popular nature of the protest has created the hope that popular aspirations will be reflected in the new system. The interim leadership that assumed power decided to introduce a parliamentary system of government. The experiment with parliamentary democracy in the face of adverse reaction from Russia and even some strong local parties is a novel one in post-Soviet Central Asia. Whether this will succeed or not

Table 2: Socio-economic Indicators, Kyrgyzstan, 2003-09

	2003	*2004*	*2005*	*2007*	*2008*	*2009 (Second Quarter)*
Unemployment % of total labour force			8.1	8.3		
Income share held by highest 20 % of population				42.6		
Income share of lowest 20 % of population				8.8		
Income share of highest 10 % of population				27.6		
Income share of lowest 10 % of population				3.9		
Life Expectancy		68	68	68	67	
External Debt (million dollars)			2,024		2,371	2,671
External Debt (% of GDP)			82		47	54
Public external borrowing (Excluding IMF), in million dollars)			92		41	320
Workers' remittances (% of GDP)			20		30	26
Govt. Expenditure (% of GDP): Transfer and subsidies			9		1.7	2.4
Govt. Expenditure (% of GDP): Wages and salaries			6		1.8	2.1
Growth rate of real GDP (in %)	7	7	0	27 (2006)		
Poverty level (% of population)	49.9	45.9	43.1	35.0		

Source: *Primechanie: Utochnili po sborniky NSK, "Kyrgyzstan b stifrakh" 2007g*; *World Bank Data*, http://data.worldbank.org/country)

Table 3: Parliamentary Election Results, Kyrgyzstan, 2007

Parties	*Votes*	*Percentage*	*Seats*
Ak Zhol	1,228,319	46.99	71
Social Democratic Party of Kyrgyzstan	55,651	5.05	11
Party of Communists of Kyrgyzstan	141,034	5.12	8
Others	Unknown	42.84	—
Total (Turnout 71.93%)		100.00	90

Source: *Inter-parliamentary Union*, http://www.ipu.org/parline-e/reports/arc/2174_07.htm.

only future events can say. But for the time being the elections of 2010 have thrown up a very balanced representation that has resulted in coalition politics. The success of any system would depend, however, on making the state responsive to the socio-economic security of the vulnerable groups of population and making the state less authoritarian in political terms.

Table 4: Kyrgyzstani Parliamentary Election Results, 2010

Party	*Percentage Won*	*Votes Cast*	*Parliamentary Seats*
Ata Jurt	8.47	257,100	28
SDPK	7.83	236,634	26
Ar-Namys	7.57	226,916	25
Respublica	6.93	210,594	23
Ata Meken	5.49	166,714	18

Source: *Kyrgyzstan. The Country in Transition*, Carnegie Endowment for International Peace, http://kyrgyzstan.carnegieendowment.org/2010/11/new-kyrgyz-parliament-represents-fraction-of-the-electorate/

Conclusion

The struggle to turn the state into a paternalistic or welfare state could take many forms. These could include radical egalitarian movements based on religion, labour movements, or movements for a liberal polity. Kyrgyzstan, a comparatively liberal state, has been the site for anti-regime protests leading to leadership change twice in a short span of five years. In fact it is the only country in the region to have done so. The mass protests that followed the 2005 parliamentary elections were intended to bring a system that would be an antithesis of what Kyrgyzstan experienced till 2005.

One important law of dialectics is known as negation of negation. The political leadership that came to power after the Soviet collapse was ousted in 2005. This however did not resolve the contradiction in the system, which needed more than just change of leadership. The second "revolution" negated the outcome of the first "revolution." In the process it heralded more radical departure from the past. It not just changed the leadership but also the post-Soviet political system. From following a presidential system, Kyrgyzstan has now become a parliamentary democracy. The success of the new political system would still depend on reorienting the role of the state and make it a socially-oriented state. The parliamentary democracy is expected to end the patronage-based regional networks and use the institutions of this system to balance the regional aspirations and interests. If that happens it would make the current synthesis an enduring one.

Notes and References

1. Pauline Jones Luong, "The future of Central Asian statehood," *Central Asia Monitor*, no. 1 (1999).
2. Richard Pomfret, *The Central Asian Economies since Independence* (Princeton and Oxford: Princeton University Press 2006) 15-18.
3. Som is the national currency of Kyrgyzstan. Very poor are those with less than 400 Soms monthly income and poor include those with 401-600 Som income.
4. *Poverty in Kyrgyzstan*, http://www.fao.org/docrep/j2603e/j2603e05.htm.
5. Timothy Edmunds, "Power and powerlessness in Kazakhstani society: ethnic problems in perspective," *Central Asian Survey* 19, no. 2 (2000): 470.
6. World Bank Data available on http://data.worldbank.org/country.
7. Anna Matveeva, "Democratisation, legitimacy and political change in Central Asia," *International Affairs* 75, no. 1 (1999).
8. *Calming the Ferghana Valley*, Preventive Action Reports, vol.4 (New York: The Century Foundation Press 1999), 75.
9. *Calming the Ferghana Valley*, Preventive Action Reports, vol.4.
10. *Central Asia HDR* 2005, 140-41.
11. "US Secretary meets Opposition," *Summary of World Broadcasts (SWB)*, part 1, SU/3819 G/1, 19 April 2000; "Two USA sponsored Kyrgyz-Uzbek-language papers launched in Kyrgyz South," *SWB*, part 1, SU/3934 G/5, 17 April 2000.
12. John Anderson, *The International Politics of Central Asia* (Manchester: 1997) 90.
13. World Bank Data available on http://data.worldbank.org/country.

24

Challenges of Institutional Transformation in Central Asia: Perspective from Uzbekistan

Mirzokhid Rakhimov

After disintegration of the USSR and the establishment of newly independent states, the change of political system became one of prominent aspects of the political reformation of the CIS countries. These changes occurred in Uzbekistan as well; however, they owed their specific features to internal and external factors. In Uzbekistan, especially at the initial stage of system renovation, as well as in many post-Soviet countries, lines of post-totalitarian authoritarianism have been obvious. In this respect, it is necessary, first, to indicate that Uzbekistan, as well as other Central Asian republics, proclaimed the creation of a democratic society based not only on universal values, but also on peculiarities of national culture and historical traditions. Thus, Prof. Rue, a renowned western political scholar, was correct in pointing out that the paternalistic nature of Asian political culture is characterized by dependence on authority, overcoming of open conflict and emphasis on stability.[1]

Secondly, in this political phenomenon a logical tendency of social development in the period of transition has been displayed. Redemption from totalitarianism demands immense efforts, step-by-step advancement, including in the initial stage, potent authoritative power which is at the same time capable of evolving towards real democracy. As a well-known American expert Prof. Martha Olcott stated "the whole complex of the entire Soviet population can only be transformed slowly."[2] This is especially true for Uzbekistan that along with the Soviet heritage it was resisting the expansion of Islamic extremism.

Establishment of a New Structure of Authority in the Republic of Uzbekistan

On 23 March 1990, the first among the leaders of union republics, Islam Karimov was elected President of Uzbekistan by majority vote in the Supreme Soviet of the UzSSR. In June 1990, the Declaration of the Sovereignty of the Republic of Uzbekistan was adopted. On 31 August 1991, the sixth session of the Supreme Soviet of the Republic was held, at which the Constitutional Law "On the Foundation of State Independence of the Republic of Uzbekistan" was adopted. For a short historical period in Uzbekistan the legal basis for the functioning of legislative, executive and judicial branches of state authority was created. The legislative branch of government was represented in the republic by the national parliament, *Oliy Majlis*, and local bodies of the representative power, *Kengashes* of People's Deputies. In the course of political reforms in the initial stage of independence, the establishment of the higher representative state organ, *Oliy Majlis* was an important step of national-democratic renovation. For the first time in Uzbekistan's history open democratic elections to the *Oliy Majlis* as well as to local representative bodies of the state authority took place on 25 December 1994.

After the expiry of the term of the *Oliy Majlis* of the first convocation in December 1999, new elections to the national parliament took place. One thousand ten candidates from five political parties, local representative bodies of power and groups of citizens contested for 250 seats in parliament. The referendum held on 27 January 2002, concerning the establishment of a parliament of two houses became a great political event; on the basis of a national referendum results, in 2002-04 new constitutional laws were adopted. Some of them are as follows: "On the referendum results and main principles of organization of a governmental authority," "On insertion of changes and additions in the Constitution of the Republic of Uzbekistan," "On the Senate *Oliy Majlis* of the Republic of Uzbekistan," "On the *Oliy Majlis* Legislative house of the Republic of Uzbekistan." Establishment of the legislative house on a constant professional basis was to promote activation of the process of legislative work, improvement of quality of adopted laws and statutory acts. In turn, establishment of the upper chamber, the Senate, as the representative body uniting in its structure the deputies of territorial subjects, the local *Kengashes*, has allowed the *Oliy Majlis*, the higher legislature, actively to influence political processes in the country, to carry out a direct connection with regions, to represent and protect their interests.

The senate consists of 100 members, 16 of whom are by appointed by the President of the country. The remaining 84 seats are occupied by representatives of the *oblast* (province), district and city legislative councils (*Kengashes*)—6 deputies from each of the 12 oblasts, Tashkent city and the Republic of Karakalpakstan. The legislative order decreed that elections to the Senate were to be held by voting by secret ballot at sessions of deputies of the *Joqorku Kenesh* or Supreme Council of the Republic of Karakalpakstan. During the 2004 elections, which was conducted in two rounds of voting (the second one took place on 9 January 2005) 120 deputies of the legislative chamber of the *Oliy Majlis* of the republic were elected. Seats in the lower chamber of the national parliament were divided between five parties and independent candidates of initiative groups of citizens. Thus, the leading positions were taken by the Liberal-Democratic Party with 21 deputies (34.2 per cent) and the People's Democratic Party with 18 deputies (23.3 per cent). Enjoying great popularity in elections of 1999, the National-Democratic Party *Fidokor* took18 seats, the Democratic Party *Milliy tiklanish* had 11 seats, Social-Democratic Party *Adolat* 10 seats, respectively. The independent candidates obtained 2 seats in the parliament.

The *Oliy Majlis* had been divided into a legislative chamber and the senate—the Lower and Upper Chambers. Essential changes have been made with regard to election legislation. According to these changes, candidates for legislative chamber are put up by political parties and initiative groups of voters, and candidates to the local *Kengash* by corresponding bodies of local political parties, self-government institutions of citizens and initiative groups of voters. The 30 per cent quota for women has been introduced for parties in nominating them as their candidates. An important stage in the development of an electoral system has been the amendments introduced in the legislative enactments on elections in 2008. The number of deputy seats increased from 120 to 150, of which 135 deputies are elected from political parties, and 15 deputy seats in legislative chamber were given to the deputies elected from Ecological Movement of Uzbekistan, proceeding from the importance and a growing urgency of problems of preservation of the environment. On 27 December 2009 new elections to the legislative chamber and the senate of the *Oliy Majlis* of the Republic of Uzbekistan took place.

Establishment of a two chamber parliament has positively affected the entire legislative process: the order and technology of elaboration and adoption of enactments were improved; scientists and experts of various fields are involved in legislative activity as experts; Public expert groups were constituted under the committees. The major core of the governmental system and the political system of Uzbekistan has been and still remains presidential form of government. According to constitutional norms, the President is elected by national poll for a period of 7 years. A President can be elected from the citizens of the Republic of Uzbekistan, should be no younger than 35 years, having a fluent command of the state language (Uzbek) and being a permanent resident on the territory of Uzbekistan for no less than 10 years directly prior the elections. One and the same person cannot be President of Uzbekistan more than two terms successively. The constitutional powers of a President are extensive. He acts as the guarantor of the constitution and human rights, represents Uzbekistan in the international relations, concludes and provides observance of international agreements and contracts, is a supreme commander in chief, etc.

However, some changes have taken place. Thus, if at the first stages of development of the country the President of the Republic of Uzbekistan was simultaneously Chairman of the Cabinet of Ministers of the state according to the new edition of the Law "On the Cabinet of Ministers of the Republic of Uzbekistan," adopted on 29 August 2003, it is the Prime Minister not the President, who has began to head it; this is certainly important as a way of further division of powers in state bodies. Those norms have been included in the constitution and legislation enactments, according to which the powers earlier belonging to the chairman of the cabinet of ministers, such as organization and operating control of the activity of the cabinet of ministers, presidency at its sessions, signing of decisions of the government adopted within their competence, are assigned to the Prime Minister.

After 1999, the next election of the President of the country took place in January 2000 and the last one on December 2007. Following were the results of the Republic of Uzbekistan Presidential elections:

- Islam Karimov (LDPU): 13,008,357 votes (88.1 %);
- Asliddin Rustamov (NDPU): 468,064 votes (3.17 %);
- Dilorom Tashmukhamedova (SDP "Adolat"): 434,111 votes (2.94 %);
- Akmal Saidov (an independent candidate): 420,815 votes (2.85 %).

Following the need for carrying out reforms for further democratization the parliament of the country directed reforms to be carried out on the order of appointment and dismissal from office of the Prime Minister, and members of the cabinet of ministers, according to which the President submits a candidate for the post of the Prime Minister for consideration and approval to *Oliy Majlis* chambers and releases him or her from office; the members of the cabinet of ministers are appointed and dismissed by the President on representation of the Prime Minister.

At the joint session of the two chambers of the *Oliy Majlis* of the Republic of Uzbekistan in November 2010, President Islam Karimov proposed that it would be necessary that the candidate for the Prime Minister be nominated by the political party which secured the greatest number of deputies in elections into the legislative chamber of the *Oliy Majlis*, or by several political parties that received equal quantity of deputy seats. In 2011 the *Oliy Majlis* introduced these changes to the constitution and other laws.

At the local level, the state authority in *oblasts*, districts and cities is represented by Councils of People's Deputies and elected *khokims*, who represents the executive power. On a new basis the system of law enforcement bodies and national safety has been created, as well as the armed forces, the ministries for foreign affairs and economic relations and other specialized establishments. Consecutive work on reforming the political system is inseparably linked with processes of democratic renovation of the whole society, for without liberalization and democratization of the state institutes none of the democratic reforms ongoing today in economic, political, humanitarian, and other spheres of vital activity of the country can be accomplished.

Specific Feature of Institutes of Civil Society in the Republic of Uzbekistan

Emergence of newly independent states of Central Asia has inaugurated new structural changes in the political life of the states of the region and their search for establishment of new system of public relations based on certain principles of democracy and a civil society, as well as national traditions and culture. The process of democratization and establishment of a civil society is carried out in conditions of difficult political, economic, ideological and geopolitical transformations. Such factors as a complex of questions of regional and international character, including the questions of civilization and inter-confessional dialogue make up a wide complex of influencing aspects for establishment of the political and public system of the countries in Central Asia.

The process of establishment of a civil society in the countries of Central Asia can be put in Hegel's words: "first, a state occurs, but the development of a civil society comes about later."[3] As is known, a multi-party system is a prominent aspect of democracy and a civil society and experience of some countries testifies to the fact that a multi-party system is characteristic of the naturally developing democratic process. In Uzbekistan, new social movements and parties began to be formed in new public realities. In particular, in 1991-2000, a number of political parties were formed, including Erk, Birlik, the People's Democratic Party, *Vatan Tarakkiyoti* (Fatherland Progress), Social Democratic Party *Adolat* (Justice), *Milliy Tiklanish* (National Revival) and National-Democratic Party *Fidokor* (Patriot). At the same time, there was transformation of parties themselves. Thus, in 2000 there was a merger of parties the two parties *Fidokor* and *Vatan Tarakkiyoti* under the title *Fidokor*. But parties like Erk and Birlik were banned. In 2003, the social movement of entrepreneurs and businessmen called Liberal-Democratic Party of Uzbekistan, holding the leading positions in national parliament of the country was shaped. The constitutional law "On strengthening the role of political parties in renovation and further democratization of public administration and country modernization" was adopted in 2006. The "Ecological Movement" was founded in 2008; however, taking into account the urgency of the problem, it is possible that in the years to come this movement can be transformed into a political party, following the example of the Green Party in Germany.

Political parties of Uzbekistan, though slowly, are gradually become an integral part of social life, and beginning to play an important role in the parliament of the country. However, the success in republican political parties' activities depends in many respects on themselves, on their active modernization and perfection of their operation and on the overall political liberalization of the country. In Uzbekistan along with the civil society structures common to many countries of the world, there is present an ancient traditional institute of self-management functions, *makhalla*, called in the national legislation as self-government institutions of citizens. The functions of a self-government institution of citizens at the local level are very wide. They are closely associated with the people and carry out various forms of public control, give targeted support to the low-income individuals, participate in organization of public services and amenities and in education of the youth. At the same time, their activity is tightly bound with local public authorities.

Currently, the total number of self-government institutions of citizens in the country accounts for more than 10 thousand. At the same time, it should be noted that the activity of *makhallas* as well as of political parties in Uzbekistan is financed mainly by the state. However, in the long run, it is necessary to expect reduction of the state financial support and increase in self-financing of the given institutes; that certainly will be a positive factor in the development of a civil society. An important place in the structure of a civil society of

Uzbekistan is taken by non-governmental public organizations (NGO) whose activity obtains an increasing significance in the resolving of basic problems of building of a democratic state and a civil society. First "sprouts" of these organizations began to make their way in Uzbekistan at the turn of the 1980s and 90s. In particular, in 1988, the Republican Children's Fund was established. In June 1991, the Association of Business Women of Uzbekistan, "*Tadbirkor ayol*" was founded. Since 1992, the Ecosan Foundation has started to operate.

Such national institutions of human rights function in the country, as Ombudsman (the parliamentary representative on human rights, a government appointee who investigates complaints by private persons against the government), the National Center on Human Rights, Institute of Public Opinion, Institute of Current Legislation Monitoring, and a large variety of other organizations. Now over 5,100 NGOs function in the Republic in various spheres of life of the society. However, there are quite a number of problems in the development of the NGO sector in Uzbekistan, including such issues as professionalism, definition of clear purposes and problems of establishments, interrelations between the NGO and the state, etc.

The situation with NGO was made important since 2003, due to the so-called "Regime changes strategy" and replacing of political elites in Ukraine, Georgia and Kyrgyzstan, when the attitude to NGOs in the CIS countries, including Uzbekistan, had sharply changed. This process became volatile after the tragic events in Andijan in 2005, and many domestic and foreign NGOs had to pass re-registration, some of whom by virtue of a number of objective and subjective reasons had been denied re-registration. However, the role of NGOs as a component of a civil society of Uzbekistan is essential and further improvement of the given sector is necessary. As a matter of fact, Uzbekistan has chosen a secular way of development. As is known, with a view to the maintenance of the tasks of revival of religion, increasing its role in the spiritual life of people in returning national-religious traditions forbidden in the Soviet period, granting holidays including, Kurban-Hait (Kurban Bayram) and Ramadan-Hait among the Muslims, Easter and Christmas among the Christians, Pesah, Purim and Hanukkah among the Jews has been introduced.

By the beginning of 2007, overall 2,227 religious organizations of 16 confessions have been registered in Uzbekistan. Of them 2,046 Muslim organizations were registered, which accounted for 92 per cent of the total number. Alongside with them there are165 Christian organizations, 8 Jewish communities, 6 Bahai communities, one society of Krishna worshippers and one Buddhist temple carry out their activity in the Republic.[4] Nevertheless, for Uzbekistan and other countries of Central Asia, the topical issues still remain the challenges and the threats of safety associated with religious extremism, inter-confessional and inter-civilization collisions. Adherents of various religions and movements seek to involve Central Asian region in their orbit and to extend their influence onto the young states. In particular, as Prof. Roy claims, an ultimate goal of Islamic parties (in Central Asia) is attainment of authority, rather than establishment of a civil society.[5] Therefore, for Uzbekistan as well as for other countries of the region it is of essentially great significance to have both the revival of religious values, and the necessity to prevent the exploitation of religion for the destructive purposes.

To sum up, the experience of the last years obviously testifies to the fact that a difficult process of formation of a civil society in Uzbekistan is evolving. During the transformative processes many difficulties were caused by a whole complex of problems. However, further liberalization of the country, creation of necessary preconditions of effective partnership among the state, and society, and strong institutions of a civil society is important for Uzbekistan. Prof. Roy is right in insisting that the civil society will be more significant, if it is based on the social structure in the process of its existence and development, rather than on abstract models taken from someone else's experience where, probably, civil culture exists.[6] Further political liberalization of Uzbekistan with due consideration of national features is the necessity for the modernization and development of the country in the conditions of globalization of the world political, economic and cultural life.

Notes and References

1. See L. Rye and M. Ruy, *Asian Power and Politics: Cultural Dimensions of Authority* (Cambridge, Mass. Harvard University Press:1985), 6.
2. M.B. Olcott, *Central Asian Second Chance* (Washington DC: The Brookings Institutions Press 2005), 156.
3. G. Hegel, *Filosofiya Prava* (Philosophy of Law) (Moscow: Misl. 1990), C.227.
4. *Pravda Vostoka*, 2007, 20 Marta.
5. Oliver Roy, *Sovetskoe nasledie I imperative zapadnoy pomoshi v novoy Centralnoy Azii\\ Grajdanskoe obshestvo v musulmanskom obshestve* (London, New York: NA 2002), 123-48.
6. Roy, *Sovetskoe nasledie*.

25

From a Union to a Region: The South Caucasus between Similarities and Differences

Marilisa Lorusso

State Building: Processes of Consolidation of Power

As the Soviet Union collapsed western observers assessed that post-Soviet countries had all the requisites to turn into modern western-type democracy. The high cultural level, the presence of a developed intelligentsia coupled by vibrant civil societies gave the impression that all the tools were available to transit to a different system of governance and living. De-sovietization itself was perceived as a demand of sovereignty inextricably interrelated with democracy. Such an assessment was based on the confidence that after a necessary period of transition post Soviet states would have become capitalistic, liberal, democratic model of nation states fully comparable with the ones that took shape in the West over the last two hundred years. Such a doctrine—described sometimes as "the science of transition"—fell in disgrace after two decades of high expectations, many of which were disappointed. The models of developments of post-Soviet societies and states can be grouped according to different trends of evolution: progressive democratization, revolutionaries, and democratic hybrids.

Progressive Democratization: Armenia

The model of democratic transition can be applied to Armenia. Such typology of transition was used in the early 1990s to describe the process taking place in approximately one hundred countries all over the world. It foresees five criteria:

- To leave dictatorial regime for a democratic one;
- Three stages: democratic unrests, collapse of the dictatorial regime, consolidation of democratic procedures and praxis;

- Elections have a special value in the process;
- The socio-cultural specificities are not relevant, this framework can be implemented anywhere;
- Once the new order is established, state building will entangle democracy building, and the two processes will mutually strength each other.

Among the South Caucasus countries, less dramatic changes have taken place in Armenia. The political confrontation remained between the margins prescribed by the constitution; no *coup d'état* or revolutions occurred and elections were held regularly. Presidential elections were in 1991, 1996, early elections in 1998, in 2003 and in 2008. Parliamentary elections were in 1995, 1999, 2003, 2007. Such stability does not imply that the transition proceeded smoothly. A remarkable exception was the episode of the shooting in the parliament (1999), which put an end to the competition for power between two political institutions: the office of the Presidency and the head of the cabinet, the Prime Minister supported by the Speaker of the National Assembly.

In 2005 President Robert Koèarjan insisted on some amendments to the constitution which were adopted after a referendum and aimed at strengthening the government he had nominated. The vote of confidence to the government, after the modification of article 74 of the Armenian Constitution, was no longer the benchmark for the government to continue. In case of lack of confidence against the programme of the government, expressed twice in a lapse of time of two months, the National Assembly itself can be dissolved by the President.[1] The National Assembly can be dissolved as well upon the proposal of its chairperson, if an imperative proposal of the government is turned down for three consecutive months,[2] for incapability to legislate or to hold ordinary sessions.[3] Beside the procedures, it should be understood that after the murder of the Prime Minister in 1999 no conflicts emerged anymore between the single-executive, that is the Presidency, and the collegial-executive, the Prime Minister and his/her government. President Serž Sargsyan *was* himself the Prime Minister, which displays that there is a double tier between the two branches of the executive power, if not a direct continuity. The weight and the political relevance of the two together definitely overwhelm the power of the legislature in leading the country.

Colour Revolutions: Georgia

The mistrust towards the transitional model and reforms as efficient tools for development led to reconsider revolution, traditionally deemed undemocratic and anti constitutional, in blatant violation of rule of law. Revolution, in its classical significance, implies a sudden change of regime which is not through elections. The regime that is breaking down no longer enjoys legitimacy and the ruling *élite* leaves the floor open to a new one, carrying new values and ideology. This shift is usually violent or accompanied by the threat of violence. Once it has seized the control of the state, the emergent ruling *élite* implements drastic and radical changes. As for its effects, a revolution can be defined so if it entails a change of the form of state or of government, i.e. from a monarchy to a republic, or from a parliamentary system to a presidential one. From this standpoint, the words of Lucan Way about the so called Colour Revolutions can be quoted:

> By most social-science definitions, these events would not be considered revolutions, but rather changes of regime or simply authoritarian breakdowns. However, for simplicity's sake and in line with most observers of the colour revolutions, I use "revolution" to refer to the postcommunist cases of authoritarian turnover.[4]

The brand "revolution" can be applied to the Colour Revolutions only to a limited extent. The grassroots takeover technique hardly had as a consequence a totally new se* of system.

As for its context, a colour revolution takes places when some pre-requisites are fulfilled. The regime in force must be authoritarian but not totalitarian. Thus opposition enjoys slight visibility and has access to one or more media with nationwide broadcast. If the country has a capitalist economic system, the opposition can also rely on private economic circles disappointed with the government. The perfect conjuncture for a colour revolution to happen is that elections, especially if they are theatre of frauds, are labelled unfair by international organizations. The ruling party, to be further discredited, must run for the elections already fragmented and having lost in the previous period some of its well known faces and supporters. Its *de jure* or *de facto* leader, who usually is the President, is at his/her last term, which opens the way to scenarios of uncertainty and internal political struggles. Government inefficiency in managing the country must be spectacular: there are cases where a pillar of statehood (i.e. territorial integrity) is at question, like in Georgia.

On the contrary the opposition, internally differentiated as it might be, is compact and transparent on its candidatures, leadership, aims. Access to resources is fundamental: media coverage, mass mobilization, supplies in case of prolonged demonstrations, distribution of gadgets and revolutionary symbols, logistic facilities; parallel vote tabulations are assets that are decisive for the success of a colour revolution. Due to such a demand, the support of international partners, non governmental organizations (NGOs) or single countries plays a primary role. While single countries may be more politically cautious, NGOs often engage more freely and openly in support and catalyze public discontent, helping the more vibrant part of the society, for example, students, to organize. For revolution makers the importance of foreign support for the revolutionary cause is not limited to organization know-how or financial help, but it becomes even more relevant on the matter of legitimacy. The would-be ruling *élite* assumes ahead of the revolution that, in case of success, the post-revolutionary regime will be accepted by the international community, that the recognition of the country will not suffer from the break of rule of law but, on the contrary the rating of the country will improve. This last factor accelerates if not democratization, then at least westernization among the political class. Another element which plays in favour of colour revolutions is the domino effect: when a revolutionary wave begins, it can expand to countries in comparable situations.

Georgia in 2003 had all the requisites. President Ševardnadze's party had lost some of its most popular faces, including the future protagonists of the Rose Revolution. The President himself was at his second mandate and expressly declared his intention not to run for presidency in line with constitutional provisions, leaving a temporary vacuum ahead. November parliamentary elections were controversial and not assessed as fair by international observers (Council of Europe Parliamentary Assembly, PACE, European Union Parliamentary Assembly, EUPA, Organization for Security and Cooperation in Europe-OSCE-Office for Democratic Institutions and Human Rights, ODIHR). *Kmara* ("Enough"), a juvenile revolutionary movement was actively engaged in promoting the anti-government mobilization. The opposition had at its disposal the friendly coverage of the national channel *Rustavi2*. At the moment of the attack the parliament building the law enforcing agencies were deployed but not used to repress protesters.

The Rose Revolution is indeed a good model for colour revolutions. The revolutionaries' declared purpose was to remove Eduard Ševardnadze's corrupt and dictatorial power and to move to a more liberal, democratic regime. In order to achieve this goal, it was suggested to turn the presidential form of government into a semi-presidential one, a step that would have restricted the almost boundless executive power. Had this initial project been accomplished, Georgian revolution would have been a revolution in the classically accepted meaning. But it was not till the war of August 2008 and the so called second wave of democratization that a mixed system was drawn by Georgian legislators, and not as a consequence of the Rose Revolution but because of the post conflict *consensus* crisis.

In fact in the constitution of 2004 the prerogatives of the President were not only left untouched, but extended. Up to then, the government was formed after the presidential elections. According to 2004 amendments, after holding consultations with the parliament, the President proposes a candidature for the position of Prime Minister. The latter has ten days to choose the members of his cabinet. Once formed it is submitted to the vote of confidence of the parliament.[5] The legislative body has to express confidence by no less of 50 per cent+1 votes calculated on the basis of the strength of the number of MPs. If the government obtains the confidence of the parliament on its composition and programme, in three days time it can be fully operational. On the other hand, the confidence can be denied to the whole cabinet or to one member.[6] In this case the single member will not be allowed to submit his/her candidacy. If the lack of confidence is expressed to the entire government, the latter can ask for a new vote of confidence after a week.[7] If the denial is repeated three times the President nominates a new candidate who in five days forms the government without his candidacy being submitted to the parliamentary vote. Then the President dissolves the Parliament and calls for new elections.[8]

This model was is clearly not semi-presidential. The discretion of the President is a key factor in case of conflicts between the collegial executive and the legislature. The former is highly dependant on the support of the President. The amendments introduced in the summer of 2010 are in the direction of balancing the powers more and reducing the arbitrary intervention of the President. The 2010 formulation of Article 80 foresees that after the parliamentary elections the President keeps the prerogative to nominate a candidate for Prime Minister on the basis of the proposals of various political groups. Within seven days the candidate presents the composition and the programme of the government for the vote of confidence. If the confidence is refused, the vote is repeated in one month's time. If the government is rejected twice, the President appoints a candidate who enjoys the support of not less than two fifths of all MPs, or the one who has more relative support in case of multiple candidatures. If a candidate so appointed again fails to gain the confidence, only then the President may dissolve the parliament and call for early elections. The discretion of the

President seems to have been restrained and the confidence of the parliament-government strengthened. So, at least as it concerns the formation and responsibility of the government, Georgia looks on the path to a mixed system. Once the new provision of Article 80 in is force in 2013, a full picture will be available. The concern expressed by the opposition is that the amendments were introduced to allow President Saakašvili to preserve his political leadership after the elapse of his second and last mandate, in 2013, that is to say, to armour the continuity of his power. He may now run for the strengthened position of Prime Minister.

Democracy Double: Azerbaijan

Both revolution and democratization describe a change, assumed to be a priority for the majority of population. The model of democratic double or hybrid does not really imply a situation in progress. It describes a transition supposed to be at its final stage, with future development as predictable for any country, not related to the Soviet legacy and a specific urgency for progression. The case under study is Russia after Putin's doctrine,[9] which is no longer claiming to be on its way to democratization but regards its present condition as a Russian variant of a modern democracy.

The definition of "democracy double" stands for a mixed system of democratic procedures—elections, multi-party system, representation, a mechanism of formal division of powers, vertically and horizontally—with beliefs and non-democratic, if not anti-democratic praxis. The basis is the refusal of relativism, together with fear of loss of control of power. Society is understood to be composed by two basic groups: electors and elected, not by a melting pot of motley social and press groups. The role of electors is to recognize legitimacy to the ruling class through the vote, so that the latter can present itself as the proper ruler of the state, at domestic and international levels. Legitimacy will be reached via elections often biased through a mixture of coercion and manipulation. From this standpoint the role played by television cannot be underestimated. I. Krastev notes: "The type of political regime […] would have been unthinkable in the pre-television age."[10] Television is the most widespread and invasive among all the media, it can be the persuading voice of the government, able to reach everybody in the intimacy of their houses. The cultural and national platforms needed to the state building process are channelled through television.

For Azerbaijan in particular, two media monitoring studies are worthy to be reported.

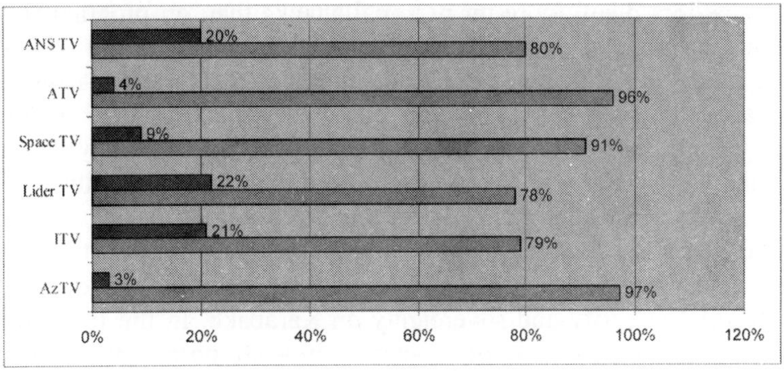

Figure 1: Television Monitoring—2005 Parliamentary Election Campaign

Note: Light dark : ruling party; dark: opposition forces.

Source: OSCE/ODIHR, EOM, *Media Monitoring,* Baku, October 2005, www.osce.org/documents/odihr/2005/11/16931_en.pdf (02/12/07).

Beyond playing a significant role in the political struggle, an additional aim is to provide society with a uniform view of the country, and make it a good flock led by a wise shepherd. Internal tensions are minimized, de-legitimized, or referred to as folkloristic phenomena, in favour of homogeneity that makes control and negotiations easier.[11] The wise shepherd is not—as it often perceived in the western press—the author of the system but a part of it, so his/her replacement would not necessary imply the collapse of the system. In his role of *Batjuška*[12] the President will approach the public opinion paternalistically and in a rather de-ideologized way, in order to be a reliable interpreter of all the citizens' identities. His institutional role of constitutional order's guarantor and at the same time of political leader will pauperize the political debate in line with the widespread contemporary trend of de-politicization of society. As a rule, he/she will stand on a populist platform, claiming to be a pragmatic leader, formally rejecting complexes and multi-factorial strategies in the name of a straight action "to resolve the real problems of citizens."

The backlash of the great ideologies' crisis of the end of the twentieth century led to a popular resentment towards political leaders, political parties and politics in general, leaving the institution often ideologically empty shells where business—much more than values and public representation—gains ground. The impoverishment of public debate and economic instability are factors that affect both majority and oppositions and that leave the floor to populist, confrontational behaviours. During the electoral campaigns competitors dwell more on personal attacks than on programmes' contents, more on claims of electoral falsification than on the view to the future. In such a context it is not surprising that "a strong man" is an appealing option. It is common sense that highly centralized power is synonymous of stability, and such an opinion is particularly shared in those countries that have suffered from periods of volatility.

Azerbaijan belongs to the group of countries that have such characteristics. Internal harsh confrontations led, in the first half of the nineties, to a disastrous situation, with much suffering, the loss of territorial integrity and sovereignty on Karabakh. In the following period, in the firm hand of Heydar Aliev some normalcy has been brought about. Stability and presidency became an inseparable binomial. The constitutional reform of 2002, pressed by Aliev himself, consolidated it to a greater extent, even more as it allowed keeping the continuity of power from father to son. The most remarkable amendments to the constitution pertained to Article 105 where it prescribed that in the event that the President is unable to exercise his/her powers, the Prime Minister will replace him. Before the reform the Speaker of the parliament was supposed to fulfil this obligation. This measure raises the question whether it was an *ad personam* amendment, as—while his health was worsening—President Aliev nominated his son Ilham as Prime Minister. The amendment of 2002 opened the way to a transition of leadership within the family.

According to amended Article 101, which was voted and approved via referendum in 2009 the provision of a maximum of two consecutive terms have been abolished. It is worthy to recall the opinion expressed by the Venice Commission of the Council of Europe about the new prescription of unlimited number of terms:

> 10. The core of the rule of law is the separation of powers. In a country with a presidential (or sometimes semi-presidential) system, power tends to be concentrated on the President, while that of the Legislature or the Judiciary is relatively weaker. Therefore, the regular change of regime through the process of election is the very method to prevent too strong a concentration of powers in the hands of the President.
> 11. A comparative survey shows that in most states with an elected president, the constitution imposes a limitation on the successive terms a president may serve. The number is

> either one or two. Limitations have been adopted both in countries where the president possesses extensive powers and in countries where the role of the president is of a more ceremonial character. At present, Belarus is the only European presidential republic which no longer limits the number of consecutive terms.[13]

Such a continuity of power, from father to son and with no time limits makes Azerbaijan resemble more an Arabian monarchy than a western republic.

A Region Divided: Nation Building and the Case of Georgia

While political processes may run independently, the same cannot be said for nation building, which might have destabilizing effects at regional level.

State building and/or Nation building?[14]

The elites of all governments found themselves in 1991-92 in the position to manage countries which were "new" ones from many points of view. Notwithstanding the legal and institutional framework they had inherited, their sovereignty was highly defective. Soviet states lacked fundamental requisites to exercise on their own territories supreme and unrestricted power and to administer their resources. They basically were deficient in fully developed fiscal systems by which services could be supplied, in proper agencies to ensure the monopoly on the use of force, in monetary and bank systems, in a clear-cut definition of the concept of citizenship if not, in some cases, in a distinct and shared certainty of who were supposed to be the citizens of the "new" states. Shortages could be detected also among other pillars of statehood, such as identification of state borders, proper governance and efficient institutions with the capacity to manage all subjects, especially in the fields previously under the direct control, *de iure atque more veterum*, of the union bodies. These limping apparatus were in charge not only of coping with the day-to-day administration but also of starting and implementing necessary reforms to transit from the Soviet system to a new one, more in line with the expectations of their citizens and of the partners they chose.

All these factors, which are linked to a process of state building, were twinned by simultaneous and parallel (or tangent?) processes of nation building. Indeed, a state is not just a mechanism, but can be more properly defined as an organism, where the legal procedures affect and are mutually affected by a society in the way it is organized, articulated and self perceived. All components which flow into the society, like a mosaic made of pieces of different ethnic, religious, linguistic, economic, political aspects, contribute to create a common identity for the community/ies settled on a territory. No human community lives without having created its own narration of history, myths, believes and language. Language in particular was an important identity marker in Soviet societies, due to the fact that they were secularized and, in late' 90s, at the beginning of their religious awakening. The process to draw a common national identity is defined nation building. The two processes of state and nation buildings were activated in all the post Soviet Republics with different degrees of intensity, according to their peculiarities, and as a consequence of the political priorities of the time.[15]

Nation Building and Citizenry

Concerning the process of *state building,* the only republic which could rely on a slightly less problematic transition was the Russian Federation. Russia basically compressed in its new statehood all the elements of USSR sovereignty (currency, army, international relations, etc.). As for the citizenship issue, being a federation for seventy years, it had developed a complex system of recognition of minorities, autonomies and self governments. Thus the federal status legacy implied a very inclusive concept of citizenship, extended to all federal citizens never mind their ethnic affiliation. The federation is *Rossiskaya* and not *"Russkaja"* (of the Russians only). The principle of *jus soli*, according to which a person is a citizen of a state if he/she is born on its territory, consolidated through the decades. The concept of Russian citizenship has been enlarged to cover, according to the most recent provisions of Russian doctrine, a positive commitment to protect Russian communities. The principle of the right to intervene to protect Russians was claimed in August 2008 when, after an escalation of skirmishes, war erupted in the district of Tskhinvali, *de jure* Georgia. Then Russian Presidency declared the right and the responsibility to protect Russian citizens living in South Ossetia.[16] The claim has been considered quite controversial and the elaboration of a precise doctrine of the extent to which the responsibility to protect can be evoked is still in progress.[17]

Except Russia, none of the post-Soviet republics was a federation, albeit in their territories there were autonomous republics (ASSR), regions (ASSO), territories and districts. Georgia is a good example of this. Till 1990 it had two ASSRs: 1. Abkhazia, autonomy based on its ethno-linguistic distinctiveness; and 2. Ajara, autonomy based on its religious belief.[18] It also had the ASSO of South Ossetia, its autonomy based on ethno-linguistic. Abkhazian and Ossetian languages have different alphabets from the Georgian one, which is unique, created in the fifth century. Ossetian belongs to a separate language family, as it is Indo-European, whilst Abkhazian and Georgian are Caucasian, pre-Indo-European languages. Identity, cultural factors and their political and juridical use played a crucial if not deciding role in shaping the outcomes of the post-independence controversies. Processes of nation and state building entered into conflict over citizenship.[19]

When on the 11 November 1990, the nationalist block of Zviad Gamsakhurdia Round Table-Free Georgia won the elections with the slogan "Georgia to Georgians," many Abkhazians and South Ossetians understood the word Georgians as the term to describe not the citizens of Georgia, but ethnic Georgians, that is to say the titular nationality of the republic. Nation building preceded state building. The latter prioritizes the protection of equality of citizens, and its discernment, as it puts at the top of the political agenda all requisites of statehood and averts any measure or behaviour that could possibly undermine the stability of the state, its territorial integrity, its sovereignty.[20] It is worthy here to underline the importance of the words discernment of equality, as the whole mechanism was highly emotionally led, and the exchanges within the society were mostly auto-representative.[21] Therefore, when in the summer of 1990 Gamsakhurdia abolished all regional parties and on 11 December the status of autonomy of South Ossetia, reacting to its breakaway threat, many deduced that Georgia was not going to be a welcoming state for minorities.

What followed was chaotic: two secessionist wars with ramification in what can be described as a civil war in Western Georgia, in the early 90s; frozen conflicts with steadily process of state and nation building in the *de facto* Republics of Abkhazia and South Ossetia, till the war in 2008, ensued by a second cease-fire and political uncertainty. Russian recognition of the two breakaway regions in August 2008 notably reduced the margins of negotiations. The unity of the citizenry of Georgia crashed against the wall of opposite nationalisms. Abkhazians and South Ossetians are undergoing a process of receiving passports, at the end of which they will be citizens of the two new, partially recognized, republics. The territorial integrity of Georgia appeared to be seriously compromised as well. One of the other main ethnic minorities in Georgia, Armenians, seems to be affected by a slow and creeping process of polarization against Tbilisi, randomly encouraged by ambiguous national policies pursued by the Georgian Government or its local branches. In 2009 Armenian President Serž Sargsjan suggested that the Armenian language be given the *status* of "regional language" in the pre-dominantly ethnic Armenian-populated region of Džavacheti, to strengthen friendship between the two countries. More than friendship concerns, the issue was the security perception of the Armenia community. In January 2009 two Georgian citizens of Armenian origins, Grigol Minasyan and Sarkis Akopjanyan were arrested in Achaltsiche (Džavakheti), under the charge of cooperating with a Belarus-based organization allegedly set up by Russia's Federal Security Service. The two men admitted being involved in espionage, but denied an additional charge of being involved in building an army.

On 6 January 2011, on the occasion of the celebration of Orthodox Christmas in the Armenian Church in Tbilisi, President Saakashvili underlined that the ethnic Armenian population of Georgia "is an integral part of Georgia's national body, Georgia's statehood development." As a bitter and ironic aftertaste, this is just an example of how sovereignty can suffer from trends meant not to damage a state, but to build it.

Notes and References

1. Art. 74.1, Constitution of Republic of Armenia.
2. Art. 74.a, Constitution of Republic of Armenia.
3. Art. 74.b and c, Constitution of Republic of Armenia.
4. L. Way, "The Real Causes of the Colour Revolutions," *Journal of Democracy* 19, no. 3 (2008): 67.
5. Art. 80.2, Constitution of Georgia 2004. Hereinafter CoG04.
6. Art. 80.3 CoG04.
7. Art. 80.4, CoG04.
8. Art. 80.5, CoG04.
9. G.P. Herd, "Russia's Strategic Choice: Conservative or Democratic Modernization?" *Geneva Centre for Security Policy, Policy Paper*, no. 2, May 2010, available at www.gcsp.ch/International-Security/Recent-Publications/Russia-s-Strategic-Choice (27/01/2011).
10. I. Krastev, "Democracy's 'Doubles'," *Journal of Democracy* 17, no. 2 (2006): 52-62.
11. About telvision, its influence and relevance in Azerbaijan, see IFES, *Public Opinion in Azerbaijan 2006,* www.ifes.org/publication/8c125401065f9250e23771fd4c3c5d1/2006%20Survey%20Report Website_11Jul2007.pdf (13/11/2008).
12. The epithet "Little father" was used for the Tsar, protector of the Russian peoples. Democracy doubles have features of populist and paternalistic

regimes in a sort of conceptual continuity with pre-revolutionary systems, although they are not to be considered a local peculiarity. Notorious cases can be detached elsewhere, e.g. South America.

13. European Commission for Democracy through Law (Venice Commission), *Opinion on the draft amendments to the Constitution of the Republic of Azerbaijan*, 78th Plenary Session, Opinion no. 518/2008, CDL-AD (2009) 010, Venice, 13-14 March 2009, www.venice.coe.int/docs/2009/CDL-AD%282009%29010-e.pdf (30/12/2010).
14. M. Lorusso, "Vent'anni di dis-Unione Sovietica. State building or nation building? Il caso della Georgia," *ISPIonline Analysis* (January 2011), www.ispionline.it/it/documents/Analysis_41_2011.pdf (31.01.2011).
15. R. Brubaker, "In the Name of the Nation: Reflections on Nationalism and Patriotism," *Citizenship Studies* 8, no. 2 (2004): 115-27.
16. For the conflict of 2008, see report of Independent International Fact Finding Mission on the Conflict in Georgia, September 2009, www.ceiig.ch/Report.html (19/12/10).
17. International Coalition for the Responsibility to Protect, *Russia's R2P* [Responsibility to protect, N.d.A.] *justification*, www.responsibilitytoprotect.org/index.php/component/content/article/133-europe/1829-international-crisis-grouprussia-vs-georgia-the-fallout. See also Crisis Group, *Russia vs Georgia: The Fallout*, Tbilisi/Brussels, Europe Report no. 195, 22 August 2008.
18. Being the last beyond the South Caucasus to be seceded to the Tsarist Empire from the Ottoman one, Ajara was a predominantely Sunni Muslim area.
19. R. Brubaker, "The Manichean Myth: Rethinking the distinction Between 'Civic' and 'Ethnic' Nationalism," available at www.sscnet.ucla.edu/soc/faculty/brubacker (20/09/07).
20. S. Smooha, *The Fate of Ethnic Democracy in Post-Communist Europe* (Budapest: ECMI 2005).
21. A. Alietti, D. Padovan, *Sociologia del razzismo* (Roma: Carocci 2003) and V. Cotesta, *Sociologia dei conflitti etnici* (Roma-Bari: Laterza 2003).

For further reading also see:

C. Brinton, *The Anatomy of Revolution* (New York: Vintage Books 1965).

R. Brubaker, "Nationhood and national question in the Soviet Union and Post-Soviet Eurasia: An institutionalist account," *Theory and Society* 23 (1994): 47-78.

T. Carothers, "The end of the Transition Paradigm," *Journal of Democracy* 13, no. 1 (2002): 5-21.

T. Diazamidze, *Status of Autonomous Regions of Abchazia and South Ossetia within Georgia (1917-1988). Collection of Political-Legal Acts* (Tbilisi: GCI Ltd. 2005).

C.H. Fairbanks, "Revolution Reconsidered," *Journal of Democracy* 18, no. 1 (2007): 42-57.

M.S. Fish, "Stronger Legislatures, Stronger Democracies," *Journal of Democracy* 17, no. 1 (2006): 5-20.

H. Hale, "Regime Cycles: Democracy, Autocracy and Revolution in Post-Soviet Eurasia," *World Politics* 58 (2005): 133-65.

F. Lanchaster, M.P. Ragionieri, *I successori dell'Impero, le Costituzioni degli ordinamenti ex-URSS*, Giuffrè (ed.) (Milano 1998).

A. Lukin, "Electoral Democracy or Electoral Clanism? Russian Democratization and Theories of Transition," *Demokratizatsiya* 7, no. 1 (1999): 93-110.

M. McFaul, "Transitions from PostCommunism," *Journal of Democracy* 16, no. 3 (2005): 5-19.

A.S. Orlov, V.A. Georgijev, N.G. Georgijeva, T.A. Sivochina, *Istorija Rossii* (History of Russia) (Moskva: Prospekt 2006).

OSCE/ODIHR, EOM, *Media Monitoring,* Baku, October 2005.

OSCE/ODIHR Needs Assessment Mission Report, *Republic of Azerbaijan Parliamentary Elections 7 November 2010,* Warsaw, 13 July 2010.

J. Rupnik, "From Democracy Fatigue to Populist Backlash," *Journal of Democracy* 18, no. 4 (2007): 17-25.

A. Rasizade, "Azerbaijan in transition to the 'New age of Democracy'," *Communist and Post-Communist Studies* 36 (2003): 345-72.

R.G. Suny, *Transcaucasia, Nationalism and Social Change* (Michigan: University of Michigan Press 1996).

Cultural Representations

26

The New Holidays in Buryatiya, or New Life to the Old Calendar Holidays

Olga V. Buraeva

S.I. Ozhegov defines *prazdnik* (holiday) as a day of celebration, set in honour or memory of someone or something; the Day of Revolution; a nonworking off day; a day especially marked by custom or church; a day of joy and festivities on the occasion of something; a day of games and entertainments. The *Great Soviet Encyclopædia* says: The holidays in the Soviet Union are established by law, dedicated to the outstanding events, traditional dates, in honour of the workers of certain professions (8 March: International Women's Day, 1, 2 May: Spring and Labour Day, 9 May: Victory Day, etc.). Thus, one may state that holiday is a multifaceted social phenomenon that reflects the life of each individual and the society as a whole.

For every person holiday is connected with a special festive situation, which impels him to participate in one or another action. The feeling of festivity is a feeling of joy, cheerfulness and elation of spirit. Holidays are always associated with a turning point or a landmark in the life of nature, society and man. The more significant is the event underlying the holiday, the greater is the urge of a person to feel his involvement into it, to express his sentiments, to combine his feelings with the feelings of others as well as of his own people. It is well-known that on holidays a person wants to be among people; in order to share his own feelings in his own way, everyone selects an object for himself to communicate from among the relatives, the friends and colleagues with whom he works, studies or enjoys spending free time, etc.

Original Paper in Russian: *Sovremennye prazdniki v Buryatii, ili novaya zhizn' starykh kalendarnykh prazdnikov*—Translated by Susmita Bhattacharya.

The holidays of Russia can be divided into the following categories:

- Church holidays, the most important of which are Christmas, *Paskha* or Easter and others;
- Calendar ritual holidays: New Year's Day, *Maslenitsa* or Pancake Week (farewell to winter), Ivan Kupala Day, Harvest Festival;
- State as well as social and political holidays;
- Profession and labour holidays (Fisherman's Day, Miner's Day, Metallurgist Day, Teacher's Day, *Militsiya* or Police Day etc.);
- Civic and private holidays or family feasts (wedding, birthday, anniversary etc.);
- Sports holidays;
- Holidays for children and teenagers;
- Memorial/Remembrance days associated with the life and creativity of great poets and writers, artists and composers;
- Jubilee celebrations of cities (City Day), regions and republics.

Debate flared up in the early nineties on the issue of streamlining the festive and memorial dates. Some suggested repealing altogether the festive and memorial dates, including the industrial holidays, while others campaigned so that there were more holidays. In some measure one may understand the supporters who negated the holidays as such, for many long years in our country those holidays have served as means to evade the sore problems, to artificially stimulate the social optimism, and even to satisfy the vanity of the leaders of one or another scale.

Whether the most active campaigners against holidays want that or not, the festive and ritual activities became significant elements of national culture at the times of totalitarianism, and it is just not possible to repudiate them. The modern man does not reject the very institution of holiday while discarding the old socio-cultural way of life, changing the calendar and making a life on new foundations; instead he preserves it because it satisfies the steady social requirements. The complexities of contemporary radical transformations in the Russian society, their uniqueness in the historical past and in the forthcoming future sharply raise the questions about a national ideology. It cannot be invented and implanted from above: such an ideology "sprouts by itself" out of predominant public sentiments.

After the disintegration of the Soviet Union, and in connection with the growth of ethnic self-consciousness of the peoples of Russia and Buryatiya, there was observed an enormous interest in one's own history, one's own traditions, and one's own festivals. Let us look at some of the festivals.

Christmas

During the years of Soviet rule one of the most popular holidays was the New Year's Day, to which some rituals earlier present in the Christmas were transferred. Among them were decorating New Year's (Christmas) fir trees, exchange of New Year's (Christmas) gifts, carrying out New Year's (Christmas) fir trees and so on. Many believers, according to the old style, observed the New Year on 13 January. During the last twenty years, there has been a revival of celebrating Christmas on 7 January along with the New Year on 31 December.

A law on celebration of the New Year according to the Lunar calendar (*Sagaalgan*) was adopted in Buryatiya in the year 1990. The tradition of celebrating the festival of *Belyi Mesyats* or White Month has already been established during the last decade. The rituals are performed in *datsans* (religious ones) and at homes (folk/popular ones). The *datsans* conduct the ceremonial services—the *khurals*, timetable of which is published in the pages of local newspapers. A cone-shaped structure of poles—a bonfire is made near the *datsans*, in which litter is burnt. The ceremony *Dugzhuuba* itself is a distinctive ritual of general purification, so the lamas do not recommend throwing rubbish into the fire. However, the people roll a body with small lump of dough, small pieces of cotton (supposedly containing impure corporal energy of the body), and cast it into the fire. Therefore, a small bonfire is made next to the large one to burn rubbish. While the bonfire burns the worshipers walk around it three times thinking of prosperity and health of the relatives. They pray to protect against ailments, with a wish for happiness and success. The people whose birth year comes according to the eastern calendar are recommended to book for a special prayer, since the regular life cycle becomes complete and starts a new one.

The next day, prayers are recited to the goddess and keeper of the faith of Lhamo, who is also the protectress of the Ivolginsk Datsan, people as well as cattle. At the dawn, when the New Year comes into its own, arrangement is made in all *datsans* for the fifteen-day long *khural*, dedicated to the Buddha's victory over the enemies of his teachings. After the New Year sets in the rituals of *Serzhem* and *Dalga* are performed. The Lama-astrologer (*zurkhaishi*) would tell the position of one's *hii morin* (winged horse), symbolizing the state of one's prosperity. Depending on the year of birth *hii morin* takes its colour. After the recital of prayers *hii morin* is hung out in a given direction. This rite is particularly popular and performed by people with great pleasure.

People start preparing for the holiday well in advance. It is necessary to put the entire household business in order for procuring firewood, hay (in rural areas). Harness is cleaned for horses, a new one is ordered. Women clean the clothes, sew new ones. All the families are engaged in cleaning the house and in the yard, throwing out the old and broken things. Then they envelop the household, livestock, house, and buildings with smoke of incense.

The Buryat people call the day before New Year as *Butuu uder*, which means closed, dark and dull day. It symbolizes the old year, going away into the darkness of time. Another rite of New Year's Eve is *Burkhan Delgeelge* (worship of the gods of home) when the altar is festively decorated. The *viands* should be placed, so that the food gets sanctified by the gods and the next day it could be eaten; *zula* (icon lamps) and *khuzhe* (sticks of fragrant herbs) are lighted up. On this day, the believers try to observe fast. It is extremely undesirable to eat meat and drink alcohol, because it mentally and physically hampers the preparation to greet the New Year and concentrating on good thoughts and actions. The housewives prepare dishes and lay them on the table in the second half of the day. The New Year begins, when in the pre-dawn darkness one can distinguish between the fingers on hands. Then greeting one's friends and relatives starts. On the first day of the holiday people greet the elders in their family—parents, uncle, aunt, brother or sister. There is a special gesture of New Year greeting, when the younger one extends both of his hands to the elders with the palms upward, and the elder puts his hands with palms down. It is as if the younger person is supporting the elder with elbows. This deeply symbolic gesture signifies the willingness of the young people to always support their elder in life. If a man and a woman are of same age, the woman is considered younger. The gifts giving ritual also has been practiced for centuries. The gift giver should hold a *khadak* [2] in his hands, and put the gift on it in the palm of his right hand or palms joined together. It is customary to accept a gift by sitting and with both hands. The festive table includes the dishes rare in everyday life like boiled sheep's head, *buuzy*, *khushuur*, black pudding, *bukhlyor*, *salamat*, cottage cheese and sour cream.

The opening days of celebration in the villages remind of carols without songs. During the days of White Month, lots of outdoor games and song competitions are conducted; they dance stirring *khorovod*[3] (*ekhor*).

The special feature of Buryatiya is that in the celebrations take part not only the representatives of Buryat ethnos but also the other ethnic groups. Holding *zemlyachestvo*,[4] a meet of the *zemlyaks*,[5] in Ulan-Ude may be considered as an innovation in the celebration of *Sagaalgan.* At first the *zemlyachestvos* of the ethnic Buryats were created on the basis of administrative-territorial principle of Buryats, but at the same time reflecting the tribal structure of the Buryat society. However, soon the *zemlyachestvo*s became a place to communicate, meet, hold various cultural events and solve the problems of the sons of the soil or the expatriates of all nationalities from the region, the Russians, Evenkis, Tatars, etc., i.e. the fellow-countrymen, united by the memory of the place of birth and residence in a particular area, by working and studying together. At present there are 26 *zemlyachestvo* operating in Ulan-Ude.

The Shamans also celebrate *Sagaalgan* in Buryatiya. Corresponding rituals are performed on the day of farewell to the old year. The Shamans prepare ablution—water added with various herbs, which wash off the bad and negative. The Shamans pray to the Eternal Blue Sky—father and the Earth—mother. The New Year begins at 5:00 am. At the margin of this time, the Shamans begin to recite prayers, and gradually go into a trance. The third rite *Dalga* is hours-long prayers for prosperity and longevity of all living things on earth. The believers bring with them meal, which, after benediction is used as food.

Maslenitsa/Pancake Week

This is an ancient Slavic holiday inherited from paganism and maintained after the adoption of Christianity. *Maslenitsa* falls in the week preceding Lent. *Maslenitsa* as though separates the two main seasons—winter and spring. The rites are also associated with send-off to the winter and welcome to the spring with songs, *khorovod*s, dances and games.

Maslenitsa is celebrated through the course of a week. Each day has its name: *Vstrecha*, *Zaigrysh*, *Lakomka*, *Razgul*, *Teschiny Vecherki*, *Zolovkiny posidelki*, *Proschenoe Voskresen'e*.[6] During meetings, people are treated with thin *bliny*.[7] Many traditional forms of *Maslenitsa* festivities were lost during the Soviet period (the send-off winter holiday was celebrated), but now they are being restored. Children riding on horses, mummers, baking pancakes on the street "with frost," hot tea, concert of the amateurs, popular winter games, fight with pillows on the balance beam, climbing a pole, the seizure of the snow town are popular and leaves no one indifferent.

At present, the Sunday dedicated to send-off *Maslenitsa*, still called Forgiveness Day, is celebrated in a bigger way. The near and dear ones ask each other for forgiveness for any offenses committed during the year. A scarecrow is made out of straw and rags especially for the send-off. It is dressed in women's clothes, put on a pole made in advance, carried along with songs and games, and then burned. The scarecrow is accompanied by the maskers, dressed in sheepskin coats turned inside out, special masks or animal skins. They dance, make faces, and touch everybody with jokes.

Paskha/Easter

The Easter rites are widely known. Most of them have survived till our days—vespers, religious procession with cross and banners, *khristosovanie*,[8] dyeing eggs, baking *kuliches*,[9] preparing *paskha.*[10] The rite of *khristosovanie* is to exchange kisses while pronouncing the Easter greeting, "Christ is Risen!" "Truly, He is Risen!" After *khristosovanie* exchanging dyed eggs takes place.

Dyed eggs are inevitable item to break fasting of *Paskha* or Easter. Many people felt that egg symbolizes the mystery of life, its fundamental principle. The symbolism of Easter eggs is even wider. Egg is one of the links of the endless chain of births and deaths. Eggs are dyed in bright colours, dominated by the shades of red.

Kulich and cheese *Paskha* are traditional set of ritual meals. *Paskha*/Easter has always been regarded as a family holiday. It is celebrated within the family circle, and then people go to the close relatives. The *Paskhal*/Easter table is set for the whole day.

At present, this holiday has been taken to the streets. People go to church for consecrating eggs, *paskha*s and *kuliches*. In the shops one can buy *kuliches* consecrated at the church. In the squares, festivities go on, performances by folklore ensembles take place, dyed eggs and *kuliches* are sold, which are not only bought by the Orthodox Russians but by other ethnic people as well.

Surkharban

This is one of the most popular holidays of Mongolian people. The customs associated with the calendar labour milestones have taken shape among the stock-breeders. *Surkharban* in the old days was observed in June on the occasion of driving away the stocks to their summer pastures. Since time immemorial, it included national sports: archery, wrestling, horse racing, as well as singers' competition. *Surkharban* is also called *Eryn Gurban Naadan* (Three games of men).

The Republic's holiday of the working people of Buryatia, devoted to the 1st anniversary of the BMASŜR,[11] took place in Verkhneudinsk,[12] on 2 August 1924. This holiday was set up to counterbalance the Buddhist and Shamanist *Obo tahilga, tailagans* and *khurals* that had been organized in the early summer. The celebrations were started at the district *Surharbans*, and since then it became a tradition to organize *Sukharbans* on the republic's anniversary day, as large sports holidays (along with the traditional form of events football, basketball, volleyball and long jump competitions were held). The shows of the winners of amateur folk and arts groups were held, festivities were organised. Today, *Sukharban* is a part of national culture of the Buryats and one of the favourite holidays of all the inhabitants of Buryatiya.

Sabuntui

This is the main labour holiday of the Tatars. In Turkic languages ?? it means a holiday or wedding of the cereals and plough. During this holiday, there have always been strong motives of humanism and friendship among the people along with the customs of celebrating the spring tillage as well as glorifying labour, strength and health. In contrast to the religious holidays that divided people into different faiths, the national holiday *Sabantui* has united them. During the Soviet times it used to be celebrated in the districts where the number of Tatars was higher.

Sabantui was celebrated in Buryatiya for the first time in 2010 at the Ethnographic Museum of the people of Trans-Baikal. The culture, traditions and cuisine of the Tatars turned out to be the spirit of *Sabantui*. The sports programme of the holiday was spectacular. The top wrestlers competed in the national Tatar wrestling *Kuresh* and the strong men in a set of power events the *Saban-Batyr*, which includes weightlifting, tug of war, and arm wrestling. The main prize, as it is also on the occasion of *Surharban*, is a ram. An area was specifically allotted for popular games—fight with sacks on a balance beam, climb a pole, buckets-race, egg-race, sack-race, breaking pots and others. The guests take part in the Tatar dances and *chastushkas*.[13]

Sabantui, like most of the holidays of the peoples of Buryatiya, has lost its exclusive Tatar colour. Rather, it has become another step towards strengthening the inter-ethnic friendship. The spectators consistently observed a striking commonality among different peoples.

The celebration was participated by the ethno-cultural centres of Buryatiya-the Armenian choreographic group "Raffaello," the Azeri "Khazar/Hazar," the Evenki "Guluvun," the Tuvan throat singing group "Arzhaan" and others.

Bol'der

This is an ancient holiday of the Evenkis, which used to be celebrated after the end of hunting season. *Bol'der* in Evenki language means "meeting." During this celebration the Evenki could boast of hunting trophies, could take part in races on deer, archery contest, could show and sell provisions and crafts. *Bol'der* was celebrated for the first time in the year 1999. The Evenki representatives from Baunt, Barguzin, Kurumkansk and Severo-Baikalsk regions of Buryatiya assembled at the celebration. In 2009, the guests from the Republic of Sakha, the Trans-Baikal and Krasnoyarsk Territories, Irkutsk oblast' joined the celebration, and the NGO *Natsional'no-kul'turnaya avtonomiya evenkov Rossiiskoi Federatsii*[14] was founded. The children ensembles, both choreographic and folk, participated in the festival *Belyi moi olen'*.[15] *Pod vechnym svetom kumalana*,[16] a performance based on Evenki legends was staged. The artisans of folk crafts presented their works in the exhibition *Evenkiiskaya raduga*.[17] The most interesting were the contest-shows on the construction of traditional *chum*,[18] on the knowledge of traditions and customs. The participants welcome the guests in beautiful national costumes, embroidered with glass beads of all colours of rainbow and adorned with furs, performed *khorovod ekhor Odera* and treat them to ethnic dishes.

For the peoples of Buryatiya and Russia holidays are an integral part of social life, which changed under the influence of political, socio-economic and cultural reforms. At different stages there emerged new holidays and most of them turned out to be ephemeral. A few have become part of the holiday calendar for many decades and centuries. Such holidays in Buryatiya are Christmas, *Sagaalgan*, *Maslenitsa* (Pancake Week), *Paskha* (Easter), *Sabantui*, *Surkharban*, *Bol'der*.

Reference

S.I. Ozhigov, N. Yu. Shvedova, *Tolkovyi slovar' russkogo yazyka: 80 000 slov i frazeologicheskikh vyrazheii*, RAS, Institut. rus. yaz. im. V.V.Vinogradova, 4th ed. (Moscow: Azbukovnik 1999).

Bol'shaya Sovetskaya entsiklopediya, (30 vols.) 3rd ed., vol. 20 (Moscow: Izd-vo Sovet. entsikl. 1975), 608.

Narodnye prazdniki na Rusi Moscow: Tsentrpoligraf 2004), 157.

L.A. Tul'tseva, *Sovremennye prazdniki i obryady narodov SSSR* (Moscow: Nauka 1985), 191.

"Vstrechaem prazdniki. Paskha," *Spetsvypusk Zastol'e*, no. 2 (2008): 98.

"Prazdniki narodov Buryatii," *Daizhest*, Ulan Ude (2010): 58.

Translator Note

1. A traditional ritual long scarf, a Buddhist symbol of hospitality, purity and compassion of the giver, beginning of a friendly and cordial relations, and compassion, a universal gift.
2. Circular dance.
3. An association of people from the same area or country; an association of fellow-countrymen a community of persons from the same land; a community of people born in one town or region.
4. Fellow-countryman.
5. Roughly can be translated as: Opening Day or Day of meeting/reception/ welcome, Game Day, Gourmand Day, Fun Day, Day of Mother-in Law's Party, Day of Sister-in-law's Party, Forgiveness Sunday respectively.
6. Pancakes.
7. Russia traditional rite of exchanging a triple kiss as Easter salutation.
8. *Kulich*-Russian Easter cakes.
9. *Paskha*-Russian/Ukrainian Easter breads.
10. The Buryat-Mongol Autonomous Soviet Socialist Republic.
11. The former name of Ulan Ude till 1934.
12. *Chastushka* is a humorous rhymed folk verse usually composed of four lines, often improvised and sung in a string of others as a folklore tradition.
13. National Cultural Autonomy of the Evenkis of the Russian Federation) was founded.
14. My White Deer.
15. Under the Eternal Light of Kumalan.
16. The Evenki Rainbow.
17. Chum is a temporary dwelling or tent of deer hides or bark, used by the nomadic Yamal-Nenets, Khanty and Todzha Tyvan people of Russia.

27

Dynamics of Transition: Films from Central Asia

Rashmi Doraiswamy

The Soviet System

The equation between the state and nation has been a complex one in the Eurasian space of Russia and Central Asia since the twentieth century. The Soviet and post-Soviet encounters between Russia and Central Asia that followed the encounter of the Tsarist period, were to have profound influences on culture. Rather than "nation-state," it is probably more apt to speak of "state-nation" in this Eurasian region. The state has defined the nation in more ways than one in this region of fluid boundaries. The creation of "fixed" territories, the creation of republics, the establishing of cultural symbols and icons was a process that was initiated by the Soviet state in conjunction with local leaders. The decolonization process from the Tsarist empire, too, was unique, for the facilitators of this process were of the same stock and neighbourhood as the colonizers; only their political persuasion was different as was the social formation they espoused: socialist and not feudalism transiting into capitalism. This process was further complemented by the creation of not just the state-nation identity, but the creation of the supranational Soviet identity. This supranational Soviet identity was in turn fed by the transnational linkages that had existed in the Eurasian region. The modern state, nation, nationalism and supranationalism in the Central Asian republics were identities that emerged in a comparatively short period of time. This process was partially repeated and also reversed after the fall of the Soviet Union. New symbols and icons from the pre-Soviet past were adopted and while the transnational linkages with the region remained, the supranational Soviet identity was rendered irrelevant in the political context of the Commonwealth of Independent States. Independence brought with it shrinkage of territory as the Soviet identity of the (supranational and national) was replaced by a wholly national identity. The historical paradox, particularly in the case of the Central Asian republics, was that there was a move towards socialist economy from predominantly feudal social structures post-1917, and post-1991, a move away from socialism into capitalism, into the processes of globalization. Through the Soviet and post-Soviet periods, the people (*narod*) have supported/complemented/negotiated/resisted imaginings of the nation by the state.

Cinema played an important role in the enlightenment project of the post-revolutionary Soviet Union. It contributed in a significant way to nation-building, prompting scholars to term the film output of the period as "cinematic nation-building." "If, as Benedict Anderson... has suggested in his classic *Imagined Communities*, the idea of a nation is in large measure imagined retrospectively, the Soviet Union offers an interesting counterpoint—that of a nation imagined prospectively. The Soviet Union literally had to be invented. As is well known, cinema was expected to play a crucial role in this process. Surely it was for such a purpose that Lenin anointed cinema the premier socialist art-form."[1] In Russia, which had a strong tradition of realism and modernism in the arts, particularly literature, cinema partook of the avant garde, leading debates in the practice and theory of the language of cinema. Film industries were set up in the republics, and directors and technicians from Russia shot films in the republics and trained local filmmakers. The shifting of the major Leningrad and Moscow studios before and during the Second World War to Tashkent and Almaty facilitated the growth of local talent and industries. One of the reasons that cinema developed later in Kyrgyzstan as compared to other Central Asian republics, was that no studios were shifted there during the War.

The integration of the erstwhile socialist bloc in Eurasia into the world economy has not been a homogenous or smooth process. The global arena itself is not a unified whole. It is uneven, comprising developed and developing countries, riven with a North-South divide and politically heterogeneous. Even within the Central Asian region, the different states are in varied state of economic development. The Eurasian landmass that had constituted the Soviet Union for seventy four years is now, as the CIS, coming to terms with the world system through each of its fifteen constituent members in different and distinct ways.

The Soviet system had over the decades created and nurtured an alternative cultural paradigm, in which the state and party played a major role in setting up and guiding culture industries. The "guidance" often turned into interference and drastic intervention, curtailing the freedom of expression of the artist. Nevertheless, the cultural formations remained vibrant and active, with a large spectrum of practitioners ranging from the officially promoted, to the critical insiders to the dissidents. The Cold War propaganda saw the valorization of the dissidents by the West and a debunking of the "above ground" art practices within the Soviet Union. Within the USSR, there was the problem of modernist tendencies in art being put on the back burner, with a privileging of realism, socialist realism in particular, as the preferred mode of representation.

Transitions

In the case of Central Asia, the twentieth century as a whole has been marked by a series of cultural transitions. It was woman who was one of the central foci of this transformation, which also dissolved the strict boundaries of the public and private spheres. It was the liberation of women—from the *parandzha* (the veil), from the cloisters of domestic space, from male polygamy into the public spaces of education and social production that was the subject of much cinematic representation in the early films made by the Russian in the republics.[2] The other important theme was the establishment of Soviet rule and the fight against the White Guards and the local feudal elites. As Dzhura Teshabaev, the well-known Uzbek critic put it: "It (i.e. Uzbek cinema-RD) never attempted to understand the contradictory and tragic character of the *basmakh* opposition to the revolution. No wonder then that 'Uzbekfilm' came to be known as 'Basmakhfilm'. This tendency was evident also in Kamil Yarmatov, although the thematic orientation of his best films is not in the opposition of 'good' commanders and 'bad' basmakh but in the romanticisation of the revolution."[3]

The representation of the problematics raised by the Russian directors in consonance with official ideology was also taken up in similar vein by local cadres, once the film industry was set up in each republic. During and after the Second War the theme of women waiting for husbands and sons to return from the front and doing the work of men or even getting into armed exploits was dealt with in literature and cinema. It was only in the period of Thaw and Stagnation that there was a break from high rhetoric to the representation of everyday emotions such as love told with a lyrical flavor or in a melodramatic mould. 1964 to 1974 is considered to be the first period of the flowering of national cinemas of the Central Asian republics. This was the time that national cadres and studios began to create their own distinctive cinemas. The second period of this flowering is during *perestroika* and *glasnost.*

The Fifth Congress of Cinematographers that was held in May 1986 fully reflected the policies of *perestroika* and *glasnost* whose effect was felt in the republics as well. Uzbek film critic Djhura Teshabaev states:

> It is now an accepted fact that the watershed between the old and the new was the unusually stormy and radical Fifth Cinematographers' Union Congress. The aim was to destroy all stereotypes and to prepare a fertile ground for new experiments. Many acknowledged "maitres" of authority who had remained unvanquished—Bondarchuk, Kulidjhanov and others—disappeared in this cataclysm; new radically oriented young directors entered the arena. Passionate appeals were made for a break, all possible declarations were announced, resounding slogans adopted, but life, as usual, dealt with everything according to its own logic. Today it is clear to everyone that appeals and intentions have given nothing in concrete terms.
>
> The change to the new model of cost accounting and economic independence has created if not total chaos then a jumble. Most of the film studios that have adopted the new model have not achieved full freedom in implementation, although censorship in principle has been abolished...
>
> Uzbekfilm Studio that was divided into four departments did not get on to new rails of cost-accounting economics. On the contrary, after a year of trying it out and reviewing it, the opinion that the new system should be rejected and the old one retained is gaining ground in the collective."[4]

If the Uzbeks did not prefer the new system of cost-accounting, the Kazakhs adapted quickly to it and by the time of the Sixth Congress of Cinematographers in April 1989 had several independent companies such as Katarsis financing and producing films. This was the time of the Kazakh New Wave, of young directors fresh out of Sergei Solovyov's Workshop at VGIK in Moscow and was taken up subjects in their films that had not been dealt with before.

In an interview I did with Talgat Temenov, one of the Kazakh New Wave directors who had studied under Sergei Solovyov in 1990, he talked of the change over to the cost-accounting and independent system that had already come into place under *perestroika*: "Goskino will no longer subsidise films because of the economic problems facing the country. The government of each republic will have to allot money on its own. The situation is very difficult for national cinemas now. People in Russia before perestroika saw very few films from the Asian Republics. ... The films that were made could not compete with productions from Mosfilm, Gorky, Dovzhenko Studios..."

There were many other trends that one witnesses in the cinemas of the republics from the 1960s onwards. These trends in many ways question and deviate from the official and "mainstream" tendencies of the time. A close analysis of some of the films also shows that the encounter of aesthetic traditions from Russia and the republics with the larger framework of socialist realism reveals many subterranean or ambivalent layers of meaning. Two of the films that gave an impetus to the Kyrgyz New Wave, for instance, were Larissa Shepitko's *Znoi* (Heat) and Andrei Mikhalkov-Kionchalovsky's *Perviy Uchitel'* (First Teacher). Both were based on Chingiz Aitmatov's stories and the paradox was that although Aitmatov was involved in the writing of the screenplays, the films were less radical and lyrical than the original stories were.[5] The directors used the themes of the stories as part of the 'Enlightenment project' that had infused the films made by Russians in Central Asia, whereas the stories took modernity unselfconsciously as a given. There were other such encounters with the outside supranational space. The "Soviet Western," a subset of the "Socialist Eastern"[6] was not only made by Nikita Mikhalkov (*At Home Among Strangers*, 1974) Vladimir Lyubomudrov (*In Search of the Wind*, 1978), Samvel Gasparov (*The Sixth*, 1981), but also by Ali Khamraev from Uzbekistan (*Seventh Bullet*, 1972) and by Bolotbek Shamsiev from Kyrgyzstan (*Red Poppies of Issyk-Kul*, 1971). There were also films that severely challenged all official dictums of socialist realism and "national in form, socialist in content": the Uzbek co-productions with India. *Ajooba* (1991) by Shashi Kapoor was a fantasy, *Alibaba and Forty Thieves* (1980) was from the 1001 Arabian Nights, and *Sohini Mahiwal* (1984) was a love legend, both directed by Umesh Mehra and Latif Faiziev from Uzbekistan. Musicals were also being made in the Soviet Union. These enjoyed immense popularity. "The Soviet musical was a coming to terms with western influence at the height of the Cold War and of creating an indigenous pop-culture.... So the Soviet musical, whatever the republic it came from, even though it dealt mainly with the situation of the staging of music, lyrical comic situations, first love and the pain of heartbreak, always had the sub-theme of nationalism! ... The more Asian version of the Soviet musical, like *Angel Wearing a Skull*

Cap from Kazakhstan or *White Piano* from Tadjikistan, have the music spread into family or fantasy situations rather than the spectacle of music performed by a group. The music in these films draws more from folk and cultural roots, as against the westernized music of the band in the others."[7]

Just as the periphery wrote back in the "Three Ps of Perestroika" (*Plakha* by Kyrgyz writer Chingiz Aitmatov, *Pozhar* by Siberian writer Valentin Rasputin and *Pechalny Detektiv* by Siberian writer Viktor Astafiev), the cinema of *perestroika* started in the republics from the periphery. *Repentance* by Tenghiz Abuladze (1984) was the beginning, the peak was *Needle* by Rashid Nugmanov and the completion was *Armavir* (1991) by Vadim Abdrashitov. According to Gulnara Abikeyeva, "The cinema of Central Asia in the period of perestroika before everything showed the world that on the territory of the Soviet Union there exist bright national cinemas and that it is from these very 'eastern provinces' that the reform and reformulation of the Soviet order occurs. When the Russian directors were busy with the critique of Soviet reality and the creation of requiems for the Soviet epoch, directors of the 'Kazakh New Wave' brought a new type of hero to the screen, showed the way for changes in aesthetic representation, started paying attention to the historical heritage of the people. Similar processes on a smaller scale were going on in all the cinemas of Central Asia. In just four years of perestroika (1988-1991) fundamentally important films, representing the change of historical periods, were made."[8]

Kazakh director Rashid Nugmanov's *Needle* (1988) captured the drug-ridden angst of the Soviet youth and its culture.[9] These were all works which were truly supranational and Soviet in spirit. They cut across national boundaries and spoke of issues that deeply troubled the Soviet Union. "In search for new eclecticism, Nugmanov dumped in one pot mannerisms and clichés, stereotypes and archetypes, from Commedia dell'Arte to early Soviet rock n roll, from Godard to Bruce Lee, just as he did with actual languages on the soundtrack, in which Russian, Kazakh, German, Italian, and English create that 'audio rug' Solovyov was dreaming about when making *Assa*. In the heat of *perestroika,* when democratization of culture had just begun, such pluralism of expressions was more than healthy for a 'cinema without cinema' overwhelmed by subject matter and largely formless."[10] The hero of the film, Moro, a dandy, played by the well-known rock star, Viktor Tsoi (a Soviet Korean from Leningrad), gave this film the kind of status Godard's *Breathless* had for the French New Wave. Rashid Nugmanov reminiscences "I directed an avant-garde, action-gangster, rock-and-drugs feature starring rock star Viktor Tsoi. When *Needle* was released, it caught fire and drew an overall audience of about 25 million. With a thousand prints in circulation, it turned out to be one of the most successful productions in Soviet film history!"[11]

By the 1980s, a genuine breakthrough had been made in the creation of a *Soviet* culture, where the culture intelligentsia of "the borderlands" or the periphery could innovatively relate not just to Western Soviet culture (from the cities of Moscow and Leningrad), but also to Western European and American culture. Modernism was indulged in on its own terms. The open climate of *perestroika* and *glasnost* also gave greater space for experimentation. Says Temenov, "We did not study under Sergei Solovyov only to shoot kisses or killings well. That can be done by anyone who knows how to put things together—the actors act, the make-up man does his job, the sound operator records and the editor edits. That kind of cinema has always and will always fare well. But that is not what we want to do."[12]

This period itself was a transition from stagnation. The fall of the Soviet Union thus occurred at a time when culturally at least the supranational identity was making its presence felt. The breakup led to an abrupt withdrawal into smaller territorial identities.

Industries after Independence

Uzbekistan

The Uzbek Government took several initiatives after the fall of the Soviet Union. Within a month after his country became independent, President Islam Karimov set up a government committee on cinema, signaling the seriousness with which the government viewed the business of cinema. Uzbek Kino is run on state budget. It produces 15 feature films a year, 20 documentaries, 10 animation films, and 60 hours of video. The government does not take the profits and earnings from films, but allows the money to be reinvested into film production. It completely finances films at the state-owned Uzbek Kino. This 100 per cent subsidy is in contrast to Russia where the state gives a 50 per cent subsidy to films in government-owned studios.

It is only because of this support that Uzbek cinema has survived, and survived well, as compared to some of the other independent states in the post-Soviet space. Some Uzbek filmmakers are now based in Moscow: Ali Khamraev is currently working on a documentary on the President of Kazakhstan, Nursultan Nazarbaev; Elyor Ishmukhamedov, who had won a major award at the International Film Festival of India during Soviet times, is also based in Moscow.

In Uzbekistan the industry retained what was good from the Soviet socialist system while adapting to the demands of a market economy. Uzbek Kino has two separate studios, for features and documentaries, and in both the government has a 51per cent stake, with the rest having been auctioned. There are five major government-owned studios: in addition to the feature and documentary studios, there is the Karakalpak Film Studio (that produces at least one documentary, feature, and one animation film annually), the *Molodyozhnoe Obedineniye* (For the Youth) and the Ecofilm Kino Studio devoted to films on the environment.

Uzbekistan also boasts of 40 private studios. While the government-owned studios shoot on film, the private ones tend to make video films. The latter are quickly made; films, on the other hand, need nearly 10-12 months. In 2006, a total of 29 feature films were made by both state-owned and private studios. While the older directors are getting back to work, there has been a spate of young filmmakers as well. "They catch the moods of the city, and of the interiors in new and interesting ways which is why even stars work with them," says director Bako Sadykov. President Karimov declared 2008 as the "Year of Youth," and young people were trained to make films. Among the private studios, the Fifth Studio is experimental. Some of the films by young directors making waves are *Yurta*, starring N Khodzhaev and *Horserider* by cameraman-turned-director Hamidullah Hasan. Other important recent films include Bako Sadykov's *Muruat,* and *Amir Timur* by Ergashev and Bako Sadykov. *Amir Timur,* the first ever film on a historical figure venerated by the Uzbeks, was released as a film and a six-part teleserial. Kamara Kamalova's *The Road under the Skies* was awarded at the Eurasia Film Festival in Kazakhstan. She returned to filmmaking after a break of many years and won the state award for her contribution to Uzbek cinema in 2007.

The *Soyuz Kinematographistov* (Union of Cinematographers/ Filmmakers) continues to function and has 300 members, including people from private studios. What distinguishes the post-Soviet film scenario is the total absence of state control over artistic expression and Soviet-style censorship. Uzbek directors remarked that there was complete creative freedom and no pressure to make propaganda films. There is also talk of reinventing the Festival of Films from Asia, Africa and Latin America that used to be held in Tashkent, a festival sorely missed by directors.

Recent films focus on the divide between the rich and the poor, a divide that has emerged very sharply after the fall of the Soviet Union. There are fantasy films such as the recent *Svenigator*, on a robot who falls in love with her maker, shown at the Eurasia Film festival in

Astana in 2008. The theme of the differing values of the provinces and hinterland and the cities is also an important theme across the post-Soviet space, including Russia and Uzbekistan. *Malenkiye Lyudi* (Small People) from Uzbekistan is a compendium of tales, depicting the conflict of values between generations and the village and city. Many films exhibit the strong influence of the Hindi cinema on the exposition of themes and on style.

The most important post-Independence Uzbek film is Yusup Razykov's *Orator*. The film's protagonist lives through all the periods of Uzbek history in the twentieth century. He is a man who can give fiery speeches in support of the Bolsheviks and draw people to the party, but remains detached from its workings and manage to lead his private life more or less untouched by the march of events in the public domain. He has three wives and the regional secretary of the communist party desires him so much that she asks him to take her on as his fourth wife. He does not, but the brief affair he has with her results in her giving birth to their son. She meets a far worse fate than his first wife who is sent to study to Kiev and returns a "modern" woman with no use for the veil. The party secretary meets a tragic fate; she dies in prison.

Tajikistan

Neighbouring Tajikistan, which had a film industry in working order till the fall of the Soviet Union and the start of the Civil War in 1991, has an industry that is still to get back on its feet. Most of its directors are working in Moscow or abroad: Jamshed Usmanov and Gulya Mirzoeva are in France; Bakhtiar Khudoinazarov is in Germany; Mairam Yusupova in Moscow; Bako Sadykov who worked in Tajik Film until independence is in Uzbekistan; Davlat Khudonazarov, who used to claim that Satyajit Ray had a great influence on him, no longer makes films but supports a studio in Tajikistan under the aegis of the Aga Khan fund.

In the Soviet period, Tajik Film Studio produced 49 films annually: 3 features, 3 television features, 1 animation, 24 documentaries, 12 newsreel production of Soviet Tajikistan, 4 satirical films *Kaltak.* Tajikistan had 1125 film theatres and projection units. Of these 274 were in the cities, 851 in the countryside.[13] The civil war and prevailing economic conditions took its toll of the film industry. Sadullo Rahimov laments the desolate condition of this studio today: "Today Tajikfilm Studios continues to have the status of a government enterprise, but runs entirely on a self-financing system. In view of the absence of any market for its products in the

Republic and in the Central Asian region as a whole, in view of the absence of updated film technology and self-sustaining creative-economic initiatives, the Film Studio is undergoing severe crisis. The only source of its present existence is the renting out of space to international organizations and the money given by foreign television companies for the screening of films of the Soviet period."[14]

Turkmenistan

Turkmen cinema had reached its peak in the '60s and '70s. Children's cinema and poetic cinema were well developed in Turkmenistan. Usman Saparov's *Little Angel Make Me Happy* won the top award in the children's section at the 1993 Berlin Film Festival. In 1996, there was a spurt of Turkmen cinema: Bairam Abdullaev and Laura Stepanskaya's poetic film *Yandim* (The Soul is Burnt Out), Biul Biul Mamedov's *Archaly Adam* (Man with the Fir-Tree), Sergei Shugarev's *Aromat Zhelany* (Scent of Desires). *Little Angel Make Me Happy* is narrated from the point of view of a German child who is left behind in the village when the parents are sent away to a camp. The children play in a deserted village and are forced to live by their wits at such a young age. The film is poignant, heart-rending and strangely optimistic in its depiction of the will, that even delicate being such as children, have to survive.

Kazakhstan

Almaty in Kazakhstan started a festival in 1991 and this has grown steadily into an important festival for the region. Named Eurasia, it has become an important event in the region for film practitioners and film buffs. This year, the festival was shifted to the new capital of Kazakhstan, Astana. It focused on Central Asian cinema for the competition section, showing films from the world in the information section. One of the most interesting films was a debut film by Daniel Salamat, *Together With Father* (*Vdvoe s Otsom*), a new generation that is Kazakh. A young boy lives alone with his father; his mother has remarried. The film has the air of neorealism. One of the most moving scenes is when the father returns with a loud woman, and wants the boy out of the small house: the boy waits for a long time on the corridor, cycling up and down the corridor, watching people come in and go out of the doors of other houses in the corridor. It is in this sequence that the theme of loneliness reaches an emotional height that the sense of "real time" characteristic of neorealism is felt.

Sergei Dvorstevoi's debut feature *Tulpan* (2008) which won the Un Certain Regard Award at Cannes, also won other awards in the

CIS. The film transposes the director's experience as a documentary filmmaker into the first feature he has made. Asa has returned from training in the navy to Betbak Dala (Hungry Steppe) in Kazakhstan. He wishes to settle down to a nomadic life as an owner of cattle, but needs to marry to do so. He goes to meet the beautiful Tulpan in her home and impress her with his knowledge of outwitting the octopus if it ever caught you. His brother-in-law who has accompanied him and the parents of the girl are not impressed with his wisdom. The girl rejects him because his ears are too big. Asa's sister, with whom he lives in a communal tent out in the steppes, has three children: a daughter whose mode of protest against her father is to sing songs loudly to irritate him, an elder son whose job is to narrate the latest world news to his father, and the youngest, a mischievous toddler. Asa's friend owns a truck of sorts, with pin-ups of naked women. He does not like to transport animals in it, but is ever ready to give a ride to Asa. Boney M's *By the River of Babylon* plays often on this truck. Animals, nature and the family live in a symbiotic relationship in this remote area of the steppes. The local and the global meet up strangely in this film—the nomadic lifestyle, the almost primordial relationship between animals, humans and nature on the one hand, and global references on the other: Prince Philip (who too has big ears), solar energy, Japanese style houses, Boney M. Segments of the film are shot in documentary style, with real time unfolding. The birthing of a lamb, the camel who bites the vet, are details of life shown with affection and humour. The global coordinates are there but there is a deep embedding in the local. The documentary feel and the sense of real time unfolding binds all the events of the narrative together.

Akhan Sataev's debut feature, *Racketeer* (2007), was one of the top box office grossers of Kazakhstan, and doing well in other parts of the CIS. Sayan is a boxer. Hs educational qualifications do not help much. After the fall of the Soviet Union, his father takes to drinking; his girlfriend ditches him for a richer guy with a car. One of the most moving scenes of the film is that of his mother sitting on the road, with her personal belonging for sale. Sayan is inducted into Ruslan's gang as an extortionist. The film traces the expansion of Ruslan's business as well as the dead end it reaches. The film, though in the genre of the gangster film, does not glamourize violence. Sayan is a quiet, restrained character, who does his job professionally, the way he would have gone about his career as a boxer had he become one.

Kyrgyzstan

Kyrgyz cinema is being resurrected on a more modest scale. In October 2008 a festival of films from the SCO countries was organized at Issyk-Kul. 2008 was the year of Chingiz Aitmatov in Kyrgyzstan. Aitmatov passed away earlier that year, but the celebrations were held by the state as planned. The awards of the Issyk-Kul Film Festival were presented at the concluding function and concert of the Year of Aitmatov in Bishkek. The well-known Kyrgyz director Bolotbek Shamsiev, who has made the largest number of film adaptations of Aitmatov's literary works, was given a lifetime achievement award.

Aitmatov has left his trace on the cinema of not just Kyrgyzstan, but of the Soviet Union and the CIS as well. Some of the films that were part of the "Kyrgyz miracle"—the New Wave of Kyrgyz cinema—were based on Aitmatov's works. His presence was felt deeply on many of the films from the region this year. *Ailanpa*, a documentary made on him during *perestroika* was released only this year. It premiered at "The Evening in Memory of Aitmatov" during the Eurasia Film Festival in Astana in September 2008. The evening opened with a short film on an akyn who sang in memory of Aitmatov. *Tengri* (Blue Heavens, 2008), by Marie-Jaoul de Poncheville (a Kyrgyz-French-German co-production) was another film that reminded one of Aitmatov's early work *Jamilia*. Set in the picturesque Tien Shan Mountains, it tells the story of two unhappily married women; one of them dies after a violent beating by her husband and the other escapes with the man she loves. They are pursued by the husband, who has become a fanatic believer and a fundamentalist. The raw energy of the woman, her passion are well portrayed by the lead actress who along with the breathtaking locales carries the film along. One of the most important films of the year in this region is Ardak Amirkulov's *Farewell Gulsary!* (*Proshai Gulsary*). The film by a Kazakh New Wave director is an adaptation of a novella by the iconic Soviet writer. It is one of the "critical insider" stories of the bane of bureaucratism, insensitivity of party officials and the lack of knowledge of local ways that mess with the life of humans and animals alike. The film won some of the top awards at the Eurasia and Issyk-Kul Film Festivals, pointing to the emotional link the works of Aitmatov have to the film fraternity in Kazakhstan and Kyrgyzstan.

The most important Kyrgyz film after independence has been *Beshkempir* by Aktan Abdykalykov. It tells the story of an adopted son of a family in the village and traces his rites of passage into adulthood. The film is in black and white and bursts into colour occasionally. The adopted son, troubled in his adolescence by the fact of his not being the progeny of the family, finds his place in the family and community when his beloved grandmother dies and he takes on the ritual responsibility of settling her accounts. Abdykalykov, a painter, has been in search of a cinematic identity that would be distinctly Kyrgyz:

> Sometime ago—I think it was Godard—said that there are cinematic nations and listed them, and there are all others, which are far from the esthetics of cinema. That hurt me. Since then I have been seeking something that would express the esthetic of Kyrgyz cinema.... Kyrgyz call it *kurak*...
>
> I would like to emphasize the unique beauty of the kurak. These bits and pieces of cloth are given away during funerals. The family buys lot of fabric, then tears it apart—approximately one elbow-length—and gives the pieces away to everybody who came to bid farewell to the deceased. This way, bits of different fabric are collected in a household. Our mothers, more often our grandmothers, sew a *kurak* from these pieces of cloth. In essence, a *kurak* accumulates memories of dead people—it becomes a patchwork of remembrance. ... I think that this essence of putting things together is very much like filmmaking."[15]

Marat Sarulu's *Song of the Southern Seas* (2008) goes into the mixed nature of blood in Central Asia. Ivan and Assan are neighbours. Ivan's son is dark, Assan's son fair. The men doubt their wives. The narrative of the film shows that there is enough mixed blood—Asian, European, Eurasian—in the people of the region to warrant the birth of children with the skin colour of the "other." A very poetic film, it shows that there are no essentialist and "pure" notions of ethnic origin, nation, people, or religion in the region. Everything is intermixed. The film uses animation to explore myths of the region—Sarulu is a trained animator as well.

Conclusion

The post-1991 newly independent Central Asian countries witnessed a collapse of their film industries. From the attitudes of the states towards their cinema industries, it is clear that they have played a crucial role in either sustaining or letting them shrink into disarray. Uzbekistan and Kazakhstan have taken their role as nurturers of the industries seriously.

Although cost-accounting in the studios had begun in the second half of the 1980s, the transition to cost-accounting under a new economic system did not happen without hiccups. In Uzbekistan, the state intervened and the industry got back on its feet with some alacrity. In Kazakhstan, the system of cost-accounting and independent studios transited far more smoothly. Since the Kazakh New Wave happened in the period immediately before independence, the New Wave spilt over into the 1990s. This enabled the Kazakh cinema, more than the others to also make their presence felt on the international scene and get foreign funds and avenues for production and distribution. Uzbekistan's loss of the Tashkent International Festival of films from Asia, Africa and Latin America, was Kazakhstan's gain. The Eurasia Film Festival started in 1991 has continued to hold an edition once in two years. Censorship that had slackened under *perestroika* lost its grip further in these states. If in Uzbekistan and in Turkmenistan, the state control over the film industry paradoxically supported and controlled it, in Kazakhstan, a happier conjuncture of state initiatives and a cinema that had drawn to itself world attention, created the possibility of a cinema culture that adapted more quickly to the international scene. It is not surprising that it is in Kazakhstan that we also witness the rise of a genre cinema that has coordinates in the genre cinema of the West. A recent example is *Racketeer*, a gangster film that did very well not only in Kazakhstan but also in the neighbouring countries of CIS. The genre cinemas of Uzbekistan, on the other hand, partake of a melodramatic style that is closer in spirit to the Hindi commercial cinema. In Tajikistan and in Kyrgyzstan, the film industries were in a bad state. While Kyrgyz cinema can still boast of a few interesting productions in the post-independence period, Tajikistan has found it more difficult to limp back to a functional normalcy.

The post-Soviet period also saw the migration of talent westwards to Moscow and abroad. Many filmmakers still nurture a longing for the Soviet Union, or for their homelands. Usman Saparov who lives in Moscow considers Turkmenistan to be his homeland. The Tajik director, Bakhtiar Khudoinazarov, in an interview to me stated that "I am Eurasian. I would have liked to live in the Soviet Union but what to do, it no longer exists. But since it no longer exists, I don't want to return. I do not understand what is going on there at all. No, I understand it, but I do not accept it."[16] Filmmakers and technicians have had to shift because of lack of finances, infrastructure, outdated equipment, differences with the political set-up (as in the case of Rashid Nugmanov, the star of the Kazakh New Wave who now lives in France). The worst case scenario is probably that of Tadjikistan. Film critic Sadullo Rahimov states "In one word, Tadjikfilm Studios—the alma mater of all the previous achievements of Tadjik cinema is growing old and nearing its end. This huge territory and significant quantity of unused buildings and equipment reminds one of cemetery. I speak of this with suffering in my heart, for the greater part of my conscious life has been spent within the four walls of this studio."[17]

Earlier most of the aspiring filmmakers from the republics were trained at VGIK; now increasingly they are studying in their own countries. The films often have the local language and Russian being spoken in them. It is problematic to categorize films according to the countries they belong to because the money comes from various sources; the actors, professional crew and directors belong to different republics. *Proshai Gulsary*, for instance, was based on Kyrgyz writer's Aitmatov's novella and the lead actor was from Kyrgyzstan. The film, however, was categorized as a Kazakh film, because the director was Kazakh. Sergei Dvortsevoi from Kazakhstan, who lives in Moscow, has a sensibility that is transnational, even when he is dealing with a traditional lifestyle in the steppes. This is as much due to his experience as a documentary filmmaker as his cosmopolitan outlook.

The themes taken up by directors in Central Asia are varied: from a re-examining of history, to the plight of minorities (Germans in Turkmenistan), to everyday life (*Dvoe s Otsom*), to ethnic identities and mixed origins, to nomadic life in the era of globalization, to literary adaptations. According to Gulnara Abikeyeva, "1997-1999 were a turning point for Central Asian cinema. Six to seven years after their declaration of independence, national cultures had truly begun to return to their traditional ethnic origins. They did this consciously, with detailed analyses of their national world views."[18] It is difficult to agree entirely with Abikeyeva, when she states that all the filmmakers from this region returned to their traditional ethnic origins, "consciously, with detailed analyses of their national worldviews." The supranational hold of the Soviet Union has left its impress on the works of directors. It is to be found in the continuing line of the Kazakh New Wave, and their new dictum of "national in form and international in content," a belief that is reflected even in the recent *Tulpan*. It is felt in *Song of the Southern Seas* that espouses a view of the *region* (and not a nation, or nationality), which like the onion, is layers of skin with no core. Even Abdykalykov pits himself against an arch-modernist like Godard to find a "national" signature in his film. The metaphor of adoption and parenthood extends to the filmmaking act itself and its many cinematic fathers and forefathers, Soviet and others that Abdykalykov draws from. The footprint of the supranational is very much present in the national acts of filmmaking. It is only in a film like *Orator* that we find a "national patriotism as against governmental patriotism."[19] This film, as against the cosmopolitanism of the other works, posits the existence of strict distinctions between the public and private realms, at odds with each other, and a patriarchal identity.

The new narratives in the cinemas of the Central Asian states are positing different kinds of nation-communities. Nurlan Amrekulov and Nurbulat Mansurov classify Kazakhstani intelligentsia into three groups, vis-à-vis the creation of an ethnocratic state: the educated Kazakh of the villages and towns, who constitute the majority and are not Russified; the Russified urban intelligentsia out of touch with Kazakh culture and the third group who have imbibed both Russian and Kazakh culture.[20] Referring to this typology Annette Bohr points out that "...this classification of the indigenous intelligentsia, which follows an urban-rural dividing line and emphasizes educational environment, can successfully be extrapolated onto the native intelligentsia of other Central Asian states. In crafting nationalizing policies contemporary Central Asian leaders are guided principally by the members of the first group as well as certain members of the third group...The primary targets of their nationalizing measures are not only ethnic Russians but also their Russified co-ethnics (*Mankurty*), whom they regard as having betrayed the national cause."[21] In the field of culture, and in cinema, in particular, these distinctions are more fluid, even if existent. Uzbek cinema is more oriented towards the first category. *Orator*, too, creates a Zhivago-like character, who negotiates his journey through tumultuous political events by remaining detached from them. He differs from Zhivago, crucially, in the fact that he is a "rustic" in an urban setting. The orator is also not a thinking or creative character like Zhivago. The film posits a private realm that is traditional and Islamic, untouched by the events of the world outside, unchanging as long as the bars on the main gate of the house can be put up. The idyllic and utopian patriarchal order within its confines is best represented in the sequence where the protagonist is bathed by his three wives. The wives live in complete harmony: so idyllic is their companionship that they do not even mind looking after the child of their husband through a fourth relationship. The husband's only grouse against "his" women to his last days are that they never heard him deliver his fiery speeches. *Orator* offers a dichotomous, or should one say, duplicitous life in which "tradition" and "modernity" remain distinct realms, not influencing or interacting with each other. Even when the first wife returns, transformed externally, subscribing now to a "western," "modern" dress code, once she is in the precincts of the house, she belongs, without any contradiction, to the "group of the wives." The story is of this past era is narrated by the child (now an adult) born of the union between the "emancipated" party worker and the traditionalist orator.

Kazakhstan's cinema represents the other end of the spectrum. This cinema has a different take on issues of "tradition" and "modernity" and the "rural-urban" divide. In Serik Aprymov's *Aksuat*, the protagonist Aman is a hardworking man, who lives in a remote area of the steppes. His brother, Kanat, a businessman from the city leaves his pregnant wife Zhanna at his brother's house, promising to come back. The wife gives birth and the brother and sister-in-law share a silent companionship. The village gossips, the brother's engagement is called off and his social networks dry up. He finally puts Zhanna and her child onto a bus for the city. This is not a simple rural versus urban, city versus *aul*, or a Russian versus Kazakh divide. "I have never seen images like those in *Aksuat*," says Gulnara Abikeyeva. "The empty winter exteriors, Kazakh's in malakhais (traditional fur hats) and cell phones, a lonely horseman in the middle of a concrete road."[22] Aman is an avid film watcher and watches foreign films when he returns home after a hard day's work. *Tulpan* too brings the "global" and the "local" together as Boney M and Japanese energy efficient houses find a place in the imagination of the inhabitants of a remote place on the steppes, where nomadism is still a way of life. Otherness comes in all forms and the daughter of the house, or rather tent, puts up a rebellion in her own way, even as the mother is surreptiously wooed by the protagonist's friend with candies. It is this intertwining that represents the paradox of Soviet development and high literacy along with the remnants of a traditional life. This, in fact, is one of the hallmarks of a post socialist state that distinguishes it from a postcolonial one: while both are characterized by economic problems and contradictions, the former is characterized by a high level of cultural literacy, which the latter is not. Sergei Dvortsevoi's *Tulpan* and Akhan Sataev's debut feature *Racketeer* point to the pathways the auteur and genre cinemas are clearing out for themselves. If Kazakhstan cinema represents a mode that is unselfconsciously realist and modernist in the same breath, Kyrgyz cinema, particularly in *Beshkempir*, represents the coming together of both the ethnic (in theme) and the transnational (in aesthetics).

The assertion by Abikeyeva that "national cultures had truly begun to return to their traditional ethnic origins" and that the artists, among others "did this consciously, with detailed analyses of their national world views" is thus open to question. The condition of the cinema industries is very different in the five republics; so are the works of the key practitioners who are in their own way coming to terms with not just the "national," but the transnational (cutting across the region and other Central Asian states), the supranational (the Soviet identity that is politically dead, but culturally alive) and the international (with linkages outside the CIS). The amalgams of these diverse forces are themselves varied, with one or the other "nationals" in dominance. If, for instance, Razykov's *Orator* has the "national" in dominance, Dvortsevoi's *Tulpan* has the national, supranational and the international interwoven into each other. Even in the assertion of national identities, there is diversity within the patriarchal ethno-religious representation of Uzbek life in *Orator* and the secular portrayal of ethnic rituals in *Beshkempir*. The heterogeneity in the experience of what has happened to the Central Asian cinema industries in the post-Soviet period as well as the practice of cinema reflects the complex interaction of what Raymond Williams termed "emergent" and "residual" cultural forms.

Notes and References

1. Noel Carroll and Sally Banes, "Cinematic Nation Building: Eisenstein's The Old and The New," in *Cinema and Nation*, Mette Hjort, Scott Mackenzie (eds.) (London: Routledge 2000), 121.
2. In Uzbekistan Mikhail Doronin's *The Second Wife* (1927), Mikhail Averbach's *Veil* (1927); in Kyrgyzstan Vasili Pronin's *Saltanat* (1955) and A Ochkin's *Tien Shan Girl* (1961); in Kazakhstan Moshe Levin's *Raikhan* (1940) and Efim Aaron's *Botagoz* (1957); in Turkmenistan Evgeny Ivanova-Barkova's *Dursun* (1940); in Tajikistan Rakhmanov and Davidson's *Zumrad* (1962).
3. Djhura Teshabaev, "A Confusing Freedom," interview by Lyubov Pelevina, *Cinemaya*, no. 8 (1990): 17.
4. Teshabaev, "A Confusing Freedom," 16.
5. For a detailed analysis of these two films see Rashmi Doraiswamy, "Encounter of Modernities," in *Cultural Histories of Central Asia*, Rashmi Doraiswamy (ed.) (New Delhi: Aakar 2009).
6. The Socialist Eastern included films such as Pierre Gaspard Huit's *The Prairie* (France-Roumania, 1968), Richard Groschopp's *Chingachgook—The Big Snake* (East Germany, 1968), Konrad Petsold's *White Wolves* (East Germany-Yugoslavia, 1969), Alfred Vohrer's *Old Surehand* (East Germany-Yugoslavia, 1965).
7. Report on the Sochi Film Festival, Rashmi Doraiswamy, *Cinemaya*, no. 49 (Autumn 2000): 50.
8. "*Perestroika v Kino Nachalas' Zdes*," in '*Natsiostroitelstvo v*

Kazakhstane I Drugikh Stranakh Tsentralnoi Azii', Gulnara Abikeyeva, Tsentr Tsentralno-Aziatskoi Kinematografii (Almaty 2006), 141.

9. "Unlike the hippie movement, which followed nothing but natural law, the punks obeyed the rules of the tough game they invented, a game that used the specific sign language of Gothic horror and 'black humour'. If the punk culture played according to defined rules, the post punk culture admits no rules at all; it plays in anything it can find. Our domestic hippies could not help overacting a bit: clearly the natural laws of the Berkeley campus and of Moscow's communal flats are quite different. The Soviet punk movement had a chance to emerge much later than in the West....The postpunk style, on the contrary, did not have any trouble finding a comfortable spot in the minds of this generation. 'The philosophy of the image' had come to replace 'natural philosophy'." Marina Drozdova, "The Dandy of the Postpunk Period or 'Goodbye, America, oh...'," in *Russian Critics on the Cinema of Glasnost*, Mikhael Brashinsky and Andrew Horton (eds.) (Cambridge: Cambridge University Press 1994), 126.
10. Mikhael Brashinsky and Andrew Horton (eds.), Editors' Commentary, in *Russian Critics on the Cinema of Glasnost* (Cambridge: Cambridge University Press 1994), 129.
11. Rashid Nugmanov, interviewed by Ron Holloway, *Cinemaya*, no 54-55 (2002): 15.
12. Talgat Temenov, "Storm over Kazakhstan," interview with by Rashmi Doraiswamy, *Cinemaya*, no. 8 (1990): 20.
13. Sadullo Rahimov, *Luch Ekrana* (Dushanbe: Kinoservis 2004): 40.
14. Rahimov, *Luch Ekrana*, 41.
15. Aktan Abdykalykov, "How to Learn to Mix Colours a la Kyrgyz," interview with by Gulnara Abikeyeva, in *The Heart of the World: Films From Central Asia* (Almaty: Complex Print House 2003), 57.
16. *Cinemaya*, no. 46 (1999): 18.
17. Rahimov, *Luch Ekrana*, 41.
18. Gulnara Abikeyeva, "Women down the Steppes," *Cinemaya*, no. 60 (2003): 10.
19. *Cinemaya*, no. 42 (1988-99): 12.
20. Referred to in Annette Bohr, "The Central Asian States as Nationalising Regimes," in *Politics of Modern Central Asia*, Bhavna Dave (ed.) (New York: Routledge 2010), 216.
21. Bohr, "The Central Asian States."
22. *Aksuat*: Review, Gulnara Abikeyeva, *Kinokultura*. http://www.kinokultura.com/CA/reviews/aksuat.html

28

The "Fall" of the Soviet Union and the "Fall" of the Socialist Realist Literary Canon

Ranjana Saxena

Introduction

The world is well into the twenty-first century, the twentieth century has receded into the past not only in the calendar terms, but also in real terms as much has changed. At the end of the twentieth century, which also happens to be the "end of an era," it was difficult to analyse and/or systemize the processes that took place during the century. Now "twenty years" after the historic 1991, it becomes imperative for us to review these changes and put them in an historical perspective.

Apart from the two World Wars, the history of the twentieth century is marked by two unprecedented socio-economic and political transformations that really shook the world. The first was the October Revolution in the year 1917 and the second was the declaration of *perestroika* or "*restructuring*" in the year 1985. The intriguing aspect of these happenings is the fact that on both occasions a comprehensive and complete systemic transition took place and had occurred within the boundaries of the same Russian geo-political space. The first incident shook the whole world by heralding in the first ever socialist state, while the second was the precursor to the collapse of the entire socialist bloc and the Soviet Union. As the emergence of the Soviet Union had transformed the politics in the whole world, especially the third world, the "*fall*" once again changed the lives of many, not only within the bounds of the erstwhile Soviet Union, but also outside.

Commenting on this a leading literary critic says that "in the last two decades we have been witness to a grand drama of the civilization. What we term as end of the 'cold war', does not only mean that the geo-political opposition between the East and West has come to an end, or the change in state boundaries, or economic systems. There is an inevitable evolution of cultural and intellectual priorities along with a rethinking of legal, ethical, behavioural norms. Though this phenomenon to some extent or other engulfs the whole world, but in the post-Soviet space it is more accentuated."[1]

A year before the fall of the Soviet Union censorship was abolished in the Soviet Union as also the 6th article in the Soviet Constitution which talked about the leading and the guiding role of the communist party. This period also saw the end of the all powerful Writers' Union. These were the times of "rethinking, reviewing, reassessing and rereading." The Russian society was deeply engrossed with its past and "*rethinking*" became its hallmark. Russian literature was no exception. Needless to say that Russian literature of the Soviet disposition formally fell apart with the fall of the Soviet Union. It would be wrong to assume that the Soviet literature or the socialist realist literature had an even trajectory from the day the term "socialist realism" was coined to describe this literature until the time its death was announced. Perhaps it may be proper to say that after the disappearance of the Soviet Union the Soviet socialist literature lost its moral grounds to existence. The "Soviet socialist literature" has been a subject of much debate and discussion throughout its existence. It has been discussed within the Soviet Union, albeit clandestinely, as well as outside. After 1991 many scholars of Russian literature began to analyse this phenomenon openly. During 1994-98, a project to study the Socialist realist canon was initiated by an international collective of scholars of Russian literature. Five conferences were conducted over four years in order to decode this phenomenon.

This essay attempts to analyse the "fall of the canon" based on the premise that (a) when we talk about Soviet literature we are talking about the Soviet socialist realist literature; (b) that the literature defined as the Soviet socialist canon did not have an unchallenged life in the former Soviet Union. Nor was it a homogenized, unchanging category. The Soviet socialist realist literature existed along with many types of Russian literature and it may be correct to say that the canon was constantly being scrutinized, tinkered with and was being challenged. So, there is no clear cut time line or specific year that can be attributed to its end.

The Beginning of the End

In terms of chronology, the "beginning of the end" can be attributed to the proclamation of the policies of *perestroika* and thereafter of *glasnost*. It was *glasnost* and the subsequent abolition of censorship that activated the Russian literary scene in the second half of the 1980s. The high point of the year 1986 was the staging of Mikhail Shatrov's play "The Dictatorship of Conscience." The play helped in establishing the dichotomy between "good Leninism" and "bad Stalinism" as the official ideological flavor of the year.

The year had also seen the publication of works like *Pozhar, Plakha, Pechalnyi dedektiv* and *Poslednaya Pastoral* by Rasputin, Aitmatov, Astafief and Adamovich respectively. These works, far removed from the socialist realist tradition, presented the reader with an "end of the world" like feeling. The starting point of Rasputin's narrative is the critical incident of the fire in the collective farm store house which pushes Ivan Petrovich, the chief protagonist, in to reviewing his times and fundamentals of the life and society. At the end of the story, after putting out the fire in the store house he simply doesn't know what to do. He seems to be faced with an endless chaos. "Ivan Petrovich kept walking, leaving the town and so it seemed to him, leaving himself, pressing further into the solitude he had found." Much in the same vein Astafief also highlights the issues related to the *fall* and degradation of the human values. The story is replete with incidents of killings, fights and rape and all kind of crimes. Aitmatov in *Plakha* depicts the times that are catastrophic and dangerously explosive in nature. The writer touches upon themes that were supposedly taboo. The title of the novel itself was symbolic in the sense that it conveyed a moral-philosophical meaning to abysmal life conditions.

The period of *glasnost* beginning from 1987 onwards up to 1989 saw the publication of almost banned and persecuted Russian literature of the past seventy years. This list included the classics of the twentieth century banned for various political reasons. Amongst them were the Russian religious and philosophical writings of the early twentieth century. *Untimely Thoughts* by Gorky, *We* by Zamyatin, *Requiem* by Akhmatova, *The Foundation Pit* and *Chevengur* by Platonov, *Dr. Zivago* by Pasternak, *Sobachye serdtse* by Bulgakov and many others were found in this list. This period also saw the publication of writings that were written during the brief phases of "thaw" but supposedly had transgressed the official limits of permitted liberalism of the "thaw." Most famous amongst them were *Sofia Petrovna* by Chukovskaya, *Gulag Archipelago* by Solzhenitsyn, and *Kolyma Tales* by Shalamov. The list is very long. At this juncture the Russian literary space acquired a drastically pluralistic character having re-assimilated within its folds "all the islands" of Russian literature that were scattered all over the world—the "Russian Berlin," the "Russian Paris," the "Russian Prague," the "Russian America" and the "Russian East." The unpublished writings of the Russian avant-garde could now see the light of the day.

During this period "the critical discussions took place around those texts, which in much traditional manner had put toward sharp political issues and proposed popular anti-totalitarian models of Soviet history."[2] This long list includes the novel *Children of Arbat* by Rybakov, Dudintsev's *White Robes*, *Faculty of Unnecessary Things* by Dombrovsky, *Disappearance* by Trifonov.

The Soviet publication industry experienced a real boom from the year 1987. The reading public was flooded with writings by writers living and dead alike. Russian literature existing under various names such as the *samizdat* or the *tamizdat* and of the internal or the external emigration—all these literature simply got rechristened as Russian literature. Some called this as a period of "cultural renaissance,"[3] while others even went to the extent to say that this was the time of the "formation of a new country and a new people."[4]

Commenting upon the logic of the Russian socio-literary thought from the days of *perestroika* to the end of the 1980s, critics Liderman and Lipavetski say that *Children of Arbat* (1986) and *Gulag Archipelago* (1990) are examples of the evolution that took place in the minds of the Russian reading public. The former concentrated on the figure of Stalin, while making a bold attempt to widen the limits of the liberalism of the "thaw." The latter is an attempt to establish the initial criminality of the Soviet regime in the readers' minds. It shows the catastrophic consequences of the October Revolution, the totalitarian nature of the communist doctrine, starting with the forefathers, i.e. from Lenin.[5] One may recall that in the beginning of *perestroika* M. Shatrov's play *Dictatorship of the Conscience* had emphasized on the "good Leninism" and "bad Stalinism" dichotomy. The play was based upon the opposition between Stalin and Lenin, who criticized Stalinism, the concept of "developed socialism" and the "stagnation period." The publication of *Gulag Archipelago* brought an end to this dichotomy. The year 1990 was declared as the Year of Solzhenitsyn and the year 1991 saw Lenin and socialism falling from grace and paving way for a new state—the Russian Federation.

A little before this the "death of the Soviet Socialist literature" was formally announced in the Soviet Union. Victor Erofeev, in the article "Soviet literature: in Memoriam" says that "in my opinion, the end has come for Soviet literature."[6] According to Erofeev Soviet literature in its later stages could be categorized under three heads:

the official, the village prose and the liberal literature. The death of Soviet literature and culture was announced by one and all. This included democrats like V. Erofeev and nationalists like Yu. Bondarev, who said that "Contemporary literature is yet not dead, but it has reached or approaching a tragic state, that is, a diabolical confusion of ideas, styles, heroes and doctrines…."[7]

Soviet Literature and the Socialist Realist Canon

While we are talking about the "death" or "disappearance" of the Soviet socialist literature, it is necessary to look into issue of what actually constituted the Soviet literature and what was the socialist realist literary canon? There are many views on what actually was the Soviet literature. One critic had rightly remarked that "in 1934 it was quite clear what Soviet literature was supposed to be; in the 1990s it is a lot less clear what it was?"[8] Another critic says that Soviet literature was something that resulted from the destruction of literary groups and members of the creative intelligentsia in the 1930s, the linking of literature to socialist production and to the myth of one happy Soviet family, and leveling of the Russian literary language to the point where there was very little to be lost in translation.[9] According to Andrei Sinyavsky, who wrote the article "What is Socialist Realism?" under the name Abram Tertz, says, "Soviet literature is the didactic novel which shows the communist metamorphosis of specific individuals and the entire collective."[10] He further adds that "many of our books are about the depiction of these moral and psychological processes directed towards the creation of the future ideal human being."[11] Precisely this was the task that the writers were supposed to accomplish in the erstwhile Soviet Union and with this aim in mind the Writers' Union had clearly defined the tenets of the new trend—socialist realism. For Sinyavsky this literature with its penchant for a positive hero and socialist optimism was closer to the idealism of classicist literature. In his opinion "with its positive hero and its spirit socialist realism is closer to the Russian 18th century, than the 19th century. Inadvertently, we have jumped over the heads of our fathers to continue the traditions of our grandfathers."[12] Further he says that the socialist realist doctrine desires that the writer depicted the reality as it should be and therefore socialist realism should have been, more appropriately, be called socialist classicism.

The genesis of the socialist realist literary canon and the dynamics of its formation, establishment, development and disappearance need to be looked into. As mentioned earlier, the "beginning of the end" commenced at the time of *perestroika* but having said that one would like to add that the Soviet literature or the Soviet literary canon was constantly being challenged by the writings which existed within the category of Soviet literature. It was being challenged by writing of the "other" nature. As rightly emphasized by Kathleen Parthe that "process of rereading and rewriting the canon began for Russians soon after Stalin's death in 1953, but the pace accelerated after 1985 when—in relatively rapid succession—the totalitarian form of government, censorship, the domination of Socialist realism, the official isolation of Soviet literature from émigré and underground works, the Writers' Union, communist party rule and finally, the Soviet state itself dissolved."[13] It was being challenged by the "village prose" from within its boundaries, by the writings about the gulag, by the *quiet lyrics* of N. Rubtsov, by the *authors' songs* of Okudzhava, Vysotsky and others. Theoretically too the canon was being challenged and was being critiqued. The article by Sinyavsky challenging the percepts of the Socialist realism has been mentioned above.

On Decoding the Socialist Realist Canon

While discussing Soviet literary canon, I am considering the classification of the life phases of the socialist realist canon given by Hans Hunter[14] in his eponymous work published in the year 2000. The critic talks about the various stages in the development of the literary canon. The critic defines the following five stages in the development of the canon:

1. Proto-canon: that is the preliminary stage of the development of the canon which provides for creation of a reservoir of texts of the canon.
2. Phase of canonization, in which the canon formulates, more or less, as a systemic whole in relation to other traditions.
3. Phase of application of the canon, when all its mechanisms come to the forefront.
4. Phase of de-canonization, during which the canon widens and looses its inevitability.
5. Post-canonization stage, which appears after the fall of the canon.

Proto-canon

The first stage in the life cycle of the socialist realist canon, i.e. the "proto-canon" covers the first decades of the twentieth century in the history of the Soviet literature. This is the stage that contains the raw material for the formation of the future "canon." The novel *Mother* written in 1906 by Gorky occupies a significant place in this category. One may recall that the principles of the socialist realist poetics were formulated in the Writer's Congress in 1934. For about two decades this novel was not touched by the critics. But at the time of the Writer's Congress the novel was hailed as an "example of the socialist didactic novel."[15] Needless to mention that Gorky's *Mother* has all the ingredients to qualify as the socialist realist novel. The novel is about the working class struggling for their bright future, puts forward the process of the formation of the "positive hero" and it is about the transformation of the mother, who moves away from spontaneous actions and reactions towards conscious revolutionary activity for the cause of the working class. Others key novels of the 1920s that fall in this category are F. Gladkov's *Cement* (1925), A. Fadeev's *The Rout* (1926).

In *Cement* the protagonists of the novel, male and female, are immersed in the construction of socialism. The male protagonist, who is the positive hero, fulfills the task of putting the devastated factory back on its feet and increasing the production despite all odds. The hero overcomes all hindrances, ideological and practical, forges ahead in the face of antagonistic forces. The female protagonist also gives up a comfort the family home, gives away her daughter in the state crèche for the sake of building socialism.

The Phase of Canonization

The second phase, i.e. the phase of canonization is the most crucial stage in the life cycle of the literary canon. In the context of the Soviet literary canon this phase covers the first half of the 1930s. In retrospective one can say that the task of canonization of the Soviet novel could not have been achieved without institutionalized support from the top. This was the period when in 1934 at the Writers Congress the slogan of "socialist realism" was given the new disposition to literature. Simultaneously, it was during this period, that all the "other" trends were given an unceremonious farewell.

Over the centuries the Russian writer shared a tumultuous relationship with the powers that be but in the twentieth century this relationship reached its "lower depth." The Soviet period in the history of Russian literature is characterized by the tendency to control and or give direction to the creativity of the Russian writer. The writers who could not fall in line with accepted socialist realist dictum either got ejected or were pushed out of the system.

The debates on the "Language Question" in 1934 and "Formalism" in 1936 are significant from the point of view of the transformation of literature and its journey from "pluralism" to a "singular idea." The debates on Language Question resulted in the disappearance of "*skaz*" and the "ornamental prose" from Russian literature as the socialist realist literature demanded clarity of style and language.

"If the 1920s was the time of constant search for a stylistic structure that would adequately depict and articulate the times; the 1930s is the period of creation and discovering this style, its fossilization, dogmatization and political canonization."[16] If the discussion on the "Language Question" established the "neutral style" as the fixed feature of the "official canon" then discussion "on formalism" ousted all other forms of description, for example, the fantasy, the science-fiction, the grotesque, etc. The discussions on the "Language Question" resolved that the socialist realist literature would be characterized "by language clarity, exactness, understandability and there would no space for formalist experimentation and naturalist perversions."[17] This was the one of the important state intervention facilitating the consolidation of the aesthetics of the socialist realist literary canon, its fundamental features being—concrete life depiction and neutral style.

The last significant intervention in this direction was the decree "on literary criticism and bibliography" in 1940 that saw the closure of the journal *Literary Critic*. This journal provided for refuge for writers like Platonov and others who were unable to fall in line with the socialist realist canon.

Phase of Application of the Canon

The most appropriate example of the period of the realization of the canon is the novel *How the Steel was Tempered* written in 1932-34 by N. Ostrovsky. *The Virgin Soil Upturned* by Sholokhov is yet another novel falling in this category. During this phase of the realization of the canon the critics played a very important role as "watch dogs" in regulating the canon principles. Many literary texts were worked upon by the editorial boards of the journals. Even Fadeev's *The Young Guard* (1945) could not evade the razor sharp eye of the editor and his scissors.

The Phase of De-canonization

The phase of de-canonization is perhaps the most vibrant and challenging period in the history of the Soviet literary canon. This period lasted for more than two decades, from 1953 to 1970. It is during this period that the socialist realist literary canon was both widened and tinkered with by literary works and critics. Writers and critics in the period began to, both, theoretically and practically, take on the canon.

Post-canonization Stage

Though the period of "thaw" that emerged after Stalin's death in 1953, was short-lived, it, nevertheless, was marked by great revelations. It was due to this period that it becomes absolutely clear that though the cold of the "thaw" was able to freeze the literary life, but it was unable to destroy the Russian literary tradition. The cultural memory appeared to be grossly harmed, but not completely destroyed. The cultural and literary logic of the period seemed to be that more the coercion, more the texts.[18] After the second congress of the Writers' Union in 1954 the literary works of M. Bulgakov, M. Zoschenko and A. Platonov, which stood outside the Soviet literary canon, began to come back to the readers. Already in 1957 Sinyavski had questioned the validity of socialist realism.

On Challenging the Socialist Realist Canon

The arrival of the village prose in Russian literature in the late '60s and the '70s of the twentieth century posed a definite challenge to the socialist realist canon. This can be considered to be the phase of post-canonization. This phase is marked by ideological and literary pluralism. The village prose touched upon taboo themes as of death, ethics and morality. At this juncture writers like Astafief, Rasputin, Shukshin, Abramov, Belov, Bondarev, Soloukhin and others appeared on the literary scene with their writings about the state of affairs in the post-war Soviet villages. These writings raised pertinent issues of the "moral degradation that reigned supreme in the society of *developed socialism*."[19] In their works these writers reject the tenets of the socialist realism and decisively move away from the *lacquered representations* of the reality. The writers touched upon various problems plaguing the Russian society: Astafief in the work *Queen Fish* expresses his concerns about the fast eroding relationship between human beings and their surroundings and reflects on the problem of consumerist attitudes towards the nature; Rasputin presents us with a powerful critique of the mindless technological progress and the generational conflict manifested in the younger generations rejection of their own peasant roots in *Farewell to Matyora*; Abramov talks about the changing character of the village polity in *Pelageya* and *Alka*. And finally the readers were posited with much talked about *shukshinian* question: So, then what's happening to us? All this was different as compared to the literature of socialist ideals. Solzhenitsyn called the village prose writers as the moral conscience keepers of their times whose basic contribution, in his opinion, lies in highlighting the existing *moral deficit*. In this prose the Soviet citizen appeared sans the epithet "Soviet," the characterization got defined in existential instead of ideological terms.[20] In this period photocopies of almost all the banned writings were available in the Soviet Union as *samizdat* versions.

Nevertheless, the exceptional impact that socialist realist canon exerted on political, social, literary and cultural movements across Africa and Asia cannot be just wished away. The literary works of this era remained source of inspiration for couple of generations in Afro-Asian national independence movement and contributed a great deal in the process of de-colonization across the world. However, this is new area of research and documentation that needs to be followed up.

After the fall of the Soviet Union a new phase began in Russian literature. This is the time of individual writers and their works in the times of changed moral-aesthetical and ideological paradigm. The 1990s was the period of "all is permissible." In post-Soviet Russia literature was no longer seen as the conscience keeper of the society and gone were the days of "literature-centrism." Commenting up on this situation, a leading Russian writer A. Varlamov remarked, "the essential character of the creative process has changed: from being a social task it has become an extremely personalized, closed up and intimate act. It is like publishing your personal papers, not aspiring to any greatness, or to any revelation." A more scathing attack came from writer Nina Sadur, who quotes Rozanov to express her views "Gentleman! You have no souls: how can there be any literature."[21]

In the year 2001 Alla Latynina, a leading critic of our times, declared that literature, even when it had the trump card of freedom on its side, entered a phase of literary twilight. The new literary reality was mesmerized by the dynamics of the market whose sole aim was to sell. Russian literature has come a long way since the days when a poet was more than a poet in Russia. Today a poet is just a poet and nothing more. Pasternak had once remarked that "great literature can exist only in collaboration with great reader." The contemporary readers' interest had suffered because of too much of skepticism as a result of high levels of moralizing of the bygone era.

At the end of the first decade of the twenty-first century the Russian literary scene, once again, looks vibrant and engaging if we take into account the presence of multiple literary prizes, literary journals: regional and metropolitan, publishing houses into consideration and do not pay attention to the fact that these prizes are sponsored by multinational corporations and big business houses. In the bygone era literary activity was supported by the State. Today these are two separate entities. A writer may not be victimized for his writing, but then the "literary word" also does not have the same power over the reader as in the bygone times.

In conclusion it could be said that if earlier in the twentieth century literature could be categorized in terms of the *dominant style* and the peripheral, today the *realist, new sentimentalist, postmodernist* and *post-realist* literatures reside side by side. In fact, the "specificity of the present literary process is the simultaneous existence (without the supremacy of one style over the another as it was in the beginning of the 20th century, when for example, modernism was perceived as the only perspective for new and fresh initiatives, or the 1930s-1950s, that saw the domination of socialist realism) of realistic, modernistic and post modernistic trends. And yet the boundaries are movable and penetrable not only within realism, modernism and post modernism but also between these literary styles."[22]

Today there are writers in Russia following varied literary styles. Many writers like Petrushevskaya, Ulitskaya, Nina Gorlanova, A, Varlamov, Andrei Volos, V. Makanin, Mariam Petrocyan, Maya Kucherskaya, Maria Rybakova and many others are keeping the flag of Russian literature afloat. The Russian literature has distinct groups of women writers, young debutant writers and so on. "The themes of the small man and woman (*malenkii chelovek*), the underground man (*podpolny chelovek*) and the superfluous man (*lishny chelovek*), that found expression in the works of writers such as Gogol, Dostoevsky, Goncharov and Chekhov among others in the nineteenth century, not only continued to be important themes in the Soviet period, but also in the post Soviet reality in the works of writers like Makanin, Petrushevskaya, Varlamov, Aitmatov and others."[23]

Notes and References

1. E. Trofimova, *On the ruins of the 'Big style': Women's literature in search of new gender constructs* (ERGON Verlag). www.ergon-verlag.de (trans. from the original Russian by the author)
2. N.L. Liderman, M.N. Lipovetsky, *Sovremennaya Russkaya Literatura* (Moscow 2001), 7.
3. A. Nove, *Glasnost in Action: Cultural Renaissance in Russia* (Boston, Mass.: Unwin Hyman 1989).

4. V. Shetliansky, *In a Meeting at St. Anthony's College* (Oxford, October 1990).
5. Liderman and Lipovetsky, *Sovremennaya Russkaya Literatura*, 8.
6. V. Erofeev, *Russkaya Literatura v zerkale kritiki* (Moscow: Academa 2003), 36.
7. Yu. Bondarev, *Apologia Literatury*, LG 24 (19 June 1991): 11.
8. K. Parthe, "What was Soviet Literature?" *The Slavic and East European Journal* 38, no. 2: 290.
9. Parthe, "What was Soviet Literature?" 291.
10. A. Sinyavsky, "What is Socialist Realism?"http://antology.igrunov.ru/authors/synyavsky/1059651903.html (trans. from the original Russian by author.)
11. Sinyavsky, "What is Socialist Realism?"
12. Sinyavsky, "What is Socialist Realism?"
13. Parthe, "What was Soviet Literature?" 290.
14. H. Gunter, "Life Phases of Socialist Realist Canon," in *The Socialist Realist Canon*, Gumanitarnoye Agenstva (St.Petersburg: Academicheski Proekt 2000): 281-88.
15. Gunter, "Life Phases of Socialist Realist Canon," 283.
16. M.M. Golubkov, *Istoriya russkoi literturi I kritiki* (Moscow: Academia, n.d.), 186.
17. Golubkov, *Istoriya russkoi literturi,* 284.
18. Parthe, "What was Soviet Literature?"
19. A.V. Schubin, *From Stagnation to Reforms—USSR from 1917-1985* (Rospen 2001), 342.
20. Liderman and Lipovetsky, *Sovremennaya Russkaya Literatura*, 55.
21. N. Sadur, V.V. Rozanov quoted by Sadur in a round table discussion "Contemporary Prose through the Eyes of the Writers," *Voprosy Literaturi*, no. 1 (1996). Available at http://magazines.russ.ru/voplit/1996/1/xx_vek1.html
22. G.L. Nefagina, *Russkaya proza kontsa XX veka* (Nauka 2005), 24.
23. Rashmi Doraiswamy, *International Studies* 44, no. 4 (2007): 315.

29

The Musical Life of Post-Soviet Turkmenistan

Shakhym Gullyev

With the collapse of the Soviet empire, the social, political, economic and cultural lives of the people of our Central Asian region, which was a part of it, have undergone drastic changes. It is very unfortunate that no positive signs have been observed in most of the cases of these changes, though history had given them a great opportunity to develop in the positive direction. The aim of this paper is to make a short excursus into the musical life of post-Soviet Turkmenistan.

In the beginning of my paper I shall make a small note: I am a citizen of Turkmenistan, Doctor of Musical Arts in Turkmenistan. It is already the tenth year now that I have been living and working in Kazakhstan. I have seen with my own eyes everything that happened in the field of musical arts of Turkmenistan during the first ten years after the disintegration of the USSR, and suffered with other progressive cultural figures. Therefore, I will speak about this period as a living witness. And while speaking on the musical life of Turkmenistan during the last ten years, I will use both the official mass media (web sites, newspapers, etc.) the information of which, unfortunately, do not always correspond to life itself as well as that of the opposition, on the basis of which materials, in spite of their commitments, one can form a picture that is at least close to reality.

The musical life of each nation is distinguished for diversity as it consists of different components: folk, oral-professional music, their place and role in the daily life of the people of the country; music by the composers of the European literary tradition and presence or absence of the performing groups associated with it; modern pop music and its performers; propagation, scientific study of all these music and many others. On the basis of this let us look at the musical life of post-Soviet Turkmenistan according to four conventional parameters: a) folk and oral-professional music; b) composers' creations; c) modern pop music; d) propagation and scientific study of all musical varieties.

Post-Soviet Transition

During the initial period (the first 5-6 years) since independence, the musical life in Turkmenistan flowed through the channel laid down in the Soviet time, peacefully, and without any particular changes.

Almost none of the genres of musical folklore (labour, ceremonial, religious and other songs, etc.), as it was even during the Soviet period, were heard any more in their natural settings. One could hear these songs only at the variety shows, or in the radio and TV performances by so-called amateur folklore groups. It was no longer the authentic folklore, but modified and meant for concert performance. The art of *bagshy* (a singer or storyteller, who render his performance with *dutar* accompaniment) and *sazanda* (the musician-instrumentalist), the main bearers of oral-professional music, continued to exist in more or less favourable conditions. They performed during family celebrations and public festivals by rendering great heroic and lyrical epics (*destan*), traditional songs and instrumental music.

The radio and TV regularly broadcasted the concerts of traditional music performed by well-known *bagshy*s and *sazanda*s as well as young performers. It was these people who were also part of the concert groups of the republic's philharmonic society as well as the regional philharmonic societies. The Turkmen National Conservatory took active part in training the young performers of traditional music by engaging the renowned masters of folk music in this effort.

While speaking about European variety of professional musical art, one should mention that its origin, evolution and development in Turkmenistan along with the formation here of the country's own school of composers (let me remind here the names of composers like Veli Mukhatov, Ashyr Kuliev, Chary Nurymov, Nury Khalmamedov, Redzhep Allayarov and many others whose musical compositions have been rendered not only in Turkmenistan, but much beyond its border) was one of the great achievements of the Soviet period, despite certain ideological pressures from above. Thanks to this the Turkmen people got acquainted with opera, ballet, symphony, oratorio, cantata and other genres of classical music, as well as solo, chamber, orchestral and other forms of rendering them.

In the early 1990s, the State Philharmonic Society named after M. Tachmuradov (it had symphonic orchestra, orchestra of national instruments, academic chorus, ensemble of national dance, numerous concert groups including the popular rock group of *Destan*) operated as before, and the Academic Theatre of Opera and Ballet named after Makhtumkuli was fully functional as well in Turkmenistan. The repertoire of these groups not only consisted of the compositions by the Turkmen composers, but also of the outstanding compositions from abroad, the Russian and Soviet classics.

By the end of the twentieth century the attitude of the authorities to the people of creativity started worsening conspicuously. The activities of many creative organizations were paralysed, and some of them, including the Union of Composers of Turkmenistan, were already shut down through the efforts of the Office of the country's President. The main reason behind such attitude towards the representatives of creative intelligentsia can be explained by the fact that during the first years of independence of Turkmenistan many composers, artists, writers, personalities of film, theatre and other fields refused to go back to the former restrictive structure, after experiencing the fresh air of freedom in creativity, inspired by Gorbachev's *glasnost* in the last Soviet years. The official Turkmen authorities found it more and more difficult to control and administer the creative process, and actively use the personalities of literature and art to glorify the ever-growing cult of personality of the first President Saparmurat Niyazov, whom, after some time, already on a statutory basis, they started referring as Saparmurat Turkmenbashi (literally—the head of the Turkmen); soon after even the word "Great" was added before his name. Here I would like to quote an excerpt from the address to Niyazov, on behalf of the students and lecturers of the State Academy of Arts of Turkmenistan on the occasion of tenth anniversary of the foundation of this educational institution:

> Our Dear Serdar (i.e. The chief—the author), you are like the legendary prophet Khydyru who lived in the golden sandy desert, Kovus the master of the misty mountains, Kiyasu the lord of stormy sea, the Great miracle man, Our Eternal Head, our dear Serdar, who has miracle power granted by the Most High, who has aroused the bright, prosperous, abundant life, the melody of eternity in the ancient and eternal Turkmen land, thanks to You the whole world today knows about the Turkmen people... our Impartial Serdar, who has been endowed by Allah with the wisdom, our Father the Great Saparmurat Turkmenbashi! [1]

The cultural policy of the state only focused on how it was perceived by Turkmenbashi himself. And his perception of it was highly original. Here are some of his arguments on opera, ballet, and classical music, made by him on 12 April 1999 at a meeting with theatre personalities:

> What is the purpose of it [opera—the author]?...Turkmen do not go to opera, they do not understand it...While working in Moscow, I had to go to the Bolshoi Theatre. I listened to "Boris Godunov," watched "Spartak," they did not excite me, I do not appreciate such kind of music. The question is, why to sing, why to shout, when these same words can be said normally, in colloquial speech...Ahmed! Musaeva! [refers to the famous soloists of ballet Akhmed Pursiyanov and Gulbahar Musaeva—the author]. Your pas de deux is not appreciated! This art is alien to the Turkmen. It not ours!.When I was attended the lectures, performances, but did not understand everything that was said and showed...sonata "Lunnaya," "Appassionato" might be listened... for once. "Othello," studying in Leningrad, season tickets used to be distributed to us, the students. I used to "Hamlet" too not more than that. See, our performances, staged after independence, are no less than the plays by Shakespeare, Moliere... We are a country of ancient culture ...[2]

Exactly two years later, President of Turkmenistan repeated almost these same words about ballet at a meeting with creative workers which was held on 3April 2001:

> If ballet is not in the blood of a Turkmen how do you want to force him to go to the ballet shows? Some people say that supposedly the people should be groomed, inculcate culture into them. But you must understand that, it is impossible to inculcate something with force what the people by nature do not accept![3]

It is especially worth mentioning that the speech of President Saparmurat Niyazov at this meeting with the creative workers became the basic "policy" document for final collapse of Turkmen literature and art. As I remember, that very day this entire speech was shown in the evening information programme of the national television. There, almost everything that had been achieved during the Soviet period was severely criticized, and it was suggested to focus only on traditional sources. His words still resonate in my ears the sense of which was roughly like this:

> Why do we need foreign classics, why do we need Shakespeare, we need the performances that tell us about the

> glorious history of the Turkmen and the happy life of the Turkmen people today.

Next day the speech was repeated, but this time with major editing, in which the name of Shakespeare and other "critical" statements apropos the world classics were no longer mentioned. One interesting detail needs special attention. The speech of the country's President at the above-mentioned meeting, held on 3 April 2001, was published in official press on 11 May 2001 just more than one month later, under the heading "Go back to the lost memory ...", that too with major editing and revisions. Here, for instance, the text is given where the President mentioned about the classics and about Shakespeare:

> Living in the USSR for seventy years, we have learned many cultures. We know about great classics of the East, Shakespeare, French writers and composers. But we do not know about the Turkmen roots. Do not think, by any means, that nationalist feelings have surged within me. I simply believe that it is difficult to judge strangers, without knowing one's own. We often forget about our own national identity.[4]

Throughout the text similar proof-reading was done. One can well imagine, how much labour was devoted and how much time was spent by numerous employees and the editor of the newspaper, in order to give a more or less decent look to the "policy" speech of the President. By the way, many other authors must have noticed that the speeches of Niyazov published in the Turkmen-language version are not always identical to that presented in the Russian version of the newspaper *Neitral'nyi Turkmenistan*.

> In the Russian-language edition they are polished, as a rule, thoroughly edited, often at the root of reworked and even added by the speechwriters. The amendment of the text goes sometimes 15-20 days. For the "Neutral Turkmenistan" is the only Russian-language newspaper in the country that is sent with the speeches of the president in many foreign countries, and, probably, it is inconvenient to represent the head of state, to put it mildly, absurd, and at times absurd. For and brought all his speech to the condition (*sic*).[5]

And even this revised text stated below clearly shows how they wanted to erase those immense achievements in the field of culture gained during the Soviet rule from the history, from the memory with the stroke of a pen, and what they were going to do with the culture and art of modern Turkmenistan. Here are some more citations from the published version of Niyazov's speech:

> We have lost our memory during seventy years. We have forgotten that Turkmen were a great people, that they had built more than 70 states... But later on their spirits declined so low that they considered themselves capable of only wandering through sands, living in squalid poor yurtas, playing on dutar and gidjak, singing mournful songs. However, today we do not intend to reconcile with the way the matter stands. Turkmen have rich and great history and they have the right to be proud of it...
>
> ...We are closing down the Mylly Tachmuradov Turkmen State Philharmonic Society, the State Folk Dance Ensemble of Turkmenistan, as well as the National Variety Art and Circus Centre of Turkmenistan, and going to build up the National Cultural Centre of Turkmenistan under the Ministry of Culture of Turkmenistan. This Centre is to accommodate the entire Turkmen culture and art. The poets, writers, musicians and sculptors would find a shelter here...
>
> ...We are closing down the Makhtumkuli Opera and Ballet Theatre, and instead going to establish the Makhtumkuli National Music and Drama Theatre...This will involve the teachers and students of the conservatories, music schools, and other artists, they would create new music, and musical as well as drama compositions. They are to attract the audience with their expertise.[6]

Turkmen traditional music also was not spared. According to the President, Turkmen musical art in the past was characterized by its richness and diversity. Numerous musical instruments were created by Turkmen (even their exact number was mentioned—72[7]), which must be revived and used everywhere! Either in concerts, or in radio or TV nobody likes to listen to *bagshi*s and *sazanda*s, who sing or perform just using *dutar* and *gidjak*. Let the *bagshi*s sing with the accompaniment of large ensembles and orchestras where many of these instruments would be heard. Solo performance on traditional musical instruments is also to be replaced, let everywhere sound the ensembles and orchestras of various instruments. As a result of this instruction by the President traditional songs and instrumental music of *bagshis* and *sazandas* stopped being heard in concerts, radio and TV in their traditional form. In other words, Turkmen traditional musical art was forcefully crammed into artificial surroundings.

Current Trend

Unfortunately, all this continues even today. Even the imagined number "72" has not yet lost its "magical" effect. For example, in one of the cabinet meetings of the ministers, the present President of Turkmenistan Gurbanguly Berdymukhamedov declared that he was dissatisfied with the fact that Turkmen musicians were confined to the arrangement of folklore legacy and imitating the popular productions of the world. The President considered that the musicians *while creating new original productions should more actively use all forms, the rich varieties and genres of musical legacy of the ancestors*. He urged the Turkmen musicians to actively bring into play all 72 Turkmen national instruments in their creative work.[8]

Pop music is the most invasive segment of musical culture of today. Unfortunately, this music in Turkmenistan, as in the other countries of our region, is hardly amenable to control, and no special attempts are observed on the part of the concerned authorities to channelize it in a positive way. On the contrary, it is being used with full force to glorify the first person of the country. Not only the singers, but also some professional composers are taking part in this process. For example, the well-known composer Redzhep Redzhepov within a short period wrote over 200 songs, which were composed on the "poems" by the poet and President Niyazov or were very much dedicated to him. And the songs heard in the annual *Yanlan, Diyarym!* Pop music competition, being held in Turkmenistan since the early 1990s, were basically eulogizing the *Great Serdar and the ongoing great achievements taking place in the country under his wise leadership*. It was repeatedly shown on television how the winners of competition were personally awarded by Saparmurat Turkmenbashi with American dollars.

There is information, that this competition *is now changing its direction—all the participants are bound to dedicate one of the songs of the competition to the new era and directly to the new leader of the nation.*[9] The latest information may be recalled:

> In the middle of April the cultural department of the capital sent out a circular to all the restaurants and cafes of Ashkhabad which organise entertaining events. From now

> on, every restaurateur was made responsible for the content of songs rendered during corporate parties, weddings and other ceremonies held in their premises. The employees of the Ministry of Culture and Broadcasting of Turkmenistan inspected the above-named establishments with a view to personally explain the document of "national importance." According to them, the songs rendered must comply with the spirit of the time, great achievements of the era of Renaissance. Simply speaking, everybody should sing about Arkadag [the support of nation—author], i.e. about the President...Many performers would have to leave their profession if they refuse to sing songs about Arkadag. But now it is very easy for less talented performers to make career in Pop music, as it is enough to sing songs praising the president.[10]

Of late, the number of so-called pop-singers in Turkmenistan is growing like mushrooms after rain, the overwhelming majority of which have neither musical education, nor vocational training (therefore it is unnecessary to especially dwell on their performing level). The strangest thing is that for some reason they are now been referred to by lofty word *bagshy*. As it is known, *bagshy* to the Turkmen is the chief bearer of Turkmen oral-professional music who sings songs, performs the great epics—*destan*s, presenting his performance with the accompaniment of self-played two-stringed plucked lute *dutar*.

This is how V.M. Belyaev, the first researcher on Turkmen music, wrote about the *bagshy* and their art back in the 1920s:

> But the private practice of music in itself does not give the status of bagshy to those who are still amateurs engaged in this art, i.e. it does not make them recognised professional traditional singers. For this status a Turkmen singer-cum-musician (only with rare exceptions a bagshy does not accompany himself with self-played dutar) must reach the high level of performance skill which does not come at once and which transforms an amateur musician into a professional musician.[11]

In earlier times, in order to deserve the right to be called *bagshy* or *sazanda* it was indeed necessary to learn from an instructor (*Khalyp*), an outstanding master of traditional oral-professional music. After attaining the perfection in the performance skill and learning repertoire under his guidance for a long time, sometimes up to 10 and more years, a pupil received his blessing (*pata*), which gave him the right to independently perform before an audience.

Speaking about pop music, one should mention about the discredit of yet another word familiar to all—"composer" (Latin *compositor*), which means an author of a musical work, that is, a person engaged in composing music. To our knowledge, the profession of a composer, among other things, presupposes the presence of creative and musical talent and requires special training (learning to compose). And in today's Turkmenistan just about everyone is engaged in song "writing." All the so-called singers are both composers and poets. And because of their songs being composed on the principle of making cocktails there is very little of Turkmen. One will hear in them mostly rhythmic intonations, melodic rotations, and sometimes the whole chunks of Azerbaijani, Turkish, Arabian, Indian and even western pop music.

Here is how the pop music has been characterized in one of the articles on the art of modern Turkmenistan:

> In the milieu of the variety performers—it is a complete mess. Popularity received only by those who are close. The competitions held every year with big pomp discover winners, but with this their official career comes to an end. Nobody takes interest in their professional growth though precisely this is the ultimate goal of competitions. And they earn their livelihood by singing in the wedding and corporate parties. Having risen financially, the pop singers at their own expenses record albums and shoot videos, which, if they are permitted, they give away for television. And if the videos are shown on television, the singers' names are not mentioned, and no interview with the artists is taken either. Art without a face—this is the main sign of the new era in Turkmenistan.[12]

Finally, let me spare a few words regarding propagation and scientific study of traditional and composers' music. In our view the area of propagation area has been most neglected. As it is known, creativity of the composer and its performance are closely related to each other. A composer cannot compose opera, ballet, symphony or other great pieces of music if he knows in advance that nobody is going to perform them. Therefore, the question does not arise at all about any full-fledged propagation of music with the closure of the opera and ballet theatre as well as other performing groups and absence of new compositions. And all that is being done in this respect by the forces of today's "semi-professional" groups who have no aesthetic or educational, rather only political, character. Two Turkmen classical operas namely *Shasenem-Garyp* by D. Ovezov and A. Shaposhnikov, *Leili-Medzhnun* by D. Ovezov and Yu. Meitus staged two years ago, by the forces of newly organized Symphonic (incomplete) Orchestra, the artists of the Music and Drama Theatre (many of whom are originally from amateur art activities and have no music education), the students and teachers of the Musical School and Conservatory, as well as by the pop singers, can be mentioned as glaring example.

These operas, already staged for several times at the Music and Drama Theatre were of amateur standard, that too not at its best. It is clear that all this is done just to "demonstrate" the world about the "revival" of opera in Turkmenistan, which was forbidden by the former authority of the country.[13] The deplorable fact is that not a single composition of great form (opera, ballet, symphony, cantata, etc.) has been written by the Turkmen composers for last 20 years. Even if it was written, they did not belong to the musical community of the country.[14]

In his "policy" speech on which we dwelt above, Saparmurat Turkmenbashi also had touched the issues of research on Turkmen music:

> Music and art of the Turkmen had no tribal affiliation. Although some people still try to divide the music according to different trends. All this happened during the last three centuries since the Turkmen were isolated and aggrieved. Turkmen have a single integral art, a common musical culture. Therefore, there is no point dividing it on the basis of tribes.[15]

However, not all scholars agree with the statement given by the President. For example, the famous known ethnologist Sergei Demidov writes:

> If to follow this logic the national music needs to be unified, denying the variety of its shades, based on the diversity of local and historical factors that were recorded in his research in the 20s even by professor Viktor Aleksandrovich Uspenskii, the well known collector of Turkmen music, one of the main heroes of the Turkmen film Tainy mukama, and by Shakhym Gullyev who defended his doctoral thesis in 1998, a lecturer of the Turkmen State Conservatory, recently forced to leave the Republic...[16]

The specific living conditions, work and life of the Turkmen who until recently preserved an isolated clan and tribal structure, have indeed left a certain imprint on their material and spiritual culture. The unique local characteristic features have been retained to this day both in colloquial dialect, clothes, ceremonies, decorative and applied arts (especially in carpet weaving), and in the musical art. This phenomenon was most distinctly reflected in the art of Turkmen *bagshy* and *sazanda*, in which, precisely on the basis of local performing characteristics, various regional-tribal styles were formed with their musical and creative traditions, artistic and aesthetic ideas, as well as practical aims and purposes.[17]

Speaking about the studies on Turkmen music in general it can be noted that there are a lot of problems in this field, which will probably be awaiting the researchers for a long time yet. The main reason is the abolition of almost all the scientific institutions in the country in due course, starting from the Academy of Sciences (earlier, the Sh. Batyrov Institute of History under the Academy of Sciences of Turkmenistan had a department of arts which was engaged in scientific researches in different areas of arts including musical art), the Higher Attestation Committee and all specialized councils on defending candidate's and doctoral dissertations. And as a result, there is lack of young specialists capable of scientific researches (some attempts are being made to revive the Academy of Sciences and other destroyed scientific structures), the careless attitude to traditional music and its bearers, malevolent attitude to the professional composers and their creativity on the part of the concerned authorities, etc.

Conclusion

Twenty years have elapsed since the superpower called USSR has ceased to exist. It is true that in that system many such things happened, which deserve criticism. But there were also many good and positive things. Therefore, denying all the achievements of Turkmen culture during the years of Soviet rule, as it is being done in today's Turkmenistan, we run the risk of splashing out the child too along with the muddy water from the bathroom. The time demands from us a solicitous attitude to the true values of our past musical culture. Practice shows it is easier to destroy, than to restore. In order to let the musical life of today's Turkmenistan return to the normal way of development active efforts are needed from the state structures as well as all the interested people. And now it would require not years, but decades.

Notes and References

1. *Neitral'nyi Turkmenistan,* no. 7 (8 January 2004).
2. V.V. Rybalov, *Turkmenskaya tragediya* (Moscow: Rossiiskoe gumanisticheskoe obschestvo 2004), 64-65.
3. *Neitral'nyi Turkmenistan* (11 May 2001).
4. *Neitral'nyi Turkmenistan* (11 May 2001).
5. Ryblov, *Turkmenskaya tragediya*, 63.
6. *Neitral'nyi Turkmenistan* (11 May 2001).
7. Naturally a question arises: why 72, and not 71 or 73 and who calculated them? Who has explored them? We know about only a few musical instruments, which are, indeed, Turkmen instruments: *dutar*, *gydzhak*, *gargy-tüyduk*, *dilli-tüydük, gopuz*... But soon an author was found, a teacher of *dutar* class in the Republic Musical School, Ovezmurad Gandymov, who named *all 72 Turkmen musical instruments* and published a whole series of articles on them during October-November 2001 in the newspaper *Neitral'nyi Turkmenistan* (for his "work" Î. Gandymov received an award worth US$5000 from the hands of the President). It is a shame to say that there were all common oriental musical instruments, which the author without any "further" " proofs termed as Turkmen musical instruments.
8. See "Prezident Turkmenistana ne dovolen estradoi," http://asiatur.com/central-asia/239-prezident-turkmenistana-ne-dovolen-yestradoj.html; IsakovaA., Muzykal'nye posidelki na Kaspii, http://www.ng.ru/cis/2010-08-04/6_kaspiy.html.
9. M. Babaev, "S novym kul'tom!" http://www.chrono-tm.org/?id=2111.
10. "Patrioticheskii repertuar dlya restoranov i kafe," http://www.chrono-tm.org/?id=3085).
11. V.A. Uspenskii, V.M. Belyaev, *Turkmenskaya muzyka* (Almaty: Fond Soros Kazahstan 2003), 43.
12. A. Yarova, "Vyzhennaya zemlya. Kul'tura nezavisimogo Tukmenistana," http://www.fergananews.com/article.php?id=6671.
13. See "Bir gezeklik opera," http://www.azathabar.org/content/article/2079618. html
14. A news, published in one of the official websites, reported on two concerts re-created by the Turkmen State Symphony Orchestra, and listed the names of compositions, performed by them in these concerts. The list included vocal and symphonic works by N. Khalmamedov, excerpts from the opera *Leili-Madzhnun* by D. Ovezov and Yu. Meitus, *Shasenem-garyp* by D. Ovezov and A. Shaposhnikova, as well as compositions by G. Bizet, J. Brahms, A. Khachaturian. As we see, there is not a single composition created by the composers of Turkmenistan since independence, i.e. during the last 20 years. See V. Baileva, *Dialogi s muzykoi i o muzyke*, http://turkmenistan.gov.tm/_rus/2008/12/24/dialogi_s_muzykoj_i_o_muzyke.html.

15. *Neitral'nyi Turkmenistan* (11May 2001).
16. S.M. Demidov, *Postsovetskii Turkmenistan* (Moscow: Natalis 2002), 115-16. Let me take this opportunity to express my gratitude to Sergei Mikhailovich for mentioning my name and referring to my research.
17. Many issues of this problem have been addressed by me in two monographs and a number of other publications. See Sh. Gullyev, *Iskusstvo turkmenskikh bakhsi: osnovy muzykal'no-poeticheskogo stroeniya* (Ashkhabad: Ilym 1985); Sh. Gullyev, *Turkmenskaya muzyka (nasledie)* (Almaty: Fond Soros-Kazakhstan 2003).

30

Musical Culture of Uzbekistan after Independence

Dilorom Karomat and Nigora Khasanova

The first half of the nineties of twentieth century was a crucial turning point for Uzbekistan. Socio-political changes and the attainment of independence marked the beginning of new era in the history of the republic. Old ideals changed and new ethical and spiritual (artistic) values were set in place. These changes, particularly, the philosophy of Sufism with its dominant spiritual content and the idea of constant moral perfection of human being and untiring search for Truth came to the forefront.[1]

The process of globalization emphasizes the necessity of awareness of cultural and spiritual values. Music, as a form of art, which is inseparably linked with internal experiences of the person has therefore found new resonances in independent Uzbekistan. On the one hand, the preservation and revival of the old musical tradition played a large role in the enrichment of an inner world and in the deepening of the cultural level of the younger generations and in familiarizing the youth with national and world musical art. On the other, omnipresence of genres of popular music, "*zatciklennost*" of young generation on it[2] and the necessity of development of popular music according to national values became evident.[3] Thus diversity is an important factor, which are shows the development and enrichment of the modern musical culture of Uzbekistan.

Today we can speak with pride about:

- the recognition by UNESCO of the cultural heritage of *Boysun*,[4] *Shashmaqom*,[5] *Katta Ashula*[6] as "Masterpieces of an oral and non-material heritage of mankind;"
- successful performances at international competitions and festivals by the different generations of performers of Uzbek traditional music, composers and musicians of the European style;[7]

- artistic tours of leading musician-virtuosos of national traditional music;[8]
- possibilities of joint international projects;[9]
- publications of research works[10] and releasing compact discs of Uzbek music;[11]
- Uzbek composers, musicologists and musicians are living, studying and working in renowned colleges, conservatoires, institutes and orchestras all over the World;[12]
- activity of immigrant musicians, for example, Bukharian Jews[13] (immigration began from the '70s to Israel and other countries of Europe and America) is a separate chapter in the process of the development of musical culture in past 20 years.

Thus the international recognition of traditional music, music composed by Uzbek composers and the musician-virtuosos school of Uzbekistan induces the national society to realize itself as the owner of traditions of high art value; but unfortunately, experts note the lack of real judges of classical arts among the audience. Nowadays experts are constantly speaking about the need to revive educational work and search for new interactive forms of dialogue with the audience in order to prepare them for understanding all kinds of music. For example, if till the last decades of the twentieth century the major aim of traditional music was preservation of repertoire, now it is has become the problem of "preservation" of its audience.[14]

In an era of rapid globalization the process of "salutary influence of music" itself has become complicated. Further complexity of the given problem in modern conditions of the republic results from the extraordinary dynamics of the concept "Uzbek music of 20th and 21st centuries." In the beginning of the twentieth century Uzbek music had an advanced system which consisted of the national monody style of professional music with an oral tradition and folklore and its own types of composition, genres, etc. By the middle of century it was enriched by the western-style polyphonic, which also possessed its own forms, genres and kinds/methods of their performance.[15]

There has also been the development of other "musical-creative kinds" (Russian musicologist Valentina Konen's term) and particularly genres of light music, which include the pop, the rock, the jazz, etc. This diversity of musical culture of Uzbekistan interferes with the perception of the audience as well as of professionals. Thus, during the twentieth and first decade of twenty-first centuries there have been constant changes in the kind of music that people have listened to and particularly in the "dominating taste" of epoch.[16]

Today, the tradition of regular acquaintance to new compositions has disappeared and listening to modern composer's creativity is possible only in the composer's anniversary concerts (often once in 5-10 years) or at concerts of festivals of symphonic and modern music. The cycle "Music and Time" (held every second Thursday of the month), two years ago was initiated by the composer Felix Yanov-Yanovskiy with the support of the museum-apartment of composer Suleyman Yudakov and the Union of composers of Uzbekistan. It has become one of the attempts to consolidate musical forces for the purpose of acquainting the youth with the history of the composer's creativity in Uzbekistan. As F.Yanov-Yanovsky comments:

> It is our old idea to make the compositions of our best composers of 20th century available to students. Unfortunately, records of the Uzbek music of that time do not exist in the libraries of Union of composers, in the conservatory neither or in radio. Many of remarkable compositions were rendering only once, but not taped or written down. Our task is to show the development of music in the 20th century. Meetings have been held with composers Rustam Abdullaev, Mustafo Bafoev, Dilorom Saidaminova, Habibullo Rakhimov. But basically we are looking at the creativity of late composers and for this we are using private records of their compositions. These are Tadzhiev, Mahmudov, Burhanov, Yudakov and others. This is aimed at showing the new generation of the creative youth what has been done before. Any kind of creativity should be based on something, on the one hand this is world classical music, and certainly, this is traditional and professional Uzbek music. In due time, a lot has been done in this direction.

In the middle of the last century musicologists of Uzbekistan established that fact that "in the musical environment the atmosphere which can promote…wide expansion of critical activity hasn't been created yet."[17] There is a sensation that this atmosphere has not been created even today because the dominating atmosphere is the information on music. Let us notice that criticism, being one of the most democratic and an effective sphere of applied musicology at the same time remains one of the less studied subjects. In the light of the points cited above one can see the necessity of the development of the musical criticism in our republic.

In this article two related aspects of the musical culture of modern Uzbekistan have been emphasized as a mirror of musical culture: 1. contest and festivals; 2. condition of musical critique.

Contests and Festivals

The government of our country has declared the restoration of national values as a priority task. This has attracted global attention to numerous unique regions of our country, where the heritage of our ancestors is still alive. The different contests and festivals which take place in Uzbekistan are becoming important events in the musical life of the country, which stimulates creative activity on the revival and preservation of traditional song and instrumental genres, which leads to synthesis of the traditional and the modern and creates interest in the search of new musical forms and expression. These events come as opportunities for cultural interactions at all levels and become a crucial factor in societal development. In addition, competitions and festivals also draw the attention of the public, the press, and other interested people like foreign representatives, experts of performing arts and the audience to become sponsors-patrons of art.

In Uzbekistan (especially in the last decades) a number of competitions and festivals have been organized. Some of them from the regional level have become international, in some other cases existing contests and festivals have been renamed while some (for various reasons) have only existed for a brief period. The regular display of the panorama of traditional and modern music (presented in composer and performing creativity) of the different countries of the world is aimed towards stimulating talented young people and contributing to the further development of national culture.

Republican Contests and Festivals

The prize *Nihol* (prize of the President of the Republic of Uzbekistan) for gifted youth in the field of art was founded according to the Resolutions of the Cabinet Ministers of the Republic of Uzbekistan (no. 334 of 25 August 2000). The award ceremony is conducted annually before Independence Day in the form of music concert presentation. According to tradition the contest is split in the following five sections: pop art, musical performance, classical music, opera and choreography. The symbol of Nihol is the gentle sprout carefully covered with palms. And *Nihol* is not a name chosen arbitrarily for this award. It indicates the development of deep roots that becomes a mighty tree with a dense crown in the course of time. Every year more than 8,000 people participate in the *Nihol* contest, held in three stages. It has to be noted that the winners of this award conquer new heights, regularly winning more awards and prizes.[18]

Competition of gifted youth *Kelajak Ovozi* (Voice of the Future)[19] is a National Youth Contest (one of the most grandiose in modern Uzbekistan). It has been held annually by Fund Forum[20] and Kamolot Public Youth Movement since 2005 (around 230,000 young talents have participated in the contest since its beginning). Today's *Kelajak Ovozi* is not a simple competition it has developed into a project directed towards revealing and supporting young talents and experts. The contest is held in four sections—architecture and design, information technologies, innovation proposals and technical development, national-applied art, literature and critique. The solemn part consists of the award ceremony of youth grant programmes. The given project has been declared the best youth project in 2010 by United Nations Information Centre in Uzbekistan (UNIC) and Fund of the United Nations in the Field of the Population (UNFPA).

Some competitions which are aimed at supporting young musicians and composers have become traditional:

> *San'at g'unchalari* for young musicians (from 1996) organized at the initiative of the International Welfare Fund Sog'lom avlod uchun (For Healthier Youth), the Ministry of Culture and Sports of Uzbekistan and the Union of Composers, in which students of musical schools from Republic Karakalpakstan, other districts and the city of Tashkent participate. For most of participants participation in this competition became the permit into the world of music.
>
> A second one is organized for young composers held annually (since 1997) in the State Conservatory by the Union of Composers of Uzbekistan together with social movement of youth Kamolot.[21]

At least two festivals are held for children.

Yangi Avlod (New Generation) is the brightest and the most cheerful (a sort of a "star factory") festival of children's creativity and one of the Fund Forum's major projects since 2004, which is supported by *Kamalak* (Rainbow) children's organization and the Ministry of National Education of Uzbekistan. The festival serves as a platform for children aged 6 to 14 to demonstrate their skills in: "A"—classical instruments (piano, strings, brass and drums); "B"—vocals (traditional (folk) singing, academic singing, pop); "C"—National Instruments

(Strings, plucked, drums); "D"—Dance (national, ballroom, sports, modern, and ballet art); "E"—Arts (crafts and fine arts); "F"—poetry, literature and theatre script. Around 72,000 young talents have participated in the festival since its beginning (in 2004 when it had only 300 participants from Tashkent and Samarkand; from 2005 it became a republican contest). Laureates received honourable prizes, presents and grants and further support from Fund Forum.

Vesna detstva (spring of childhood) is conducted among art collectives of children's school of music and art. Children demonstrate their skill in singing of pop music, dance and performing on the Uzbek national musical instruments.

The main aim of carrying out several competitions and festivals, which are dedicated to fixed events (like Independence Day or celebration of city's anniversary) are propagation of national popular music, instilling the feeling of patriotism among the younger generation and also stimulation of poets and composers for the creation of new original songs related with historical traditions, values and ceremonies of Uzbekistan. These are

- competition of pop singers *Qalbimda Vatan madhi* (Love for the country—in my heart), devoted to the 2200th anniversary of Tashkent and the national holiday of *Navruz*. It is organized by popular music association "Uzbeknavo," the National Broadcasting Company of Uzbekistan, Fund of Development of Popular Musical Art, *Kamolot* and the Union of Composers of Uzbekistan. This competition had involved over 2000 professional and amateur singers/musicians and collectives between the age of 6 till 40 years old. Competition has been held since December 2008 stage by stage in the Republic Karakalpakstan, in all districts and the city of Tashkent. Over two months the entire country is engaged in singing songs and rendering the melodies devoted to native land, beauty of our capital, to friendship and love and *Navruz*.
- Competition *Yagonasan, muqaddas Vatan*! (You are only one, the sacred Native land!), devoted to Independence. It is organized on the initiative of the Ministry of Culture and Sports of Uzbekistan, together with popular music association "Uzbeknavo," the Unions of Writers and Composers, and also the Republican Centre of Spirituality. One of features of this creative competition is that any singer/musician, not limited by age and a trade, could become its participant. Competition is been held since June 2009 stage by stage over Uzbekistan.

- Competition for the best song "Uzbekistan—my Native land" is regularly held since 1996 in the entire republic. Since 1998 it has been held as a public festival of songs.
- Festival *Navqiron Samarqandga ta'zim* (Bow to eternally young Samarkand) among the folk-ethnographic collectives, devoted to the city's 2750th anniversary. About twenty collectives have taken part in the festival.
- Festival in Khiva named "Culture of ancient Khoresm" had collected the representatives of more than 20 countries. The forum's main objective was attracting the attention of tourists through various programmes. Interest was generated by the performances of regional musical drama theatre named after Ogahi, regional puppet theatre, performance of folk-ethnographic ensembles "Khiva navolari" and "Jilo."

Some of festivals had been held in the republic during several months. One of them was named Davr sadolari (2003, 2008). Among the organizers of this grandiose project were the Union of Composers of Uzbekistan, the State Conservatory and Creative-Production Association "Uzbektheatre." This festival demonstrated achievements of the Uzbek musical art and creativity of the Uzbek composers for the last years and usually organizes more than 30 concerts, which are: evenings/concerts of symphonic, chamber, vocal (soloist, cantata, oratory), children's music; concerts of Bastakor's (composers in traditional monody style) music; musical drama, opera and ballet art. Festivals bring into its activity almost all stages as in the capital as well in some districts of the Republic. Under the umbrella of this festival research and practical conference are organized which are dedicated to problems of composer's creativity and performing art.

Several republican contests and festivals as well as ethno musical contests continued since Soviet times, but now they have come under a new frame.

- Contest among young performers, since 1968, once in two years amongst specialized secondary education institutions of music and art.
- Contest named after M. Kariyakubov, since 1986, once in three years amongst music schools and schools of art.
- Contest named after M. Ashrafi, since 1987, once in three years amongst music schools and schools of art.
- Ethno musical contest of the performers of Alla (Lullaby) is conducted once in two years since 1991.

- Competition of Katta ashula is conducted from 1984 once in two years. Last one was in Marghilon in 2009.
- Republican contest of folk group/ensembles, songs and dancing, conducted since 1994, once in three years.
- Republican contest of Bakhshi and Aqins, conducted since 1986, once in two years.
- Festivals of folk-ethnographic groups, conducted since 1990, once in two-three years.
- Festivals of Lapar and Ulan performers, conducted since 2005, once in two years.

Also several regional contests have been organized among them: *Zarb*-2007,[22] *Iste'dod*-2011, *Bahor taronalari* ('Melodies of spring'). Others are dedicated to performance of Uzbek traditional music only, like "Asrlar sadosi" named after À. Abdurasulov (Samarkand), K. Ataniyazov (Urgench) and M. Uzakov (Marghilon).

Musical "surprise," which was not mentioned in colourful pamphlets, became the most unexpected moment for the listeners in the festival named "the Present to Mozart." This was dedicated to the celebration of the 250th birth anniversary of the great composer Wolfgang Amadeus Mozart. This festival was performed by a chamber orchestra of "Turkiston" and was held in the State Conservatory of Uzbekistan, on October 3-8, 2006. The art producer and the conductor of the orchestra, Honoured Artist of the Uzbekistan, Eldar Azimov remarked "Anniversary of Wolfgang Amadeus Mozart is widely celebrated all over the world. We have chosen the festival as a form because it allows us the possibility to capture all spectrums of instrumental concerts of Mozart." As a part of the performance, suddenly the lights were put off and music emanated from various corners of the hall amidst the silence. This was unexpected and a talented interpretation of the music of Mozart. Musicians played while in motion and transported the audience to a world of beautiful music. In the height of surprise the musicians danced as they exited the stage while playing on the instruments even while they moved behind the curtain. "The reason behind the interpretation was to encourage the audience not only listen to the music but also deeply appreciate and feel each instrument and Mozart's music from their hearts."[23]

Actor's song festival, which is artistic interpretation of songs, held special place in the hearts of the Uzbek listeners. For three years Mark Vail's capital theatre "Ilhom" conducted the festival of a song named after Qourqmas Muhitdinov (2008, 2009, 2011). The third festival (April 2011) was devoted to the 70th anniversary of the birth of great Russian (Soviet) actor Andrey Mironov (famous because of the films "Diamond Hand," "My friend Ivan Lapshin" and others), who has brought to perfection the genre of actor's song.[24]

At least two republican contests of vocalists named after M. Uzakov and J. Sultanov respectively have been conducted since 1997 annually. Also a competition of vocalists (2002, 2005, 2007, 2009) is organized devoted to the memory of Nazira Ahmedova, the outstanding opera singer of the twentieth century and the national actress of Uzbekistan. It is organized by the Ministry of Culture and Sports of Uzbekistan, the Union of Composers, the International Musical Welfare Fund named after Talibdzhan Sadykov and the State Conservatory. It became international from 2009, since it included participants from Ukraine, Kazakhstan, Tajikistan and China.

International Contests and Festivals

These international contests and festivals will add a fresh impetus to the promotion and strengthening of mutual cultural and humanitarian cooperation. The main aims and objectives of almost all the festivals is to popularize the best achievements of national music art, to preserve and develop great traditions of people, to encourage talents in musical and vocal sphere, as well as to spread them for further international creative ties in order to strengthen cultural-spiritual cooperation.

Music Festival "Sharq Taronalari" ("Melodies of Orient") is one of the biggest festivals in Central Asia since 1997 held at Registan Square in Samarkand every two years (24-31 August 1997, 1999, 2001, 2003, 2005, 2007, 2009, 2011). Within the framework of festival a research conference dedicated to problems of traditional and modern music has been organized.[25]

As was mentioned above the UNESCO proclaimed the cultural space of Boysun as a Masterpiece of the Oral and Intangible Heritage of Humanity. From 2002 till 2006 open folklore festival named *Boysun Bahori* is held every May with the support of UNESCO and Uzbek Government. The best folk ensembles and individual performers from throughout Uzbekistan gather for three days of enthusiastic and entertaining shows and competitions.

Festival of traditional culture named *Asrlar Sadosi* (Echo of Centuries) differs in historical and cultural orientation and has become a kind of continuity of a previously existing festival. Since 2008 it became the annual high-profile event, which sought to demonstrate the entire diversity of Uzbek culture—national music, dances, applied art, costumes and cuisine. This festival is a collaborative effort between the Fund Forum and UNESCO Tashkent Office. The festival culminates in a gala concert.[26]

Contest of *Maqom*-performers named after Yunus Rajabiy is conducted since 1991 amongst young performers once in two years. This contest actually started in the Soviet period in 1983. From 1991 it became an international contest because of the inclusion of Tajikistan and Azerbaijan.

Festival Tashkent-jazz (1968, 2008, 2011) again had a place forty years later after the first festival in a capital's concert hall named "Turkiston" on 24 May 2008. It achieved great success. Organizers were led by the board of the Tashkent jazz club. They intended to make it traditional and conducted it in the capital of independent Uzbekistan every two-three years.[27]

International festival of modern music "Ilhom-20" was directly devoted to composer's creativity (annually, from 1996 till 2005). This festival was held at Tashkent and in Samarkand and was literally a "child" (a result of personal communications) of Uzbek composer Dmitriy Yanov-Yanovskiy, who was an art director of the Ilkhom-20. With considerable financial and technical support of the Open Society Fund Assistance-Uzbekistan (Sores Fund), and also other international, humanitarian and republican organizations, a main idea of the festival was to display of a panorama of composer's modern music of the twentieth century and performing art of the countries of Europe, the USA, republics of the former USSR and countries of Central Asia in Uzbekistan. Actually programmes have been focused on the best achievements of known composers with global renown. The purpose was to present global music to Uzbek listeners. Festivals have in many respects changed the world of modern music in Uzbekistan. These have organized creative meetings and master classes (in some way this tradition can be seen in Ilkhom's ensemble named "Omnibus," which has master classes for young composers named "Omnibus Laboratorium"); have presented thousand pieces of music (ten festivals included 120 concertos where 660 pieces were performed, 67 of them announced as "World Premiere" and the rest as "First Performance in Uzbekistan." Sixty ensembles and soloists visited the republic to participate in the festivals). CDs were recorded and released in the wake of all festivals.[28]

The Black Box Music and Visual Arts Festival have been conducted in Ilkhom theatre since 2006. It has been organized in cooperation with Goethe-Institute in Tashkent. Organizers of Black Box Festival are considering one of the main problems of the consolidation of young and independent artists of Uzbekistan. In the course of this festival the spectators of Tashkent had a great chance to be acquainted with the creativity of contemporary young poets, artists and musicians.[29]

The festival of opera in Uzbekistan *Toshkent bahori* (the Tashkent's spring; 2007, 2011) has been organized by the Ministry of Culture and Sports Affairs of Uzbekistan, the Fund Forum, Creative Association "Uzbektheatre" and Theatre of Opera and Ballet named after Alisher Navoi with support from the embassies of Italy, Belarus, Ukraine, Russia, Bulgaria and Azerbaijan. The festival has called for the definition of the place of opera and ballet art in the country and aimed for the further development and popularization of opera art in Uzbekistan.[30] For ten days, the festival offers to theatre/opera fans opportunities to see international and local professionals at play.

The festival, which was devoted to the 150th anniversary of the birth of great Italian composer Giacomo Puccini, was organized in Navoi theatre from 6 May till 11 May 2008. This became an extraordinary event both for fans of classical music and for actors. Organizers of the given project were the Ministry of Culture and Sports of Uzbekistan, Creative Association "Uzbektheatre," Fund Forum, Theatre of Opera and ballet named after A. Navoi with assistance of embassies of Italy and Russian Federation.[31] World famous opera singers have presented to listeners Puccini's most well-known operas like *La Boheme*, *Tosca*, *Madam Butterfly*.

The festival of ensembles and orchestras of national musical (reconstructed) instruments was conducted in Tashkent (2001, 2005 and 2009). This festival became very important for musicians and students for further popularization of all kinds of music between Uzbek listeners and for stimulation in rendering in reconstructed traditional musical instruments.

The capital of Uzbekistan has organized at least five rock music events or festivals with different names. One of the most remembered was "Children of Colours" (conducting from 1999 till 2001). "Creating Legends" and an annual festival of rock-music "Uzfest" (2005, 2006, 2007, 2008), international "IOSIS FEST" and "IlhomRokFest"[32] all of which played their own role in the process of developing musical culture in country.

In the understanding and appreciation of music by the audience mass media plays an important role. Here the role of musical critique is significant.

The Musical Critique

The musical cultural life of Uzbekistan is presented and discussed in the mass media in all its diversity.[33] Almost all modern state mass media prefer an "informational" method of presenting the material ("what-where-when" in which the analytical component is completely absent). There are many domestic bloggers who announce and analyse all events of cultural life, but unfortunately, the majority of authors have no special music education. This is why musical criticism (or writings and reviews by professional musicians) assumes importance since it is directed to perfection of the ethical and aesthetical world of the modern person and his understanding of musical culture.

At the beginning of the review on the condition of musical criticism in modern Uzbekistan, it is necessary to make a small deviation and to look at the '80s of last century.[34] In doing so it is clear that many of the problems, which have become aggravated today, had already been revealed at that time.

When we considered this decade, which is in fact a tiny piece in a centuries-old history of the Central Asian region, we see that it has to concentrate in itself numerous contradictions of political life and numerous cardinal changes practically in all spheres of social being. One of the main tendencies of cultural life of the given period was the revival of monody genres and concentration of public attention around the problems of Oriental classical music. Here we would like to note the measures described in the most significant spheres of musical art. The editorial conversation/discussion in the journal *Soviet Music* named "The musicians of Uzbekistan speak"[35] has been used as the core of analysis of the situation.

The conversation which took place in the middle of '80s has drawn our attention first of all because such "meetings" where prominent representatives of Uzbek musical culture, such as composers, musicologists, and conductors took part and where several problems/issues were brought to the forefront was rare. Here, the basic tendencies in musical life of the country, lack of spheres of musical activity, attempts to find solutions to problems were discussed and plans for further development made. Among the positive developments that were marked was the activization of traditional monody art sharply amplified and progressing interest of composers to professional forms of a heritage (according to experts it is one of the most remarkable and fruitful tendencies practiced by modern composer); intensive development of symphonic genres, etc. Among the designated negative tendencies were recession in development of applied genres; absence of consecutive popularization of national repertoire; a question of preparation/raising/teaching of performers; problem of audience.

Among the problems of Uzbek musical science the following were identified: a lack of use of historical sources relating to data on music; insufficient professionalism of musicologists; absence of fundamental/serious sociological studies/researches (related with perception of the new creative phenomena by general public); search of effective ways for familiarization with wide circle of listeners (as much as it is possible).

In this discussion participants of the conversation had noticed the following points, which were related with musical criticism:

- a problem of "survival" of critique writings/reviews on pages of domestic journals and newspapers (according to musicologist, professor T.Gafurbekov);
- the absence of musical publicism (according to conductor, Professor Z.Khaknazarov);
- flat/categorical and groundless critical statements (according to composer, late M. Tadzhiev);
- imperfection of the criteria of an estimation, unavailability of musicologists for critical activity (according to musicologist, Dr. G. Kuznetsova);
- necessity of operative critical responses, weighty, convincing judgements (according to composer, late S. Babaev);
- stereotype of critical statements (under form, language, style); a neutrality of estimations; weak illumination by criticism of current musical life (according to musicologist, Dr. N. Yanov-Yanovskaya);
- the domination of informative and descriptive materials, which are "remarkable" by unreasonable praises that testifies to indifference of critics to condition of art (according to musicologist, Prof. F. Karomatov).

Looking into musical-critical article/works of the first half of '90s of the twentieth century we saw musicologists still attempting to designate the major problems of the present time. These were the comprehension and a sober estimation of the past historical stage; a search for the ways of organic coexistence/balance between two musical branches of national culture; preservation and the further development of the Uzbek musical art in all its forms.

From the above discussion we can conclude that in the first decade of '90s of the past century the condition of musical critique was:

- the authors of articles and reviews were basically students of Tashkent State Conservatoire (students were trained for musical critique) and journalists with a general profile;
- essential changes in sphere of the publications, caused by general-political changes, where editions were renamed, others

ceased to exist, and some appeared for the first time in the beginning of '90s. However special musical editions still had not made an appearance;

- in the sphere of genre one can see the prevalence of the information-descriptive materials "issued" in different genres.

The thematic/subjects are practically the same, as it was in '80s, though some recession of interest to the composer's creativity in the beginning of '90s was discovered, which was caused by a common cultural situation.

From the second half of '90s and till 2006 all the tendencies mentioned above remained. However, to traditional mass-media sources were added internet editions/sites. Also an attempt was undertaken to publish the newspaper *Musiqa* in the State Conservatory of Uzbekistan but it did not receive the status of official publication. The official site of the State Conservatory could become an original megaphone of musical criticism; however that has not happened. "The News" heading is seldom updated, so the information on concerts and events is available only in the conservatory itself. Announcements of other events can be found in several internet sites, including the www.imhoart.uz. But it is "a drop in the sea" which, certainly, cannot fill the lack of the serious periodical journals or a newspaper devoted directly to problems of musical art.

In 2004 a journal named *Musical Academy*[36] published the material "The musicians of Uzbekistan speak: twenty years later ..."[37] This became in some ways a continuation of the conversation which took place in 1985. That is one of the reasons why our review of musical critique began from the article in the '80s. It would be interesting to compare the situation of musical culture in '80s with the present situation. In the discussion by composers and musicologists were added that of performers, such as M. Gumarov (the senior lecturer of a department of a special piano of the State Conservatory of Uzbekistan) and K. Muhitdinov (soloist of the Opera and Ballet Theatre named after A. Navoi, head of department of the academic singing and opera preparation of the State Conservatory of Uzbekistan).

Many questions discussed in 1985 still remained unsolved. Coming back to results of the analysis of the practical activities of critics of Uzbekistan, we notice that the revealed omissions reduce its efficiency and "scientific diagnostics." The scientific research/study potential of criticism remains unclaimed. "The art criticism, without depending on their nature, is vitally real and the driving factor of the public. Moreover, there are periods when critical activity is more important in moments of 'art crisis' or 'social crisis', when the lack of balance between perception and creativity level causes temporary 'inflow' of creative energy, till such time as the crisis is not resolved, and balance between the artist and environment is not restored."[38] This is one such period. On the one hand, there is the problem of coexistence of two traditions in Uzbek music on the other hand, specificity of market economy, naturally, caused displacement of valuable orientations and in this situation the material factor becomes dominant with all that it implications.

There is necessity not just to ascertain the facts, but also to try and find effective ways to change the current situation. In our opinion, a scientific study of the problems of musical criticism is necessary today. We would like to name some theoretical problems of musical criticism in Uzbekistan, which are the most pressing: the problem of perception and understanding of music; musical criticism as estimated judgement; the place of musical criticism in art and musical life of a society.

In conclusion we would like to stress that criticism, while being one of the most democratic and effective spheres of applied musicology, also remained at the same time one of least studied. One of the reasons for the lack of fundamental works on it is the shortage of critique and critics. And it is especially surprising that many of the actual problems of modern "criticology/critiqueology," for example, a problem of perception of music have been developed in due time by the Central Asian Encyclopaedists like Al-Farabi, Ibn Sina and others. The comprehension and studying of deep successive communications of modern musical criticism with the richest aesthetic heritage of the Middle East is one of the directions in the formation of musical critique in Uzbekistan. The development of the understanding (with the coordinated activity of musicologists of different generations) that musicology is not only applied to the history and the theory of music, but also its critique, as its most dynamical and socially significant sphere is important.

Notes and References

1. N.Yanov-Yanovskaya, the Preface (O morfologii sovremennoy uzbekskoy musyki), in *Uzbekskaya muzyka na styke stoletiy (XX-XXIvv.): tendentsii, problemi*, N.S.Yanov-Yanovskaya (ed.) (Tashkent 2008).
2. The term was suggested by N.S.Yanov-Yanovskaya.

3. Besides traditional three-component layers as folklore, professional (masterpiece) art music and creative work of Bastakor's in today's Uzbekistan there is also the composer's music, Jazz and several types of popular music. There are important tasks before all of them and pop song particularly, which are concerned with increasing of level and perfection of quality of the text and musical maintenance of pop songs. Research and practicals have been conducted dedicated to pressing questions of development of pop music (in the State conservatory of Uzbekistan, 2009, organized by the Ministry of Culture and Sports Affairs, Academy of the State and Public building under President of Republic of Uzbekistan and the National Broadcasting Company), seminars and round tables (in a television complex Bunyodkor: "Modern pop music on the air of electronic mass media: problems, ways of perfection, prospect," 2007; in pop music's association of "Uzbeknavo" in 2011, has passed a round table dedicated to performing Rap music, in which participated responsible officials, and also critics, poets, composers, executors, editors of radio stations and representatives of mass-media), have taken part art conversations.
4. The Boysun territory is located on the ridge of Boysuntog, the southwest spur of the Gissar Mountains in the district of Boysun, Uzbekistan. In March 2001 and 2008 UNESCO proclaimed the cultural space of Boysun as a Masterpiece of the Oral and Intangible Heritage of Humanity. For more information see: http://en.wikipedia.org/wiki/Boysun
5. *Shashmaqom* is heritage of Tajik and Uzbek people. This is cycle or multipart suite of "Six Maqam-s" ((Pers-Arab. Six Maqam-s (musical modes) and named Rost, Buzruk, Navo, Dugoh, Segoh and 'Iraq for the scale in which they are composed) was formed in Bukhara apparently in eigheenth century and based on medieval 12 Maqam System. Every maqam consisting of two large divitions: instrumental (mushkilot, Arab. "difficulties") and vocal (Nasr, Pers. "prose"), each of them contains five basic parts. Inscribed in 2008 on the Representative List of the Intangible Cultural Heritage of Humanity (originally proclaimed in 2003).
6. *Katta Ashula* (literally 'big song') is a type of traditional song, is peculiar traditional style and manner of singing in Fergana Valley. It is singing in rhythmically free style and in high register by two and more (up to five) singers by turn without instrumental accompaniment. On 30 September 2009 it was included by UNESCO within 76 forms of cultural self-expression into the Representative list of a non-material cultural heritage of mankind. See: http://www.unesco.org/culture/ich/index.php?RL=00288
7. More than three hundred young performers of Uzbekistan are world famous, being winners of prestigious international musical competitions and festivals. We name only some of them: performers of traditional

music: M.Yulchieva (The first prize, *Sharq tarionalari* 1997), N. Sattorova (Grand-Prix, *Sharq Taronalari*, 1999); pianists: late A. Sultanov (1995-13th International competition of F.Chopin, 2nd award), A. Malikova (the International competition in Munich, Gran-pri.1993) S. Judenich (June 2001-11th International competition of pianists of a name of Van Kliberna, I place, a gold medal), E.Mursky (1994-the International competition "National forces", London, heist award: Grand prix the princess of Great Britain Diana), F. Husanov (1997-Competition in Salt Lake City, the USA, 2nd place, 2002-the International competition in Naples, I award), E.Nebolsin (winner of Grand prix of the international competition in Spain) (for more information see http://uspenka.zn.uz/laureaty; also some of them can be listen on http://www.youtube.com); opera soloists: D.Piyozov (Grand prix in the International competition "Romansiada," Moscow, 2010), Bobomurod Hudajkulov (3d place at 2nd International competition of conductors named after Stefan Turchak in Kiev, November 2010); With prizes of the international composer's competitions are awarded Felix Yanov-Yanovsky, Dm. Yanov-Yanovsky ("Lakrimoza" for a soprano and a string quartet has been noted by jury of 4th International competition of a sacred music in Freiburg; for the play "Presentiment" he was awarded by the International prize ALEA III in Boston in 1992; has won the Special prize of the International Nantes film festival for music to a film "Kammmi" (the director-D.Faiziev, 1992ã.), D.Saidaminova. One of the young musicians, Nodir Hoshimov, in the 17 years old was entered into the List of four best young violinists of the world. Being graduated on Liceum named after V.Uspenskiy, now he is trained at Kalambussky university of the USA, is the winner of the State grant of the President of Republic of Uzbekistan and musician Vladimir Spivakov's International welfare fund, and also competitions of violinists in Lithuania, Czechia, Romania, China, Russia, the USA. In 2007 Fund Forum has let out a DVD-disk with concerts of Nodir Hoshimov.

8. M. Yulchiyeva (vocal, France, Spain, Belgium, Italy, Norway, Finland, the Netherlands, Germany, Switzerland, the USA, Brazil, Morocco, Korea and India), late T.Alimatov (Tanbur, sato and dutar), A.Ismailov (gijak), Ì.Sattarova (vocal) and others.
9. Uzbek chamber orchestra of national (reconstructed) musical instruments *Sog'diana* (the art producer and conductor F.R. Abdurahimova) had joint programmes together with ensemble of the Bavarian music (Germany) and with Scottish fate-folk group *Iron Horse* and with ensembles of national instruments of Japan and India and with ensemble Samulnori (South Korea). Participated in joint programs of Found Forum.
10. Have been republished in A.Fitrat's book *O'zbek musiqa tarihi*; Mullah Bekzhop Rahman oghli, Muhammad Yusuf Devonzoda, *Khorezm*

musiqa tarihi; a number of new monographic researches were published: R. Abdullaev, *Obryadovaya muzyka narodov Centralnoy Azii*, R.Yunusov *Maqoms and Mugams*; A.Nazarov, *Faroby va Ibn Sina i'qa' haqida*; O.Ibragimov, *Maqom va Makon* ; textbooks and manuals: H. Azimov, *Shkola igri na fortepiano* (based on a material of the Uzbek music),etc; "The sound world of Karakalpaks" from a series Dialogue of Cultures of the Central Asia (the Program on culture and art of the Swiss Agency on development and cooperation); the Catalogue of Uzbek musical instruments by O. Tashmatova, *Khorezm tanbur notatsiyasi*, etc.

11. *The Uzbek instrumental music's art*, CD-disk of Turgun Alimatov, Radio France Studios, Paris, France (05/1995), in 1999, republished in Switzerland; World Music From Uzbekistan with Monâjât Yultchieva; Samarkand and Beyond: Music of Central Asia by Mashriq Dilnura and Abror Zufarov 2007; a disc of national classic music "Tashkent: Voices and Sounds, " which is dedicated to the 2,200th anniversary of Tashkent city prepared by Fund Forum of Art and Culture of Uzbekistan; the French publishing house HARMONIA MUNDI has let out two author's disks of composer D. Yanov-Yanovskiy, etc.; with support of the Swiss Cooperation Bureau (RACP) recorded the unique CD of a music (compositions) of composers of the Central Asia for chamber orchestra by the State chamber orchestra of *Turkiston*, etc.
12. Rasulova Lola (a piano, b.1977), in 1999-2000 raised qualification at university POWEN the cities of Glazboro (USA); Nebolsin Eldar (pianist, b.1974) teaches in Musical Academy of the Princess of Sofia in Spain; Abdullaev Rustam (pianist, b.21.08.1980) teaches piano in district's cultural house "Kreiskulturhaus"—Brandenburg, Germany; Halikov Daniel (violinist, b.1984) works in an orchestra of opera theatre in New York. S. Judenich has finished Musical Academy of the Princess of Sofia in Spain. The qualification raised in Italy at the skill higher school, in conservatory of Kansas City (USA). Composer D.Yanov-Yanovskiy in 2002 has received the grant from corporation Siemens and the Invited composer in North central college in the State of Illinois USA and he has spent two months in USA as "the invited composer," 2010-11, etc.
13. See Theodore Levin, *The Hundred Thousand Fools of God* (Bloomington, Indiana: Indiana University Press 1999); A. Djumayev, "Musical Traditions and Ceremonies of Bukhara," *Anthropology of the Middle East* 3, no. 1 (Spring 2008): 52–66; A. Volosevich, "*Hay Nozanin*": *Muzykal'nyy fenomen vyjivaniya bukharskih evreyev*, Fergana.ru, 12.03.2009.
14. This became a global problem and the same processes one can found in other regions of world. According to researcher R. Abdullayev's opinion, the system of traditional music of Uzbeks has been destroyed

by this time. The main reason that the education system, which exists nowadays brings up musicians of "*notation*" type, who have not developed a deep knowledge of traditional aesthetics, the theory and history of Oriental music, laws of classical poetry and improvisation. See Rustam Abdullaev, *Uzbekskaya traditsionnaya muzyka kak chast' sovremennosti,* in Yanov-Yanovskaya (ed.), *Uzbekskaya muzyka.*

15. Natalia Yanov-Yanovskaya, *Odna kul'tura – dve traditsii, Pravda Vostoka,* 26.08.1997. So complexities of perception of composer's creativity in our country "are aggravated with specific factors: tradition of hearing of such music simply wasn't existing till recent time." See Yanov-Yanovskaya, *Pervaya i osnovnaya..., Sovetskaya muzyka* 2 (1989): 5.
16. Roman Gruber, "O Muzykal'noy kritike kak predmete teoreticheskogo i istoricheskogo izucheniya," col.: *Kritika i muzykoznaniye*, no. 3 (Leningrad 1987), ñ.245.
17. *Muzykal'naya kritika v Uzbekistane* (Tashkent 1984), c.165.
18. For example, piano player Fazliddin Husanov was awarded Prize Nihol in 2002. Also he is a winner of International Piano Contest of Central Asia and Kazakhstan (Ashgabat, Turkmenistan); 5th Junior Gina Bachauer International Piano Competition (Salt Lake City, USA); International Festival de St. Pons (France); an International Piano Contest (London, Great Britain); an International Contest (Naples, Italy); an International Piano Contest (Germany), 1st place and Absolute Title; Shizuoka International Contest (Japan); an International Piano Contest (Sicily, Italy); 3rd Rahmaninov International Competition (Los Angeles, USA) etc.; since 2000, he has taught special piano at Wales Conservatory (Great Britain).
19. *Kelajak Ovozi*, http://kelajakovozi.uz/. Age of participants from 15 to 25 years, who wish to declare itself on all republic, and also to receive real financial and encouragement for realization of their projects, winners of republican round can be entered/admitted into high schools/ colleges directly without any exams/tests. For example the winners were: Behzod Abduraimov (the diploma, 2005; Nowadays Behzod continues study at musical university "Park" (the USA)).
20. For more information about Fund Forum, see www.fondforum.uz; http://gulnarakarimova.com; their chairman Gulnara Karimova appears as the author of the several projects like *Yangi Avlod*, *Asrlar sadosi,* etc. The winners successfully performed and participated at the festivals and acted in the show-programs and cultural activities of the Fund Forum over the world.
21. In one of his interviews the composer Felix Yanov-Yanovskiy has mentioned that nowadays in conservatory are training more than 50 students on specialization "composition".

22. Since ancient times rhythmical sound of *doira* (framed drum) always foretold the beginning of the big holidays and joyful events.
23. Uzbekistan today [http://ut.uz. Shahlo Rasulova, *Pyat vecherov prinosheniya Motsartu*, 27.10.2006.
24. http://www.ilkhom.com/russian/news//, Festival of an actor's song named after Qourqmas Muhitdinov.
25. http://sharqtaronalari.uz.
26. For the first time the festival was held in 2008 in Kitab (Kashkadarya). In 2009 it was held in Aqkurgan and Bostanlyq (Tashkent district) and has been devoted to 2200th anniversary of Tashkent; 2010-Ichan-Qala, the most ancient part of Khiva (Korazm), Bukhara. See http://www.fondforum.uz/ru/news/, http://www.orexca.com/rus/asrlar_sadosi.shtml.
27. See http://jazz.uz/festival.
28. See A. Djumaev, *Tashkentskiy festival sovremennoy muzyki: popytka osmysleniya v kontekste kul'turnogo protsessa,* http://cultureuz.net/music/ajumaev/jumaev03.html; Ilkhom-20, festival of modern music, cancelled in Tashkent, 4/27/2006, Fergana.ru; http://cultureuz.net/music/ilchomxx05.html; was realized in five CDs, where the first one was dedicated to selected compositions of festival from 1996 till 2001.
29. http://www.ilkhom.com/russian/new, Black Box; http://www.omni busensemble.asia/
30. *Toshkent bahori* is a unique forum of eminent masters of classical music, opera and ballet who came together in Tashkent. Within the limits of festival outstanding figures both of opera and ballet art gave master classes and seminars on theatrical management.
31. 2008 was declared by UNESCO the "Year of Puccini" in Italy. The festival was brightened by the names of stars like Irina Arkadeva, Michael Vekua and the favourite of Uzbek spectator Hibly Gerzmavy from Russia, Ombretta Makki, Eddi de Nadai and Dominiko Minini.
32. See Zerkalo XXI, 2006–10: Pavel Kravets, *Uzfest -2006: v Tashkente prohodit rok-festival*, 18.08. 2006; Julia Korchagina, *Uzfest-2007*, 11.09. 2007; *Eleksir vechnoy molodosti*? 24.09.2008. The festival was organized with support of representation of fund UNFPA in Uzbekistan and the cellular company "U cell" and was passed under the slogan "youth Music–Year of Youth." In total within the limits of festival eight rock groups performed. They are five from Tashkent and three foreign (from Russia and France). Approximately twelve thousand persons were present at the programme.
33. They can be divided into following sections conditionally:
    - Festivals and contests;
    - Musical heritage of Uzbek people;
    - Talented youth;
    - Opera, ballet, Music in theatre (Ilkhom, Muqmiy, Operetta)

- Concerts of orchestras *Turkiston, Sog'diana, Solisti Uzbekistana* etc.;
- Concerts programms in the State Conservatoire of Uzbekistan;
- Musical evenings, concerts in Catholic Church, The Tashkent Diocesan Management of Russian Orthodox Church, in conference hall of The Tashkent and Central Asian Metropolitanate;
- Popular music, rock, jazz etc.;
- Concerts of foreign musicians of classical and popular music;
- Initiations of embassies in realisation of joint programmes;
- Music in different kind of occasions, as Art Exhibitions, celebrates of Independence day, Navroz, etc.;
- Conferences and round tables related to Musical culture.

34. See monograph *Muzykal'naya kritika v Uzbekistane* (Tashkent 1984).
35. *Sovetskaya Muzyka* 8 (1985): 5-26.
36. Post-Soviet name of journal *Sovetskaya Muzyka.*
37. *Muzykal'naya Akademiya* 1 (2004): 63-76.
38. Gruber, *O Muzykal'noy,* c. 234.

Neighbourhoods

31

Gaps in the Fence: Negotiating Grassroots Relations in the Sino-Soviet Borderlands (1983–1993)

Sören Urbansky

Border regions are places where, at times, relations between countries as perceived by the elites in the foreign ministries differ strongly from the realities of everyday life for the local residents. At times, the latter are inclined to challenge aims of the former for their personal benefit. This article examines the development of the Sino-Soviet and Sino-Russian relations at the border from the post-Brezhnev years to the early 1990s. It explores how the border between the two countries changed its character through policies adopted by the centres and bottom-up strategies in the peripheral border regions. Did local initiatives accelerate processes of diplomatic rapprochement between the two sides? Which contact zones can be found in the border settlements during time under study? The article argues that at the still heavily guarded border between China and the USSR the first signs of disintegration appeared years before Moscow and Beijing decided to re-open the border officially, almost a decade before the Soviet empire collapsed. This in turn accelerated *informal* economic activities at the periphery. The borderland soon slipped out of the centre's control.

The study will take a local focus on the two border settlements of Manzhouli and Zabaikal'sk. The construction of the Chinese Eastern Railway at the turn of the twentieth century transformed the border region from a remote imperial periphery into a centre of cross border economic exchange. Manzhouli was founded as a railway settlement. It soon became the major economic hub for Sino-Russian commerce, and remains so to the present day.

I attempt three tasks with this essay. First, in a brief historical survey, I attempt to analyse the 1980s as a diplomatic era within the history of Sino-Soviet relations. Second, I try to shed light on the growing centre-based (*formal*) political and economic reconciliations between the two countries and how they affected the borderlands. Third, I try to analyse how with the slackening control at the border and the simultaneous political and economic power break down of the Soviet centre, (*informal*) cross-border contacts increased.

Rapprochement from Above

With the Chinese attack on Vietnam and the Soviet Union's intervention in Afghanistan in 1979, relations between Moscow and Beijing again went downhill. They evoked an increase of Soviet ground forces in the Far Eastern strategic theatre. Yet, there were also signs of a cautious rapprochement between the two countries. Yuri Andropov's fifteen months interregnum from 1982 to 1984 was insufficient to achieve a fundamental break with inflexible Soviet foreign policy during the period of *zastoi*. Nevertheless, it proved to be receptive towards a more pragmatic Soviet China policy. After Andropov's demise, his cautious initiatives were continued, even though proponents of retaining the previous policy of containing the PRC had the upper hand in Moscow until Mikhail Gorbachev came to power. When Deng Xiaoping returned to Chinese leadership in 1978, China's foreign policy towards the USSR made obvious changes. Worsening Sino-US relations under Ronald Regan accelerated a new Chinese approach to *Weltpolitik*. In 1982, at the Twelfth CCP Congress, the Chinese leadership declared that China would pursue an independent foreign policy and would refrain from allying with either superpower.[1]

One of Gorbachev's prime concerns upon taking office in March 1985 was to enhance relations with Beijing. The Kremlin's new foreign policy agenda explicitly addressed the resolution of what Chinese officials call the "Three Obstacles" (*san da zhang'ai*) to normalization.[2] Border talks, suspended since 1978, resumed in early 1987. During *perestroika* a consensus emerged in Soviet foreign policy elite to refocus resources on economic reform rather than on costly international conflicts. The Soviet elite were much less concerned with Chinese military threat. In their eyes, China, like the capitalist world, was not inherently militaristic and aggressive any longer, making cooperation possible. Congruent reform efforts in the PRC and in the USSR contributed to the development of cooperation and trust. The Sino-Soviet summit in mid-May 1989 in Beijing became the symbolic breakthrough in the relations. Both sides agreed to the resumption of relations between the two communist parties, and to base bilateral relations on peaceful coexistence.[3]

Re-Establishing Contacts in the Borderlands

In order to understand the dynamics of the Sino-Soviet borderlands one must do more than merely explain changes in the bilateral diplomacy of the metropolis. What impact did rapprochement have on the political, economic and cultural ties in the shared periphery? Already before Gorbachev's ascendance to power Moscow and Beijing took steps to ease political tensions on the cultural level. The Sino-Soviet Friendship Association (SSFA) restored contacts in 1983. The societies resumed some of their activities in the capitals. Exhibitions and educational evenings paying homage to writers or historical dates of the neighbouring country were organized. The first top-level delegations commuted between Moscow and Beijing. Exchanges of students and tourist delegations began in 1984.[4]

The Soviet-Chinese Friendship Society (SCFS) also began to restore activities of its affiliates in the border regions. Together with Blagoveshchensk, Pogranichnaya and Nakhodka, Zabaikal'sk was added to the list newly established local branches.[5] The SCFS-Presidium urged regional staff to hold an inauguration meeting at Zabaikal'sk already in the first quarter of 1984. It was followed by a regional conference in Chita to elect local branch president, vice-president and secretary.[6] The first official delegation of the local Manzhouli branch of the SSFA spent a brief 24-hour-visit to Zabaikal'sk in November 1984 to commemorate October Revolution 67th anniversary. Five Chinese and five Soviet professionals met, locals mainly working for border-sensitive cargo companies like "Soyuzvneshtrans" and "Sinotrans." The programme included a tour of Zabaikal'sk middle school, two movie screenings, and the participation in the October Revolution celebration demonstration.[7] Zabaikal'sk delegates already had visited Manzhouli one month earlier during the People's Republic of China's 35th anniversary ceremonies.[8]

Central and regional authorities in Moscow and Chita remained traditional in their ways of organizing "friendship." The CPSU regional party committee advised its Zabaikal'sk subordinates to commemorate crucial historical dates of the CCP and the Chinese revolution.[9] The following year's exchanges of delegations on 1 October and 7 November continued in the well-tried scheme and took place in a "cordial atmosphere."[10] Sometimes they were prepared by an unofficial working meeting which took place some days earlier. During their meetings in the autumn of 1985, Chinese delegation members expressed repeatedly their preparedness to expand cultural and professional activities and to come together "not just during anniversaries."[11] They proposed to include "meetings between veterans, women, youth, working experience exchanges of teachers, agronomists etc." The Soviet side had to slow the enthusiasm of its Chinese partners indicating that "all activities are orientated according to relations between the two central organizations." It was the Moscow-based CPSU that had to sanction activities of the regional Soviet-Chinese Friendship Societies and regional government exchanges.[12]

Cross-border contacts were expanded cautiously by the Soviets. By 1986, railway delegations accompanied the friendship association representatives during fall festivities in Manzhouli.[13] That very year, Moscow and Beijing allowed for the first time members of the two local friendship associations to come together for substantial working meetings.[14] Especially the three-day visits of the Chinese to Zabaikal'sk in August 1986 and of four Soviet friendship delegates in the fall of 1987 to Manzhouli proved fruitful. The cultural façade of the programme, of film screenings, concerts and kindergarten visits or gatherings at veteran's clubs, was kept. But economic issues prevailed on the agenda. Chinese delegates visited the sovkhoz "Stepnoi" and the firm "Agroprom."[15] In a brief article the local Soviet newspaper *Zabaikal'ets* informed its local readership about the meetings.[16] In return, Chinese hosts showed their Soviet guests the coalmines of Zhalainuo'er, a chemical plant in Manzhouli and then took them on a walk through the city. Local Chinese television reported. Manzhouli's CCP Vice-Secretary Wu Yihan used each and every occasion to express his hope "that the visit will stimulate deeper contacts between the two border regions in economic and cultural sphere." What Wu had in mind was local cross-border cooperation between Manzhouli and Zabaikal'sk in culture, sports; meetings between labour union activists, organized tourists groups, but most importantly, direct cross-border trade.[17]

For the first time in their three decades of history[18] both friendship societies became more than just a stage of display for state-sanctioned friendship. At least for the Chinese side, both organizations were to become agencies of economic cooperation. Just one month after the Soviet delegates had taken a stroll through Manzhouli, Vice Party Secretary Wu again visited Zabaikal'sk. He took the chance to make his ideas more explicit than ever before. Wu offered to set up a Chinese canteen in Zabaikal'sk staffed and supplied from across the border and invited the Soviets to open a Russian lunchroom in Manzhouli.

While inspecting the new dormitory for Chinese railway men at the train station of Zabaikal'sk, Wu proposed to send more Chinese workers permanently to meet the increased need for labourers for the loading of freight cars.[19]

Indeed, the increase in freight railway traffic over the border was one of the first visible signs of mending economic ties between the two countries. At the train station in Zabaikal'sk, international freight rates between 1981 and 1985 had more than tenfold. Bilateral trade caused chaos on the tracks and at the cargo terminals. Transport proved to be inadequate.[20] Clogged tracks in fact were a good sign. Since the early 1980s, China's leadership had urged Moscow to expand contacts beyond the cultural folklore. In October 1982, the two sides held negotiations on the resumption of cross border business in Khabarovsk. Two agreements were signed in April 1983, restoring border trade between the Soviet Far East and Heilongjiang Province, as well as between Eastern Siberia and Inner Mongolia. CCP General Secretary Hu Yaobang envisioned in a Heihe speech China's northernmost border city as a second Shenzhen: "Shenzhen in the South, Heihe in the north—they should take off side by side."[21] Between 1983 and 1988, cross-border trade increased by a tremendous 4,000 per cent. Since business started off from almost zero, these figures are more impressive than the facts. Even in 1990, bilateral trade represented a small percentage of about three percent of total foreign trade. It never matched expectations, due to shortages of exportable goods in both countries.[22] The USSR mainly exported cement, fertilizer, pharmaceuticals, motorcycles, refrigerators, and imported agricultural commodities and textiles.[23]

Yet, until the late 1980s, almost all the border trade and traffic was by rail and the increase in bilateral business ran largely *through* the border settlements but barely affected peoples' lives in Zabaikal'sk and Manzhouli. Breakthrough in regional trans-border collaboration brought about an official economic agreement in 1988. The protocol on organization of direct cross-border trade, economic, and technical cooperation between Zabaikal'sk region and the city of Manzhouli was signed on 15 April 1988. It set the legal, financial and administrative frame for future contacts. Main areas of professional cooperation were joint companies, technical exchange, delivery of Chinese building materials, assistance in construction and allocation of labour force, and Soviet delivery of raw materials. Since both countries did have nonconvertible currencies and neither wanted to expend precious reserves of hard currency, transactions were largely carried out in barter trade. A mixed trade-economic working commission replaced the rather inflexible channel of the friendship associations. The board held its first meeting in Zabaikal'sk in mid-July.[24] Local SSFA and SCFS branches had proved to be inappropriate for quick economic development. They lost their status as discreet diplomatic channels. Subsequently friendship associations returned to fulfil their original assignment. They again became agents of cultural exchange.[25]

Both sides would profit from economic exchange. The Soviets needed Chinese labour to overcome the state of stagnation. In Zabaikal'sk, most buildings dated back to the 1950s. Lethargic workers, a prevalent lack of materials, as well as antiquated cranes and excavators left canalization and housing projects unfinished. Even small but prestigious works such as the station's archway were incomplete.[26] The first Chinese construction projects built by some 250 workers of the Ha'erbin Railway Administration started in 1988 and included a dairy, several apartment buildings, a canteen, and a gymnasium with an indoor-pool in Zabaikal'sk.[27] Some regional papers such as *Zabaikal'ets* soon praised the neighbour's effort: "Our Chinese friends help us to solve our housing problems. There is a great demand for their goods."[28] Agriculture became another important field of cooperation. Manzhouli peasants were waiting to cultivate potatoes and other crops in the vicinity of Zabaikal'sk. "Our Soviet neighbours would like to learn to produce melons the way we do here," told Manzhouli mayor Xu Shaoan to a *Time* journalist in 1988. Soviet agriculture was still mostly collectivized, centrally planned, and inefficient. Siberian farmers would learn Chinese techniques for planting, growing and harvesting. For Dmitri Krolov, a Soviet regional trade official from Zabaikal'sk, it was of mutual benefit. "Business is booming. We manufacture what they want, they grow what we want."[29] Local cross-border tourism was also to be facilitated.[30] Zabaikal'sk soon became one of the symbols in a nationwide discourse of mending friendship. The remote dwelling was portrayed as a border-post, which "had been asleep for years now and wakes-up again."[31] "Zabaikal'sk-border-station" reads the headline in an *Izvestiia* front-page top story, with a photograph depicting two smiling cargo managers, one Soviet and one Chinese.[32]

Nevertheless, although development had been "above expectations," Manzhouli's mayor, named the lack of a highway checkpoint as the major weak point in a Soviet newspaper. Local politicians of both sides of the border were eager to solve it, but still they had to wait for central approval.[33] Authorities in Moscow again remained hesitant. Backing would have meant loss of control. Road traffic is primarily individual, while trains are operated by the state.

During first years of *perestroika* formal and informal relations remained limited to very narrow zones of contact and a relatively small circle of railway workers, customs officers and local cadres. Friendship organizations continued to monitor contacts between the people of both sides. Activities of SCFS Zabaikal'sk local branch among locals who did not work in the sphere of transport were negligible. These SCFS members, librarians, teachers, doctors had virtually "no contact with PRC citizens." Officials aimed to improve the situation, e.g. by enhancement of teaching Chinese in First Zabaikal'sk middle school.[34] A group of teachers from Zabaikal'sk region's village schools was invited to celebrate Teachers Day with some of their Chinese colleagues in Manzhouli on 10 September 1989. By that time professional exchanges in other disciplines, between doctors, agronomists had been established, delegations at International Children's Day, International Women's Day, and the like were exchanged and bi-national sports events had been organized.[35] Only from April to September 1990, did Manzhouli's SSFA and Zabaikal'sk's SCFS local branches agree to meetings of at least ten delegations of teachers, mothers, translators, health care workers, and veterans.[36] By that time, most members of Chita oblast's insignificant Chinese diaspora had also spent time with relatives in their homeland or were visited by Moscow based Chinese diplomats.[37]

Lifting Barriers

With Beijing and Moscow mending their bilateral relations, international travel was fostered. Tourism was not as exclusive as in the early 1970s anymore, when just a handful of westerners crossed the border every year.[38] Yet, in the late 1980s international train travel still remained something for the privileged. In 1988 it was a fancy Swiss-owned "Nostalgie Istanbul Orient Express Company" train, which drew much attention from international to local audiences. A *New York Times* advertisement praised the 20,000 US-Dollar, 19-day sojourn from Paris to Hong Kong as a travel experience, "as it was experienced by the royalty of yesteryear."[39] The Japanese broadcaster, "Fuji" produced a two-hour documentary about the journey to the East. *Zabaikal'ets* covered the four-hour stop at the Soviet terminus in great detail. It described the authentic in-1924-built train cars and the way passengers entertained themselves at the station during their brief stopover.[40]

In 1988, when the luxury train passed the border, it marked the quiet before the storm. Within just two years the number of passengers on international trains tripled (Table 1). Facilities of the train station

苏联赤塔州后贝加尔斯克区
苏中友好协会后贝加尔斯克区分会：

根据中苏友好协会同苏中友好协会1988——1989年合作计划，满洲里市中苏友好协会邀请苏中友好协会后贝加尔斯克区分会以会长为首的友协代表团一行五人（包括两名工作人员）于1988年8月22日至24日对满洲里市进行友好访问。

中国内蒙古自治区满洲里市
中苏友好协会
一九八八年七月二十六日

Figure 1: Letter of invitation from the Manzhouli branch of the SSFA sent to their Zabaikal'sk peers

Source: GAChO, fond P-6748, opis' 34, delo 316, l. 29

of Zabaikal'sk were not made for such high numbers of passengers. At times, two hundred to three hundred passengers crowded the smelly station "with no place to rest or snack."[41] Immigration procedures remained much the same as in the 1950s. After the 6,293 kilometres from Moscow to Zabaikal'sk, the train was taken away so that the bogies on all cars could be changed. Meanwhile, passengers turned in their visas and filed into the station building in Zabaikal'sk with its Corinthian pillars, to exchange their leftover roubles for dollars.[42] After two to three hours, the railway journey continued. At slow speed, trains passed the giant slogan "USSR builds Communism [*SSSR stroit kommunizm*]" to reach Manzhouli after 15 minutes.

Table 1
International Train Passengers (all nationalities) Crossing the Border at Manzhouli-Zabaikal'sk[43]

Passengers	*PRC-bound*	*USSR-bound*	*Total*
1966	–	–	34,255*/ r–
1970	5,944	5,418	11,130*/11,362
1975	6,007	5,030	16,230*/11,037
1980	4,102	2,740	6,972*/6,842
1985	8,780	5,595	14,375
1986	9,786	5,532	15,318
1987	9,295	5,422	14,717
1988	9,125	6,879	16,004
1989	15,017	12,204	27,221
1990	20,925	20,761	41,686
1991	35,474	32,048	67,522
1992	40,451	36,154	76,605
1995	20,027	9,343	29,370

Sources: Figures are from Soviet sources. GAChO, fond R-604, opis' 25, delo 88, ll. 1-3 (1966); delo 112, l. 6 (1970); delo 214, l. 5 (1975); delo 313, l. 6 (1980).

Winds had changed on both sides of the border. Douglas Fetherling, a Canadian writer who in spring 1990 travelled the Trans-Siberian, was surprised: "Foreigners were even allowed to take photographs of the platform, an activity forbidden at many another, less sensitive facilities of the Soviet Railways." In Manzhouli, passengers exchanged the freshly retrieved dollars for Chinese Foreign Exchange Certificates at the station. Fetherling experienced the Chinese immigration and customs officials who climbed aboard as "courteous as well as efficient." He even had a chat with a young customs inspector who asked him if he might sit down and join him in a conversation to practice his English.[44]

It was not only the western adventurer that took the train from Moscow to Beijing. The route became increasingly popular among Chinese and Soviets. By 1991, it was almost impossible to obtain tickets for the Beijing-bound train in Chita. The train ran once a week and was mostly booked-up. People in Chita oblast' usually had to take the local train to Zabaikal'sk to cross the border by bus to Manzhouli, where they eventually would get on a Chinese train. Nevertheless, crossing into China was still not an easy task. "It takes forever for people to cross the border. Many camp at the train station.

Figure 2. First official meeting of Russian and Chinese veterans in Manzhouli in 1990 (*Komsomolets Zabaikal'ia*, 16 May 1990)

There are too few train tickets, and too few cars pass the highway checkpoint," *Zabaikal'skii Rabochii* quoted a Soviet customs official. To meet increasing demand, Chinese and Soviet railways agreed to add an additional passenger car from Chita to Beijing. In summer, the train was scheduled to run twice a week.[45] A regular shuttle bus between Zabaikal'sk-Manzhouli started to commute in August 1991.[46]

With growing cross-border traffic and increasing economic activities a dark side of relaxed controls reoccurred at the border. Smuggling undeniably never ceased to exist. Even at the height of political tensions, smuggling occurred on a small scale.[47] Banned from official public discourse for decades, by 1990 the subject did reappear in Soviet media. Customs inspections at Zabaikal'sk checkpoint became a popular topic for newspaper features.[48] In 1990 an article in *Zabaikal'ets* explained the etymology of *kontrabanda*, the Russian term for smuggling: "It has Italian origins. 'Kontra' means against, 'banda' means state decree." The newspaper informs the readers of some popular hideaways on Beijing-Moscow trains: lipsticks in sealed cigarette packs, electronic watches wrapped in toilet paper, jewellery in thermos cups, and—in the opposite direction—rouble bills squirreled away in the window frame of the train car lavatory.[49] Not only Soviet and Chinese nationals were involved in smuggle. In June 1990, the "Polish pearl necklace scandal" became a widely discussed incident in local and regional papers. Polish nationals, mainly university students, used their academic holidays for a shopping tour to the People's Republic. That June at the train station in Zabaikal'sk, at least 15 delinquents were nabbed by Soviet customs and send to the KGB prison in Chita. The Poles had acquired pearl necklaces in Chinese bazaars, which they intended to sell on black markets at stations along the Trans-Siberian border, in their native Poland and, probably, on *the* European bazaar of that time: at Berlin's long deserted Potsdamer Platz. On 24 June, Soviet customs made their biggest discovery of 49 kilos of pearls. Due to a different pricing system in China and the USSR, the Soviet customs estimated the overall value with the absurd amount of almost 2.5 million roubles.[50]

"Run on the Freight Wagons"

Economic disruption across the country and political power breakdown in Moscow fostered a dramatic increase in Sino-Soviet cross-border contacts and, in the end, led to a state that was close to anarchy. Many of the shortages in consumer goods and food products in the Russian border regions were compensated through imports from Chinese border cities. In 1992, not only the number passengers on international trains had peaked. By that time, the Sino-Russian shuttle trade had expanded rapidly. In 1993, the border trade of Heilongjiang Province conducted with Russia accounted for one third of the overall Sino-Russian trade balance. Beijing's policies accelerated this trend. China granted four border cities (Manzhouli, Heihe, Suifenhe, Hunchun) the right to establish economic cooperation zones. These zones were aimed to stimulate foreign investment, technology exchanges and labour exports. They were also encouraged to improve their service industries.[51]

The arguably most important precondition for this trend was a slackening Soviet control at the border to China. With the end of communism in the USSR and its disintegration as a state, the border zone regime was lifted in December 1991. People did not need special permits to enter Zabaikal'sk any longer. It was not the decision makers in Moscow any longer who presided over the movements across the border. Cross-border tourism soon challenged the control of the centre. Contact zones between the Russians and the Chinese were not limited to the train station any more. Anyone could travel, not just the privileged people who crossed the border for job reasons. Zabaikal'sk, the once sleepy border dwelling, transformed into a heaven-on-earth for the new post-soviet caste of *biznesmeny*. They came from all corners of the former Soviet empire.

Train tickets to the border station were sold out. The railway administration pulled two passenger carriages to a holding siding to enlarge the station hotel's capacity. Within several days all beds were fully booked.[52]

It was no longer state sanctioned commissions which organized trade between the two countries. Beginning in early 1992, people of both nations took barter trade into their own hands. By that time around roughly 1,500 Chinese nationals crowded Zabaikal'sk permanently. In the streets, on the tracks, even in the passenger waiting hall, soon everywhere Russians "bartered gold for ... 'adidas'." Locals dressed no longer in Soviet grey or brown but in Chinese loudly coloured dresses. Tolerated by local authorities, the small square in front of the station building was converted into a bazaar and emerged as the centre of the grassroots economy. The vernacular named it the "Five-Kopeks." Seeing that it was fenced in, one journalist came up with a term that suited it better: "cage."[53]

Another valve leaked. Since the late 1980s, motor traffic between Zabaikal'sk and Manzhouli largely expanded. While in 1988 a total of 15 to 20 cars daily were cleared by the customs figures within three years multiplied up to 300 vehicles per day. Every month about 12,000 people used the highway border crossing in 1991, twice as many as railway passengers. Until 1992, when the Manzhouli-Zabaikal'sk highway border crossing was finally officially opened, the checkpoint remained makeshift lacking appropriate customs facilities. The head of the Soviet customs at the highway checkpoint, Vladimir Buriakov, admitted that smugglers were caught "almost every day."[54] Smugglers were as creative as in the past. One Chinese truck driver hid rouble bills in the air filter of his *Dongfeng* truck. Russians accused the Chinese contract workers of being the most vigorous smugglers. "After finishing their jobs [in the USSR,] Chinese citizens carry many export-restricted items home to their motherland." If one article is allowed "they" convey ten to 15.[55]

In the end it was not the Chinese truck driver or contract worker but the "tourist" that challenged the Russian border control. By summer in 1992, Zabaikal'sk had become the largest motorcar checkpoint along the Sino-Russian border. Cross-border tourism increased exceptionally. Newly established private travel agencies started to offer trips to China. For many Chita citizens a trip to China became as common as going fishing or mushrooming.[56] When things visibly went out of control, central authorities pulled the emergency brake. They ordered the crossing-point to be closed in early August

1992. Only official delegations and goods could pass. An official statement read that the checkpoint had never been sanctioned for private border crossing.[57] Instantly, prices for Chinese goods skyrocketed. Crowds of Chinese day-trippers waited in Manzhouli. Countless people from all former Soviet republics and Eastern Europe waited in Zabaikal'sk to cross the border. In the turmoil of the disintegration of the USSR, commands from Moscow impressed only a few. People at the border came up with new ways of acquiring China-made western lifestyle.

> Everything started with people sick of their monotonous existence in front of deserted shop windows. They turned eyes to the railway tracks, with its cargo trains and considered their freight to be 'humanitarian aid'. During that moment among parts of the population the 'Run on the freight wagons'-war cry was born. Very soon it became evident, that looting the cargo trains was not a difficult task.[58]

The lift of state export-monopoly in April 1989, led to an increase of train cars for customs clearance in the late 1980s. The first theft of railway cargo was reported.[59] Thereafter, dimensions changed. In 1992 up to 2,000 wagons with imports from China waited simultaneously to be cleared by the Russian customs. The train station of Manzhouli was clogged with goods cars too.[60] Now, shoes, bikes, electronic devices, vodka, cigarettes, and other expensive goods were left almost unprotected for months. "Sidings lack an ordinary fencing, there is just one guard per one thousand wagons, the floodlights do not work, and the only two surveillance cameras are out of service."[61] Railway staff did not prevent burglary but instead assisted the raiders.[62] The once isolated border settlement turned into the heart of the crime scene of the whole province. According to Russian media, looting started as early as spring 1992, and lasted at least for ten months.[63] Media reported regularly on lootings, gunfights, and moral decay, on how people exchanged conscience for a pair of sneakers.

> Children abandoning school, adults their jobs, the disabled and the retired blank out their indispositions, railway men ignoring their duties. All rush on the freight depots mercilessly plundering goods wagons [...]. They seize everything from condoms to leather jackets and fur coats.

> Disgusted by nothing they get on the car, take off Soviet clothes to dress in Chinese garments.[64]

Families and entire school classes raided the cars. The herdsman, Apilov, seized with his wife and daughter, Oksana, 107 leather jackets and sets of sportswear as well as 45 bottles of vodka. Local youth, among them nine year olds, looted in organized groups.[65] Pupils established market economy on the schoolyard. They dealt with everything that was carried off the trains.[66] Zabaikal'sk soon bred its home grown filthy rich. The biggest braggarts gathered around "Victory Street" (*ulitsa Pobedy*) which is next to the tracks. Residents soon gave it the by-name "Millionaire's Street" (*ulitsa Millionerov*).[67] Disorder culminated in December 1992, when Zabaikal'sk looked similar to a front line village. The sound of machine guns shelled the dwelling. People were killed.

In early January, 1993, provincial authorities in Chita re-established the border zone control. Like from the 1930s onwards, only locals, visitors with proper documents, and passengers bound for China were allowed to enter Zabaikal'sk region.[68] An extremely cold winter brought life to a standstill and may have contributed to the reduced influx of soldiers of fortune.[69] Only in spring 1993, authorities were able to fully re-establish control. Some sources estimated the losses in the billions.[70] Freight depots were fenced in, observation towers and additional floodlight poles built. Authorities announced the number of casualties within the settlement to be seven people dead and eleven people seriously injured. Figures in the region lay significantly above.[71] Bazarov, a local resident, was shot for stealing six featherbeds. Police searched the corpse and found 72,217 roubles and a tear gas cylinder. During winter, police and military detained suspects numbering in the hundreds (in February 1993, more than three thousand were taken into custody). Many of them were prosecuted for theft.[72] Still, probably most were never put on trial. Many became "national heroes" among their peers.[73]

Conclusion

Diplomatic rapprochement went along with lifting barriers at the shared border, which had been sealed since the Sino-Soviet conflict during the 1960s and 1970s. It was decided in Moscow and in Beijing that also regional friendship society branches would resume their work. Since 1984, delegates from Zabaikal'sk and Manzhouli shook hands after the centre had decided about the "when," the "who," and the "how." The Chinese side pressured the Soviets to go beyond festivity folklore. Within years, delegations' agendas had shifted from cultural to economic itineraries. The friendship society exchanges had proved to be a crucial diplomatic tool to revive formal economic ties in the borderlands during the early period. Yet, already by 1988, friendship societies had been replaced by trade-economic working commissions. Both sides profited from cross-border cooperation. As a consequence, zones of contact between the people of both countries widened. It was not only the customs inspector or train conductor, who crossed the border to have restricted contact to his colleagues from the other side, but also Chinese farmers and construction workers that now poured into the Soviet borderland. Number of passengers on international trains swelled too and twice a week gave the once tightly protected train stations at the border a polyglot charm. Yet, all these were formal and remained under state command. As soon as political weakness and economic disorder reached the periphery, the shift from formal to informal came almost overnight. Bottom-up initiatives now negotiated relations at the border. The spring and summer of 1992 saw a flood of shuttle trade tourists, which was halted by Moscow in August. Angry about the lost freedom, people went for arbitrary law and began to loot the trains. The border was closed again, but with a weak centre nothing was formal.

Notes and References

1. Elizabeth Wishnick, *Mending Fences. The Evolution of Moscow's China Policy from Brezhnev to Yeltsin* (Seattle: University of Washington Press 2001), 73-97.
2. First, the Soviet Union's invasion of Afghanistan, second, its support for the Vietnamese occupation of Cambodia, and third, and certainly most important for the topic of this paper, the issue of Soviet military presence in Mongolia and along the border to China. See Wishnick, *Mending Fences*.
3. See Wishnick, *Mending Fences*, 98-113.
4. See Wishnick, *Mending Fences*, 79. First delegations from Chita oblast' had visited Haila'er and Harbin as early as 1983. See *Zabaikal'skii Rabochii*, 22 December 1987.
5. See GAChO, fond P-6748, opis' 34, delo 89, ll. 1-4. There were a total of 23 local subdivisions in the USSR in 1986. See GAChO, fond P-6748, opis' 34, delo 193, l. 4.
6. See GAChO, fond P-6748, opis' 34, delo 89, ll. 9-10.

7. See GAChO, fond P-6748, opis' 34, delo 89, ll. 37, 41, 43.
8. See GAChO, fond P-6748, opis' 34, delo 89, ll. 42.
9. See GAChO, fond P-6748, opis' 34, delo 193, ll. 9-12.
10. GAChO, fond P-6748, opis' 34, delo 145, ll. 19-23, quote on l. 20.
11. See GAChO, fond P-6748, opis' 34, delo 145, ll. 42-43, quote on l. 42.
12. GAChO, fond P-6748, opis' 34, delo 145, ll. 29-32, 34-35, quotes on l. 30. See also Wishnick, *Mending Fences*, 117.
13. See GAChO, fond P-6748, opis' 34, delo 193, l. 20.
14. See GARF, fond R-9576, opis' 20, delo 5099, l. 1.
15. See GAChO, fond P-6748, opis' 34, delo 193, ll. 23-27.
16. See *Zabaikal'ets* (13 September 1986).
17. GAChO, fond P-6748, opis' 34, delo 246, ll. 8-11, 13, quote on l. 9.—See also *Zabaikal'ets*, 29 October 1987.
18. For an official brief history see *Zabaikal'ets*, 29 October 1987.
19. See GAChO, fond P-6748, opis' 34, delo 246, ll. 12-14, 25.
20. Soviet railroads remained the main employer in Zabaikal'sk with ca. 1,300 staff in 1985. In 1981 and 1982 up to 3,500 freight wagons per year were dispatched, during the first eleven months of 1985 the number of cars rose to 33,242 cars. The more than 250 railway men working at the cargo terminal were too few to manage the task and had to be temporarily reinforced by workers from other railway departments. See GAChO, fond P-1710, opis' 1, delo 70, l. 103, 112. Dispatch coordination problems, shortage of railway staff remained a problem well into the late 1980s. It continually caused holdups of international freight traffic and, according to its director, brought "Zabaikal'sk station near to collapse". *Zabaikal'ets*, 3 August 1989.
21. "*Nan Shen, bei Hei, biyi qifei.*" Quoted in Wishnick, *Mending Fences*, 84.
22. See Wishnick, *Mending Fences*, 103, 117.
23. See *Zabaikal'ets*, 30 September 1986.
24. See GAChO, fond P-6748, opis' 34, delo 316, ll. 1-8, protocol on ll. 1-3. See also *Zabaikal'ets*, 14 May 1988 and 23 July 1988.
25. See e.g. the three-day programme of Manzhouli SSFA-delegates visiting Zabaikal'sk region in July 1989. It primarily consisted of sports, recreation and cultural activities. GAChO, fond P-6748, opis' 34, delo 378, ll. 12-14.
26. See *Zabaikal'ets*, 12 August 1986. Zabaikal'sk's unappealing appearance led to heated discussions in the local paper. See *Zabaikal'ets*, 31 May 1988.
27. See GAChO, fond P-6748, opis' 34, delo 316, ll. 12-15. See also *Zabaikal'ets*, 23 July 1988.
28. *Zabaikal'ets*, 7 October 1988. See also *Zabaikal'skii Rabochii*, 2 July 1989; *Komsomolets Zabaikal'ia*, 7 July 1989; *Zabaikal'skaia Magistral'*, 16 July 1988, 23 July 1988, and 12 December 1989.

29. *Time*, 18 July 1988. In 1989 Chinese construction workers erected some buildings in the sovkhoz "Krasnii Velikan." A group of 40 Chinese peasants arrived during spring at the sovkhoz to assist during planting season. See *Zabaikal'skii Rabochii*, 26 February 1989; *Zabaikal'skii Rabochii*, 2 June 1989.
30. See GAChO, fond P-6748, opis' 34, delo 316, ll. 16-18.
31. *Zabaikal'skii Rabochii*, 22 April 1988.
32. *Izvestiia*, 4 May 1988.
33. *Zabaikal'skii Rabochii*, 1 October 1989.
34. See GAChO, fond P-6748, opis' 34, delo 246, ll. 16-18, quote on l. 16.—Since 1980 pupils of all nine grades were taught Chinese language in First Zabaikal'sk middle school. See GAChO, fond P-6748, opis' 34, delo 316, l. 26.
35. See GAChO, fond P-6748, opis' 34, delo 378, ll. 8-10, 15. See also *Zabaikal'ets*, 28 November 1989.
36. See GAChO, fond P-6748, opis' 34, delo 452, ll. 2, 24. See also *Zabaikal'ets*, 8 September 1990; *Komsomolets Zabaikal'ia*, 16 May 1990.
37. See *Zabaikal'skii Rabochii*, 1 October 1989.
38. According to Soviet statistics, between 1966 and 1976 only two US citizens had crossed the border officially by train at Zabaikal'sk. Now they were counted in dozens, later hundreds. See table in my dissertation (forthcoming).
39. *New York Times,* 10 August 1988. See also *New York Times,* 29 Mai 1988.
40. See *Zabaikal'ets*, 24 September 1988.
41. *Zabaikal'ets*, 24 July 1990.
42. See Douglas Fetherling, *Year of the Horse. A Journey through Russia and China* (Toronto: Stoddart 1991), 98-99.
43. Figures according to *Manzhouli shi zhi*, Huhehaote: Neimenggu renmin chubanshe, 1998, 673-74. The same statistics are reprinted in *Manzhouli zhan zhi. 1901-2001* (Beijing: Zhongguo tiedao chubanshe 2002), 143.
44. Fetherling, *Year of the Horse*, 98-99, quotes on 99.
45. See *Zabaikal'skii Rabochii*, 30 May 1991.
46. See *Zabaikal'skii Rabochii*, 3 August 1991.
47. Various items were smuggled, although political propaganda materials prevailed. See *Manzhouli haiguan zhi. 1949-1999* (Huhehaote: Yuanfang chubanshe 1999), 93-95, 133-36.
48. See e.g. the one page report in *Komsomolets Zabaikal'ia*, 16 September 1990. See also the feature of cargo train inspection in *Zabaikal'skaia Magistral'*, 17 May 1990.
49. *Zabaikal'ets*, 29 May 1990.

50. In 1990 in China the market price for one necklace of river pearls (*rechnoi zhemchug*) was two to 50 yuan. The official Soviet price was terrific 50 rubles per gram. Import was restricted to 200 grams per person. See *Zabaikal'ets*, 10 July 1990. See also *Zabaikal'skaia Magistral'*, 28 July 1990. For Berlin's "Polenmarkt" see Karl Schlögel, "Polenmarkt," *Lettre* 86 (2009).
51. See Wishnick, *Mending Fences*, 159-63. See also *Manzhouli shi zhi*, 620-21.
52. See *Zabaikal'skii Rabochii*, 9 April 1992.
53. The illustrating photograph, a bird's-eye view of the bazaar, depicts a huge crowd of people. See *Zabaikal'skii Rabochii*, 23 June 1992.
54. *Zabaikal'ets*, 26 June 1991. See also *Manzhouli shi zhi*, 233-34, 238.
55. *Zabaikal'ets*, 29 May 1990. According to Soviet newspapers, vodka, cosmetics, shoes, and cassette players were popular illegal import items among Chinese workers for sale on Soviet black market. See *Zabaikal'skaia Magistral'*, 17 May 1990.
56. See *Komsomolets Zabaikal'ia*, 22 August 1992.
57. See *Zabaikal'skii Rabochii*, 8 August 1992.
58. *Zabaikal'skii Rabochii*, 22 December 1992.
59. The reform of the USSR customs system in late 1988 terminated state monopoly on exports. Beginning on 1 April 1989 all USSR companies and trade organizations were allowed foreign trade. New regulations caused chaos at the customs frontiers. See *Zabaikal'ets*, 13 July 1989. By the end of 1989 already hundreds of goods wagons were waiting for customs clearance at Zabaikal'sk station and burglaries occasionally occurred. See *Zabaikal'ets*, 28 November 1989.
60. See *Manzhouli shi zhi*, 230-32.
61. *Zabaikal'skii Rabochii*, 9 April 1992. Every shift had ten to 13 guards patrolling 15 kilometers of freight cars. See *Zabaikal'skaia Magistral'*, 1 March 1994.
62. For example, railway staff informed plunderers about wagons with expensive freight. See *Zabaikal'skaia Magistral'*, 2 March 1993.
63. First reports about train lootings appeared in April 1992. See *Zabaikal'skii Rabochii*, 9 April 1992.
64. *Zabaikal'skii Rabochii*, 19 January 1993.
65. See *Zabaikal'skii Rabochii*, 19 January 1993.
66. See *Zabaikal'skii Rabochii*, 22 December 1992.
67. See *Zabaikal'skii Rabochii*, 22 December 1992.
68. See "O vremennom polozhenii spetsial'nogo rezhima vezda i propuska v Zabaikal'skii raion Chitinskoi oblasti," *Zabaikal'skii Rabochii*, 7 January 1993. See also *Zabaikal'skaia Magistral'*, 12 January 1993.
69. Schools, kindergartens, shops, the regional hospital were shut down for

weeks. The local newspaper *Zabaikal'ets* was not printed for months. See *Zabaikal'skii Rabochii*, 24 February 1993.

70. For example, *Zabaikal'skaia Magistral'* believes the losses to be about 2 billion rubles. See *Zabaikal'skaia Magistral'*, 1 March 1994.
71. According to *Zabaikal'skaia Magistral'* between November 1992 and March 1993 48 people were killed in Zabaikal'sk region. See *Zabaikal'skaia Magistral'*, 22 May 1993.
72. See *Zabaikal'skii Rabochii*, 13 May 1993. Members of all professions, military servants, pupils were among the arrested. See *Zabaikal'skii Rabochii*, 19 January 1993.
73. *Zabaikal'skii Rabochii*, 1 October 1993.

32

Extra-Legal Practices of Natural Resource Management in the Russian Far East

Natalia P. Ryzhova

The *Strategy for the Development of the Far East and Baikal Region*, adopted in 2009, underscored that the concentration of resources of "global importance" makes the Far East alluring to all states, especially to the countries of the Asia Pacific region. The *Strategy* further mentioned about the importance of creating a *special normative-legal base*, different from the rest of Russia:

> In this connection it is required to have special normative-legal basis determined by special terms of the policies of price, tariff, customs, taxes, ... as well as that of finance and budget, which would ensure the economic growth. [1]

Thus, the raw materials specialization in the APR is being intensified and the necessity of institutionalized innovations (of the special terms of different policies) being talked about. Both of these are justified, but the current experience of institutional reforms in Russia show that because of poor assessment of the informal restraints prevailing at the time of introduction of innovations, the imported/constructed institutions often turn out to be ineffective, or quite destructive.[2] Considering from this point of view the specifically institutional innovations in the field of exploitation of natural resources, evidently should think about the less-studied phenomenon of extra-legal nature management in the Siberian and Far Eastern regions: illegal logging, smuggling of fish and seafood, poaching practices to procure objects of flora and fauna. The extra-legal use of forests has been studied the most to date,[3] but the issue of extra-legal export of wild plants, nephrite, derivatives, seafood and fish products still remains primarily relevant to the journalists, rather than the scientific texts.

The published works, mainly within the scope of juridical sciences, often contains reference to the particular character of economic motivation of the Chinese entrepreneurs, engaged in these spheres of activity:

> The barbaric attitude to the wildlife of Russia on the part of the Chinese citizens, temporarily residing in the Russian Federation is of particular concern. It is no longer a secret, that one of the main objectives of a substantial number of Chinese citizens visiting the Far East is, if not poaching itself, but purchasing animals, plants, their parts and derivatives from the local inhabitants, obtained by illegal means to subsequently smuggle out.[4]

I am not aware of any research, which has been done on the basis of the Russian empirical materials and focused on the comparative study of economic motivation of foreign entrepreneurs, leading their activity in Russia. And the works, which refer to the illegal activities as their objective, have not compared the practices of the Chinese entrepreneurs with those from Russia or other countries. With this turn of events, when one side is *victim*, and the other is *predator*, using archaic technology, the analytical projection is distorted. After all, in reality, along with Chinese *fisherman and poacher* there appears Russian *fisherman with net*, with Chinese *smuggler,* zealously work Russian *shadow supplier* of furs and timber.

This work aims at systemization of the extra-legal practices of nature management, associated with the export of natural resources to China, attempts to explain the authoritative institutional decisions, and evaluates the transformation of the informal restraints on adoption of such decisions.

There are various terms to define the activities that go beyond the bounds of legality (informal, unaccounted, criminal, shadow, unofficial, etc.). The areas of their application are diverse, although many of the concepts overlap. The fact relevant for this study is that informality does not have any negative assessment and is perceived as an evidence of the dynamic character of the entrepreneurial activities of people, which the *centralized structures tried to take away from them*,[5] as a reaction of the population to the rigid behaviour of the state that survives at the cost of delegating to a small elite the privileges of legal participation in economic activities.[6] The term 'extra-legal', - that is, the activities which exists apart from the legal norms in force, but not necessarily contrary to them - is especially accurate within the bounds of such a conceptual approach. It underscores that tax evasion or seizure of a piece of land for gold mining is the consequence of resistance to the pressure of a *predatory state*, and the opportunity to get profits by means of evading this pressure.[7]

The official publications of the Federal Security Service (FSB) and the Federal Customs Service (FTS) of the Russian Federation put up on the relevant Internet sites serve as the main source.[8] The decision to choose these databases are determined by the fact that both the Services are officially accountable for representation of the fight that is going on in Russia against smuggling and other illegal practices of trafficking natural resources. This representation is limited by many objective and subjective factors, for instance, the internal directives on customs regulation or the external ones, i.e. those coming from the federal centre, on the frequency and nature of connections with the general public. Nevertheless, these same restraints may be interpreted as advantages of the database, in the light of solving the given problems, as the formal directives are not only by specific power of actions, but also by corresponding discursive practices. Accordingly, the change in the frequency of official reports on punishments or the references in the reports to the increased number of prosecutions, as well as the changes in severity of punishments may be regarded as signals, intended for updating extra-legal practices.

The analytical reports, presentations and publications by experts served as another important source as well for systemization of the extra-legal practices. The total number of selected cases, i.e. the reports by the Federal Customs, and Federal Security Services, is 78. The Services reported that in 48 cases Chinese citizens were apprehended for smuggling, in one case it was a Kazakh citizen, in 15 Russian and mixed groups (Russo-Chinese groups) were operating in the remaining 14 cases.

The resources on smuggling of which the reports are made:

- fish and caviar of sturgeon and auk varieties, as well as seafood (43.9%);
- objects of wild flora (ginseng, fern); fauna (frogs, deer, wild boar, furs, derivatives) (27.9%);
- timber and timber products (20.5%);
- minerals (gold, nephrite) (7.7%).

However, in contrast to these figures reflecting the official representation by the respective Services of their activities, the customs statistics on illegally exported resources to China point out, that the predominant among them is timber, both in value and number registered for customs violations.

Fish and Seafood Trade

The fish and seafood (trepang/sea cucumber, crab and sea scallop) trade, which is run by bypassing the formal regulations, on the border of Amur and in the rivers of the Amur basin, as well as in the coastal waters, of course, has a long history.[9]

Since extra-legal economic activities aim at avoiding the costs associated with observance of laws and administrative regulations, one may say that extra-legal trade in the border river began at the time when formal regulations on the use of natural resources of the Far East were created in the Russian empire. Of course, there were *illegal* (i.e., violating the legislation), criminal cross-border practices at the turn of the nineteenth-twentieth centuries: in particular, associated with the Chinese subjects catching especially valuable species of fish in the inland Russian waters and exploiting the indigenous population for this purpose. However, until 1 January, 1913, i.e. until the duty-free trade in an area within 50-versts was abolished, the fishing in the Amur River was of rather *illegal* (i.e. unregulated by the legislation in force) nature: the Chinese harvested, bought up and free of duty exported all kinds of resources, including fish.[10]

The prohibitions introduced during the Soviet and other periods, contributed to the development of extra-legal practices:

> In our assessment the effective impact of all these prohibitions is very weak ... when there was really a few of them (till the mid-1990s), the fishermen did not release the by-catch yellowcheek carp (it is silly to release dead or half-dead fishes). Moreover, it was impossible to keep track of every fisherman, and many people of Amur consider yellowcheek carp a delicacy. As it was difficult during the Soviet times to officially sell "Red Book" (rare and endangered) species, yellowcheek carps as by-catch of the fisheries were bit by bit taken away to the homes of fishermen.[11]

Taken away to homes was just one of the forms of the informal economy of the Soviet time.[12] The fish taken away to home (just like any other commodity) became an item of monetary and non-monetary forms of exchange. Once emerged extra-legal practice eventually became consolidated, and the change in formal regulations (for instance, transition to market) only made the ground for its transformation. In fact, during the collapse of the economy, when the Far-Eastern fishermen, just like other workers, did not get salaries for months, a survival mechanism was formed by itself. As a result of this and other reasons various extra-legal practices became intensified.

The main extra-legal practices of the present-day fishery in the Far East include:

1. Those associated with fishing (for commercial and non-commercial purposes): bribery to the controlling officials, who ensure extra-legal trade; fishing without registration of documents for personal consumption including protected species of fish caught by prohibited means of fishing etc.; exploitation and appropriation of the right to unrestricted trade by the representatives of indigenous and minority nationalities for industrial purposes; small-scale industrial fishing by unregistered brigades (being organized both in the RF and the PRC); non-observance of border regime, throwing fishing nets in the Russian waters; reciprocal exchanges with the controlling authorities (the inspectors, responsible for law enforcement, themselves can earn their livings from fish and, at the personal level of arrangements can ascertain *permitted* and *prohibited* forms of violations; the strength of such formal contracts are determined by the '*you to me—and I to you*' relations, far beyond monetary exchanges);
2. Those associated with implementation: purchasing of extra-legally procured fish products, *legalizing it* by means of fake documents for sending it to China; smuggling of roes, including fertilized live ones, for the purposes of consumption and breeding; smuggling of fish products, including those, catch of which is prohibited; extra-legal dispatch of fish products to the point-of-sale terminals; processing of fish and seafood, caviar for small-scale industrial purposes (dressing, salting, packing), without properly registered documents to run such business; establishing enterprises to run illegal trafficking of fish products, registered under fake identity; trading without documents or with false documents (including under the guise of confiscated products by the organizations of fish protection).

The study of extra-legal economy always encounters difficulties to estimate its volumes in absolute and/or relative terms. According to the data by Amurrybvod poaching catch in the Amur River exceeds the legal one by 2-3 times.[13] Probably, these estimates are not correct. This way, the official catch of Amur chum salmon in the year 1999 was less than one thousand tons, but according to the methodically based estimate by the TINRO specialists, in the 1990s the consumer fishing of autumn chum salmon in the Amur basin, with the length of 1200 km. was almost 9 thousand tons.[14] That is, there is already a gap of 9 times, but to this must be added the extra-legal transfer of sturgeon along with caviar, and other fishes (Chinese perch or auha, yellowcheek carp, sheatfish etc.) as well. As per the minimal estimate by TINRO, the illegal catch of only sturgeon and that too just in the course of the 1990s was not less than 750 tons. Thus, the excess of extra-legal transfer of fish over that of the officially registered was not less than ten times.

The researchers statistically prove that China has been constantly exploiting the bio-resources of the bordering rivers more actively than Russia, the reason behind which is, of course, greater density of population of the Chinese lands.[15] But, despite greater activeness of the Chinese fishermen, their economic activities in their own inland waters mostly take place within the bounds of formal regulations, stipulated by Chinese legislation. On the contrary, in Russia, the extra-legal catches exceed the official ones, and the volume of poaching, in particular, of sturgeons that are prohibited to catch, has been constantly increasing.

From the legal point of view there are major differences between the activities of Russian amateur and professional groups of fishermen, and they have become more significant after the institutional innovations. But, under no circumstances, the Chinese fishermen, who are earning their livings on the Russian territory, can be referred as 'amateurs'. Nevertheless, the motivational logic is extremely important for institutional analysis. Therefore, let us try to understand, how far the extra-legal fishery is of commercial (for sale) or private nature.

Out of 34 reports by the FSB and FTS, 16 showed that it was a group of people who had been detained. However, it is not always clear from a report, whether the violation is a manifestation of individual strategy or it ensures the realisation of certain operation in a business plan. For instance, the following citation reports about a specific *Chinese citizen*, and at the same time, the volume and price of the export consignment indicates the commercial nature of the operation:

> Yesterday, the officers of the FSB Department of the EAO foiled an attempt to smuggle a large consignment of Amur sturgeon and kaluga to China. In one of the private homes of Birobidzhan 1300 kg of fish was detected. According to the house owner, the fish was concealed by a Chinese citizen, who promised to export the consignment to PRC by this week. Sergei Dorofeev, the officer of the FSB Public Relations Department, stated that the cost of the fish, which the Chinese most probably had acquired from poachers, is estimated at about 130 thousand roubles. In China it would be higher by many times.[16]

On the other hand, if it is reported that a group of offenders have been detained, their affiliation to the commercial structure is not stated:

> Two citizens of China have been sentenced to three months imprisonment by the court of the Amur Oblast for violating the state border of Russia. The Oblast Department of FSB reported that in June the border guards had detained the Chinese while poaching fish in the Svobododenskii raion, 118 km from the upper Amur on the Russian bank. A wooden rowing boat and fishing gears were seized from them. The court sentenced the offenders to three months imprisonment serving the term in colony-settlement. Taking into consideration the detention in custody during preliminary investigation the term of imprisonment of the convicts has already been covered. Hence, they were released and left the territory of Russia.[17]

The qualitative content-analysis shows that it is better to categorize the extra-legal practices into two groups of private and commercial, depending on the motivation rather than the number of participants. The most common practice of private (i.e. non-commercial) use of cross-border natural resources by the Chinese is fishing in the opposite (Russian) bank. The urge of the Chinese fishermen to catch fish on the Russian territory is due to the earlier fishing grounds of China being considerately regulated by dams and degraded by industrial pollutions, the wild populations of fish being legally caught in a practically unrestricted manner for many years, both for industrial purposes and household needs, culminating in the disappearance of many species of fish. On the Russian side, the legal trade has always remained limited, and the industrial as well as agricultural pollution has always been low.

There have been dramatic changes in the regulation of fishing, staring from the year 2004: they aimed at increasing control, reducing illegal trade, separating amateur from commercial fishing—i.e. tightening legislation by making fundamental and radical changes. The Federal Law No. 166 FL "On the fishery and conservation of aquatic biological resources" and other legal acts along with it (in particular, regulating the receipt of industrial quotas and permits, the identification of areas, etc) were adopted in 2004, and the Water Code of Russian Federation No. 74-FL dated 03.06.2006—in 2006.

The official database of the FSB and FTS *reacted* to the institutional innovations by increasing the number of reports on violation uncovered (in 2004 and especially in 2006). In 2006 they covered almost one-third of all the reports. The most possible explanation of this was the change in the means of enforcement (both through greater diligence in detaining the offenders and through public awareness of the *broad masses*).

However, the fact that extra-legal practices continued to exist after the adoption of these institutional decisions is *on hand*; and on the basis of reports of FTS and FSB the changes in the volume of extra-legal operations can be judged (towards their significant increase by the end of the period under study). On the whole, a comparison between the reports of the beginning and the end of the 2000s shows the change in the organisational methods of extra-legal activities—from individual violations on a small scale to big organised groups. In 2002, a consignment of 2 tonnes of sea cucumber was the largest one, and in 2009 one report informed about a consignment of some 20 tons of the same item.

The report of 2002 stated:

> A large consignment of smuggled dried sea cucumber has been seized at the Primorskii krai on the Russian-Chinese border. ... The truck was detained at the Poltavskii customs post and was delivered to the Ussuriiskii customs terminal. The customs officers discovered a stash in one of the walls of the container truck. It contained, according to preliminary estimate, around 2 tons of dried trepang, which was packed in sacks of 15-20 kg. Such a large consignment of dried trepang seized last time was more than two years ago. The container has been confiscated and a criminal case for smuggling has been lodged.[18]

The 2009 report informed:

> 6 criminal cases have been right away filed by the investigators of the Far Eastern Operational Customs House against a criminal group, which was carrying out smuggling of dried sea mushrooms. ... Then the first criminal case was against two Russians, for making false documents and trying to use them to smuggle out to China a consignment of dried sea-mushrooms amounting to almost 20 tons. In the course of operational investigations conducted 10 more criminal cases were filed against these citizens, and thereafter there were collected evidences that a whole organised group was involved in the smuggling of sea mushrooms and functions were set for each member of the group. Thus, the organiser of the crime is a Chinese citizen, who financed the illegal trafficking of goods to his homeland, and also instructed a female Russian citizen who was part of the criminal gang, to make forged documents, required for customs clearance. And two Russian female citizens were engaged in running the illegal trade and processing of the sea-mushrooms, as well as organising the dispatch of the sea-mushrooms from the Sakhalin Island to Primorskii krai. Thereafter they were passing on the goods to their counterpart, who was engaged in making documents for customs clearance and in directly acquiring customs clearance of sea-mushrooms by submitting forged documents to the customs authorities. During the period of its criminal activities the group, with the help of forged documents, was able to smuggle out dried sea-mushrooms worth more than 3 million roubles.[19]

This way, both the Chinese and Russians actively take part in the rapacious use of fish resources. The extra-legal practices of fishing are based on traditions and historical continuity, and consequently, there exist social norms ensuring the legitimacy (recognition) of extra-legal regulations. The range of motivations of the participants of cross-border exchanges is quite wide and includes both commercial purpose and motivations of personal consumption. The tightening of legal enforcement had no impact on the extra-legal practices (rather influenced towards deterioration of the situation).

Objects of Wild Flora and Fauna

During 2000-2010, the objects of wild fauna and flora illegally smuggled out to China from the territory of the Far East included frog, deer, wild boar, fur and derivatives of wild fauna (17.6 per cent of reports from the FSB ad FTS database), as well as ginseng and brake (10.3 per cent). The reports on detention of Chinese nationals were predominant in the FSB and FTS database, 21 cases being against them and 1 case was against a Russian citizen.

In this sense the historical *continuity* of extra-legal practices is obvious, as even 100 years ago the rich natural resources were actively involved in commercial turnover, directly bypassing the then existing formal regulations by both the Chinese nationals and Russian immigrants.

At present, poaching takes place in all the territories of the Far East, and this kind of economic activity is reported as carried out by

> inhabitants of the settlements in the rural areas, amateur hunters, having high speed motor vehicle servicemen and border guards, ... posted in the frontiers or in remote garrisons.[20]

The elk, brown and Himalayan bears, musk-deer, sable, species of sturgeon and salmon fish are targets of poaching in the Khabarovsk krai and Jewish Autonomous Region; in the Primorskii krai, it is the Himalayan bears, musk-deer, Amur tiger, trepang, species of salmon; in the Amur oblast' species of sturgeon, river otters, etc.[21] Of course, it is not that the extra-legal trade is entirely done for subsequent sale of products in China—part of it is directly consumed by the hunters' households, and part of it is sold in the domestic market.

The typification of extra-legal practices, associated with trafficking of the objects of wild flora and fauna literally is the same as the practices mentioned above for catching fish and seafood, although their prevalence varies in relation to each other. If the most frequent reports on cross-border irregularities in the practices associated with acquisition and trafficking of fish are connected with the violation of border regime, much less frequently are reports on illegal border crossing as regards harvesting of frogs, bile etc:

> 'The Chinese national, who was detained the day before with the help of a watch dog, has been taken into temporary detention of the Khasanskii border patrol. The border guards have sent a letter in the name of the Commander of the Jilin Military District of PRC demanding to tighten the control over its borders'[22];

> Two Chinese poachers, who had placed traps on the deer tracks, were detained in Primor's on Monday by the border guards in the Ussuri taiga;[23]
>
> The Russian border guards have arrested three Chinese fern collectors, who had illegally crossed the border in the south of Primor'e. Two women and a man have been taken into temporary detention of the Khasanskii border patrol for the hearing'[24].

The objects of flora and fauna are involved in the extra-legal cross-border trafficking primarily through their harvest (purchase) for further dispatch to China. The advertisements for purchase and sale of bear paws and bile, musk of musk-deer, as well as wild ginseng are published in the Amur, Primor'e and Khabarovsk newspapers and Internet websites. The cross-border extra-legal practices are mainly prevented during the customs checking within the bounds of customs check posts:

> The officials of the Khasanskii customs post … detected 22 cylindrical cellophane briquettes with derivatives (frog fat) in the structural cavities of the bus, concealed from customs control. …such a large consignment—almost 27 kg, is detained for the first time. As per the most modest estimates the market value of the frog fat may be more than 1.8 million roubles'; 'an attempt to smuggle out bear paws to China through the Russian-Chinese border was foiled at the "Border Rail and Freight" checkpoint in Primor'e. … Three boxes containing nine bear paws were found among the logs in one of the trucks laden with timber'.[25]

The most common items detained by the customs during 2001-2010, were wild ginseng and derivatives (musk of musk-deer, bear paws, etc.). It is clear that the extra-legal practices in respect of both the products are supported by the cultural traditions of oriental medicine, and it is equally obvious, that for most of the Russians, this product has no intrinsic value, which in the absence of a free market for these goods, contributes to a highly specific method of pricing, and as a consequence the possibility of obtaining additional profits.

At present the enforcement regarding the regulation of trafficking of the objects of endangered fauna is relatively mild, in particular, for criminal proceedings the amount for the detected violations mush be raised to 1500 thousand roubles. In the recent years there were no significant changes, directly concerning the regulation of this kind of economic activity.

There has been significant changes in the legal regulation of hunting and trafficking of the objects of wild fauna with the adoption of the law *On Hunting and on Conservation of Game Resources* (209-FZ dt 24 July 2009), as well as due to the changes in the Forest Code. The law "On Hunting" just like the other normative-legal acts in the sphere of nature management has become the *fundamental institutional innovation*, since the basic motivation for hunting activities changed, accentuating the commercial component (practically leading to the necessity of privatisation of hunting grounds) and *forgetting* about the traditions and culture of hunting in Russia, about that implication that a *forest, a river, a pasture and a farmland has for the inhabitants of the rural areas, especially in remote regions of the country.*[26]

> Nothing can be done in Siberia as half of the population are hunters and fishermen, and they are extremely concerned about the fate of their hunting grounds, which, in view of the adoption of this bill, will be subject to privatisation, they are so alarmed, that they have already worked out a draft of their own, and it has already been adopted on the very first reading'; 'neither any ecological organisation, nor any hunting ground of the regions supported the draft on hunting. The law would ruin the entire system of hunting in Russia, and in this system not a single hunting farm would be able to purchase any land at the auction. No one is interested in this law other than rich people. The draft is designed not for the benefit of the real hunters, but focused on the rich, cash bags, poachers and so called «helicopter pilots». The law would introduce norms that would dramatically change the procedure of granting the right to use the objects of wildlife and their habitat.[27]

The introduction of new formal regulations did not reflect in the FTS and FSB reports on the extra-legal practices: the information in 2004 and 2010 are practically the same. No information on the amount of damage was reported till 2005. The average estimated damage amounted to 1297 thousand roubles, the highest damage was estimated at 7500 thousand roubles (by the way, it was registered in 2010):

> Since the early August the customs officials of the region have foiled 4 attempts of smuggling out ginseng. Cases of administrative offences were filed against three of them, given the small volume of the contraband, as well as the Ussuri customs officials filed one criminal case against a Chinese citizen, who was trying to smuggle out more than 2 kgs of root, worth more than 7.5 and a half million roubles.[28]

S.N. Lyapustin and others[29] have informed about the increase in the number of criminal cases filed for smuggling the objects of flora and fauna, which according to the authors, gives evidence to the *improved quality of work of the operational and investigating units of the DVTU and the Far Eastern Operational Custom House*. In our view, this may also indicate an increase in the smuggling, in the ineffectiveness of the adopted institutional decisions, and other external factors, such as decline in the overall living standard of the population, increase in the number of unemployed, etc.

Thus, in the regions of the Far East the extra-legal natural resource management in respect of the objects of flora and fauna is wide spread; these practices are based on both the Russian and Chinese cultural traditions. The people are involved in extra-legal catching and preying at the level of everyday routine, which implies the support of entrenched social norms. The extra-legal cross-border trafficking is also motivated by the resource rent extraction by commercial set-ups. The changes that occurred in the formal regulations of hunting were incremental in nature; there is no reason to expect that they will be able to instantly change the existing informal constraints.

Forest Management

The FTS and FSB database reported 15 times on the practices associated with extra-legal timber export. Most of the reports go the years 2009 and 2010. Largely it was the Russian nationals having registered business who were caught for smuggling.

This kind of extra-legal natural resource management in the Siberian and Far Eastern regions has been studied and described in the literature relatively better than others;[30] number of variants to systemize the extra-legal practices, including undocumented and documented ones, have been suggested. The first ones in particular include: logging by the local population for their personal needs; felling, carried out by citizens or unregistered groups to subsequently sell the timber; felling, carried out by companies close to the officially workable sites, or in inaccessible places, rarely visited by inspecting authorities in a larger volume than what is indicated in the permit; felling, illegally done according to the plan of "official selective felling." And the felling, illegal as well, but done with documents: obtaining permits for lumbering in areas, where it is prohibited, or not stipulated by existing law; obtaining permits for logging in violation of existing regulations; inserting customised changes in the forest management documentation formally allowing to lumber, but prohibiting it until such changes are made.

The timber exporters (both the Chinese and Russians), use the above mentioned practices for timber harvesting, or purchase the timber thus harvested, and then apply extra-legal practices to smuggle out the goods:

- giving double, triple commission contracts during timber export;
- legalization of the illegally purchased timber by means of its formal dealing through some sellers and buyers;
- overestimation of timber, going through customs, in comparison with registered documents, and others.

The common business plan is that both the exporter and importer is the same Chinese company, for which a Chinese phony company gets registered. It harvests and delivers the timber, using the aforementioned extra-legal practices, the export prices being generally lower than the world price, lower than the Chinese domestic market and even unusually lower than the harvesting cost (to minimise the tax on profit).

Since 2007 the forest legislation has significantly changed, a new Forest Code was introduced, whose main objective was to improve the profitability of forest resources. The basic innovation of the forest legislation was transfer of power from the federal to the regional level, as well as assignment of the whole complex of forest management activities on tenant in the form of encumbrances (in exchange for unspecified preferences). The Code immediately became a target of criticism by the business circle (and not only from forest trade but also large state-owned corporations—because most of the energy, and even oil and gas infrastructure passes through forest land).

The export control legislation has changed as well. For instance, the rate of export duty on round timber was 6.5 per cent of customs value till July 2007, after which it was to increase up to 20 per cent, from April 2008—25 per cent, and from January 2009 it was to be 80 per cent. The global economic crisis deterred the introduction of prohibitive duties (the increase stopped at 15 per cent). These institutional innovations led to the reduction of the volume of production—mainly because of the reduction in the volume of export, sharp aggravation of social problems and growth of unemployment in the forest villages, and general decline in the forest sector. For example, the physical volume of export of the Amur region in 2009 decreased by 64 per cent as Japan, Hong Kong and South Korea stopped buying Amur timber, and China's share increased up to 98 per cent. Since the more developed countries traditionally are very demanding to the confirmation of legality of timber, it has become another incentive to increase extra-legal turnover.

In general, the whole set of institutional changes did not lead to the expected results. At the meeting of the presidium of the State Soviet on the improvement of state regulation in the sphere of environment protection the director of the World Wildlife Fund of the Russian Federation remarked the following:

> We know what the consequences of introduction of the Forest Code were—at times, according to the official data alone, illegal felling increased, and the analysis of satellite images shows a far more grave scenario.[31]

The FTS and FSB started reporting on the detected irregularities in the forest management during 2009, and in 2010 far more frequently, than before (more than half of the cases occurred precisely during these two years); generally the reports concerned the check points, located in Kabarovskii and Primorskii krais. The maximum amount of loss was 19.5 million roubles, minimum being 65 thousand roubles, and in an average it was around 6 million roubles. All informative reports give the evidence of offences committed during trafficking timber through the customs check points. Only one report gave the evidence of trafficking through the zone outside the customs checking, and that too the trafficking was done by an individual person (a Kazakh national was smuggling out in a Kamaz car 32 cubic metres of lumber without any knowledge to the customs check point in the region of the zone of Mikhailovskii customs post of the Altai Customs). As a rule, the volume of extra-legal deals was considerably high: in any case on an average it amounted to about 3 thousand cubic metres (the report on the largest violation involved 10.5 thousand cubic metres of timber).

The detected offences were generally committed by the firms registered in the name of Russian citizens (by the limited liability companies), but nevertheless the notes also pointed to the activities carried out jointly with Chinese nationals. The following informative report is probably, the most *symbolic* which has been confirmed by the results of our field research conducted earlier:

> The Investigations Division of the Khabarovsk Customs at once filed 10 criminal cases under article 188 part 1 of the Criminal Code of the RF (Smuggling). The items involved in the crime were various kinds of timber, including the valuable species. In most of the cases ash and oaks as well as linden, aspen, birch and firs were being smuggled out to China. All the goods, roughly to the tune of 5.5 thousand cubic metres, were being taken out from Russia to the PRC during the year 2007 by a limited liability Russian company using forged documents. The total value of the items involved in the crime was more than 17.5 million roubles.[32]

Thus, the unbending motivation of extra-legal forest management, focussing on acquiring and maximising the resource rents, by registered business houses, and tightening of formal institutional restrictions yield other than intended effects. One of the significant effects is the growth of social instability and unemployment in the remote areas.

Precious Metals and Semi-precious Stones

The official database of the FSB and FTS reports the least about the cross-border extra-legal exchanges of metals and minerals: they are reported 6 times and all the reports go to 2008 and 2009. The main smuggling item was gold, but there was also report about illegal export of nephrite, silver and platinum.

Since the 1960s stringent measures were introduced in the USSR to control illegal transfer of foreign exchange assets (including gold); the illegal transfer included any transactions with industrial gold, along with its transfer for refining, and artisanal mining was completely excluded. In addition to this, severity punishments and other methods of enforcement (for instance, supervising the production, guarding, and transporting the gold from each mine to the refinery by the KGB officials) excluded free trafficking of gold. The criminal practices (theft), of course, continued to exist, but they were an exception.

The types of extra-legal users at the present time (rather than categorization of practices, as in other forms of economy, mentioned above) include:

- plunderer (as a rule, the employees of the industrial enterprises, selling stolen industrial gold from enterprises);
- individual self-employed, *predators* (this is the people of surrounding villages adjacent to goldmine carrying out artisanal mining without registered documents);
- "gold diggers"-"predators" (this is an organization, without any official permission for gold processing at the site);
- "gold diggers," who extract gold on the basis of a permit issued by a "license holder", but keep a part of gold "on the side", along with the "license holder";
- "gold diggers" and "license holders", who are engaged in extraction beyond the formally defined site;
- license holders, selling gold "on the side", that is, not handing it to the state refinery;
- intermediaries, i.e. the buyers and sellers of gold through extra-legal arrangements within the RF and abroad.

The 1990s marked the beginning of extra-legal trafficking of gold,[33] when, during the post-reform crisis the state did not always settle accounts with the enterprises on time for the gold given to the refinery.

The adopted Laws "On Subsoil" (1992) and "On Precious Metals and Stones" (1998) aimed at the legislative regulation of large deposits of gold, as it included multi-stage exploration, development of feasibility study of temporary and permanent conditions, approval of reserves in SRC or CRC, coordination of projects, approval of technological losses etc. Technogenic areas, small areas, especially in the remote areas, to which place it is not profitable to construct roads, braided (i.e. river) placers were not introduced in industrial turnover. However, the former workers as well as the residents of the nearby villages began to extra-legally exploit those mines, the reserves of which had been exhausted and the enterprise had been closed down. In this regard the regions of Siberia and the Far East (Buryatiya, Magadan, Irkutsk, Amur Oblast, Khabarovskii krai) are very frequently discussed in the official meetings at various levels and in the materials of mass media.

Since 1999, the Duma has been discussing about the possibility of introducing the sites with non-industrial reserves into turnover for private individuals to work in them without business registration and obtaining a license (so called "law on *volnoprinositelstvo*"). the Law "On precious Metals and Precious Stones" (№41-FZ) was adopted in 2003, which allowed the mining of gold in technogenic and small placers. But for this operation licenses were required as before, and for obtaining them it was necessary to prepare around 23-26 documents, with their mandatory approval in the federal authorities.[34] The officially declared motivation for adopting the "law on *volnoprinositelstvo"* was connected with the necessity to ensure job and legal means of livelihood to the inhabitants of remote areas, for whom such formal barriers practically close the possibility to legalize the ongoing extra-legal trade. The reluctance of the authorities to pass this legislation is due to the pressure from the big business as well as the anxieties of the central authorities to lose control over revenues and the declaration of possible growth of illegal turnover is because of the manifestation of incentives to the of industrial gold.

According to the media reports, the volume of illegal trafficking of gold varies from 10 per cent (15-20 tons per year—according to the estimate of the Union of Gold Producers of Russia) to 30 per cent-50 per cent (as per the estimate by the Union of Participants of the Market of Precious metals and precious stones).[35] Currently the chance to legalize (to hand over for refining) the gold extracted through artisanal mining or "beyond the bounds of license" is thin, and subsequently, part of it should be implemented outside the country.

We have not come across any estimate of the volume of illegal cross-border exchange towards Russia from China, but there is evidence of gold being smuggled out to China in a number of reports, and judging by the dates of the published information, this kind of activity intensified after 2005:

> Criminal case filed against two citizens of China. ... During the time of investigation the staff of the Regional Department of the FSB seized 2,5 kg of native gold;
> More than 2 kg of scrap silver was seized from a Chinese citizen at the customs post of the Poltavka of Usurriiskii Customs;
> On November 11, a resident of Zabaikalskii Krai was detained while making an attempt to cross the Russo-Chinese border, from whom 6,48 kg of industrial gold was seized;
> a Chinese national attempted to take out 3435 gms of placer gold to China under his clothes and inside his boots;
> a proposal for illegal transportation of precious metal in the form of native placer gold through the customs post in return of cash payment was received from an unidentified person;
> there is almost 3 kg of pure gold of 998 hallmark in this consignment.It was procured by a Chinese named Dun Lyufan from an unknown person.[36]

Thus, the spectrum of incentives for extra-legal mining of gold includes providing the population living in remote villages with the means of livelihood. The institutional changes for recognising the right to/private gold mining, lobbied by some regions, but discarded by the Central authorities for 10 years, are essentially emollients, which contradict the general trend of change in the formal regulations in the area of nature management. Moreover, the proposed innovations rely on the existing informal constraints, though they do not have the signs of continuity. The active involvement of gold in the cross-border Russo-Chinese exchange, apparently, has a short history.

Findings

On the whole it may be said, that the formal structures for exploitation of natural resources have become more stringent during the 2000s. The only exception has been the legislation in the sphere of trafficking of gold and precious stones, where attempts were made in the last ten years to lessen the legal barriers. The example of extra-legal economic activities in forestry, fisheries, hunting, and fishing reveal that intensification of legal pressure by the state did not promote their legalization. And the instance of proposed and regularly discarded institutional innovations in the sphere of gold mining with the support of informal restraints (the prevailing social norms and regulations), shows that the small-scale unprofessional activities of natural resources' exploitation are at variance with the interests of big state-owned corporations or state-supported companies. Greater attention to build legal frameworks that are adequate to the interests of big business is also connected, though not exclusively, with the substantially large amount of revenues potentially generated for the federal budget by big business. The government, aiming at intensification of centralization, is not ready to create legal frameworks for the small business either, because this would mean expansion of rights and freedoms of the regional and local authorities.

As regards the accuracy of the specifications of property rights this issue is meant for another research, because the so-called problem of common pool resources, a characteristic feature for a number of natural resources discussed in this paper, whose solution lies in the solution of the dilemma of public choice, in coordination with public and private interests. The attempts to minimize the problems of poaching hunting through specification of property rights, for instance, by introducing a new Law On Hunting for formal right to privatisation of hunting resources, does not look promising, because here again the existing system of informal social relations is not taken into account.

The presence of Chinese market has been an essential, but not the only incentive for cross-border actors (the Russians and Chinese are practically the same) to implement commercial, but not legally registered, exploitation of natural resources. The increase in the volumes of contraband, the change in the business patterns towards their extension are clear indicators of this process. There is no reason to expect any reduction in the volumes of extra-legal cross-border exchanges in view of toughening the formal regulations.

Notes and References

1. Rasporyazhenie Pravitel'stva Rossiskoi Federatsii No 2094-r. *Strategiya sotsial' no-ekonomicheskogo razvitiya Dal' nego Vostoka i Baikal' skogo regiona na period do 2025 g.,* 08 Dec 2009.
2. Viktor M. Polterovich, "Transplantatsiya ekonomicheskikh institutov", *Ekonomicheskaya nauka sovremennoi Rossii,* (2001) no. 3.
3. *Sheingauz, Alexander S. 'Prirodopol'zovanie rossiiskogo Dal'nego Vostoka v aspekte svyazei s Severo-Vostochnoi Aziei: problemy i perspektivy',* Vestnik DVO RAN, no 3, 2005; Crowley, R.M. "Stepping on to a moving train: the collision of illegal logging, forestry policy, and emerging free trade in the Russian Far East," *Pacific Rim Law and Policy Journal*, no. 14 (April 2005): 425-50.
4. S.N. Lyapustin, P.V. Fomenko, *Bor'ba s kontrabandoi ob'ektov fauny i flory na Dal' nem Vostoke Rossii* (Vladivostok: Izdatelstvo Apel'sin 2003).
5. Kit Hart, "The Idea of Economy: Six Modern Dissenters", in *Beyond the Marketplace: Rethinking Economy and Society*, R. Friedland and A. Robertson (eds.) (N.Y.: Aldine de Gruyter, 1990), p. 158.
6. Hernando De Soto, *The Other Path*, J. Abbott (Trans.) (N.Y.: Harper and Row 1989).
7. Alexandro Portes, "Neformal'naya ekonomika i ee paradoksy," *Ekonomicheskaya sotsiologiya,* T. 4, no 5 (2003): 5.
8. Otbor sluchaev osuschestvlyalsya na ofitsial'nykh saitakh ukazannykh sluzhb (http://fsb.ru/and http://www.customs.ru/ru) po kluchevym slovam "Kitai" i "resurs" (za period 2001-2009 gg. Polnost'yu i za 9 mes. 2010g.)
9. Sergei N. Lyapustin, "Bor'ba s kontrabandoi ob'ektov fauny i flory na Dal'nem Vostoke. Istoricheskii aspect", *Vestnik DVO RAN,* no 5 (2006): 170-74.
10. S.N. Lyapustin, P.V. Fomenko, *Bor'ba s kontrabandoi ob'ektov fauny i flory na Dal' nem Vostoke Rossii* (Vladivostok: Izdatelstvo Apel'sin, 2003).

11. G. Novomodnyi, S. Zolotukhin, P. Sharov, *Amurskie ryby: bogatsvo i krizis. Analiticheskii obzor* (Vladivostok: Izd-vo Apel'sin 2004), 19.
12. A. Katsenelinboigen, "Svetnye rynki v Sovetskom Soyuze," *Ekonomicheskaya teoriya prestuplenii i nakazanii*, Vyp. 4, Bibliografiya (Moscow: RGGU, 2002).
13. V.N. Koshelev, V.E. Ostrovskii, V.P. Ovsiannikov, N.N. Semenchenko, "Presnovodnye i morskie bioresursy Khabarobskogo kraya," *Gosudarstvennyi doklad "O sostoyanii i ob okhrane okruzhayuschei sredy Khabarovskogo kraya v 2008 gody"*, Ministerstvo Ekonom. razvitiya i vneshnikh svyazei Khabarovskogo kraya, Khabarovsk (rukopis'). http://www.adm.khv.ru/invest2.nsf/ecology_ru/2731E837E08BA4F4CA25767300197269?OpenDocument
14. G. Novomodnyi, S. Zolotukhin, P. Sharov, *Amurskie ryby,* 19.
15. Novomodnyi, Zolotukhin, Sharov, *Amurskie ryby*, 19.
16. http://www.fsb.ru/fsb/comment/ufsb/single.htm!id=10311774@fsbComment.html.
17. http://www.fsb.ru/fsb/comment/ufsb/single.htm!id=10315092@fsbComment.html.
18. http://webserver.customs.ru/ru/sea_activity/actions/index.php?&date286=200510&id286=8625
19. http://dvtu.customs.ru/ru/reviews/index.php?&date695 =200906&id695=25964
20. S.N. Lyapustin, N.V. Pervushina, P.V. Fomenko, *Nezakonnyi oborot ob'ektov fauny i flory na dal'nem Vostoke (2007-2009)*, WWF, WWF, TRAFFIC, PTA. (Vladivostok: Izdatel'stvo Apel'sin) 2010), 25.
21. Lyapustin, Pervushina, Fomenko, *Nezakonnyi oborot ob'ektov fauny i flory*, 24.
22. http://www.fsb.ru/fsb/comment/ufsb/single.htm!id=10314002@fsbComment.html, 11K
23. http://www.fsb.ru/fsb/comment/ufsb/single.htm!id=10313794@fsbComment.html
24. http://www.fsb.ru/fsb/comment/ufsb/single.htm!id=10314371@fsbComment.html
25. http://www.fsb.ru/fsb/comment/ufsb/single.htm!id%3D10316364@fsbComment.html
26. http://piterhunt.ru/library/articles/ofitsialno/khoteli_kak_luchshe_a_poluchilos_kak_vsegda.htm
27. http://piterhunt.ru/library/articles/ofitsialno/khoteli_kak_luchshe_a_poluchilos_kak_vsegda.htm
28. http://www.customs.ru/ru/press/news_dvtu/index.php?id286=33757
29. Lyapustin, S.N., Pervushina, N.V., Fomenko, P.V., *Nezakonnyi oborot ob'ektov fauny i flory*, 8.
30. O. Olimpieva, Z. Pachenkov, Solov'eva, *Neformal'naya ekonomika lesopolzovaniya: uchastniki, praktiki, otnosheniya (na osnove*

materialov issledovaniya Irkutskoi oblasti), MONF. Seriya "Nezavisimoi ekonomisheskii analiz" (Moscow 2005).

31. http://www.kremlin.ru/transcripts/7872
32. http://customs.ru/ru/press/news_dvtu/index.php?id305=3771&date286=200803&id286=18909
33. P.U. Afanas'ev, N.B Trubnikov, P.Yu. Afanasiev, N.B. Trubnikov, *Vitok zolotoi spirali: Iz istorii zolotobobychi na yuge Rossiskogo Dal'nego Vostoka* (Blagoveshchensk: Zeya 2008).
34. http://www.vslux.ru/node/5182
35. http://www.rosbalt.ru/2010/09/21/773778.html
36. http://www.jewellerynews.ru/

33

Looking beyond Geographic Neighbours: Post-Soviet Mongolia's "Third Neighbour" Policy

Sharad K. Soni

Sandwiched between Russia and China, Mongolia has had a long history of having been controlled by both of its two giant neighbours until the collapse of the former Soviet Union, which paved the way for gaining "real" independence. It all began with the post-Soviet democratic transition in Mongolia that led to the adoption of a new constitution which came into force on 12 February 1992. And with that in independence Mongolia's legacy of dependence led it to reach beyond geographic constraints to cultivate relationships with countries far away. Consequently, in June 1994 Mongolia made radical changes in its national security and foreign policies by adopting two key documents—National Security and Foreign Policy Concepts. It thus shifted from a "satellite" foreign policy of dependence on Moscow to what Ulaanbaatar describes as an "independent, non-aligned, multi-pillar, open" foreign policy. The policy was formulated in such a manner that it can ensure the security and prosperity of the country both internally and externally by "forming with influential countries in the region and in the world a network of relationships based on the interdependence of political, economic and other interests." In essence, Mongolia adopted a spirited posture of gracious defiance, rejecting dependence on Russia or China and reaching out to countries that can counterbalance the inclinations and serve as a check on the economic, political, and strategic ambitions of Moscow and Beijing. In other words, the National Security Concept and the Concept of Mongolia's Foreign Policy, articulated a policy of balance that is known as the "third neighbour" policy.

It is against this backdrop that this paper seeks to make a deeper understanding of how post-Soviet Mongolia's security and foreign policies have been formulated and implemented with an emphasis on the "third neighbour policy". While doing so it also examines the state of Mongolia's mutually beneficial cooperation in diverse areas with the major "third neighbour" countries, particularly the United States and India. Besides, it also deals with the Russian and Chinese response to such policy.

Mongolia's Security and Foreign Policies

The last decade of the twentieth century witnessed many ups and downs at the global level beginning with the collapse of one of the world's superpowers, the Soviet Union, which eventually resulted in the rapid democratization of most of the former Soviet satellite countries. Mongolia too found itself suddenly out of the Soviet orbit that meant no more ideological and material support it had for almost 70 years from the big brother on the northern side. Consequently, a chronic economic recession started thus giving way to quite a new thinking among the leaders, policy planners and academics in this thinly populated country, i.e. to embark on the establishment of democracy and market-oriented economy. As such policies and planning began to be formulated with a focus on a rapid shift in priorities, both at the internal as well as external levels. All this has been done with the sole aim of bringing out democratic changes in the country's internal and external policies in order to ensure overall security, particularly in the socio-economic and strategic fields. The 1990s, thus, saw Mongolia going for not only the social and economic changes, but also writing a new constitution and installing the democratically-elected governments.[1] As part of such changes, the seven decades old unilateral foreign policy was discarded that was dictated from Moscow and was based on ideological relations and "close comprehensive cooperation" with the former Soviet Union and other COMECON countries.[2] Beginning with the adoption of a new constitution Mongolia also reformulated its national security and foreign policy, taking into account the ongoing international developments.

While Article 1 of the new constitution of 1992 clearly states that "the fundamental purpose of State activities is the ensurance of democracy, justice, freedom, equality, national unity and respect for law," Article 10 exclusively deals with the foreign policy matters, stipulating that "Mongolia shall adhere to the universally-recognized norms and principles of international law and pursue a peaceful foreign policy."[3] In practical terms, it implies that Mongolia has opted for an open foreign policy, free from past ideological constraints.[4] Strikingly, it also points to the concerns of the Mongolian policy-makers who realized that Mongolia's national security could only be ensured by securing international guarantees "through a combination of unilateral, bilateral and multilateral measures."[5] Consequently, in June 1994 Mongolia adopted three basic documents—National Security and Foreign Policy Concepts as well as the Military Doctrine, which were interlinked and all together aimed at achieving favourable internal and external conditions for ensuring vital national interests, i.e. the existence of the Mongolian people and their civilization, the country's independence, sovereignty, territorial integrity, inviolability of state frontiers, relative economic independence, sustainable ecological development and national unity.[6]

Similarly, Mongolia's foreign policy too revolves around the national interests in the first place. As stipulated in the Foreign Policy Concept, Mongolia's foreign policy priority focuses on "safeguarding of its security and vital national interests by political and diplomatic means, and creating a favourable external environment for its economic, scientific and technological development."[7] One of the main characteristics of what is termed as a Mongolia's "multi-pillar" foreign policy is its pragmatism, and therefore, it relies on ongoing international political reality as well as the trends of international economic development. However, Mongolia's foreign policy aims at ensuring the security and prosperity of the country both internally and externally by "forming with influential countries in the region and in the world a network of relationships based on the interdependence of political, economic and other interests."[8] To this end, the Foreign Policy Concept provides general principles as follows:

- Mongolia shall pursue an open and non-aligned foreign policy;
- While following a policy of creating realistic interest of developed countries in Mongolia, it will seek to avoid becoming overly reliant or dependent on any particular country…;
- Mongolia will not interfere in the disputes between its neighboring countries unless the disputes affect Mongolia's national interests; and
- Mongolia shall pursue a policy of refraining from joining any military alliance or grouping, allowing the use of its territory or air space against any other country, and the stationing of foreign troops or weapons, including nuclear or any other type of weapons of mass destruction in its territory.[9]

As such Mongolia began focussing its attention towards developing political and economic cooperation with a host of countries such as the United States as well as those in Europe and the Asia-Pacific region. In the past few decades, Mongolia's desire of promoting cooperation with the countries of North East Asia as well as its own integration with this region has evolved to a great extent. It is more so because during the period of democratic reforms especially in the mid-1990s when no single nation came forward to be understood in real terms as Mongolia's "Third Neighbour," Ulaanbaatar's thinking took a definite turn to forge a new relationship with northeast Asia that went beyond economic ties to include political concerns.[10] Currently, in line with its national security and foreign policy objectives Mongolia has not only been trying to maintain balanced relations with Russia and China but also looking beyond these two neighbours to forge mutually advantageous ties with other countries that may well be treated as "Third Neighbours".

Evolution of "Third Neighbour" Policy

The "Third Neighbour" policy came into being as a policy of balancing Mongolia's two geographic neighbours, resulting from the country's internal and external objectives as specified in the "National Security Concept" and "Foreign Policy Concept." Today Mongolian diplomacy is indeed characterized by the "Third Neighbour" policy. The term "third neighbour" was coined by the then US Secretary of State James A. Baker in a statement given in August 1990 while visiting Mongolia. He referred to the United States as Mongolia's third neighbour. It was a rhetorical gesture to support the nation's first move towards democracy as the first free elections were held in Mongolia in July of that year. However, such a fresh idea, forgotten in Washington, was quickly picked up and reinterpreted by the Mongolian elite and policy makers, who for centuries had never thought of anything beyond a pawn between the Russians and Chinese. The term began to be used in Mongolian media and scholarly works and remained so throughout the 1990s. But it was not reciprocated in the United States until the late 1990s. Alicia Campi, a well-known Mongolist and diplomat recalls that the American officials at the first American bilateral conference in Washington, DC in the late 1990s declared that their Mongolian counterparts could refer to the United States as a "third neighbour."[11]

By then, Mongolian foreign policy already affirmed that Mongolia will focus its attention on developing friendly relations with states beyond its geographic neighbours. This policy was then titled as the "third neighbour policy" under which Mongolia could strive to overcome its physical geographical location and increase its security internationally. In simple words, as the Mongolian President Nambaryn Enkhbayar described the "third neighbour" policy in 2007 while delivering his address to the audience at the Centre for Strategic and International Studies, Washington DC, "it means that Mongolia will no longer be dependent only on one neighbor but rather on as many countries and international institutions as possible…including first of all the US, international organizations and other stakeholders which support our democratic nation building and development."[12] He clearly remarked that "multi-pillar foreign policy concept is the outcome of our aspirations not to be isolated, but to be open, and it brings about the necessity to develop "neighborly" relations with such important players at the international arena as the US, Europe, Japan, India, the UN and others, thus securing the independence of the country."[13] Hence, the so-called "third neighbour" policy easily explains the "multipillarity, complexity and openness of Mongolia's foreign policy [which] undoubtedly attracted attention of the regional and world community, and the country's position on the international arena has been strengthened substantially."[14]

In order to understand the "third neighbour" policy more substantially, its review in retrospect clearly points to its being a "collective socio-psychological consensus" that the Mongolian state and society reached in the aftermath of the 1989-90 democratic revolution. It is based on the self-perception of a small state with experience of subservience to big geographic neighbours and an indigenous culture, sometimes seen as the "northernmost extension of the Indosphere," flanked by three of the world's great civilizations: Christendom, Islam, and Confucian East Asia. Besides, this virtual "third neighbourhood" derives from historically close ties and friendliness with other countries which are often based on shared values, common interests or even simply societal sympathy. In this context, one could identify third neighbours like India, which has eloquently been described as Mongolia's "spiritual neighbour" due to the fact that much of Mongolia's intellectual and cultural heritage, particularly Buddhism stems from the subcontinent; and Japan, owing to the fact that it has been the largest Official Development Assistance (ODA) provider to Mongolia for latter's economic growth as well as the intense cultural and humanitarian relations that the two counties have which could be seen through pro-Japanese attitude of Mongolian society.

The United States and a cohort of western democracies certainly fall into this category as well, as does South Korea, which is one of Mongolia's largest trading partners and Canada, the second largest foreign investor in Mongolia after China. All these "third neighbours" are indeed fellow democracies and strong economies that may bring added value to Mongolia's acts of "cautious" balancing of Russia and China and the projection of Mongolia's place in the international arena with its "new regional identity of a Northeast Asian country."[15] In fact, Mongolian integration into the Northeast Asian region has been described by the Mongolian policy makers and economists as the best ever opportunity for not only the country to develop and prosper but also to balance China's economic and political influence.[16] This is more so because Northeast Asia has been considered as Mongolia's natural economic territory, and in a more specific term, as coined by Robert Scalapino, a "regional Third Neighbour."[17] The whole exercise of reviewing Mongolia's "third neighbour" policy, thus, raises some serious questions, such as (a) Will the much flaunted "third neighbour" policy work and be efficient or is it merely an elaborate trap for foreign investors? and (b) Can Mongolia secure its security both economic as well as strategic by forging ties with such "third neighbour" countries that arouse geopolitical anxieties in Russia, China, or both? The following paragraphs seek to find out possible answers.

The "Third Neighbour" Actors

As already pointed out that despite Russia and China being the heavyweights in the region, Mongolia has resolved since the mid-1990s to embrace "third neighbour" countries as it recognizes that diverse foreign and trade relations are an element of broader stability. And it has indeed succeeded in forging growing relationships with a roster of "third neighbour" countries prepared to underwrite a portion of Mongolia's development, invest, and encourage the democratic transition/consolidation that is under way. Such "third neighbour" countries include, among others, the United States of America, India, Japan, South Korea, Canada, and the European Union.

The United States

One of the main "third neighbour" actors to which Mongolia has looked is the United States of America whose comparative power, wealth, democracy-and distance from Mongolia-make the US a much-valued source of support and security.[18] In more than two decades now since the US and Mongolia established diplomatic relations on 27 January 1987, the US has made its presence felt by paying much attention, especially after Ulaanbaatar came out of being a so called "satellite" of Moscow. Baker's 1990 visit to Mongolia was followed by a number of visits by American political and military luminaries including George W. Bush who became the first sitting US President to visit Mongolia in

2005. During his visit Bush reiterated that the United States is "proud to be called" Mongolia's "third neighbor." At that point of time Bush was understood to have used this term, partly in recognition of the successes of Mongolia's democratization efforts and partly in recognition of Mongolia's support to US efforts in the global war on terror. Mongolia has also received considerable economic and military assistance from the US. The United States Agency for International Development (USAID) has provided approximately $173 million in grants since 1991. The US and Mongolia undertook a military-to-military relationship in 1991 that has, thus far, resulted in more than $36.4 million in assistance to the Mongolian Armed Forces. In addition, more than 600 Peace Corps volunteers have served in Mongolia and the US has offered support for the education of Mongolian students and exchange visitors in the United States.[19]

The US Government has also been instrumental in spurring support for Mongolia from private foundations, international organizations, and the American business community. In October 2007, when Mongolian President Nambaryn Enkhbayar visited USA, he received Washington's pledge of an additional US $ 285 million in aid from the Millennium Challenge Account (Millennium Challenge Account 2007). Mongolia is currently America's 175th largest trading partner with a total trade turnover of $55 million that includes US exports of worth $41 million, and imports $15 million during 2009.[20] The rationale for US largesse toward Mongolia is considered to be the recognition that the two states have "shared values and common strategic interests."[21] In addition, the US has established a collaborative military-to-military relationship with the Mongolian Armed Forces. The stated focus of this relationship has been to help modernize and professionalize the Mongolian military and to help train it to assume international responsibilities as part of peacekeeping operations in regions of need. In October 2007, Mongolia deployed troops and engineers to Iraq for the eighth time and stated that they would "persist until the end alongside" the US army in Iraq.[22] This is in sharp contrast to other US allies who have reduced troop numbers or have completely withdrawn soldiers from Iraq. In 2001, they held a humanitarian rescue exercise code named "Balance Magic." However, in 2003, the two sides renewed their previous practice of small-scale military maneuvers to hold large-scale "Khaan Quest" joint military exercise every summer in Mongolia.

The "Khaan Quest" exercises were expanded into a multinational peacekeeping military exercise in 2006 in which soldiers from seven nations of Mongolia, the United States, Bangladesh, India, Thailand,

Tonga and Fiji participated. Though China expressed dissatisfaction over such exercises, it came forward along with Russia, Malaysia and Japan to participate as observer states in 2007 "Khaan Quest."[23] Since then such exercises have been continuing annually. The "Khaan Quest" exercise in 2010 has been an international platoon-and company-level training event culminating in a company-level field training exercise supporting peacekeeping operations, particularly to tackle challenges like insurgency, terrorism, crime and ethnic conflict.[24] However, one may think that perhaps at first glance on the world map Mongolia does not seem to be a country of strategic importance outside Russia and China, then why is Mongolia being considered as strategically important to the US. According to Kaplan, "we live in an era when 'anyplace can turn out to be strategic' and after 9/11 Central Asia, including Mongolia, became 'strategic' to the US."[25]

There are other examples, too, of growing interaction between the people of Mongolia and the United States in very many ways, which have been motivated by a broad spectrum of civic, cultural, spiritual and scientific interests. And such interaction, as American Ambassador to Mongolia, Jonathan Addleton emphasized in his speech on 29 October 2009, "is by no means simply a one-way street, solely involving Americans living and working in Mongolia."[26] In sharp contrast, what he meant was that "growing Mongolian communities in the United States in places like California, Colorado and Virginia further strengthen the US-Mongolia relationship," and that "over the long term, such connections ensure that the US-Mongolia partnership is not simply based on 'official,' government-to-government but is also rooted in more personal ties that are durable and lasting." By any measure, the United States is an important partner of Mongolia and since the establishment of diplomatic relations, the Mongolia-US relationship has become broader and deeper. But still American assistance on some specific areas would prove to be vital for Mongolia particularly to (a) achieve sustainable development through private investment (b) strengthen democracy and good governance (c) ensure both internal and external security and (d) boast people-to-people contacts.

India

Another important country being perceived by Mongolia as its "third neighbour" is India in both regional and international contexts, particularly in the context of India's role in promoting a multipolar security structure in Asia. Mongolia's proximity with

India is being perceived not only as a window to the outside world, but also as a factor to balance off the equation with China. The Mongolians admit India's positive influence on them and desire that the strong cultural relationship between the two should be translated into a strategic partnership.

Though geographically far apart, India and Mongolia have had civilisational links spanning over a period of 2700 years. These links are fascinating, intense and inseparable; transcending all human activities from language, literature, religion, medicine, and folklore to culture and traditions. Given such a rich legacy of interaction, assimilation and exchanges, it is but natural that the two countries have established very close and friendly relations in modern times so much so that they are known as "spiritual" neighbours. Mongolia has been in close contact with India not only on the basis of their traditional relationship but on the basis of post-cold war realities as well for mutual benefits in diverse areas. Ever since the two countries signed the Treaty of Friendly Relations and Cooperation in 1994, a solid foundation was laid down for further development of bilateral relations and cooperation on regional and international relations. It was in January 2001 when the then Mongolian President N. Bagabandi visited India, new agreements in areas of information technology, defence and legal matters were signed. However, the 2009 visit of newly elected Mongolian President to India changed the extent and pattern of their bilateral relations. Pursuing its "third neighbour" policy Mongolia drew its attention towards India so much so that both countries began defining their geostrategic interests.[27] With Mongolian President Ts. Elbegdorj choosing India (not Russia or China as tradition has been in the past) for his first official trip abroad after assuming office in June 2009, Delhi appeared to be on the right track in the strategic imagination of Ulaanbaatar to emerge as one of Mongolia's third neighbours.

Since Mongolia is critical for a rising India's Asian strategy, the two countries needed to upgrade their bilateral ties to comprehensive partnership. This is evident from the fact that in 2009 both sides signed a comprehensive partnership treaty to cooperate in developing Mongolian uranium mining with a MoU on the "peaceful use of radioactive minerals and nuclear energy." Mongolia is the sixth country to sign such a civil nuclear pact with India after the United States, France, Russia, Kazakhstan and Namibia. The fact that such a deal was signed with India, as opposed to Russia or China who already have high stakes in the Mongolian mining sector reflects two important considerations:[28] (a) Mongolia recognizes the need to develop economic ties with a diverse group of countries as outlined in its security and foreign policy concepts; and (b) signing such a pact with India is a direct usage of the third neighbour concept allowing for continued neutrality between Mongolia and its physical neighbours. As India's own demand for imported natural resources multiplies manifold, Mongolia may prove to be a natural and long-term economic partner. In return, Mongolia can benefit considerably from India's advancement in different areas like IT and telecommunications.

As regards trade relations it may be pointed out that Mongolia is landlocked between China and Russia, and therefore, goods have to be shipped through ports in China or Russia which increases freight rates and also delay in delivery schedule. This has been the primary reason as to why the bilateral trade between India and Mongolia has not developed to the desired extent, though bilateral trade between the two countries in 2009 was recorded as US $12.7 million, of which US $11.7 million formed Indian exports to Mongolia. Today both sides are involved in several activities in political, economic and cultural fields including further expansion of their defence ties as well as annual joint military exercises. Defence cooperation and relations between the militaries of the two countries has seen a steady growth over the last decade with the first joint exercise in 2004. The second joint exercise was held in 2005 at the Counter Insurgency and Jungle Warfare School at Vairnagte, Mizoram while another exercise held in Mongolia in September 2008. The latest two-week exercise in counter-insurgency took place in Belgaum in December 2010. Nearly 30 officers and personnel of the Mongolian armed forces participated in this workout called "Nomadic Elephant" along with 50 officers and personnel of the Indian Army in counter-terrorism environment.

Mongolia's strategic location as a geographical bridge between Central Asia and Northeast Asia could provide an impetus as having more than one strong ally there could be beneficial to Indian interests in the whole region. Moreover, India's traditional South Asian centric security policies are being stretched out into East Asia and the Pacific as well as a northward movement into Central Asia.[29] Miliate is of the opinion that "with an ever increasing liberal interpretation of regional security it may well be the case that East Asia as a division could expand into South Asia and northward to include Russia and Mongolia, bringing into question the whole issue of geographical divisions in an increasingly transnational world."[30] Besides, India's "Look-East" policy, which was designed to strengthen its engagement with the Asia-Pacific as a whole, has somehow remained concentrated on its immediate neighborhood in Southeast Asia; other regions, especially

Northeast Asia, have not received the desired attention, and hence now is the time for India to begin looking at Northeast Asia. However, it remains to be seen whether Mongolia-India synergy would indeed benefit New Delhi in its engagement with Northeast Asia to the extent of becoming a major player in this region in order to contain the power politics being played by China, especially in the integration process.[31]

Japan

Another "third neighbour" has been Japan, with which Mongolia maintains "comprehensive partnership." Japan is the largest Official Development Assistance (ODA) provider to Mongolia since 1970s after the normalization of diplomatic relationship between the two sides. Between 1991 and 2003, Japan provided Mongolia a total of US 6.5 billion in aid, US $ 2.2 billion in technological support, and US $ 3.4 billion loan.[32] During this period Japan also hosted eight of the 10 conferences of countries providing ODA to Mongolia. In 2004, Japanese ODA to Mongolia further increased to amount to a cumulative total of US $ 1.22 billion. In 2006, when Japanese Prime Minister Koizumi Junichiro visited Mongolia, he gave US $3.3 million, including grant aid to Mongolia for a Project on Human Resource Development Scholarship. As per the statistics from Japanese Foreign Ministry, in terms of economic cooperation Japan's aid to Mongolia has reached about US$2.18 billion in 2008 that accounts for approximately one third of total aid for Mongolia by foreign countries and international organizations.[33] As for the sectoral distribution, most of the aid flows are in the infrastructure development. Transport ranks as the largest sectoral recipient followed by mining and energy sectors. In September 2010, during a visit to Mongolia by the Japanese Foreign Minister Katsuya Okada, Mongolian President Elbegdorj acknowledged that "the aid and loan from the Government of Japan contributed greatly to the reform and strengthening of democracy in Mongolia." The Mongolia-Japan joint statement issued during the visit of Mongolian President to Tokyo in November 2010 on the agreement of developing the bilateral relations on the principles of strategic partnership has now become vital for future cooperation between the two sides in key areas of mutual benefits. At present Mongolia is more interested in developing their bilateral relations in the field of mining particularly uranium, rare earth elements, and technology, besides producing the value-added products from minerals for export purposes.[34]

South Korea

Since Mongolia does not have any political issues or unresolved misunderstandings with South Korea,[35] it actively seeks to advance its "partnership of good neighborliness, peace and cooperation" with the latter which is also a significant aid provider to Mongolia. The two countries work together to fight sand storms and desertification that have intensified in Northeast Asia due to climate change. However, the most important aspect of Mongolia-South Korea relations is human exchanges. South Korea hosts the largest number of Mongolian overseas workers, whose remittances contribute greatly to the livelihoods of their families in Mongolia. Moreover, the number of travelers between the two countries has already reached at 200,000 a year.[36] Besides, due to an ever-growing South Korean business in Mongolia Seoul now ranks the third largest investor in the country. This has been further emphasized by the Mongolian Ambassador to South Korea during a recent interview with Korea IT Times, when he said that "during the last few years, the South Korean government has been intensely expressing its interest to cooperate and invest in Mongolian mining and power generation sectors," and that "Korea Resource Corporation Consortium, governed by state owned giant enterprise of Korea, which covers 11 countries of the world, has also been proposing its cooperation with our [Mongolia's] Tavan Tolgoi project."[37] Being a third neighbour actor South Korea holds an enormous potential to expand bilateral cooperation in several key sectors of Mongolia. That is also because of many positive factors influencing the bilateral cooperation, such as geographical proximity and minimal time difference between the two countries as well as South Korea's huge investment potential due to its highly developed economy and technologically advanced industrial base.

Canada

As Mongolia's "third neighbour" Canada ranks the second largest source of foreign investment in Mongolia after China. However, its main commercial interest in Mongolia remains to be mining investment.[38] According to Canadian government sources, the two sides are also making efforts to expand their bilateral trade into new sectors such as agriculture and construction, which is evident from the fact that MoUs have been signed between Mongolian agencies and Agriculture and Agri-Food Canada and the Standards Council of Canada. The Canadian International Development Agency provides funding to Canadian and multilateral organizations active in Mongolia, and supports development projects of Mongolian NGOs in order to resolve problems of poverty and economic development. In addition, the International Development Research Centre has supported projects in Mongolia in the field of information technology. Canada's Investment Cooperation Programme (INC) is contributing to Canadian private sector initiatives supporting Mongolia's community and economic development. The Public Service Commission of Canada has also signed a MoU with the Civil Service Commission of Mongolia on cooperation in matters related to public service reforms. Significantly, Mongolia sends its police officers to Canada for training in the investigation of major crimes including the financial ones.

The European Union

The European Union (EU) and its member-countries are also considered to be an important "third neighbour" of Mongolia, particularly from the trade and economic point of view. In fact, Mongolia's relationship with the EU is based on the Trade and Economic Cooperation Agreement of 1993 which provides a legal framework for their cooperation. Besides, EU's development assistance to Mongolia is being given to support its agricultural sector and rural development. Since 2005 Mongolia enjoys EU 'GSP+' incentive, which allows Mongolia a duty free and quota-free access to the EU for Mongolia's 7200 products.[39] However, as Batbold Sukhbaatar, Minister of Foreign Affairs and Trade of Mongolia states, Mongolia is looking for a Partnership and Cooperation Agreement with the EU because "such an agreement would enable the two sides to move beyond trade and economic interaction and pursue broader cooperation in areas such as environment, education, science, finance and justice."

Russian and Chinese Response

As Mongolia's "third neighbour" policy is becoming truly effective, the two powerful geographic neighbours feel that they are missing out and their influence may diminish within Mongolia. But the fact of the matter is that China is Mongolia's largest trading partner, followed by Russia. While Russia supplies almost all of Mongolia's oil, China controls its access to ports. Both are also major investors and both have their eyes firmly fixed on Mongolia's mineral wealth. Hence, both Moscow and Beijing remain concerned to ensure that the other does not dominate Mongolia. Recently there has been growing Chinese and Russian concerns about US-Mongolian military cooperation, particularly about the Khaan Quest joint exercises. Russia, concerned about the US influence anywhere on its periphery, has pushed back against Washington's moves and in 2008 started its own series of military exercises, under the "Darkhan rubric", besides pledging a military aid worth $7 million to Mongolia. Similar concerns were shown by China against the US and also against India's participation in the 2006 Khaan Quest, alleging that "India is trying to expand its military resources to establish a potential base in Mongolia."[40] However, it was nothing but a baseless allegation published on 25 March 2006 in the Chinese government-controlled newspaper Qingnian Cankao.

At the same time there is no denying of the fact that since Mongolia is completely encircled by China and Russia, its traffic and communication with the outside world has no option but to pass through one of the two geographic neighbours. If China or Russia refuses to open up airspace or seaports to Mongolia, then its multi-national joint exercises with other countries and the successful arrival of the related personnel and equipment would be cut off. Besides, the main foundation of Mongolia's external economy also lies in good relations with China and Russia because the trade costs associated with Mongolia's use of Chinese and Russian railways and highways depend on the corresponding preferential rights bestowed by these two great powers.[41] Interestingly, in 2006, Mongolia and Russia agreed to move from "traditionally good-neighborly partnership" to "strategic partnership." On the other side, once in a state of stagnation, Mongolia's relationship with China is nowadays the one that is dynamic and capitalises on good-neighbourliness, mutual trust and partnership in which extensive trade and economic cooperation plays the central role. However, Mongolia as a young democracy, cautious of past subordination to Moscow and China's hunger for natural resources, also sees diversifying its international ties as the best guarantee of its political and economic independence.

It is to be noted that among Mongolia's greatest third neighbours are states that are, themselves, democratic states and several of which have had pre-existing friction with either Russia or China or both. Since 1990, Russia and China have generally accepted Mongolia's independent identity and with some apprehensions its military relations with other states. Bearing in mind that this acceptance marks a break from past practice, Mongolians are justified in worrying about how long it may sustain. After all, Chinese are vigilant about the prospect of Mongolia's encirclement. Russians are especially unsettled by the prospect of a democratic state on their border entangled with powerful Western democracies, notably the United States. This is what Wachman describes as "the geopolitical gambit,"[42] thus raising the question, whether Mongolia would be able to secure its security both economic as well as strategic by forging ties with such "third neighbour" countries that arouse geopolitical anxieties in Russia, China, or both?

Conclusion

By pursuing its "third neighbour" policy Mongolia has been able to attract several key actors including the USA, India, Japan, South Korea, Canada and the EU which may reduce a little bit influence and position of Russia and China in Mongolia. But it seems impossible in the near future that they would be able to change an outright dependency of Mongolia on the Russian oil supply or 75 per cent supply of food stuffs from China. At the moment, over 50 per cent of the foreign investment in Mongolia comes from China. The US sees an independent Mongolia as a stabilizing buffer between Russia and China, but if Mongolia's economy is absorbed by China's, how much political independence it retains may simply be a matter of opinion. No one expects China to be happy with an independent Mongolia, but pursuing the "third neighbour" policy and maintaining equidistance in relations with Russia and China is a significant way out to peaceful existence. While Mongolians consider Russian activities in Mongolia as their geostrategic needs of balancing China, Russians still see Mongolia as a buffer against a rising China. In other words, in a unipolar world, the multi-pillar policy or for that matter the "third neighbour" policy should aim at ensuring security, both economic and strategic, by trying to overcome related challenges. So far, Mongolia's delicate balancing act has worked. Yet, the best way to ensure that Mongolia's two neighbours respect her independent identity, as John J. Tkacik stresses, "is to integrate that isolated land into regional and global security structures like the Asia-Pacific Economic Cooperation forum, the Northeast Asia Cooperation Dialogue, NATO's Partnership for Peace, and, of course, the OSCE's Asian Partner for Development Programme."[43] Moreover, it is the obligation of Mongolia's "third neighbour" actors to lend their support in these efforts.

Notes and References

1. Ariunsanaa Tunjin, "Mongolia's National Security and Nuclear-Free Policy," *Korean Journal of Defense Analysis* 15, no. 1 (2003): 10
2. Alan J.K. Sanders, "Foreign Relations and Foreign Policy," in *Mongolia in Transition: Old Patterns, New Challenge*, O. Bruun, and O. Odgaard (eds.) (Richmond, Surrey: Routledge/Curzon 1997), 219.

3. See *The Constitution of Mongolia,* Ulaanbaatar, 1992 (Articles 1 and 10).
4. For more details see Sharad K. Soni, "Mongolia's Security Thinking and Outside World: A Reappraisal," *Bimonthly Journal on Mongolian and Tibetan Current Situation* 15, no. 6 (2006):7-39.
5. Ministry of Defence of Mongolia, *Mongolian Defence White Paper, 1997-1998* (Ulaanbaatar 1998), 29.
6. See "Concept of National Security of Mongolia," *Strategic Digest* 26, no. 2 (1996):173.
7. See "Concept of Mongolia's Foreign Policy," *Strategic Digest* 26, no. 2 (1996):188.
8. "Concept of Mongolia's Foreign Policy."
9. "Concept of Mongolia's Foreign Policy," 189.
10. Alicia Campi, "Mongolia in Northeast Asia—the New Realties," *The Mongolian Journal of International Affairs*, no. 12 (2005):51.
11. See Alicia J. Campi, "Mongolia's Foreign Policy Vision for Eurasia," paper presented at a Jamestown Foundation Seminar, 10 November 2010, 2. Moreover, as Alicia Campi opines, the events of 9/11, 2001 and the increased attention attached to the rise of international terrorism encouraged the US "to completely recalculate its strategic interests and embrace the Third Neighbor relationship, at least politically, with Mongolia."
12. "Mongolia's Foreign Policy: Efforts towards Regional Peace and Security," Address by Nambaryn Enkhbayar, President of Mongolia at the Centre for Strategic and International Studies, Washington DC, USA, 23 October 2007.
13. "Mongolia's Foreign Policy," Address by Nambaryn Enkhbayar.
14. A. Tuvshintugs, "Mongolia's National Security: Past, Present and Future Perspectives," in *Mongolia in the 21st Century: Society, Culture and International Relations,* K. Warikoo and Sharad K. Soni (eds.) (New Delhi and London: Pentagon 2010), 76.
15. Sharad K. Soni, "China's Periphery Policy: Implications for Sino-Mongolian Relations," *India Quarterly* 65 no. 3(2009): 254-55.
16. Alicia Campi, "U.S. Policy towards Mongolia since Diplomatic Relations in 1987," in Warikoo and Soni (eds.), *Mongolia in the 21st Century*, 251.
17. Robert Scalapino, "The Political Process in Northeast Asia and Mongolia's Challenge," unpublished paper presented at Mongolia-U.S. Bilateral Conference, *Mongolia-U.S. Comprehensive Partnership in the Context of North East Asia: Challenges and Opportunities,* Washington, 28 February 2005, cited in Warikoo and Soni (eds.), *Mongolia in the 21st Century.*
18. Alan M. Wachman, *Mongolia's Geopolitical Gambit: Preserving a Precarious Independence While Resisting "Soft Colonialism"*, EAI Fellows Programme Working Paper Series 18, Seoulm The East Asia Institute, 2009.

19. For more on Mongolia's quest for its relationship with third neighbours, see Sharad K. Soni, "Post-1991 Mongolia: A Paradigm for Peaceful Democratic Transition," in *Communities, Institutions and 'Transition' in Post-1991 Eurasia*, Suchandana Chatterjee and Anita Sengupta (eds.) (Delhi: Shipra Publications and Maulana Abul Kalam Azad Institute of Asian Studies 2011), 274-76.
20. Office of the US Trade Representative, *http://www.ustr.gov/countries-regions/china/mongolia.*
21. United States, "Joint Statement between Mongolia and the United States of America", 21 November 2005, *http://www.whitehouse.gov.*
22. Wang Peiran, "Mongolia's Delicate Balancing Act," *China Security* 5, no. 2 (2009):21.
23. Sharad K. Soni, "India-Mongolia Relations: Implications for Regional Cooperation in North East Asia," *Mongolian and Tibetan Quarterly* 18, no. 2 (2009): 57.
24. P. Shinebayar, "Khaan Quest 2010 Starts," *UB Post*, 10 August 2010.
25. R.D. Kaplan, "Supremacy by Stealth," *The Atlantic Monthly*, July/August 2003, *http://www.theatlantic.com/issues/2003/07/kaplan.htm*
26. Speech by Ambassador Designate to Mongolia, Jonathan Addleton on "US-Mongolia Relations: Looking Forward, Looking Back," delivered on 29 October 2009 at the Opening of American Center for Mongolia Studies, University of Wisconsin at Madison, http://mongolia.usembassy.gov/speech_102909.html
27. Ranjan Gupta "India and Mongolia: A Geostrategic Perspective," *Regional Security Issues and Mongolia*, no. 6 (1999): 30.
28. Brandon Joseph Miliate, *India's Role in Mongolia's Third Neighbor Policy*, SIT Study Abroad: Mongolia, ISP Collection, (2009), 18.
29. Miliate, *India's Role*, 17.
30. Miliate, *India's Role.*
31. Sharad K. Soni, "The Importance of Mongolia in India's Engagement with Northeast Asia," in *Sino-Indian Relations: Challenges and Opportunities for 21st Century*, Sudhir Kumar Singh (ed.) (New Delhi: Pentagon Press 2011), 295.
32. See Li Narangoa, "Mongolia and Preventive Diplomacy," *Asian Survey* 49 no. 2 (2009): 373-74.
33. P. Shinebayar, "Mongolia, Japan vow to boost Partnership," *UB Post*, 3 September 2010.
34. The Office of the President of Mongolia, Public Relations and Communications Division, "President Elbegdorj Expresses Mongolia's interest to Produce Ready Made Products instead of Exporting Mineral Resources," 5 January 2011.
35. "The Ties that bind with Korea and Mongolia," *Korea IT Times*, 25 March 2010, *http://www.koreaittimes.com/story/8141/ties-bind-korea-and-mongolia*

36. "The Ties that bind with Korea and Mongolia."
37. "The Ties that bind with Korea and Mongolia."
38. Government of Canada, "Canada-Mongolia Bilateral Relations," 15 November 2010, *http://www.canadainternational.gc.ca/mongolia-mongolie/bilateral_relations_bilaterales/index.aspx?lang=eng*
39. See Batbold Sukhbaatar, "Mongolia's Relations with Russia And China and its Third Neighbor Policy: Relations with U.S, Japan," speech delivered at Hudson Institute, Washington DC, 8 June 2009, http://www.hudson.org/files/documents/Batbold_Speech.pdf
40. "Mongolia to become Strategic Military location," 29 May 2006, *http://mongolia.neweurasia.net/?p=226*
41. Peiran, "Mongolia's Delicate Balancing Act," 25.
42. Wachman, *Mongolia's Geopolitical Gambit*, 9.
43. John J. Tkacik, Jr., "Mongolia's Current Political Situation: Implications for the OSCE," *Heritage Lectures*, no. 1098 (15 September 2008): 4.

34

Mongolia in the Post-Soviet Space

Viktor B. Bazarov

At the end of the twentieth century the Mongolian society passed through the path of democracy and changing the model of social development. With the transition of Mongolia to the new market relations, the economy of the country suffered the most severe crisis, as also did the other countries of the former Soviet Union. It reached its peak during the years from 1990 to1995. There were many factors that caused this crisis, the main among them being the collapse of the socialist economic system, liquidation of planned and centralized economy, interruption of world economic relations, and accordingly the termination of investment component and subsidies from the Russian Federation.

The Mongolian enterprises that were engaged in export totally lost their traditional buyers because of the collapse of the socialist bloc, upon which, in fact, depended the entire export production of Mongolia's industry. The imports declined sharply and the supply of manufactured goods and food stuffs from other countries virtually stopped. Under these conditions, there occurred commodity deficit, further aggravated by the rapid withdrawal from Mongolia of the Soviet army contingent comprising over 100 thousand people with their family members. At the same time, the specialists numbering more than 150 thousand people along with their families began to move out from Russia and other countries of the former USSR. By Mongolian standards, a huge mass of people poured into the stores, sweeping off from the shelves everything that was available, as the civilized exchange market was not yet in operation and the only way to keep savings was to purchase goods. In fact, within a very short time all goods, both the imported products as well as the goods of the domestic manufacturers were sold out.

Original Paper in Russian: *Mongoliya v postsovetskom prostranstve*—Translated by Susmita Bhattacharya.

The situation became extremely difficult with the essential commodities disappearing from the shelves. The administration of the capital city of Ulan Bator brought the provisions under food rationing system. In the beginning of 1993, a resident of the capital per month received 2.3 kg of 1st grade flour, 1.7 kg of 2nd grade flour and 2 kg of meat.[1]

However, this did not change the situation. The food problem intensified, it was impossible to provide bare subsistence through rationing system. The shops had only "black salt" and virtually no provisions were there. As such there was no market of provisions, and speculation as well as small shuttle trade with Russia and China became predominant. In these circumstances, the government liberalized the prices of food products and thereby passed the issue of food security on the shoulders of the population.

Another serious problem was the progressing unemployment. Bankruptcy and commercial insolvency of the industrial sector of the economy generated multitudes of skilled unemployed people. At the end of January 1993, the number of unemployed people marked as "skilled worker" was 23.1per cent of the total number of the unemployed. Due to acute crisis in the sector, a large number of workers in the manufacturing industry abandoned their jobs and moved to small entrepreneurship and trade. While in 1990 the number of workers employed in the manufacturing sector was 1, 23,400, it declined to 67,300 in 1995.[2] A number of citizens started leaving for other countries in search of livelihood and just in 1993 alone 39,190 citizens of Kazakh nationality left their homeland and moved to the neighbouring Kazakhstan in search of fortune.

The internal political situation got worse more and more and crisis engulfed every sphere of the society. In these circumstances, there loomed the danger of collapse of public order, and in 1992 in view of the plight of the country the Great State Khural issued a decree "On basic directions of activities of the State to maintain public order,"[3] which, though, did not produce the desired effect on the public order situation. Simultaneously, the Government of Mongolia took actions, dictated by the course of the objective process of transition to market economy. Thus, in 1990s it launched mass privatization of livestock and partial privatization of state enterprises, which created the prerequisites for the development of small and medium business. In 1993, the private sector of the Mongolian economy produced 60 per cent of GDP. There was an increase in the total cattle heads of privatized livestock, which had almost entirely passed to the private hands. If in 1990 there were 25.8 million heads of cattle in the country, in 1995 it was 28.5 million, in 1999 it was 33.6 million and now it is approximately 40 million.[4]

But after mass privatization of livestock, primarily owned by the agricultural cooperatives of socialist type and state farming, the agrarian sector that was not ready for this became dominated by the market forces. The grain production dropped sharply and the country became dependent on imported wheat. The cattle heads of livestock increased, but the technology to protect it from adverse natural phenomena remained unchanged. In fact, almost every winter there was a massive loss of livestock.

Road to Revival: Foreign Aid

In order to stabilize the social structure it was needed to revive the economy by pouring external financial aids into it. Due to the fact that the state of Mongolia was up on the track of democratic development and because of its open foreign policy concept, the rest of the world responded to its call for assistance quite fast.

The donor states, led by Japan started rendering extensive assistance and giving credit to Mongolia with a view to stabilize its economy. Japan provided 50 per cent of the entire donor revenues, the USA 11 per cent, PRC 9 per cent,[5] along with Russia, Germany, the World Bank and Asian Development Bank.[6] In August 1993, the ADB President Mr. Kimimasa Tarumizu made a visit to Mongolia, who jointly with the Prime Minister P. Zhasrai studied the way to most effectively utilize the first part of the soft loan of US $30 million, which was granted on interest-free basis to Mongolia for 40 years. During the years from 1993 to1996 Mongolia received US$ 10 million through UNDP for the implementation of 10 projects.

Since 1991, the Republic of Korea has been providing grant aid, allocating US $200 thousand per year with the purpose of supporting Mongolia's transition to market economy and widening the cooperation between the two countries.[7] In November 1993, the US rendered grant to Mongolia, by sending 123 tons of goods necessary for production: explosives for coal mines, the wheels dump trucks, equipment for power stations and other necessary materials, which made it possible to raise the extraction of coal from the open-pit mines of Baganuur, Sharyngol, as well as to increase the production of electricity and thermal energy at the power plants of Darkhan and Ulan Bator.

During 1991-93 the USA, Japan, Denmark, Holland and Italy provided Mongolia with US $ 27.5 million worth of commodity aid, including provisions and essential commodities (sugar, rice, vegetable oil, milk powder, matches, cotton fabrics, school supplies).[8] In the beginning of the 1990s, at the request of the Government of Mongolia the United States supplied 30 thousand tons wheat of worth US $ 9 million.[9]

At the same time, 20 tons of food commodities were received from Japan: rice, sugar, flour, milk powder, as well as 10 thousand sets of clothing, meant for the livestock breeders of those *aimaks*[10] that were suffering from natural disasters. In the spring of 1994, as gratuitous aid Japan sent to Mongolia 140 tons fertilizers and 21 tractors with all hinged instruments worth 20 million yen.[11]

Starting from 1993, there have been fundamental changes in the use of credit and humanitarian aids allocated to Mongolia by the donor countries as well as international credit and financial organizations. If in 1991-92 only 10 per cent of the loan and humanitarian aids was allocated for developing and financing the medium and long-term projects, by the mid-'90s the share of funding the projects increased to 60 per cent.[12]

The joint Mongolian-Japanese research project *Shirokaya step'*[13] is of obvious interest, which is gratuitously being financed by Japan. The participants in the project are engaged in prospecting to locate valuable, rare polymetals and other minerals through more than 500 thousand sq. km territory of the southern, south-eastern and eastern parts of Mongolia. The samples of ores extracted during the joint expeditions were sent for analysis to Japan. Subsequently, the project expanded, got the name *Zolotaya step'*,[14] and covered almost the entire territory of Mongolia.

For the implementation of the projects to reform the economy of Mongolia, substantial assistance was rendered by the European Union (EU) with which the diplomatic relations had already been established in the late 80s. In 1993, the economic and trade cooperation agreement was signed with the EU. In the next two years the EU financed ECU € 8 million to the projects, which aimed at developing small and medium business in the sector of agricultural products processing.[15]

The G-7 Conference in London (July 1991) expressed its approval and support to the political reforms in Mongolia and its "open door" policy. Thereby, a feasible base was founded to provide the country with coordinated financial aid from the industrially developed countries. The first meeting of the group of donor countries was held in October 1991 at Tokyo, after which the international financial assistance to the country started to be implemented under the aegis of UNDP and Japan became its coordinator. It was mentioned in the Mongolian press that one-third of the entire amount of the donor aid

(US $ 600 million) during 1991-97 was granted by Japan.[16] From 1991 to 1999, Tokyo acted for 7 times as initiator of the meeting of the group of countries and international organizations that provide financial assistance to Ulan Bator. One of the recent meetings was held at Ulan Bator in June 1999. During the period from 1997 to 2000 the Japanese Government provided Mongolia with an unplanned assistance amounting to 12.4 billion yen (US $12 million).[17] During this period Mongolia received US $ 1.3 billion from the donors' group. And besides, 40 per cent of this amount was provided gratis. These resources provide 70 per cent of investments in the country's economy. In December 2004, the Government of Japan worked out and approved a new program of assistance to Mongolia, which aimed at "training the professional personnel, improving the market mechanisms, developing agriculture and infrastructure, as well as protecting the environment."[18] Tokyo has been playing a substantial role in the Asian Development Bank on the matters of allocating credits to Ulan Bator.

In its turn, Mongolia supplies copper, molybdenum concentrate, goat's hair, knitted garments, horse meat to Japan, while imports production equipment, machinery and consumer goods. The total turnover between the two countries exceeds US $ 51 million. In Mongolia, 76 enterprises are operating with Japanese investments of worth US $ 32.5 million.

The growth of direct investments in Mongolia's economy, which by 1999 reached US $ 300-350 million and the advancement of Switzerland as the main buyer of Mongolian exports, in addition to the expansion of the donors' assistance and credits give evidence of economic interest of the West towards Mongolia.

The Downturn of Foreign Assistance

However, foreign injections also have its negative side. The policy to attract foreign credits has led to a sharp increase in the external debt of Mongolia, which is causing justified sense of anxiety among the public. It is quite clear that foreign investors has not been suffering from altruism and, in particular, have great interest on the issue related to mining mineral resources, which are rich in Mongolia. Thus, the famous Mongolian political analyst G. Tumurchuluun, while calling the developed countries "best friends of the small countries," at the same time emphasizes that the political and economic integration "leads to reduction of their autonomy and sovereignty."[19] There is no doubt that assistance from the international financial organizations and donor countries played a crucial role in rescuing Mongolia from actually impending economic disaster and creating the necessary economic conditions for the development of dynamic relations in the domestic market and the inclusion of Mongolia in the system of world market relations. However, this assistance, first of all, creates a real threat to the national security and, secondly, it is unable to fully compensate the loss of such a powerful source of financial, economic, military and political support as the assistance from the former USSR.

But with the disintegration of the Soviet Union, the vector of international relations of Mongolia with the world community has changed. For Mongolia it was of prime importance to normalize relations, in particular, with neighbouring China. After the long years of confrontation, mutual suspicion and distrust, when the Mongolian People's Republic was forced to shield itself under the Soviet "military umbrella," being seriously afraid of its southern neighbour. There was a substantial improvement of international relations between Mongolia and the People's Republic of China in the 1990s, as a result of which China became the biggest investor and external economic partner of Mongolia.

Conclusion

This way, Mongolia survived the exit from the system of the then existing relations in a situation of profound systemic crisis that forced it to radically reconsider its mutual relations with the contemporary world political systems. The need to overcome the crisis objectively led Mongolia to forced appellation to the world community, since the traditional partners were not ready to restore the former relations and could not actively support even the bases of livelihood of the country. The collapse of the world system of socialism and the disintegration of the Soviet Union were the prerequisites for independent self-determination of Mongolia in the contemporary world. The world community, especially the developed countries of the West and the East Asia rendered assistance in the making of a self-reliant Mongolian state initially by an enormous humanitarian as well as financial and economic aid, and then in the formation of political and economic programs. This helped to create the base for exit from the critical situation, transition to market relations and gradually setting into the world economic relations. In the political sphere the conditions were created for irreversible process of becoming a democratic state. These processes were consolidated in the form of free participation of a large number of countries in deciding the future destiny of Mongolia, which stared being considered by many as a reliable prospective outpost in the Eurasian space. At the same time, great attention was paid to the question of the country's natural resources, for more active mobilization of those to the needs of global economy.

As a result of the transformation processes, Mongolia changed the form of its political power and took the path of recognizing the fundamental world values. It created a new economic structure based on different forms of ownership. There emerged a new financial system, acting on the basis of new principles and standards. The democratization of public life through a new constitution increased the interest in traditional spiritual values, history, religion and achievements of nomadic civilisation. A multiparty political system has been formed, which reflects the whole spectrum of public interests. Mongolia has become member of several influential international organisations whose activities give evidence of development of integration processes in the regional as well as global scales, and Mongolia has established relations with more than 140 countries and carried out economic cooperation in one way or another with 70 out of them.

Notes and References

1. Udo Barkman, *Politicheskie partii i demokraticheskie protsessy v Mongolii* (Ulan Bator 2004), 21.
2. *Statisticheskie dannye* (Ulan Bator 2000), 197.
3. See *Gosudarstvennyi vestnik* (Ulan Bator 1992), 34.
4. *Istoriya Mongolii, XX vek.*, Institut vostokovedeniya RAN, 2007, 347.
5. *Istoriya Mongolii*, 349.
6. Ganzhurov V. Ts., *Rossiya-Mongoliya (istoriya, problemy, sovremennost')* (Ulan-Ude 1997); Ganzhurov V. Ts., *Rossiisko-mongol'skie otnosheniya (1980-1995 gg.) (istoriya, problemy, sovremennost'*), 148.
7. *Byulleten' ekonomichesoi informtsii*, Ulan Bator, Ministerstvo infrastruktury Mongolii, (August1993), 19.
8. *Mongol'skii vestnik* (19 yanvarya (January) 1993).
9. *Ardyn Erkh* (27 yanvarya (January) 1992).
10. An *aimak* or *aimag* (Mongolian) is the first level administrative subdivision in Mongolia—translator's note.
11. *Byulleten' ekonomichesoi informtsii*, Ulan Bator, Ministerstvo infrastruktury Mongolii, (May1994), 12.
12. *Ardyn Erkh*, (27 aprelya (April) 1994).
13. Broad/Wide steppe—translator's note.
14. Gold steppe—translator's note.

15. *Zasgiin gazryn medee* (22 oktyabrya (October) 1944).
16. *Mongol Ulsyn Gadaan Hariltsaany Yaamnii Medeeliin Tovkhimol*, no. 161561 (31 March1999).
17. *Unen* (15 fevralya (February) 2000).
18. "Pravitel'stvo Yaponii utverdilo programmu pomoschi Mongolii," *Novosti Mongolii* (27 dekabrya (December) 2004).
19. G. Tumurchuluun, "External Factors of Development: Human Security," paper at the Conference *Geopolitical Environment and National Development of Mongolia*, Ulaanbaatar, 9 May, 2000, 12.

35

The Legacy of the Ottoman Diplomacy in Central Asia and the Parallels with Modern Turkey

Roza Abdykulova

Since the break-up of the USSR, five republics in Central Asia achieved their independence. Since that time, these countries have been establishing diplomatic ties with foreign countries. Similarly, a large number of countries in the world have been establishing diplomatic relations with the newly independent countries of Central Asia. The Republic of Turkey is one of the first countries which recognized the sovereignty of the Central Asian republics and established close relations in the field of humanities, culture, economy and politics. This was primarily due to the cultural ties of Turkey and four of the Central Asian states except Tajikistan. Though the extent and nature of relations of Turkey with each of the Central Asian countries varied, one common thing between them is that Turkey has started playing an active role in the economic and political development of these countries.

However, it is worth mentioning that relation with Turkey is not a new phenomenon. It is true that during the period of the former USSR, due to deliberate policies of Moscow to separate the Central Asian republics from Turkey's influence, the relations with Turkey had become very distant. Previously, the khanates in Central Asia had close diplomatic relations with the Ottoman Empire, the predecessor of the Turkish Republic. There are a large number of archival sources documenting these relations. Examples for this can be found at the documents in the Ottoman State Archives,[1] in the Oriental Institute of the Uzbek Academy of Sciences, and in the Kyrgyz State Archive.[2]

The first communication between the Ottoman empire and Central Asian Khanates was the missive informing that Yavus Sultan Selim Shah Ismail was defeated in 1514 (the war Chaldyran in 1514). This letter was sent to the Uzbek's governor Kuchkinchi Khan. Iran was an obstacle between the Ottoman empire and Central Asian Khanates in that period, but in nineteenth century Russia became an obstacle between them. As the Ottoman empire expected Central Asian Khanates to help it during the war with Russia, when Russia began its policy of conquest, Central Asian Khanates expected the Ottoman empire to help them and appealed to it. Due to the fact that geographically they were located far from each other, they could not help each other in time. The Ottoman empire considered the governors of Central Asian Khanates to be supportive, but the Khanates were not at such level so as to help them. Especially, after Russian conquest of Tashkent, the relationship between the Ottoman empire and Central Asian Khanates got worse since Tashkent was the centre of Turkistan during that period.

The process of breaking down of the empire began even though the Ottoman empire took measures for its survival. During this period the internal factor that further accelerated it was the strikes of the minorities and the external factor was the attack of foreign countries to its territory. The reforms (Tanzimat, Islahat, I, II, Meshrutiet) of that time could not preserve the empire from breaking down. Despite that, the Ottoman empire was still a force in the nineteenth century. The sultan of the Ottoman empire used a special writing style while writing to the governors of the other countries in epistolary style of diplomatic letters. For example, the sultan used encomium like "happy", "hero", "kind", "fighting for religious (*Jihad*) and for the home country (*Gaza*)" to Central Asian Khanates. It is possible to find the context of the letter translated into the Ottoman language and sent to the sultan although they weren't so widespread.

Ottoman Connections

In fact, diplomatic relations between Central Asian states and Ottoman empire began in the sixteenth century and continued until the beginning of the twentieth century. Four sovereign states/khanates in Turkestan (Khiva, Bukhara, Kokand and Kashgar) had close relations. Khiva and Bukhara established relations in the sixteenth century, Kokand in the beginning of the eighteenth century and Kashgar in the ending of the nineteenth century. But for the Ottoman empire this period was the period of protecting and saving the country from its enemies, while for the Central Asian states (Turkestan in general terms) it was a political period of being conquered by the Russian empire.

At the end of nineteenth century the Ottoman empire, constantly changing for about 700 years, lost its territory in Africa, Asia and part of Europe and was confined to the territory of the Turkish Republic. At the beginning of nineteenth-twentieth centuries religious link between the Ottoman empire and Central Asia was strong due to the fact that the sultan was assumed to be heir of the Islamic world on religious and humanitarian relations. We come across information that Central Asian governers took "relic" (the things which belonged to prophet Muhammed) from time to time, and future pilgrims, who were going to Mecca, went through Istanbul, and religious books were sold there. As for humanitarian relations, an expert coming from Central Asia to teach Persian language worked in the Ottoman empire; it is interesting to note that publishing houses of Ottoman letters were sent to Central Asia for fighting against illiteracy.

At the beginning of nineteenth-twentieth centuries Turkistan was dependent on Russian empire in regards to policy; there were many political events, there was a exchange with countries like Russia and England in matters of policy. Yet, unlike them the Ottoman empire had maintained kinship relations with Turkistan for about five centuries. Unlike the policy of England, Russia and China with respect to Turkistan, the Ottoman empire's relationship helped khanates in time and could only urge it to unite them. Central Asian states considered the Ottoman empire to be heir of the the Islamic World. Because the sultan of the Ottoman empire Yavus Sultan Selim won Egypt, he had sacred things taken which belonged to Prophet Muhammed. From this time the Ottoman empire began to be introduced as Halifat.

Pilgrims, governors, sheikhs asked for the private belongings of Prophet Muhammed and used them in their own interests on different purpose. According to the information of the researchers of the strikes in Andijan, the Ottoman empire used the sacred belongings as weapons during the Central Asian bad political situation. But from the information taken from archive materials this information can be refuted by us. Economically, governors of Central Asian states used to ask for weapons, military instructors and military clothes from the Ottoman empire.

In the first half of nineteenth century Emirate of Bukhara, among Central Asian States, maintained close diplomatic ties with the Ottoman empire. It sent envoys to Istanbul several times in order to get official documents allowing it to rule the other Central Asian khanates. The second half of nineteenth century was a very difficult historical time for Central Asian states because Russian empire captured Central Asia at that time. Central Asian states asked for help from the Ottoman empire during this period. The Ottoman empire being busy with defending its own territory and trying to preserve the country from enemies could not help it. Geographically, being far from it could not help them. Having realized the situation, some of the Central Asian governors asked only for weapons, military instructors and military clothes from the Ottoman empire. Despite it, gifts between the Ottoman empire and Central Asian khanates and intercommunication between ambassadors strengthened their friendship.

During Russo-Turkish War, the Ottoman empire expected Central Asian states to help it. But as noted above, they could not help it in time. At the beginning of twentieth century Central Asian states collapsed, their relationship with the Ottoman empire weakened sharply and relationship was maintained only in religious and humanitarian aspects. Now being conquered by Russia, Russian schools were opened in Central Asia. Besides, some literate people among the local population began to open schools and madrasas. These schools and madrasas, however, got books and brochures for teaching the Ottoman language and Islam.

Archival Documentation

The pre-Soviet relations of Turkey with the Central Asian states have not been researched systematically until now. Therefore, I conducted research using the archival documents in Central Asia and Turkey to conduct historiographical study of these relations. An analysis was made of the epistolary genre of letters of the Ottoman empire and Central Asian countries. Especially the information was given to the terminology of the Ottoman empire's official letters. Having divided the main archival documents thematically into some parts the information from those documents were compared with historical writings and the historical facts from other research work. The study provided with new historical knowledge and research, especially in Kyrgyzstan as these kinds of studies could not be conducted during the Soviet period due to ideological/political reasons.

The archive materials provided information about political, economic and cultural relations between Central Asian states (khanates) and Ottoman empire. However, the main factor was religious as the Ottoman empire was caliphate (legacy) of the Muslim world in the nineteenth century. The Muslims of Central Asia looked at Turkey as a bridge to Islam and many Muslims from Central Asia went to Mecca through Istanbul. The Muslims from Central Asia also brought from Arabia via Turkey or from Turkey itself various religious/sacred items (e.g., artifacts belonging to the Prophet Mohammad, books, Quran, Hadids) which further strengthened the religious ties between Turkey and Central Asia.

Attention has not been paid properly to ties between the Ottoman empire and Central Asian khanates by historians. Some researches were conducted restrictedly as they researched only one country. Scientists from Central Asia have not taken heed of this problem yet. With respect to Turkey, this problem was researched by Zeki Veli Togan,[3] Baymyrza Hayit[4] and Mehmet Saray[5] who were first researchers of common Turkish history. Zeki Veli Togan is considered to be the most important historian who wrote the common Turkistan history in Turkey. In his work Today's *Turkistan where the Turks live and Resent History* (reprinted 1981), he wrote about the geographical location and administrative structure of Turkistan, its position before and after sixteenth century, during Russian empire and also about culture of Turkistan. That is, he wrote the history of Turkistan from the beginning till the 1920s. There is information about condition of khanates concerned with research. Zeki Veli Togan's second important work is named *Region of the Turks, History of Turkistan* (reprinted Istanbul, 1980). History of Turkistan is written from a broad perspective and contains information relevant to this research.

Baymirza Hait's work, *History of the Turkistan States National Struggle* was devoted to describing political events from the beginning of nineteenth to twentieth centuries, especially, policy of Russian empire about capturing Turkistan, fighting and strikes against it. Basically, it gives information about the years of difficult political situation of Central Asia.

Mehmed Saray's work, *Political Relationship between the Ottoman Empire and Turkistan's Khanates during Russian Capturing* (reprinted Ankara, 1994) contained history from 1775 to 1875. Besides, it gives information about political state of Central Asian khanates generally, and we learn about some archive documents related to our subject. It should be noticed that Bukhara among other Central Asian states was far higher politically. Saray's work, *History of New Turkish Republics* (reprinted Istanbul, 1996) tells the history of today's Azerbaijan, Kazakhstan, Uzbekistan and Kyrgyzstan from the beginning till current times.

Archival documents concerned with this subject were found in the chapter named "Hatt-I Humayun" where there were writings of the sultans of the Ottoman empire and in the chapter named "Name-I Humayun" where there were letters written by the sultans of the Ottoman empire to governors of other countries and in the chapter where there were decisions of Ministry of the Foreign Affairs and in the archive Yildiz built in nineteenth century as well as the decision of the Council, chief vizier's decision, decision of the foundations (the role of the foundations during the Ottoman empire was very important, even they could solve some problematic matters of the government), the decision on Foreign Political Issues and the decision of the Ministry of Internal Affairs.There are not only missives between the khanates and the sultans in the archival documents but also different decision and news related to political events of that time. Comparing historical information (travelogues, reports) with archive materials, it is possible to analyse political, social and economic conditions of that period.

The matters in archive documents concerned with diplomatic relations between the Ottoman empire and Central Asian khanates were devoted to political, economic, religious and humanitarian relations. If we examine their contents, there are responses to letters of the sultan of the Ottoman empire, to the Khokand khanate's governor (1820), the translation of the letter into the Ottoman language sent by Khokand khanate's governor Madaly Khan to the sultan of the Ottoman empire (1839), the translation of the letter into the Ottoman language sent by Khokand khanate's governor Kudayar Khan to the sultan of the Ottoman empire (1847), the writing of the chief vizier to the sultan where he says that Turkman tribes from Bukhara and Khiva applied to the Ottoman empire for help against Russia (1870), the writing of the Ministry of Foreign Affairs of the Ottoman empire refuting the information about the sultan's contribution of the Ottoman empire during Andijan uprising (1898), the document concerned with matters of setting up two large armies and increasing the number of the soldiers joining all military departments of Turkistan, Caspian and Jetisuu regions and naming them General Governorate of Turkistan generally (1899), the translation of the letter into the Ottoman language where Kulu bey talks about political condition of Kashar Khanates to the sultan of the Ottoman empire (1879), the document related to the matter of sending weapons and military clothing to Khokand Khanate (1868), coming of the ambassador from Khokand with presents and letters to Istanbul and his request to the sultan of the Ottoman empire to send specialists of iron business (1848), the document concerned with governor of Issar's contribution of money sent to build Hijaz railway (1899), the writing of the general secretary of the Ottoman empire to chief vizier about supplementing shortage of ambassador Mir Kuban from Khokand while setting off Mekka, the decision of the Council of the Ottoman empire concerned with this matter and the translation of the letter into the Ottoman language written by Khokand Khanate to the sultan of the Ottoman empire (1852), the document about the Ottoman empire's sultan's monetary contribution to the ambassador of the Khiva Khanate who was setting of Mekke (1841), the order given to send a single beard of the prophet Muhammed again to Khokand from the Ottoman empire, Khokand ambassador's asking a single beard of the prophet Muhammed again (1860), Hadji Meylibek from Khokand asked "Lilye saadet" (Muhammed prophet's a single beard) (1851), Kashkar Kazi (Muslim Judge) asked Muhammed prophet's a single beard from the Ottoman empire (1895), people whose name were Sheikhulislam Haji Ahmet from Khokand were given a present named "governer's present"which was gratuity from the sultan of the Ottoman empire (1850), lists of the religious books to be sent from the Ottoman empire to Bukhara Emirate (1820), the decision about publishing several books with the Arabic letters from the Ottoman empire and sending them to Central Asia (1906), the copy of permision asking the teacher, from Fergana, who teached the Persian language to return to home country (1849), application of Haji Muhammed Rasul, who was from Turkistan, where he asked to let him to be granded civil rights of the Ottoman empire (1915) etc.

Archive material also exists about the building of the Hicaz railway from Asian khanates by Shabdan Baatyr[6] and Astanakul Kushbegi.[7] We know that help was received from the Indian Muslims. This document has been found in the Kyrgyz State Archive.

The pre-Soviet relations between Turkey and Central Asia were the main areas of concern for the Soviets as they tried to separate the two as far as possible so that to create socialist republics with no religious and cultural ties with Turkey. The change from the Latin to Cyrillic in the Central Asian states was one of the tools that Moscow used to achieve its goal.

Relations between Turkey and Central Asia

Presently, it is possible to observe parallels between contemporary Turkey and Ottoman empire's relations with Central Asia. However the relations between modern Turkey and Central Asian Turkic republics are not based on religion, but on language and on relations in the field of economics and politics. Central Asian Turkic world has been establishing diplomatic links with neighbouring countries such as Russia, China as well as Turkey. After the collapse of the USSR Turkic summits were organized in the Turkic world (Turkey, Kyrgyzstan, Kazakhstan, Uzbekistan, Azerbaijan and Turkmenistan).

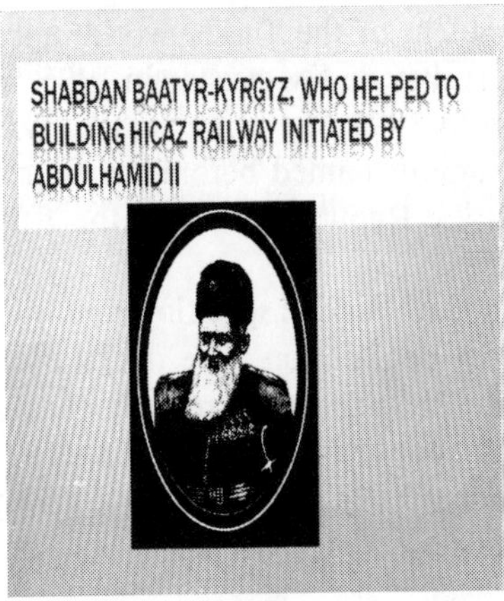

Figure 1: Shabdan Baatyr

Figure 2. Astanakul Kushbegy-Uzbek

Figure 3. Certificate of Shabdan Baatyr

Turkic summits considered the problem of the Turkic world since 1992. Five Congresses was held in Turkey, in Kyrgyzstan in 1995, in Uzbekistan in 1996, in Kazakhstan in 1998, the ninth summit was held in Azerbaijan in 2009. The summit named before the fourth summit of the President of the Turkic Republic, became the fifth summit of Turkish speaking countries.

The tenth summit of heads of state of Turkish speaking countries in Istanbul ended with signing of a declaration. The declaration emphasized deepening ties among the Turks and an increase in mutual cooperation, to enhance cultural and economic relations, to uncover a common historical heritage. Economically, the primary target of the two fields is transportation and energy.

The main topics of the summit were:

- to develop closer relations among the Turkish peoples, to strengthen friendly and constructive relations among the Turkish republics;
- to increase the positive contribution of the Turkish-speaking countries serving for international peace and stability;
- to convert geography of the countries into a cooperative, prosperous, stable and peaceful zone;
- to provide perception of the reality of Eurasia much more strongly;
- to contribute to the Turkish-speaking countries, which was celebrating independence of the fifteenth anniversary;
- to increase the activities of states acting in common on international platforms and on the world geopolitics.

The targets were:

- to found a permanent secretariat;
- to develop a common alphabet of the Turkish world;
- to prepare a comparative dictionary of Turkish dialects;
- to create a common history curriculum and create common history book;
- to establish the joint Institute of Turkic history;
- to create the energy policies to link the Turkic world;
- to include Bishkek into Almaty-Istanbul train and public transport network and to enhance support to Baku-Tbilisi-Kars-Ahıskalı railway construction;
- to revive the Silk Road in a real sense;

- to develop multilateral and bilateral cooperation in various fields among countries;
- to advance transport and communications projects, trade and economic relations;
- to found partner institutions to preserve common cultural heritage;
- to promote cooperation between ministries of education and universities;
- to enhance mutual exchange of scholarship students;
- to establish exchange and the circulatory system for high school-university student;
- to establish a General Assembly;
- to exchange ideas on various regional and international issues among countries and to seek compromise.

It is a good indication of relationship according to today's political direction that Kyrgyzstan, one of the Central Asian countries is entering the system of parliament using the experience of Turkey. After the collapse USSR Central Asian sovereign states (Turkic) have had close diplomatic links with Turkey not only in economics and politics but also in the religious sphere. Turkey and Central Asian Turkic Republic share the same language, ancestry, religion and historical root. All share diplomatic relations with Turkey.

We can conclude with examples of the following table:

Ottoman Empire-Central Asia	*Turkey-Central Asian States*
Political relations-1916 Turkestan	Political relations-Turkic summit (Kurultai)
Cultural relations: there are some archive documents with request to send them books as Muallim Sharsha, Tarihi Islam, Kuran, Taharat, Muntahab, Muhtasar Cografya, Tarihi Anbiya	Cultural relations: opening of universities, cultural organizations
Economic relations: there are some archive documents with request to send them weapon, arms	Economic relations: trade
Religion: Hicaz Railway (Indian Muslims helped with findings of the railway serving in purpose of Hajj to Mecca)	Religion: Influence to spread Islam in Central Asian states played more important role Afghanistan, Pakistan than Turkey

Notes and References

1. Belgelerle Osmanlı-Turkistan İlishkileri. (XVI-XX. Yuzyıllar). *TC. Bashbakanlik Devlet Arshıvlerı Genel Mudurlugu* Osmanlı Arshivi Daire Bashkanlıgı Yayın Nu: 70, (Ankara 2004); Kutukoglu, Mubahat; Osmanlı Belgelerinin Dili. (Diplomatik) (İstanbul 1998); Osmanlı Devleti ile Kafkasya, Turkistan ve Kırım Hanlıkları Arasındaki Munasebetlere Dair Arshiv Belgeleri, *T.C. Bashbakanlik Devlet Arshıvlerı Genel Mudurlugu* Osmanlı Arshivi Daire Bashkanlıgı Yayın Nu: 3, (1687-1908 Yılları Arası) (Ankara 1992).
2. Certificate of Shabdan Baatyr given by Ottoman empire. Kyrgyz State Archive.
3. Zeki Veli Togan, *Bugunku Turkili Turkistan ve Yakın Tarihi, Enderun Kitabevi, 2. Baskı* (Ankara:1981); Turk İli, *Turkistan Tarihi* (Istanbul 1980); Umumi Turk Tarihine Girish, *Enderun Kitabevi* (Istanbul 1980).
4. Baymyrza Hayit, *Turkistan Devletlerinin Milli Mucadeleleri Tarihi, TTK Basımevi* (History of the Turkistan States National Struggle) (Ankara: 1995).
5. Mehmet Saray, *Rus İshgali Devrinde Osmanlı Devleti ile Turkistan Hanlıkları Arasındaki Siyasi Munasebetler (1775-1875)* (Political Relationship between the Ottoman empire and Turkistan's Khanates during Russian Capturing) (Ankara: TTK Yay 1994); History of New Turkish Republics (reprinted Istanbul, 1996).
6. Shabdan Baatyr-Kyrgyz helped to building Hicaz Railway initiated by Abdulhamid II.
7. Astanakul Kushbegy-uzbek helped to building Hicaz Railway initiated by Abdulhamid II.

For further reading see:

Archival documents

Hatt-i Humayun (Governor's decision and writings) №36579
Hatt-i Humayun (Governor's decision and writings) №36565
Name-i Humayun (Governor's official missives) №11/253
Decisions of Ministry of Foreign Affair №2206-2
Decision taken in Council no. 1627
Decisions taken from archive Yildiz no. 179/128

Edited books

Alpargu Mehmet, *Turkistan Hanlıkları*, Turkler, C. 8, Yeni Turkiye Yayınları, (Ankara, 2002), ss. 557-605.

Atalar Munir, *Osmanlı Devletinde Surre-i Humayun ve Surre Alayları*, Diyanet İshleri Bashkanlıgı Yayınları (Ankara: 1999).

Belgelerle, *Osmanlı-Turkistan İlishkileri* (XVI-XX. Yuzyıllar). TC. Bashbakanlyk Devlet Arshivleri Genel Mudurlugu. Osmanlı Arshivi Daire Bashkanlıgı Yayın Nu: 70 (Ankara: 2004).

Daglı Yucel-Ucer Cumhure, *Tarih Chevirme Kılavuzu*, 24 Ekim 1786-16 Kasım 2077, (Ankara:1997).

Devellioglu Ferit, *Osmanlıca-Turkche Ansiklopedik Lûgat, Aydın Kitabevi Yayınları* (Ankara: 2000).

Mehmet Emin Efendi, *İstanbul'dan Orta Asya'ya Seyahat*. T.C. Kultur Bakanlıgı Yayınları, (Ankara 2000).

Osmanlı Devleti ile Kafkasya, *Turkistan ve Kırım Hanlıkları Arasındaki Munasebetlere Dair Arshiv Belgeleri*, T.C. Basgbakanlyk Devlet Arshivleri Genel Mudurlugu. Osmanlı Arshivi Daire Bashkanlıgı Yayın Nu: 3, (1687-1908 Yılları Arası) (Ankara: 1992).

A. Chaikovsky, *Dalekoe proshloe Turkestana*. (S-Petersburg: 1896).

36

Central Eurasia: Relevance for India from Geopolitical and Economic Perspectives

Nivedita Das Kundu

In recent years, after the disintegration of the Soviet Union the relatively new geopolitical term Central Eurasia, has gained popularity. The term Central Eurasia is normally applied to Azerbaijan, Armenia, Georgia, Kazakhstan, Kyrgyzstan, Tajikistan, Turkmenistan, and Uzbekistan, which are treated as a single geopolitical area. However, the logic suggests that if the physical dimensions of the continent's parts are put aside, then the geographic Eurasia as a continent consists of two parts of the world, that is, Europe and Asia. Traditionally, Central Eurasia as a geographic concept relates to the territory between the Bosporus in the west and the Uighur autonomous region in the east and from the Kazakh steppe in the north to Afghanistan in the south. There is even wider interpretation of Central Eurasia, which also includes the Black Sea region.[1] Geographically, Central Eurasia almost completely covers Central Asia and the Caucasus.

Central Eurasia consists of mostly Turkic-speaking people—mainly Tatars, Bashkirs, Azeris, Turkmen, Kyrgyz, Kazakhs, Uyghurs. They all share the heritage of the common Turkic language. Their language includes not just the lexicon and grammar but also texts, proverbs idioms and sometimes even part of oral epics, such as the *Alpamysh* derived from a linguistically transmitted common Turkic heritage. The influence of Iranian language and culture is the second important determinant here. Languages and cultures of Iran (Persian), Tajikistan (Tajik) and Afghanistan (Dari) are all represented in this region which has impacted on the culture and civilizations of the region.[2]

The heritage of Arabic language is also quite prominent here. The Arabic heritage is inseparable from the Iranian and Turkic heritage. This suggests a unique combination of determinants characterizing Central Eurasia. Geopolitical as well as economic factors are the ways and the means, but the linguistic-cultural factors provide the explanatory narrative for the people sharing them.

In Central Eurasia different global and regional players are actively involved in politics. The significance of this region increased mainly due to its geo-strategic location, natural resources and rich cultural heritage which became noticeable mainly after the collapse of the Soviet Union and when these states became independent sovereign states. It is also due the Islamic terrorist activities in the region that received international attention, immediately after 9/11 terrorist attack which also increased US interest in the region.[3] Recently, Central Eurasia has acquired a central role in international power politics. While dealing with Central Eurasia, it is pertinent to see what relevance it bears to the reality of power politics that is being witnessed today. These states that are the members of the Commonwealth of Independent States (CIS) today are in various stages of political or economic transition. Some are vibrant democracies whereas others are centralized totalitarian regimes.

Driven by India's security and increasing energy needs, India has emerged with a high profile in Central Eurasian region because of its long standing special relationship with the erstwhile Soviet Union and its links with Central Eurasia in terms of security and trade. India also tried to become a major factor in shaping and organizing the Central Eurasian region. The states of Central Eurasia also showed keenness to develop close relations with India due to India's economic growth and geopolitical influence.

The focus of this article is on the relevance of "Central Eurasia" and its significance in the regional/international power politics and economics. The prevalent discourse is about the region's importance mainly due to its geo-strategic location, natural resources and rich cultural heritage. While dealing with this region's relevance for India and examining its geopolitical and economic perspective the major question that comes up is that, can India play a significant role in the region? What factors are working in India's favour in the region? What are the constraints? To what extend can India be seen as a Central Eurasian player? What strategy can India devise to engage these countries meaningfully and effectively? The article argues that Central Eurasia with its central place in regional and international politics also connects western and eastern civilizations, in spite of having a distinct character that is not exclusively Russian or Asian. In this article an attempt has been made to point to specific factors of the region and also determine the future scenarios. The article also provides some policy recommendations for India to improve its relations with the region.

Identifying Central Eurasia

The two distinct parts of Central Eurasia are Caucasus and Central Asia. The contemporary geopolitical interpretation of the term "the Caucasus" came up when Russia conquered the region. It is also known as "the Trans-Caucasus/South Caucasus," that is, the part of the region found beyond the main Caucasian range if viewed from Russia and "the Northern Caucasus," the territory to the north of the Trans-Caucasus and the mountain range.[4] The southern limits of the Caucasus were always identified by the Russian empire's southern state border in the Caucasus. The border change was amply illustrated by the case of Kars of the late nineteenth century, when the Russian empire detached it by force from the Ottoman Empire and it came to be known as part of the Caucasus. The entire territory of the North Caucasus, which consists of the piedmont and mountainous areas, comprises of part of the Russian Federation (RF). The piedmont area comprises of the following RF region: the Krasnodar and Stavropol territories, the Astrakhan and Rostov regions and the Republic of Kalmykia. The mountainous areas are the Republics of Adigey, Daghestan, Ingushetia, Kabardino-Balkaria, Karachaevo-Cherkessia, North Ossetia-Alania and Chechnya.[5]

In Soviet times the Central Asian region was called *Sredniaia Azia* (Middle Asia). The latter includes Kyrgyzstan, Tajikistan, Turkmenistan, Uzbekistan and Kazakhstan. Western scholars mostly use the term "Central Asia," while some Russians have not yet dropped the old term "Middle Asia." Another term, "Greater Central Asia," is more recently used.[6] Recently this term has been given more exact geopolitical specification and applied to the five former Soviet republics including Afghanistan.

Centrality of Central Eurasia

One may begin with the twentieth century British geopolitical theory of Halford J. Mackinder who called Central Eurasia as the Eurasian "Heartland" to specify the region's geopolitical and geo-strategic importance in global politics. Mackinder was of the opinion that the one, who would control this region, would also control the whole world. Indeed, with the end of cold war and disintegration of the Soviet Union, Central Eurasia has developed as an important geo-strategic and geo-economic region in world politics.[7] Central Eurasia, however, suffers from localized conflicts as well as economic distress. Ethnic tensions continue in many of these states, making the region susceptible to instability and threatening its political and economic development. Its location between Russia, China, Iran, Turkey, and Afghanistan make the region a focal point for foreign powers as well as potential conflict between them.[8] The US, EU, China, Japan, Pakistan, Saudi Arabia, and Israel are all interested in the region. Here a new "Great Game" is quite predictable.

Unlike the Great Game of the nineteenth century, which was played out between the British empire and the Tsarist Russia, the post-cold war Great Game involves not only states but also non-state actors, international organizations, transnational oil corporations (TNOCs), etc. Active in the region in military security terms is the US and NATO. NATO also runs military programmes in Central Eurasian states in the context of the Partnership for Peace Programme (PfP). The Organization for Security and Cooperation in Europe (OSCE) is also active in the region. Another significant multilateral organization coming up in the region in a big way is the Shanghai Cooperation Organization (SCO). This can be a possible counterbalance in the region with the western organizations. The SCO set up in August 1996, including Russia, China, Kazakhstan, Kyrgyzstan, Tajikistan, and Uzbekistan as main members of the organization now expanded its agenda.[9] The agenda of the SCO is based mainly on the economic cooperation, but now also working towards curbing drugs trafficking and terrorist activities in the region focusing on the security concerns of the region. The Russian factor is still very strong in the Central Eurasian states' political, economic as well as the energy sectors. Today lot of study is going on to understand the problems and prospects of this region including the three South Caucasian States (Azerbaijan, Armenia, and Georgia) and the five Central Asian states (Kazakhstan, Kyrgyzstan, Tajikistan, Turkmenistan, and Uzbekistan).

Geopolitics of Oil and Gas

The Central Eurasian region's oil and gas reserves could be a major contribution to socio-economic development and transition of the region. The new Caspian littoral states (Azerbaijan, Kazakhstan, and Turkmenistan) together with Russia and Iran have one of the world's largest oil and gas reserves, which makes them significant to global markets.

Estimates of proven and possible oil reserves across the whole Caspian area, excluding Russia and Iran, run up to 190 billion barrels of oil. Its proven gas reserves are estimated at 196 trillion cubic feet. The Trans-Afghanistan Pipeline (Turkmenistan-Afghanistan-Pakistan-India) is a proposed natural gas pipeline being developed by the Asian Development Bank.[10] This pipeline (TAPI) will transport Caspian Sea's natural gas from Turkmenistan through Afghanistan into Pakistan and then to India. The Indian Government has approved Inter-Governmental Agreement and Gas Pipeline Framework Agreement for TAPI pipeline project at a summit meeting of the four participating nations at Ashgabat to import natural gas through Turkmenistan-Afghanistan-Pakistan-India pipeline on 11 December 2010. Turkmenistan will supply gas from its South Yoloten-Osman field and state-owned gas utility GAIL India has entered into a Gas Sales and Purchase Agreement (GSPA) with Turkmenistan's national oil firm Turkmengaz during the Summit in Ashgabat.[11] Another significant pipeline connection of the region is the Baku-Tbilisi-Ceyhan (BTC) pipeline; these pipelines can become a major energy resource for India. But the political situation in these countries might make their smooth operation difficult.

Security Concerns

Central Eurasian states are particularly sensitive to security issues as they lack the experience that comes from independent statehood. They have not had the opportunity to develop a definite culture for strategic and security planning or for policy engineering. Furthermore, all these newly independent states feel insecure and quite uncertain about their security interests and priorities. They tend to underestimate certain security threats, exaggerate others and sometimes even overlook vital factors in national security planning.[12] Their strategic visions and calculations are mainly based on historical events with reference to ethnic lines.

Since the collapse of the Soviet Union, all the Central Eurasian states had common threat of terrorist activities mainly emanating from the neighbouring Afghanistan, which is becoming one of the major security threats to the region. Rise of militancy and extremism and the cross-border infiltration of terrorist groups into their territories is causing severe concern for the whole Central Eurasian space.[13] Refugees from Afghanistan move towards Central Eurasian region and get influenced by developments in Afghanistan and create disturbances in Central Eurasian states.

Another significant security threat towards the region is drug trafficking. Afghanistan's drug production flows to Europe through Central Eurasia. Afghan drug trafficking has become the most serious threat to the security of the whole Eurasian region including Russia.

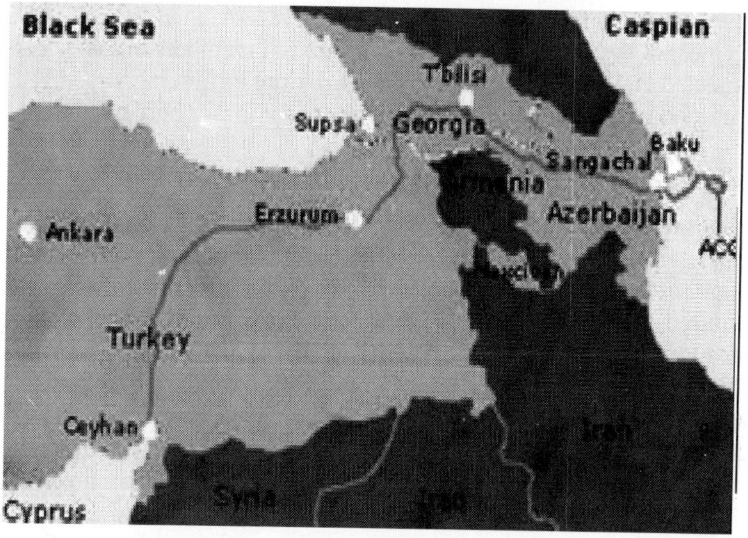

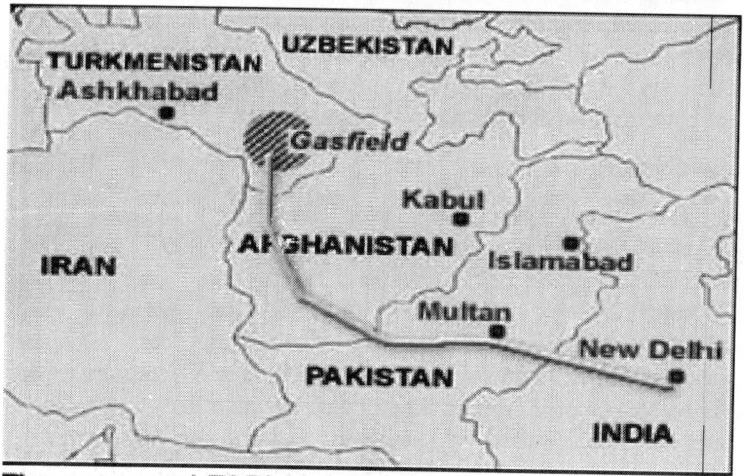

The proposed TAPI gas pipeline

Map 1. Maps Showing BTC and TAPI Pipelines

Source: http://www.google.co.in/imgres?imgurl=http:///SUsptBMSszI/AF8/QdjKTP1wQLs/s1600/BTC_pipeline.gif&imgrefurl=http://defenceforumindia.com/showthread.&http://www.google.co.in/imgres?imgurl=http://www.viewsbuzz.com/wp-content/uploads/2010/12/tapi-/tapi-gas-pipeline-project-map

The action plan from Russia called for joint SCO-Afghan operations.[14] As most of the Central Eurasian states are full members of SCO, it is expected that the joint operation can curb drug trafficking, organized crime, combat laundering of drug money and improve border controls.

Forging Relations between India and Central Eurasia

India's relations with Central Eurasia are based on strong civilizational links. India has deep interest in the region as its extended neighbourhood and also due to its security concerns and energy requirements. India maintains relatively high profile in the region because of its long-standing special relationship with the erstwhile Soviet Union and its links with Central Eurasia in terms of age-old trade and economic relations through silk route. The areas of interest as far as Central Eurasia is concerned include nationalist policy, civil society issues and urban development issues. India has been active in Central Eurasia, although China was quicker off the mark in developing close relationship with post-Soviet Central Eurasia than India.[15] However, all visits to the region by senior Indian politicians have been treated as significant events. India has strong diplomatic presence in the region. Significant and deep cultural contacts between them have also existed for past many years.

India-Central Asia

Central Asia is an important region for India for its vital geo-strategic location. The five landlocked republics of Central Asia—Uzbekistan, Kazakhstan, Kyrgyzstan, Tajikistan and Turkmenistan—are in India's neighbourhood or extended neighbourhood. The region not only connects Asia to Europe, but is also rich in natural resources. It occupies a special place in India's foreign policy priorities. Its importance to India today is not merely civilizational, but also geo-political and economic.[16] India's attempt has always been to increase political, cultural and economic ties with the Central Asian republics (CARs).

Since 1991, India-CAR relations have come a long way. Though numerous political and economic changes have taken place in the recent past in these states, the relationship between India and CAR has gone beyond this level to the level of strong political and security cooperation. There is significant common interest on the basis of which India and CAR can accelerate future cooperation. India-CAR relations are aimed to counter common threats to their security, namely religious extremism. The fight against terrorism is one major area of cooperation. Both CAR-India shares the view that the problem of drug trafficking and threat of weapons of mass destruction (WMD) are to be addressed jointly. On the situation in Afghanistan both hold similar views. India and the states of CAR have signed number of agreements to improve their relationship and cooperate in economic and energy sectors.[17] Both India and CAR have similar approaches towards major international and regional issues. New strategic options as well as new security realignments in the region have emerged.

India is also taking an initiative to provide satellite based tele-education and tele-medicine connectivity between India and CAR which would be a demonstration of cutting edge technological and human resource cooperation between them. Uzbekistan would become an important connecting point in the transport corridor, the route connecting India with Central Asia via Mumbai-Chah Bahar-Zaranj-Delaran-Herat-Naibabad-Khairaton-Termez and further has high potential for success.[18]

India's approaches to secure a niche for itself in Central Asian hydrocarbons have so far been unsuccessful. New Delhi had earlier tried to secure a share in the Kurmangazy field of Kazakhstan, but lost to China. However, it is hoped that India's present energy diplomacy would mark a breakthrough and will help ONGC Videsh and the Gas Authority of India Limited (GAIL) to put their plans of investment in CARs on the fast track.[19] As far as increasing the cooperation on nuclear energy is concerned it is going to increase. Among five Central Asian states, Uzbekistan is reported to have vast quantities of uranium and India is examining the option of buying uranium from Uzbekistan for its nuclear energy production requirements.

All CAR states have expressed their support for India's demand for permanent member status of the extended United Nations Security Council (UNSC). After the events of 11 September 2001, India has also started building military technical cooperation with this region. India is engaged with the states of CAR in intelligence sharing, sharing of joint military experience and providing training and assistance to Central Asian forces. Both India and Central Asia have economic complementarities in terms of natural resources; human resources and markets, which if exploited can broaden cooperation. Opportunities for joint ventures in banking, insurance, agriculture, information technology and in pharmaceuticals also exist. The Indian pharmaceutical industry has done well in all the CAR states. Today, it accounts for nearly a quarter of the imports into the region. Indian industrialists have also registered an impressive presence in the steel and construction sectors there.[20] India is exploiting its expertise in the construction of small and medium-sized hydroelectric plants mainly in Kyrgyzstan and Tajikistan, which have substantial hydropower potential.

With Central Asian energy reserves being estimated at 2.7 per cent of world oil reserves (between 13 and 15 billion barrels) and 7 per cent of natural gas reserves (around 270 to 360 trillion cubic feet, mainly in two big fields Kashagan and Tengiz), the region has a potential to become future energy hub for India. The main hydrocarbon deposits are in Kazakhstan, Turkmenistan and Uzbekistan. These Central Asian states with energy potential have agreed to cooperate with India in the fields of oil and natural gas exploration and production. On 26 April 2006, India's GAIL and Ministry of Petroleum signed an MOU to conduct oil and gas exploration in Uzbekistan. Uzbekistan has also agreed to allocate geological territory to Indian companies to explore its hydrocarbon resources. The work is in progress between GAIL and *Uzbekneftogas* to build facilities in Uzbekistan to produce LPG (liquefied petroleum gas).

In the field of defence, India acquired six Ilyushin-78 in-flight refuelling aircraft from Uzbekistan. Indian aircrafts are being regularly serviced at the Chekalov aircraft plant in Tashkent in Uzbekistan.[21] Indian experts have also been involved in repairing military aircrafts in Tajikistan.

India and Central Asian states together are carrying on dialogue to develop the human resource potential in the region. India has shown its desire to build major software development centre and light motor vehicles manufacturing sector in Central Asia. India being observer in Shanghai Cooperation Organization (SCO) has opened up further opportunities for cooperation with the CARs in areas like security, communication and economic integration. There has been a strong opinion in favour of India's integration with Central Asia and observer status for the CARs in South Asian Association for Regional Cooperation (SAARC).[22] India's membership in the Economic Cooperation Organization (ECO), which is also expected to develop soon, could also strengthen India's economic relationship with the CARs.

The overall outlook on the region suggests that for India there is an enormous scope and potential to engage in meaningful and fruitful political-economic cooperation with five states of CAR. Tourism, diplomacy, defence, education, food processing, and products related to small-scale industries offer considerable potential for cooperation. The region could be used as a ground for joint ventures for producing goods and commodities for export to the wider world.

India-South Caucasus

Friendly relationships between India and South Caucasus have existed for more than four thousand years. Affinities of culture, language and mythology brought these two regions closer. As far back as the fifth century Armenian traders regularly traded in Indian muslin, spices, precious stones and herbs. Many Armenians who became citizens of India were traders, government servants and academics. Some Armenians were even involved in India's independence movement and even served in the Indian army. Armenians were mostly resident of Chennai, Mumbai, Kolkata and Surat but currently there are hardly hundred Armenians in India, mostly in Kolkata. In Chennai, the first Armenian Constitution was written.[23] Today, the main concern of the Armenian Church Committee of Kolkata is to preserve the Armenian heritage and properties such as the Armenian College and Philanthropic Academy. India and Armenia are both keen to cooperate with each other in politico-security and economic spheres.

India's relationship with Azerbaijan is also very old. The *Atesgah* monument near Baku, with Sanskrit and Gurmukhi wall inscriptions, is a surviving proof of the ancient relationship between India and Azerbaijan. Trade was carried on between the two countries over the Silk Route. Master craftsmen from Tabriz, principal city of Iranian Azerbaijan were involved in the construction of the Taj Mahal. India and Azerbaijan established diplomatic relations on February 1992.

Much of the trade in Indian items with Azerbaijan is carried out in UAE, which does not get reflected in the trade statistics. However, many Indian pharmaceutical companies are successfully competing with their European companies for the Azeri market. Bharat Heavy Electricals Limited (BHEL) has sanctioned a project for *Azenergy*, a government undertaking, for the supply and installation of power generators for the Mingechevir Power Plant in Azerbaijan. Aluminium Ore and Concentrate from Gujarat has supplied raw material to the aluminium plants in Ganja and Sumgait, which has contributed largely to the quantum jump in India's exports to Azerbaijan. During the Soviet period, the educational institutions in Azerbaijan were a favourite destination for Indian students. Currently there are over 500 Indian students in Azerbaijan mainly pursuing medical and technical studies. Indians make their presence felt in various sectors in Azerbaijan even today.[24] If the oil and gas industry in Azerbaijan takes off as a global energy supplier in the near future, this development can be of immense benefit for India.

Bilateral relations between India and Georgia are also significant. Georgia has consistently supported India's position on

Jammu and Kashmir and India's candidature to the UN Security Council. Both sides have emphasized the need to combat international terrorism and separatism. Georgia also supports India's draft Comprehensive Convention on International Terrorism (CCIT). Georgia's unstable political situation has slowed down the growth in trade and economic cooperation between the two countries. India's main exports to Georgia are pharmaceuticals and consumer durables. Imports comprise of metals like aluminium, copper and ferrous. Indian construction company Punj Lloyd was a major sub-contractor in 2004-05 for the construction of Georgian part of the Baku-Tbilisi-Ceyhan (BTC) oil pipeline. Indian automobile company Mahindra and Mahindra's MUV Bolero is assembled at the Kutaisi Auto Plant in Georgia and doing good business there. Mahindra's Scorpio also did good business in Georgia. India's expertise and experience could be useful to Georgia in the small and medium size industries such as in light engineering, IT, agriculture, e.g. in silkworm rearing, tea, high-yield wheat varieties and in dryland farming.[25] There is also a huge scope to cooperate in science and technology and in the health sector.

In the recent conflict between Georgia and Russia where two breakaway territories of Georgia, South Ossetia and Abkhazia declared independence on 26 August 2008 with Russian support, India's official viewpoint was:

> India has a long-standing and consistent policy on the issue of recognition. Recognition is normally accorded on the basis of a country having a defined territory, a duly constituted government in charge, which is accepted by the people and which has effective control over an area of governance. It has been India's consistent position that the sovereignty and territorial integrity of all countries should be fully respected by all states.[26]

However, in Georgia's case India was upset by the sudden escalation of the conflict and loss of human lives and hope for an early restoration of normalcy in the region.

Future Scenarios

Scenarios for Central Eurasia have been developed here to widen perspectives and explore uncertain aspects of the future of the region. Scenarios also lead to new opportunities. Particularly, the issues like the shift from resource dependence to economic diversification; economic reforms and formation of effective governance could help bringing in various changes in the systems during next decade. The range of such possible scenarios is huge of which five are mentioned here.

Scenario One

By 2021, resource extraction will remain as an important part of Central Eurasia's economy. Good economic policies could lead to inflow of foreign direct investment outside the energy sector while any failure to diversify Central Eurasia's economy could well lead to the "petro-state phenomenon," leading to huge income inequality, capital flight and social tensions.

Scenario Two

Central Eurasian states are likely to be challenged by the twin pressures of growing population and a lack of arable land and water resources. The economic and demographic challenges can negatively impact the environment, compounding the current degradation caused by the high rates of "dirty" resource extraction. Also, states with the limited supplies of natural resources would face challenges to develop effective service industries.

Scenario Three

Ethnic unrest mostly arising due to xenophobia and economic difficulties would destabilize the region. Particularly susceptible are the northern Caucasus including Chechnya, Dagestan and Ingushetia, may prove insoluble and could persist in one form or another till 2021 which could affect the bordering states of South Caucasus causing severe civil unrest.

Scenario Four

The West will continue to pursue self-centred foreign policy objectives in the region. This also could give rise to the aggressive nationalist politicians (due to anti-western rhetoric) that would lead to more rift with the west.

Scenario Five

Central Eurasia's relations with China would deepen. This could happen due to Chinese economic investments in the region. China in collusion with Russia will counterbalance the US interests in the region.

Recommendations for India

Keeping in mind above mentioned scenarios the following policy recommendations are put forward:

1. Work towards improving relations with the Central Eurasian region in politico-economic and security sectors through regular interaction at the higher decision making level.
2. Work closely with the three CARs bordering Afghanistan (Uzbekistan, Tajikistan and Kazakhstan) to curb security threats emanating from Afghanistan.
3. Try to revive the silk route and improve trade and economic cooperation with these states.
4. Try to develop close contacts with the multilateral organizations currently active in the region.
5. Formulate strong energy policy to intervene in this region's energy sector as this region has the potential to provide India energy security.
6. Try to resolve differences with Beijing that is aligned with Central Asia and thisb creates a powerful alignment in the region.
7. Look for ways to assist CARs in areas of IT and S&T sector, which could improve their economic profile beyond natural resources.
8. Revive India's strong civilizational links based on religious ties (like Buddhism) in the Caspian Sea region.
9. Look for ways to utilize India's soft power to get closer to the region.
10. Look for ways to increase people-to-people contacts and information sharing.

Notes and References

1. *Central Eurasian Studies Review*, available at http://www.cesr-cess.org/CESR_contribution.html accessed on 16 February 2011.
2. Richard Lugar, "Energy Security: Cause for Cooperation or Competition?" 90th Anniversary Leadership Series, The Brooking Institution, 13 March 2006, http://www.brookings.edu/comm/events/20060313.pdf; also see Adrian Pabst, "Central Eurasia in the Emerging Global Balance of Power," *American Foreign Policy Interest* 31, no. 3 (May 2009): 166-76

3. T. Firdous, "India and Central Asia," in *Central Asia Introspection*, M.A.Kaw and A.A. Banday (eds.) (Srinagar: Crown Press 2006), 321-22.
4. Yekaterina Kuznetsova, "The Near Abroad: Increasingly far away from Russia," *Russia in Global Affairs* 3, no. 1 (January-March 2005): 27.
5. *Bolshaia Sovetskaia Entsiklopedia* (Moscow: Sovetskaia Entsiklopediia 1977), 255.
6. Nacelenia Rossia, *Edzegodniyie Demographicheskie Doklad*, Center Demographicheskie Chelavieka, Moscow, 1993, 15-20.
7. Tomohiko Uyama (ed.), *Empire, Islam and Politics in Central Eurasia*, Slavic Eurasian Studies, no. 14 (Sapporo, Hokkaido University 2007): 376.
8. Fault line of Conflict in Central Asia and the South Caucasus, RAND Document, RAND Publications, 2003.
9. Svante E. Cornell, "Security Threats and Challenges in Caucasus after 9/11," in *Eursaia in Balance: The US and the Regional Power Shift*, Ariel Cohen (ed.) (Aldershot: Ashgae Publishing Ltd. 2005), 44.
10. Anita Singh, "India's Relations with Russia and Central Asia," *International Affairs*, 71, no. 1 (January 1995): 69.
11. Daily News Analyses, "Government approves signing pact for TAPI gas pipeline project," 11 December 2010.
12. "Nationalism and Ethnic Conflicts in Transcaucasia in Comparative Perspective,"www.geocities.com; also see Zurab Davitashvilki, "The Ethno Political Situation in the Caucasus and the Problem of Oil in Transportation," http://ourworld.compuseve.com
13. Afghanistan and Regional Security, http://www.globalsecurity.org/military/world/afghanistan/opium.htm, accessed on 17 February 2011
14. Kim Sengupta, "Afghanistan: Russia steps in to help NATO," *The Independent World News*, 27 October 2010.
15. M.S. Roy, "India's Interest in Central Asia," *Strategic Analysis* 34, no. 12 (March 2001): 2273-89.
16. "India-Central Asia Economic Relations," A Report of RIS/CII Seminar RIS-DP # 94/2005, May 2005.
17. "India looking for energy supplies in Central Asia," 13 September 2006, available at http://www.asianews.it/index.php?art=7200&l=en
18. S. Blank, "India: the new Central Asian Player," availableatwww.eurasianet.org/departments/insight/articles/eav062606a.shtml.
19. Naira Mkrtchyan, "Armenians in India and Indians in Armenia," in *India-Eurasia: The Way Ahead*, S. Paramjit Sahai (ed.) (Chandigarh: CRRID 2008), 203-05.
20. Naira Shovgaryan, "Cultural Links between Armenia and India," in Sahai (ed.), *India-Eurasia*, 258-60.
21. Azerbaijan, Report of Embassy of India, available at http://meaindia.nic.in/foreignrelation/azerbaijan.htm, 2007.

22. Zhang Deguang, "Generalising Experience, Deepening Cooperation, Leading the SCO towards New Great Achievements," available at www.sectsco.org., accessed on 15 February 2011.
23. Mkrtchyan, "Armenians in India," in Sahai (ed.), *India-Eurasia.*
24. Sadiqoglu Afet, *Azerbaijan-Hindustan Relations* (Baku: Nurlan 2009), 5-8.
25. Afet, *Azerbaijan-Hindustan Relations.*
26. Eurasian Division Report, MEA, 2009.

Migration Patterns

37

Overcoming the "New Borders": Labour Migrants from Central Asia to Russia

Viktor I. Dyatlov

The disintegration of the USSR has not cut down the scales of day-to-day contacts between the people in its former space. And what is more, it has rather increased them. This paradox is explained by the formation of massive flows of labour migrants to Russia, particularly from the countries of Central Asia. By the scales it is comparable to the influx of labour migrants from China. At the same time, of course, there are essential distinctions in proportions between various cities and regions. Already by now the regular, temporary and seasonal labour migrants from Tajikistan, Uzbekistan and Kirghizstan have become important factors in the economy of Russia, a matter of intent attention of the host society. The mass and day-to-day contacts stimulated the formation of steady stereotypes as a tool of communication.

Migration Infrastructure

The first-comers, the "pioneers" of mass labour migration from Central Asia have been the inhabitants of Tajikistan, the Tajiks by their ethnic affiliation. They were pushed to migrate by the short-lived but extremely bloody civil war of the early 1990s. The mass flow of refugees (about one million people just for the CIS countries) paved the way for labour migrants.[1] The post-war economic dislocation and economic backwardness in general created the push-out factor that had already been long-standing and powerful by this time. The refugees organically became labour migrants.

Original Paper in Russian: *Preodolevaya "novye granitsy": trudovye migranty iz Tsentral'noi Azii v Rossii*—Translated by Susmita Bhattacharya.

They formed their "niche" also in the labour market. As newcomers, they could not count on the startling potentialities of the natives from the Caucasus who had massively assimilated Siberia ever since the Soviet times and accumulated substantial material resources, experience, as well as business and social connections. The very first Tajik labour migrants in fact started from zero, virtually from scratch. Therefore, they could only count on the sectors of most unattractive, dirty and poorly-paid occupations and employment. Doctors, scientists, lecturers, skilled workers, people with secondary and higher education turned unskilled labourers. A Tajik loader in the market, a seasonal construction labourer-worker became typical figures, even iconic ones. The city dwellers, the people with education and profession, with experience of life and studies outside their native places were the first to pave the way, along which subsequently moved their relatives and fellow-countrymen from villages and small towns.

They quickly formed a migration infrastructure—from organizing traffic to rendering intermediary services in the Russian cities. Its base consists of a stratum of various intermediaries and organizers. First of all are the "gang leaders"—the people forming groups of migrants ("gang") to execute certain jobs. In those groups they usually recruit their relatives, fellow-countrymen, and the people they personally know as well as who are well-known. The "gang leader" finds job in one of the Russian cities, enters into a formal or informal contract with the employer, settles all difficult problems related to official registration of papers and naturalization, supervises the production process, receives all the payments and distributes a part of it among the gang members. He manages all the inevitable conflicts with the representatives of the authorities, especially the militia, the employers and solves all the problems of day-to-day life (house rent, treatment, transferring their earnings to home, etc.). If the gang is small—he himself works at the construction site, but if it is big he only deals with organization. He has complete and absolute authority over the members of the gang and takes the responsibility before them for the success of a working season. For all this he gets a significant portion of the entire money earned (sometimes up to one half of it). To become a gang leader it is necessary to have substantial resources: construction profession, organizing capacities, leadership qualities, good knowledge of Russian language and contacts in the host society as well as authority in the homeland.

Sometimes, the intermediary and organizational functions are performed by a former migrant who has settled in one of the Russian cities. His status (Russian citizenship or residential permit) and his network of social contacts as well as acquaintances in the new homeland become additional resources. He might carry out the same functions, as a "gang leader" does, but often for a number of gangs.

The leaders and active workers of national-cultural societies that have been founded in the majority of large Russian cities turn out to be special type of intermediaries. The national-cultural societies are those social organizations that are based on ethnic criterion and intended for the development and strengthening of national culture as well as to protect the ethnic interests of their members. Implicitly they claim the role of representative of interests of the entire ethnic group and are often recognized as such by the local authorities. The local officials as well as the politicians regularly consult with the leaders of these societies, and their opinion is taken into account while solving the problems related to the migrants. The opportunity of such constant dialogue provides the elite of these societies unique intermediary resources.

The specificity of the intermediary networks and structures that have been formed is their flexibility as well as ability to branch out on the one hand, and their informal nature on the other. They have shown a high degree of efficiency and played a decisive role in the migration process. Their activities are aimed at gaining profit, but it would be wrong to consider them as purely market-based institution, just a mechanism of production and sale of intermediary services. Their flexibility and efficiency are largely determined by the fact that they form a patron-client relationship. The recipient not just pays (and pays highly) for the services, but also falls into the bondage of the "gang leaders" and other intermediaries. This way, a stable mechanism of social control and hierarchy of power is formed. From among the patrons there has already emerged quite a rich and influential migrant elite, efficiently blend fitting in with the host society.

Migration from Central Asian Republics

By the size as well as social and economic impact on the country, Saodat Olimova and Muzaffar Olimov consider the present scales of migration in Tajikistan as unprecedented.[2] According to a survey of 2007 (the times on the eve of the economic crisis), the volume of labour migration was more than 700 thousand people. It involves a sizeable section of Tajikistan's population numbering 7 million people, half of them being children and young people under 18. Every third household in the country has at least one member working abroad. In spite of the fact that the geography of the migration flows from

Tajikistan encompasses a number of countries (Kazakhstan, Ukraine, China, UAE, Afghanistan, USA), the labour migration has mainly been oriented towards the Russian Federation (97 per cent of the total number of migrants). The migrants work in such segments as construction (74.1per cent of the total migrants), trade (10.8 per cent), industry (4.8 per cent), agriculture (5.4 per cent) and other sectors (public utility services, education, etc. 4.8 per cent).

As a whole, the labour migration from Tajikistan is adapted to the needs and conditions of the labour market of the Russian Federation. The climatic conditions explain the seasonal prevalence of labour in Russia, which is particularly a characteristic feature for construction, mining industry, agriculture, retail street trade and public catering, i.e. those sectors where the majority of the migrants from Tajikistan work. A survey in 2007 showed that 73.1 per cent of the migrants work abroad seasonally, i.e. from February-March to October-November. The specificity of both the living condition as well as work in Russia, and the job of the seasonal labourers at home in Tajikistan, contribute to the formation of large-scale seasonal migration. The no-visa-required condition, developed transport connectivity between Tajikistan and Russia, low wages of the migrants in Russia preventing the workers to bring their families with them are also important factors. Within a short period, migration has become a structural feature of the economic and social life of Tajikistan. Within the span of 2006-08, the volume of remittances transferred by the labour migrants to Tajikistan increased from 1 billion to 2.6 billion dollars (by 2.6 times). According to the data by the National Bank of the Republic of Tajikistan, the volume of remittances in 2008 amounted to 46 per cent of the GDP of the country.

A few years later, the inhabitants of the neighbouring Uzbekistan, the migration potential of which is much higher than that of Tajikistan, began to move following the Tajiks, partly depending on the migration infrastructure built by them. And now, in many Siberian cities (for example, in Irkutsk) they have come to the top by the figure of officially registered labour migrants, outstripping the previously predominant Chinese.

According to L. Maksakova's assessment Russia accounts for more than one half of the total volume of labour migration from Uzbekistan, that is, not less than 400-450 thousand people. The labour migrants from Uzbekistan work in almost all the regions of Russia. The main spheres of their activities are construction (23 per cent), trade (18 per cent), services (19 per cent), as well as agriculture, industrial enterprises, transport.[3] There also exist higher estimates of the number of Uzbek migrants—up to 600-800 thousand people. It is difficult to give exact figures of their number due to the flaw in the record-keeping system, large seasonal mobility of the migrants and substantial illegal component. The academician Rustamzhon Abdullaev, referring to the Director of the Federal Migration Service of Russia Konstantin Romodanovskii, affirms that there were some 2 million citizens of Uzbekistan on the territory of the Russian Federation in 2008.[4] The volumes of remittances from Russia tell about the scales of labour migration and its significance. According to the Central Bank data, the total amount in 2010 was $2,835 billion. By this index, Uzbekistan ranked first among the CIS countries.[5]

Simultaneously, there was an intensive migration process from Kyrgyzstan. Sergei Naryshkin, the head of the administration of the president of Russian Federation, cited the official figures that in 2010 up to 600 thousand Kirghiz were working in the Russian Federation. But officially only 1,13,143 among them had the right to work in the Russian Federation. One-third of the labour migrants from Kyrgyzstan were involved in construction, 14.2 per cent in the sphere of services, 13.2 per cent in trade, 12.1per cent in manufacturing activity, 9 per cent in the sphere of transport and communication, and 5.7 per cent in agriculture. Their remittances this year accounted for $1.2 billion (according to the Ministry of Labour, Employment and Migration of Kyrgyzstan).[6] Many of them are actively and quite successfully engaged in trading business. As market dealers the Kyrgyz people have become an appreciable part of the urban communities. Special Kyrgyz rows of stalls have come up in the markets of many Siberian cities.

Formation of Attitudes and Stereotypes

The mass labour migrations are economically necessary and useful both for the countries of Central Asia and Russia. However, it does not remove the complexity of the problem of human communications, mutual adaptation of the peoples with vastly different cultures. The mass arrival of new people and formation of a new social phenomenon demanded establishment of a mechanism of adaptation to this of the people of the host society. And it was impossible to do without developing attitudes and forming stereotype. The myths and stereotypes took shape so fast and entrenched in the public consciousness so firmly for the simple and important reason that they were needed. This is an indispensable method for determining the place of the new peoples and new groups in the hierarchy of relationships and statuses. Through them a model of attitudes takes shape and functions. This is a tool of ideological mobilization and struggle for power; a tool to decide bureaucratic, regional or corporate interests. But the changes in attitude of the host society towards the migrants, would also change the structure of stereotypes, intensity of the presence of fears and animosity in them. The stereotype is, first of all, development of attitude. This is not so much a heuristic view, as evaluating and a way to streamline the social information. This is a sphere of a priori to/unscientific knowledge. Therefore, by condition stereotypes do not require critique of sources, verification, internal logic and consistency of separate postulates. But precisely it is they, and not positive scientific knowledge that shape the attitude of the society as well as authorities to the process of migration and the migrants. The stereotypes are structured mainly around xenophobic complexes, while reflecting the attitude prevalent so far towards the migrants.

The pioneering role of the Tajiks and their massive day-to-day and constant presence in the host society formed the "image of a Tajik." This word itself is full of new connotations. On the one hand, for the inhabitants of Russia it remains as an accustomed ethnonym and a name for an inhabitant of Tajikistan (that was formed during the Soviet times). On the other, however, it is now extended to all the natives from Central Asia, coming to Russia in search of job, mostly temporary and seasonal. Practically, it has become a synonym for the word *gasterbeiter* or "guest worker" which promptly entered into the mass language practice and became generally accepted term. There appeared set phrases like "Tajik labour" or "Tajik salary;" "To work like a Tajik does" and even "To work as a Tajik."

And the reason for this is not only the fact that very few people in the host society makes distinction between, say, a Tajik and an Uzbek. Now "Tajik" has become a mass and familiar figure, a part of daily life as well as day-to-day occurrence. He is remembered when one needs to hire a person on less money for a temporary job (to renovate apartment, for instance). The information about the "reliable Tajiks," that is about those who can do a job not only at cheap rate but also competently, spread flawlessly through informal channels, through acquaintances and relatives. It presupposes personal contacts with the migrants, and that also means formation of attitude.

Accordingly, an image and stereotype of "Tajik" is also formed. Naturally, he is a native of Central Asia, though not necessary actually a Tajik. Even with the numerical predominance of the Uzbeks, for example, they are practically absent in the public opinion and consciousness in this capacity though everybody, of course, knows about the existence of Uzbekistan and the Uzbeks. He is in no way a Russian or, according to the widespread definition, "Russian-speaking." In the process, it is implied that the person is not a European. Neither is he a Korean or German, whose ancestors were brought to Central Asia by Stalin's deportations. At this point, the racial characteristics are clearly implied though it is not verbalized, and often not realized. Nevertheless, the word "blacks" is used everywhere in xenophobic texts.

Sometimes, the ethnic Kyrgyz and Kazakhs are deduced beyond the frames of the category of "Tajik." The reasons may be different. The important fact for the formation of the image of a Kyrgyz is, as mentioned earlier, that many of them are actively and quite successfully engaged in trading business.[7] As market traders Kyrgyz have become an appreciable part of the urban communities in the recent years. Special Kyrgyz rows of stalls have appeared in the retail and cash-and-carry markets of many Siberian cities. This gets set by the local residents and creates stimulus for an attitude towards them precisely as Kyrgyz. But when they are engaged in unskilled physical job (especially in the sphere of community services) it does not happen and at this point they are "Tajiks."

Kazakhs are a separate problem. This is an important issue largely for the Western Siberia and the Volga region. They are classic labour migrants, although their number is not so big as the Tajiks and Uzbeks. But there are also a lot of indigenous people (in Kulunda, Gornyi Altai). In large Siberian cities (especially in Omsk) there are many Kazakhs who have settled here even since the Soviet period. They are already indigenous citizens, the people who have been deeply integrated into the Russian culture, the Russian citizens.[8] This prevents the shaping of a uniform stereotype in relation to them and considers all of them through the model of "Tajiks." Within the frameworks of post-colonial and post-imperial historiographical tradition being formed in Kazakhstan, inevitably ideologized, this situation has been expressed by G. Mendikulova [9] as how rigidly it separates the Kazakhs of "diaspora" (that is the migrants and their descendants) and the Kazakhs of irredenta (the Kazakhs living outside of modern Kazakhstan thanks to the movement of borders). This creates the classic ideologeme "divided nation," also emphasized by the choice (extremely controversial) of terms.

Thus, the stereotype of "Tajik" is formed by not only, perhaps also even by so many, ethnic connotations. It is essentially important that he is a labour migrant, "*gastarbeiter*." Here is a person, who is not just a visitor, but temporary, "migratory bird." His understanding is not disturbed by the fact that many migrants come to the same place for a span of many years, grow into a system of local social connections and relationships. And sometimes they also stay back here to live permanently, bring their families here or (more often) acquire them on the spot. Nevertheless, still they are characterized by temporality. This also implies the dubious status of their stay and work in Russia ("illegal migrants"). There is serious ground for this, since until recently the majority of the seasonal migrants from Central Asia did not have the permission to get engaged in labour activities. Following the liberalization of this procedure in 2006 their number has decreased, but it still remains significant. Whenever the degree of their integration crosses certain border, they cease to be "Tajiks" although fully aware of their Tajik origin and culture.

In the eyes of the social surroundings "Tajik" is a person of second category, low-status and deprived of rights, without any claim for a place in the social hierarchy, ready for any job, on the whole, anything for the sake of earnings. He is not even at the bottom of the social ladder—he is outside of it. As early as in the 1990s, I heard quite a common operational use of the word "slave" with reference to them from the officials dealing with the migration processes. This way they defined for themselves the status and place of the latter in the society. In the recent years, though, this word seems to have disappeared from their lexicon.

At the base of stereotype formation lies attitude. As compared with the Chinese and native Caucasians, with regard to a "Tajik," there is more rejection as well as desire to keep aloof rather than fear. They are afraid of "Tajiks" not only as labour migrants, but also competitors for workplaces, alternative resources. But this competitor seems to be weak. He is not supported by the might of power, energy, diligence and numerical strength, which they are afraid of about the Chinese. Neither do they have, as ascribed to the "Caucasians," the aggressiveness, willingness and capacity to use physical strength as well as resources of the corrupt state machinery.

The most important component of the growing migrant-phobic complex in Russia is to accuse the migrants of mass criminalization. The press always finds a way to highlight the cases when certain crime is perpetrated by a migrant. Especially when it comes to crimes against a person—murders, robberies, rapes. Frequently the proposition of migration threat is reasoned by it. Extremely rare and almost unnoticed attempts are made to compare the levels and patterns of criminality among the migrants with equivalent indicators of the population of the host society. As soon as the economic crisis began, there appeared a lot of alarmist statements by the politicians, journalists, officials that the migrants who remained without work would right away switch to criminal activities and that an enormous surge of criminality was awaiting Russia. The lonely voices of the professionals, who put such a prospect into question, submerged in this chorus. When the surge of criminality did not happen, this hysterical propaganda campaign abruptly came to an end.

In the complex of "criminal migrant" the "Tajiks" have a special place. They are accused of drug-trafficking. In the mass-media there has been constructed a fixed and strong semantic chord: the Tajik labour migrants have been equated with the traffic of drugs. On numerous nationalist websites a common chain is constructed: deadly threat to the society from narco-business—instances of Tajiks' involvement in it—charge of narco-trade against all the Tajiks call for their expulsion from Russia.[10] Frequent attempts are made to link the labour migration of the "Tajiks" with the threat of "Islamic extremism" and "Islamic terrorism." So far, however, it has not received any warm response from the common man.

There has not been developed any fear in the society towards an individual migrant and the "Tajiks" as a whole. Predominant is a condescending aloofness. They look at them as representatives of some other world, as "people out of glass." It is already several years that my students have been taking interview of the migrants within the framework of their training course. They carry it out in very diverse ways, but after this very many of them are genuinely surprised: "it turns out that they are also the same kind of people just as we are." Perhaps, the fundamental and accentuated aloofness as well as rejection are means of their own psychological support in a situation of an obvious and unfair inequality; a means to reconcile with the existence of a number of "slave."

Conclusion

The new migration situation in Russia, despite its short duration, has already demonstrated striking dynamics. The migrants from Central Asia have taken such a huge place in the life of the Russian society and have been such a unique phenomenon that it demanded to create both one's own, individual attitude and a stereotype. The Tajik of the Soviet era (an inhabitant of one of the union republics and a representative of one of the nationalities) was replaced by "Tajik." Its main attribute has become the word *gastarbeiter*, which entered the Russian language and went in mass use only in the 1990s. Until then it was extremely rarely used as a term in special literature. Originating in Germany, apparently, most completely and adequately it reflected the society's perception of the problem and attitude towards it. It reflected, in particular, the radical shift from the ethnic to migrant principle of stereotypization. It has been remarkably formulated in the heading of an article in the *Komsomol'skaya Pravda*, the most widely circulated and read newspaper of Russia, "Ect' takaya natsional'nost'—"gastarbaitery."[11] A book entitled "*Gastarbaiter*" enjoyed resounding success.[12]

The basic features of new stereotype are being drawn from the huge bulk of various latest texts. Gastarbeiter is a newcomer, not a local person, a "migrant" who has come from abroad to work, earn money and then to go away. His ethnicity, culture, country of origin and personal qualities are of no interest to anybody. His presence is not much desirable, it irritates, but one has to reconcile with him because there must be someone to do the dirty and low-paying jobs. He should "know his place," and this is the place that remains outside the social hierarchy of the host society. The less he is seen the better it is. The name Ravshan that came along with the Tajiks has been gradually becoming a common name and losing its ethnic binding. Now this is the name of a migrant, a "*gastarbeiter*/guest worker," a "Tajik." As was told by a chief of small construction in Moscow to the correspondent of *Izvestiya*, "the main advantage with the Ravshans against the Ivans is that you can easily 'throw' them 'away' ('throw away', that is, to deceive, not to return money-the author).[13]

In a popular television show "Our Russia" two comic "*gastarbeiters*/guest workers" Jamshud and Ravshan quite spitefully and venomously comment upon the current realities of Russian life. These are not the images of the Tajiks, (though this television show rouses great discontent in Tajikistan), but of the "*gastarbeiters*/guest workers," of the people who are strangers, newly arrived and detached.[14] This detachment, in fact, enables them to see and comment particularly sharply on the absurdity of many situations that are common for "their people." The fact itself that the "*gastarbeiters*/ guest workers" have become television heroes, also speaks about how massive and familiar has become their presence, and the image formed and easily understandable by everybody.

With the image of a "migrant," a "*gastarbeiter*" is inextricably linked migrant-phobia, which gradually has been replacing the previously predominant ethno-phobia. In the massive and ubiquitous presence of migrants many people, as also in the countries of Western Europe and the USA, see a threat of erosion of the "civilisational foundations," the basic and fundamental categories of culture. This fear is that the inevitable changes associated with the massive presence of the culturally alien migrants might change the host society so much that the latter would vanish into its former kind.[15]

The migration process has been distinguished in powerful dynamics. It forms new realities, radically transforms the old ones. It frightens and irritates many (often the majority of them) representatives of the host society. The presence of migrants creates new conflicts, gives new forms and values to the old ones. And it is extremely important, so that the image of a "Tajik" does not become a permanent stigma, so that the current situation does not form a virtual, but no less a stable ghetto out of this.

Notes and References

1. V. Dyatlov, "Tadzhiki v sovremennom Irkutske: Pervoprokhodtsy novoi migratsionnoi volny?" *Perspektivy migratsii korennykh narodov Tsentral'noi Azii v Rossiyu* (Novosibirksk: Novosibirkskii gosudarstvennyi universitet 2003), 152.
2. S. Olimova and M. Olimov, "Migratsiya iz Tadzhikistana v krizis: pervaya zarisovka s natury," *Demoskop Weekly*, no. 415-16 (22 March-4 April 2010).
3. L. Maksakova, "Uzbekistan v sisteme mezhdunarodnykh migratsii," in *Postsovetskie transformatsii: otrazhenie v migratsiyakh*, Zaionchkovskaya Zh. and Vitkovskaya G.S. (eds.) (Moscow: IT Adamant' 2009), 323-49; *Demoskop Weekly*, no. 415-16 (22 March-4 April 2010).
4. R. Abdullaev, "Uzbekistan: vyzovy, ugrozy, problemy i resheniya-II," Internet journal *Kapital strany* (15 March 2010). www.kapital-rus.ru › articles/article/176564/.
5. www.b2blogger.com/pressroom/release/90444.html
6. http://news.mail.ru/politics/2950953/; http://news.mail.ru/economics/5336203/
7. V. Agadjanian, A. Nedoluzhko, G. Kumskov, "Eager to Leave? Intentions to Migrate Abroad among Young People in Kirgizstan," *International Migration Review* 42, no. 3 (2008): 620-51; A. Kurtov, "Geometriya politiki," *Nezavisimaya gazeta Dipkur'er* (13 January 2003); V. Petrova, "Novyi prodovol'stvennyi rynok poyavitsya v Irkutske," *Vostochno-Sibirskaya Pravda*, 9 October 2008.
8. V. Dyatlov, S. Ryazantsev (ed.), *Stabil'nost' i konflikt* v *rossiiskom prigranich'e. Etnopoliticheskie protsessy v Sibiri i na Kavkaze* (Moscow: Nauchno-obrazovatel'nyi forum po mezhdunarodnym otnosheniyam 2005); E. Sadovskaya, *Migratsiya v Kazakhstane na rubezheXXI vèka: novye tendentsii i perspektivy* (Almaty 2001); E. Larina, O. Naumova, "Kosh-Agachskie kazakhi-migranty," *Vestnik Evrazii*, no. 2 (2008): 44-65; A. Bondarenko, "Rossiiskie kazakhi ob'edinilis' v Samare," *Nezavisimaya gazeta-Regiony*, 25 June 2007.
9. G. Mendikulova, *Kazakhstanskaya diaspora: istoriya i sovremennost'* (Almaty: Vsemirnaya assotsiatsiya kazakhov 2006).

10. See for instance Novosti Ekaterinburga: Ekaterinburg On.Line: Otkrytoe pis'mo po povodu tadzhikov poluchil segodnya gubernator Sverdlovskoi oblasti Eduard Rossel', http://www.e1.ru/news/spool/news_id-265267-section_id-15.html
11. There exists such a nationality-*gastarbeiters* (guest worker)—translator's note. See D. Steshin, "Est' takaya natsional'noct'—gastarbaitery," *Komsomol'skaya Pravda*, 17 July 2007.
12. E. Bagirov, *Gastabaiter* (Moscow: Populyarnaya literatura 2007).
13. *Izvestiya*, 6 October 2008.
14. G. Sapozhnikova, "Dzhamshud, Ravshan i tadzhiskie obidy na Rossiyu," *Komsomol'skaya Pravda*, 26 May 2009; V. Nikonov, "Nauka yvazhat," *Izvestiya*, 29 July 2009.
15. S. Huntington, *Kto my? Vyzovy amerikanskoi natsional'noi identichnosti* (Moscow: AST Publishing House 2008).

38

Demographic Transition in North Asia: Paradoxes of History

Vladimir A. Isupov

Demographic transition is a global process all over the world. It has already been completed in Europe, North America and some of the Asian countries. In a number of Asian countries it has entered the stage of its rapid development. But many countries in the Asian continent are yet to go through this difficult and, in certain sense, painful path connected with the radical breakdown of entire socio-cultural relations and ties.

Northern Asia, territorially being a part of Russia, in general, has completed the demographic transition. It is interesting to follow how the demographic transition developed there, because it shows what might be in store for other Asian countries.

The concept of demographic transition was developed during the years 1909-34 by the French demographer A. Landry. But strictly speaking the term "demographic transition" belongs to the American demographer F. Notestein. The demographic transition, which marked a radical transformation of the entire demographic subsystem of society, became a major event in the history of the population of the Asiatic Russia of the twentieth century. It signified a change in the type of reproduction of population during which the traditional type of reproduction, with its high mortality and fertility went into the historical non-existence, giving way to a rational (modern) type of reproduction with its inherent reduced parameters of mortality and fertility. In connection with this, the efficiency of action of all the social mechanisms regulating the production of immediate life significantly increased.

Original Paper in Russian: *Demograficheskii perekhod v Severnoi Azii: paradoksy istorii*—Translation by Susmita Bhattacharya.

According to the generally accepted theoretical views, the reduction in mortality opens the first phase and only after that follows the reduction in fertility. Thus, for determining the initial phase of demographic transition it is extremely important to find the starting point of decrease in mortality. This article seeks to highlight this issue. Since the modernization of mortality at first affects the cities and then spread to the villages, we would turn to the urban population in search of the initial state of the demographic transition. The task is difficult because of the fact that the demographic transition in our country during the twentieth century took, as writes V.B. Zhiromskaya, an irregular character.[1] Its indicators now appeared, now disappeared. Eventually, it determined the peculiarity of the "Russian-Soviet" variety of demographic transition.

The process of modernization of mortality as an inalienable element of demographic transition has been quite exhaustively described in scientific literature.[2] Conceptually it is based on the theory of epidemiologic transition, formulated by A. Omran.[3] At the foundation of his doctrine lies the idea, according to which the radical changes in the structure of causes of mortality are the base of changes in the parameters of mortality. It is basically the socio-historical process of redistribution of the causes of mortality from the predominance of exogenous factors caused by the influence of adverse living conditions of people (infections, respiratory diseases, gastrointestinal diseases) to the endogenous ones (cardiovascular and other diseases caused by natural aging of the human body) as well as quasi-endogenous (oncological ailments) ones. The shift of mortality to the older age groups seems to be the consequence of a profound structural reconstruction of the causes of mortality. Accordingly, the life span of the generations increases. Thus, in fact, the reduction in mortality is not so much a quantitative change as it is a fundamental transformation of all its qualitative characteristics.

The empirical parameters of demographic transition in certain regions of Russia have been presented in the scientific literature in an extremely fragmentary manner. Even in the most thoroughly researched studies the authors, as a rule, confine themselves to comparative indicators of mortality and life span before and after the demographic transition along the line: such used to be before and such has become now. As a result, the historical process is basically either dropped out of the scope of scientific observation or painted in so bold strokes that the details disappear. Meanwhile, the elicitation of details, based on painstaking analysis of numerous statistical sources often leads to unexpected results. Conducting this kind of specific-historical research is a job not so much of the demographers, but primarily of all the historians who know the methods of source-study analysis. The historical demography must show its worth in the long run.

Demographic Transition in Siberia

In the historical demographic literature till now there is no definite answer to the phenomenon of demographic transition in Siberia. In the late nineteenth and early twentieth centuries, evidence points to fact that traditional type of reproduction of the population was predominant in Russia, and all the more, in her eastern regions, fundamentally being based on the patriarchal way of life of the majority of the Russians. According to an estimate by V.A. Zverev, the dynamics of overall coefficient of mortality in the cities of the Western Siberia (in the borders of Tomsk, Tobol'sk and Akmolinsk guberniyas/provinces) presented the following figures:

Table 1: Overall Coefficient of Mortality in the Cities of the Western Siberia

Year	*Coefficient of Mortality (‰)**
1893-1895	35.0
1902-1905	33.0
1906-1909	40.3
1910-1914	33.1

* Here and further the overall mortality rates have been cited in promille (from Lat. Pro mille) of per 1000 people of the population, as it is customary in historical demography, by a special sign ‰.

Source: A. Omran, "Epidemiologicheskii aspect teorii estestvennogo dvizheniya naseleniya," *Problemy narodonaseleniya. O demograficheskikh problemakh stran Zapada* (Moscow 1979), 73.

Without questioning the reliability of the figures and accuracy of calculations of such a knowledgeable historian as V.A. Zverev, let us note that a reader does not find any significant reduction in the mortality rate of the above-mentioned data. During the years 1893-1914 it oscillated to one or the other side, but never went down below 30%. In our opinion, the difference between the mortality rates of the years 1893-95 and 1910-14 lay in the random fluctuations and was not so significant in order to draw a conclusion that this was the beginning of the process of demographic modernization. An authoritative demographer as R.I. Sifman refuted the fact of reduction of mortality in Siberia between the years 1901 and 1913.[4] No fundamental changes in the mortality rate during that period, immediately preceding the revolution has been registered, even in the more "advanced" European Russia, in terms of demographic modernization. According to P.M. Dmitrieva and E.M. Andreev, for two decades immediately preceding the revolution, there were no dramatic changes in the mortality rate—there was its highly insignificant and fluctuating decrease only among certain age groups.[5]

But most importantly the overall coefficient of mortality cannot be used as an evidence of initiation of the process of demographic transition. It is too unsophisticated an instrument, highly dependent on the distorting effects of structural factors. Identification of demographic transition presupposes an indispensable study of such nodal characters of modernization of mortality, such as transformation of the structure of causes of death rate as well as its age parameters and, ultimately, the indicators of life expectancy.[6] Until this work is done, the conclusion about the beginning of the demographic transition based on the overall factors of natural movement of the population remains unfounded.

Problems of Modernizing Demographic Transition

Before the outbreak of the First World War the parameters of mortality in Siberia were of extremely archaic nature. Because of incomplete statistics of population movement in the Russian Empire during the early twentieth century, we have at our disposal relatively reliable information on the structural indicators of mortality only in Omsk, the largest city in the region at that time.[7] According to the data meticulously prepared by V.E. Klyachkin, in the year 1913 the overall mortality in Omsk was 29.3% and the rate of child mortality reached 31.9%.[8] The share of the deceased children below 5 years of age exceeded 57% in the total number of death.[9] The increased child mortality caused the prevalence of death among the groups dying at the early age. The main reasons for the high mortality—both general and infant—were infectious and gastrointestinal as well as respiratory diseases. Suffice it to say, that out of every 1,000 born 159 children below the age of 1 year died of gastro-intestinal disorders, 57 of pneumonia and 28 children of infections (measles, scarlet fever, whooping cough, etc.). Among the adults, the major causes of death were tuberculosis, typhoid, dysentery and pneumonia.[10] The factors of so-called endogenous and quasi-endogenous etiology were relegated to the distant periphery of the structure of causes of death. And if on the eve of the World War II, such a structure of mortality was predominant in the largest Siberian city, then what would have been happening in the remote corners of the region?

These figures are fairly sound evidence of the existence of such phenomenon, which the Polish demographer E. Rosset, following the Frenchman A. Sauvy, cleverly called "demographic primitivism."[11] And it is unlikely, that in the year 1913, 845 Siberian physicians,[12] scattered across the vast territory, populated by people untrained in sanitary health, could meet the global challenge of providing epidemiological transition.

In this light, it seems that the assertions about development of the process of demographic modernization in Siberia at the turn of the nineteenth-twentieth centuries are not substantiated by statistical facts, and consequently are unproven. At the same time, one cannot but take into account the undeniable socio-economic and cultural progress, which was characteristic for Siberia in the early twentieth century, connected with the construction of the Trans-Siberian Railway, peasant resettlements and accelerated urbanization. But even taking this into account, one can only talk about the formation of separate, extremely poorly expressed prerequisites (mainly in the cities), which in the future, under favourable circumstances, could give a start to the full-scale modernization process of mortality. But this "future" was not destined to become a reality—Russia entered an era of wars and revolutions. The process of accumulation of prerequisites necessary for a reversal of the demographic transition, not only slowed down but, on the contrary, made themselves felt clearly regressive trends.

The next, and as it turned out, another fruitless attempt to modernize the demographic subsystem of Siberia was made in the second half of the 1920s. But even during these years, the factors of exogenous origin were predominant among the causes of mortality of the inhabitants of Siberia. Suffice it to say that, in 1928, the proportion of the people died of infectious diseases was 25% out of the total number of the deceased in the cities of Siberian krai.[13] These deaths occurred mainly through such diseases as measles, diphtheria, whooping cough, dysentery, typhus and typhoid, and tuberculosis. The Siberian people even died of such "medieval" diseases like smallpox and cholera. As before, the statistics recorded numerous deaths from gastro-intestinal diseases and diseases of the respiratory organs. The widely spread exogenous factors of death led to the mortality of infants whose immature organism had lower immunity exceed the number of death of 70-year old men.[14] In 1926 the coefficient of child mortality rate[15]in the cities of Siberian krai was 24.2%.[16] And what is more, out of every 100 children who died at the age of 1 year, 23 died of diarrhoea and enteritis, 16 of pneumonia, 4 of dysentery, 3 of whooping cough, and 2 of measles.[17]

The archaic structure of the causes of mortality, ultimately, determined the low life expectancy of the population. The life expectancy of the urban population of Siberia during 1926-27 was only 38 years,[18] and the major factors reducing the life expectancy were of exogenous origin. According to the estimates made by R.I. Biryukova for the population of the USSR as a whole, during 1926-27, the increased mortality from tuberculosis reduced the potential life expectancy of the population almost by 5 years, from scarlet fever by 1.5, from dysentery by 0.6, and from typhoid by 0.4 years.[19] No such data exists on Siberia, but this does not essentially affect the findings. Thus, the structural indicators of mortality in the second half of the 1920s differed a little from the analogous characterstics, recorded before the beginning of the World War II, which was in fact found in his study by V.E. Klyachkin.[20]

Undoubtedly, during the NEP the infectious and gastrointestinal disease declined. This was a result of the overall stabilization of the internal political situation in connection with the introduction of NEP, some rise in the material well-being of the population, spreading of sanitary culture among the mass of the people and the state activities for the development of public health. Accordingly, in the structure of the causes of death, the exogenously determined mortality slowly but steadily declined, the indicators of infant mortality decreased and life expectancy increased. The fact that not a single person died in the region from such dangerous diseases like cholera and plague in those years, and that during 1925-27 the death from smallpox in urban areas at once decreased by two times, gives evidence that the first stage of epidemiological transition in Siberia was taking shape (albeit weakly) in the second half of the 1920s.[21] Altogether, this is a strong evidence of real and not imaginary start of the demographic modernization.

However, the process that had hardly begun once again got interrupted. The forced industrialization and collectivization through violent means started in the USSR. The brutal internal political line of Stalin, eventually caused a demographic crisis, which during 1932-33 developed into a massive disaster. In these circumstances, regressive trends prevailed in the dynamics of the demographic subsystem of the Soviet society. Hunger and chronic malnutrition, growth of epidemics, collapse of the public health system, forced deportation of the peasants not only resulted in mass extinction of the population, but practically preserved the mortality inherent in the traditional type of reproduction of the population, and what is more, in its worst manifestations. During 1933, in the structure of causes of death in the cities of Western Siberia, the infectious and parasitic diseases took the main place—they accounted for almost 30 per cent of deaths. The ailment of digestive system accounted for 20 per cent, and of respiratory organs 13 per cent.[22] In the official nomenclature of the causes of death appeared one line: "diseases of malnutrition."[23] It was in fact a structure of mortality, corresponding to the medieval society, but by no means of the twentieth century.

The demographic situation in the USSR became somewhat stable only after it got over some of the obvious consequences of starvation during 1932-33. But even during the late 1930s and early 1940s the fundamental changes in the dynamics of mortality compared with the 1920s are not recorded by statistical sources. During the late 1930s and early 1940s the mortality of archaic type prevailed in the Western Siberia with an obvious predominance of exogenously determined causes, which is confirmed by the statistical data, presented in the Table 2.

Thus, in 1940, almost 14 per cent of deaths occurred due to tuberculosis, over 16 per cent by pneumonia, almost 15 per cent by toxic dyspepsia and acute gastroenterocolitis; about 13 per cent by measles in the Altai krai (the situation here reflected the trend across Siberia).

Table 2. The Structure of Causes of Death of the Urban Population of the Altai Krai[24] (% of the Total)

Causes of death	*1940* г.	*1942* г.	*1944* г.
Typhoid, paratyphoid, and typhus	0.8	2.2	1.6
Measles	12.6	3.0	1.2
Scarlet Fever	0.6	1.2	0.0*
Whooping Cough	1.3	1.2	0.6
Diphtheria	1.0	1.8	0.8
Dysentery	1.4	3.5	0.6
Hemocolitis	0.9	0.7	0.1
Tuberculosis	13.9	14.1	18.8
Cancer	2.8	2.3	4.6
Arteriosclerosis	0.9	0.9	1.6
Heart Disease	6.4	12.3	16.7
Pneumonia	16.1	13.9	10.0
Toxic dyspepsia	8.3	5.4	1.6
Acute gastroenterocolitis	6.5	3.4	2.2
Carbuncle, furuncle, phlegmon, abscess	0.1	0.2	0.2
Other and uncertain causes of death	26.4	33.9	39.3
Altogether	100.0	100.0	100.0

* Index of less than 0.1 per cent.

Source: Current Archives of the State Committee on Statistics of the Altai Territory.

Nevertheless, the end of the 1930s and the beginning of the 1940s can be assessed as a period when once again began the weak process of formation of the preconditions that prepared the approaching demographic transition. The government, apprehensive of epidemics that had washed away the labour force, adopted a series of measures to tackle the number of infectious and gastrointestinal cases and, in particular, tightened the health legislation. Roughly by the end of 1930s, the Soviet people adapted to all eventualities caused by fluctuations in the political line. It did not take long to have its impact. The life expectancy of the population of the USSR during the years 1938-39 reached 47 years of age.[25] In 1940, the overall coefficient of mortality of the urban population of Western Siberia dropped to 20.7%.[26]

However, this barely incipient sprout of demographic transition was once again crushed. From the very beginning of the Great Patriotic War, the index of mortality of the logistic population began to increase rapidly, which was caused by the failure in organizing evacuation, deterioration of the living conditions, spreading of infectious and gastrointestinal diseases, and respiratory diseases. In 1941, 22 people died out of every 1000 urban population of Western Siberia, in 1942 it was 26.[27] The proportion of deaths from infectious and gastrointestinal diseases in 1942 increased significantly, even with respect to the anything but successful 1940. In 1942, the share of the deceased from typhoid, paratyphoid, scarlet fever and dysentery in the Altai krai was more than double compared to 1940. The share of people who died of typhus right away rose by 7 times. The causes of death of endogenous origin were relegated to the sidelines.

Of course, this situation was not something typical just for the Altai krai. It covered the whole territory of Western Siberia. In 1942, the proportion of typhoid and typhus in the structure of the causes of death of the citizens of the Omsk oblast' reached 1.1 per cent, dysentery and hemocolitis 5.1 per cent, toxic dyspepsia and acute gastroenterocolitis almost 12 per cent, measles, scarlet fever, whooping cough and diphtheria over 5 per cent, tuberculosis 16.1per cent, pneumonia almost 16 per cent.[28] Of the overall number of people who died in 1942 in the Novosibirsk oblast', the proportion of deaths from typhus was 1.3 per cent, from major paediatric infections almost 8 per cent, from dysentery and hemocolitis over 4 per cent, tuberculosis almost 16 per cent, from pneumonia 15.8 per cent, from toxic dyspepsia and acute gastroenterocolitis over 11 per cent.[29] The demographic situation in Western Siberia did not differ from that, which was prevailing in general all over the logistic regions of the country. Thus, in 1942, the proportion of deaths in the RSFSR due to acute infections reached 13 per cent, chronic infections 12 per cent, respiratory diseases 16 per cent, toxic dyspepsia and acute gastroenterocolitis 11per cent.[30]

Nevertheless, the historical paradox is that the first significant results in the modernization of mortality in Russia were received in the logistic regions of the USSR during the Great Patriotic War. At the end of 1942 and the beginning of 1943, the demographic subsystem of Western Siberia entered a qualitatively new stage in its history. Since then, the mortality rate of the population in logistiic regions very rapidly began to decline. During 1942-1945 the overall coefficient of mortality rate of the urban population of Western Siberia decreased by 2.5 times.[31]

The reasons varied for such unusual phenomenon as decline in the mortality rate in the logistic regions of a country leading a war that was the most severe in its history and which accompanied sharp deterioration in the living conditions. In order to understand the crux of the processes that radically changed the direction of the demographic development of Western Siberia, let us once again turn to the analysis of the structure of causes of death of the urban population. As evidenced by the data in Table 2, during 1942-44 the proportion of deaths due to the causes of exogenous origin, such as measles, scarlet fever, whooping cough, dysentery, pneumonia, toxic dyspepsia, acute gastroenterocolitis noticeably decreased in urban settlements of the Altai krai. Simultaneously, the proportion of deaths due to endogenously and quasi-endogenously determined causes like cardiovascular diseases and malignant tumors increased. Consequently, during the war, the process of qualitative reformation of the structure of causes of death began in the cities of Western Siberia.

Since it was often the children and young people who died of the diseases of exogenous natuare and the older people of the diseases of endogenous and quasi endogenous origin, the major outcome of this process was gradual shift of mortality from the range of younger ages to the older ones.

Table 3 clearly demonstrates that the mortality rate in 1940 was concentrated mainly in the pediatric age group up to 5 years. During the years of war there was a clear trend of shift of mortality to the age groups above 40 years. And if, in the Altai krai the proportion of those who died at the age 40 years and above accounted for 21.2 per cent before the war, in 1945 it was more than half, in the Omsk oblast' it was 22 per cent and 48 per cent respectively. Meanwhile, in 1940 the share of deaths below the age of 5 years in the Altai krai accounted for 66 per cent and 22 per cent in 1945, in the Omsk oblast' it was 63 per cent and 22 per cent respectively.

Table 3. The Age Structure of the Deceased (in %)

Age (years)	*Altai krai **		*Omsk oblast'**	
	1940 r.	1945 r.	1940 r.	1945 r.
0-4	65.7	22.4	63.0	22.0
including below the age of 1 year	40.6	13.1	41.2	12.1
5-9	2.7	4.5	2.6	4.9
10-14	1.6	2.5	1.9	2.7
15-19	1.6	4.2	1.9	4.6
20-24	1.3	3.6	1.5	4.4
25-29	2.0	2.7	2.1	2.9
30-34	2.1	4.6	2.2	4.3
35-39	2.2	4.5	2.2	4.6
40-44	2.0	5.0	2.1	5.2
45-49	1.8	4.6	2.0	4.8
50-54	1.7	4.5	1.9	5.0
55-59	2.0	5.1	2.2	5.3
60 and above	13.7	31.6	14.2	27.8
Age is not specified	0.5	0.2	0.2	1.5
Altogether	100.0	100.0	100.0	100.0

*According to the administrative-territorial structure of the corresponding ages.
Source: Current Archives of the State Committee on Statistics of the Altai Territory; GAOO, F.2122, Op. 1, D. 1133, L. 22; D. 1141, L. 30-30 ob.

Advancing through the age scale, the mortality age became higher, which was the most important demographic consequence of the reduction in deaths from infectious and gastrointestinal diseases. The children and young people increasingly survived till the older ages. It is ironic, but most likely the life expectancy of the logistic population of Western Siberia (excluding the losses in war) increased during the years of the Great Patriotic War. The process of aging of the mortality, of course, was not typical only for Western Siberia, but for all the regions of the RSFSR, which were not subjected to occupation, as has been substantiated by the latest historical and demographic studies.[32] One of the many paradoxes of Soviet demographic history is that the process of modernization of mortality had started during the period of Great Patriotic War, and more precisely at the turn of 1942-43, when it was possible not only to stop the sharp increase in mortality of the logistic population, but achieve its reduction. It would be impossible without the tough and even brutal measures taken by the Stalinist state. The authorities in the face of terrible threat had to take the steps that they should have done back in the 1920s and 1930s, but what they cynically ignored while solving the industrial, military and political problems. However, this forced paternalistic socio-demographic policy in the war years aimed at adaptation of the population to semi-starved existence in the damp and cold barracks, by means of improving health care and maximum tightening of sanitary control turned out to be quite effective. Against the backdrop of low level of material support and increased morbidity it enabled to reduce the infant mortality and somewhat reduce the mortality among the older generations, especially among men.

This kind of pragmatic policy was not an outcome of the "Stalinist" care for the people, but it had its own purpose to increase the working capacity of those employed in the production and to maximise the number of people fit to serve the army. In the hierarchy of values ??of the communist government the actual solution of the problem of super-mortality, as before, remained at one of the last places after the military, economic and political goals. But objectively, this strategy yielded the result that, apparently, was not expected even by the creators of the Soviet socio-demographic policy. This incidental branch of Stalinist paternalism, in fact, became a major "demographic achievement" of the war years. The result was a paradoxical situation in which, as noted by the French scholar of the demographic history of Russia A. Blum, the mortality rates were "too low for the existing economic situation."[33] On our part, let us add that the mortality rate in the logistic regions of the USSR was paradoxically low for the level of material well-being of the population that was typical for that hard time. This turns the demographic history of our country into such a specific and exclusively "Soviet" phenomenon, which, apparently, will not be reproduced in any other country of the world.

Thus, in the demographic history of Western Siberia we find that a number of attempts were made to switch over to rational type of reproduction. But the three out of them were unsuccessful. Only the fourth time managed to "Get the height." This kind of "march on the spot" that held back the demographic modernization and, ultimately, caused a noticeable lag of the Soviet Union and then also of Russia from the developed countries of Europe and North America was certainly an indirect (and sometimes direct) consequence of political decisions, and repeatedly plunged the country into demographic disaster during the course of the twentieth century.

Notes and References

1. *Naselenie Rossii v XX veke: Istoricheskie ocherki очерки*, T. 3, Kn. 1, 1960-1979 (Moscow 2005), 269.
2. A.G. Vishnevskii, *Demograficheskaya revolyutsiya* (Moscow 1976); Vosproizvodstvo *naseleniya i obschestvo: Istoriya, sovremennost', vzglyad v buduschee* (Moscow 1982); *Vosproizvodstvo naseleniya SSSR*

(Moscow 1983); *Demograficheskaya modernizatsiya Rossii*, 1900-2000 (Moscow 2006).

3. A. Omran, "Epidemiologicheskii aspect teorii estestvennogo dvizheniya naseleniya," in *Problemy narodonaseleniya. O demograficheskikh problemakh stran Zapada* (Moscow 1979).
4. R.I. Sifman, "Dinamika chislennosti naseleniya Rossii za 1897-1914 gg.," in *Brachnost', rozhdaemost', smertnost' v Rossii i v SSSR*, Sb. Statei (Moscow1977), 72-3.
5. R.M. Dmitrieva and E.M. Andreev, "Snizhenie smertnosti v SSSR za gody Sovetskoi vlasti," in *Brachnost', rozhdaemost'*, 31-32.
6. Life expectancy is the number of years on an average that an individual is expected to live from a generation born on the stipulation that throughout the life of this generation the mortality rate will remain unchanged—the author.
7. V.E. Klyachkin, *Estestvennoe dvizhenie naseleniya goroda Omska po parallel'nym dannym za 1913, 1916, 1923-1926 gg.* (Omsk 1928).
8. Klyachkin, *Estestvennoe dvizhenie naseleniya*, 6.
9. Klyachkin, *Estestvennoe dvizhenie naseleniya*, 8.
10. Klyachkin, *Estestvennoe dvizhenie naseleniya*, 13, 18.
11. E. Rosset, *Prodolzhitel'nost' chelovecheskoi zhizni* (Moscow 1981), 16-17.
12. *Statisticheskie materialy po sostoyaniyu narodnogo zdraviya i organizatsii meditsinskoi pomoschi v SSSR za 1913-1923 gg.* (Moscow1926), 132, 134, 136.
13. *Statistika Sibiri*, Vypusk 3 (Novosibirsk 1930), 66-7.
14. "Smertnost' i prodolzhitel'nost' zhizni naseleniya SSSR, 1926-1927 gg.," *Tablitsy smertnosti* (Moscow, Leningrad 1930), 136-37.
15. The coefficient of child mortality rate is the number of infants died below one year of age out of every 1000 born.
16. *Estestvennoe dvizhenie naseleniya v Sibkrae za 1925-27* gg. (Novosibirsk 1930), 26.
17. *Estestvennoe dvizhenie naseleniya v Sibkrae*, 25.
18. "Smertnost' i prodolzhitel'nost' zhizni, 136-37.
19. R.I. Biryukova, "Tablitsy smertnosti po prichinam smerti," in *Problemy demogreficheskoi statistiki* (Moscow1959), 339.
20. Klyachkin, *Estestvennoe dvizhenie naseleniya*, 7-36.
21. Естественное движение населения в Сибкрае… С. 49, 54-71.
22. GARF, F. A-374, Op. 23, D. 222, L. 1-2.
23. GARF, F. A-374, Op. 23, D. 222, L. 1-2.
24. Materials on the Altai krai provide good opportunities to compare in the chronological aspect, because the administrative borders of the krai almost did not change during the entire Great Patriotic War.
25. *Naselenie SSSR*, Spravochnik, (Moscow 1983), 68.
26. *Naselenie Rossii za 100 let (1897-1997),* Stat. sbornik (Moscow 1998), 86, 130.

27. V.I. Isupov, *Glavnyi resurs Pobedy. Lyudskoi potentsial Zapadnoi Sibiri v gody Vtoroi mirovoi voiny (1939-1945 gg.)* (Novosibirsk 2008), 114.
28. GARF, F. A-373, Op. 11, D. 161, L. 2-2 ob.
29. GANO, F. 11, Op. 2, D. 736, L. 40-40 ob.
30. V.I. Isupov, *Demograficheskie katastrofy i krizisy v Rossii v pervoi polovine XX veka: Istoriko-demograficheskie ocherki* (Novosibirsk 2000), 156.
31. Isupov, *Glavnyi resurs Pobedy*, 114.
32. O.M. Verbitskaya, *Naselenie* rossiiskoi derevnii v 1939-1959 gg. *Problemy demograficheskogo razvitiya* (Moscow 2002), 130; G.E. Kornilov, "Ural'skoe selo i voina," *Problemy demograficheskogo razvitiya* (Ekaterinburg 1993), 69.
33. A. Blum, *Rodit'sya, zhit', i umeret' v SSSR* (Moscow 2005), 110.

39

Migration Processes in the Post-Soviet Space (Russia and Central Asian Region)

Sayan Darzhaev

Today the migration processes are integral part of world development, and the post-Soviet space occupies a special place in the migration map of the world. An intensive expansion of the migration process was observed in the beginning of the 1990s, in connection with the disintegration of the Soviet Union. Therefore by the end of the twentieth century, the phenomenon of migration became a component factor of all the global issues. This demanded new approaches to migration policy that contributes in achieving and maintaining the balance of interests of international actors, who are participating to regulate the migration processes in the post-Soviet space. In the 1990s the problems related to the regulation of migration of people went beyond the scope of demographic policy and demanded new sets of approaches as well as joint efforts of different state departments and social organizations. The effects of migration are apparent in various spheres: political, social, economic, cultural and psychological and others. Moreover, these effects are both positive as well as negative in nature and thereby become source of conflicts. All this determines the topicality of studying the problems of migration in the post-Soviet space. In 1995, the migration in all the countries of Central Asia took place predominantly within the limits of each country. Nevertheless, quite a large number of people arrived in and left the CIS countries. The largest number of migration, both in absolute and relative terms, took place in Kazakhstan, the migration network of which with the former countries of the USSR surpassed the similar network of the rest of all four countries of Central Asia taken together.

If we consider the total number of migrants from Central Asia to the countries of the former USSR during the period since its disintegration (1991-96), in Kazakhstan it was 1,375, 880, in Kyrgyzstan 3,81, 130 and in Uzbekistan 691,340 (no data available for Tajikistan and Turkmenistan).[1] As it is evident from the above data, the number of migrants from Kazakhstan during the said period was more than that of Uzbekistan and Kyrgyzstan taken together. The migrants from these republics of Central Asia mostly went to Russia. According to the available statistics, their number during this period was more than 2.5 million, including: 12,69,119 people from Kazakhstan, 3,06,594 from Kyrgyzstan, 2,89,077 from Tajikistan, 1,07,298 from Turkmenistan, and 5,81,707 from Uzbekistan.[2]

Almost half of all migrants arrived from Kazakhstan. In relative terms, compared to the total population also the number of those who left Kyrgyzstan amounted to a high proportion while in absolute terms it exceeded even the number of migrants from Tajikistan, which at that time was engulfed in civil war. The outflow of population from Turkmenistan and Uzbekistan to Russia for every 10000 population was approximately the same, since the former is almost five times less than the later, both in terms of outflow of its people to Russia, and in terms of its total population.

As per the data of the *Goskomstat* of the Russian Federation, a declining trend was observed in the number of people who arrived during 1994-95 and the first half of 1996 from all the republics of Central Asia. In its turn, the outflow from Russia to Kazakhstan and Uzbekistan increased in 1995 compared with the year 1994. But even in their migration networks with Russia during these years all the republics of Central Asia sustained large negative balance, i.e. not increase, rather migration loss, the aggregate estimate of which in 1995 was more than 3,62000 people (in favour of Russia).[3] The overwhelming majority of the migrants from Central Asia to Russia were Russian. There were a lot of Ukrainians, Tatars and Bashkirs. A segment of German and Jewish population left Central Asia and arrived in Russia. A certain, though quite insignificant, number of migrants were representatives of local nationalities, and each group of migrants from all the five republics having all five nationalities. At the same time, the titular nationality in each of the republics represented to a great extent.

The social changes in recent times fundamentally changed the political and social situation in the former Soviet republics, and millions of people became forced migrants. Close and intensive migration network was built between Russia and the states of Central Asia. And besides, while Russia and Kazakhstan were exchanging primarily the migrants who are moving to a permanent place of residence, all the other republics were suppliers of cheap and unskilled labour, firstly to Russia, and next to Kazakhstan. The statistics show that about 6,00,000 citizens of Tajikistan and 3,50,000 citizens of Kyrgyzstan are labour migrants, with more than 80 per cent of them going to Russia for earnings, and the rest to Kazakhstan.[4] The main sources of labour migration flows from the region are the three states of Uzbekistan, Tajikistan and Kyrgyzstan. According to various estimates, at the end of 2005, in Russia, there were 1.8 to 3.5 million labour migrants from the countries of Central Asia, nine-tenth of whom arrived from the above-mentioned countries.[5]

In the post-Soviet period de-urbanization has gained momentum in all the countries of Central Asia. It was especially high in Tajikistan, Uzbekistan and in Kyrgyzstan, in the first of which today almost three-fourth live in rural areas, and in the other two almost two-third of the entire population. The degradation of the educational system led to the fact that the majority of the native population have low level of education. At the same time, the people of Central Asia has a favourable age structure of labour resources—more than one-third are children in the age group of 14 years and nearly 60 per cent people are of working age group.[6] In contrast to the developed countries that have experienced migration boom and are not connected with permanent immigration, Russia encountered intensive migration flows at a time, when her economic base was in a critical situation. Migration, having acquired a distinct ethno-social character during the past few years, brings adjustments in the lives of local *sotsiums*, influences the policy taken by the sovereign states, and primarily changes the individual characteristics of those, who are forced to move to other territories in search of peaceful life and better future. At the moment, the Russian Government is facing the following problems: how to make foreign policy as regards the countries, which have Russian speaking populations; what to do with the immigrants, refugees and displaced persons in the territory of Russia; how to respond to the ongoing "brain drain" from the Russian Federation; what to do in order to attract the highly qualified personnel; and how to regulate labour migration. As per the scales of international migration the post-Soviet space has occupied the second place in the world after the USA. The flow of foreign labour force, despite some restrictive measures, may increase in the near future. In the opinion of the specialists of the World Bank, Russia as a receiving country has already received a huge effect of the mass and cheap labour migrants. Thanks to the migrants in Russia there were fewer bankruptcies of the enterprises, new kinds of business have developed, and growth of investments in construction got stimulated. Simultaneously the migration has also been creating certain problems. Illegal migration is leading to a rise in crime and has become a "breeding ground" for corruption. The real problem for the authorities is the non-payment of taxes by the illegal migrants and the unaccounted remittances of the migrants. Nevertheless, according to the specialists of the World Bank, there are rather positive aspects than negative ones for Russia in the inflow of labour migrants.[7] In general, the processes of mass movement of people in the Central Asian region annually involves up to four million people, or more than 15 per cent of the able-bodied population, out of which not less than three million constantly reside in the territory of Russia. In the conditions of present-day crisis the number of labour migrants to Russia from Central Asia has not significantly declined, though less than half of them are working legally. It is interesting that in spite of the measures to increase the effectiveness of migration policy within the CIS (Commonwealth of Independent States), taken since the year 2006, the situation with the Central Asian migrants remains difficult. The main challenge in this is the absence of legal status of one and half to two million foreign citizens in the territory of the RF. At the same time the number of each Central Asian diaspora implies its further increase, which in the next five years might bring the total number of the native people from Central Asia in Russian Federation up to six million people, i.e. to the level that would be able to paralyse the functioning of the migration structures of Russia.

According to data by the experts in the field of migration policy, not less than 80% migrants, working in Russia, are originally from the countries of the former USSR. At present there is no alternative in Russia to fill the man-power resources, except at their expense. Today, not a single construction either private or state can do without involving foreign workers; in the capital, generally, they work as janitors, general labourers and are engaged in other heavy, but not so prestigious jobs. The negative aspect of the modern migration situation in Russia is the huge gap in skill level between the emigrants and the immigrants. It is usually high with the emigrants from Russia and low with the immigrants. As the researchers point out, the positive effects of the influx of population from the near abroad to Russia is, first of all, the reduction in the labour shortage caused by the demographic crisis in the country. It is precisely this migration influx from the former republics of the USSR that to a considerable extent compensates for the loss of able-bodied population of the Russian Federation as a result of depopulation. There is dearth of man-power in some sectors of the Russian economy, especially in those jobs that do not require high skills and pay low wages. The labour migrants partially make up this shortage. *The foreign labour force often fills up the vacancies, which are not prestigious for the Russian citizens and therefore not in demand among the local population.* In addition, the efficiency and quality of work of the foreign labour force is sufficiently high, and the *competition from it gives good guidelines and incentives to the local population.*[8] On the whole, this facilitates the development of the service sector, and has a positive effect on the quality of life of the entire population. The Central Asian migrants are not so burdensome to the Russian budget. On the social welfare of the migrants Russia spends significantly less money, than, for instance, Western Europe.

At the same time, only about 1 million 700 thousand citizens of different states are officially registered to work in Russia. According to the law "On Legal Status of Foreign Citizens in the Russian Federation" the labour migrants notify the Federal Migration Service (FMC) about their stay once a year. The work permit must be registered within 10 working days (standard two weeks), but this actually takes at least one month. As a result, many employers either do not register the migrants officially, or tritely buy work permits through numerous brokerage firms. Besides, according to various statistical data, today there are 2 to 4 million illegal migrants in Russia. From the legal point of view the illegal migrants are subject to a much greater risk. After all, such a migrant can be offered a disproportionately lower wage than a citizen of Russia, or not to be paid at all, or to be partially paid. The employers are well aware that the migrants do not have any protection and they will not approach any law enforcing authorities, labour inspections, court, etc. By the way, some law enforcement officers themselves consider the illegal migrants as one of the sources of their income. The procedure of mass legalization could certainly break these negative processes. This is much more advantageous to Russia than forced deportation of the illegal migrants to their homeland. The USA and the European countries (Italy, Belgium, and Germany) have passed immigration amnesties more than once. And even a poor country like Poland has recently announced amnesty for immigrants. Experience shows, that for any state it is much more useful to get taxes into its exchequer from the migrant workers than to process their fines, deportations and engender corruption in the ranks of the officials. The Federal Migration Service (FMC) already has positive experience of expedited procedure of legalisation of the labour migrants. Thus, as per the data of the expert of the State Duma of the RF, Rauf Verdeev, in 10 regions of Russia, the representatives of the Service themselves help the illegal migrants to process migration cards. Such spot actions have already enabled to cover more than 200 thousand people, but this is obviously not enough. The practice, in our opinion, should be continued and drastically expanded. The important positive aspect is that in the last three years the leaders of all the Central Asian states, especially Kazakhstan and Kyrgyzstan, have increased their attention on optimization of institutional control in the area of trans-border migration processes. However, practically there is no development of inter-regional coordination of migration policy. As for the Russian vector, the institutionalization of inter-governmental cooperation in the field of migration policy has been achieved only in the mutual cooperation between Russia and Uzbekistan, who by now have ratified three special agreements concerning the fight against illegal migration, the status of labour migrants, and their readmission. Realizing the considerable acuteness of the problems, the Kyrgyz and Tajik authorities are striving, first of all, not to reduce the migration flow of their own citizens, secondly, to secure special resolutions for increasing the quotas for labour migrants in various regions of Russia. Kazakhstan, on its part, is concentrating mainly on the issues concerning seasonal migrants in its southern border areas, which are considered in the context of protecting the territorial integrity of the state. Evaluating the factors of labour migration of the inhabitants of Central Asia in the CIS space, it is necessary to underscore that mass movements of regional labour force has not solved the key contradictions of the Central Asian societies, rather in many cases has undermined the prospects of their elimination. The constant outflux of up to half the male population of Tajikistan and about one third of Kyrgyzstan is blocking any plans for rejuvenating any actual production sector. In the case of Uzbekistan, the trend of "dispersion" of labour resources of young ages, which has become steady, is severely limiting the possibilities of modernization of the Uzbek economic system, both in general and in its key segments. Besides, shadow structures of interaction between exporters and importers of labour forces have been formed everywhere in the countries of Central Asia whose incomes are comparable with the revenues from the major items of the state budget, but are out of the purview of state control. On the Russian side, the growth of negative phenomena associated with the labour migrants from Central Asia is due to purely criminal challenges and due to the fact that in the past few years they have become one of the most stable segments of shadow employment of the Russian Federation. It is also significant that illegal migrants from the far abroad enter Russia through the "Central Asian corridor" and the problem of migrants in general has become a popular proposition of the Russian politicians, who appeal to the protesting potential of the electorate. Thus, the number of migrating human resources from Central Asian region and the lack of effective control over their flows are intensifying the contradictions between the current and strategic objectives of the state authorities in the CIS space. The labour of the migrants is making noticeable contribution in solving the economic problems of both the sending and receiving countries, but the system to counteract the negative effects of migration processes is not yet sufficiently effective. The formats to deal with migration processes in the post-Soviet space remain in a nascent stage. As far as the Central Asian side is concerned, the Russian authorities probably are to encounter the prospects of maintaining considerable flow of migrants from all the countries of the region, even including Turkmenistan. Therefore, such aspects as, improvement of special training of the staff, intensification of attention to the widening of the flows of labour migrants from the countries of Central Asia in the provincial Russian cities, and measures to support the dialogue of the Central Asian states on the issues of inter-regional labour migration. Moreover, in the process of developing bilateral cooperation with the countries of Central Asia, it would be appropriate to include, as a separate item of the agenda, the question of teaching Russian language amidst the titular population. The consequences of the current foreign labour migration from the countries of Central Asia should be considered from the perspective of both the sending (countries of the Central Asian region) and the receiving sides—Russia. As the International Labour Office experts observed, "... because international migration depends on the linkages between sending and receiving countries and is itself a means of interaction between the two, determinants and consequences cannot be looked at from a single country perspective."[9] The Russian specialists, arguing the policy objectives in the field of migration and settlement, first of all distinguish the task of finding the most preferred contingents of migrants, who can most easily integrate into the Russian ethno-cultural environment. The basic aim of the activities is *normalization of the migration inflows, attracting the migrants, who do not pose any threat to its national security.*[10] The experts point to the need of *a sound migration policy, without closing the doors for immigration that is desirable on demographic considerations, but also not keeping the doors open too wide and uncontrolled.*[11] The Concept of Demographic Development of the Russian Federation during the period till the year 2015, among the priorities in the field of migration indicates the necessity of attracting immigrants to the Russian Federation, primarily from the CIS member states. It is believed that the migrants from Central Asia are preferred on the basis of geopolitical considerations, since those countries of this region, from which mostly the migrants come, do not have a common border with Russia. The intense migration processes is an objective characteristic of the modern world. In this respect the CIS space also is no exception. I would like to express my hope that the multilateral and bilateral cooperation among the post-Soviet states would facilitate to reduce the number of migration challenges to their development.

Notes and References

1. "Rynok truda v stranakh Sodruzhestva Nezavisimykh Gosudarstv v tsifrakh i diagrammakh," *Statisticheskii Sbornik* (Moscow: Mezhdunarodnyi komitet Sodruzhestva Nezavisimykh Gosudarstv 1996), 15.
2. *Sodruzhestvo Nezavisimykh Gosudarstv v 1996 godu, Statisticheskii Ezhegodnik,* Mezhdunarodnyi komitet Sodruzhestva Nezavisimykh Gosudarstv (Moscow 1997), 16-17.
3. *Sodruzhestvo Nezavisimykh Gosudarstv v 1996 godu*, 16-17.
4. A.S. Chesnokov, "Migratsionnaya politika i migratsionnye protsessy v stranakh ShOS", in A.S. Chesnokov (ed.), *Izvestiya Ural'skogo gosudarstvennogo universiteta* 3, no. 80 (2010): 154.
5. K. Borishpolets, A. Babajanov., "Migratsionnye riski stran Tsentral'noi Azii", in Аналитические записки Analiticheskie zapiski MGIMO (U) MID, Russia, Vyp. 2 (22), (Moscow 2007): 4.
6. *Sodruzhestvo Nezavisimykh Gosudarstv v 2003 godu, Statisticheskii Ezhegodnik,* Statkomitet SNG (Moscow 2004): 102.
7. Mansoor Ali, Quillin Bryce (eds.), *Migration and Remittances: Eastern Europe and the Former Soviet Union* (Washington, D.C.: World Bank 2007), 19.
8. G. Vitkovskaya, S. Panarin (eds.), *Migratsiya i bezopasnost' v Rossii* (Moscow: Interdialekt Plyus 2000), 104.
9. R.E. Bilsborrow, Hugo Graeme, A.S. Oberai, Zlotnik Hania, *Statistika Mezhdunarodnoi Migratsii: Rekomendatsii po sovershenstvovaniyu system sbora dannykh* (Moscow: Academia 1999), 6. Quoted from the original book in English *International migration statistics: Guidelines for improving data collection systems* (Geneva: International Labour Office 1997), 6-7.
10. L.L. Rybakovskii, *Kontseptsiya demograficheskoi politiki: (metodologicheskie voprosy)* (Moscow: Ekon-Inform 2002), 25.
11. Vitkovskaya and Panarin (eds.), *Migratsiya i bezopasnost' v Rossii*, 104.

40

Age and Gender Structure of the Population of the Countries of Asia: General and Specific

Yana A. Kuznetsova

Key Indicators of Demographic Development of the World's Population

For studying the general trends and specificities of age structure of the countries of Asia, which is the purpose of this study, it is necessary to start by examining the main indicators of the demographic development in the world: fertility, mortality and types of reproduction of the population, etc.

The current regional differences in the growth of world population are due to the socio-economic and demographic developments of the twentieth century, especially in its second half. First of all, they are characterized by intense growth of population of the developing countries, in contrast to significant reduction in the growth rate of population of the developed countries of the world (Map. 1).

Mankind reached the first billion around the year 1830, after 100 years (1939 г.) the second, the third after 20 years (1960 г.), the fourth after 15 years (1975), and the fifth after 12 years (1987).

After the Second World War the nations of Asia and Africa, Central and South America having attained their independence, got the opportunities to widely utilize the achievements throughout the world in the spheres of medicine and public health. With the help of the world community (the UNO, WHO and others) the countries succeeded in eliminating many of the epidemic diseases, which had taken the lives of tens of thousands of people. As a result, within the next decades the mortality of population began to decrease significantly, which, along with maintaining a high birth rate led to a sharp increase in natural growth. At the expense of the Asian and Africa countries, the world's population began to increase sharply.

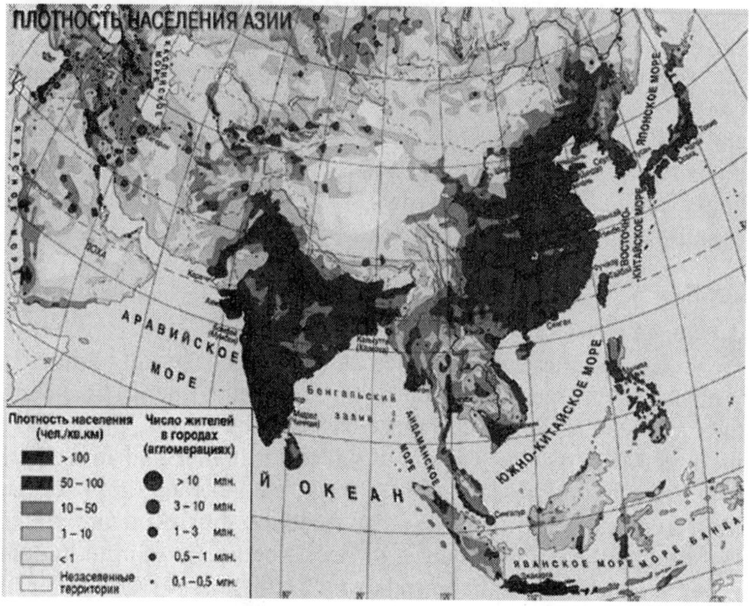

Map 1. Density of Population of Asian Countries

Source: http://baigigitov.narod.ru/

In the 1990s the world population increased daily by 2,54,000 people. The industrially developed countries accounted for less than 13,000 of this total, and the developing countries shared the remaining 2,41,000: 10 per cent were in Latin America, 20 per cent in Africa, and 60 per cent of this total were in Asia.[1]

In the year 2000, the most populated countries of Asia were China with 1.3 billion people, India with 1 billion people, Indonesia (200 million), Bangladesh (150 million), Pakistan (140 million) and Japan (125 million).[2]

The dynamics of the world population and also the specificities of the age and gender composition are, first of all, determined by the process of reproduction. It is the correlation of fertility and mortality rates that ensures uninterrupted rejuvenation and replacement of human generations.

The demographers mark out two types of reproduction, which have characteristic features. The first type of population reproduction (the contemporary one) is distinguished by low indicators of fertility, mortality, natural growth, in addition to stabilization of the number of population and process of population "ageing" (i.e. increase of ratio of old people in the total population). This is the characteristic type of the developed countries of Europe, CIS, North America, Australia and Japan.

The second type of reproduction of the population (the traditional one) is characterized by high natural growth due to high birth rate and relatively low indicators of mortality rate, as well as constant increase of population number, and the major proportion of the total being young people. This type is distinctive for the developing countries of Africa, Latin America, and the entire Overseas Asia.

On an average, the total coefficient of fertility rate in the world is 23%,[3] including 26% in the developing countries and 11% in the developed ones.

In Europe and North America the indicator of fertility birth rate is higher by 1.4 times, in Asia by 2.3 times, in Latin America (including the Caribbean region) by 2.5 times, in Africa by 4 times, particularly in West Africa where it is about 4.5 times higher and in Central America by 4.6 times. In terms of birth rate indicator, not only the large regions (continents) are at variance, but even the states constituting them. For instance, the total coefficient of birth in Asia is 26 %, with Oman and Yemen having the highest (44%), and Japan with the lowest (10%). A similar situation prevails in Africa, where the total coefficient of birth rate equals to 40%, the highest coefficient being in Mali and Angola (51%) and the lowest in Mauritania (17%).[4]

The general trend in the world population is a transition to birth control within the family and gradual decrease in birth rate. Let us mention that in the countries of Asia and Africa this transition is taking place slowly.

The total birth rate coefficient is quite contrasting in the post-Soviet space as well. In 2000, it did not exceed 10% in the Russian Federation, Ukraine, Latvia, Estonia and Belarus, about 15% in Lithuania, Georgia, Armenia, Moldova, Kazakhstan, and 20% in Azerbaijan. The indicator reached 22%-26% only in the countries of Central Asia (Uzbekistan, Kyrgyzstan, Tajikistan, and Turkmenistan).[5] The religious factor had significant influence in such sharp differentiation, along with the time difference in transition from traditional population reproduction to modern one and other socio-economic factors.

From the viewpoint of reproduction of world population, the total fertility coefficient (the number of children to each woman during the entire period of her fertile age) is an important indicator. On an average it was about 2.9 in the world by the year 2000. The declining trend of birth rate has been noticed: the general pattern, on an average reduced it to 3% in the world just in two years (1998-99). Currently, the total coefficient of birth rate in the developing countries has reached 3.3, and in the developed ones did not exceed 1.6.[6]

In comparison with Europe this indicator in North America exceeds by 1.4 times, and by 2 times in Asia, 2.1 times in Latin America (including in the Caribbean region) and in Africa by 4 times higher, including 4.3 times higher in East Africa and 4.6 times in Central Africa.

Among the post-Soviet states the total fertility coefficient did not exceed 1.3 in Ukraine, Belarus and Estonia, 1.2 in the Russian Federation and Latvia (the number of children to each 100 women during the entire period of her fertile age was within the range of 120-130), while even for simple reproduction of the population it was not has not necessarily been less than 210 children.[7]

The mortality coefficient has undergone a major transformation towards a decline to the extent of human development associated with the elimination of mass epidemics, improvement of medical knowledge, decrease in the frequency of devastating wars and a number of other progressive changes for the better. In spite of this, the total coefficient of mortality still differs from continent to continent and from country to country. In 1998 it was 15% in Africa, including 18% in East Africa, 16% in West and Central Africa, 7% in Latin America, 8% in North America and Asia, 1% in Europe, while 13 % in East Europe.[8]

Poor health care and tough socio-economic conditions are the main factors that contribute to the high mortality rate in the developing countries. In the developed countries, they are the deformed age structure of the population, environmental pollution with hazardous substances and adverse social phenomena (drug addiction, prostitution, road accidents and others).

In year 2000, the highest indicator of mortality among the countries of the post-Soviet space was in Ukraine (15%), followed by the Russian Federation and Latvia (14%), Belarus and Estonia (13%), Moldova and in Lithuania (12%), and Kazakhstan (10%). Whereas, less than 10% has been observed in Tajikistan, Uzbekistan, Turkmenistan, Kyrgyzstan, Armenia, Azerbaijan, and Georgia.[9]

The coefficient of infant mortality represents highly specific indicator of intensity of mortality in contrast to the overall coefficient. It is absolutely justified to consider this as one of the vital aspects of development of the society, and in general precisely on the basis of this the development level of healthcare system of a country is assessed.

In 2000, on an average 58 children up to the age of 1 year died to each 1000 births in the world, including 64 in the developing region and 8 in the developed one. This indicator is high in Africa (91%), especially in East Africa (104%) and Central Africa (103%), followed by Asia (57%) and Latin America (36%). It is low in Europe (10%) and North America (7%).[10]

The coefficient of infant mortality among the countries of the erstwhile USSR is relatively low in Estonia and in Lithuania (10%), followed by Belarus, Armenia, Ukraine, Latvia, the Russian Federation and Georgia (12%). Comparatively it is high in Azerbaijan, Moldova, Kazakhstan, Uzbekistan and Kyrgyzstan (19-28%), and it is especially high in Tajikistan (32%) and Turkmenistan (42%).[11]

The correlation between fertility and mortality gives an idea about the natural growth of population. In case fertility exceeds mortality, the growth of reproduction of population, as a rule, is guaranteed. And on the contrary, if there is more death than birth, with other conditions being unchanged, depopulation is inevitable. This would lead to an absolute natural decline in the population. Thus, in the end of the twentieth century, the natural growth of population on an average was 14% to each 1000 people in the whole world. However, in this correlation the difference between the developed (1%) and the developing (17%) regions amounted to 16%.

Africa made a distinction (25%) among the continents with high natural population growth, especially Central Africa (30%) and West Africa (29%), followed by Latin America, the Caribbean region (18%), and Asia (15%). The North America was characterised with low indicator (6%), and Europe with a negative one, especially East Europe (minus 4%).[12]

By the end of twentieth century, the depopulation among the post-Soviet states was observed in Ukraine and Latvia (minus 6%), the Russian Federation (minus 5%), Belarus and Estonia (minus 4%), and Lithuania (minus 1%). Despite the declining trend in fertility rate, the demographic pattern ensuring growth of population reproduction was the characteristic feature of the countries of Central Asia (Uzbekistan, Tajikistan, Kyrgyzstan, and Turkmenistan).[13]

All the above mentioned demographic trends in the world at the end of the twentieth century testifies the presence of specific characteristics and contrasts in the dynamics of development of different countries and continents. The traditional type of population reproduction has been maintained in the developing countries, which led to a sharp rise in the population and so-called demographic explosion. On the other hand, the low fertility rate and "ageing" population have led to the depopulation and demographic crisis in the developed countries.

Distribution of World Population by Gender

The gender structure of the world population has distinctive features. The issue of gender imbalance in various countries has become the most pressing in this direction. Let us note that in childhood, both in the world as a whole and in specific regions, the male babies are predominant. This is explained by the fact that worldwide per year on an average male births exceed the female births by 4 million. In the able-bodied age similar predominance sustains throughout the world, but in half of the regions, the balance swings in favour of women. As to the elderly age, the balance everywhere in this group is in favour of the women. For instance, the sharp predominance of women in the CIS by almost 16.5 million is first and foremost explained by the impact of the First World War, civil war and to a great extent the Second World War, as well as the very long lifespan of the women in the CIS countries. Roughly the same reasons influenced the gender composition of the population in the Europe, where in all the countries, other than Ireland and Iceland, women are in majority. Their predominance is particularly high in Austria and FRG.

Sharp swing in the gender composition is not a characteristic feature for the countries of Africa, and in the overwhelming majority of these countries the number of men and women are almost equal. Nevertheless, some predominance of males is observed in the northern and Arab-Muslim part of the continent, while women are majority, for instance, in East Africa. In North America, as a region of relatively new colonization and mass influx of immigrants—primarily men—the male population predominated for a long time. But gradually the swing in favour of women was observed initially in the US and then in the 1970s in Canada. This, in particular, concerned the elderly. In Latin America, as in Africa, the number of men and women are almost equal. In Australia, as a country with continuing mass influx of immigrants, till the early 1970s the males were dominant as in Canada. Thereafter a slight swing in favour of the women was observed. In the developed countries the males are predominant in rural areas and women in the cities, whereas in the developing countries it is on the contrary—the female population is in majority in the rural areas and men in the cities.

The Characteristic Features of the Age-Gender Structure of the Countries of Asia

The current "demographic explosion" in the countries of Asia has significant characteristics. The rapid population growth in Europe was primarily due to socio-economic changes, i.e. it followed the economic growth and progressive changes in the social sphere. Just an opposite scenario is observed in the Asian countries: the rapid growth of population considerably overtakes the economic and social development, thus exacerbating the already difficult problems of employment, social sphere, provision of food, ecology.

Yet another distinctive feature of the current "demographic explosion" is its super-cardinality in comparison with the last century. The decline of the level of mortality is occurring much faster in the developing countries, which with the high level of fertility that has been more prolonged than in Europe, will lead to a more intense demographic growth, having huge accumulative effect. The population growth in the Asian countries, observed during 1970-1990s, exceeded by more than twice the maximum level attained in due time by Europe.

The current "demographic explosion" also encompasses quite a large part of the world population, and directly or indirectly affects the entire world community, by turning a local demographic problem into one of the global problems of modern times.

It should also be noted that the Asian countries are characterized by almost universal predominance of male population. The only exceptions are Japan, Indonesia, Myanmar, Yemen, Israel and Cyprus. Numerically the highest balance in favour of males is in South and East Asia (in India by 24 million, in Pakistan by 4.5 million, in China by 31 million). The predominance of males is also characteristic for all the Arab-Muslim countries of South-West Asia. This is explained by a number of reasons, including the highest mortality of women due to early marriage, frequent child-birth, constant hard labour at the working place and home. The social transformations of the twentieth century are just beginning to influence the gender composition of the Asian population.

At the beginning of the twenty-first century, the power of the current "demographic explosion" mostly continued to be supported by a very young age structure of the population of Asian countries (Fig. 1).

The youngest country is Pakistan, where people aged 65 years and above comprise only 3 per cent of the population, and children up to 14 years account for about *2/5* of the total population (Table 1).

The median age of the population of Pakistan as well as some neighbouring countries like Iran, Iraq and others does not exceed 18-20 years (Table 2).

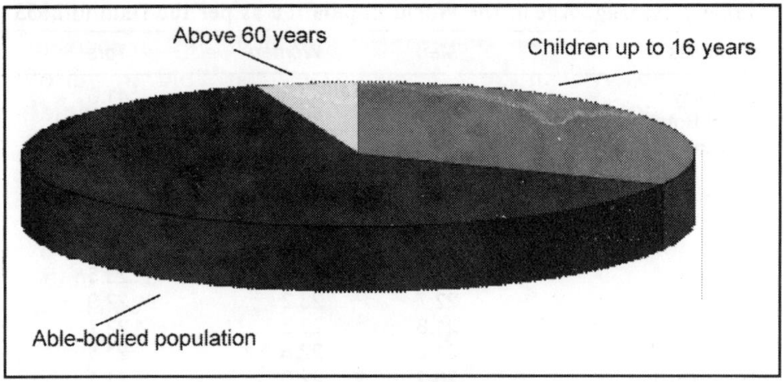

Fig. 1. The Age Structure of the Population of the Asian Countries at the End of the 20th Century

Source: http://www.mir-geo.ru/aziya/k/nasel/vozr-stru

Table 1. The Dynamics of World Population According to age (%)

Country	*2000*			*2005*		
	Up to 14 years (%)	*From 15 to 64 years (%)*	*65 years and above (%)*	*Up to 14 years (%)*	*From 15 to 64 years (%)*	*65 years and above (%)*
Pakistan	41.00	55.00	4.00	39.60	56.30	4.10
Iraq	42.00	55.00	3.00	40.00	57.00	3.00
Tajikistan	42.00	54.00	4.00	38.50	56.70	4.80
Turkmenistan	38.00	58.00	4.00	35.7	60.20	4.10
Uzbekistan	37.00	58.00	5.00	33.50	61.70	4.80
Kyrgyzstan	36.00	58.00	6.00	31.60	62.30	6.20
India	34.00	62.00	4.00	31.20	63.90	4.90
Mongolia	34.00	62.00	4.00	28.70	67.70	3.70
Iran	34.00	61.00	5.00	27.10	68.00	4.90
Kazakhstan	27.00	65.00	8.00	23.70	68.40	7.90
China	25.00	68.00	7.00	21.40	71.00	7.60
USA	21.25	66.11	12.64	20.60	67.00	12.40
Great Britain	19.00	65.00	16.00	17.70	66.50	15.80
Russia	18.00	69.00	13.00	14.60	71.30	14.20
Germany	16.00	68.00	16.00	14.40	66.70	18.90

Source: http://www.chinalist.ru/facts/index.php?p_lang=0

The demographic transition to the modern type of reproduction has been taking place at a very slow pace. These countries have not made significant progress in reducing the annual growth of population and fertility.

Table 2. Average Age of the World Population as per the Data of 2003

Countries	*Men*	*Women*	*Total*
Germany	39.9	42.8	41.3
Great Britain	37.3	39.5	38.4
Russia	34.7	40.3	37.6
USA	34.5	37.1	35.8
China	31.2	31.7	31.5
Kazakhstan	26.6	29.7	28.2
India	24.1	24.2	24.1
Mongolia	23.2	23.9	23.5
Iran	22.7	23.2	22.9
Kyrgyzstan	21.8	23.6	22.7
Uzbekistan	21.2	22.5	21.8
Turkmenistan	20.2	22.0	21.1
Pakistan	19.7	20.0	19.8
Tajikistan	19.0	19.6	19.3
Iraq	18.9	19.1	19.0

Source: http://worldgeo.ru/asia

India (the second most populated country in the world after China) also continues to have high rate of population growth. Each year almost 25 million babies are born in India. The high fertility has been and still remains the main driving force behind the population explosion. In the process, the population explosion makes it gravely complicated to solve the basic economic and social challenges faced by the country. During 1901-91 the average population density in India grew from 27 to 267 persons per sq.km. At the same time, it is observed, that India was perhaps the first among the developing countries which actively began to launch the idea of family planning on an international scale back in the 1930s. The correlation of genders in India is characterized by the following figures:

- at birth—112 boys per 100 girls;
- up to the age of 15—110 boys per 100 girls;
- 15-64 years—106 males per 100 females;
- above 65 years—90 males per 100 females.

The correlation throughout the country on an average equals to 106 males per 100 females.[14]

The children and young people up to 18 years represent a large section of India's population (Tables 1, 2). The median age of the population of India in 2003 was equal to 24.66 years, being almost the same for males and females (males: 24.64, females: 24.67).[15]

The most populated country in the world is China. For the last 60 years the population of China increased by 2.5 times, from 540 million to 1.328 billion people. At present, the annual growth is almost 7-8 million people, and because of the population growth it requires more than 25 per cent growth in the national revenue.[16]

The males considerably exceeding the female population (519.4 million, or 51.5 per cent, and 488.7 million, or 48.5 per cent respectively) is the feature of the structure of China's population.[17] In the PRC the number of men exceeds that of women by 30.7 million. There are 106 men per 100 women. There are a number of provinces and regions in China where male population highly exceeds female population. In contrast to India, the PRC is characterized by less proportion of children in the entire population (26 per cent and 34 per cent respectively).[18] This is due to the successful implementation in China of the policy of encouraging families with fewer children. The age structure of China's population is characterized by intense process of growth of proportion of the group of working-age people. In the late 1960s, the young age group accounted for 43 per cent of China's population.[19] However, as a result of the birth-control measures the ratio of the population up to 15 years has slightly decreased, and that of the age group from 65 years and above has relatively increased (Table1). China's population aged 15 to 64 years increased by 72.2 million in absolute terms during the period 2000-07, i.e. from 889.3 to 961.5 million.[20] The average age of China's population is 31.5 years (men—31.2, women—31.7).[21]

The political developments of the first half of the 1990s and the disintegration of the USSR caused some reduction in the fertility indicator of the former Soviet republics—the states of Trans-Caucasus and Central Asia (Tables 1, 2). However, by the end of the 1990s the fertility rate still remained very high especially in Central Asia in comparison with the other post-Soviet European states. The indigenous population of these states, especially in the rural areas, still retains the traditional type of reproduction. Here, the demographic transition to the modern type of reproduction has just begun, Kazakhstan and Kyrgyzstan are characterized by more intense process of transition, which is due to the presence of numerous Russian-speaking population. In the 1990s, the coefficient of reproduction in the Central Asian states was: 1.264 in Kazakhstan, 1.702 in Kyrgyzstan, 2.281 in Tajikistan, 1.880 in Turkmenistan, and 1.867 in Uzbekistan.[22]

In the year 2000, the Central Asian countries were also characterized by a high total fertility indicator (on an average 3.5 or 4.0 children per woman, which is even higher than Bangladesh, Vietnam, Malaysia, Mongolia), as well as the presence of fairly young age structure.[23] Tajikistan, Uzbekistan, Turkmenistan and Kyrgyzstan were among them. In 2002, the annual growth of population in Turkmenistan was by 1.82 per cent, in Uzbekistan by 1.63 per cent, in Tajikistan by 2.13 per cent. In Kazakhstan the population increased quite slowly, per year altogether by 0.17 per cent. The average age of the population of these countries is 28.2 years.[24] The youngest population lives in Tajikistan and in Turkmenistan, where the average age is 23 years.[25]

The Demographic Situation in the Countries of Europe

Along with the demographic explosion observed during the second half of the twentieth century, there emerged demographic crisis with all its severity during 1970s-80s and especially in the 1990s that primarily affected the developed countries of the world. The crux of the current demographic crisis is sharp deterioration in the development of population, which is reflected in sharp decline of population growth in the developed countries, as well as certain crisis of the institution of family, some deterioration in the quality of population growth, and its demographic ageing.

The trend towards a sharp drop of fertility as observed in the developed countries of the world is substantially below the level that ensures normal reproduction of the population. In addition to the process of depopulation, the decline in fertility leads to a significant demographic ageing of the population or increase in the proportion of elderly and old people, reduction of labour resources and increase of the "economic burden" on the economically active population.

The current process of depopulation and natural population loss, which is characteristic for Russia as well, the demographic crisis that started from 1991 has not been overcome. However, the average age of Russia's population is slightly higher (37.6) than Germany (41.3), Great Britain (38.4) and other European countries (Tables 1, 2).

The origins of the European demographic decline dates back to the years 1914-18, which was the beginning of the end of world colonial system. Later on, the change of the vector of demographic growth intensified: there was population growth in the colonial countries due to the decline in its mortality, while the drop in fertility continued in Europe.

The Second World War, which engendered both the direct losses of population and exacerbated the decline of fertility in Europe, became the driving force behind the collapse of the colonial system. The paradox of acceleration of this process was the rapid post-War growth of the European economy, which called forth the wave of re-immigration of the European population of the colonies to their historical homeland.

In the second half of the twentieth century, a new global trend distinctly emerged, which may be called "reverse colonisation" of the former metropolises or centres of empire.

The overpopulation of the developing countries as a consequence of demographic boom and steady fall in fertility of the "old industrial" countries, with high standard of living and social safeguards created a situation, when a stream of migrants from among the indigenous inhabitants of the former colonies rushed to Europe following the wave of reverse migration of white colonialists during the years 1950-60. It is significant that the historical and economic relations were maintained—the process of resettlement took the same path, as it happened in the nineteenth century, but in the opposite direction; in addition the process of decolonization in many respects became easier by the cultural and linguistic legacy of the colonial era. Thus, in Great Britain there is a very large number of emigrants from India, in France already up to 20 per cent of its population are the natives of the former African colonies (Algeria, Tunisia, Morocco); the traditional aspiration of Germany for Turkey and the Balkans has led to the prevalence there of such immigrants, like the Turks, Kurds and Croatians. The migration processes that are going on in the territory of the countries of Central Asia are of a similar nature.

Thus, as per the calculations of the demographers, if the number of Muslim population in France will increases from 20 to 30 per cent by the year 2020 as a consequence of migration, then, given the demographic expansion, it will exceed 50 per cent, i.e. the French will become an ethnic minority in their own historical territory.[26]

The continuous depopulation and external migration-demographic expansion are threatening the indigenous population of Europe with the repetition of the same fate as had been faced by the aborigines of America: turning into national minority and then, at the best being excluded to the social periphery.

The Trend of Demographic Development in Russia

At the current stage of development the demographic situation in Russia, and in the Asian macro-region, in particular, is characterized by adverse dynamics: declined fertility, high mortality, and outflux of population.

The population of the eastern regions declined from 52.1 million in 1995 to 50 million in 2002.[27] This figure decreased by about another 2 million in 2009. According to various predictions, the stable population in the Asian parts of Russia would not exceed 32 million by 2015.[28]

In comparison with other European countries the age and gender structure of the population of Russia, including Siberia as a whole, is characterized by more favourable composition (Table 3). In spite of the constant outflux of the population (mostly the young and able-bodied) the average age in the Siberian regions was also slightly younger than that of the Russian Federation in general. In 2002, throughout the Russian Federation it was 37.1 (including 34.1 for men and 39.8 for women), in Siberia it was equal to 35.1 (including 32.3 for men and 37.8 for women).[29]

We also note that among the national regions of Siberia the average age of male and female populations was even less (Table 4). This is primarily due to the persistent high indicators of natural growth

Table 3. Distribution of Population in Russian Federation According to Age Census 2002 (%)

Age of population	*Russian Federation*			*Siberian Federal Okrug*		
	Total	*Men*	*Women*	*Total*	*Men*	*Women*
Under the able-bodied age (up to 14 years)	18.1	19.9	16.6	19.6	21.3	18.0
Able-bodied age (15-64 years)	61.3	66.3	56.9	62.3	66.4	58.7
Older than the able-bodied age (more than 65 years)	20.5	13.7	26.4	18.1	12.3	23.3

Source: http://www.perepis2002.ru/index.html?id=11

Table 4. Average Age of Population of National Regions of the Siberian Federal Okrug Census 2002 (%)

National Regions	*Total Population*	*Men*	*Women*
Republic of Altai	30.5	29.0	32.0
Republic of Buryatiya	31.6	29.4	33.9
Republic of Tyva	25.5	24.3	26.7
Republic of Khakassia	34.6	32.0	37.2
Altai Krai	37.2	34.3	39.8
Evenk Autonomous Okrug	31.4	31.5	31.3
Dolgano-Nenets Autonomous Okrug	30.6	29.7	31.5
Ust-Ordyn Autonomous Okrug	30.2	28.5	31.9
Agin-Buryat Autonomous Okrug	28.1	26.7	29.7

Source: http://www.perepis2002.ru/index.html?id=11

of the population (families with many children) and low mobility, which are the characteristics of the autochthonous population, preserving the traditional lifestyle.

Nevertheless, the issues related to economic development and ensuring human resources for the vast and poorly developed spaces of this region still remains unsolved. To some extent they are filled by the labour migrants from Central Asia, as well as the migrants from the neighbouring over-populated Republic of China, who each year more and more actively have been starting to assimilate the empty spaces across the border of Siberia.

Thus, the countries of Asia at the current phase are characterized by predominance of youth in their population structure. Given the fact that the bulk of the contingent of labour and educational migration are within the range of 20 to 40 years, the migration potential of the population of the countries of Asia will not decrease in the near future. The ageing population of the industrialized countries is supplemented by the migrants from Asia. And what is more, it is the people of reproductive age who are their main migration contingent, and therefore the growth of ethnically alien communities is being facilitated not only by migration (linear growth of numbers), but also by the unlimited natural growth.

Notes and References

1. A.P. Kuznetsov, *Geografiya naseleniya i khozyaistva mira* (Moscow: Izd. Drofa 1998), 17-18.
2. http://www.ongeo.ru/population
3. Here and further the overall demographic rates have been cited in promille (from Lat. Pro mille) of per 1000 people of the population, as it is customary in historical demography, by a special sign ‰.
4. http://www.mediaget.ru/referat/referat/56250/
5. S.N. Nekhoroshkov, *Demografiya* (Novosibirsk 2005), 80-81.
6. http://www.mediaget.ru/referat/referat/56250/
7. http://kaig.ru/
8. http://www.mediaget.ru/referat/referat/56250/
9. Nekhoroshkov, *Demografiya*, 82.
10. http://www.mediaget.ru/referat/referat/56250/
11. http://www.demoscope.ru/dem-98/g6.html
12. http://www.mediaget.ru/referat/referat/56250/
13. http://www.mediaget.ru/referat/referat/56250/
14. http://worldgeo.ru/asia/ind/
15. M. Gracheva, "Sovremennaya demograficheskaya situatsiya v Indii i istorii ee demograficheskoi politiki," http://www.demoscope.ru/weekly/2010/0425/student03.php#_FNR_56#_FNR_56.

16. Xin Yuan, "Naselenie Kitaya na rubezhe XXI veka. Trudnosti, ozhidayuschie naselenie Kitaya v XXI veke, vzglyad na rozhdaemost', a takzhe na chislennost'i starenie naseleniya," http://www.demoscope.ru/weekly/2002/073/analit04.php
17. E. Bazhenova, "Naselenie Kitaya v epokhu modernizatsii i ekonomicheskikh reform," *Problemy Dal'nego Vostoka*, no. 5 (2009): 212-29.
18. Bazhenova, "Naselenie Kitaya v epokhu modernizatsii."
19. Yuhua Chen, "Naselenie Kitaya na rubezhe XXI veka. Problemy korrektirovki politiki rozhdaemosti v Kitae," http://www.demoscope.ru/weekly/2002/073/analit05.php
20. A.G. Larin, *Kitaiskie migrant v Rossii. Istoriya i sovremennost'*, (Moscow: Vostochnaya kniga 2009), 344-45.
21. Larin, *Kitaiskie migrant v Rossii.*
22. http://www.demoscope.ru/dem-98/g6.html
23. "Demograficheskie pokazateli stran mira," 2000 g., *Geografiya PS*, no. 33: 11-22.
24. V. Perevedentsev, *Migratsiya v ritme vremeni* (Moscow 2005), 34.
25. E. Shcherbakova, "Srednii vozrast naseleniya povsemestno uvelichivaetsya," http://www.demoscope.ru/weekly/2006/0235/barom03.php
26. A. Kudryavtsev, "Musul'mane vo Frantsii," *Rossiya i musul'manskii mir*, no. 11 (2002): 155-68.
27. V.A. Lamin, M.M. Efimkin, "Naselenie vostochnykh raionov Rossii v global'nykh demograficheskikh protsessakh," *Migratsionnye protsessy v aziatskoi Rossii v kontse XIX-XXI vv.* (Novosibirsk: Parallel' 2009), 210.
28. Lamin and Efimkin, "Naselenie vostochnykh raionov Rossii," 211.
29. *Perepis'naseleniya Rossii*, 2002.

Contributors

Oleg A. Donskikh, Professor, Department of Philosophy, Novosibirsk, Russia.

Vsevolod Bashkuev, Research Fellow, Institute of Mongolian, Buddhist and Tibetan Studies, Siberian Branch of the Russian Academy of Sciences, Ulan Ude.

Zuhra Altymyshova, Faculty of Letters, Kyrgyz-Turkish Manas University, Bishkek/Kyrgyz Republic.

Marina N. Baldano, Professor, Head of the Department of History, Ethnology and Sociology, Institute for Mongolian, Buddhist and Tibetan Studies of SBRAS, Ulan Ude.

Svetlana Baldano, Research Scholar, Institute for Mongolian, Buddhist and Tibetan Studies of SBRAS, Ulan Ude.

Isenbike Togan, Professor, Turkish Academy of Sciences, Bogazici University, History Department Istanbul, Turkey.

Tatiana Shaumian, Head, Centre for Indian Studies, Institute of Oriental Studies, Russian Academy of Sciences.

Büşra Ersanlı, Professor, Department of Political Science and International Relations, Marmara University, Istanbul, Turkey.

Yunus Emre Gürbüz, Faculty of Communication, Kyrgyz-Turkish Manas University, Bishkek, Kyrgyz Republic.

Denis Ananyev, Fellow, Institute of History, SBRAS, Novosibirsk and part-time Fellow of Specialized Educational and Scientific Centre, Novosibirsk State University.

Shirin Akiner, Senior Fellow of the Cambridge Central Asia Forum, University of Cambridge, and Research Associate at the School of Oriental and African Studies, University of London, UK.

Timur Dadabaev, Associate Professor, Graduate School of Social Sciences and Humanities, University of Tsukuba, Japan.

İlhan Şahin, Professor, Faculty of Letters, Kyrgyz-Turkish Manas University, Bishkek.

Kishimjan Eshenkulova, Kyrgyz-Turkey Manas University, Bishkek/ Kyrgyz Republic.

Hikoyat Salimova, Research Fellow, Center for Business and Economic Research Ball State University, USA.

Preeti Das, Assistant Professor, Centre of Russian and Central Asian Studies, School of International Studies, Jawahalal Nehru University, New Delhi, India.

Pinar Akcali, Associate Professor, Department of Political Science and Public Administration Middle East Technical University, Ankara, Turkey.

P.L. Dash, Professor of International Relations and India Chair, University of World Economy and Diplomacy, Tashkent, Uzbekistan.

Michael Fredholm, Senior Researcher and Lecturer, Stockholm International Program for Central Asian Studies, Stockholm University, Sweden.

Didier Chaudet, Lecturer at Sciences Po, Paris.

Debidutta Aurobinda Mahapatra, Research Associate, Centre for Central Eurasian Studies, University of Mumbai.

Darima Amogolonova, Doctor of Sciences (History), Associate Professor, Department of Philosophy, Cultural and Social Anthropology and Religious Studies, Institute for Mongolian, Buddhist and Tibetan Studies, Siberian Branch, Russian Academy of Sciences, Ulan Ude.

R.G. Gidadhubli, Professor and Former Director and currently Adjunct Faculty, Centre for Eurasian Studies, University of Mumbai, India.

Ajay Kumar Patnaik, Professor, School of International Studies, Jawaharlal Nehru University, India.

Mirzokhid Rakhimov, Head of Contemporary History and International Relations Department of the Institute of History of the Academy of Sciences and also Associate Professor at Tashkent Pedagogical University, The Institute of History Uzbek Academy of Sciences, Tashkent, Uzbekistan.

Marilisa Lorusso, Associate Researcher, Genova University and Osservatorio Balcani e Caucaso, Italy.

Olga V. Buraeva, Research Fellow and Head of the Ethnology group, Department of History, Ethnology and Sociology, Institute of Mongolian, Buddhist and Tibetan Studies, SBRAS, Ulan Ude.

Rashmi Doraiswamy, Professor (Central Asia), Academy of International Studies, Jamia Millia Islamia, New Delhi.

Ranjana Saxena, Associate Professor and Head, Department of Slavonic and Finno-Ugrian Studies, University of Delhi.

Shakhym Gullyev, Professor of Zhetysu State University named after I. Zhansugurov, Taldykorgan, Kazakhstan.

Dilorom Karomat, Fellow, Maulana Abul Kalam Azad Instiute of Asian Studies, Kolkata.

Nigora Khasanova, Uzbek musicologist and musician, Turkestan Orchestra, Tashkent.

Sören Urbansky, Research Associate and Lecturer (East Asian History), Department of History at the University of Freiburg/Germany; Ph.D. candidate at the University of Heidelberg/Germany within the Cluster of Excellence Asia and Europe in a Global Context.

Natalia P. Ryzhova, Head, Candidate of Science (Economics), Amur Laboratory for Economic and Social Studies of Far Eastern Branch of Russian Academy of Science, Blagoveshchensk.

Sharad K. Soni, teaches at Central Asian Studies Programme, Centre for South, Central, Southeast Asian and Southwest Pacific Studies, School of International Studies, Jawahalal Nehru University, New Delhi, India.

Viktor B. Bazarov, Junior Scientific Researcher, Institute of Mongolian, Buddhist and Tibetan Studies, SBRAS, Ulan Ude.

Roza Abdykulova, Faculty of Letters, Kyrgyz-Turkish Manas University, Bishkek, Kyrgyz Republic.

Nivedita Das Kundu, Foreign Policy Analyst, Assistant Director, Research and Publication Division. Indian Council for Social Science Research, New Delhi.

Viktor I. Dyatlov, Doctor of Historical Sciences, Professor, Department of History and International Relations, Irkutsk State University, Irkutsk.

Vladimir A. Isupov, Head of the Department of History and Demography Studies, Institute of History, SBRAS, Novosibirsk.

Sayan Darzhaev, Senior Scientific Researcher, Doctor of Historical Sciences, Institute of Mongolian, Buddhist and Tibetan Studies, SBRAS, Ulan Ude.

Yana Y. Kuznetsova, Candidate of History, Researcher, Department of History and Demography Studies, Institute of History, SBRAS, Novosibirsk.

Index